A KIERKEGAARD ANTHOLOGY

A
KIERKEGAARD
ANTHOLOGY

Edited by Robert Bretall

PRINCETON UNIVERSITY PRESS

PRINCETON, NEW JERSEY

To
DAVID F. SWENSON
Late Professor of Philosophy in the University of Minnesota
and
WALTER LOWRIE, D.D.
Devoted Laborers
in the
Kierkegaardian vineyard

PREFACE

The selections in this book have been chosen, first, with a view to the only kind of reading which the editor of an anthology has any right to expect; but secondly, in the hope that possibly a few persons may read it through from beginning to end. So read, it gives a picture of Kierkegaard's intellectual and spiritual development from the age of twenty-one (the date of the first passage from the *Journals*) until his death a little over twenty years later. This picture is traced by the hand of S.K. himself in the excerpts taken from his various works and ar-ranged (with one or two exceptions) in chronological order.

In pointing this out I have no thought of competing with the biographies of Kierkegaard in English which already exist, particu-larly the two excellent ones by Dr. Walter Lowrie; neither do I believe that S.K.'s works are unapproachable save through the temporal course of his "life." I am wholly in sympathy with Dr. Philip Merlan in his contention that "to understand Kierkegaard, it is by no means necessary to find out the history of his engagement, whether his father did or did not curse God, and so forth; nay . . . we can understand him even if we resign ourselves never to learning when, why, with whom, and whether while intoxicated or not, he was in a brothel. It is, on the contrary, obvious that we cannot understand his life unless we have understood his writings." My selections are arranged chronologically because they had to be arranged in some order and the chronological seemed less arbitrary or at any rate less open to objection than any "systematic" schemework that might be imposed upon them; but also because in this way it becomes possible for those with little or no previous knowl-edge of S.K. to become acquainted with him through his works. The very few "facts" about his life which help one to understand the works I have tried to outline in the introductions to the different books; but even these are by no means indispensable and, if they do not aid the reader, I would strongly urge him to let S.K. speak entirely for himself.

Among the works from which excerpts have been taken will be found one with the inviting title, *The Point of View for My Work as an Author*. Perhaps another editor would have placed this first, as I seriously considered doing; yet there is a good reason for *not* having this "point of view," illuminating as it is, too clearly in mind while reading the early "aesthetic" works, and I would beg the reader not to go snooping into this section before he has reached the period of the *Concluding Postscript* at least.

The order of the selections is the order of *publication* rather than the order of writing (the latter being doubtful in some cases), with the following exceptions: (1) *The Point of View* and most of the *Journal* passages come approximately at the time they were written, whereas they were published posthumously; (2) the *Journal* excerpts used to preface the different works are out of chronological order entirely, as is also the long passage, "My Relation to 'Her'," telling the story of S.K.'s love affair, which I have placed at the time of the events related. The address on "The Unchangeableness of God" was among the last things S.K. published, although it was delivered in a Copenhagen church some four years previously. Harking back as it does to S.K.'s favorite Scripture text and the first on which he ever wrote, this seemed the most fitting conclusion to the whole anthology.

By choosing passages that are relatively self-contained and suffer less than others from being lifted out of context, I have sought to mitigate the harshness of S.K.'s judgment upon me for laying "violent hands" on his works, as he once predicted would be done. Even so, I am afraid that if ever I meet him in heaven, he is going to turn a reproachful yet forgiving countenance in my direction! In most cases I believe that I have given a correct impression of the entire work from which a part has been taken; yet in the *Stages on Life's Way* this principle did not prevent me from giving the opening and closing parts of the "Banquet" scene apart from the intervening speeches of the participants and apart from anything in the other two divisions of the book. In self-justification I can only say that I happen to find the included portions very beautiful indeed and the rest of the book (especially the interminable "Quidam's Diary") on the whole rather dull. Admirers of the "Diary"—and there are many—will certainly condemn me for this, and it would have been easy enough to conceal my opinion by choosing a few of the more interesting passages; but in view of the many other things which clamored for inclusion, I simply could not bear to use material about which I am less than enthusiastic.

It would indeed be un-Kierkegaardian, as well as untrue, to claim that within the limits indicated this collection is not very largely a personal one. I have chosen passages which interest me, and which I think may have an interest for others. Since S.K. considered himself a "poet" rather than an "apostle," it is quite in order to express the hope that these others will get as much pleasure from the selections as I have had in making them. I hope also that a goodly number may, like the Hegelians satirized by S.K., feel themselves inclined to "go further"— into Kierkegaard, and not beyond Christianity!

It is now my privilege to mention the names of some who, in one way and another, have helped me in the preparation of this book. The moving spirit behind it was Mr. Datus Smith, Director of the Princeton University Press, whose enthusiasm for Kierkegaard goes far beyond the bounds of the publishing business, in which medium, however, it has been very effectively expressed. Another Princetonian, Dr. Walter Lowrie, has very kindly granted permission to use his translations and such of his notes as I saw fit, and has spent no few hours with me smoothing out difficulties in the text. As probably the greatest living authority on Kierkegaard, he was the logical person to prepare this anthology, and I can only say that the readers of this book have been the losers by his not electing to do so. Mrs. David F. Swenson, widow of the late Professor Swenson, has likewise allowed me to use the translations of her late husband and to quote from some of his notes and excellent introductions. Mrs. Swenson is now engaged in revising the text of the *Concluding Unscientific Postscript*, and I have had the benefit of her suggestions in the passages from this most important of S.K.'s works. Dr. Fritz Kaufmann, formerly of Northwestern University and now at the University of Buffalo, has been of assistance in both specific and general ways. Although I had been acquainted with S.K. for several years, it was in a graduate seminar of Dr. Kaufmann's three years ago that I received a new impetus to the study of Kierkegaard. In this seminar was another Kierkegaardian, Dr. Paul S. Minear, then of Garrett Biblical Institute, now of Andover Newton Theological School, who gave me the benefit of his and some of his students' suggestions one evening. To them is hereby dedicated the "Deer Park" passage from the *Postscript!*

Among others to whom I have shown the plan of the book at various stages and from whose good counsel I have profited are the Reverend Howard Johnson of St. John's Church, Washington, D.C., a man whose acquaintance with Kierkegaard is comprehensive and profound; Professor Philip Merlan of Scripps College in California, from whose illuminating article on S.K. I have already quoted; Mr. George de Huszar of the *Encyclopaedia Britannica*, a political scientist who studies Kierkegaard for "relaxation," and who will shortly bring

out a valuable edition of the "aesthetic works"; M. Denis de Rougemont, the discerning author of *Love in the Western World* and *The
Devil's Share,* and my former teachers at Union Theological Seminary,
Professor Paul Tillich and Professor Richard Kroner, to both of whom
I am greatly indebted. Two of my faithful friends, Miss Nadine Mack
and Miss Joyce Blackburn, have made suggestions about specific parts
of the manuscript and have helped in reading the proofs, as have also
Mr. de Huszar, Miss Maud Nosler, and Mr. and Mrs. Theodore Brad-
shaw.

I am indebted to the Oxford University Press, to the Augsburg
Press, and to Harper and Brothers for permission to quote from translations bearing their imprint.

The frontispiece showing Kierkegaard at his "high desk" is taken
from an oil painting in the Frederiksborg Museum. It was painted by
Luplau Janssen. It appears in Walter Lowrie's volume *Kierkegaard*
(Oxford University Press) and is reproduced here from a photograph
kindly furnished by Dr. Lowrie.

In supplying notes, I have been guided by pragmatic rather than
logical principles. There is much in Kierkegaard that requires comment and explanation, but I have confined myself to elucidating those
passages which are most essential for the understanding of S.K.'s central
thoughts. In identifying the notes, the following convention has been
observed: those written by Kierkegaard himself are marked (K); notes
taken over from Lowrie are designated by (L), those from Swenson by
(S), those from Dru by (D); and where no initial appears, the note is
by the present editor.

On this, the 100th anniversary of the publication of the great *Unscientific Postscript,* I should like to conclude by quoting a paragraph
from the Introduction to that work:

"It is not impossible that one who is infinitely interested in his
eternal happiness may sometime come into possession of it. But it is
surely quite impossible for one who has lost a sensibility for it (and
this can scarcely be anything else than the infinite interest) ever to
enjoy an eternal happiness. If the sense for it is once lost, it may be impossible to recover it. The foolish virgins had lost the infinite passion
of expectation. And so their lamps were extinguished. Then came the
cry: 'The bridegroom cometh.' Thereupon they run to the market-
place to buy new oil for themselves, hoping to begin all over again,
letting bygones be bygones. And so it was, to be sure, everything was

forgotten. The door was shut against them, and they were left outside; when they knocked for admittance, the bridegroom said: 'I do not know you.' This was no mere quip in which the bridegroom indulged, but the sober truth; for they had made themselves strangers, in the spiritual sense of the word, through having lost the infinite passion."

May the words of this book help to rekindle that "infinite passion" in the hearts of many!

ROBERT WALTER BRETALL

Phoenix, Arizona
27 February 1946

CONTENTS

Contents

INTRODUCTION

My whole life is an epigram calculated to make people aware.—THE JOURNALS (1848)

ONE hundred years ago in the city of Copenhagen there lived a man—
"fantastic," eccentric in many of his ways and ideas, deeply sensitive
and morally courageous—whom the English-speaking world is now
coming to recognize as one of the most important literary figures of
the nineteenth century and one of the greatest, most individual thinkers of all time. These are broad claims and they cannot be wholly
substantiated by a book like the present one; a certain amount of
evidence may, however, be presented for the benefit of those who would
like this evidence collected in one volume rather than distributed over
some two dozen. Such is the purpose of this anthology.

Kierkegaard's "time" has come; his position in the history of
Western thought is in one sense assured. The past decade has seen the
publication in English of all his major works, whereas not a single complete translation existed previously. He has been called "the greatest
Protestant Christian of the 19th century"[1] and "the profoundest interpreter of the psychology of the religious life . . . since St. Augustine"[2]
(to quote only two appraisals out of many). Although the fourteenth
edition of the *Encyclopaedia Britannica* has about 125 words on S.K., it
may be assumed that the next edition will have several times as many,
while the Communists have recently found him worthy of long and
violent denunciation.[3]

The tardy recognition of Kierkegaard's genius is attributable, first
to the fact that he wrote in a minor language, and secondly to at least
two characteristics of the writings themselves: their individuality of
form, whereby they resist being pigeonholed in the established literary
genres; and their content, which went strongly against the grain of
most philosophical and religious thought at the time, and only later
could be recognized for its essential modernity. Time and again history
has rewarded those who swim against the current and oppose the
thought-patterns of their age, rather than those who, in one way or
another, allow themselves to be borne along on the tide of "contemporary thought"; and Kierkegaard's passionate opposition to the intel-

[1] H. A. Reinhold, "Soren Kierkegaard" in *The Commonweal*, Vol. xxxv, p. 608
(April 10, 1942).
[2] Reinhold Niebuhr.
[3] See the new Soviet philosophical dictionary. For the relation between Kierkegaard
and Karl Marx see also Herbert Marcuse, *Reason and Revolution*.

lectualism and aestheticism of his era is paying him rich dividends today.

Almost totally neglected by his contemporaries—or, when he was not neglected, scorned and treated as a dangerous fanatic—Kierkegaard remained in obscurity until more than two decades after his death, when he was discovered by the Danish critic, Georg Brandes. Himself an agnostic—and confirmed in his agnosticism by S.K.'s uncompromising portrayal of Christianity—Brandes saw in the *Concluding Unscientific Postscript* "not only a new book, but a new *kind* of book"; and through Brandes Kierkegaard's fame began to spread through Germany as well as Scandinavia,[4] the complete works being translated into German around the turn of the century. The way had been prepared by Schopenhauer and Nietzsche, and Kierkegaard added new impetus to the great revolt against Hegelian philosophy—though in point of time he had been one of the very first to react against Hegel's intellectualism and to launch the counter-movement in the direction of temporality, concreteness and the "individual." In America William James was a part of this movement, and in France Henri Bergson; but in Germany the new trend took the name of "existentialism," with Kierkegaard—the Kierkegaard of the *Unscientific Postscript*—as its acknowledged forerunner. It is this Existentialism—developed and elaborated by a number of contemporary philosophers, but especially by Karl Jaspers and Martin Heidegger—which is having so extraordinary a vogue in France at the present time.[5]

To point out all this is perhaps unnecessary, and certainly it is un-Kierkegaardian; for if ever a man discounted popularity on principle, it was S.K. He held that to read a man's works because of the reputation he has acquired is to read them in a way that prevents or at least seriously hinders one from reacting to them independently; and in his own life he carried this principle to fantastic extremes. While he was at work night and day on some of his greatest books, he would not fail to put in an appearance at the theater every evening "for just ten minutes, no more," so that people would go on thinking of him as the desperate dilettante he actually had been in his earlier youth.

---

[4] One of the Scandinavians to be deeply influenced by S.K. was the great dramatist Henrik Ibsen—though the nature of this influence has been subject to much debate. See Werner Möhring, *Ibsen und Kierkegaard*; Miguel de Unamuno, *Perplexities and Paradoxes*, pp. 51–57. One is reminded of Unamuno's saying that he learned Danish in order to read Ibsen, and was rewarded by reading Kierkegaard.

[5] See "Existentialism: a Preface," by Jean Wahl in *New Republic,* 113: 442-444 (October 1, 1945); "Existentialism," *Time,* 47: 28–29 (January 28, 1946).

Later on this inverted pretense was dropped; but the only "authority" he ever coveted was the authority his words might have as they echoed through the consciousness of that "solitary individual" to whom they were all dedicated.

II

Putting aside, therefore, the opinions of others, we may well ask ourselves what foundation there is for considering Kierkegaard one of the intellectually and spiritually great. One quality of his mind is indeed undeniable—viz. its enormous *range*. Within this volume are included (1) a masterly short novel, the well known *Diary of the Seducer*, together with the humorous part of another novel, *Repetition*; (2) the "Banquet" scene from *Stages on Life's Way*, which has been hailed as the modern counterpart of Plato's *Symposium*; (3) the subtle, abstruse thinking of the *Philosophical Fragments* (an ironical title, as the reader will discover) and its great successor, the *Unscientific Postscript;* (4) the absorbing and astonishingly modern psychology of "despair" in *The Sickness unto Death*;[6] (5) the analysis of "the public" and the levelling process of modern society—an adumbration of Ortega y Gasset's "mass man"—in *The Present Age;* (6) the various beautiful and moving religious discourses, the tone of which moves constantly from impassioned utterance to the strictest dialectic and back again; and finally (7) the terse and biting satire of S.K.'s final period, in *The Attack upon "Christendom"* and many of the *Journal* passages. Further divisions and subdivisions could be made, but these are enough to show in a general way how many strings S.K. had to his bow. Incredible as it may sound, it is difficult to think of any writer, ancient or modern, who had as many—or who used them any more effectively.

For Kierkegaard does not merely cover all of these different fields; he is penetrating in each of them, with the penetration born of his one overmastering desire to become clear about himself through incessant reflection and self-analysis. It was a way that led through suffering known only to himself, though we can appreciate something of what it cost to become "the exception" and to be "sacrificed" for the edification of mankind. It was a way that led through conflict and the bitterness of estrangement, but it was also a way that led to

---

[6] *The Concept of Dread*, Kierkegaard's other great psychological work, is not represented here.

peace and joy. "Humanly speaking, what a painful thing thus to be sacrificed! . . . But on the other hand God knows well . . . how to make it so blessed a thing to be sacrificed, that among the thousands of divers voices which express, each in its own way, the same thing, his also will be heard, and perhaps his especially, which is truly *de profundis*, proclaiming: God is love. . . ." [7]

S.K. does not want us to be dazzled by the individual excellences— literary, philosophical, or otherwise—which abound in his works; for they are by-products, existing incidentally to the main design of a life which was identical with what it gave to the world—an unbroken fabric whose unity is the more amazing the more we see of its diversity. If purity of heart, in Kierkegaard's beautiful formula, is "to will one thing," then purity of mind is to think one thing—"not to have many thoughts, but to have one thought" (like Socrates, who "always said the same thing") and that one absolute. Early in life [8] he made the discovery that one must "find a truth which is true *for me*—the idea for which I can live and die." When S.K. wrote these words in his *Journal* he already suspected what his "idea" was, and before long he had become certain. The idea was Christianity; and his one thought was "what it means to be a Christian—in Christendom."

III

To those who would question this choice of theme—and, having traced the various influences which led S.K. to choose it, perhaps flatter themselves that they had "explained" Kierkegaard and need not trouble themselves about him further—to these gnostics the answer comes in the form of a *tu quoque*. It is impossible to reach an absolute beginning, and there is no such thing as "presuppositionless thought." The man who pretends that his view of life is determined by sheer reason is both tiresome and unperceptive: [9] he fails to grasp the elementary fact that he is not a pure thinker, but an *existing individual*. To one who has chosen Christ, says S.K.: "the only possible objection would be: but you might possibly have been saved in another way. To that he cannot answer. It is as though one were to say to some one in love, yes, but you might have fallen in love with another girl; to which he would have to answer: there is no answer to that, for I only know

[7] *Journals*, 1260.
[8] See p. 5.
[9] S.K. found him essentially comic: see pp. 200-203.

that she is my love. The moment a lover can answer that objection he is *eo ipso* not a lover; and if a believer can answer that objection he is *eo ipso* not a believer." [10]

"Existential thinking" begins at a definite point, which others may regard as arbitrary but which is not at all arbitrary for the thinker himself, since it expresses his "ultimate concern" [11] as an existing individual; it is quite simply "the idea for which he would be willing to live and die." And his task is to understand the multiplicity of things from this particular point of view. It is true that Adolf Hitler was an existential thinker, of sorts; so are most of the inmates of insane asylums. To this charge, so frequently brought against existentialism, there is a pragmatic answer—and another answer, which applies to Christianity alone. The pragmatic answer consists simply in pointing out that the false "ultimates" refute themselves in experience: they lead to the disintegration of a personality and not to its unification. The other answer is that Christianity by definition excludes irrationalism: the "choice" here cannot possibly be arbitrary, because it is the choosing of Eternity in time.

Both of these answers are implied in Kierkegaard, yet he would have been loath to use them, for in doing so one steps out of the faith-relationship, which has "objective uncertainty" as its correlate. "The lover who can answer the objection is *eo ipso* not a lover, and the believer who can answer the objection is *eo ipso* not a believer." Knowledge and faith, for Kierkegaard, are polar opposites: knowledge is objectively certain, but it deals only with "the possible," i.e. the hypothetical (cause and effect, condition and conditioned, premise and conclusion); faith is highly uncertain, but only by taking the "leap" and exercising it does one come into contact with actuality— the actuality of one's own being. "The only reality accessible to any existing individual is his own ethical reality. To every reality outside the individual, even his own *external* reality, his highest valid relation is cognitive; but knowledge is a grasp of the possible and not a realization of the actual; the knowledge of actualities transmutes them into possibilities, and the highest intellectual validity of knowledge is attained in an even balancing of alternative possibilities with an absolutely open mind." [12]

This "even balancing" is what Kierkegaard accomplishes in such

---

[10] *Journals*, 922.
[11] The term is Paul Tillich's, but the thought is Kierkegaardian.
[12] David F. Swenson, *Something about Kierkegaard*, pp. 105–106.

works as *Either/Or, Stages on Life's Way, Fear and Trembling,* and *Philosophical Fragments.* In each of these books alternatives are delineated, but no choice is made between them: this is left up to the reader, the "existing individual" for whom alone the choice can have significance. For Kierkegaard to choose on behalf of his readers would be meaningless; this is why he did not want any "disciples." Like Socrates, he employed "indirect communication" when he was dealing in terms of *knowledge*; but in his religious discourses he addresses the reader directly, using every available means to persuade him to become a Christian.

IV

What is it, then, to become a Christian—in Christendom? In *The Point of View for my Work as an Author* S.K. tells us that the whole of his authorship centers about this one question; everything he wrote is relevant to it—even the *Diary of the Seducer*—and he proceeds to show us how. I do not wish to anticipate his explanation here; but briefly, S.K.'s great insight was into the fact that a Christian environment, far from helping one to become a Christian, puts special obstacles in the way, and particularly two—the *aesthetic* obstacle and the *speculative* obstacle.

In the early ages of Christianity, to be a Christian meant to separate oneself from the crowd—to do what was not easy to do, humanly speaking. It meant an effort, it meant sacrifice; it *cost something.* Today, says Kierkegaard, the situation is exactly the opposite: one becomes a Christian by the easiest and most natural of processes. Not only have the sacraments of the Church been formalized to the point where they are little more than social functions (so that a christening and a cocktail party go hand in hand); but even these formalities are no longer necessary, since it is assumed that "everyone is a Christian" who lives in a "Christian" land. The tragedy that "nowadays all are Christians" is a real one, since the idea of being or becoming a Christian is thereby emptied of the significance it originally had. It is for this reason, and this reason alone, that Kierkegaard attacks "the aesthetic way of life," [13] the way of feeling and enjoyment, the way of "immediacy"; and it is important to realize this. His assault has nothing to do with Puritanism or with any doctrine that pleasure is wrong

[13] S.K. uses the word "aesthetic" in its etymological sense of *feeling.* (Greek αἰσθάνομαι, "to feel.")

per se. The aesthetic, he said, "has not to be abolished but *dethroned*"; it must cease to be the motivating power of a man's life, and it must be removed from the sanctuary of religion. This again does not mean that one should not take pleasure in worshiping God; it means that the worship must go back to something which is not aesthetic to begin with—not simply "doing the natural thing" in a "Christian" society, or in any way following the path of least resistance. When Christianity is made so attractive that pretty nearly everyone accepts it as a matter of course, then one can be sure it is not true Christianity that is being presented—not the Christianity of Him who made the taking up of one's cross the condition of discipleship.

The second obstacle to becoming a Christian in Christendom is the *speculative* one. Not only may people accept the Gospel (or what they think to be the Gospel) because it is made easy and attractive for them; but they may accept it because it is made to appeal to their intellects as logical or reasonable—i.e. as *sanctioned by human reason.* But "the reasonableness of Christianity" is treason to Christianity because it subjects the self-revelation of the infinite God to finite human standards. Abhorrent to S.K. above all else was the condescending attitude of the Hegelian philosophers of his day, who were continually "going further" than Christianity—i.e. from a supposed higher vantage-point looking down upon such doctrines as the Incarnation and the Atonement and showing that they were indeed true—if one understood them in a certain sense, etc. S.K. felt that one should either give up Christianity altogether—or else accept it as what it claims to be, the ultimate truth about human existence, a truth which man could not have discovered for himself. In order to show that the Hegelians were on the wrong track he brought to the fore the *paradoxical* quality of Christian truth and the fact that, so far from appearing true to the human intellect, it constitutes an "offense" [14] to our intellectual faculty as such. The central notion of the Christian faith—the idea of *God in time*—is purely and simply a contradiction, for God is by definition eternal. The early Christians knew that their faith was not intellectually respectable, and they believed against the understanding; the modern Christian, after hearing the sermon of a Liberal Protestant clergyman or reading a Catholic treatise on "natural theology," is tempted to believe because his understanding assents to what is presented. But to believe because the understanding assents is in reality *not to believe.*

Kierkegaard's treatment of faith *vs.* reason opens up perspectives

[14] See *Training in Christianity.*

into the history of philosophy which can hardly be entered here, and I wish merely to suggest that his position is not quite what it may appear to be on the surface. The advent of Christianity posed a new problem for philosophy, a solution of which was reached in the medieval synthesis of St. Thomas Aquinas: faith and reason were harmonized by carefully delineating their respective spheres. This synthesis was broken up by the centrifugal and individualistic forces of the Renaissance, with the result that reason (in one form or another, patently or disguised) tended to gain the upper hand. This was true of the English Empiricists almost as much as of the great Continental Rationalists Descartes, Spinoza, and Leibnitz; only in the radical skepticism of David Hume does the element of "belief" (very much secularized in form) come to assert itself once more. Kant put an end to the pretensions of the older rationalism, but with his doctrine of the thing-in-itself and the transcendental Ego paved the way for a new and bolder rationalism—that of Hegel. It was against this that S.K. reacted so violently, and for this very reason he sometimes swings to the opposite extreme and appears to be a fideist who would cut himself off completely from the intellect and its claims. Here as elsewhere he was a "corrective," providing the emphasis which was needed at the time; but his considered viewpoint was not fideistic. As we shall see, he himself was capable of the most abstract thinking: in the *Journals* he speaks of using the understanding in order to believe *against* the understanding, and this was precisely his aim. As Lowrie says, he was essentially a "Catholic Christian"[15]—understanding the word "catholic" in its broadest sense as the opposite of sectarianism and one-sidedness of every sort.

But S.K. was also a Protestant, and the whole tenor of his thought points toward a new and distinctively Protestant synthesis, parallel to the medieval Catholic one. In the "philosophical theology" of Paul Tillich we can see the beginnings of such a synthesis, and Tillich's work owes much to Kierkegaard. Without S.K.'s passionate protest against the rationalizing theology of his day, and without his conception of existential thinking, the way to such a synthesis could hardly have been opened.

I am not at all sure, however, that he would appreciate this role. He emphatically did not want to be embalmed and tucked away in "a paragraph of universal history," however important the paragraph might be. His appeal is ever to the living individual, the solitary,

---

[15] *A Short Life of Kierkegaard*, p. 219.

concerned individual who, not unmindful of his eternal destiny, seeks an absolute direction for his life amid the relativities of time. To such a one Kierkegaard speaks—indirectly at first, then directly and with mounting eloquence. And such a one can hardly fail to listen.

WHAT is a poet? A poet is an unhappy being whose heart is torn by secret sufferings, but whose lips are so strangely formed that when the sighs and the cries escape them, they sound like beautiful music. His fate is like that of the unfortunate victims whom the tyrant Phalaris imprisoned in a brazen bull and slowly tortured over a steady fire; their cries could not reach the tyrant's ears so as to strike terror into his heart; when they reached his ears they sounded like sweet music. And men crowd about the poet and say to him: "Sing for us soon again"; that is as much as to say: "May new sufferings torment your soul, but may your lips be formed as before; for the cries would only frighten us, but the music is delicious." And the critics come, too, and say: "Quite correct, and so it ought to be according to the rules of aesthetics." Now it is understood that a critic resembles a poet to a hair; he only lacks the suffering in his heart and the music upon his lips. Lo, therefore, I would rather be a swineherd from Amager, and be understood by the swine, than be a poet and be misunderstood by men.—*Either/Or*

"THE SACRIFICE," THE CORRECTIVE

As a skillful cook says with regard to a dish in which already a great many ingredients are mingled: "It needs still just a little pinch of cinnamon" (and we perhaps could hardly tell by the taste that this little pinch of spice had entered into it, but she knew precisely why and precisely how it affected the taste of the whole mixture); as an artist says with a view to the color effect of a whole painting which is composed of many, many colors: "There and there, at that little point, there must be applied a little touch of red" (and we perhaps could hardly even discover that the red is there, so carefully has the artist suppressed it, although he knows exactly why it should be introduced). So it is with Governance.

Oh, the Governance of the world is an immense housekeeping and a grandiose painting. Yet He, the Master, God in heaven, behaves like the cook and the artist. He says: "Now there must be introduced a little pinch of spice, a little touch of red." We do not comprehend why, we are hardly aware of it, since that little bit is so thoroughly absorbed in the whole. But God knows why.

A little pinch of spice! That is to say: Here a man must be sacrificed, he is needed to impart a particular taste to the rest.

These are the correctives. It is a woeful error if he who is used for applying the corrective becomes impatient and would make the corrective normative for others. That is the temptation to bring everything to confusion.

A little pinch of spice! Humanly speaking, what a painful thing thus to be sacrificed, to be the little pinch of spice! But, on the other hand, God knows well him whom He elects to use in this way, and then He knows also how, in the inward understanding of it, to make it so blessed a thing for him to be sacrificed, that among the thousands of divers voices which express, each in its own way, the same thing, his also will be heard, and perhaps especially his which is truly *de profundis*, proclaiming: God is love. The birds on the branches, the lilies in the field, the deer in the forest, the fishes in the sea, countless hosts of happy men exultantly proclaim: God is love. But beneath all these sopranos, supporting them as it were, as the bass part does, is audible the *de profundis* which issues from the sacrificed one: God is love.—*The Journals*

A KIERKEGAARD ANTHOLOGY

THE JOURNALS (1834–1842)

TRANSLATED BY ALEXANDER DRU

Oh, the sins of passion and of the heart—how much nearer to salvation than the sins of reason!
. . . What our age needs is education. And so this is what happened: God chose a man who also needed to be educated, and educated him *privatissime,* so that he might be able to teach others from his own experience.—THE JOURNALS

In reading the works of Kierkegaard it is desirable (though by no means necessary) to know something of his life. Judged by almost any standard, it was a singularly uneventful one—if by "events" we mean external happenings. He went to Berlin four times—otherwise his 42 years were passed entirely in Copenhagen. He led rather a wild life as a student at the University—and he was converted. He was in love—and for no apparent reason he renounced the girl and never married. A popular magazine caricatured him, and he became an object of public ridicule. In the last year of his life he launched a pamphleteering attack on the Danish State Church, in the midst of which he died. These are almost the only "events" of any importance; yet his life was one of the most dramatic ever known, because of the depth and power of his "reflection." Everything took place inside his soul, and what others would regard as trivial, or to be forgotten as soon as possible, was in him enhanced and magnified and "penetrated" by thought until it yielded the richest of poetic and philosophical treasures. None of his thinking is calm, judicious, or "objective"; it all begins from his own subjectivity—his inner torment, his particular, individual "concern"—and it terminates in what is at once the accentuation and the resolution of this ferment. Here is "Existentialism," of which Kierkegaard is justly regarded as the father; but here is something older and greater than that—an individual man, highly gifted but terribly "alone," struggling not with external forces, but with himself—and God.

As intimated in the Preface, this anthology seeks to give a more or less continuous picture of S.K. and what he was thinking (the two being really one) from the time of the first entries in the *Journals* until his death some twenty years later. From the age of 21 onward, he can tell his own story; those unfamiliar with the early years of his life may welcome the brief account by Walter Lowrie in his introduction to *The Point of View* (p. xiv):

"S.K. was born in Copenhagen on 5 May 1813, the youngest child of an elderly father who, coming as a poor peasant boy to the city, had acquired considerable wealth as a merchant and had retired from his business to brood over his sins. The father was a man of strong character, with considerable intellectual ability, who brought up his children sternly in the fear of God.

"In *The Point of View* S.K. says enough about his 'crazy upbringing' as a child. But the period of his youth, and the ten years passed in the university, he barely refers to as his *vita ante acta*, with the mere hint that he walked, alas, 'even in the path of perdition.' In fact, he lived for several years a disorderly life, in revolt against his father and against God. A gradual return in the direction of 'his old home' (i.e. the Christian position) culminated, on his 25th birthday, 5 May 1838 . . . in a thorough reconciliation with his father, which was followed a few days later (19 May at 10:30 A.M.) by a very striking and effectual experience of conversion, which he speaks of in his *Journal* as an 'indescribable joy.' His father died soon after, leaving him a considerable fortune. Thereupon, largely out of deference to his father's wish, he began to apply himself seriously to the study of theology, the faculty in which he had long been inscribed, and two years later he passed his examination *cum laude*. He never became a pastor, yet almost to the end of his life he thought of this as a possibility and cherished it as an ideal."

Already we are ahead of our story. The first few of the following *Journal* passages antedate S.K.'s conversion; soon we reach the crucial entry relating to the conversion itself (a document that has been compared to the famous paper sewed in Pascal's doublet) and the one describing "the great earthquake" in his relation to his father. (See *infra*, pp. 10 and 11.) When we come to the period of S.K.'s one and only love, I have let him tell the story in words written much later (1849) and not published until long after his death.

1834

Nov. 25. The stone which was rolled before Christ's tomb might appropriately be called *the philosopher's stone* because its removal gave not only the pharisees but, now for 1800 years, the philosophers so much to think about.

Nov. 25. Faith, surely, implies an act of the will, and moreover not in the same sense as when I say, for instance, that all apprehension implies an act of the will; how can I otherwise explain the saying in the New Testament that whatsoever is not of faith is sin.[1]

Dec. 23. Should a great man be judged according to different principles from other men? People have often answered this question with Yes, but I think No. For a great man is great because he is a chosen instrument in the hand of God; but the moment he imagines that it is he himself who is acting, that he can look into the future and with that in mind let the end ennoble the means—then he is small. Rights

[1] Rom. 14:23 (D).

and duties are valid for all and their transgression can no more be excused in the great than in politics, though people imagine that states are allowed to do wrong. Certainly wrongs such as these have often produced beneficial results, but for that we have to thank providence and not this man or that state.

1835

How bewildering the contemplation of life often is when seen in all its richness, when we look at the astonishing variety of ability and disposition, from the man who has grown so inwardly familiar with God that like John of old he may be said to lie upon the divine breast, to the man who in his bestial brutality misunderstands and wants to misunderstand all the deeper emotions, from the man who sees through the historical process with the eyes of a lynx and almost dares to set the hour, to him for whom even the simplest thing is difficult; or else we realize the inequality of rank and position, at one moment enviously feeling the lack of what has been given to others, at another time with a thankful melancholy seeing how much has been given to us which has been denied to others—and then a cold philosophy tries to explain it all from pre-existence and does not see it as the unending pageantry of life with its motley play of colors and its infinite variety.

July 29. As one goes from the inn through Sortebro across the bare fields that run along the coast, about a mile and a quarter to the north one comes to the highest point in the district, to Gilbjerg. It has always been one of my favorite places. And as I stood there one quiet evening as the sea struck up its song with a deep and calm solemnity, whilst my eye met not a single sail on the vast expanse of water, and the sea set bounds to the heavens, and the heavens to the sea; whilst on the other side the busy noise of life subsided and the birds sang their evening prayer—the few that are dear to me came forth from their graves, or rather it seemed to me as though they had not died. I felt so content in their midst, I rested in their embrace, and it was as though I were out of the body, wafted with them into the ether above—and the hoarse screech of the gulls reminded me that I stood alone, and everything vanished before my eyes, and I turned back with a heavy heart to mix in the busy world, yet without forgetting such blessed moments.—I have often stood there and looked out upon my past life and upon the different surroundings which have exercised their power upon me; and the pettiness which so often gives offense in life, the numerous mis-understandings too often separating minds which if they properly understood one another would be bound together by indissoluble ties, vanished before my gaze. Seen thus in perspective only the broad and powerful outline showed, and I did not, as so frequently happens to me, lose myself in the moment, but saw everything as a whole and was strengthened to understand things differently, to admit how often I had blundered, and to forgive others.

As I stood there, without that feeling of dejection and despondency which makes me look upon myself as the enclitic of the men who usually surround me, and without that feeling of pride which makes me into the formative principle of a small circle—as I stood there alone and forsaken, and the power of the sea and the battle of the elements reminded me of my own nothingness, and on the other hand the sure flight of the birds recalled the words spoken by Christ: Not a sparrow shall fall on the ground without your Father: then all at once I felt how great and how small I was; then did those two mighty forces, pride and humility, happily unite in friendship. Lucky is the man to whom *that* is possible at every moment of his life; in whose breast those two factors have not only come to an agreement but have joined hands and been wedded—a marriage which is neither a *mariage de convenance* nor a *mésalliance,* but a tranquil marriage of love held in the most secret chamber of a man's heart, in the holy of holies, where there are few witnesses but where everything proceeds before the eyes of Him who alone witnessed the marriage in the Garden of Eden—a marriage which will not remain unfruitful but bears blessed fruits, as may be seen in the world by an experienced observer; for like cryptogams among plants, they withdraw from the notice of the masses and only the solitary inquirer discovers them and rejoices over his find. His life will flow on peacefully and quietly, and he will neither drain the intoxicating cup of pride nor the bitter chalice of despair. He has found what the great philosopher—who by his calculations was able to destroy the enemy's engines of war—desired, but did not find: that Archimedean point from which he could lift the whole world, the point which for that very reason must lie outside the world, outside the limitations of time and space.

Gilleleie, August 1, 1835

. . . What I really lack is to be clear in my mind *what I am to do, not* what I am to know, except in so far as a certain understanding must precede every action. The thing is to understand myself, to see what God really wishes *me* to do; the thing is to find a truth which is true *for me,* to find *the idea for which I can live and die.* What would be the use of discovering so-called objective truth, of working through all the systems of philosophy and of being able, if required, to review them all and show up the inconsistencies within each system; what good would it do me to be able to develop a theory of the state and combine all the details into a single whole, and so construct a world in which I did not live, but only held up to the view of others; what good would it do me to be able to explain the meaning of Christianity if it had *no* deeper significance *for me and for my life;* what good would it do me if truth stood before me, cold and naked, not caring whether I recognized her or not, and producing in me a shudder of fear rather than a trusting devotion? I certainly do not deny that I still recognize an *imperative of understanding* and that through it one can work upon men, *but it must be taken up into my life,* and *that* is what I now recognize as the most important thing. That is what my soul longs after, as the African desert thirsts for water. That is what I lack, and that is why I am left standing like a man who has rented a house and gathered all the furniture and household things together, but has not yet found the beloved with whom to share the joys and sorrows of his life. . . . It is this divine side of man, his inward action, which means everything—not a mass of information, for that will certainly follow and then all that knowledge will not be a chance assemblage, or a succession of details without system and without a focusing point. I too have certainly looked for such a center. I have looked in vain for an anchorage in the boundless sea of pleasure and in the depth of understanding; I have felt the almost irresistible power with which one pleasure reaches out its hand to the next; I have felt the kind of meretricious ecstasy that it is capable of producing, but also the *ennui* and the distracted state of mind that succeeds it. I have tasted the fruit of the tree of knowledge and often delighted in its taste. But the pleasure did not outlast the moment of understanding and left no profound mark upon me. It seems as though I had not drunk from the cup of wisdom, but had fallen into it. I have searched with resignation for the principle of my life, by trying to believe that since all things proceeded according to unalterable laws things could not be otherwise, by dulling my ambition and the antennæ of my vanity. And because I could not adapt everything to my own mind I withdrew, conscious of my own ability, rather like a worn out parson resigning with a pension. What did I find? Not my Self, which was what I was looking for (thinking of my soul, if I may so express it, as shut in a box with a spring-lock which external circumstances, by pressing upon the lock, were to open).—And so the first thing to be decided was the seeking and finding of the Kingdom of Heaven. But just as a heavenly body, if we imagine it in the process of constituting itself, would not first of all determine how great its surface was to be and about which other body it was to move, but would first of all allow the centripetal and centrifugal forces to harmonize its existence, and then let the rest take its course—similarly, it is useless for a man to determine first of all the outside and afterwards fundamentals. One must know oneself before knowing anything else (γνῶθι σέαυτον). It is only after a man has thus understood himself inwardly and has thus seen his way, that life acquires peace and significance. . . .

And so I stand once again at the point where I must begin my life in a different way. I shall now try to fix a calm gaze upon myself and begin to act in earnest; for only thus shall I be able, like the child calling itself "I" with its first conscious action, to call myself "I" in any deeper sense.

But for that patience is necessary, and one cannot reap immediately where one has sown. I shall bear in mind the method of the philosopher[2] who bade his disciples keep silence for three years after which time all would come right. One does not begin feasting at dawn but at sunset. And so too in the spiritual world it is first of all necessary to work for some time before the light bursts through and the sun shines forth in all its glory. For although it is said that God allows the sun to shine upon the good and the wicked, and sends down rain upon the just and the unjust, it is not so in the spiritual world. And so the die is cast— I cross the Rubicon! This road certainly leads me *to strife;* but I shall not give up. I will not grieve over the past—for why grieve? I will work on with energy and not waste time grieving, like the man caught in the quicksands who began by calculating how far down he had already sunk, forgetting that all the while he was sinking still deeper. I will hurry along the path I have discovered, greeting those whom I meet on my way, not looking back as did Lot's wife, but remembering it is a hill up which we have to struggle.

Oct. 9. The same thing happens to Christianity, or to becoming a Christian, as to all radical cures, one puts it off as long as possible. . . .

[2] Pythagoras.

When I look at a number of particular phenomena in the Christian life it seems to me that Christianity, instead of giving men strength— yes, that compared to the pagans such individuals are bereft of their manhood by Christianity and are as geldings to the stallion.

1836

I have just returned from a party of which I was the life and soul; wit poured from my lips, everyone laughed and admired me—but I went away—and the dash should be as long as the earth's orbit ——————————————— and wanted to shoot myself.

'Sdeath, I can abstract from everything but *not from myself*. I cannot even forget myself when I am asleep.

Is it true that I should not laugh at my own jokes?

The omnipresence of wit.

Sept. 11. Everything is a question of ear—the rules of grammar— the dictates of the law—a thorough-bass—the philosophical system— and therefore the next life is also represented as nothing but music, a great harmony—may my life's discord soon end in it. . . .

What Schleiermacher calls "Religion" and the Hegelians "Faith" is at the bottom nothing but the first immediate condition for every-thing—the vital fluidum—the spiritual atmosphere we breathe in— and which cannot therefore with justice be designated by those words. . . .

The bourgeois mind is really the inability to rise above the absolute reality of time and space, and as such is therefore able to devote itself to the highest objects, e.g. prayer, only at certain times and with certain words. That is what Hoffman has always known how to bring out so excellently.

Dec. 11. When the dialectical period (the romantic) in history is over (a period which I could certainly very aptly call the period of individualism) social life will begin to play its part in the highest sense, and ideas such as "state" (e.g. as it existed among the Greeks; "church" in the older Catholic sense) must necessarily return richer and fuller than before, that is to say enriched by all the values which the surviving differences of individualism can give to the idea, so that the individual means nothing as such, but everything as a link in the chain. That is why the concept "church" is becoming more important, the concept of a definite objective faith etc., just as the tendency to found societies is a forerunner, though till now a bad one, of this movement. . . .

One thought succeeds another; just as one is thought and I want to write it down, comes a new one—hold on, catch it—madness—insanity!

Above all I hate the half educated—how often, when I go into society, I purposely go and sit down so as to talk with some old spinster who simply lives in order to retail family gossip, and listen with the greatest seriousness to all she can rattle off.

Most of all I like to talk with old women who retail family gossip, after them with lunatics—least of all with very sensible people.

1837

The idea, the view of life, of knowing all evil, which a gnostic sect made its own, is profound; only one must be susceptible to what is suggested by things, because those who are not baptized see things which others do not see.

Yes, I believe I would give myself to Satan so that he might show me every abomination, every sin in its most frightful form—it is this inclination, this taste for the mystery of sin.

Faust did not want to know evil in order to rejoice that he was not so bad (only the bourgeois does that), but on the contrary he wants to feel all the sluices of sin opening within his own breast, the whole immense realm of possibilities, nothing else matters compared with that. He wants to be disappointed in his expectations. . . .

July 9. . . . A situation.
A man wishes to write a novel in which one of the characters goes mad; while working on it he himself goes mad by degrees, and finishes it in the first person.

It must be terrible, on the day of judgment, when all souls come back to life—to stand there utterly *alone,* alone and *unknown* to all, all.

I am a *Janus bifrons*; I laugh with one face, I weep with the other.

But humor is also the joy which has overcome the world.

There are men who are wanting in the comparative, they are as a rule the most interesting.

Paganism never gets nearer the truth than Pilate: What is truth? And with that crucifies it.

July 14. The bourgeois always jump over one fact in life, which is why they are always a parody of those above them. . . . Morality is to them the highest, far more important than intelligence; but they have never felt enthusiasm for greatness, for talent even though in its abnormal form. Their *ethics* are a short summary of police ordinances; for them the most important thing is to be a useful member of the state, and to air their opinions in the club of an evening; they have never felt homesickness for something unknown and far away, nor the depth which consists in being nothing at all, of walking out of Nørreport with a penny in one's pocket and a cane in one's hand; they have no conception of the point of view (which a gnostic sect made its own) of getting to know the world through sin—and yet they too say: one must sow one's wild oats (*wer niemals hat ein Rausch gehabt, er ist kein braver Mann*); they have never even had a glimpse of the idea which is behind that saying, after one has forced one's way through the hidden and mysterious door into that "dark realm of sighs," [3] which in all its horror is only open to foreboding—when one sees the broken victims of seduction and inveiglement, and the tempter's coldness.

People reproach others for fearing God too much. Quite rightly, for in order really *to love God* it is necessary to have *feared* God; the bourgeois' love of God begins when vegetable life is most active, when the hands are comfortably folded on the stomach, and the head sinks back into the cushions of the chair, while the eyes, drunk with sleep, gaze heavily for a moment towards the ceiling.

Aug. 31. What a typical example in the history of the human heart is that Jewish trait which, when things went badly for them in the world, transformed their hopes of a saviour into the expectation of a worldly Messiah. How it recalls those dreams of wealth which is to heal and calm, of a happy marriage, of success in some particular career.
Every Christian has had his earthly Messiah.

Oct. 7. How dreadful it is when everything historical vanishes before a diseased probing of one's own miserable history! Who is to show us the middle course between being devoured by one's own reflections, as

[3] Görres: *Die teutschen Volksbücher,* p. 61. (D)

though one were the only man who ever had existed or ever would exist, and—seeking a worthless consolation in the *commune naufragium* of mankind? That is really what the doctrine of an *ecclesia* should do.

The reason why I far prefer the autumn to the spring is because in the autumn one looks up to heaven—in spring at the earth.

1838

Feb. 9. Sometimes, there is such a tumult in my head that it feels as though the roof had been lifted off my cranium, and then it seems as though the hobgoblins had lifted up a mountain and were holding a ball and festivities there—God preserve me!

April 14. . . . Life can only be explained after it has been lived, just as Christ only began to interpret the Scriptures and show how they applied to him—after his resurrection.

These last few days I have been reading Görres' *Athanasius* not only with my eyes but with my whole body—with a throbbing heart.

People hardly ever make use of the freedom which they have, for example, freedom of thought; instead they demand freedom of speech as a compensation.

The noble alley of the Fathers, in whose shade I can still sometimes find rest.

The fact that God could create free beings *vis-à-vis* of himself is the cross which philosophy could not carry, but remained hanging from.

May 19. Half-past ten in the morning. There is *an indescribable joy* which glows through us as unaccountably as the Apostle's outburst is unexpected: "Rejoice, and again I say, Rejoice."—Not a joy over this or that, but full jubilation "with hearts and souls and voices": "I rejoice over my joy, in, by, at, on, through, of and with my joy"—a heavenly refrain which suddenly breaks in upon our ordinary song, a joy which cools and refreshes like a breeze, a breath of air from the trade wind which blows from the plains of Mamre to the everlasting habitations.

July 7. God creates out of *nothing*—wonderful, you say: yes, to be sure, but he does what is still more wonderful: he makes saints out of sinners.

Dec. 31.[4] The Lord cometh, even though we have to wait for him, he cometh even though we grow as old as Anne, as gray as Simon . . . but we must wait for him in *his* house.

25 Years Old

. . . Then it was that the great earthquake occurred, the terrible revolution which suddenly forced upon me a new and infallible law of interpretation of all the facts. Then I suspected that my father's great age was not a divine blessing but rather a curse, that the outstanding intellectual gifts of our family were only given to us in order that we should rend each other to pieces: then I felt the stillness of death grow around me when I saw in my father an unhappy man who was to out-live us all, a cross on the tomb of all his hopes. There must be a guilt upon the whole family, the punishment of God must be on it; it was to disappear, wiped out by the powerful hand of God, obliterated like an unsuccessful attempt, and only at times did I feel a little alleviation in the thought that my father had been allotted the task of calming us with the consolation of religion, of ministering to us so that a better world should be open to us even though we lost everything in this world, even though we were overtaken by the punishment which the Jews always called down upon their enemies: that all recollection of us should be utterly wiped out, that we should no longer be found.

Inwardly torn asunder as I was, without any expectation of leading a happy earthly life . . . , without hope of a happy and comfortable future—as this naturally springs from and inheres in the historical con-tinuity of family life—what wonder then that in desperate despair I grasped at nought but the intellectual side in man and clung fast to it, so that the thought of my own considerable power of mind was my only consolation, ideas my only joy, and mankind indifferent to me.

1839

The whole of existence frightens me, from the smallest fly to the mystery of the Incarnation, everything is unintelligible to me, most of all myself; the whole of existence is poisoned in my sight, particularly myself. Great is my sorrow and without bounds; no man knows it, only God in heaven, and he will not console me; no man can console

[4] S.K.'s father had died during the interval between this passage and the pre-ceding one.

me, only God in heaven and he will not have mercy upon me.—Young man, you who still stand at the beginning of the way, if you have not gone astray, O be converted, turn to God, and taught by him your youth will be strengthened to the work of manhood; you will never experience what he must suffer who, after having wasted the strength and courage of his youth in rebellion against Him, must now, exhausted and powerless, begin a retreat through desolate and devastated provinces surrounded on all sides by the abomination of desolation, by burned towns and the delusive expectations of smoking sites, by trampled down prosperity and broken strength, a retreat as slow as a bad year, as long as eternity monotonously broken by the sound of the complaint: these days please me not.

Aug. 8. Genius, like a thunderstorm, comes up against the wind.

Sept. 6. Most men think, talk, and write as they sleep, eat, and drink, without ever raising the question of their relation to the idea; this only happens among the very few and then that decisive moment has in the very highest degree either the power to compel (genius), or it paralyzes the individual with anxiety (irony).

Mysticism has not the patience to wait for God's revelation.

1840

July 18. If the claim of philosophers to be unbiased were all it pretends to be, it would also have to take account of language and its whole significance in relation to speculation, for therein speculation has a medium which it did not itself choose; and what the eternal mystery of consciousness is for speculation, as the unity of natural qualifications and the qualification of freedom, such also is language, being partly something originally given, partly that which develops freely. And just as the individual, however freely he may develop, can never reach the point at which he becomes absolutely independent, since true freedom on the contrary consists rather in freely appropriating that which is given, and consequently in being absolutely dependent through freedom, so too with language, and moreover we sometimes find the mistaken tendency of not wishing to accept language as the freely appropriated "given," but of giving it to oneself, whether this shows itself in the very highest regions, where it easily ends in silence [the negation of language], or in personal isolation in complete gibberish. Perhaps the history of the Babylonian confusion of tongues might also be explained as an arbitrary attempt to constitute an arbitrarily formed common language, which attempt was bound to split up into the wildest differences because it lacked the common denominator which holds everything together, for here *totum est parte sua prius,* which they did not understand, holds good.

The Journey to Jutland

July 19, 1840—August 6, 1840.

After the individual has given up every effort to find himself outside himself in existence, in relation to his surroundings, and when after that shipwreck he turns towards the highest things, the absolute, coming after such emptiness, not only bursts upon him in all its fullness but also in the responsibility which he feels he has.

I am always accused of using long parentheses. Reading for my examination [5] is the longest parenthesis I have known.

The heaths of Jutland [6] must of all places be suited to develop the spirit powerfully; here everything lies naked and uncovered before God, and there is no room for the many distractions, the many little crevices where consciousness can hide and where seriousness has such difficulty in running down one's scattered thoughts. Here consciousness must firmly and scrupulously close itself around itself. And on the heaths one may say with truth: "Whither shall I flee from thy presence?"

End of Journey

It requires moral courage to grieve; it requires religious courage to rejoice.

1841

It requires more courage to suffer than to act, more courage to forget than to remember, and perhaps the most wonderful thing about God is that he can forget man's sins.

[5] His examination for the theological degree, undertaken out of respect for his father.

[6] It was here that S.K.'s father, while still a boy, is said to have cursed God—this being the sin that he could not forget "even when he was 70 years old."

My doubt is terrible.—Nothing can withstand it—it is a cursed hunger and I can swallow up every argument, every consolation and sedative—I rush at 10,000 miles a second through every obstacle.

It is a positive starting point for philosophy when Aristotle says that philosophy begins with wonder, not as in our day with doubt. Moreover the world will learn that the thing is not to begin with the negative, and the reason why it has succeeded up to the present is that it has never really given itself over to the negative, and so has never seriously done what it said. Its doubt is mere child's play.

The idea of philosophy is mediation [7]—Christianity's is the paradox.

How beautiful, how true and how heartfelt are the words of J. Boehme where he says: in the moment of temptation the thing is not to have many thoughts, but to hold fast to *one* thought.[8] God give me strength.

My relation to "her" [9]

August 24, 1849. Infandum me jubes, Regina, renovare dolorem [10]
Regina Olsen—I saw her first at the Rørdams. I really saw her there before, at a time when I did not know her family. . . .
Even before my father died I had decided upon her. He died (Aug. 9, 1838). I read for my examination. During the whole of that time I let her being penetrate mine.
In the summer of 1840 I took my theological examination.
Without further ceremony I thereupon called at their house. I went to Jutland and perhaps even at that time I was fishing for her, e.g. by lending them books in my absence and by suggesting that they should read certain passages.
In August I returned. The period from August 9 till the beginning of September I used in the strict sense to approach her.

[7] The reconciliation of opposites, the principle on which Hegel's system was founded.
[8] Cf. pp. 270–281.
[9] This account was sent to Regina Olsen on S.K.'s death, together with all the papers relating to their engagement. They were edited under her supervision, but not published until after her death, by Raphael Meyer in 1904 under the title *Kierkegaardske Papirer: Forlovelsen.*
[10] "Thou biddest me, Regina, renew the unspeakable grief." This sentence in purest Latin style is a good illustration of S.K.'s classical propensities, even in a highly personal document of this sort.

On September 8 I left my house with the firm purpose of deciding the matter. We met each other in the street outside their house. She said there was nobody at home. I was foolhardly enough to look upon that as an invitation, just the opportunity I wanted. I went in with her. We stood alone in the living room. She was a little uneasy. I asked her to play me something as she usually did. She did so; but that did not help me. Then suddenly I took the music away and closed it, not without a certain violence, threw it down on the piano and said: "Oh, what do I care about music now! It is you I am searching for, it is you whom I have sought after for two years." She was silent. I did nothing else to make an impression upon her; I even warned her against myself, against my melancholy. When, however, she spoke about Schlegel[11] I said, "Let that relationship be a parenthesis; after all the priority is mine." (N.B. It was only on the 10th that she spoke of Schlegel; on the 8th she did not say a word.)

She remained quite silent. At last I left, for I was anxious lest someone should come and find both of us, and she so disturbed. I went immediately to Etatsraad Olsen.[12] I know that I was terribly concerned that I had made too great an impression upon her. I also feared that my visit might lead to a misunderstanding and even hurt her reputation.

Her father said neither yes nor no, but he was willing enough, as I could see. I asked for a meeting: it was granted to me for the afternoon of the 10th. I did not say a single word to persuade her. She said, Yes.

I immediately assumed a relation to the whole family, and turned all my virtuosity upon her father whom, moreover, I have always loved.

But inwardly, the next day I saw that I had made a false step. A penitent such as I was, my *vita ante acta*,[13] my melancholy, that was enough.

I suffered unspeakably at that time.

She seemed to notice nothing. On the contrary her spirits were so high that once she said she had accepted me out of pity. In short, I have never known such high spirits.

In one sense that was the danger. If she does not take it more to heart, I thought, than her own words betray: "if she thought I only came from force of habit she would break off the engagement at once"; if she does not take it more to heart, then I am saved. I pulled myself

---

[11] The man Regina married eventually.
[12] "State Councillor" Olsen, Regina's father.
[13] "My past life."

together again. In another sense I must admit my weakness, that for a moment she vexed me.

Then I sent my whole strength to work—she seriously gave way and precisely the opposite happened, she gave herself unreservedly to me, she worshiped me. To a certain extent I myself bear the guilt of that. While I perceived the difficulty of the position only too clearly, and recognized that I must use the maximum of strength in order if possible to burst through my melancholy, I had said to her: "Surrender to me; your pride makes everything easier for me." A perfectly true word; honest towards her, melancholy and treacherous towards myself.[14]

And now of course my melancholy awoke once more. Her devotion once again put the whole "responsibility" upon me on a tremendous scale, whereas her pride had almost made me free from "responsibility." My opinion is, and my thought was, that it was God's punishment upon me.

I cannot decide clearly what purely emotional impression she made upon me. One thing is certain: that she gave herself to me, almost worshiping me, asking me to love her, which moved me to such an extent that I was willing to risk all for her. How much I loved her is shown by the fact that I always tried to hide from myself how much she had moved me, which however really has no relation to the passions. If I had not been a penitent, had not had my *vita ante acta,* had not been melancholy, my union with her would have made me happier than I had ever dreamed of being. But insofar as I was what, alas, I was, I had to say that I could be happier in my unhappiness without her than with her; she had moved me and I would have liked, more than liked, to have done everything.

But there was a divine protest, that is how I understood it. The wedding. I had to hide such a tremendous amount from her, had to base the whole thing upon something untrue.

I wrote to her and sent her back the ring. The letter is to be found word for word in the "psychological experiment."[15] With all my strength I allowed that to become purely historical; for I spoke to no one of it, not to a single man; I who am more silent than the grave. Should the book come into her hands I wanted her to be reminded of it.

[14] To some extent she suspected my condition, for she often answered: "You are never happy; and so it is all one to you whether I remain with you or not." She also once said to me that she would never ask me about anything if only she might remain with me. (K)

[15] A part of the *Stages* by Frater Taciturnitus.

What did she do? In her womanly despair she overstepped the boundary. She evidently knew that I was melancholy; she intended that anxiety should drive me to extremes. The reverse happened. She certainly brought me to the point at which anxiety drove me to extremes; but then with gigantic strength I constrained my whole nature so as to repel her. There was only one thing to do and that was to repel her with all my powers.

During those two months of deceit I observed a careful caution in what I said directly to her from time to time: "Give in, let me go; you cannot bear it." Thereupon she answered passionately that she would bear anything rather than let me go.

I also suggested giving the appearance that it was she who broke off the engagement, so that she might be spared all offense. That she would not have. She answered: if she could bear the other she could bear this too. And not unsocratically she said: In her presence no one would let anything be noticed and what people said in her absence remained a matter of indifference.

It was a time of terrible suffering: to have to be so cruel and at the same time to love as I did. She fought like a tigress. If I had not believed that God had lodged a veto she would have been victorious.

And so about two months later it broke. She grew desperate. For the first time in my life I scolded. It was the only thing to do.

When I left her I went immediately to the Theater because I wanted to meet Emil Boesen. (That gave rise to what was then said in Copenhagen, that I had looked at my watch and said to the family that if they had anything more in their minds would they please hurry up as I had to go to the theater.) The act was finished. As I left the stalls Etatsraad Olsen came up to me and said, "May I speak to you?" We went together to his house. "It will be her death, she is in absolute despair." I said, "I shall calm her down; but everything is settled." He said, "I am a proud man and I find it difficult to say, but I beg you, do not break with her." He was indeed a noble-hearted man; I was deeply moved. But I did not let myself be persuaded. I remained with the family to dinner. I spoke to her as I left. The following morning I received a letter from him saying she had not slept all night, and asking me to go and see her. I went and tried to persuade her. She asked me: "Are you never going to marry?" I answered, "Yes, perhaps in ten years' time when I have sown my wild oats; then I shall need some young blood to rejuvenate me." That was a necessary cruelty. Then she said, "Forgive me for the pain I have caused you." I answered: "It is for me to ask forgiveness." She said: "Promise to think of me." I did so. "Kiss me," she said. I did so, but without passion. Merciful God!

And so we parted. I spent the whole night crying on my bed. But the next day I behaved as usual, wittier and in better spirits than ever. That was necessary. My brother told me he wanted to go to the family and show them that I was not a scoundrel. "If you do, I will put a bullet through your head," which is the best proof of how deeply concerned I was.[16] I went to Berlin. I suffered greatly. I thought of her every day. Until now I have kept my promise and have prayed for her at least once and often twice a day, in addition to the other times I might think about her.

When the bonds were broken my thoughts were these: either you throw yourself into the wildest kind of life—or else become absolutely religious, but it will be different from the parson's mixture. . . .

1842

Disjecta Membra

May, 1842. . . . And it was the delight of his eyes and his heart's desire. And he stretched forth his hand and took hold of it, but he could not retain it; it was offered to him, but he could not possess it alas, for it was the delight of his eyes and his heart's desire. And his soul was near to despair; but he chose the greater suffering, of losing it and giving it up, to the lesser, which was to possess it without right; or to speak more truly . . . he chose the lesser suffering of being without it rather than to possess it at the cost of his peace of soul . . . and strange to relate, it came to pass that it was for his good.

[16] In a letter to Emil Boesen forbidding him to contradict the malicious stories being circulated about the engagement, S.K. refers to the above episode.

EITHER/OR: A FRAGMENT OF LIFE

PUBLISHED BY VICTOR EREMITA (1843)

TRANSLATED BY DAVID F. SWENSON, LILLIAN MARVIN SWENSON, AND WALTER LOWRIE

There are many people who reach their conclusions about life like schoolboys: they cheat their master by copying the answer out of a book without having worked the sum out for themselves.

A man who cannot seduce men cannot save them either.—THE JOURNALS

As WE HAVE SEEN (*supra*, p. 18), S.K. took refuge in Berlin after the breaking off of his engagement to Regina. Here he attended Schelling's anti-Hegelian lectures, patronized the theater, and worked diligently on a strange, enigmatic book which, though published under a pseudonym, was eventually to make him famous. Actually he had begun the book in Copenhagen, while he was still engaged to Regina but had already determined to give her up. Under these poignant circumstances he produced "The Aesthetic Validity of Marriage" in Vol. ii; in Berlin he wrote the long essay on "Equilibrium," and after returning to Copenhagen turned out the papers of the Aestheticist in Vol. i (save for a few fragments which were already in existence). The whole prodigious work was put on paper in about eleven months.

The title of the book, says Lowrie, "in a certain sense is more important" than the book itself. "It became the name by which S.K. was commonly known to the man in the street. It represented in fact precisely what he stood for: a decisive choice between practical alternatives" (*Short Life of Kierkegaard*, p. 151). "Either/Or" was S.K.'s answer to Hegel's concept of "mediation," i.e. the preservation of contradictory ideas—"thesis" and "antithesis" —in a "synthesis" which includes and somehow reconciles them both. For this principle of "both—and" Kierkegaard had already acquired an unyielding hatred. In a rhetorical moment he exclaims, "Either/or is the word at which the folding doors fly open and the ideals appear—O blessed sight! Either/or is the pass which admits to the absolute—God be praised! Yea, either/or is the key to heaven." . . . "Both—and is the way to hell."

Because the alternatives it presents—the life of calculated enjoyment and the life of self-realization through moral decision—are left strictly such, *Either/Or* brings into prominence "that form of communication which Kierkegaard erected into a category, namely 'indirect' communication." In this form "the reader is asked a question, not furnished with an answer. . . . The ethicist is not decked out with a superior dialectical skill" (as in Plato's dialogues); "on the contrary, the aestheticist appears to be unquestionably the more brilliant mind. . . . Hence it becomes clearer precisely in what the ethicist differs from the aestheticist, namely in the quality of his pathos and in his more calm and secure assurance with respect to the problems of life; a moral and existential superiority is not confused with a merely intellectual giftedness; the choice offered becomes a choice of character, not of brains" (Swenson, Introduction to the *Philosophical Fragments*, pp. xvi–xvii). A hint, however, of the direction in which the author looks for a solution of the problem is provided by the concluding section of the book, a sermon by a country parson, a friend of Judge William's, on "The Edification Implied in the Thought that as against God We Are Always in the Wrong."

If, as Matthew Arnold put it, morality is three-fourths of life and sex one-half of morality, the contents of *Either/Or* are justly proportioned. Vol. 1, containing the papers of "A," the aestheticist, opens with a group of aphorisms (Diapsalmata) in which the theme of despair is prominent, and continues with essays on "The Immediate Stages of the Erotic, or the Musical Erotic" (in which Kierkegaard's enthusiasm for Mozart is given an outlet) and "The Ancient Tragical Motive as Reflected in the Modern"; "Shadowgraphs," a psychological study of certain heroines of reflective grief (Marie Beaumarchais, Donna Elvira, Margaret in *Faust*); "The Unhappiest Man," an oration; a review of Scribe's comedy, "The First Love"; "The Rotation Method," a super-sophisticated study in applied hedonism; and finally the renowned "Diary of the Seducer," a condensation of which is here reproduced.

This Diary is not to be taken as autobiographical, Kierkegaard's own sex experience (aside of course from the Regina episode) having been, in all probability, of a grosser and more commonplace variety. (See Lowrie's *Kierkegaard*, p. 132.) In a sense "A" is Kierkegaard, or one aspect of him; the author of the Diary, however, is not "A" (who merely edits it), but "Johannes the Seducer," whom we shall meet again in the *Stages on Life's Way*. Johannes could pretty well qualify as the most ultra-refined "wolf" in all literature. The reality, to him, is little or nothing; what matters is "always to have the *idea* on one's side" and to make of the moment "a little eternity," completely self-contained. Like all hedonists, he aims so to order things that his experience of them is enhanced and sharpened to the uttermost. "Everything must be savored in slow draughts" and so he "squanders his opportunities on a frightful scale," deliberately remaining at the *schwärmerisch* stage for weeks. His knowledge of women is amazing (though debatable), but he is no less an artist than a psychologist, and once the stage has been carefully set, the consummation follows with telling swiftness.

After the somewhat "hectic eloquence" of the Diary, Judge William's letters (addressed to his "young friend," i.e. "A") come as a not unwelcome contrast. The Judge is no Puritan, and his sense of humor, if more rarely exhibited, is at least as great as "A's"; but above all he is ethically sound, and he tries to show "A" the error of his ways. The first letter, with its interesting analysis of romantic love, is an able attack on "the love-is-heaven-but-marriage-is-hell school of thought," which both "A" and Johannes represent in different degrees. The second letter is a more general treatment of the ethical problem from the standpoint of the centrality of *choice* or decision. "Here there is unfolded an ethic somewhat in the Kantian spirit, except that the rigid separation of duty from inclination is corrected, and that the abstract formalism . . . of Kant is replaced by a rich concreteness. Judge William is not so much the theorist unfolding a doctrine, as he is a mature personality attempting to help and influence a friend" (Swenson, *op. cit.*, p. xv). Here also is the first formulation of many a theme which will reappear, elaborated or transformed, in S.K.'s later writings (e.g. the idea of self-acceptance and of the ethical primacy of the will). The letters of Judge William (especially the second) would be enough to prove Kierkegaard's boldness and originality as a thinker, but these letters are far from being his last word on any of the subjects represented.

VOL. I:

THE ROTATION METHOD

AN ESSAY IN THE THEORY OF SOCIAL PRUDENCE

Chremylos: You get too much at last of everything.
　　　　　Of love,
Karion: 　　　of bread,
Chremylos: 　　　　　of music,
Karion: 　　　　　　　and of sweetmeats.
Chremylos: Of honor,
Karion: 　　　cakes,
Chremylos: 　　　　　of courage,
Karion: 　　　　　　　and of figs.
Chremylos: Ambition,
Karion: 　　　barley-cakes,
Chremylos: 　　　high office,
Karion: 　　　　　lentils.

(Aristophanes' *Plutus, v. 189ff.*)

STARTING from a principle is affirmed by people of experience to be a very reasonable procedure; I am willing to humor them, and so begin with the principle that all men are bores. Surely no one will prove himself so great a bore as to contradict me in this. This principle possesses the quality of being in the highest degree repellent, an essential requirement in the case of negative principles, which are in the last analysis the principles of all motion. It is not merely repellent, but infinitely forbidding; and whoever has this principle back of him cannot but receive an infinite impetus forward, to help him make new discoveries. For if my principle is true, one need only consider how ruinous boredom is for humanity, and by properly adjusting the intensity of one's concentration upon this fundamental truth, attain any desired degree of momentum. Should one wish to attain the maximum momentum, even to the point of almost endangering the driving power, one need only say to oneself: Boredom is the root of all evil. Strange that boredom, in itself so staid and stolid, should have such power to set in motion. The influence it exerts is altogether magical, except that it is not the influence of attraction, but of repulsion.

In the case of children, the ruinous character of boredom is universally acknowledged. Children are always well-behaved as long as they are enjoying themselves. This is true in the strictest sense; for if they sometimes become unruly in their play, it is because they are already beginning to be bored—boredom is already approaching, though from a different direction. In choosing a governess, one therefore takes into account not only her sobriety, her faithfulness, and her competence, but also her aesthetic qualifications for amusing the children; and there would be no hesitancy in dismissing a governess who was lacking in this respect, even if she had all the other desirable virtues. Here, then, the principle is clearly acknowledged; but so strange is the way of the world, so pervasive the influence of habit and boredom, that this is practically the only case in which the science of aesthetics receives its just dues. If one were to ask for a divorce because his wife was tiresome, or demand the abdication of a king because he was boring to look at, or the banishment of a preacher because he was tiresome to listen to, or the dismissal of a prime minister, or the execution of a journalist, because he was terribly tiresome, one would find it impossible to force it through. What wonder, then, that the world goes from bad to worse, and that its evils increase more and more, as boredom increases, and boredom is the root of all evil.

The history of this can be traced from the very beginning of the world. The gods were bored, and so they created man. Adam was bored because he was alone, and so Eve was created. Thus boredom entered the world, and increased in proportion to the increase of population.

Adam was bored alone; then Adam and Eve were bored together; then Adam and Eve and Cain and Abel were bored *en famille;* then the population of the world increased, and the peoples were bored *en masse.* To divert themselves they conceived the idea of constructing a tower high enough to reach the heavens. This idea is itself as boring as the tower was high, and constitutes a terrible proof of how boredom gained the upper hand. The nations were scattered over the earth, just as people now travel abroad, but they continued to be bored. Consider the consequences of this boredom. Humanity fell from its lofty height, first because of Eve, and then from the Tower of Babel. What was it, on the other hand, that delayed the fall of Rome, was it not *panis* and *circenses?* [1] And is anything being done now? Is anyone concerned about planning some means of diversion? Quite the contrary, the impending ruin is being proclaimed. It is proposed to call a constitutional assembly. Can anything more tiresome be imagined, both for the participants themselves, and for those who have to hear and read about it? It is proposed to improve the financial condition of the state by practicing economy. What could be more tiresome? Instead of increasing the national debt, it is proposed to pay if off. As I understand the political situation, it would be an easy matter for Denmark to negotiate a loan of fifteen million dollars. Why not consider this plan? Every once in a while we hear of a man who is a genius, and therefore neglects to pay his debts—why should not a nation do the same, if we were all agreed? Let us then borrow fifteen millions, and let us use the proceeds, not to pay our debts, but for public entertainment. Let us celebrate the millennium in a riot of merriment. Let us place boxes everywhere, not, as at present, for the deposit of money, but for the free distribution of money. Everything would become gratis; theaters gratis, women of easy virtue gratis, one would drive to the park gratis, be buried gratis, one's eulogy would be gratis; I say gratis, for when one always has money at hand, everything is in a certain sense free. No one should be permitted to own any property. Only in my own case would there be an exception. I reserve to myself securities in the Bank of London to the value of one hundred dollars a day, partly because I cannot do with less, partly because the idea is mine, and finally because I may not be able to hit upon a new idea when the fifteen millions are gone. . . .

All men are bores. The word itself suggests the possibility of a subdivision. It may just as well indicate a man who bores others as one who bores himself. Those who bore others are the mob, the crowd, the in-

[1] Bread and circuses.

finite multitude of men in general. Those who bore themselves are the elect, the aristocracy; and it is a curious fact that those who do not bore themselves usually bore others, while those who bore themselves entertain others. Those who do not bore themselves are generally people who, in one way or another, keep themselves extremely busy; these people are precisely on this account the most tiresome, the most utterly unendurable. This species of animal life is surely not the fruit of man's desire and woman's lust. Like all lower forms of life, it is marked by a high degree of fertility, and multiplies endlessly. It is inconceivable that nature should require nine months to produce such beings; they ought rather to be turned out by the score. The second class, the aristocrats, are those who bore themselves. As noted above, they generally entertain others—in a certain external sense sometimes the mob, in a deeper sense only their fellow initiates. The more profoundly they bore themselves, the more powerfully do they serve to divert these latter, even when their boredom reaches its zenith, as when they either die (passive form), or shoot themselves out of curiosity (the active form).

It is usual to say that idleness is a root of all evil. To prevent this evil one is advised to work. However, it is easy to see, both from the nature of the evil that is feared and the remedy proposed, that this entire view is of a very plebeian extraction. Idleness is by no means as such a root of evil; on the contrary, it is a truly divine life, provided one is not himself bored. Idleness may indeed cause the·loss of one's fortune, and so on, but the high-minded man does not fear such dangers; he fears only boredom. The Olympian gods were not bored, they lived happily in happy idleness. A beautiful woman, who neither sews nor spins nor bakes nor reads nor plays the piano, is happy in her idleness, for she is not bored. So far from idleness being the root of all evil, it is rather the only true good. Boredom is the root of all evil, and it is this which must be kept at a distance. Idleness is not an evil, indeed one may say that every human being who lacks a sense for idleness proves that his consciousness has not yet been elevated to the level of the humane. There is a restless activity which excludes a man from the world of the spirit, setting him in a class with the brutes, whose instincts impel them always to be on the move. There are men who have an extraordinary talent for transforming everything into a matter of business, whose whole life is business, who fall in love, marry, listen to a joke, and admire a picture with the same industrious zeal with which they labor during business hours. The Latin proverb, *otium est pulvinar diaboli,*[2] is true enough, but the

[2] "Idleness is the devil's pillow."

devil gets no time to lay his head on this pillow when one is not bored. But since some people believe that the end and aim of life is work, the disjunction, idleness-work, is quite correct. I assume that it is the end and aim of every man to enjoy himself, and hence my disjunction is no less correct. . . .

Now since boredom, as shown above, is the root of all evil, what can be more natural than the effort to overcome it? Here, as everywhere, however, it is necessary to give the problem calm consideration; otherwise one may find oneself driven by the demoniac spirit of boredom deeper and deeper into the mire, in the very effort to escape. Everyone who feels bored cries out for change. With this demand I am in complete sympathy, but it is necessary to act in accordance with some settled principle.

My own dissent from the ordinary view is sufficiently expressed in the use I make of the word "rotation." This word might seem to conceal an ambiguity, and if I wished to use it so as to find room in it for the ordinary method, I should have to define it as a change of field. But the farmer does not use the word in this sense. I shall, however, adopt this meaning for a moment, in order to speak of the rotation which depends on change in its boundless infinity, its extensive dimension, so to speak.

This is the vulgar and inartistic method, and needs to be supported by illusion. One tires of living in the country, and moves to the city; one tires of one's native land, and travels abroad; one is *europamüde,* and goes to America, and so on; finally one indulges in a sentimental hope of endless journeyings from star to star. Or the movement is different but still extensive. One tires of porcelain dishes and eats on silver; one tires of silver and turns to gold; one burns half of Rome to get an idea of the burning of Troy. This method defeats itself; it is plain endlessness. And what did Nero gain by it? Antonine was wiser; he says: "It is in your power to review your life, to look at things you saw before, but from another point of view."

My method does not consist in change of field, but resembles the true rotation method in changing the crop and the mode of cultivation. Here we have at once the principle of limitation, the only saving principle in the world. The more you limit yourself, the more fertile you become in invention. A prisoner in solitary confinement for life becomes very inventive, and a spider may furnish him with much entertainment. One need only hark back to one's schooldays, when aesthetic considerations were ignored in the choice of one's instructors, who were consequently very tiresome: how fertile in invention did not one prove to be! How entertaining to catch a fly and hold it imprisoned under a nut shell, watching it run around the shell; what pleasure, from cutting a hole in the desk, putting a fly in it, and then peeping down at it through a piece of paper! How entertaining sometimes to listen to the monotonous drip of water from the roof! How close an observer does not one become under such circumstances, when not the least noise nor movement escapes one's attention! Here we have the extreme application of the method which seeks to achieve results intensively, not extensively.

The more resourceful in changing the mode of cultivation one can be, the better; but every particular change will always come under the general categories of *remembering* and *forgetting*. Life in its entirety moves in these two currents, and hence it is essential to have them under control. It is impossible to live artistically before one has made up one's mind to abandon hope; for hope precludes self-limitation. It is a very beautiful sight to see a man put out to sea with the fair wind of hope, and one may even use the opportunity to be taken in tow; but one should never permit hope to be taken aboard one's own ship, least of all as a pilot; for hope is a faithless shipmaster. Hope was one of the dubious gifts of Prometheus; instead of giving men the foreknowledge of the immortals, he gave them hope.

To forget—all men wish to forget, and when something unpleasant happens, they always say: Oh, that one might forget! But forgetting is an art that must be practiced beforehand. The ability to forget is conditioned upon the method of remembering, but this again depends upon the mode of experiencing. Whoever plunges into his experiences with the momentum of hope, will remember so that he cannot forget. *Nil admirari* [3] is therefore the real philosophy. No moment must be permitted a greater significance than that it can be forgotten when convenient; each moment ought, however, to have so much significance that it can be recollected at will. Childhood, which is the age which remembers best, is at the same time most forgetful. The more poetically one remembers, the easier one forgets; for remembering poetically is really only another expression for forgetting. In a poetic memory the experience has undergone a transformation, by which it has lost all its painful aspects. To remember in this manner, one must be careful how one lives, how one enjoys. Enjoying an experience to its full intensity to the last minute will make it impossible either to remember or to forget.

[3] To wonder at nothing.

For there is then nothing to remember except a certain satiety, which one desires to forget, but which now comes back to plague the mind with an involuntary remembrance. Hence, when you begin to notice that a certain pleasure or experience is acquiring too strong a hold upon the mind, you stop a moment for the purpose of remembering. No other method can better create a distaste for continuing the experience too long. From the beginning one should keep the enjoyment under control, never spreading every sail to the wind in any resolve; one ought to devote oneself to pleasure with a certain suspicion, a certain wariness, if one desires to give the lie to the proverb which says that no one can have his cake and eat it too. The carrying of concealed weapons is usually forbidden, but no weapon is so dangerous as the art of remembering. It gives one a very peculiar feeling in the midst of one's enjoyment to look back upon it for the purpose of remembering it.

One who has perfected himself in the twin arts of remembering and forgetting is in a position to play at battledore and shuttlecock with the whole of existence.

The extent of one's power to forget is the final measure of one's elasticity of spirit. If a man cannot forget he will never amount to much. Whether there be somewhere a Lethe gushing forth, I do not know; but this I know, that the art of forgetting can be developed. However, this art does not consist in permitting the impressions to vanish completely; forgetfulness is one thing, and the art of forgetting is something quite different. It is easy to see that most people have a very meager understanding of this art, for they ordinarily wish to forget only what is unpleasant, not what is pleasant. This betrays a complete one-sidedness. Forgetting is the true expression for an ideal process of assimilation by which the experience is reduced to a sounding-board for the soul's own music. Nature is great because it has forgotten that it was chaos; but this thought is subject to revival at any time. As a result of attempting to forget only what is unpleasant, most people have a conception of oblivion as an untameable force which drowns out the past. But forgetting is really a tranquil and quiet occupation, and one which should be exercised quite as much in connection with the pleasant as with the unpleasant. A pleasant experience has as past something unpleasant about it, by which it stirs a sense of privation; this unpleasantness is taken away by an act of forgetfulness. The unpleasant has a sting, as all admit. This, too, can be removed by the art of forgetting. But if one attempts to dismiss the unpleasant absolutely from mind, as many do who dabble in the art of forgetting, one soon learns how little that helps. In an unguarded moment it pays a surprise visit, and it is then invested with all the forcibleness of the unexpected. This is absolutely contrary to every orderly arrangement in a reasonable mind. No misfortune or difficulty is so devoid of affability, so deaf to all appeals, but that it may be flattered a little; even Cerberus accepted bribes of honey-cakes, and it is not only the lassies who are beguiled. The art in dealing with such experiences consists in talking them over, thereby depriving them of their bitterness; not forgetting them absolutely, but forgetting them for the sake of remembering them. Even in the case of memories such that one might suppose an eternal oblivion to be the only safeguard, one need permit oneself only a little trickery, and the deception will succeed for the skillful. Forgetting is the shears with which you cut away what you cannot use, doing it under the supreme direction of memory. Forgetting and remembering are thus identical arts, and the artistic achievement of this identity is the Archimedean point from which one lifts the whole world. When we say that we *consign* something to oblivion, we suggest simultaneously that it is to be forgotten and yet also remembered.

The art of remembering and forgetting will also insure against sticking fast in some relationship of life, and make possible the realization of a complete freedom.

One must guard against *friendship*. How is a friend defined? He is not what philosophy calls the necessary other, but the superfluous third. What are friendship's ceremonies? You drink each other's health, you open an artery and mingle your blood with that of the friend. It is difficult to say when the proper moment for this arrives, but it announces itself mysteriously; you feel some way that you can no longer address one another formally. When once you have had this feeling, then it can never appear that you have made a mistake, like Geert Westphaler,[4] who discovered that he had been drinking to friendship with the public hangman. What are the infallible marks of friendship? Let antiquity answer: *idem velle, idem nolle, ea demum firma amicitia,*[5] and also extremely tiresome. What are the infallible marks of friendship? Mutual assistance in word and deed. Two friends form a close association in order to be everything to one another, and that although it is impossible for one human being to be anything to another human being except to be in his way. To be sure one may help him with money,

---

[4] In Holberg's comedy of that name. (L)

[5] "To wish and not to wish the same thing—this at last is firm friendship."

assist him in and out of his coat, be his humble servant, and tender him congratulations on New Year's Day, on the day of his wedding, on the birth of a child, on the occasion of a funeral.

But because you abstain from friendship it does not follow that you abstain from social contacts. On the contrary, these social relationships may at times be permitted to take on a deeper character, provided you always have so much more momentum in yourself that you can sheer off at will, in spite of sharing for a time in the momentum of the common movement. It is believed that such conduct leaves unpleasant memories, the unpleasantness being due to the fact that a relationship which has meant something now vanishes and becomes as nothing. But this is a misunderstanding. The unpleasant is merely a piquant ingredient in the dullness of life. Besides, it is possible for the same relationship again to play a significant role, though in another manner. The essential thing is never to stick fast, and for this it is necessary to have oblivion back of one. The experienced farmer lets his land lie fallow now and then, and the theory of social prudence recommends the same. Everything will doubtless return, though in a different form; that which has once been present in the rotation will remain in it, but the mode of cultivation will be varied. You therefore quite consistently hope to meet your friends and acquaintances in a better world, but you do not share the fear of the crowd that they will be altered so that you cannot recognize them; your fear is rather lest they be wholly unaltered. It is remarkable how much significance even the most insignificant person can gain from a rational mode of cultivation.

One must never enter into the relation of *marriage*. Husband and wife promise to love one another for eternity. This is all very fine, but it does not mean very much; for if their love comes to an end in time, it will surely be ended in eternity. If, instead of promising forever, the parties would say until Easter, or until May-day comes, there might be some meaning in what they say; for then they would have said something definite, and also something that they might be able to keep. And how does a marriage usually work out? In a little while one party begins to perceive that there is something wrong, then the other party complains and cries to heaven: faithless! faithless! A little later the second party reaches the same standpoint, and a neutrality is established in which the mutual faithlessness is mutually cancelled, to the satisfaction and contentment of both parties. But it is now too late, for there are great difficulties connected with divorces.

Such being the case with marriage, it is not surprising that the attempt should be made in so many ways to bolster it up with moral supports. When a man seeks separation from his wife, the cry is at once raised that he is depraved, a scoundrel, etc. How silly, and what an indirect attack upon marriage! If marriage has reality, then he is sufficiently punished by forfeiting this happiness; if it has no reality, it is absurd to abuse him because he is wiser than the rest. When a man grows tired of his money and throws it out the window, we do not call him a scoundrel; for either money has reality, and so he is sufficiently punished by depriving himself of it, or it has none, and then he is, of course, a wise man.

One must always take care not to enter into any relationship in which there is a possibility of many members. For this reason friendship is dangerous, to say nothing of marriage. Husband and wife are indeed said to become one, but this is a very dark and mystic saying. When you are one of several, then you have lost your freedom; you cannot send for your traveling boots whenever you wish, you cannot move aimlessly about in the world. If you have a wife and perhaps a child, it is troublesome; if you have a wife and children, it is impossible. True, it has happened that a gypsy woman has carried her husband through life on her back, but for one thing this is very rare, and for another, it is likely to be tiresome in the long run—for the husband. Marriage brings one into fatal connection with custom and tradition, and traditions and customs are like the wind and weather, altogether incalculable. In Japan, I have been told, it is the custom for husbands to lie in childbed. Who knows but the time will come when the customs of foreign countries will obtain a foothold in Europe?

Friendship is dangerous, marriage still more so; for woman is and ever will be the ruin of a man, as soon as he contracts a permanent relation with her. Take a young man who is fiery as an Arabian courser; let him marry, he is lost. Woman is first proud, then she is weak, then she swoons, then he swoons, then the whole family swoons. A woman's love is nothing but dissimulation and weakness.

But because a man does not marry, it does not follow that his life need be wholly deprived of the erotic element. And the erotic ought also to have infinitude; but poetic infinitude, which can just as well be limited to an hour as to a month. When two beings fall in love with one another and begin to suspect that they were made for each other, it is time to have the courage to break it off; for by going on they have everything to lose and nothing to gain. This seems a paradox, and it is so for the feeling, but not for the understanding. In this sphere it is particularly necessary that one should make use of one's moods; through them one may realize an inexhaustible variety of combinations.

One should never undertake any *business*. If you do, you will become a mere *Peter Flere,* a tiny little cog in the machinery of the body politic; you even cease to be master of your own conduct, and in that case your theories are of little help. You receive a title, and this brings in its train every sin and evil. The law under which you have become a slave is equally tiresome, whether your advancement is fast or slow. A title can never be got rid of except by the commission of some crime which draws down on you a public whipping; even then you are not certain, for you may have it restored to you by royal pardon.

Even if one does not engage in business, one ought not to be inactive, but should pursue such occupations as are compatible with a sort of leisure, one should engage in all sorts of breadless arts. In this connection the self-development should be intensive rather than extensive, and one should, in spite of mature years, be able to prove the truth of the proverb that children are pleased with a rattle and tickled with a straw.

If one now, according to the theory of social jurisprudence, varies the soil—for if he had contact with one person only, the rotation method would fail as badly as if a farmer had only one acre of land, which would make it impossible for him to fallow, something which is of extreme importance—then one must also constantly vary himself, and this is the essential secret. For this purpose one must necessarily have control over one's moods. To control them in the sense of producing them at will is impossible, but prudence teaches how to utilize the moment. As an experienced sailor always looks out over the water and sees a squall coming from far away, so one ought always to see the mood a little in advance. One should know how the mood affects one's own mind and the mind of others, before putting it on. You first strike a note or two before evoking the pure tones, and see what there is in a man, the middle tones follow later. The more experience you have, the more readily you will be convinced that there is often much in a man which is not suspected. When sentimental people, who as such are extremely tiresome, become angry, they are often very entertaining. Badgering a man is a particularly effective method of exploration.

The whole secret lies in arbitrariness. People usually think it easy to be arbitrary, but it requires much study to succeed in being arbitrary so as not to lose oneself in it, but so as to derive satisfaction from it. One does not enjoy the immediate, but rather something which he can arbitrarily control. You go to see the middle of a play, you read the third part of a book. By this means you insure yourself a very different kind of enjoyment from that which the author has been so kind as to plan for you. You enjoy something entirely accidental; you consider the whole of existence from this standpoint; let its reality be stranded thereon. I will cite an example. There was a man whose chatter certain circumstances made it necessary for me to listen to. At every opportunity he was ready with a little philosophical lecture, a very tiresome harangue. Almost in despair, I suddenly discovered that he perspired copiously when talking. I saw the pearls of sweat gather on his brow, unite to form a stream, glide down his nose, and hang at the extreme point of his nose in a drop-shaped body. From the moment of making this discovery, all was changed. I even took pleasure in inciting him to begin his philosophical instruction, merely to observe the perspiration on his brow and at the end of his nose.

The poet Baggesen says somewhere of someone that he was doubtless a good man, but that there was one insuperable objection against him, that there was no word that rhymed with his name. It is extremely wholesome thus to let the realities of life split upon an arbitrary interest. You transform something accidental into the absolute, and as such, into the object of your admiration. This has an excellent effect, especially when one is excited. This method is an excellent stimulus for many persons. You look at everything in life from the standpoint of a wager, and so forth. The more rigidly consistent you are in holding fast to your arbitrariness, the more amusing the ensuing combinations will be. The degree of consistency shows whether you are an artist or a bungler; for to a certain extent all men do the same. The eye with which you look at reality must constantly be changed. The Neo-Platonists assumed that human beings who had been less perfect on earth became after death more or less perfect animals, all according to their deserts. For example, those who had exercised the civic virtues on a lower scale (the men of detail) were transformed into busy animals, like bees. Such a view of life, which here in this world sees all men transformed into animals or plants (Plotinus also thought that some would become plants) suggests rich and varied possibilities. The painter Tischbein sought to idealize every human being into an animal. His method has the fault of being too serious, in that it endeavors to discover a real resemblance.

The arbitrariness in oneself corresponds to the accidental in the external world. One should therefore always have an eye open for the accidental, always be *expeditus* if anything should offer. The so-called social pleasures for which we prepare a week or two in advance amount to so little; on the other hand, even the most insignificant thing may accidentally offer rich material for amusement. It is impossible here to go into detail, for no theory can adequately embrace the concrete. Even the most completely developed theory is poverty-stricken compared with the fullness which the man of genius easily discovers in his ubiquity.

VOL. I:

DIAPSALMATA[1]

AD SE IPSUM

LET others complain that the age is wicked; my complaint is that it is wretched, for it lacks passion. Men's thoughts are thin and flimsy like lace, they are themselves pitiable like the lacemakers. The thoughts of their hearts are too paltry to be sinful. For a worm it might be regarded as a sin to harbor such thoughts, but not for a being made in the image of God. Their lusts are dull and sluggish, their passions sleepy. They do their duty, these shopkeeping souls, but they clip the coin a trifle, like the Jews; they think that even if the Lord keeps ever so careful a set of books, they may still cheat Him a little. Out upon them! This is the reason my soul always turns back to the Old Testament and to Shakespeare. I feel that those who speak there are at least human beings: they hate, they love, they murder their enemies, and curse their descendants throughout all generations, they sin.

These two familiar strains of the violin! These two familiar strains here at this moment, in the middle of the street. Have I lost my senses? Does my ear, which from love of Mozart's music has ceased to hear, create these sounds; have the gods given me, unhappy beggar at the door of the temple—have they given me an ear that makes the sounds it hears? Only two strains, now I hear nothing more. Just as they burst forth from the deep choral tones of the immortal overture,[2] so here they extricate themselves from the noise and confusion of the street, with all the surprise of a revelation.—It must be here in the neighborhood, for

---

[1] Διαψάλματα, musical interludes; *ad se ipsum*, to himself.
[2] The Overture to *Don Giovanni*.

now I hear the lighter tones of the dance music.—And so it is to you, unhappy artist pair, I owe this joy.—One of them was about seventeen, he wore a coat of green kalmuck, with large bone buttons. The coat was much too large for him. He held the violin close up under his chin, his hat was pressed down over his eyes, his hand was hidden in a glove without fingers, his fingers were red and blue from cold. The other man was older; he wore a chenille shawl. Both were blind. A little girl, presumably their guide, stood in front of them, her hands tucked under her neckerchief. We gradually gathered around them, some admirers of this music: a letter carrier with his mailbag, a little boy, a servant girl, a couple of roustabouts. The well appointed carriages rolled noisily by, the heavy wagons drowned out the strains, which by snatches flashed forth. Unhappy artist pair, do you know that these tones are an epitome of all the glories of the world?—How like a tryst it was!

The essence of pleasure does not lie in the thing enjoyed, but in the accompanying consciousness. If I had a humble spirit in my service, who, when I asked for a glass of water, brought me the world's costliest wines blended in a chalice, I should dismiss him, in order to teach him that pleasure consists not in what I enjoy, but in having my own way.

I feel as if I were a piece in a game of chess, when my opponent says of it: That piece cannot be moved.

My life is absolutely meaningless. When I consider the different periods into which it falls, it seems like the word *Schnur* in the dictionary, which means in the first place a string, in the second, a daughter-in-law. The only thing lacking is that the word *Schnur* should mean in the third place a camel, in the fourth, a dust-brush.

Wine can no longer make my heart glad; a little of it makes me sad, much makes melancholy. My soul is faint and impotent; in vain I prick the spur of pleasure into its flank, its strength is gone, it rises no more to the royal leap. I have lost my illusions. Vainly I seek to plunge myself into the boundless sea of joy; it cannot sustain me, or rather, I cannot sustain myself. Once pleasure had but to beckon me, and I rose, light of foot, sound and unafraid. When I rode slowly through the woods, it was as if I flew; now when the horse is covered with lather and ready to drop, it seems to me that I do not move. I am solitary as always; forsaken, not by men, which could not hurt me, but by the happy fairies of joy, who used to encircle me in countless multitudes, who met acquaintances everywhere, everywhere showed me an opportunity for pleasure. As an intoxicated man gathers a wild crowd of youths about him, so they flocked about me, the fairies of joy, and I greeted them with a smile. My soul has lost its potentiality. If I were to wish for anything, I should not wish for wealth and power, but for the passionate sense of the potential, for the eye which, ever young and ardent, sees the possible. Pleasure disappoints, possibility never. And what wine is so foaming, what so fragrant, what so intoxicating, as possibility!

Music finds its way where the rays of the sun cannot penetrate. My room is dark and dismal, a high wall almost excludes the light of day. The sounds must come from a neighboring yard; it is probably some wandering musician. What is the instrument? A flute? . . . What do I hear—the minuet from *Don Juan!* Carry me then away once more, O tones so rich and powerful, to the company of the maidens, to the pleasures of the dance.—The apothecary pounds his mortar, the kitchen maid scours her kettle, the groom curries the horse and strikes the comb against the flagstones; these tones appeal to me alone, they beckon only me. O! accept my thanks, whoever you are! My soul is so rich, so sound, so joy-intoxicated!

My grief is my castle, which like an eagle's nest is built high up on the mountain peaks among the clouds; nothing can storm it. From it I fly down into reality to seize my prey; but I do not remain down there, I bring it home with me, and this prey is a picture I weave into the tapestries of my palace. There I live as one dead. I immerse everything I have experienced in a baptism of forgetfulness unto an eternal remembrance. Everything finite and accidental is forgotten and erased. Then I sit like an old man, grey-haired and thoughtful, and explain the pictures in a voice as soft as a whisper; and at my side a child sits and listens, although he remembers everything before I tell it.

The sun shines into my room bright and beautiful, the window is open in the next room; on the street all is quiet, it is a Sunday afternoon. Outside the window, I clearly hear a lark pour forth its song in a neighbor's garden, where the pretty maiden lives. Far away in a distant street I hear a man crying shrimps. The air is so warm, and yet the whole town seems dead.—Then I think of my youth and of my first love— when the longing of desire was strong. Now I long only for my first longing. What is youth? A dream. What is love? The substance of a dream.

Something wonderful has happened to me. I was carried up into the seventh heaven. There all the gods sat assembled. By special grace I was granted the favor of a wish. "Will you," said Mercury, "have youth, or beauty, or power, or a long life, or the most beautiful maiden, or any of the other glories we have in the chest? Choose, but only one thing." For a moment I was at a loss. Then I addressed myself to the gods as follows: "Most honorable contemporaries, I choose this one thing, that I may always have the laugh on my side." Not one of the gods said a word, on the contrary, they all began to laugh. Hence I concluded that my request was granted, and found that the gods knew how to express themselves with taste; for it would hardly have been suitable for them to have answered gravely: "It is granted thee."

VOL. I:

DIARY OF THE SEDUCER

Sua passion' predominante
e la giovin principiante—
DON GIOVANNI, ARIA NO. 4[1]

April 4

CAUTION, my beautiful unknown! Caution! To step out of a carriage is not so simple a matter, sometimes it is a very decisive step. I might lend you a novel of Tieck's in which you would read about a lady who in dismounting from her horse involved herself in an entanglement such that this step became definitive for her whole life. The steps on carriages, too, are usually so badly arranged that one almost has to forget about being graceful and risk a desperate spring into the arms of coachman and footman. Really, coachmen and footmen have the best of it. I really believe I shall look for a job as footman in some house where there are young girls; a servant easily becomes acquainted with the secrets of a little maid like that.—But for heaven's sake, don't jump, I beg of you! To be sure, it is dark; I shall not disturb you; I only pause under this street lamp where it is impossible for you to see me, and one is never embarrassed unless one is seen, and of course if one cannot see, one cannot be seen. So out of regard for the servants who might not be

---

[1] "His ruling passion is the fresh young girls"—from the "Catalogue" aria of Leporello in *Don Giovanni*.

strong enough to catch you, out of regard for the silk dress with its lacy fringes, out of regard for me, let this dainty little foot, whose slenderness I have already admired, let it venture forth into the world, and dare to trust that it will find a footing. Should you tremble lest it should not find it, or should you tremble after it has done so, then follow it quickly with the other foot, for who would be so cruel as to leave you in that position, so ungracious, so slow in appreciating the revelation of beauty? Or do you fear some intruder, not the servants of course, nor me, for I have already seen the little foot, and since I am a natural scientist, I have learned from Cuvier [2] how to draw definite conclusions from such details. Therefore, hurry! How this anxiety enhances your beauty! Still anxiety in itself is not beautiful, it is so only when one sees at the same time the energy which overcomes it. Now! How firmly this little foot stands. I have noticed that girls with small feet generally stand more firmly than the more pedestrian large-footed ones.

Now who would have thought it? It is contrary to all experience; one does not run nearly so much risk of one's dress catching when one steps out of a carriage as when one jumps out. But then it is always risky for young girls to go riding in a carriage, lest they finally have to stay in it. The lace and ribbons are wasted, and the matter is over. No one has seen anything. To be sure a dark figure appears, wrapped to the eyes in a cloak. The light from the street lamp shines directly in your eyes, so you cannot see whence he came. He passes you just as you are entering the door. Just at the critical second, a side glance falls upon its object. You blush, your bosom becomes too full to relieve itself in a single sigh; there is exasperation in your glance, a proud contempt; there is a prayer, a tear in your eye, both are equally beautiful, and I accept both as my due; for I can just as well be the one thing as the other.

But I am still malicious—what is the number of the house? What do I see? A window display of trinkets. My beautiful unknown, perhaps it may be outrageous in me, but I follow the gleam. . . . She has forgotten the incident. Ah, yes, when one is seventeen years old, when at that happy age one goes shopping, when every object large or small that one handles gives one unspeakable pleasure, then one easily forgets. She has not even seen me. I am standing at the far end of the counter by myself. A mirror hangs on the opposite wall; she does not reflect on it, but the mirror reflects her. How faithfully it has caught her picture, like a humble slave who shows his devotion by his faithfulness, a slave for

[2] French scientist who affirmed that from a single bone the whole animal could be constructed. (S)

whom she indeed has significance, but who means nothing to her—who indeed dares to catch her, but not to embrace her. Unhappy mirror, that can indeed seize her image but not herself! Unhappy mirror, which cannot hide her image in its secret depths, hide it from the whole world, but on the contrary must betray it to others, as now to me. What agony, if men were made like that! And are there not many people who are like that, who own nothing except in the moment when they show it to others, who grasp only the surface, not the essence, who lose everything if this appears, just as this mirror would lose her image, were she by a single breath to betray her heart to it?

And if a man were not able to hold a picture in memory even when he is present, then he must always wish to be at a distance from beauty, not so near that the earthly eye cannot see how beautiful that is which he holds and which is lost to sight in his embrace. This beauty he can regain for the outward sight by putting it at a distance, but he may also keep it before the eyes of his soul, when he cannot see the object itself because it is too near, when lips are closed on lips.— Still, how beautiful she is! Poor mirror, it must be agony! It is well that you know no jealousy. Her head is a perfect oval, and she bends it a little forward, which makes her forehead seem higher, as it rises pure and proud, with no external evidence of intellectual faculties. Her dark hair wreathes itself softly and gently about her temples. Her face is like a fruit, every plane fully rounded. Her skin is transparent, like velvet to the touch, I can feel that with my eyes. Her eyes—well, I have not even seen them, they are hidden behind lids armed with silken fringes which curve up like hooks, dangerous to whoever meets her glance. Her head is a Madonna head, pure and innocent in cast; like a Madonna she is bending forward, but she is not lost in contemplation of the One. A variety of emotions finds expression in her countenance. What she considers is the manifold, the multitude of things over which worldly pomp and splendor cast their glamour. She pulls off her glove to show the mirror and myself a right hand, white and shapely as an antique, without adornment, and with no plain gold ring on her fourth finger. Good!— She looks up, and how changed everything is, and yet the same; the forehead seems lower, the oval of her face a little less regular, but more alive. She is talking now with the salesman, she is merry, joyous, chatty. She has already chosen two or three things, she picks up a fourth and holds it in her hand, again she looks down, she asks what it costs. She lays it to one side under her glove, it must be a secret, intended for—a lover?—But she is not engaged.—Alas, there are many who are not engaged and yet have a lover; many who are engaged, and who still do not have one. . . .

Ought I to give her up? Ought I to leave her undisturbed in her happiness?—She is about to pay, but she has lost her purse.—She probably mentions her address, I will not listen to it, for I do not wish to deprive myself of surprise; I shall certainly meet her again in life, I shall recognize her, and perhaps she will recognize me; one does not forget my side glance so easily. Her turn will come when I am surprised at meeting her in circles where I did not expect to. If she does not recognize me, if her glance does not immediately convince me of that, then I shall surely find an opportunity to look at her from the side, and I promise that she will remember the situation. No impatience, no greediness, everything should be enjoyed in leisurely draughts; she is pointed, she shall be run down.

5th day

I like that! Alone in the evening on Eastern Street! Yes, I see the footman is following you. Do not believe I think so ill of you as to think you would go out quite alone; do not believe that I am so inexperienced that in my survey of the situation I did not notice this sober figure. But why in such a hurry? You are still a little anxious, you can feel your heart beating; this is not because of an impatient longing to get home, but because of an impatient fear streaming through your entire body with its sweet unrest, and hence the swift rhythm of your feet.—But still it is a splendid, priceless experience to go out alone—with the footman behind. You are sixteen years old, you are a reader, that is to say, you read novels. You have accidentally in going through your brothers' room caught a word or two of a conversation between them and an acquaintance, something about Eastern Street. Later you whisked through several times, in order if possible to get a little more information. All in vain. One ought, it would seem, if one is a grown-up girl, to know a little something about the world. If without saying anything, one could only go out with the servant following. No, thank you. What kind of a face would Father and Mother make up, and, too, what excuse could one give? If one were going to a party, it would afford no opportunity, it would be a little too early, for I heard August say, between nine and ten o'clock. Going home it would be too late, and then one must usually have an escort to drag along with one. Thursday evening when we return from the theater would seem to offer a splendid opportunity, but then we always go in the carriage and have Mrs.

Thomsen and her worthy cousins packed in with us. If one ever had a chance to drive alone, then one could let down the window and look around a bit. Still, it is always the unexpected that happens. Today my mother said to me: "You have not yet finished your father's birthday present; to give you time to work undisturbed, you may go to your Aunt Jette's and stay until tea time, and I'll send Jens to fetch you!" It was really not a very pleasing suggestion, for Aunt Jette is very tiresome; but this way I shall be going home alone with the servant at nine o'clock. Then when Jens comes he will have to wait till a quarter of ten before leaving. Only I might meet my brother or August—that wouldn't be so good, for then I should probably be escorted home—Thanks, I prefer to be free—but if I could get my eye on them, so that they did not see me. . . .

Now, my little lady, what do you see, and what do you think I see? In the first place, the little cap you have on is very becoming, and quite harmonizes with the haste in your appearance. It is not a hat, neither is it a bonnet, but rather a kind of hood. But you cannot possibly have worn that when you went out this morning. Could the servant have brought it, or could you have borrowed it from your Aunt Jette?—Perhaps you are incognito.—You should not lower the veil completely if you are going to make observations. Or perhaps it is not a veil, but only a piece of lace. It is impossible to tell in the dark. Whatever it is, it conceals the upper part of your face. Your chin is really pretty, a little too pointed; your mouth is small, open a trifle—that is because you have gone so fast. Your teeth—white as snow. That is the way it should be, teeth are of the utmost importance; they are a life-guard, hiding behind the seductive softness of the lips. The cheeks glow with health. If one tips one's head a little to the side, it might be possible to get a glimpse under the veil or lace.

Look out! An upward glance like that is more dangerous than a direct one. It is as in fencing; and what weapon is so sharp, so penetrating, so flashing in action, and hence so deceptive, as the eye? You feint a high quart, as fencers say, and attack in second; the swifter the attack follows the feint, the better. The moment of the feint is indescribable. The opponent, as it were, feels the slash, he is touched! Aye, that is true, but in quite a different place from where he thought. . . . Indefatigable she goes on, without fear and without reproach. Look out! Yonder comes a man; lower your veil, let not his profane glance besmirch you. You have no idea—it will perhaps be impossible for you for a long time to forget the disgusting fear with which it touched you—you did not notice, as I did, that he had sized up the situation. Your servant is set upon as the nearest objective.—There, now you see the consequences of going out alone with a servant. The servant has fallen down. At bottom it is laughable, but what will you do now? That you should turn back and assist him in getting to his feet is impossible, to go on with a mud-stained servant is disagreeable, to go alone is dangerous. Look out! the monster approaches.—You do not answer me. Just look at me, is there anything about me to frighten you? I simply make no impression at all upon you. I seem to be a good-natured person from quite a different world. There is nothing in my speech to disturb you, nothing to remind you of the situation, no movement that in the least approaches too near you. You are still a little frightened, you have not yet forgotten the attempt of that sinister figure against you. You feel a certain kindliness toward me, the embarrassment that keeps me from looking directly at you makes you feel superior. It pleases you and makes you feel safe. You are almost tempted to poke a little fun at me. I wager that at this moment you would have the courage to take my arm, if it occurred to you.—So you live on Storm Street. You curtsy to me coldly and indifferently. Have I deserved this, I who rescued you from the whole unpleasantness? You regret your coldness, you turn back, thank me for my courtesy, offer me your hand—why do you turn pale? Is not my voice unchanged, my bearing the same, my glance as quiet and controlled? This handclasp? Can then a handclasp mean anything? Aye, much, very much, my little lady; within a fortnight I shall explain it all to you, until then you must rest in the contradiction that I am a good-natured man who, like a knight of old, came to the assistance of a young girl, and that I can also press her hand in a no less good-natured manner.

April 7

"All right! Monday at one o'clock at the Exhibition." Very well, I shall have the honor of appearing at a quarter to one. A little rendezvous. Last Saturday I finally put business aside, and decided to call upon my business friend, Adolph Bruun. Accordingly I set out about seven o'clock for Western Street where someone had told me he was living. However, I did not find him, not even on the third floor after I had puffed my way up. When I turned to go downstairs, my ear caught the sound of a musical feminine voice saying, "Then on Monday at one, at the Exhibition, when everybody is out, for you know I never dare to see you at home." The invitation was not for me, but for a young man who was out of the door in a jiffy, so fast that my eyes could not even follow him, to say nothing of my feet. Why do they not have light on stairways? Then I might perhaps have found out whether it would be worth while to be so punctual. Still, if there had been a light, I probably should not have heard anything. What *is* is rational,[3] and I am and remain an optimist. . . . Now which one is she? The place swarms with girls, to use Donna Anna's expression.[4] It is exactly a quarter to one. My beautiful unknown! I wish your intended were as punctual as I am, or perhaps you would rather not have him come fifteen minutes too early. As you will, I am at your service in every way. "Charming enchantress, witch or fairy, let your cloud vanish," reveal yourself; you are probably already here, but invisible to me; betray yourself, for otherwise I dare not expect a revelation. Could there perhaps be several here on a similar errand? Possibly so, for who knows the way of a man, even when he goes to an exhibition?—There comes a young girl through the front room, hurrying faster than a bad conscience after a sinner. She forgets to give up her ticket, the doorkeeper detains her. Heaven preserve us! Why is she in such a hurry? It must be she. Why such unseemly impetuosity? It is not yet one o'clock. Remember that was the time you were to meet your beloved. Are you on such occasions entirely indifferent as to how you look, or is it a case of putting your best foot forward? When such an innocent young damsel goes to a rendezvous, she goes about the matter like a madman. She is all of a flutter. Meanwhile I sit here comfortably in my chair and look at a delightful painting of a rural scene.

She is the child of the devil, the way she storms through all the rooms. You must learn to conceal your anxiety a little. Remember the advice given to the young Lisbed:[5] "Is it becoming for a young girl to show her feelings like that?" Now of course this meeting is an innocent one.—A rendezvous is generally regarded by lovers as a most beautiful moment. I even remember as clearly as if it were yesterday the first time I hastened to the appointed place, with a heart as true as it was ignorant of the joy that awaited me; the first time I knocked three times, the first time a window opened, the first time a little wicket gate was unfastened by the unseen hand of a girl who hid herself as she opened it; the first time I hid a girl under my cloak in the light summer night. There is still much illusion blended in this judgment. The re-

---

[3] A leading tenet of Hegelian philosophy.
[4] *Don Giovanni:* "There he comes, who always swarms with girls." (S)
[5] In Holberg's *Erasmus Montanus.* (S)

flective third party does not always find the lovers most beautiful at this moment. I have witnessed rendezvous where although the girl was charming and the man handsome, the total impression was almost disgusting, and the meeting itself was far from being beautiful, although I suppose it seemed so to the lovers. As one becomes more experienced, he gains in a way; for though one loses the sweet unrest of impatient longing, he gains ability in making the moment really beautiful. I am vexed when I see a man with such an opportunity, so upset that mere love gives him delirium tremens. It is caviar to the general. Instead of having enough discretion to enjoy her disquiet, to allow it to enhance and inflame her beauty, he only produces a wretched confusion, and yet he goes home joyously imagining it to have been a glorious experience.

But where the devil is the fellow? It is nearly two o'clock. He surely is a fine fellow, this lover! Such a scoundrel, to keep a lady waiting for him! Now I, on the contrary, am a very dependable man! It might indeed be best to speak to her as she now passes me for the fifth time. "Pardon my boldness, fair lady. You doubtless are looking for your family. You have hurried past me several times, and as my eyes followed you, I noticed that you always stop in the next room; perhaps you do not know that there is still another room beyond that, possibly you might find your friends there." She curtsied to me, a very becoming gesture. The occasion is favorable. I am glad the man has not come; one always fishes best in troubled waters. When a young girl is emotionally disturbed, one can successfully venture much which would otherwise be ill-advised. I bow to her as politely and distantly as possible; I sit back again in my chair, look at my landscape, and watch her out of the corner of my eye. To follow her immediately would be too risky; it might seem intrusive to her and put her on her guard. At present she believes that I addressed her out of sympathy, and I am in her good graces.—I know very well that there is not a soul in that inner room. Solitude will be beneficial to her. As long as she sees many people about, she is disturbed; when she is alone, she will relax. Quite right that she should stay in there. After a little I shall stroll by; I have earned a right to speak to her, she owes me at least a greeting.

She has sat down. Poor girl, she looks so sad, I believe she has been crying, at least she has tears in her eyes. It is outrageous—to make such a girl cry. But be calm, you shall be avenged, I will avenge you, he shall learn what it means to wait.—How beautiful she is, now that her conflicting emotions have subsided and her mood is relaxed. Her being is a harmony of sadness and pain. She is really captivating. She sits there in a traveling dress, and yet she was not going to travel; she wandered out in search of joy, and it is now an indication of her pain, for she is like one from whom gladness flees. She looks like one who had forever said farewell to the beloved. Let him go! The situation is favorable, the moment beckons. Now may I express myself so that it will seem as if I think that she is looking for her family, or a party of friends, and yet warmly enough to make every word significant to her feelings, thus I get a chance to insinuate myself into her thoughts.—Now may the devil take the scoundrel! There is a man approaching, who undoubtedly is he. Now write me down as a bungler if I cannot shape the situation as I want it. Yes indeed, a little finesse brings one well out of it. I must find out their relationship, bring myself into the situation. When she sees me she will involuntarily have to smile at my believing that she was looking for someone quite different. That smile makes me an accomplice, which is always something.—A thousand thanks, my child, that smile is worth much more to me than you realize; it is the beginning, and the beginning is always the hardest. Now we are acquainted, and our acquaintance is based on a piquant situation; it is enough for me until later. You will hardly remain here more than an hour; in two hours I shall know who you are, why else do you think the police maintain a directory?

9th day

Have I gone blind? Has the inner eye of my soul lost its power? I have seen her, but it is as if I had seen a heavenly vision, so absolutely has her image again vanished from me. Vainly have I exerted all the power of my soul to recall this image. If I were to meet her again, then I should recognize her instantly, even among a hundred other girls. Now she has fled away, and my soul's eye vainly seeks to overtake her with its longing.—I was walking along the shore boulevard, apparently unconcerned and indifferent to my surroundings, although my roving eye let nothing pass unnoticed, when I saw her. My eye fixed itself steadfastly upon her, it paid no attention to its master's will. It was impossible for me to direct its attention to the object I wished to look at, so I did not look, I stared. Like a fencer who becomes frozen in his pass, so was my eye fixed, petrified in the one appointed direction. It was impossible for me to look away, to withdraw my glance, impossible for me to see because I saw too much. The only thing I have retained is that she wore a green cloak; that is all, that is what one may call catching the cloud instead of Juno; she slipped away from me as Joseph did from Potiphar's wife, and left only her cloak behind. She was accompanied by a middle-aged lady, presumably her mother. I can describe her from top to toe, and that although I glanced at her only *en passant*. So it goes. The girl made an impression upon me, and I have forgotten her; the other made no impression upon me, and I can remember her.

14th day

I scarcely recognize myself. My mind is like a turbulent sea, swept by the storms of passion. If another could see my soul in this condition, it would seem to him like a boat that buried its prow deep down in the sea, as if in its terrible speed it would rush down into the depths of the abyss. He does not see that high on the mast a look-out sits on watch. Roar on, ye wild forces, ye powers of passion! Let your dashing waves hurl their foam against the sky. You shall not pile up over my head; serene I sit like the king of the cliff. . . .

Turkey gobblers flare up when they see red; so it is with me when I see green, whenever I see a green cloak; and then my eyes often deceive me, and sometimes all my hopes are frustrated by the livery of a porter from Frederik's Hospital.

May 15

. . . It was on the path between the north and east gates, about half past six. The sun had lost its intensity, only the memory of it remained in a mild radiance spreading over the landscape. Nature breathed more freely. The lake was calm, smooth as a mirror, the comfortable houses on Bleachers' Green were reflected in the water, which farther out was dark as metal. The path and buildings on the other side were lighted up by the faint rays of the setting sun. The sky was clear and bright, only a single fleecy cloud floated unnoticed across it, best seen by looking at the lake, beyond whose shining surface it was lost to view. Not a leaf moved.—It was she! My eye had not deceived me, even if the green coat had done so. Although I had long been prepared for this moment, it was still impossible for me to control a certain excitement, a rising and falling, like the song of the lark soaring above the adjacent fields. She was alone. Again have I forgotten how she was dressed, and yet now I have a picture of her. She was alone, preoccupied, manifestly not with herself but with her thoughts. She was not thinking, but the quiet play of her thoughts wove a picture of longing before her soul, a picture which held a certain foreboding, unclarified as a young girl's many sighs. She was at her most adorable age. A young girl does not develop in the sense that a boy does; she does not grow, she is born. A boy begins to develop at once, and takes a long time for the process; a young girl takes a long time in being born, and is born full-grown. Therein lies her infinite richness; at the moment she is born she is full-grown, but this moment of birth comes late. Hence she is twice born, the second time when she marries, or rather, at this moment she completes her birth, at that moment she is first really born. It is not only Minerva who sprang full-grown from the head of Jupiter, not only Venus who rose in all her beauty from the depths of the sea; every young girl is like this if her womanliness has not been destroyed by what men call development. She does not awaken by degrees, but all at once; meantime she dreams the longer, if people are not inconsiderate enough to arouse her too early. But her dream has infinite richness.

She was preoccupied not with herself, but in herself, and this preoccupation afforded infinite rest and peace to her soul. Thus is a young girl rich; to embrace this richness makes one himself rich. She is rich although she does not know that she possesses anything; she is rich, she is a treasure. Quiet peace broods over her, and a little melancholy. She was light to look upon, as light as Psyche who was carried away by the Zephyrs, even lighter, for she carried herself away. Let the theologians dispute about the ascension of the Madonna; that does not seem inconceivable to me, for she no longer belonged to the world; but a young girl's lightness is incomprehensible and baffles the law of gravity.— She noticed nothing, and for that reason believed herself unnoticed. I kept my distance from her and absorbed her image. She walked slowly, no precipitancy disturbed her peace or the quiet of her surroundings. A boy sat by the lake fishing. She stood still and watched the cork floating on the water. She had not walked very fast, but she wanted to cool off. She loosened a little scarf that was fastened about her neck under her shawl; a soft breeze from the water fanned her bosom, white as snow, and yet warm and full. The boy did not seem to like to have anyone watch his catch, he turned around and looked her over with a rather phlegmatic glance. He really cut a ridiculous figure, and I did not wonder that she began to laugh at him. How youthfully she laughed! If she had been alone with the boy, I do not believe she would have been afraid to fight with him. Her eyes were large and radiant; when one looked into them they had a dark luster which suggested an infinite depth, impossible to fathom; pure and innocent it was, gentle and quiet, full of mischief when she smiled. Her nose was finely arched; when I saw her profile, her nose seemed to merge into her forehead, which made it look a little shorter, a little more spirited.

She walked on, I followed. Fortunately there were many strollers on the path. While I exchanged a word or two with one and another of my acquaintance, I let her gain a little on me, and then soon overtook her again, thus relieving myself of the necessity of walking as slowly as she did, while keeping my distance. She went toward Eastgate. I was anxious to get a nearer view without being seen. On the corner stood a house from which I might be able to do so. I knew the family, and consequently needed only to call upon them. I hurried past her at a rapid pace, as if I had not noticed her in any way. I got a long way ahead of her, greeted the family right and left, and then took possession of the window that looked out upon the path. She came, I looked and looked, while at the same time I carried on a conversation with the tea party in the drawing room. Her walk readily convinced me that she had not taken many dancing lessons, and yet there was a pride in it, a natural nobility, but a lack of attention to details in herself. I got to see her one more time than I had counted on. From the window I could not see very far along the path, but I could see a pier extending out into the lake, and to my great surprise I caught sight of her again out there. It occurred to me that perhaps she lived out here in the country, that perhaps her family had a summer home here.

I was on the point of regretting my call, for fear that she might turn back and I thus lose sight of her, indeed the fact that she was already at the far end of the pier indicated that she would soon turn back and disappear, when she reappeared close by. She was walking past the house, and in great haste I seized my hat and stick in order, if possible, to pass her and then again fall behind as many times as might be necessary, until I found out where she lived—when in my haste I happened to jostle the arm of a lady who was just about to serve tea. A frightful screaming arose. I stood there with my hat and stick, anxious only to get away. To turn the incident off and motivate my retreat, I exclaimed pathetically: "Like Cain, I shall be banished from the place where this tea was spilled!" But as if everything had conspired against me, my host conceived the preposterous idea of continuing my remarks, and declared loudly and solemnly that I should not be allowed to go a single step until I had enjoyed a cup of tea, and had also served the ladies with tea in place of that which was spilled, thus setting everything right again. Since I was perfectly certain that under the circumstances my host would consider it courteous to detain me by force, there was nothing I could do except to stay.—She had vanished!

16th day

How beautiful it is to be in love, how interesting to know that one is in love. Lo, that is the difference. I could become embittered at the thought that for a second time I have lost sight of her, and yet in a certain sense it pleases me. The image I now have of her shifts uncertainly between her actual and her ideal form. This picture I now summon before me; but precisely because it either is reality, or the reality is the occasion, it has a peculiar fascination. I am not impatient, for she certainly lives in the town, and that is enough for me at present. This possibility is the condition of her image appearing so clearly— everything should be savored in slow draughts. And should I not be content, I who regard myself as a favorite of the gods, I who had the rare good fortune to fall in love again? That is something that no art, no study can effect, it is a gift. But having been fortunate enough to start a new love affair, I wish to see how long it can be sustained. I coddle this love as I never did my first. The opportunity falls to one's lot seldom enough, so if it does appear, then it is in truth worth seizing; for the fact is enough to drive one to despair, that it requires no art to seduce a girl, but that one is fortunate to find one worth seducing. . . .

19th day

So her name is Cordelia. Cordelia! That is a lovely name, and that, too, is of importance, since it is often very embarrassing to have to use an ugly name in connection with the tenderest predicates. I recognized her a long way off; she was walking with two other girls on the left side. Their pace seemed to indicate that they would soon stop. I stood on a street corner and read a poster, while constantly keeping an eye on my unknown. They took leave of each other. The two had evidently gone a little out of their way, for they took an opposite direction. She came on toward my corner. When she had taken a few steps, one of the other girls came running after her, calling loudly enough for me to hear: Cordelia! Cordelia! Then the third girl came up, and they stood with their heads together for a secret conference, which I tried in vain to hear. Then all three laughed and went away somewhere more hastily in the direction the two had taken before. I followed them. They went into a house on the Strand. I waited a long time since it seemed probable that Cordelia might soon return alone. However, that did not happen.

Cordelia! That is a really excellent name, and it was also the name of King Lear's third daughter, that remarkable girl who did not carry her heart on her lips, whose lips were silent while her heart beat warmly. So it is with my Cordelia. She resembles her, I am certain of that. But in another way she does wear her heart on her lips, not in the form of words, but more cordially in the form of a kiss. How healthily full her lips were! Never have I seen prettier ones.

That I am really in love I can tell among other things by the reticence with which I deal with this matter, even to myself. All love is secretive, even faithless love, when it has the proper aesthetic factor in it. It never has occurred to me to desire a confidant or to boast of my affairs. So I am almost glad that I did not find out where her home is, but only a place where she often comes. Perhaps on account of this I have also come a little nearer to my goal. I can, without attracting her attention, start my investigations, and from this fixed point it will not be difficult to secure an approach to her family. Should this circumstance, however, appear to be a difficulty—*eh bien!* It is all in the day's work; everything I do, I do *con amore;* and so too I love *con amore.*

20th day

Today I got some information about the house into which she disappeared. It belongs to a widow by the name of Jansen, who is blessed with three daughters. I can get an abundance of information there, that is to say, insofar as they have any. The only difficulty is in understanding this information when raised to the third power, for all three talked at once. Her name is Cordelia Wahl, and she is the daughter of a sea captain. He died some years ago, and her mother also. He was a very hard and austere man. She now lives with an aunt, her father's sister, who resembles her brother, but who otherwise is a very respectable woman. This is good as far as it goes, but for the rest, they know nothing about the house. They never go there, but Cordelia often visits them. She and the two girls are taking a course in cooking at the Royal Kitchen. For this reason she usually comes there early in the afternoon, sometimes in the morning, but never in the evening. They live a very secluded life.

Thus her story ends. There appears to be no bridge by which I can slip over into Cordelia's house. . . .

22nd day

Today I saw her for the first time at Mrs. Jansen's. I was introduced to her. She did not seem to care much about it, or to pay any attention to me. I made myself as inconspicuous as possible in order to observe her the better. She stayed only a moment, she had merely called for the daughters on the way to cooking school. While the two Miss Jansens were getting their wraps, we two were alone in the room. With a cold, almost supercilious indifference I made some remark to her, to which she replied with a courtesy altogether undeserved. Then they left. I could have offered to accompany them, but that might have set me down as a ladies' man, and I am convinced that she is not to be won that way.—On the contrary, I preferred to leave a moment after they had gone, but to go more rapidly than they, and by another street, but likewise in the direction of the cooking school, so that just as they turned into Great Kingstreet I passed them in the greatest hurry, without even a greeting or other recognition, to their great astonishment.

30th day

Everywhere our paths cross. Today I met her three times. I am conscious of her slightest movement, when and where I shall meet her; but this knowledge is not used to secure a meeting with her; on the contrary, I squander my opportunities on a frightful scale. A meeting which has cost me many hours of waiting is thrown away like a mere bagatelle. I do not meet her, I touch only the periphery of her existence. If I know that she is going to Mrs. Jansen's, then my arrival does not coincide with hers, unless I have some important observation to make. I prefer to arrive a little early at Mrs. Jansen's and then to meet her, if possible, at the door or upon the steps, as she is coming and I am leaving, when I pass her by indifferently. This is the first net in which she must be entangled. I never stop her on the street; I may bow to her, but I never come close to her, but always keep my distance. Our continual encounters are certainly noticeable to her; she does indeed perceive that a new body has appeared on her horizon, whose orbit in a strangely imperturbable manner affects her own disturbingly, but she has no conception of the law governing this movement; she is rather inclined to look about to see if she can discover the point controlling it, but she is as ignorant of being herself this focus as if she were a Chinaman. It is with her as with my associates in general: they believe that I have a multiplicity of affairs, that I am always on the move, and that I say with Figaro, "one, two, three, four intrigues at the same time, that is my delight." I must first know her and her entire intellectual background before beginning my assault. Most men enjoy a young girl as they do a glass of champagne, in a single frothing moment. Oh yes, that is all right, and in the case of many young girls it is really the most one can manage to get; but here there is more. If the individual girl is too frail to endure the clearness and transparency, oh well, then one enjoys the obscurity; but she can evidently endure it. The more one can sacrifice to love, the more interesting. This momentary enjoyment is, if not in a physical yet in a spiritual sense, a rape, and a rape is only an imagined enjoyment; it is like a stolen kiss, a thing which is rather unsatisfactory. No, when one can so arrange it that a girl's only desire is to give herself freely, when she feels that her whole happiness depends on this, when she almost begs to make this free submission, then there is first true enjoyment, but this always requires spiritual influence. . . .

June 3rd

Even yet I cannot decide how she is to be understood. Therefore I wait very quietly, very inconspicuously—aye, like a soldier on vedette duty who throws himself on the ground and listens for the faintest sound of an approaching enemy. I really do not exist for her in any real sense, not only not in a negative relationship, but simply not at all. Even yet I have not dared to experiment.—To see her was to love her, that is the way it is described in novels—aye, it is true enough, if love had no dialectics; but what does one really learn about love from novels? Sheer lies, which help to shorten the task. . . .

The question is always whether her femininity is strong enough to become reflective, or whether it is only to be enjoyed as beauty and charm; the question is whether one dares to tense the bow more strongly. It is indeed a wonderful thing to find a pure immediate femininity, but if one dares to attempt a change, then one gets the interesting. In such a case it is always best simply to provide her with a suitor. Some people are superstitious enough to believe that this would be injurious for a young girl. If she is, indeed, a very fine and delicate plant whose charm is her crowning quality, then it might always be best for her never to hear love mentioned, but if this is not the case, it is an advantage, and I should never hesitate to bring forward a suitor, providing there were none. This suitor must not be a mere caricature, for then nothing is gained; he must be a respectable young man, attractive if possible, but not a man big enough for her passion. She looks down on such a man, she gets a distaste for love, she almost doubts her own reality, when she feels what her destiny might be and sees what reality offers. If this is love, she says, and not something else, then it is nothing to boast about. Her love makes her proud, this pride makes her interesting, it penetrates her being with a higher incarnation; she is also approaching her downfall, but all this constantly makes her more and more interesting. However, it is always best to find out about her acquaintances first, to see whether or not there might be such a suitor. Her own home furnishes no opportunity, or as good as none, but still she does go out, and such a one might be found. To provide a suitor before knowing this is altogether inadvisable. To allow her to compare two equally insignificant suitors might be bad for her. I must find out whether there may not be such a lover in the offing, one who lacks the courage to storm the citadel, a chicken thief who sees no opportunity in such a cloistered house. . . .

5th day

I did not have to go far after all. She visits at the home of a wholesale merchant, Baxter by name. Here I found not only Cordelia, but also a man who appears very opportunely. Edward, the son of the house, is dead in love with her, one needs only half an eye to see that, when one looks at his two eyes. He is in business with his father, a good-looking young man, quite pleasant, somewhat bashful, which last I think does not hurt him in her eyes.

Poor Edward! He simply does not know how to go about his courtship. When he knows that she is to be there in the evening, then he dresses for her sake alone, puts on his new dark suit with collar and cuffs, just for her sake, and cuts an almost ridiculous figure among the quite commonplace company in the drawing-room. His embarrassment is almost incredible. If it were assumed, Edward would become a very dangerous rival. Embarrassment needs to be used very artistically, but it can be used to great advantage. How often have I not used it to fool some little maiden. Girls generally speak very harshly about bashful men, yet secretly they like them. A little embarrassment always flatters a young girl's vanity, she feels her superiority, it is earnest money. When you have lulled them to sleep, when they believe that you are ready to die from embarrassment, then you have an opportunity to show that you are very far from that, that you are very well able to shift for yourself. By means of bashfulness, you lose your masculine significance, and therefore it is a relatively good means of neutralizing sexuality. Then when they notice that this shyness was only assumed, they are ashamed, they blush inwardly, and feel very strongly that they have certainly gone too far. It is the same as when people continue too long to treat a boy as a child.

7th day

We are fast friends now, Edward and I; a true friendship, a beautiful relationship, exists between us, such as has not been seen since the palmiest days of Greece. We soon became intimates, then; after having lured him into many conversations about Cordelia, I made him confess his secret. It goes without saying that when all secrets are being revealed, this one is included with the others. Poor fellow, he has already sighed a long time. He dresses up every time she comes, then accompanies her home in the evening; his heart beats fast at the thought of her arm resting on his, they walk home, gaze at the stars, he rings her bell, she disappears, he despairs, but hopes for better luck next time. He has not even had the courage to set foot over her threshold, he who has had such excellent opportunities. Although personally I cannot refrain from making fun of Edward, there is still something really beautiful in his childishness. Although I ordinarily imagine myself to be fairly familiar with the very epitome of the erotic, I have never observed this condition in myself, this fear and trembling—that is, to the degree that it takes away my self-possession, for otherwise I know it well enough, but only as tending to make me stronger. Someone may say that I have never been in love; perhaps. I have taken Edward to task, I have encouraged him to rely on my friendship. Tomorrow he is going to take a decisive step, he is going to call on her personally. I have led him to the desperate idea of inviting me to go with him; I have promised to do so. He regards this as an extraordinary display of friendship. The occasion is just what I wish it to be, we invade the house through the door. Should she have the slightest doubt as to the meaning of my conduct, my appearance will confuse everything.

I have never before been accustomed to preparing myself for my part in a conversation; now this becomes necessary in order to entertain the aunt. I have assumed the disinterested task of conversing with her, thereby covering Edward's loving advances toward Cordelia. The aunt formerly lived in the country, and by my own prodigious studies of agricultural literature, coupled with the aunt's information drawn from experience, I am making definite progress in insight and efficiency.

When I sit thus in the comfortable living room, while she like a good angel diffuses her charm everywhere, over everyone with whom she comes in contact, over good and evil alike, then I sometimes become out of patience with myself; I am tempted to rush forth from my hiding place; for though I sit there, visible to everyone in the living room, still I am really lying in ambush. I am tempted to grasp her hand, to take her in my arms, to hide her in myself, for fear someone else should take her away from me. Or when Edward and I leave in the evening, when in taking leave she offers me her hand, when I hold it in mine, it sometimes becomes very difficult to let the bird slip out of my hand. Patience—*quod antea fuit impetus, nunc ratio est* [6]—she must be quite otherwise ensnared in my web, and then suddenly I let the whole power of my love rush forth. We have not spoiled that moment for ourselves by tasting, by unseemly anticipation—for which you must thank me, my Cordelia. I work to develop the contrast, I tense the bow of love to wound the deeper. Like an archer, I release the string, tighten it again, listen to its song, my battle ode, but I do not aim it, I do not even lay the arrow on the string.

When a small number of people are frequently together in the same room, a sort of easy pattern soon develops, in which each one has his own place and chair; thus a picture of the room is formed which one can easily reproduce for himself at will, a chart of the terrain. It was that way with us in the Wahl home; we united to form a picture. In the evening we drink tea there. Generally the aunt, who previously has been sitting on the sofa, moves over to the little work table, which place Cordelia in turn vacates. She goes over to the tea table in front of the sofa, Edward follows her, I follow the aunt. Edward tries to be secretive, he talks in a whisper; usually he does it so well that he becomes entirely mute. I am not at all secretive in my outpourings to the aunt—market prices, a calculation of the quantity of milk needed to produce a pound of butter; through the medium of cream and the dialectic of buttermaking, there comes a reality which any young girl can listen to without embarrassment, but, what is far rarer, it is a solid, reasonable, and edifying conversation, equally improving for mind and heart. I generally sit with my back to the tea table and to the ravings of Edward and Cordelia. Meanwhile I rave with the aunt. And is not Nature great and wise in her productivity, is not butter a precious gift, the glorious result of nature and art! I had promised Edward that I would certainly prevent the aunt from overhearing the conversation between him and Cordelia, providing anything was really said, and I always kept my word. On the

[6] What before was impulse is now method. (S)

other hand, I can easily overhear every word exchanged between them, hear every movement. This is very important to me, for one cannot always know how far a desperate man will venture to go. The most cautious and faint-hearted men sometimes do the most desperate things. Although I have nothing at all to do with these two people, it is readily apparent that Cordelia constantly feels that I am invisibly present between her and Edward. . . .

Our relationship is not the tender and loyal embrace of understanding, not attraction; it is the repulsion of misunderstanding. My relationship to her is simply nil; it is purely intellectual, which means it is simply nothing to a young girl. The method I am following has extraordinary advantages. A man who approaches as a gallant awakens mistrust and encounters resistance. I escape all such suspicions. She is not on guard against me, instead she regards me as a trustworthy man who is fit to watch over a young girl. The method has but one drawback, namely, it is tedious, but it can, therefore, only advantageously be used against an individual when the interesting is to be the reward. . . .

Soon I hope that I shall have brought her to the point of hating me. I have presented a perfect picture of a confirmed bachelor. All I talk about is sitting at my ease, being comfortably lodged, having a competent servant, friends of good standing whom I can rely upon as intimates. Now if I can induce the aunt to abandon her agricultural interests, then I can interest her in these, in order to get a more direct occasion for irony. One can laugh at a bachelor, even have sympathy for him; but a young man who has any spirit at all shocks a young girl by such conduct. The entire significance of sex, its beauty and its poetry, are destroyed.

So the days go on, I see her but I do not talk with her, I talk with the aunt in her presence. Occasionally at night it occurs to me to give my love air. Then wrapped in my cloak, with my hat pulled down over my eyes, I go and stand outside her window. Her bedroom looks out over the yard, but since it is a corner house, it can be seen from the street. At times she stands a moment at the window, or she opens it, looks up at the stars, unseen by anyone except the one she would least of all believe was watching her. In these hours of the night I steal about like a wraith, like a wraith I haunt the place where she lives. Then I forget everything, I have no plans, no calculations, I throw reason overboard, I expand and strengthen my chest by deep sighs, an exercise which I need in order not to suffer from the systematized routine of my life. Some are virtuous by day, sinful at night; I dissemble by day, at night I am sheer desire. If she could see me here, if she could look into my soul—if!

. . . One would not believe it possible to calculate the developmental history of a soul so accurately. It shows how wholesome Cordelia is. She is in truth a remarkable girl. She is quiet and modest, unpretentious, but unconsciously there is in her a prodigious demand. This was evident to me today when I saw her enter the house. The slight resistance that a gust of wind can offer awakens, as it were, all the energy within her, without arousing any fight. She is not a little insignificant girl who slips between your fingers, so fragile that you almost fear that she will go to pieces if you look at her; but neither is she a showy ornamental flower. Like a physician I can therefore take pleasure in observing all the symptoms in her case history.

Gradually I am beginning to approach her in my attack, to go over to more direct action. Were I to indicate this change on my military map of the family, I should say that I have turned my chair so that my side is toward her. I have more to do with her, I address remarks to her and elicit an answer from her. Her soul has passion, intensity, and without being foolish or vain, her reflections are remarkably pointed, she has a craving for the unusual. My irony over the foolishness of human beings, my ridicule of their cowardice, of their lukewarm indolence, fascinate her. She likes well enough to guide the chariot of Apollo across the arch of heaven, to come near enough to earth to scorch people a little. However, she does not trust me; hitherto I have discouraged every approach on her part, even intellectually. She must be strong in herself before I let her take rest in me. By glimpses it may indeed look as if it were she whom I would make my confidante in my freemasonry, but this is only by glimpses. She must be developed inwardly, she must feel an elasticity of soul, she must learn to evaluate the world. What progress she is making, her conversation and her eyes easily show me. I have only once seen a devastating anger in her. She must owe me nothing, for she must be free; love exists only in freedom, only in freedom is there enjoyment and everlasting delight. Although I am aiming at her falling into my arms as it were by a natural necessity, yet I am striving to bring it about so that as she gravitates toward me, it will still not be like the falling of a heavy body, but as spirit seeking spirit. Although she must belong to me, it must not be identical with the unlovely idea of her resting upon me like a burden. She must neither hang on me in the physical sense, nor be an obligation in a moral sense. Between the two of us only the proper play of freedom must prevail. She must be mine so freely that I can take her in my arms.

July 3rd

... As a woman, she hates me; as an intelligent woman, she fears me; as having a good mind, she loves me. Now for the first time I have produced this conflict in her soul. My pride, my defiance, my cold ridicule, my heartless irony, all tempt her, not as if she might wish to love me; no, there is certainly not a trace of such feeling in her, least of all toward me. She would emulate me. What tempts her is a proud independence in the face of men, a freedom like that of the Arabs of the desert. My laughter and singularity neutralize every erotic impulse. She is fairly at ease with me, and insofar as there is any reserve, it is more intellectual than feminine. She is so far from regarding me as a lover, that our relation to each other is that of two able minds. She takes my hand, presses it a little, laughs, pays some attention to me in a purely Platonic sense. Then when irony and ridicule have duped her long enough, I shall follow that suggestion found in an old verse: "The knight spreads out his cape so blue, and begs the beautiful maiden to sit thereon. . . ."

Today my eyes have for the first time rested upon her. Someone has said that sleep can make the eyelids so heavy that they close of themselves; perhaps my glance has a similar effect upon Cordelia. Her eyes close, and yet an obscure force stirs within her. She does not see that I am looking at her, she feels it, feels it through her whole body. Her eyes close, and it is night; but within her it is luminous day.

Edward must go; he has reached the very end. At any moment I may expect him to go to her and make a declaration of love. There is no one who knows this better than myself, who am his confidant, and who assiduously keeps him overexcited so that he can have a greater effect upon Cordelia. To allow him to confess his love is still too risky. I know very well that she will refuse him, but that will not end the affair. He will certainly take it very much to heart. This would perhaps move and touch Cordelia. Although in such a case I do not need to fear the worst, that she might start over again, still her self-esteem would possibly suffer out of pure sympathy. If this should happen, it frustrates my whole plan concerning Edward.

. . . One could think of several methods by which to surprise Cordelia. I might attempt to raise an erotic storm, powerful enough to tear up trees by the roots. By its aid I might try, if possible, to sweep her off her feet, snatch her out of her historic continuity; attempt, in this agitation, by stealthy advances to arouse her passion. It is not inconceivable that I could do this. . . . However, that would be all wrong from the aesthetic standpoint. I do not enjoy giddiness, and this condition is to be recommended only when one has to do with a girl who can acquire poetic glamour in no other way. Besides, one misses some of the essential enjoyment, for too much confusion is also bad. Its effect upon Cordelia would utterly fail. In a couple of draughts I should have swallowed what I might have had the good of for a long time, moreover what with discretion I might have enjoyed more fully and richly. Cordelia is not to be enjoyed in over-excitement. I might perhaps take her by surprise at first, if I went about it right, but she would soon be surfeited, precisely because this surprise lay too close to her daring soul.

A simple engagement is the best of all the methods, the most expedient. If she hears me make a prosaic declaration of love, *item* asking for her hand, she will perhaps believe her ears even less than if she listened to my heated eloquence, absorbed my poisonous intoxicants, heard her heart beat fast at the thought of an elopement.

The curse of an engagement is always on its ethical side. The ethical is just as tiresome in philosophy as in life. What a difference! Under the heaven of the aesthetic, everything is light, beautiful, transitory; when the ethical comes along, then everything becomes harsh, angular, infinitely boring. An engagement, however, does not have ethical reality in the stricter sense, as marriage does; it has validity only *ex consensu gentium*.[7] This ambiguity can be very serviceable to me. It has enough of the ethical in it so that in time Cordelia will get the impression that she has exceeded the ordinary bounds; however, the ethical in it is not so serious that I need fear a more critical agitation. I have always had a certain respect for the ethical. I have never given any girl a marriage promise, not even in jest. Insofar as it might seem that I have done it here, that is only a fictitious move. I shall certainly manage it so that she will be the one who breaks the engagement. My chivalrous pride scorns to give a promise. I despise a judge who by the promise of liberty

[7] By consent of the people in general.

lures an offender into a confession. Such a judge belittles his own power and ability.

Practically, I have reached the point where I desire nothing which is not, in the strictest sense, freely given. Let common seducers use such methods. What do they gain? He who does not know how to compass a girl about so that she loses sight of everything which he does not wish her to see, he who does not know how to poetize himself into a girl's feelings so that it is from her that everything issues as he wishes it, he is and remains a bungler; I do not begrudge him his enjoyment. A bungler he is and remains—a seducer, something one can by no means call me. I am an aesthete, an eroticist, one who has understood the nature and meaning of love, who believes in love and knows it from the ground up, and only makes the private reservation that no love affair should last more than six months at the most, and that every erotic relationship should cease as soon as one has had the ultimate enjoyment. I know all this, I know too that the highest conceivable enjoyment lies in being loved; to be loved is higher than anything else in the world. To poetize oneself into a young girl is an art, to poetize oneself out of her is a masterpiece. Still, the latter depends essentially upon the first.

23rd day

. . . The decisive moment is approaching. I might address myself to the aunt in writing, asking for Cordelia's hand. This is indeed the ordinary procedure in affairs of the heart, as if it were more natural for the heart to write than to speak. What might decide me to choose this method is just the philistinism in it. But if I choose this, then I lose the essential surprise, and that I cannot give up. . . .

On my side there is nothing now to obstruct the engagement. Consequently I go ahead with my wooing, though no one realizes it but myself. Soon will my humble person be seen from a higher standpoint. I cease to be a person and become—a match; yes, a good match, the aunt will say. She is the one I am most sorry for; she loves me with such a pure and sincere agricultural love, she almost worships me as her ideal. . . .

31st day

Today I have written a love letter for a third party. I am always happy to do this. In the first place it is always interesting to enter into a situation so vividly, and yet in all possible comfort. I fill my pipe, hear about the relationship, and the letters from the intended are brought out. The way in which a young lady writes is always an important study to me. The lover sits there like a fathead, he reads her letters aloud, interrupted by my laconic comments: She writes well, she has feeling, taste, caution, she has certainly been in love before, and so on. In the second place I am doing a good deed. I am helping to bring a couple of young people together; after that I balance accounts. For every pair I make happy, I select one victim for myself; I make two happy, at the most only one unhappy. I am honorable and trustworthy. I have never deceived anyone who has taken me into his confidence. Little fools always fail there. Well, it is a lawful perquisite. And why do I enjoy this confidence? Because I know Latin and attend to my studies, and because I always keep my little affairs to myself. And do I not deserve this confidence? Indeed I never misuse it.

August 2

The moment came. I caught a glimpse of the aunt on the street, and so I knew she was not at home. Edward was at the custom-house. Consequently there was every likelihood of Cordelia's being at home alone. And so it was. She sat by her work-table occupied with some sewing. I have very rarely visited the family in the forenoon, and she was therefore a little disturbed at seeing me. The situation became almost emotional. She was not to blame for this, for she controlled herself fairly well; but I was the one, for in spite of my armor she made an uncommonly strong impression upon me. . . . She was really charming, childlike, and yet adorned with a noble maidenly dignity that inspired respect. However, I was soon again dispassionate and solemnly stolid, as is proper when one would do the significant as if it were the insignificant. After a few general remarks, I moved a little nearer to her and began my petition. A man who talks like a book is exceedingly tiresome to listen to; sometimes, however, it is quite appropriate to speak in that way. For a book has the remarkable quality that you may interpret it as you wish. One's conversation also acquires the same quality, if one talks like a book. I kept quite soberly to general formulas. It cannot be denied that she was as surprised as I had expected. To describe how she looked is difficult. Her expressions were so variable, indeed much like the still unpublished but announced commentary to my book, a commentary which has the possibility of any interpretation. One word, and she would have laughed at me, one word, and she would have been moved, one word, and she would have fled from me; but no word crossed my lips, I remained stolidly serious, and kept exactly to the ritual.—"She had known me so short a time." Good heavens! such difficulties are encountered only in the narrow path of an engagement, not in the primrose path of love.

Curiously enough. When in the days preceding I surveyed the affair, I was rash enough and confident enough to believe that, taken by surprise, she would say yes. That shows how much thorough preparation amounts to. The matter is not settled, for she neither said yes, or no, but referred me to her aunt. I should have foreseen this. However, I am still lucky, for this outcome is even better than the other.

The aunt gives her consent, about that I never had the slightest doubt. Cordelia accepts her advice. As regards my engagement, I do not boast that it is romantic; it is in every way very matter of fact and commonplace. The girl doesn't know whether to say yes or no; the aunt says yes, the girl also says yes, I take the girl, she takes me—and now the story begins.

3rd day

So now I am engaged; so is Cordelia, and that is all she needs to know about the whole matter. If she had a girl friend she could talk freely with, she might perhaps say: "I don't really understand what it all means. There is something about him that attracts me, but I can't really make out what it is. He has a strange power over me, but I do not love him, and perhaps I never shall; on the other hand I can stand it to live with him, and can therefore be very happy with him; for he certainly will not demand so much if one only bears with him." My dear Cordelia! Perhaps he may demand more, in return for less endurance.—Of all ridiculous things imaginable, an engagement is the most ridiculous. Marriage, after all, has a meaning, even if this meaning does not please me. An engagement is a purely human invention which by no means reflects credit upon its inventor. It is neither one thing nor the other, and it has as much to do with love as the scarf which hangs from a beadle's back has to do with a professor's gown. Now I am a member of this honorable company. That is not without significance, for, as Trop [8] says, it is only by first being an artist that one acquires the right to judge other artists. And is not a fiancé also a make-believe artist?

Edward is beside himself with rage. He is letting his beard grow, he has hung away his dark suit, which is very significant. He insists on talking with Cordelia in order to describe my craftiness to her. It is an

[8] In Heiberg's *The Reviewer and the Beast*. (S)

affecting scene: Edward unshaven, carelessly dressed, shouting at Cordelia. Only he cannot cut me out with his long beard. Vainly I try to bring him to reason. I explain that it is the aunt who has brought about the match, that Cordelia perhaps has a warmer feeling for him, that I am willing to step back if he can win her. For a moment he wavers, wonders whether he should not shave his beard in a new way, buy a new black suit, then the next instant he abuses me. I do everything to keep on good terms with him; however angry he is with me, I am certain he will take no step without consulting me; he does not forget how helpful I have been to him in my role as mentor. And why should I wrest his last hope from him, why break with him? He is a good man; who knows what may happen in the future?

What I now have to do is, on the one hand, to get everything in order for getting the engagement broken, thus assuring myself of a more beautiful and significant relation to Cordelia; on the other hand, I must improve the time to the uttermost by enjoying all the charm, all the loveliness with which Nature has so abundantly endowed her, enjoying myself in it, still with the self-limitation and circumspection that prevents any violation of it. When I have brought her to the point where she has learned what it is to love, and what it is to love me, then the engagement breaks like an imperfect mold, and she belongs to me. This is the point at which others become engaged, and have a good prospect of a boring marriage for all eternity. Well, let others have it. . . .

> *Auf heimlich erröthender Wange*
> *Leuchtet des Herzens Glühen.*

She sits on the sofa by the tea table, I in a chair by her side. This position has the advantage of being intimate and yet detached. So tremendously much depends upon the position, that is, for one who has an eye for it. Love has many positions, this is the first. How regally Nature has endowed this girl: her pure soft form, her deep feminine innocence, her clear eyes—all these intoxicate me. I pay her my respects. She cheerfully greets me as usual, still a little embarrassed, a little uncertain: the engagement still makes our relationship somewhat different, just how she does not know. She shook hands with me, but not with her usual smile. I returned the greeting with a slight, almost imperceptible pressure. I was gentle and friendly without being erotic.—She sits on the sofa by the tea table. I sit in a chair by her side. A glorified solemnity diffuses itself over the situation, a soft morning radiance. She is silent;

nothing disturbs the stillness. My eyes steal softly over her, not with desire, in truth that would be shameless. A delicate fleeting blush passes over her, like a cloud over the meadow, rising and receding. What does this blush mean? Is it love? Is it longing, hope, fear; for is not the heart's color red? By no means. She wonders, she is surprised—not at me, that would be too little to offer her; she is surprised, not at herself, but in herself—she is transformed within. This moment demands stillness, therefore no reflection shall disturb it, no intimation of passion interrupt it. It is as if I were not present, and yet it is just my presence that furnishes the conditions for her contemplative wonder. My being is in harmony with hers. When she is in this condition, a young girl is to be worshiped and adored in silence, like some deities. . . .

I cannot regret the time that Cordelia has cost me, although it is considerable. Every meeting has demanded long preparation. I am watching the birth of love within her. I am even almost invisibly present when I visibly sit by her side. My relation to her is that of an unseen partner in a dance which is danced by only one, when it should really be danced by two. She moves as in a dream, and yet she dances with another, and this other is myself, who, insofar as I am visibly present, am invisible; insofar as I am invisible, I am visible. The movements of the dance require a partner, she bows to him, she takes his hand, she flees, she draws near him again. I take her hand, I complete her thought as if it were completed in herself. She moves to the inner melody of her own soul; I am only the occasion for her movement. I am not amorous, that would only awaken her; I am easy, yielding, impersonal, almost like a mood. . . . . .

So now the first war with Cordelia begins, in which I flee and thereby teach her to triumph in pursuing me. I constantly retreat before her, and in this retreat I teach her, through myself, to know all the power of love, its unquiet thoughts, its passion, what longing is, and hope, and impatient expectation. As I thus set all this before her in my own person, the same power develops correspondingly in her. It is a triumphal procession. I lead her in it, and I also am the one who dithyrambically sings praises for her victory, as well as the one who shows the way. She will gain courage to believe in love, to believe that it is an eternal power, when she sees its mastery over me, sees my emotions. She will believe me, partly because fundamentally what I do teach is true. If this were not the case, then she would not believe me. With every movement of mine, she becomes stronger and stronger: love is awakening in her soul, she is becoming initiated into her significance as a woman. Hitherto I have not set her free in the ordinary meaning of the word. I do it now, I set her free, for only thus will I love her. She must never suspect that she owes this freedom to me, for that would destroy her self-confidence. When she at last feels free, so that she is almost tempted to break with me, then the second war begins. Now she has power and passion, and the struggle becomes worth while to me. The temporary results may be what they will. If she becomes dizzy with pride, if she should break with me—oh, well, she is free; but she shall yet be mine. That the engagement should bind her is foolishness; I will have her only in her freedom. Let her forsake me, the second war is just beginning, and in this second war I shall be the victor, just as certainly as it was an illusion that she was the victor in the first. The more abundant strength she has, the more interesting for me. The first war was a war of liberation, it was only a game; the second is a war of conquest, it is for life and death.

Do I love Cordelia? Yes. Sincerely? Yes. Faithfully? Yes—in an aesthetic sense, and this also indicates something important. What good would it do this girl to fall into the hands of some numskull, even if he were a faithful husband? What would she then become? Nothing. Someone has said that it takes a little more than honesty to get through the world. I should say that it takes something more than honesty to love such a girl. That more I have—it is duplicity. And yet I really love her. Rigidly and abstemiously I watch over herself, so that everything there is in her, the whole divinely rich nature, may come to its unfolding. I am one of the few who can do this, she is one of the few who is fitted for this; are we not then suited to one another?

Is it sinful of me that, instead of looking at the preacher, I fix my eye on the beautiful embroidered handkerchief you hold in your hand? Is it sinful for you to hold it thus? It has your name in the corner.— Your name is Charlotte Hahn? It is so fascinating to learn a lady's name in such an accidental manner. It is as if there were a helpful spirit who mysteriously made me acquainted with you.—Or is it perhaps not accidental that the handkerchief was folded just right for me to see your name?—You are disturbed, you wipe a tear from your eye, the handkerchief again hangs carelessly down.—It is evident to you that

I am looking at you, not at the preacher. You look at the handkerchief, you notice that it has betrayed your name.—It is really a very innocent matter that one should get to know a girl's name.—Why do you take it out on the handkerchief, why do you crumple it up? Why are you angry? Why angry at me? Listen to what the preacher says: "No one should lead a man into temptation; even one who does so unwittingly, has a responsibility, he is even in debt to the other, a debt which he can discharge only by increased benevolence."

My Cordelia!

Love loves secrecy—an engagement is a revelation; it loves silence—an engagement is a public notice; it loves a whisper—an engagement is a proclamation from the housetops; and yet an engagement, with my Cordelia's help, may be an excellent trick for deceiving the enemies. On a dark night there is nothing more dangerous to other ships than hanging out a lantern, which is more deceptive than the darkness.

Thy Johannes.

She sits on the sofa by the tea table. I sit by her side; she holds my arm, her head weighed down by many thoughts rests on my shoulder; she is so near me, and yet so far away. She resigns herself to me, and yet she does not belong to me. Even yet she resists me, but this is not sub-jectively reflective; it is the ordinary feminine resistance, for woman's nature is renunciation in the form of resistance.—She sits on the sofa by the tea table, I sit by her side. Her heart is beating, yet without passion; her bosom moves, yet not in disquiet; sometimes she changes color, yet in an easy transition. Is that love? By no means. She listens, she under-stands. She listens to the winged word, she understands it as her own; she listens to another's speech as it echoes through her; she understands this echo also, as if it were her own voice, which is manifest to her and to another. . . .

Cordelia becomes more and more indignant whenever we go to my uncle's house.[9] She has several times requested that we should not go there again; there is no help for her, I always know how to find an excuse. Last night when we left she pressed my hand with unusual pas-sion. She had probably felt tortured at being there, and it was no won-

[9] At the uncle's house were always to be found several engaged couples, as explained in an earlier entry.

der. If I did not always get some amusement out of watching the artificiality of these artistic performances, it would be impossible for me to stand it. This morning I received a letter from her wherein she, with more wit than I had expected from her, ridiculed the engagements. I have kissed that letter; it is the dearest one I have received from her. Rightly so, my Cordelia, this is the way I wish it. . . .

My Cordelia!

Outside the door stands a little carriage which to me is large enough for the whole world, since it is large enough for two; hitched to it are a pair of horses, wild and unmanageable as the forces of nature, impatient as my passion, spirited as your thoughts. If you are willing, I shall carry you away, my Cordelia! Only command it. Your command is the word which loosens the reins and the lust of flight. I carry you away, not from one person to another, but out of the world. Rear, horses! The carriage rises, the horses rear up almost above our heads; we ride heavenward through the clouds; they bluster about us; is it we who are sitting still while all the world is moving, or is it our daring flight? Does it make you dizzy, my Cordelia? Then hold fast to me; I do not become dizzy. One never becomes giddy in a spiritual sense when one thinks only of a single thing,[10] and I think only of you—in the physical sense one is never giddy if one fastens the eyes on a single object. I look only at you. Hold fast; if the world passes away, if our comfortable carriage vanishes beneath us, we still hold each other close, floating in the harmony of the spheres.

Thy Johannes.

It is almost too much. My servant has waited six hours, I myself have waited two, in the wind and rain, just to meet that dear child, Charlotte Hahn. She is in the habit of visiting an old aunt of hers regularly every Wednesday between two and five. Today she doesn't come, just when I was so eager to see her. And why? Because she puts me in a very definite mood. I bow to her, she curtsies to me in a manner at once indescribably worldly, and yet so divine; she almost stops, sinks nearly to the ground, looking all the time as if she might ascend to heaven. When I look at her, my mind is at once solemn and yet filled with desire. As for the rest, the girl does not interest me in the least. All I want is this greeting, nothing more, even if she were willing to give it. Her greet-

---

[10] A foreshadowing of one of S.K.'s profoundest themes. Cf *supra*, pp. 14 and 270–281.

ing creates a mood in me, and it is this mood which I then squander on Cordelia. . . .

My letters do not fail of their purpose. They develop her mentally, if not erotically. For that purpose I must not use letters but notes. The more the erotic is to come out, the shorter they should be, but the more positively they should stress the erotic side. However, in order not to make her sentimental or soft, irony must again stiffen her emotions, while yet giving her an appetite for the nourishment dearest to her. The notes vaguely and remotely suggest the absolute. As soon as this suspicion begins to dawn in her soul, the relation is ruptured. By my resistance the suspicion takes form in her soul, as if it were her own thought, her own heart's impulse. This is just what I want. . . .

My Cordelia!

Speak—I obey. Your wish is a command. Your prayer is an all-powerful invocation, every fleeting wish of yours is a benefaction to me; for I obey you not like a servile spirit, as if I stood outside of you. When you command, then your will increases, and with it I myself; for I am a confusion of the soul which only awaits your word.

Thy Johannes.

My Cordelia!

Because I have loved you so short a time you almost seem to fear that I may have loved someone before. There are manuscripts on which the trained eye immediately suspects an older writing, which in the course of time has been superseded by insignificant foolishness. By means of chemicals this later writing may be erased, and then the original stands out plain and clear. So your eye has taught me to find myself in myself. I let forgetfulness consume everything which does not concern you, and then I discover a very old, a divinely young, original writing—then I discover that my love for you is as old as myself.

Thy Johannes.

My Cordelia!

People say that I am in love with myself; I don't wonder, for how could they notice that I am in love, since I love only you? How could anyone suspect it, since I love only you? I am in love with myself, why? Because I am in love with you; for I love you truly, you alone, and everything which belongs to you, and so I love myself because this myself belongs to you, so if I cease to love you, I cease to love myself. What is, then, in the profane eyes of the world an expression of the greatest egoism, is for your initiated eyes an expression of purest sympathy; what is for the profane eyes of the world an expression for the most prosaic self-preservation, is in your sacred sight an expression for the most enthusiastic self-annihilation.

Thy Johannes.

My Cordelia!

Mine, what does this word signify? Not what belongs to me, but what I belong to, what contains my whole being, which is mine insofar as I belong to it. My God is not the God who belongs to me, but the God to whom I belong, and so again when I say my native land, my home, my calling, my longing, my hope. If you had not been immortal before, then would this thought, that I am thine, break through Nature's accustomed course.

Thy Johannes.

. . . Last evening the aunt had a little party. I knew Cordelia would have her knitting-bag with her, so I had hidden a little note in it. She dropped it, picked it up, read it, and showed both embarrassment and wistfulness. One should never fail to take advantage of such opportunities. It is incredible how much it can help. The note had nothing of importance in it, but it became infinitely significant to her when she read it under such circumstances. She had no chance to talk with me; I had arranged it so that I had to escort a lady home. Consequently Cordelia had to wait until today. It is always best to give an impression time to sink into her soul. It always looks as if I were very attentive. This gives me the advantage of everywhere being in her thoughts, of everywhere surprising her. . . .

Love has many positions; Cordelia makes good progress. She is sitting on my knee, her arm, soft and warm, encircles my neck; she rests upon my breast, light, without bodily weight; her soft form hardly touches me; like a flower her graceful figure twines about me, freely as a ribbon. Her eyes are hidden behind her lashes, her bosom is of a dazzling whiteness like snow, so smooth that my eye cannot rest upon it, would glance off, if her bosom did not move. What does this agitation mean? Is it love? Perhaps. It may be its anticipation, its dream. It still lacks energy. She embraces me elaborately, as the cloud the glorified, casually as a breeze, softly as one caresses a flower; she kisses me as dispassionately as heaven kisses the sea, softly and quietly as the dew kisses a flower, solemnly as the sea kisses the image of the moon.

So far I should call her passion a naïve passion. When the change comes, and I begin to draw back in earnest, then she will really muster all her resources in order to captivate me. She has no way to accomplish this except by means of the erotic, but this will now appear on a very different scale. It then becomes the weapon in her hand which she swings against me. Then I have the reflected passion. She fights for her own sake because she knows that I possess the erotic; she fights for her own sake in order to overcome me. She develops in herself a higher form of the erotic. What I taught her to suspect by inflaming her, my coldness now teaches her to understand, but in such a way that she believes she discovered it herself. Through this she will try to take me by surprise; she will believe that her boldness has outstripped me, and that she has thereby caught me. Then her passion becomes determinate, energetic, conclusive, logical; her kiss total, her embrace firm.—In me she seeks her freedom, the more firmly I encompass her, the better she finds it. The engagement is broken. When this happens, then she needs a little rest, so that this wild tumult may not bring out something unseemly. Then her passion gathers itself again, and she is mine. . . .

An ancient philosopher has said that if a man were to record accurately all of his experiences, then he would be, without knowing a word of the subject, a philosopher. I have now for a long time lived in close association with the community of the engaged. Such a relationship ought then to bear some fruit. I have considered gathering all the material into a book, entitled: *Contribution to the Theory of Kissing,* dedicated to all tender lovers. It is, too, quite remarkable that no such work on this subject exists. If, then, I am fortunate in being prepared, I also remedy a long-felt want. Could this lack in literature be due to the fact that philosophers do not consider such matters, or that they do not understand them? I am able to offer one suggestion immediately. The perfect kiss requires a man and a girl as the participants. A kiss between men is tasteless, or what is worse, has a bad taste. Next, I believe a kiss comes nearer the ideal when a man kisses a girl than when a girl kisses a man. When in the course of years there has come about an indifference in this relation, then the kiss has lost its significance. This is true about the domestic kiss of marriage with which married people dry each other's lips in lieu of a napkin, as they say "you are welcome." If the difference in age is very great, then the kiss is without idea. I re-

member that in a girl's school in one of the provinces, the senior class had
a peculiar byword: "to kiss the judge," an expression connoting only
agreeable ideas. It had originated in this way: The schoolmistress had
a brother-in-law who lived in her house. He was an elderly man, had
been a judge, and took advantage of his age to kiss the young girls.
The kiss ought to be the expression of a definite passion. When a
brother and sister who are twins kiss each other, it is not a true kiss. This
also holds true of kisses given during Christmas games, as well as of the
stolen kiss. A kiss is a symbolic action which is unimportant when the
feeling it should indicate is not present, and this feeling can only be
present under certain conditions.

If one wishes to classify the kiss, then one must consider several
principles of classification. One may classify kissing with respect to the
sound. Here the language is not sufficiently elastic to record all my
observations. I do not believe that all the languages in the world have
an adequate supply of onomatopoeia to describe the different sounds I
have learned to know at my uncle's house. Sometimes it was smacking,
sometimes hissing, sometimes sticky, sometimes explosive, sometimes
booming, sometimes full, sometimes hollow, sometimes squeaky, and so
on forever. One may also classify kissing with regard to contact, as in
the close kiss, the kiss *en passant,* and the clinging kiss. . . . One may
classify them with reference to the time element, as the brief and the
prolonged. With reference to the time element, there is still another
classification, and this is the only one I really care about. One makes a
difference between the first kiss and all others. That which is the subject of this reflection is incommensurable with everything which is
included in the other classifications; it is indifferent to sound, touch,
time in general. The first kiss is, however, qualitatively different from
all others. There are only a few people who consider this. . . .

There is a difference between spiritual love and physical. Hitherto I
have chiefly tried to develop the spiritual in Cordelia. My physical presence must now be something different: not only an accompanying
mood, it must be a temptation. I have in these days been constantly
preparing myself by reading the celebrated passages in *Phaedrus* concerning love. It electrifies my whole being and is an excellent prelude.
Plato really understood about love.

. . . Today we were at a party. We had not exchanged a word with
each other. We were leaving the table; a servant came in and informed

Cordelia that a messenger wished to speak with her. This messenger was from me, he brought a letter which explained the meaning of a remark I had made at the table. I had managed to introduce it into the general table conversation so that Cordelia, although she sat at a distance from me, must necessarily overhear it and not understand it. The letter was calculated with this in mind. Had I not been fortunate enough to give the conversation this turn, then I should have been ready at the right time to confiscate the letter. When she returned to the room, she had to tell a little fib. Such things consolidate the erotic mystery, without which she cannot progress on her appointed way.

Jacta est alea.[11] Now the change begins. I was with her today, quite carried away by an idea that has always engaged my thought. I had neither eyes nor ears for her. The idea was interesting in itself, and it fascinated her. Besides, it would have been wrong to begin this new plan of action by treating her coldly. Now when I have left her and the idea no longer interests her, she will readily discover that I was different from what I used to be. That she should come to realize this change when she is by herself makes it more painful to her; it acts more slowly but more earnestly upon her. She cannot immediately flare up, and so when the opportunity does come, she has already imagined so much that she cannot find expression for it all at once, but will retain a residuum of doubt. Unrest increases, the letters cease, the erotic nourishment is diminished, love is ridiculed as laughable. Perhaps she gets along for a short time, but in the long run she cannot endure it. Then she wishes to captivate me by the same means I had used with her, by means of the erotic. . . .

Today I was with Cordelia. With the speed of thought I adroitly directed the conversation to the same subject we had considered yesterday, in order again to arouse ecstasy within her. "There is something I really should have said yesterday; it occurred to me after I had gone." That succeeded. As long as I am with her she enjoys listening to me; when I have gone, she realizes that she has been cheated and that I am indeed changed. In this way one extends his credit. This method is underhanded but very adequate, like all indirect methods. She can very well argue to herself that the things I talk about can really engross me, that they even interest her for the moment, and yet I defraud her of the real erotic. . . .

[11] "The die is cast."

Now she lets drop numerous remarks which clearly indicate that for her part she is tired of our engagement. They do not pass my ear unheeded, they are the scouts of my plans in her soul, who give me enlightening hints; they are the ends of the thread by which I weave her into my plan.

My Cordelia!

You complain about the engagement. You think our love does not need an external bond which exists only to hinder. In that I immediately recognize my wonderful Cordelia! In truth, I admire you. Our external union is only a separation. And yet there is a wall between us that separates us like Pyramus and Thisbe. Even now the consciousness of men is disturbing. Only in contrast is there liberty. When no outsider suspects the love, then it first gets significance. When every stranger believes that the lovers hate each other, then first is love happy.

Thy Johannes.

. . . Woman will always offer an inexhaustible fund of material for my reflection, an eternal abundance for observation. The man who feels no impulse toward the study of woman may, as far as I am concerned, be what he will; one thing he certainly is not, he is no aesthetician. This is the glory and divinity of aesthetics, that it enters into relation only with the beautiful: it has to do essentially only with the literature which is beautiful, with the sex which is beautiful. It makes me glad and causes my heart to rejoice when I represent to myself how the sun of feminine loveliness spreads out its rays in an infinite manifoldness, splitting itself up in a confusion of tongues, where each individual woman has her little part of the whole wealth of femininity, yet so that her other characteristics harmoniously center about this point. In this sense feminine beauty is infinitely divisible. But the particular share of beauty which each one has must be present in a harmonious blending, for otherwise the effect will be disturbing, and it will seem as if Nature had intended something by this woman, but had not realized her plan.

My eyes can never weary of surveying this peripheral manifold, these scattered emanations of feminine beauty. Each particular has its little share and yet is complete in itself, happy, glad, beautiful. Every woman has her share: the merry smile, the roguish glance, the yearning look, the drooping head, the exuberant spirits, the calm sadness, the deep foreboding, the prophetic melancholy, the earthly homesickness, the unbaptized movements, the beckoning brows, the questioning lips, the mysterious forehead, the ensnaring curls, the concealing lashes, the heavenly pride, the earthly modesty, the angelic purity, the secret blush, the light step, the graceful airiness, the languishing posture, the dreamy yearning, the inexplicable sighs, the willowy form, the soft outlines, the luxuriant bosom, the swelling hips, the tiny foot, the dainty hand.— Each woman has her own, and the one does not merely repeat the other. And when I have gazed and gazed again, considered and again considered this multitudinous variety, when I have smiled, sighed, flattered, threatened, desired, tempted, laughed, wept, hoped, feared, won, lost—then I shut up my fan, and gather the fragments into a unity, the parts into a whole. Then my soul is glad, my heart beats, my passion is aflame. This one woman, the only woman in all the world, she must belong to me, she must be mine. Let God keep Heaven, if I could keep her. I know what I choose; it is something so great that Heaven itself must be the loser by such a division, for what would be left to Heaven if I keep her? The faithful Mohammedans will be disappointed in their hopes when in their Paradise they embrace pale, weak shadows; for warm hearts they cannot find, all the warmth of the heart is concentrated in her breast; they will yield themselves to a comfortless despair when they find pale lips, dim eyes, a lifeless bosom, a limp pressure of the hand; for all the redness of the lips, and the fire of the eye, and all the restlessness of the bosom, and the promise of the hand, and the foreboding of the sigh, and the seal of the kiss, and the trembling of the touch, and the passion of the embrace—all, all are concentrated in her, and she lavishes on me a wealth sufficient for a whole world, both for time and eternity. . . .

I shall now for variety's sake attempt, myself being cold, to think woman as cold. I shall attempt to think woman under her category. Under what category must she be conceived? Under being for an other. . . . Woman shares this category with nature and, in general, with everything feminine. Nature as a whole exists only for an other; not in the teleological sense, so that one part of nature exists for another part, but so that the whole of nature is for an Other—for the Spirit. In the same way with the particulars. The life of the plant, for example, unfolds its hidden charms in all naïveté, and exists only for an other. In the same way a mystery, a charade, a secret, a vowel, and so on, has being only for an other. And from this it can be explained why when God created Eve, He let a deep sleep fall over Adam; for woman is the dream of man. In still another way the story teaches that woman is a being for an other. It tells, namely, that Jehovah created Eve from a rib taken from the side of man. Had she been taken from man's brain, for example, woman would indeed still have been a being for an other; but it was not the intention to make her a fantasy, but something quite different. She became flesh and blood, but this causes her to be included under nature, which is essentially being for an other. She awakens first at the touch of love; before that time she is a dream. Yet in her dream life we can distinguish two stages: in the first, love dreams about her; in the second, she dreams about love.

When woman is determined as virginity, she is thereby characterized as being for an other. Virginity is, namely, a form of being which, insofar as it is a being for itself, is really an abstraction and only reveals itself to another. The same characterization also lies in the concept of female innocence. It is therefore possible to say that woman in this condition is invisible. As is well known, there existed no image of Vesta, the goddess who most nearly represented feminine virginity. This form of existence is, namely, jealous for itself aesthetically, just as Jehovah is ethically, and does not desire that there should be any image, or even any conception of one. This is the contradiction, that the being which is for an other *is* not, and first becomes visible, as it were, by the interposition of an other. Logically, this contradiction will be found to be quite in order, and he who knows how to think logically will not be disturbed by it, but will be glad in it. But whoever thinks illogically will imagine that whatever is a being for an other exists, in the finite sense in which one can say about a particular thing: that is something for me.

This being of woman (for the word existence is too rich in meaning, since woman does not persist in and through herself) is rightly described as charm, an expression which suggests plant life; she is a flower, as the poets like to say, and even the spiritual in her is present in a vegetative manner. She is wholly subject to nature, and hence only aesthetically free. In a deeper sense she first becomes free by her relation to man, and when man courts her properly, there can be no question of a choice. Woman chooses, it is true, but if this choice is thought of as the result of a long deliberation, then this choice is unfeminine. Hence it is, that it is a humiliation to receive a refusal, because the individual in question has rated himself too high, has desired to make another free without having the power.—In this situation there is deep irony. That which merely exists for another has the appearance of being predominant: man sues, woman chooses. Woman is in the idea the vanquished, man the victor, and yet the victor bows before the vanquished; but this is quite natural, and it is only awkwardness, stupidity and lack of erotic sensibility, to seek to set one's self above that which immediately reveals itself in this fashion. It has also a deeper ground. Woman is, namely, substance; man is reflection. She does not therefore choose independently; man sues, she chooses. But man's courtship is a question, and her choice only an answer to a question. In a certain sense man is more than woman, in another sense he is infinitely less.

This being for an other is the true virginity. If it makes an attempt to be a being for itself, in relation to another being which is being for it, then the opposition reveals itself in an absolute coyness; but this opposition shows at the same time that woman's essential being is being for an other. The diametrical opposite to absolute devotion is absolute coyness, which in a converse sense is invisible as the abstraction against which everything breaks, without the abstraction itself coming to life. Femininity now takes on the character of an abstract cruelty, the caricature in its extreme form of the intrinsic feminine brittleness. A man can never be so cruel as a woman. Consult mythologies, fables, folktales, and you will find this view confirmed. If a natural principle is to be described, whose mercilessness knows no limits, it will always be a feminine nature. Or one is horrified at reading about a young woman who callously allows all her suitors to lose their lives, as so often happens in the folk-tales of all nations. A Bluebeard slays all the women he has loved on their bridal night, but he does not find his happiness in slaying them; on the contrary, his happiness has preceded, and in this lies the concrete determination; it is not cruelty for the sake of cruelty. A Don Juan seduces them and runs away, but he finds no happiness at all in running away from them, but rather in seducing them; consequently it is by no means this abstract cruelty.

Thus the more I reflect on this matter, the more I see that my practice is in perfect harmony with my theory. My practice has always been impregnated with the theory that woman is essentially a being for an other. Hence it is that the moment has here such infinite significance; for a being for an other is always the matter of a moment. It may take a longer, it may take a shorter time before the moment comes, but as soon as it has come, then that which was originally a being for an other assumes a relative being, and then all is over. I know very well that husbands say that the woman is also in another sense a being for an other, that she is everything to her husband through life. This is something that we must leave to the husbands. I really believe that it is something which they mutually delude one another into believing. Every class in life generally has certain conventional customs, and especially certain conventional lies. Among these must be reckoned this sailor's yarn. To understand it at the moment is not so easy a matter, and he who misunderstands it naturally acquires such a boredom for the rest of his life. The moment is everything, and in the moment, woman is everything; the consequences I do not understand. Among these consequences is also the begetting of children. Now I fancy that I am a fairly consistent thinker, but if I were to think myself crazy, I am not a man who could think this consequence; I simply do not understand it—to understand it probably one must be a husband. . . .

How Cordelia engrosses me! And yet the time is soon over; always my soul requires rejuvenescence. I can already hear, as it were, the far distant crowing of the cock. Perhaps she hears it too, but she believes it heralds the morning.—Why is a young girl so pretty, and why does it last so short a time? I could become quite melancholy over this thought, and yet it is no concern of mine. Enjoy, do not talk. The people who make a business of such deliberations do not generally enjoy. . . .

Have I been constantly faithful to my pact in my relation to Cordelia? That is to say, my pact with the aesthetic. For it is this which makes me strong, that I always have the idea on my side. This is a secret, like Samson's hair, which no Delilah shall wrest from me. Simply and directly to betray a young girl, that I certainly could not endure; but that the idea is set in motion, that it is in its service that I act, to its service that I dedicate myself, this gives me a strictness toward myself, abstemiousness from every forbidden enjoyment. Has the interesting always been preserved? Yes, I dare say it freely and openly in this secret conversation with myself. Even the engagement was interesting, exactly because it did not offer that which one generally understands by the interesting. It preserved the interesting by the fact of the outward appearance being in contradiction to the inner life. Had I been secretly bound to her, then it would have been interesting only in its first potentialities. This, however, is interesting in another potentiality. . . . The engagement is broken, but in such a way that she herself breaks it, in order to raise herself to a higher sphere. So it should be; this is, in fact, the form of the interesting which will occupy her most.

Sept. 16

The bond is burst; longing, strong, daring, divine, she flies like a bird which now for the first time gets the right to stretch its wings. Fly, bird, fly! In truth if this royal flight were a withdrawal from me, then my pain would be infinitely deep. As if Pygmalion's love were again turned to stone, so would this be for me. Light have I made her, light as a thought, and why should not this, my thought, belong to me! That would be a cause for despair. A moment earlier it would not have mattered, a moment later it would not trouble me, but now—now—this now, which is an eternity to me! But she does not fly away from me. Fly, then, bird, fly; soar proudly on your wings, glide through the soft realms of the air, soon I shall be with you, soon I shall hide myself with you in a profound solitude!

The aunt was somewhat taken aback by the news. However, she is too detached to wish to coerce Cordelia, although I, partly to lull her to a sounder sleep, partly to fool Cordelia a little, have made some attempt to get her to interest herself in my behalf. As for the rest, she shows me much sympathy; she does not suspect how much reason I have for deprecating all sympathy.

She has received permission from her aunt to spend some time in the country; she will visit a family. It happens very fortunately that she cannot immediately give herself up to excessive moods. She will still, for some time, be kept tense by all kinds of external criticism. I maintain a desultory communication with her by means of letters, so our relationship is sustained. She must now be strengthened in every way; especially, it is best to permit her to make a few eccentric flights to show her contempt for mankind in general. Then when the day for her departure arrives, a trustworthy man will appear as coachman. Outside the gate my confidential servant will join them. He will accompany her to her destination and remain with her to render attention and assistance in case of need. Next to myself I know no one who is better fitted for this than John. I have myself arranged everything out there as tastefully as possible. Nothing is lacking which can in any way serve to delude her soul and to soothe it with a sense of well-being.

. . . Spring is the most beautiful time of the year to fall in love; autumn the most beautiful to reach the goal of one's desires. There is a sadness in the autumn which well corresponds to the movement with which the thought of a fulfillment of one's desires courses through one. Today I have been out in the country where some day Cordelia will find surroundings that are attuned to her soul. For myself I do not desire to participate in her surprise and pleasure over this; such erotic conditions would only enervate her soul. If she is alone there, she will pass her time in revery, everywhere she will see allusions, hints, an enchanted world, but all this would lose its significance if I were with her; it would cause her to forget that, for us, the period of time when such things enjoyed in fellowship have significance, is past. This environment must not like a narcotic ensnare her soul, but constantly incite it to rise up, because she sees it as a play, which has no significance in comparison with that which is to come. I even intend in these days which still remain to visit this place more often, in order to retain my mood.

My Cordelia!

Now I call you mine in truth, no external sign reminds me of my possession.—Soon I call you mine in truth. And when I hold you fast in my arms, when you entwine me in your embrace, then we need no ring to remind us that we belong to each other, for is not this embrace a ring, which is more than a sign. And the more firmly this ring encloses us, the more inseparably it knits us together, the greater our freedom, for your freedom consists in being mine, as mine in being yours.

Thy Johannes.

My Cordelia!

Soon, soon you are mine. When the sun closes its spying eye, when history is over and the myths begin, then I not only fling my cloak about me, but I fling the night about me like a cloak, and hasten to you, and harken to find you, not by the sound of footfalls, but by the beating of your heart.

Thy Johannes.

My Cordelia!

What, frightened? When we keep together, then are we strong, stronger than the world, stronger even than the gods themselves. You know there once lived a race of people on the earth [12] who were indeed men, but who were each self-sufficient, not knowing the inner union of love. Yet they were mighty, so mighty that they would storm heaven. Jupiter feared them, and divided them so that from one came two, a man and a woman. Now, if it sometimes happens that what had once been united are united again in love, then is such a union stronger even than Jupiter. They are not only as strong as the individuals were, but even stronger, for love's union is an even higher union.

Thy Johannes.

[12] Cf. the speech of Aristophanes in Plato's *Symposium,* Chaps. 14–15. (S)

Sept. 24

The night is still—the clock strikes a quarter before twelve. The watchman by the gate blows his benediction out over the countryside, it echoes back from Bleacher's Green—he goes inside the gate—he blows again, it echoes even farther.—Everything sleeps in peace, everything except love. So rise up, ye mysterious powers of love, gather yourselves together in this breast! The night is silent—only a lonely bird breaks this silence with its cry and the beat of its wings, as it skims over the dewy field down the glacial slope to its rendezvous—*accipio omen!* How portentous all nature is! I read the omen in the flight of birds, in their cries, in the playful flap of the fish against the surface of the water, in their vanishing into its depth, in the distant baying of the hounds, in a wagon's faraway rumble, in footfalls which echo in the distance. I do not see specters in this night hour; I do not see that which has been, but that which will be, in the bosom of the sea, in the kiss of the dew, in the mist that spreads out over the earth and hides its fertile embrace. Everything is symbol, I myself am a myth about myself, for is it not as a myth that I hasten to this meeting? Who I am has nothing to do with it. Everything finite and temporal is forgotten, only the eternal remains, the power of love, its longing, its happiness. Now my soul is attuned like a bent bow, now my thoughts lie ready like arrows in my quiver, not poisoned, and yet able to blend themselves with the blood. How vigorous is my soul, sound, happy, omnipresent like a god.—Her beauty was a gift of nature. I give thee thanks, O wonderful Nature! Like a mother hast thou watched over her. Accept my gratitude for thy care. Unsophisticated was she. I thank you, you human beings, to whom she was indebted for this. Her development was my handiwork—soon I shall enjoy my reward.—How much have I not gathered into this one moment which now draws nigh. Damnation—if I should fail!

I do not yet see my carriage.—I hear the crack of the whip, it is my coachman.—Drive now for dear life, even if the horses drop dead, only not a single second before we reach the place.

Sept. 25

Why cannot such a night be longer? If Alectryon[13] could forget himself, why cannot the sun be equally sympathetic? Still, it is over now, and I hope never to see her again. When a girl has given away everything, then she is weak, then she has lost everything; for a man

[13] Ares' friend who stood guard at the rendezvous of Ares and Aphrodite, but fell asleep, so that they were surprised by the sun-god and Hephaestus. (S)

guilt is a negative moment, for a woman it is the value of her being. Now all resistance is impossible, and only as long as that is present is it beautiful to love; when it is ended there is only weakness and habit. I do not wish to be reminded of my relation to her; she has lost the fragrance, and the time is past when a girl suffering the pain of a faithless love can be changed into a heliotrope.[14] I will have no farewell with her; nothing is more disgusting to me than a woman's tears and a woman's prayers, which alter everything and yet really mean nothing. I have loved her, but from now on she can no longer engross my soul. If I were a god, I would do for her what Neptune did for a nymph, I would change her into a man.

It would, however, really be worthwhile to show whether one might not be able to poetize himself out of a girl, so that one could make her so proud that she would imagine that it was she who tired of the relationship. It could become a very interesting epilogue, which, as a matter of observation, might have psychological interest, and along with that enrich one with many erotic observations.

VOL. II:

THE AESTHETIC VALIDITY OF MARRIAGE

... This might seem a superfluous investigation, something which everyone is willing to concede, since it has been pointed out often enough. For through many centuries have not knights and adventurers undergone incredible pains and trouble in order to come to harbor in the quiet peace of a happy marriage? Have not novelists and novel readers worked their way through one volume after another in order to stop with a happy marriage? And has not one generation after another endured the troubles and complications of four acts if only there was some likelihood of a happy marriage in the fifth? However, by these prodigious efforts very little has been accomplished for the glorification of marriage, and I doubt very much if by the reading of such works any man has been made capable of performing the task he set himself, or has felt oriented in life. For this precisely is the pernicious, the unwholesome feature of such works, that they end where they ought to begin. After the many fates they have overcome the lovers finally sink into one another's arms. The curtain falls, the book ends; but the reader is none the

---

[14] As happened to Clytie when the sun-god became untrue to her. (S)

wiser. For truly (assuming that the first flame of love is present) it requires no great art to have courage and shrewdness enough to fight with all one's might for the good which one regards as the only good; but on the other hand it surely requires discretion, wisdom, and patience to overcome the lassitude which often is wont to follow upon a wish fulfilled. It is natural that to love in its first outflaming it seems as if it could not suffer enough hardships in acquiring possession of the beloved object, yea, that in case there are no dangers present it is disposed to provide them in order to overcome them. Upon this the whole attention is directed in plays of this sort, and as soon as the dangers are overcome the scenery shifter knows well what he has to do. Hence it is rather rare to see a wedding on the stage or to read of one, except in case the opera or the ballet holds in reserve this factor, which may well furnish an occasion for some sort of dramatic galimatias, for a gorgeous procession, for the significant gesticulations and the heavenly glance of a ballet dancer, for the exchange of rings, etc.

The truth in this whole exposition, the real aesthetic element, consists in the fact that love is represented as a striving, that this feeling is seen fighting its way through opposition. The fault is that this struggle, this dialectic, is entirely external, and that love comes out of this fight quite as abstract as when it entered into it. When once there awakens an apprehension of love's proper dialectic, an apprehension of its pathological struggle, of its relation to the ethical, to the religious, verily one will not have need of hard-hearted fathers or ladies' bowers or enchanted princesses or ogres and monsters in order to give love plenty to do. In our age one rarely encounters such cruel fathers or such frightful monsters, and insofar as modern literature has fashioned itself in conformity with the antique, money has become essentially the opposition medium through which love moves, and again we sit patiently through the four acts if there is a reasonable prospect of a rich uncle dying in the fifth.

However, it is rather seldom one sees such productions and, generally speaking, modern literature is fully occupied with making fun of the abstract conception of immediate love which was the subject of the romantic novelists. . . . Taking it all in all, it is remarkable how voracious modern poetry is, and for a long time it has been living on nothing else but love. Our age reminds one vividly of the dissolution of the Greek city-state: everything goes on as usual, and yet there is no longer any one who believes in it. The invisible spiritual bond which gives it validity no longer exists, and so the whole age is at once comic and tragic—tragic because it is perishing, comic because it goes on. For it is always the imperishable which sustains the perishable, the spiritual which sustains the corporal; and if it might be conceived that an exanimate body could for a little while continue to perform its customary functions, it would in the same way be comic and tragic. But only let our age go on consuming—and the more it manages to consume of the substantial value contained in romantic love, with all the more consternation will it some day, when this annihilation no longer gives pleasure, awaken to the consciousness of what it has lost and despairingly feel its misfortune.

We will now see whether the age which demolished romantic love has succeeded in putting anything better in its place. First, however, I will indicate the mark by which romantic love may be known. One might say in one word that it is *immediate:* to see her was to love her; or, though she saw him only once through a slit in the shuttered window of her chamber, nevertheless from this instant she loved him, him alone in the whole world. Here I ought properly, according to agreement, leave place for a few polemical outbursts in order to promote in you [1] the secretion of bile which is an indispensable condition for the wholesome and profitable appropriation of what I have to say. But for all that I cannot make up my mind to do so, and for two reasons: partly because this is a rather hackneyed theme in our time (and honestly it is incomprehensible to me that in this instance you want to go with the current, whereas ordinarily you go against it); and partly because I really have conserved a certain faith in the reality of romantic love, a sort of reverence for it, accompanied by some feeling of sadness. . . . After all, is it not beautiful to imagine that two beings are meant for one another? How often one has felt the need of reaching out beyond the historical consciousness, a longing, a nostalgia for the primeval forest which lies behind us. And does not this longing acquire a double significance when with it there is associated the conception of another being which also has its home in these regions? Hence every marriage, even one which was entered upon after reflective deliberation, feels the need, at least in certain moments, of such a foreground. And how beautiful it is that the God who is spirit loves also the love which is earthly. The fact that among married people there is great deal of lying in this respect I am very ready to concede to you, and also that your observations in this field have amused me; but one ought never to forget the truth that is

---

[1] "A," the Aestheticist, to whom Judge William's letters are addressed.

in it. Perhaps one or another man may think that it is better to exercise his own sovereign discretion in the choice of "his life's companion," but such an opinion discloses a high degree of narrow-mindedness and a foolish self-importance on the part of the understanding, with no inkling of the fact that romantic love is by its very nature *free*,[2] and that its greatness consists precisely in this quality.

Romantic love shows that it is immediate by the fact that it follows a natural necessity. It is based upon beauty, in part upon sensuous beauty, in part upon the beauty which can be conceived through and with and in the sensuous. . . . In spite of the fact that this love is essentially based upon the sensuous, it is ennobled by reason of the consciousness of eternity which it embodies; for what distinguishes all love from lust is the fact that it bears an impress of eternity. The lovers are sincerely convinced that their relationship is in itself a complete whole which never can be altered. But since this assurance is founded only upon a natural determinant, the eternal is thus based upon the temporal and thereby cancels itself. Since this assurance has undergone no test, has found no higher attestation, it shows itself to be an illusion, and for this reason it is easy to make it ridiculous. People should not, however, be so ready to do this, and it is truly disgusting to see in modern comedy these experienced, intriguing, dissolute women who know that love is an illusion. I know of no creature so abominable as such a woman. No debauchery is so loathsome to me and nothing is so revolting as to see a lovable young girl in the hands of such a woman. Truly this is more terrible than to imagine her in the hands of a club of seducers. It is sad to see a man who has learned to discount every substantial value of life, but to see a woman on this false path is horrible. Romantic love, however, as I have said, presents an analogy to morality by reason of the presumptive eternity which ennobles it and saves it from being mere sensuality. For the sensual is the momentary. The sensual seeks instant satisfaction, and the more refined it is, the better it knows how to make the instant of enjoyment a little eternity.[3] The true eternity in love, as in true morality, delivers it, therefore, first of all from the sensual. But in order to produce this true eternity a determination of the will is called for. Of this I shall say more later.

Our age has perceived very clearly the weak points of romantic love, and its ironical polemic against it has sometimes been thoroughly amus-

[2] This "freedom," however, is a false or capricious freedom—as the next sentence shows.

[3] Cf. "The Seducer's Diary," *passim*.

ing; whether it has remedied its defects and what it has put in its place, we shall now see. One may say that it has taken two paths, one of which is seen at the first glance to be a false one, that is, an immoral path; the other is more respectable, but to my mind it misses the deeper values of love, for if love is in fact founded upon the sensuous, every one can easily see that this "immediate" faithfulness of theirs is foolishness. What wonder then that women want emancipation—one of the many ugly phenomena of our age for which men are responsible. The eternal element in love becomes an object of derision, the temporal element alone is left, but this temporal again is refined into the sensuous eternity, into the eternal instant of the embrace. What I say here applies not only to a seducer here and there who sneaks about in the world like a beast of prey; no, it is appropriate to a numerous chorus of highly gifted men, for it is not only Byron who declares that love is heaven, marriage is hell. It is very evident that there is in this a reflection, something which romantic love does not have. For romantic love is quite willing to accept marriage too, willing to accept the blessing of the Church as a pretty adjunct to the festivity, without attaching to it any real significance on its own account. By reason of its disposition to reflection the love here in question has with a terrible firmness and induration of mind made up a new definition of what unhappy love is, namely, to be loved when one no longer loves—the opposite of loving without requital. And verily, if this tendency were aware what profundity is implied in these few words, it would itself shrink from it. For apart from all the experience, shrewdness and cunning this definition reveals, it contains also a presentiment that conscience exists. So then the moment remains the principal thing, and how often one has heard these shameless words addressed by such a lover to a poor girl who could love only once: "I do not demand so much, I am content with less; far be it from me to require that you shall continue to love me to all eternity, if only you love me at the instant when I wish it." Such lovers know very well that the sensuous is transient, they know also what is the most beautiful instant and therewith they are content.

Such a tendency is, of course, absolutely immoral; yet on the path of thought it brings us in a way nearer our goal, forasmuch as it lodges a formal protest against marriage. Insofar as the same tendency seeks to assume a more decent appearance it does not confine itself merely to the single instant, but extends this to a longer period, yet in such a way that instead of receiving the eternal into its consciousness it receives the temporal, or it entangles itself in this opposition between the temporal and the eternal by supposing a possible alteration in the course of time.

It thinks that for a time one can well enough endure living together, but it would keep open a way of escape so as to be able to choose if a happier choice might offer itself. This reduces marriage to a civil arrangement; one need only report to the proper magistrate that this marriage is ended and another contracted, just as one reports a change of domicile. Whether this is an advantage to the State I leave undecided—for the individual in question it must truly be a strange relationship. Hence one does not always see it realized, but the age is continually threatening us with it. And verily it would require a high degree of impudence to carry it out—I do not think this word is too strong to apply to it—just as on the part of the female participant in this association it would betray a frivolity bordering on depravity.

There is, however, an entirely different disposition of mind which might get this notion into its head, and that is a disposition which I would deal with here more especially, since it is very characteristic of our age. For in fact such a plan may originate either in an *egoistic* or in a *sympathetic melancholy*. . . . The egoistic sort fears, of course, for its own sake, and like all melancholy it is self-indulgent. It has a certain extravagant deference for the thought of an alliance for the whole life, and a secret horror of it. "What assurance has a man that he will not change? Perhaps this being whom I now adore may change; perhaps fate may subsequently bring me into association with another being who for the first time would be truly the ideal I had dreamt of." Like all melancholy it is defiant and knows that it is, thinking "perhaps precisely the fact that I tie myself to one person by an irrevocable bond may make this being whom otherwise I should love with my whole soul intolerable to me; perhaps, perhaps, etc." The sympathetic melancholy is more painful and at the same time rather nobler: it is fearful of itself for the sake of the other. "Who knows so surely that I may not change? Perhaps what I now regard as good in me may vanish; perhaps that by which I now captivate the loved one, and which only for her sake I wish to retain, may be taken from me, and there she stands then, deluded, deceived; perhaps a brilliant prospect opens for her, she is tempted, she does not withstand the temptation. Great God! I should have that upon my conscience! I have nothing to reproach her for, it is I who have changed, I forgive her everything if only she can forgive me for being so imprudent as to let her take a step so decisive. I know indeed in my heart that so far from talking her into it I rather warned her against me; [4] I know that it was her free resolution, but perhaps it was precisely this warning which tempted her, which let her see in me a better being than I am, etc., etc."

It is easy to see that such a way of thinking is no better served by an alliance for five years than by one of ten, or even by an alliance such as Saladin formed with the Christians, for ten years, ten months, ten weeks, ten days, and ten minutes; indeed, is no better served by such an alliance than by one for the whole life. One sees very well that such a way of thinking feels only too deeply the significance of the saying, "Sufficient unto the day is the evil thereof." It is an attempt to live every day as though that day were the decisive one, an attempt to live as though every day were a day of examination. Hence, when one finds in our times a strong disposition to abolish marriage, this is not as in the Middle Ages because the unmarried life is regarded as more perfect, but the reason of it is cowardice and self-indulgence. It is also evident that such marriages as are contracted for a definite time are of no avail, since they involve the same difficulties as those which are contracted for a whole life, and at the same time are so far from bestowing the required strength for living that on the contrary they enervate the inner power of married life, relax the energy of the will, and diminish the blessing of confidence which marriage possesses. It is also clear at this point, and will subsequently become more so, that such associations are not marriages, inasmuch as, though contracted in the sphere of reflection, they have not yet attained the consciousness of the eternal which morality has and without which such an association is not marriage. There is also something upon which you will agree with me entirely, for how often and how surely have your mockery and your irony hit the mark when you were denouncing what you call "fortuitous love affairs" and the "bad infinity" of love—when one is looking with his sweetheart out of the window, and that instant a young girl turns the corner into another street, and it occurs to him, "It is with her I am really in love," but when he would follow her trace he is again unsettled, etc.

The other expedient, [5] the respectable way, would be the marriage of convenience. The mere mention of it shows that reason intervenes, and that we have entered the sphere of reflection. One person and another, and you among them, have always made a dubious face at the union

---

[4] As S.K. warned Regina against himself.
[5] I.e. the second substitute for romantic love. Cf. p. 84.

here implied between immediate love and the calculating understanding; for really, if one were to show respect for linguistic usage, it ought to be called a marriage of common sense. Especially are you accustomed, with an ambiguous use of words, to recommend "respect" as a solid foundation for the marriage relation. It shows how thoroughly reflective this age is, that it must help itself out with such a compromise as a marriage of convenience. Insofar as such an association waives all claim to real love it is at least consistent, but at the same time it thereby shows that it is not a solution of the problem. A marriage of convenience is therefore to be regarded as a sort of capitulation, necessitated by the complications of life. But how pitiful it is that this should be the only comfort that is left to the poetry of our age, the comfort of despairing; for it is evidently despair which makes such an alliance acceptable. It is contracted, therefore, more likely by persons who no longer are chickens, and who also have learned that love is an illusion and its realization at the most a *pium desiderium*. What it therefore has to do with is life's prose, subsistence, and social standing.

Insofar as it has neutralized the sensuous factor in marriage it appears to be moral, but it nevertheless remains a question whether this neutralization is not just as immoral as it is unaesthetic. Even when the erotic is not entirely neutralized, it is nevertheless disheartened by a cool common-sense consideration that one must be prudent, not be too quick in sorting and rejecting, that life after all never presents the ideal, that it is quite a respectable match, etc. The eternal, which (as has been shown above) is properly a part of every marriage is not really present here; for a common-sense calculation is always temporal. Such an alliance is therefore at once immoral and fragile. Such a marriage of convenience may assume a prettier form when the motive is somewhat higher. In such a case it is a motive foreign to the marriage which decides the matter—as, e.g. when a young girl, out of love for her family, marries a man who is in a position to rescue it. But precisely this outward teleology shows clearly that we cannot seek here a solution of the problem. At this point I might perhaps aptly deal with the manifold motives to marriage about which there is a great deal of talk. However, I prefer to reserve this subject for another place,[6] where also, if possible, I may be able to make this talk hold its tongue.

We have now seen how romantic love was built upon an illusion, that

[6] The "Observations on Marriage" in the *Stages*.

the eternity it claims was built upon the temporal, and that although the knight of romantic love was sincerely convinced of its absolute durability, there nevertheless was no certainty of this, inasmuch as its trials and temptations have hitherto been in a medium which was entirely external. Such being the case, it was able with a pretty piety to accept marriage along with love, although, after all, this acquired no very deep significance. We have seen how this immediate and beautiful but also very naïve love, being embodied in the consciousness of a reflective age, must become the object of its mockery and of its irony; and we have seen too what such an age was capable of substituting for it. Such an age embodied marriage in its consciousness and in part declared itself on the side of love in such a way as to exclude marriage, in part on the side of marriage in such a way as to exclude love. Hence, in a recent play a sensible little seamstress, speaking of the love of fine gentlemen, makes the shrewd observation, "You love us but you don't marry us; the fine ladies you don't love, but you marry them."

. . . However many painful confusions life may still have in store, I fight for two things: for the prodigious task of showing that marriage is the transfiguration of first love, that it is its friend, not its enemy; and for the task (which to others is very trivial but to me is all the more important) of showing that my humble marriage has had such a meaning for me, so that from it I derive strength and courage to fulfill constantly this task. . . .

Let us now glance at the relation between romantic and conjugal love. Romantic love remains constantly abstract in itself, and if it is able to acquire no external history, death already is lying in wait for it, because its eternity is illusory. Conjugal love begins with possession and acquires inward history. It is faithful. So is romantic love—but now note the difference. The faithful romantic lover waits, let us say, for fifteen years—then comes the instant which rewards him. Here poetry rightly sees that the fifteen years can very well be concentrated. It hastens on, then, to the moment. A married man is faithful for fifteen years, yet during those fifteen years he has had possession, so in the long succession of time he has acquired faithfulness. But such an ideal marriage cannot be represented, for the very point is time in its extension. At the end of the fifteen years he apparently got no further than he was at the beginning, yet he has lived in a high degree aesthetically. His possession has not been like dead property, but he has constantly been acquiring his possession. He has not fought with lions and ogres, but with the most dangerous enemy—with time. For him eternity does not come afterwards as in the case of the knight, but he has had eternity in time. He alone, therefore, has triumphed over time; for one can say of the knight that he has killed time, as indeed a man constantly wishes to kill time when it has no reality for him. But this is never the perfect victory. The married man, being a true conquerer, has not killed time but has saved it and preserved it in eternity. The married man who does this truly lives poetically. He solves the great riddle of living in eternity and yet hearing the hall clock strike, and hearing it in such a way that the stroke of the hour does not shorten but prolong his eternity—a contradiction as profound but far more glorious than the situation described in a well known tale of the Middle Ages which tells of an unhappy man who awoke in hell and cried out, "What time is it?" and the devil answered, "An eternity." And now even if this is something which cannot be represented in art, let it be your comfort as it is mine that the highest and most beautiful things in life are not to be heard about, nor read about, nor seen but, if one will, may be lived. When, then, I willingly admit that romantic love lends itself more aptly to artistic representation than does conjugal love, this is not by any means to say that the latter is less aesthetic than the former; on the contrary, it is more aesthetic. In one of the tales of the Romantic School [7] which evinces the greatest genius, there is one character who has no desire to write poetry like the others among whom he lives, because it is a waste of time and deprives him of the true enjoyment; he prefers to live. Now if he had had the right conception of what it is to live, he would have been the man for me.

Conjugal love has its foe in time, its triumph in time, its eternity in time, and so it would have its problems, even if I were to imagine it free from all the so-called external and internal trials. Generally, it has these too; but if one were to interpret them rightly, one must observe two things: that these trials are constantly inward determinants; and that they constantly have in them the determinant of time. It is easy to see that for this reason, too, conjugal love cannot be represented. It constantly drags itself back inwardly, and (to use the expression in a good sense) it constantly drags along in time; but what is to be represented by reproduction must let itself be lured out, and its time must be capable of abbreviation. You may convince yourself of this more thoroughly by considering the predicates commonly applied to conjugal love. It is faithful, constant, humble, patient, long-suffering, indulgent, sincere, contented, vigilant, willing, joyful. All these virtues have the character-

[7] Fr. Schlegel's *Lucinde.* (L)

istic that they are inward qualifications of the individual. The individual is not fighting with external foes but fights with himself, fights out love from within him. And they have reference to time, for their truth does not consist in being once for all, but in being constantly what they are. And by these virtues nothing else is acquired, only they themselves are acquired. Conjugal love does not come with any outward sign, like "the rich bird" with whizzing and bluster, but it is the imperishable nature of a quiet spirit.

Of this fact you and all natures born for conquest have no conception. You are never in yourselves, but constantly outside yourselves. Yea, so long as every nerve in you is aquiver, whether when you are stealing softly about, or when you step out boldly and Janizary music within you drowns out your consciousness—then you feel that you are living. But when the battle is won, when the last echo of the last shot has died away, when the swift thoughts, like a staff officer hurrying back to head-quarters, report that the victory is yours—then, in fact, you know nothing more, you know not how to begin; for then, for the first time, you are at the true beginning.

What you, therefore, under the name of custom abhor as unavoidable in marriage is merely the historical factor in it, which in your perverted eye acquires such a terrifying aspect.

But what is this thing you are accustomed to think of as not merely annihilated but profaned by the "custom" which is inseparable from conjugal love? Generally you think of what you call "the visible sacred symbol of the erotic," which, as you say, "like all signs or tokens, has in itself no importance but depends for its significance upon the energy, the artistic bravura and virtuosity, themselves proofs of inborn genius, with which it is executed." "How disgusting it is," you say, "to see the languor with which such things are performed in married life, how perfunctorily, how sluggishly it is done, almost at the stroke of the clock—pretty much as among the tribe the Jesuits discovered in Paraguay, which was so sluggish that the Jesuits found it necessary to ring a bell at midnight as a welcome notice to all husbands, to remind them thereby of their marital duties. So everything is done on time, as they are trained to do it." Let us at this point agree that in our meditation we shall not let ourselves be disturbed by the fact that there is a great deal to be seen in existence which is ludicrous and preposterous; let us simply see whether it is necessary and, if so, learn from you the way of salvation. In this respect I dare not expect much from you; for like the Spanish knight of the doleful countenance you are fighting, though in a different sense, for a vanished time. For as you are fighting for *the moment* against *time,* you actually are fighting for what has vanished. Let us take an idea, an expression, from your poetic world, or from the real world of first love: "the lovers *look* at one another." You know very well how to underscore this word "look" and to put into it an infinite reality, an eternity. In this sense a married couple who have lived together for ten years and have seen one another daily cannot "look" at one another. But might they not therefore be able to look lovingly at one another? Now here we have again your old heresy. You have got to the point of limiting love to a certain age, and limiting love for one person to a very short period of time. Thereupon, like all conquering natures, you seek recruits in order to carry out your experiment—but this, indeed, is the very deepest profanation of the eternal power of love. This, indeed, is despair. However you turn and twist, you must admit that the gist of the matter is to preserve love in time. If this is impossible, then love is an impossibility. Your misfortune is that you recognize love simply and solely by these visible signs. If they are to be repeated again and again, and must be accompanied, you are to note, by a morbid reflection as to whether they continually possess the reality they once had by reason of the accidental circumstance that it was the first time, it is no wonder you are alarmed and that you associate these signs and "gesticulations" with things of which one dare not say *decies repetita placebunt*;[8] for if that which gives them value was the characteristic qualification "the first time," a repetition is indeed impossible. But healthy love has an entirely different worth: it is in time that it accomplishes its work, and therefore it will be capable of rejuvenating itself by means of these outward signs, and (what to me is the principal thing) it has an entirely different conception of time and of the significance of repetition.

I have shown in the foregoing discussion that conjugal love has its conflict in time, its victory in time, its blessing in time. I then regarded time merely as simple progression; now I shall show that it is not merely a simple progression in which the original datum is preserved, but a growing progression in which the original datum increases. You who have made so many observations will certainly grant that I am right in making the general observation that men are divided into two great classes: those who predominantly live in hope, and those who predominantly live in recollection. Both have a wrong relation to time. The healthy individual lives at once both in hope and in recollection, and only thereby does his life acquire true and substantial continuity. So,

[8] "Ten times repeated, they will please." (Horace, *Ars. Poetica,* 365.)

then, he has hope and does not wish, like those who live off recollection, to return backward in time. What, then, does recollection do for him? For after all, some influence it surely must have. It sets a cross over the note of the instant—the further back recollection goes, and the more frequent the repetition, the more crosses there are. Thus, if in the present year the individual experiences an erotic moment, this is enhanced by the fact that he recollects it in the preceding year, etc. In a beautiful way this has also found expression in married life. I do not know what may now be the age of the world, but you know as well as I that people are accustomed to say that first comes the golden age, then the silver age, then the copper age, then the iron age. In marriage this is inverted: first comes the silver wedding, then the golden wedding. Is not recollection really the point of such a wedding? And yet the marriage terminology declares that this is still more beautiful than the first wedding. Now you must not misunderstand this—as you would do, for instance, if you might be pleased to say, "Then it would be best to get married in the cradle in order to begin promptly with one's silver wedding and have hope of being the first inventor of a brand-new term in the vocabulary of married life." You yourself presumably perceive the fallacy of your witticism, and I shall not dwell upon it any further. What I would remind you of, however, is that the individuals are in fact not merely living in hope; they constantly have in the present both the one and the other, both hope and recollection. At the first wedding hope has the same effect that recollection has at the last. Hope hovers over them as the hope of eternity which fills the moment to the brim. You also will perceive the correctness of this when you reflect that if one were to marry merely in the hope of a silver wedding, and then hoped and hoped again for twenty-five years, one would be in no state to celebrate the silver wedding when the twenty-fifth year came around, for indeed one would have nothing to recollect, since with all this hoping everything would have fallen apart. Moreover, it has often occurred to me to wonder why, according to the universal usage and way of thinking, the state of single blessedness has no such brilliant prospects, that on the contrary, people rather turn it to ridicule when a bachelor celebrates a jubilee. The reason, doubtless, is that in general it is assumed that the single state never can rightly grasp the true present, which is a unity of hope and recollection, and that therefore, bachelors are for the most part addicted either to hope or to recollection. But this again suggests the correct relation to time which common estimation also attributes to conjugal love.

There is also something else, however, in married life which you characterize by the word "custom": "its monotony," you say, "the total lack of events, its everlasting vacuity, which is death and worse than death." You know that there are neurasthenics who may be disturbed by the slightest noise, who are unable to think when someone is walking softly across the floor. Have you observed that there is also another sort of neurasthenia? There are people so weak that they need loud noise and a distracting environment in order to be able to work. Why is this, unless for the fact that they have no command over themselves, except in an inverse sense? When they are alone their thoughts disappear in the indefinite; on the other hand, when there is noise and hubbub around them, this compels them to pit their will against it. It is for this reason you are afraid of peace and quietness and repose. You are within yourself only when there is opposition, but therefore you are never within yourself. That is to say, the moment you assimilate opposition there is quiet again. Therefore you do not dare to do so. But then you and the opposition remain standing face to face, and so you are not within yourself.

The same thing, of course, applies here which we noted earlier in the case of time. You are outside yourself and therefore cannot dispense with "the other" as an opposition; you believe that only a restless spirit is alive, whereas all men of experience think that only a quiet spirit is truly alive; for you, an agitated sea is the image of life, for me it is still deep waters. Often I have sat by a bit of purling water. It is always the same, the same soft melody, the same green plants on its floor, swaying beneath its quiet waves, the same little creatures running about at the bottom, a little fish which glides under the protection of the overhanging flowers, spreading out its fins against the current, hiding under a stone. How monotonous, and yet how rich in change! Such is the home life of marriage: quiet, modest, purling—it has not many *changements,* and yet like that water it purls, yet like that water it has melody, dear to the man who knows it, dear to him above all other sounds because he knows it. It makes no pompous display, and yet sometimes there is shed over it a luster which does not interrupt its customary course, as when the moonbeams fall upon the water and reveal the instrument upon which it plays its melody. Such is the home life of marriage. But in order to be seen thus and to be lived thus it presupposes the one quality which I shall mention to you. I find it mentioned in a poem by Oehlenschläger upon which, at least in time gone by, I know you set great store. For the sake of completeness I shall transcribe the whole of it:

How much must come together in the world
That love's enchantment may be brought to pass!
First the two hearts which know each other well,
Then charm which doth accompany them both,
The moon then casting its bewitching beams
Through the beech forests in the early spring,
Then that these two can meet there all alone—
Then the first kiss—and then . . . their innocence.

You too are given to eulogizing love. I will not deprive you of that which is not indeed your property, for it is the property of the poet, but which, nevertheless, you have appropriated; but since I too have appropriated it, let us share it: you get the whole poem; I, the last words: "their innocence."

Finally, there is still another side to married life which has often given you occasion for attack. You say, "Conjugal love conceals in itself something quite different. It seems so mild and heartfelt and tender, but as soon as the door is closed behind the married pair, then before you can say Jack Robinson out comes the word *duty*. You may deck out this scepter as much as you will, you can make it into a Shrovetide rod, it still remains a rod." I deal with this objection here because it also is due essentially to a misunderstanding of the historical factor in conjugal love. You would have it that either obscure powers or caprice are the constituent factors of love. As soon as consciousness comes forward to join them this enchantment vanishes. But this consciousness is conjugal love. To express it quite crudely—in place of the wand with which the director of the orchestra indicates the tempo for the graceful attitudes assumed in the dance of first love, you show us the unpleasant stick of the policeman. First of all you must concede to me that so long as there is no alteration in first love (and this, we have agreed, is contained in conjugal love) there can be no question of the strict necessity of duty.[9] So the fact is, you do not believe in the eternity of first love. Here we are back again at your old heresy: it is you who so often assume to be the knight of first love, and yet you do not believe in it, yea, you profane it. So because you do not believe in it, you dare not enter into an alliance which, when you no longer are *volens* may compel you *nolens* to remain in it. For you, therefore, love is obviously not the highest thing, for otherwise you would be glad there was a power capable of compelling you to

[9] I.e. no question of duty in the strict sense of being bound to do what one does not truly want to do.

remain in it. You will, perhaps, make answer that this remedy is no remedy; but to that I will remark that it depends upon how one looks at the matter.

This is one of the points to which we constantly return—you, as it seems, against your will and without being quite clear what it involves, I with full consciousness of its significance: the point, namely, that the illusory or naïve eternity of first or romantic love cancels itself out, in one way or another. Just because you try to retain love in this immediate form, try to make yourself believe that true freedom consists in being outside oneself, intoxicated by dreams, therefore you fear the metamorphosis, not regarding it as such but as something altogether heterogeneous which implies the death of first love, and hence your abhorrence of duty. For, of course, if duty has not already subsisted as a germ in first love, it is absolutely disturbing when it makes its appearance. But such is not the case with conjugal love. Already in the ethical and religious factors it has duty in it, and when this appears before it, it is not as a stranger, a shameless intruder, who nevertheless has such authority that one dare not by virtue of the mysteriousness of love show him the door. No, duty comes as an old friend, an intimate, a confidant, whom the lovers mutually recognize in the deepest secret of their love. And when he speaks it is nothing new he has to say, and when he has spoken the individuals humble themselves under it, but at the same time are uplifted just because they are assured that what he enjoins is what they themselves wish, and that his commanding it is merely a more majestic, a more exalted, a divine way of expressing the fact that their wish can be realized. It would not have been enough if he had encouraged them by saying, "It can be done, love can be preserved"; but when he says, "It shall be preserved," there is in that an authority which answers to the heartfelt desire of love. Love drives out fear; yet when love is for a moment fearful for itself, fearful of its own salvation, duty is the nutriment of all others love stands in need of; for it says, "Fear not, you shall conquer," speaking not futuristically, for that only suggests hope, but imperatively, and in this lies an assurance which nothing can shake.

So then you regard duty as the enemy of love; I regard it as its friend. You will, perhaps, be content at hearing this declaration, and with your customary mockery will congratulate me on such an interesting and uncommon friend. I, on the other hand, will by no means be satisfied with this reply, but will take the liberty of carrying the war into your own territory. If duty, once it has appeared in consciousness, is an enemy of love, then love must do its best to conquer it; for you, after all, would not think of love as a being so impotent that it cannot vanquish every opposition. On the other hand, you think that when duty makes its appearance it is all over with love, and you think also that duty, early or late, must make its appearance, not merely in conjugal love but also in romantic love; and the truth is that you are afraid of conjugal love because it has in it duty to such a degree that when it makes its appearance you cannot run away from it. In romantic love, on the other hand, you think this is all right, for as soon as the instant arrives when duty is mentioned, love is over, and the arrival of duty is the signal for you, with a very courtly bow, to say farewell. Here you see again what your eulogies of love amount to. If duty is the enemy of love, and if love cannot vanquish this enemy, then love is not the true conqueror. The consequence is that you must leave love in the lurch. When once you have got the desperate idea that duty is the enemy of love, your defeat is certain, and you have done just as much to disparage love and deprive it of its majesty as you have done to show despite of duty, and yet it was only the latter you meant to do. You see, this again is despair, whether you feel the pain of it or seek in despair to forget it. If you cannot reach the point of seeing the aesthetical, the ethical, and the religious as three great allies, if you do not know how to conserve the unity of the diverse appearances which everything assumes in these diverse spheres, then life is devoid of meaning, then one must grant that you are justified in maintaining your pet theory that one can say of everything, "Do it or don't do it—you will regret both." . . .

If you hold fast what I have set forth in the foregoing treatise, just as I have expounded it, you will easily perceive that in holding fast to the inwardness of duty in love I have not done so with the wild alarm which sometimes is displayed by men in whom prosaic common sense has first annihilated the feelings of immediacy and who then, in their old age, have betaken themselves to duty, men who in their blindness cannot express strongly enough their scorn of the purely natural, nor stupidly enough sing the praise of duty—as though with this it was different from what you call it. Of such a breach between love and duty I, thank God, know nothing; I have not fled with my love into wild regions and deserts where in my loneliness I return to savagery, neither have I asked all my neighbors what I should do. Such isolation and such participation are equally mad. . . . But I have not been afraid of duty; it has not appeared before me as an enemy which would disturb the bit of happiness and joy I had hoped to preserve through life; rather it has appeared before me as a friend, the first and only confidant of our love.

But this power of having constantly a free outlook is the blessing bestowed by duty, whereas romantic love goes astray or comes to an
impasse because of its unhistorical character.

VOL. II: EQUILIBRIUM

BETWEEN THE AESTHETICAL AND THE ETHICAL

IN THE COMPOSITION OF PERSONALITY

My Friend,

What I have so often said to you I say now once again, or rather I
shout it: Either/or, *aut/aut*. . . . There are situations in life where it
would be ridiculous or a species of madness to apply an either/or; but
also, there are men whose souls are too dissolute (in the etymological
sense of the word) to grasp what is implied in such a dilemma, whose
personalities lack the energy to say with pathos, Either/or. Upon me
these words have always made a deep impression, and they still do,
especially when I pronounce them absolutely and without specific reference to any objects, for this use of them suggests the possibility of
starting the most dreadful contrasts into action. They affect me like a
magic formula of incantation, and my soul becomes exceeding serious,
sometimes almost harrowed. I think of my early youth, when without
clearly comprehending what it is to make a choice I listened with childish trust to the talk of my elders, and the instant of choice was solemn
and venerable, although in choosing I was only following the instructions of another person. I think of the occasions in my later life when I
stood at the crossways, when my soul was matured in the hour of decision. I think of the many occasions in life less important but by no
means indifferent to me, when it was a question of making a choice.
For although there is only one situation in which either/or has absolute
significance, namely when truth, righteousness, and holiness are lined
up on one side, and lust and base propensities and obscure passions and
perdition on the other; yet it is always important to choose rightly, even
as between things which one may innocently choose; it is important to
test oneself, lest some day one might have to beat a retreat to the point
from which one started,[1] and might have reason to thank God if one had
to reproach oneself for nothing worse than a waste of time. In common

---

[1] A leading ethical idea of S.K.'s is the "reversal" of one's path which is necessary
in order to undo the effects of evil. Cf. pp. 103–104, 346–347; see also *Journals*, 635.

parlance I use these words as others use them, and it would indeed be a foolish pedantry to give up using them. But sometimes it occurs, nevertheless, that I become aware of using them with regard to things entirely indifferent. Then they lay aside their humble dress, I forget the insignificant thoughts they discriminated, they advance to meet me with all their dignity, in their official robes. As a magistrate in common life may appear in plain clothes and mingle without distinction in the crowd, so do these words mingle in common speech—when, however, the magistrate steps forward with authority he distinguishes himself from all. Like such a magistrate whom I am accustomed to see only on solemn occasions, these words appear before me, and my soul always becomes serious. And although my life now has to a certain degree its either/or behind it, yet I know well that it may still encounter many a situation where the either/or will have its full significance. I hope, however, that these words may find me in a worthy state of mind when they check me on my path, and I hope that I may be successful in choosing the right course; at all events, I shall endeavor to make the choice with real earnestness, and with that I venture, at least, to hope that I shall the sooner get out of the wrong path.

And now as for you—this phrase is only too often on your lips, it has almost become a byword with you. What significance has it for you? None at all. You, according to your own expression, regard it as a wink of the eye, a snap of the fingers, a *coup de main,* an abracadabra. At every opportunity you know how to introduce it, nor is it without effect; for it affects you as strong drink affects a neurasthenic, you become completely intoxicated by what you call the higher madness. "It is the compendium," you say, "of all practical wisdom, but no one has ever inculcated it so pithily (like a god in the form of a puppet talking to suffering humanity) as that great thinker and true practical philosopher who said to a man who had insulted him by pulling off his hat and throwing it on the floor, 'If you pick it up, you'll get a thrashing; if you don't pick it up, you'll also get a thrashing; now you can choose.'" You take great delight in "comforting" people when they have recourse to you in critical situations. You listen to their exposition of the case and then say, "Yes, I perceive perfectly that there are two possibilities, one can either do this or that. My sincere opinion and my friendly counsel is as follows: Do it, or don't do it—you will regret both." But he who mocks others mocks himself, and your rejoinder is not a mere nothing but a profound mockery of yourself, a sorry proof how limp your soul is, that your whole philosophy of life is concentrated in one single proposition, "I say merely 'Either—or.'" [2] In case this really was your serious meaning, there would be nothing one could do with you, one must simply put up with you as you are and deplore the fact that melancholy [literally, heavy-mindedness] or light-mindedness had enfeebled your spirit. Now on the contrary, since one knows very well that such is not the case, one is not tempted to pity you but rather to wish that some day the circumstances of your life may tighten upon you the screws in its rack and compel you to come out with what really dwells in you; that they may begin the sharper inquisition of the rack which cannot be beguiled by nonsense and witticisms. Life is a masquerade, you explain, and for you this is inexhaustible material for amusement; and so far, no one has succeeded in knowing you; for every revelation you make is always an illusion, it is only in this way that you are able to breathe and prevent people from pressing importunately upon you and obstructing your respiration. Your occupation consists in preserving your hiding-place, and that you succeed in doing, for your mask is the most enigmatical of all. In fact you are nothing; you are merely a relation to others, and what you are you are by virtue of this relation. To a fond shepherdess you hold out a languishing hand, and instantly you are masked in all possible bucolic sentimentality. A reverend spiritual father you deceive with a brotherly kiss, etc. You yourself are nothing, an enigmatic figure on whose brow is inscribed, *Either—or*. "For this," you say, "is my motto, and these words are not, as the grammarians believe, disjunctive conjunctions; no, they belong inseparably together and therefore ought to be written as one word, inasmuch as in their union they constitute an interjection which I shout at mankind, just as boys shout 'Hep' after a Jew."

Now although nothing you say in that style has the slightest effect upon me, or, if it has any effect, it is at the utmost the effect of arousing a righteous indignation, nevertheless for your own sake I will reply to you. Do you not know that there comes a midnight hour when every one has to throw off his mask? Do you believe that life will always let itself be mocked? Do you think you can slip away a little before midnight in order to avoid this? Or are you not terrified by it? I have seen men in real life who so long deceived others that at last their true nature could not reveal itself; I have seen men who played hide and seek so long that at last in madness they disgustingly obtruded upon others their secret thoughts which hitherto they had proudly concealed.

[2] The Aestheticist is surely not entitled to the mark of disjunction, though Kierkegaard himself made no such distinction since he did not employ the mark in either case.

Or can you think of anything more frightful than that it might end with your nature being resolved into a multiplicity, that you really might become many, become, like those unhappy demoniacs, a legion, and you thus would have lost the inmost and holiest thing of all in a man, the unifying power of personality? Truly, you should not jest with that which is not only serious but dreadful. In every man there is something which to a certain degree prevents him from becoming perfectly transparent to himself; and this may be the case in so high a degree, he may be so inexplicably woven into relationships of life which extend far beyond himself, that he almost cannot reveal himself. But he who cannot reveal himself cannot love, and he who cannot love is the most unhappy man of all. My young friend, suppose there was no one who troubled himself to guess your riddle—what joy, then, would you have in it? [3] But above all, for your own sake, for the sake of your salvation— for I am acquainted with no condition of soul which can better be described as perdition—stop this wild flight, this passion of annihilation which rages in you; for this is what you desire, you would annihilate everything, you would satiate the hunger of doubt at the expense of existence. To this end you cultivate yourself, to this end you harden your temper; for you are willing to admit that you are good for nothing, the only thing that gives you pleasure is to march seven times around existence and blow the trumpet and thereupon let the whole thing collapse, that your soul may be tranquilized, yea, attuned to sadness, that you may summon Echo forth—for Echo is heard only in emptiness.

However, I am not likely to get further with you along this path; moreover, my head is too weak, if you would put it that way, to be able to hold out, or, as I prefer to say, too strong to take pleasure in seeing everything grow dizzy before my eyes. I will therefore take up the matter from another side. Imagine a young man at the age when life really begins to have significance for him: he is wholesome, pure, joyful, intellectually gifted, himself rich in hope, the hope of every one who knows him; imagine (yea, it is hard that I have to say this) that he was mistaken in you, that he believed you were a serious, tried and experienced man from whom one could confidently expect enlightenment upon life's riddles; imagine that he turned to you with the charming confidence which is the adornment of youth, with the claim not to be gainsaid which is youth's privilege—what would you answer him?

[3] "Without knowing it, the neurotic person is in the dilemma of being incapable of loving and yet being in great need of love from others." (Karen Horney, *The Neurotic Personality of Our Time,* p. 107.)

Would you answer, "I say merely 'Either—or' "? That you would hardly do. Would you (as you are wont to express it when you would indicate your aversion to having other people vex you with their affairs of the heart), would you stick your head out of the window and say, "Try the next house"? Or would you treat him as you do others who ask your advice or seek information from you, whom you dismiss as you do the collector of tithes by saying that you are only a lodger in life, not a householder and paterfamilias? No, you would not do this either. A young man with intellectual gifts is the sort of thing you prize only too highly. But in the case I suppose, your relation to the youth is not just what you would have wished, it was not an accidental encounter which brought you in contact with him, your irony was not tempted. Although he was the younger, you the older man, it was he, nevertheless, who by the noble quality of his youth made the instant serious. It is true, is it not, that you yourself would like to be young, would feel that there was something beautiful in being young but also something very serious, that it is by no means a matter of indifference how one employs one's youth, but that before one there lies a choice, a real either/or. You would feel that, after all, the important thing is not to cultivate one's mind but to mature one's personality. Your good nature, your sympathy, would be set in motion, in that spirit you would talk to him; you would fortify his soul, confirm him in the confidence he has in the world, you would assure him that there is a power in a man which is able to defy the whole world, you would insist that he take to heart the importance of employing time well. All this you can do, and when you will, you can do it handsomely.

But now mark well what I would say to you, young man—for though you are not young, one is always compelled to address you as such. Now what did you do in this case? You acknowledged, as ordinarily you are not willing to do, the importance of an either/or. And why? Because your soul was moved by love for the young man. And yet in a way you deceived him, for he will, perhaps, encounter you at another time when it by no means suits your convenience to acknowledge this importance. Here you see one of the sorry consequences of the fact that a man's nature cannot harmoniously reveal itself. You thought you were doing the best for him, and yet perhaps you have harmed him; perhaps he would have been better able to maintain himself against your distrust of life than to find repose in the subjective, deceitful trust you conveyed to him. Imagine that after the lapse of several years you again encountered him: he was lively, intellectual, daring in his thought, bold in his expression, but your ear easily detected doubt in his soul, you conceived a suspicion that he had acquired the questionable wisdom: "I say merely Either—or." It is true, is it not, that you would be sorry for him, would feel that he had lost something, and something very essential? But for yourself you will not sorrow, you are content with your ambiguous wisdom, yea, proud of it, so proud that you will not suffer another to share it, since you wish to be alone with it. And yet you find it deplorable in another connection, and it is your sincere opinion that it was deplorable for the young man to have reached the same wisdom. What a monstrous contradiction! Your whole nature contradicts itself. But you can only get out of this contradiction by an either/or, and I who love you more sincerely than you loved this young man, I who in my life have experienced the significance of choice, I congratulate you upon the fact that you are still so young, that even though you always will be sensible of some loss, yet if you have, or rather if you will to have the requisite energy, you can win what is the chief thing in life— win yourself, acquire your own self.[4]

Now in case a man were able to maintain himself upon the pinnacle of the instant of choice, in case he could cease to be a man, in case he were in his inmost nature only an airy thought, in case personality meant nothing more than to be a kobold, which takes part indeed in the movements, but nevertheless remains unchanged; in case such were the situation, it would be foolish to say that it might ever be too late for a man to choose, for in a deeper sense there could be no question of a choice. The choice itself is decisive for the content of the personality, through the choice the personality immerses itself in the thing chosen, and when it does not choose it withers away in consumption. For an instant it is as if, for an instant it may seem as if the thing with regard to which a choice was made lay outside of the chooser, that he stands in no relationship to it, that he can preserve a state of indifference over against it. This is the instant of deliberation, but this, like the Platonic instant,[5] has no existence, least of all in the abstract sense in which you would hold it fast, and the longer one stares at it the less it exists. That which has to be chosen stands in the deepest relationship to the chooser and, when it is a question of a choice involving a life problem, the individual must naturally be living in the meantime; hence it comes

[4] Cf. *The Sickness unto Death,* where this theme is treated at length from a religious point of view.

[5] *Parmenides,* Chap. 19, defines the "now" as the border between the "before" and the "after." (L)

about that the longer he postpones the choice the easier it is for him to alter its character, notwithstanding that he is constantly deliberating and deliberating and believes that thereby he is holding the alternatives distinctly apart. When life's either/or is regarded in this way, one is not easily tempted to jest with it. One sees, then, that the inner drift of the personality leaves no time for thought-experiments, that it constantly hastens onward and in one way or another posits this alternative or that, making the choice more difficult the next instant, because what has thus been posited must be revoked. Think of the captain on his ship at the instant when it has to come about. He will perhaps be able to say, "I can either do this or that"; but in case he is not a pretty poor navigator, he will be aware at the same time that the ship is all the while making its usual headway, and that therefore it is only an instant when it is indifferent whether he does this or that. So it is with a man. If he forgets to take account of the headway, there comes at last an instant when there no longer is any question of an either/or, not because he has chosen but because he has neglected to choose, which is equivalent to saying, because others have chosen for him, because he has lost his self.

You will perceive also in what I have just been saying how essentially my view of choice differs from yours (if you can properly be said to have any view), for yours differs precisely in the fact that it prevents you from choosing. For me the instant of choice is very serious, not so much on account of the rigorous cogitation involved in weighing the alternatives, not on account of the multiplicity of thoughts which attach themselves to every link in the chain, but rather because there is danger afoot, danger that the next instant it may not be equally in my power to choose, that something already has been lived which must be lived over again. To think that for an instant one can keep one's personality a blank, or that strictly speaking one can break off and bring to a halt the course of the personal life, is a delusion. The personality is already interested in the choice before one chooses, and when the choice is postponed the personality chooses unconsciously, or the choice is made by obscure powers within it. So when at last the choice is made, one discovers (unless, as I remarked before, the personality has been completely volatilized) that there is something which must be done over again, something which must be revoked, and this is often very difficult. We read in fairy tales about human beings whom mermaids and mermen enticed into their power by means of demoniac music. In order to break the enchantment it was necessary in the fairy tale for the person who was under the spell to play the same piece of music backwards without making a single mistake. This is very profound, but very difficult to perform, and yet so it is: the errors one has taken into oneself one must eradicate in this way, and every time one makes a mistake one must begin all over.

Therefore it is important to choose and to choose in time. You, on the contrary, have another method—for I know very well that the polemical side you turn toward the world is not your true nature. Yea, if to *deliberate* were the proper task for a human life, you would be pretty close to perfection. I will adduce an example. To fit your case the contrasts must be bold: either a parson/or an actor. Here is the dilemma. Now all your passionate energy is awakened, reflection with its hundred arms lays hold of the thought of being a parson. You find no repose, day and night you think about it, you go to church three times every Sunday, pick up acquaintance with parsons, write sermons yourself, deliver them to yourself; for half a year you are dead to the whole world, you can now talk of the clerical calling with more insight and apparently with more experience than many who have been parsons for twenty years. When you encounter such men it arouses your indignation that they do not know how to get the thing off their chests with more eloquence. "Is this enthusiasm?" you say. "Why, I who am not a parson, who have not consecrated myself to this calling, speak with the voice of angels as compared with them." That, perhaps, is true enough, but nevertheless you have not become a parson. Then you act in the same way with respect to the other task, and your enthusiasm for art almost surpasses your clerical eloquence. Then you are ready to choose. However, one may be sure that in the prodigious thought-production you were engaged in there must have been lots of waste products, many incidental reflections and observations. Hence the instant you have to choose, life and animation enter into this waste mass, a new either/or presents itself—jurist, or perhaps advocate, as this has something in common with both the other alternatives. Now you are lost. For that moment you are at once advocate enough to be able to prove the reasonableness of taking this third possibility into account. So your life drifts on.

After you have wasted a year and a half on such deliberations, after you have with admirable energy exerted to the utmost the powers of your soul, you have not got one step further. You break the thread of thought, you become impatient, passionate, scolding and storming, and then you continue: "Either hairdresser, or bank teller; I say merely either—or." What wonder, then, that this saying has become for you an offense and foolishness—that it seems, as you say, as if it were like the arms attached to the iron maiden whose embrace was the death penalty. You treat people superciliously, you make sport of them, and what you have become is what you most abhor: a critic, a universal critic in all faculties. Sometimes I cannot help smiling at you, and yet it is pitiful to see how your really excellent intellectual gifts are thus dissipated. But here again there is the same contradiction in your nature; for you see the ludicrous very clearly, and God help him who falls into your hands if his case is similar to yours. And yet the whole difference is that he perhaps becomes downcast and broken, while you on the contrary become light and erect and merrier than ever, making yourself and others blissful with the gospel: *vanitas vanitatum vanitas,* hurrah! But this is no choice, it is what we call in Danish letting it go, or it is mediation like letting five count as an even number. Now you feel yourself free, you say to the world, farewell.

> *So zieh' ich hin in alle Ferne,*
> *Ueber meiner Mütze nur die Sterne.*[6]

Therewith you have chosen—not, to be sure, as you yourself will admit, the better part. But in reality you have not chosen at all, or it is in an improper sense of the word that you have chosen. Your choice is an aesthetic choice, but an aesthetic choice is no choice. The act of choosing is essentially a proper and stringent expression of the ethical. Whenever in a stricter sense there is question of an either/or, one can always be sure that the ethical is involved. The only absolute either/or is the choice between good and evil, but that is also absolutely ethical. The aesthetic choice is either entirely immediate, or it loses itself in the multifarious. Thus when a young girl follows the choice of her heart, this choice, however beautiful it may be, is in the strictest sense no choice, since it is entirely immediate. When a man deliberates aesthetically upon a multitude of life's problems, as you did in the foregoing, he does not easily get one either/or, but a whole multiplicity, because the determining factor in the choice is not accentuated, and because when one does not choose absolutely one chooses only for the moment, and therefore can choose something different the next moment. The ethical choice is therefore in a certain sense much easier, much simpler,

---

[6] "So fare I forth to realms afar, over my cap naught but the stars." The couplet is somewhat inaccurately quoted from a poem entitled "Freisinn" in the first book of Goethe's *Westöstlicher Divan.* For this identification I am indebted to my former teacher, Professor Harvey W. Hewett-Thayer of Princeton.

but in another sense it is infinitely harder. He who would define his life task ethically has ordinarily not so considerable a selection to choose from; on the other hand, the act of choice has far more importance for him. If you will understand me aright, I should like to say that in making a choice it is not so much a question of choosing the right as of the energy, the earnestness, the pathos with which one chooses. Thereby the personality announces its inner infinity, and thereby, in turn, the personality is consolidated. Therefore, even if a man were to choose the wrong, he will nevertheless discover, precisely by reason of the energy with which he chose, that he has chosen the wrong. For, the choice being made with the whole inwardness of his personality, his nature is purified and he himself brought into immediate relation to the eternal Power whose omnipresence interpenetrates the whole of existence. This transfiguration, this higher consecration, is never attained by that man who chooses merely aesthetically. The rhythm in that man's soul, in spite of all its passion, is a *spiritus levis*.[7]

So, like a Cato, I shout at you my either/or, and yet not like a Cato, for my soul has not yet acquired the resigned coldness which he possessed. But I know that only this incantation, if I have the strength for it, will be capable of rousing you, not to an activity of thought, for of that you have no lack, but to earnestness of spirit. Perhaps you will succeed without that in accomplishing much, perhaps even in astonishing the world (for I am not niggardly), and yet you will miss the highest thing, the only thing which truly has significance—perhaps you will gain the whole world and lose your own self.

What is it, then, that I distinguish in my either/or? Is it good and evil? No, I would only bring you up to the point where the choice between the evil and the good acquires significance for you. Everything hinges upon this. As soon as one can get a man to stand at the crossways in such a position that there is no recourse but to choose, he will choose the right. Hence if it should chance that, while you are in the course of reading this somewhat lengthy dissertation, you were to feel that the instant for choice had come, then throw the rest of this away, never concern yourself about it, you have lost nothing—but choose, and you shall see what validity there is in this act, yea, no young girl can be so happy in the choice of her heart as is a man who knows how to choose. So then, one either has to live aesthetically, or one has to live ethically. In this alternative, as I have said, there is not yet in the strictest sense any question of

---

[7] "Light breathing." (L)

a choice; for he who lives aesthetically does not choose, and he who after the ethical has manifested itself to him chooses the aesthetical is not living aesthetically, for he is sinning and is subject to ethical determinants even though his life may be described as unethical. Lo, this is, as it were, a *character indelebilis* impressed upon the ethical, that though it modestly places itself on a level with the aesthetical, it is nevertheless that which makes the choice a choice. And this is the pitiful thing to one who contemplates human life, that so many live on in a quiet state of perdition; they outlive themselves, not in the sense that the content of life is successively unfolding and now is possessed in this expanded state, but they live their lives, as it were, outside of themselves, they vanish like shadows, their immortal soul is blown away, and they are not alarmed by the problem of its immortality, for they are already in a state of dissolution before they die. They do not live aesthetically, but neither has the ethical manifested itself in its entirety, so they have not exactly rejected it either; they therefore are not sinning, except insofar as it is sin not to be either one thing or the other; neither are they ever in doubt about their immortality, for he who deeply and sincerely is in doubt of it on his own behalf will surely find the right, and surely it is high time to utter a warning against the great-hearted, heroic objectivity with which many thinkers [8] think on behalf of others and not on their own behalf. If one would call this which I here require selfishness, I would reply that this comes from the fact that people have no conception of what this "self" is, and that it would be of very little use to a man if he were to gain the whole world and lose himself, and that it must necessarily be a poor proof which does not first of all convince the man who presents it.

My either/or does not in the first instance denote the choice between good and evil, it denotes the choice whereby one chooses good *and* evil/or excludes them. Here the question is under what determinants one would contemplate the whole of existence and would himself live. That the man who chooses good and evil chooses the good is indeed true, but this becomes evident only afterwards; for the aesthetical is not the evil but neutrality, and that is the reason why I affirmed that it is the ethical which constitutes the choice. It is, therefore, not so much a question of choosing between willing the good *or* the evil, as of choosing to *will,* but by this in turn the good and the evil are posited. He who chooses the ethical chooses the good, but here the good is entirely abstract, only its being is posited, and hence it does not follow by any

[8] E.g. the Hegelians.

means that the chooser cannot in turn choose the evil, in spite of the fact that he chose the good. Here you see again how important it is that a choice be made, and that the crucial thing is not deliberation, but the baptism of the will which lifts up the choice into the ethical. The longer the time that elapses, the more difficult it is to choose, for the soul is constantly attached to one side of the dilemma, and it becomes more and more difficult, therefore, to tear oneself loose. And yet this is necessary if one is truly to choose.

TWO EDIFYING DISCOURSES

BY S. KIERKEGAARD (1843)

TRANSLATED BY DAVID F. SWENSON AND LILLIAN MARVIN SWENSON

I am a poet. But I was made for religion long before I became a poet.

If an Arab in the desert were suddenly to discover a spring in his tent, and so would always be able to have water in abundance, how fortunate he would consider himself—so too, when a man who *qua* physical being is always turned towards the outside, thinking that his happiness lies outside him, finally turns inward and discovers that the source is within him; not to mention his discovering that the source is his relation to God.—THE JOURNALS

"ONLY the truth that edifies is truth for thee." When Kierkegaard wrote these, the concluding words of *Either/Or*, he was wresting from his own experience a truth which sums up his life and work, and at the same time setting the theme for a whole group of writings, radically different from *Either/Or* and his other poetic, "aesthetic" works, and to be published concurrently with these. While the aesthetic works were signed with fantastic pseudonyms, these "edifying discourses" were from the outset acknowledged as his own: they were by "S. Kierkegaard," which meant that they set forth the highest truth he knew at the time of writing them, whereas the pseudonymous works afforded only single aspects or perspectives of that truth. The reader does not always rejoice in this procedure of S.K.'s—his way of stating something with the greatest earnestness, which *already* he knows to be only a partial truth. It is the method of the poet rather than of the philosopher or religious prophet; and "poet" was the title S.K. claimed for himself to the end of his days. Its justification lies in the truism that one cannot say everything at once—and penetrate very deeply. To put it otherwise, truth is "dialectical," composed of elements seemingly at variance with one another—only seemingly, because of our standpoint in "existence"; but this standpoint is inescapable for us as human beings. The Truth wherein all truths are reconciled is for God alone; yet a "relationship" to this Truth is possible for human beings. The relationship is not that of knowledge, as philosophy (and many forms of religion) suppose; the relationship is *faith*.

To expound this relationship in such a way that others may be persuaded to enter into it is the aim of the *Edifying Discourses*, a set of which was published to "accompany" each of S.K.'s larger "aesthetic" writings. The words "edifying" and "edification" are liable to scare readers away nowadays; but Kierkegaard uses them in their etymological sense. The discourses are for "upbuilding" the individual in faith, or for building up faith within the individual. In reality they are sermons, and high examples of the homiletic art; but Kierkegaard was averse to calling them such, since he felt that he had no authority to preach. (He did preach on a few occasions in Copenhagen churches, as we shall see later on.)

Generally speaking, the *Discourses* represent an "immanent religiousness" (as S.K. was to characterize it three years later in the *Unscientific Postscript*) and not the "paradoxical religiousness" which he came to understand as the heart of Christianity. In this sense the *Discourses* do not give us Kierkegaard's mature view of religion; but there is nothing in them that he would have repudiated later. One must understand God as immanent in man and nature before one can understand Him as "the absolute Paradox."

The present discourse (of which about one-half is here reproduced—the complete translation is to be found in *Edifying Discourses*, Volume 1) is one of two which "accompanied" *Either/Or* rather tardily, being published some three months later; hereafter S.K. arranged it so that the discourses came out on the same day as the pseudonymous works of which they were the complement. The text is Kierkegaard's favorite one, and he returned to it several times in later years—most memorably in "The Unchangeableness of God," the final selection in this book. That which stands at the beginning of the religious writings stands also at the end, and the reader may find it worthwhile, when the time comes, to compare the two passages.

PRAYER

FROM Thy hand, O Lord, do we receive everything! Thou stretchest out Thy powerful hand and takest the wise in their foolishness. Thou openest it, Thy gentle hand, and satisfiest whatever lives with blessing. And even if it seems that Thine arm is shortened, then do Thou increase our faith and our confidence, so that we may hold Thee fast. And if it sometimes seems that Thou dost withdraw Thine hand from us, oh, then we know that it is only so because Thou dost close it, that Thou dost close it only in order to conceal the more abundant blessing within it, that Thou dost close it in order again to open it and satisfy everything which lives with Thy blessing. Amen.

EVERY GOOD AND EVERY PERFECT GIFT
IS FROM ABOVE

Every good gift and every perfect gift is from above and cometh down from the Father of lights, with whom is no variableness, neither shadow of turning. Of his own will begat he us with the word of truth, that we should be a kind of first-fruits of his creatures. Wherefore, my beloved brethren, let every man be swift to hear, slow to speak, slow to wrath: for the wrath of man worketh not the righteousness of God. Wherefore lay apart all filthiness and superfluity of naughtiness, and receive with meekness the engrafted word, which is able to save your souls.—JAMES 1:17–22

EVERY *good and every perfect gift is from above and cometh down from the Father of lights, with whom is no variableness, neither shadow of turning.* These words are so beautiful, so eloquent, so moving, that it was certainly not the fault of the words if they found no entrance to the listener's ear, no echo in his heart. They are by an apostle of the Lord, and insofar as we ourselves have not felt their significance more deeply, we still dare have confidence that they are not loose and idle words, not a graceful expression for an airy thought, but that they are faithful and unfailing, tested and proved, as was the life of the apostle who wrote them. They are said not incidentally but with special emphasis, not in passing but accompanied by an earnest admonition: "Do not err, my beloved brethren." We dare then set our confidence in their having not only power to lift up the soul, but also strength to sustain it, these words which sustained an apostle through a stormy life. They are spoken in connection with other words: it is in order to warn against the fearful error of believing that God would tempt a man, in order to warn against the foolishness of a heart that would tempt God, that the apostle says: "Do not err, my beloved brethren." We dare then assure ourselves that the word is also mighty in explaining the folly, mighty in halting the erring thought.

Every good and every perfect gift is from above and cometh down from the Father of lights, with whom is no variableness, neither shadow of turning. These words are again and again repeated in the world, and yet many go on as if they had never heard them, and it would perhaps have affected them disturbingly if they had heard them. Carelessly they go on their way, a friendly fate makes everything so easy for them, every wish is fulfilled, all their undertakings are successful. Without knowing how it comes about, they are in the midst of the life movement, a link in the chain which connects a future with a past. Unconcerned about how it happened, they are borne along on the wave of the present. Resting in the natural law that lets a human life develop in the world in the same way that it spreads a carpet of flowers over the earth, they live happy and satisfied amid the changes of life, wishing at no moment to extricate themselves from it, giving everyone his honest due: thanksgiving to the one to whom they ascribe the good gifts, help to the needy in the way they believe is useful to him. That there are good and perfect gifts they know well; they also know whence these come; for the earth gives its increase, and heaven sends the early and the late rain, and family and friends consider it best for them; and their plans, wise and intelligent, succeed as is natural since they themselves are wise and intelligent. For them life holds no riddle, and yet their life is a riddle, a dream, and the apostle's earnest admonition, "Do not err," does not make them pause; they have no time to pay attention to it nor to the words, any more than the wave gives heed as to whence it comes or whither it goes. Or if some individuals among them, considering higher things, gave heed to the apostle's words, they would soon be through with them. They let their thought for a moment occupy itself with the words, and then they said: "Now we have understood them, bring us some new thoughts which we have not understood." Nor would they have been wrong; for the apostle's words are not difficult, and yet they proved thereby, in that after having understood them they wished to abandon them, that they had not understood them.

Every good and every perfect gift is from above and cometh down from the Father of lights, with whom is no variableness, neither shadow of turning. These words are so soothing, so comforting, and yet how many were there who really understood how to suck the rich nourishment from them, how to appropriate them! Those concerned, those whom life did not permit to grow up and who died as babes, those whom it did not suckle on the milk of prosperity, but who were early weaned from it; the sorrowing, whose thought attempted to penetrate through the changing to the permanent—those were conscious of the apostle's words and gave attention to them. The more completely they could sink their souls in them, could forget everything in them, the more they felt themselves strengthened and made confident. Still it soon appeared that this strength was a delusion; no matter how much confidence they gained, they still did not gain the strength to comprehend life; sometimes the troubled mind and the bewildered thought resorted again to that rich consolation, sometimes they felt again the contradiction. At last, perhaps, it seemed to them that these words were almost dangerous to their peace of mind. They awakened a confidence in them which was constantly being disappointed. They gave them wings which could indeed lift them up to God, but which could not help them in their walk through life. They did not deny the inexhaustible comfort of the words, but they almost feared this comfort even when they praised it. If a man owned a magnificent jewel, a jewel which he never denied was magnificent, he might take it out from time to time and rejoice over it; but soon he would say: I cannot adorn myself with this for daily use, and the festal occasions on which it would really be appropriate I wait for in vain. So then he would put the jewel away, and would sadly consider the fact that he owned such a jewel, but that life gave him no opportunity to find happiness in displaying it.

So they sat in their quiet sorrow: they did not harden themselves against the consolation of the word; they were humble enough to acknowledge that life is a dark saying, and as in their thought they were swift to listen to see if there might be an explanatory word, so were they also slow to speak and slow to wrath. They did not presume to give up the word; they longed only for the opportune hour to come. If that came, then they would be saved. Such was their belief; and indeed it might happen. . . . Or is there only a spirit who bears witness in heaven, but no spirit who bears witness on earth! Heaven only knows, and the spirit which flees from earth, that God is good; the earthly life knows nothing about it! Is there then no mutual harmony between what happens in heaven and what happens on the earth! Is there joy in heaven, only sorrow on earth, or is it only said that there is joy in heaven! Does God in heaven take the good gifts and hide them for us in heaven so that we may sometime receive them in the next world?

Perhaps you spoke in this way in your heart's bewilderment. You did not demand that for your sake there should be given signs and wonderful manifestations, you did not childishly demand that every one of your wishes should be fulfilled; only you begged for a testimony early and late, for your troubled soul treasured one wish. If this were fulfilled, then everything would be well; then would your thanks and your praise be unceasing, then would the festal occasion come, then would you with all your heart bear testimony to the word, that every good and every perfect gift comes from above. But lo, that was denied you; and your soul became restive, tossed about by the passionate wish. It became defiant and angry. You did not impatiently cast off the leading-strings of humility, you had not forgotten that you are on earth and God in heaven. With humble prayers and burning desires you sought, as it were, to tempt God: This wish is so important to me; my joy, my peace, my future, all depend on this; for me it is so very important, for

God it is so easy, for He is all-powerful. But the wish was not fulfilled. Vainly you sought rest; you left nothing untried in your unfruitful restlessness; you ascended the dizzy heights of anticipation to see if a possibility might not appear. If you believed that you saw such a possibility, then you were immediately ready with prayers, that by the help of these you might create the actual from the apparent. Still it was an illusion. You descended again and gave yourself up to the stupefying exhaustion of sorrow, while time went on as it always does. And the morning came, and the evening, but the day you desired did not dawn. And still you made every effort, you prayed early and late, more and more fervently, more and more temptingly. Alas, it still did not come to pass! And you gave up, you would dispose your soul to patience, you would wait in quiet longing, if only your soul might be assured that eternity would bring you your wish, bring you that which was the delight of your eyes and your heart's desire.[1] Alas, this certainty too was denied you. But when the busy thoughts had worked themselves weary, when the fruitless wishes had exhausted your soul, then perhaps your being became more quiet, then perhaps your heart, secretly and un-noticed, had developed in itself the meekness which received the word which was implanted in you and which was able to save your soul, that every good and perfect gift cometh from above.

Then you acknowledged in all humility that God had certainly not deceived you, since He accepted you, since He accepted your earthly wishes and foolish desires, exchanged them for you and gave you instead heavenly consolation and holy thoughts; that He did not treat you unfairly when He denied you your wish, but for compensation created this faith in your heart; when instead of the wish, which even if it could do everything was at most able to give you the whole world, He gave you a faith through which you gained God and overcame the whole world. Then you recognized with humble gladness that God was still the almighty Creator of heaven and earth, who had not only created the world out of nothing, but had done the even more miraculous—out of your impatient and unstable heart He had created the incorruptible essence of a quiet spirit. Then ashamed you confessed that it was good, so very good for you, that God had not permitted Himself to be tempted; then you understood the apostle's admonition and its relation to the error that wishes to tempt God. Then you per-

[1] Cf. *Journals, supra*, p. 18. This whole paragraph is an echo of S.K.'s experience with Regina—and also an anticipation, for he still believed in the "possibility" of getting her back, a possibility that was to be rudely shattered just two months after the publica-tion of this discourse by the news of Regina's engagement to Schlegel.

ceived how foolish your conduct had been. You wished that God's ideas about what was profitable to you might be your ideas, but you also wished that He might be the almighty Creator of heaven and earth, so that He might rightly fulfill your wish. And yet if He were to share your ideas, then must He cease to be the almighty Father. You would in your childish impatience, as it were, corrupt God's eternal Being, and you were blind enough to delude yourself, as if God in heaven did not know better what was profitable to you than you yourself; as if you would not sometime discover with terror that you had wished what no man would be able to bear if it came to pass. For let us a moment speak foolishly and with human wisdom. If there was a man in whom you rightly had confidence, because you believed he wished for your welfare; but you had one conception about what would be advantageous to you, he another—is it not true, you would then seek to persuade him, you would perhaps beg and adjure him, to fulfill your wish; but if he continued to deny you, you would cease to beg him, you would say: If now I influenced him by my prayers to do what he does not regard as right, then it would be even more terrible, that I had been weak enough to make him equally weak, since then I should have lost him and my confidence in him, even if, in a moment of intoxication, I had called his weakness affection.

Or perhaps this was not the case with you; you were perhaps too old to cherish childish conceptions about God, too mature to think humanly about Him; you would perhaps influence Him by your defiance. That life was a dark saying you readily confessed, but you were not, in accordance with the apostle's warning, swift to hear whether there might be an explanatory word; you were, contrary to his admonition, swift to wrath. If life is a dark saying, then let it be so, you would not concern yourself about the explanation—and your heart was hardened. Your appearance was perhaps calm, perhaps friendly, your speech even benevolent, but in your heart, in the secret workshop of your thoughts, you said—no, you did not say it, but you heard a voice which said: God does tempt a man. And the coldness of despair chilled your spirit, and its death brooded over your heart. If sometimes life again stirred within you, then there raged wild voices, voices which did not belong to you, but which still sounded from within you. For why was your complaint so violent, why was your shriek so penetrating, why were even your prayers so challenging? Was it not because you believed that your sufferings were so great, your sorrows so crushing, and because of this your complaint so just, your voice so mighty, that it must resound through heaven and call God forth from His hidden depth, where, as it seemed to you, He sat calm and indifferent, paying no attention to the world and its fate? But heaven is closed to such presumptuous speech, and it is written that God is tempted of no man. Impotent was your speech, impotent as your thought, as your arm was impotent; and heaven did not hear your prayer.

But, then, when you humbled yourself under God's powerful hand and, crushed in spirit, groaned: "My God, my God, great is my sin, greater than can be forgiven," then heaven again opened, then did God, as a prophet writes, look down upon you from the window of heaven and say: Yet a little while; yet a little while, and I will renew the forms of earth—and lo, your form was renewed, and God's merciful grace had produced in your barren heart the meekness which receives the word. Then you humbly acknowledged before God that God tempts no man, but that everyone is tempted when he is seduced and drawn away by his own desire, just as you were tempted by proud and arrogant and defiant thoughts. Then you were terrified at your error in thinking that the idea that God tempts a man could make life explicable; for then life would become to you a dark saying, as you listened to this explanation, which, as you must confess, simply made everything inexplicable. Then you acknowledged, humble and ashamed, that it was well that God did not allow Himself to be tempted, that He was the almighty God, able to crush every presumptuous thought; well that you, in your despair, should not have found an explanation of life's dark saying which any man would be able to insist upon. . . .

Did you do this, my hearer? Then, although the outward man perished, the inward man was renewed. Then you understood that every good and every perfect gift is from above if it is received with thankfulness; you understood that repentance is a returning of thanks not only for punishment but also for the dispensation of Providence. . . . As the Lord Himself says: Yet today, so the apostle of the Lord says: Yet today is every good and every perfect gift from above, and comes down from the Father of lights, with whom is no variableness, neither shadow of turning; yet today, and that although He is the same today as He was yesterday.

Every good and every perfect gift is from above and cometh down from the Father of lights, with whom is no variableness nor shadow of turning. These words are so beautiful, so eloquent, so moving; they

are so soothing and so comforting, so simple and comprehensible, so
refreshing and so healing. Therefore we will beseech Thee, O God,
that Thou wilt make the ears of those who hitherto have not regarded
them, willing to accept them; that Thou wilt heal the misunderstanding heart by the understanding of the word, to understand the word;
that Thou wilt incline the erring thought under the saving obedience of
the word; that Thou wilt give the penitent soul confidence to dare to
understand the word; and that Thou wilt make those who have understood it more and more blessed therein, so that they may repeatedly
understand it. Amen.

FEAR AND TREMBLING: A
DIALECTICAL LYRIC

BY JOHANNES DE SILENTIO (1843)

TRANSLATED BY WALTED LOWRIE

Therefore faith hopes also in this life, but . . . by virtue of the absurd, not by
virtue of the human understanding.

The paradox in Christian truth is invariably due to the fact that it is truth as it
exists for God. The standard of measure and the end is superhuman; and there is only
one relationship possible: faith.—THE JOURNALS

S.K. leaves us in no doubt of the fact that all his pseudonymous works
were written "for Regina"; this is true, however, in different degrees and in
different ways. *Fear and Trembling* has perhaps the most direct relationship
of all, for it "reproduced my own life." Just as Abraham was called upon to
sacrifice Isaac, his most dearly beloved, so S.K. was impelled to give up
Regina—i.e. to do something he could not explain and something "immoral"
in the strict sense of the word. The parallel is clear enough, once we
come to think of it; but nobody would be likely to think of it who did not
know S.K.'s tragedy from the inside. This was just the sort of situation that
appealed to S.K.'s love of mystification, and he made the most of it in the
name of the "author," Johannes de Silentio, and in the motto which he
chose for the title page, a quotation from Hamman: "What Tarquinius
Superbus spoke in his garden with the poppies was understood by his son,
but not by the messenger." [1] That is to say, Regina would understand his book
if nobody else did.

[1] Alluding to the old Roman story in which Tarquinius, not wishing to trust the
messenger who had come from his son asking what he should do with the people of
Gabii, took the messenger into the garden and struck off the heads of the tallest poppies—
meaning that the son was to bring about the death of the most eminent men in the city.

The significance of *Fear and Trembling*, however, is in no way lessened or limited by the personal circumstances of its creation. Just as the *Divine Comedy* transcends its political motivation in the Italy of the fourteenth century, so does *Fear and Trembling* rise high above the Regina episode into the region of universality which is artistic greatness—the region wherein that which is most *individual* and that which is most *universal* coincide. The criterion of truth here is precisely the opposite of that used in science. Science appeals to sense-data which can be perceived by anyone; art appeals to what is found by the individual in his particularity, with just this personal make-up and just this special experience of the world, *when this experience is penetrated by reflection* as it was in Kierkegaard's case. The element of "personal bias," which constitutes a reproach to the scientist, is a precondition for understanding in the larger sense. "Truth is subjectivity," as Kierkegaard himself was to proclaim a little later on.

Fear and Trembling remained one of S.K.'s favorite works, and six years later he wrote in his Journal: "Oh, when once I am dead—then *Fear and Trembling* alone will give me the name of an immortal author. Then it will be read, then too it will be translated into foreign tongues; and people will almost shudder at the frightful pathos of the book. . . ." The pathos, however, is lightened by some of S.K.'s most delightful humor, as in the portrait of the Knight of Faith *versus* the Knight of Infinite Resignation, here reproduced. The latter is the ancient Stoic or the modern Romantic hero who renounces everything (cf. Goethe's *"Entbehren sollst du, sollst entbehren!"*), with no hope of ever getting it back; he forswears the finite and lives constantly in the infinite. The Knight of Faith, on the other hand, gives up everything just as the Knight of Infinite Resignation does, but at the same time he believes, "by virtue of the absurd," that he will gain it back in the end, and he lives in a manner corresponding to this assumption. He makes the "double movement" of renouncing the finite yet continuing to live in it, so that whereas the Knight of Infinite Resignation is always "incommensurable" with everyday bourgeois life, the Knight of Faith has nothing remarkable about him, and looks and acts "like a tax-collector." Be it noted that Johannes de Silentio does not pretend to be a Knight of Faith; as a poet he is necessarily a Knight of Infinite Resignation, who nevertheless admires the Knight of Faith (e.g. Abraham) from afar, as a being he cannot comprehend.

S.K. wrote both *Fear and Trembling* and *Repetition* in less than two months, during his second stay in Berlin. At that time he still hoped, like Abraham, to receive the finite back—i.e. to be able to marry Regina after all. He was in for a rude shock on his return to Copenhagen, for he found Regina engaged to Schlegel. This result, which was right in line with his intention of "getting her underway for marriage with another," was received by S.K. at the time with mixed emotions, but he later described it as a "thunderstorm" which cleared the atmosphere. Of *Repetition* he had to rewrite the conclusion, in line with this latest turn of events. *Fear and Trem-bling* was allowed to stand (though at least one passage seems to have been added; see p. 124 and footnote), but the "religion of hidden inwardness" underlying the conception of the knight of faith was only two years later (in the *Unscientific Postscript*) to be replaced by a rather different account of "what it means to be a Christian."

THE KNIGHT OF FAITH AND THE KNIGHT
OF INFINITE RESIGNATION

. . . ABRAHAM I cannot understand, in a certain sense there is nothing I can learn from him but astonishment. If people fancy that by con-sidering the *outcome* of this story [1] they might be moved to believe, they deceive themselves and want to swindle God out of the first move-ment of faith, the infinite resignation. They would suck worldly wisdom out of the paradox. Perhaps one or another may succeed in that, for our age is not willing to stop with faith, with its miracle of turning water into wine; it goes further, it turns wine into water.

Would it not be better to stop with faith, and is it not revolting that everybody [2] wants to go further? . . . Would it not be better that they should stand still at faith, and that he who stands should take heed lest he fall? For the movements of faith must constantly be made by virtue of the absurd, yet in such a way, be it observed, that one does not lose the finite but gains it every inch. For my part I can well describe the movements of faith, but I cannot make them. When one would learn to make the motions of swimming one can let oneself be hung by a swimming-belt from the ceiling and go through the motions (describe them, so to speak, as we speak of describing a circle), but one is not swimming. In that way I can describe the movements of faith, but when I am thrown into the water, I swim, it is true (for I don't belong to the beach-waders), but I make other movements, I make the movements of infinity, whereas faith does the opposite: after having made the movements of infinity, it makes those of finiteness. Hail to him who can make those movements, he performs the marvelous and I shall never grow tired of admiring him, whether he be Abraham or a slave in Abraham's house; whether he be a professor of philosophy or

[1] The story of Abraham and Isaac.
[2] Notably Hegel and his followers.

a servant-girl, I look only at the movements. But at them I *do* look and do not let myself be fooled, either by myself or by any other man. The knights of the infinite resignation are easily recognized: their gait is gliding and assured. Those on the other hand who carry the jewel of faith are likely to be delusive, because their outward appearance bears a striking resemblance to that which both the infinite resignation and faith profoundly despise—to Philistinism.

I candidly admit that in my practice I have not found any reliable example of the knight of faith, though I would not therefore deny that every second man may be such an example. I have been trying, however, for several years to get on the track of this, and all in vain. People commonly travel around the world to see rivers and mountains, new stars, birds of rare plumage, queerly deformed fishes, ridiculous breeds of men—they abandon themselves to the bestial stupor which gapes at existence, and they think they have seen something. This does not interest me. But if I knew where there was such a knight of faith, I would make a pilgrimage to him on foot, for this prodigy interests me absolutely. I would not let go of him for an instant, every moment I would watch to see how he managed to make the movements, I would regard myself as secured for life and would divide my time between looking at him and practicing the exercises myself, and thus would spend all my time admiring him.

As was said, I have not found any such person, but I can well think him. Here he is. Acquaintance made, I am introduced to him. The moment I set eyes on him I instantly push him from me, I myself leap backwards, I clasp my hands and say half aloud, "Good Lord, is this the man? Is it really he? Why, he looks like a tax-collector!" However, it is the man after all. I draw closer to him, watching his least movements to see whether there might not be visible a little heterogeneous fractional telegraphic message from the infinite, a glance, a look, a gesture, a note of sadness, a smile, which betrayed the infinite in its heterogeneity with the finite. No! I examine his figure from tip to toe to see if there might not be a cranny through which the infinite was peeping. No! He is solid through and through. His tread? It is vigorous, belonging entirely to finiteness; no smartly dressed townsman who walks out to Fresberg on a Sunday afternoon treads the ground more firmly; he belongs entirely to the world, no Philistine more so. One can discover nothing of that aloof and superior nature whereby one recognizes the knight of the infinite.

He takes delight in everything, and whenever one sees him taking part in a particular pleasure, he does it with the persistence which is the mark of the earthly man whose soul is absorbed in such things. He tends to his work. So when one looks at him one might suppose that he was a clerk who had lost his soul in an intricate system of bookkeeping, so precise is he. He takes a holiday on Sunday. He goes to church. No heavenly glance or any other token of the incommensurable betrays him; if one did not know him, it would be impossible to distinguish him from the rest of the congregation, for his healthy and vigorous hymn-singing proves at the most that he has a good chest. In the afternoon he walks to the forest. He takes delight in everything he sees, in the human swarm, in the new omnibuses, in the water of the Sound; when one meets him on the Beach Road one might suppose he was a shopkeeper taking his fling, that's just the way he disports himself, for he is not a poet, and I have sought in vain to detect in him the poetic incommensurability. Toward evening he walks home, his gait is as indefatigable as that of the postman. On his way he reflects that his wife has surely a special little warm dish prepared for him, e.g. a calf's head roasted, garnished with vegetables. If he were to meet a man like-minded, he could continue as far as East Gate to discourse with him about that dish, with a passion befitting a hotel chef. As it happens, he hasn't four pence to his name, and yet he fully and firmly believes that his wife has that dainty dish for him. If she had it, it would then be an invidious sight for superior people and an inspiring one for the plain man, to see him eat; for his appetite is greater than Esau's. His wife hasn't it—strangely enough, it is quite the same to him. On the way he runs across another man. They talk together for a moment. In the twinkling of an eye he erects a new building, he has at his disposition all the powers necessary for it. The stranger leaves him with the thought that he certainly is a capitalist, while my admired knight thinks, "Yes, if the money were needed, I dare say I could get it."

He lounges at an open window and looks out on the square on which he lives; he is interested in everything that goes on, in a rat which slips under the curb, in the children's play, and this with the nonchalance of a girl of sixteen. And yet he is no genius, for in vain I have sought in him the incommensurability of genius. In the evening he smokes his pipe; to look at him one would swear that it was the grocer over the way vegetating in the twilight. He lives as carefree as a ne'er-do-well, and yet he buys up the acceptable time at the dearest price, for he does not do the least thing except by virtue of the absurd.[3] And yet, and yet I could become furious over it—for envy, if for no other reason—because the man has made and every instant is making the movements of infinity. With infinite resignation he has drained the cup of life's profound sadness, he knows the bliss of the infinite, he senses the pain of renouncing everything, the dearest things he possesses in the world, and yet finiteness tastes to him just as good as to one who never knew anything higher. . . . And yet, and yet the whole earthly form he exhibits is a new creation by virtue of the absurd. He resigned everything infinitely, and then he grasped everything again by virtue of the absurd. He constantly makes the movements of infinity, but he does this with such correctness and assurance that he constantly gets the finite out of it, and there is not a second when one has a notion of anything else.

It is supposed to be the most difficult task for a dancer to leap into a definite posture in such a way that there is not a second when he is grasping after the posture, but by the leap itself he stands fixed in that posture. Perhaps no dancer can do it—but that is what this knight does. Most people live dejectedly in worldly sorrow and joy; they are the ones who sit along the wall and do not join in the dance. The knights of infinity are dancers and possess elevation. They make the movements upward, and fall down again; and this too is no mean pastime, nor ungraceful to behold. But whenever they fall down they are not able at once to assume the posture, they vacillate an instant, and this vacillation shows that after all they are strangers in the world. This is more or less strikingly evident in proportion to the art they possess, but even the most artistic knights cannot altogether conceal this vacillation. One need not look at them when they are up in the air, but only the instant they touch or have touched the ground—then one recognizes them. But to be able to fall down in such a way that the same second it looks as if one were standing and walking, to transform the leap of life into a walk, absolutely to express the sublime and the pedestrian—that only the knight of faith can do, and this is the one and only prodigy.

But since the prodigy is so likely to be delusive, I will describe the movements in a definite instance which will serve to illustrate their relation to reality, for upon this everything turns. A young swain falls in love with a princess,[4] and the whole content of his life consists in

[3] That which runs counter to human experience and human understanding in general. Here, the "absurdity" of living simultaneously in the infinite and the finite.

[4] The princess is Regina and the whole passage a dramatization of the Regina episode.

this love, and yet the situation is such that it is impossible for it to be realized, impossible for it to be translated from ideality into reality. The slaves of paltriness, the frogs in life's swamp, will naturally cry out, "Such a love is foolishness. The rich brewer's widow is a match fully as good and respectable." Let them croak in the swamp undisturbed. It is not so with the knight of infinite resignation: he does not give up his love, not for all the glory of the world. He is no fool. First he makes sure that this really is the content of his life, for his soul is too healthy and too proud to squander the least thing upon a mere inebriation. He is not cowardly, he is not afraid of letting love creep into his most secret, his most hidden thoughts, to let it twine in innumerable coils about every ligament of his consciousness; if the love becomes an unhappy love, he will never be able to tear himself loose from it. He feels a blissful rapture in letting love tingle through every nerve, and yet his soul is as solemn as that of the man who has drained the poisoned goblet and feels how the juice permeates every drop of blood—for this instant is life and death.

So when he has thus sucked into himself the whole of love and absorbed himself in it, he does not lack courage to make trial of everything and to venture everything. He surveys the situation of his life, he convokes the swift thoughts, which like tame doves obey his every bidding, he waves his wand over them, and they dart off in all directions. But when they all return, all as messengers of sorrow, and declare to him that it is an impossibility, then he becomes quiet, he dismisses them, he remains alone, and then he performs the movements. If what I am saying is to have any significance, it is requisite that the movement come about normally. So for the first thing, the knight will have power to concentrate the whole content of life and the whole significance of reality into one single wish. If a man lacks this concentration, this intensity, if his soul from the beginning is dispersed in the multifarious, he never comes to the point of making the movement; he will deal shrewdly in life like the capitalists who invest their money in all sorts of securities, so as to gain on the one what they lose on the other—in short, he is not a knight at all. In the next place the knight will have the power to concentrate the whole result of the operations of thought into one act of consciousness. If he lacks this intensity, if his soul from the beginning is dispersed in the multifarious, he will never get time to make the movements, he will be constantly running errands in life, never enter into eternity, for even at the instant when he is closest to it he will suddenly discover that he has forgotten something for which he must go back. He will think that to enter eternity is possible the next instant, and that also is perfectly true, but by such considerations one never reaches the point of making the movements, but sinks deeper and deeper into the mire.

So the knight makes the movement—but what movement? Will he forget the whole thing? (For in this too there is indeed a kind of concentration.) No! For the knight does not contradict himself, and it is a contradiction to forget the whole content of one's life and yet remain the same man. To become another man he feels no inclination, nor does he by any means regard this as greatness. Only the lower natures forget themselves and become something new. . . . The deeper natures never forget themselves and never become anything else than what they were. So the knight remembers everything, but precisely this remembrance is pain, and yet by the infinite resignation he is reconciled with existence. Love for that princess became for him the expression of an eternal love, assumed a religious character, was transfigured into a love for the Eternal Being, which did to be sure deny him the fulfillment of his love, yet reconciled him again by the eternal consciousness of its validity in the form of eternity, which no reality can take from him. Fools and young men prate about everything being possible for a man. That, however, is a great error. Spiritually speaking, everything is possible, but in the world of the finite there is much which is not possible. This impossible, however, the knight makes possible by expressing it spiritually, but he expresses it spiritually by waiving his claim to it. The wish which would carry him out into reality, but was wrecked upon the impossibility, is now bent inward, but it is not therefore lost, neither is it forgotten. At one moment it is the obscure emotion of the wish within him which awakens recollections, at another moment he awakens them himself; for he is too proud to be willing that what was the whole content of his life should be the thing of a fleeting moment. He keeps this love young, and along with him it increases in years and in beauty.

On the other hand, he has no need of the intervention of the finite for the further growth of his love. From the instant he made the movement the princess is lost to him. He has no need of those erotic tinglings in the nerves at the sight of the beloved, etc., nor does he need to be constantly taking leave of her in a finite sense, because he recollects her in an eternal sense, and he knows very well that the lovers who are so bent upon seeing "her" yet once again, to say farewell for the last time, are right in being bent upon it, are right in thinking that it is the last time, for they forget one another the soonest. He has comprehended the deep secret that even in loving another person one must be sufficient unto oneself. He no longer takes a finite interest in what the princess is doing, and precisely this is proof that he has made the movement infinitely. Here one may have an opportunity to see whether the movement on the part of a particular person is true or fictitious. There was one who also believed that he had made the movement; but lo, time passed, the princess did something else, she married [5]—a prince, let us say; then his soul lost the elasticity of resignation. Thereby he knew that he had not made the movement rightly; for he who has made the act of resignation infinitely is sufficient unto himself. The knight does not annul his resignation, he preserves his love just as young as it was in its first moment, he never lets it go from him, precisely because he makes the movements infinitely. What the princess does cannot disturb him, it is only the lower natures which find in other people the law for their actions, which find the premises for their actions outside themselves.

If on the other hand the princess is like-minded, the beautiful consequence will be apparent. She will introduce herself into that order of knighthood into which one is not received by balloting, but of which everyone is a member who has courage to introduce himself, that order of knighthood which proves its immortality by the fact that it makes no distinction between man and woman. The two will preserve their love young and sound; she also will have triumphed over her pains, even though she does not, as it is said in the ballad, "lie every night beside her lord." These two will to all eternity remain in agreement with one another, with a well-timed *harmonia praestabilita*,[6] so that if ever the moment were to come, the moment which does not, however, concern them finitely (for then they would be growing older), if ever the moment were to come which offered to give love its expression in time, then they will be capable of beginning precisely at the point where they would have begun if originally they had been united. He who understands this, be he man or woman, can never be deceived, for it is only the lower natures which imagine they were deceived. No girl who is not so proud really knows how to love; but if she is so proud, then the cunning and shrewdness of all the world cannot deceive her.

---

[5] This passage was evidently added after S.K. learned of Regina's engagement—and after he had had time to cool off.

[6] Preestablished harmony, the principle of Leibnitz's philosophy.

In the infinite resignation there is peace and rest; every man who will, who has not abased himself by scorning himself (which is still more dreadful than being proud) can train himself to make these movements. The infinite resignation is that shirt we read about in the old fable. The thread is spun under tears, the cloth bleached with tears, the shirt sewn with tears; but then too it is a better protection than iron and steel. The imperfection in the fable is that a third party can manufacture this shirt. The secret in life is that everyone must sew it for himself, and the astonishing thing is that a man can sew it fully as well as a woman. In the infinite resignation there is peace and rest and comfort in sorrow—that is, if the movement is made normally. It would not be difficult for me, however, to write a whole book, were I to examine the various misunderstandings, the preposterous attitudes, the deceptive movements, which I have encountered in my brief practice. People believe very little in spirit, and yet making these movements depends upon spirit, it depends upon whether this is or is not a one-sided result of a *dira necessitas*, and the more this is present, the more dubious it always is whether the movement is normal. . . . However, in our time people concern themselves rather little about making pure movements. In case one who was about to learn to dance were to say, "For centuries now one generation after another has been learning positions, it is high time I drew some advantage out of this and began straightway with the French dances"—then people would laugh at him; but in the world of spirit they find this exceedingly plausible. What is education? I should suppose that education was the curriculum one had to run through in order to catch up with oneself, and he who will not pass through this curriculum is helped very little by the fact that he was born in the most enlightened age.

The infinite resignation is the last stage prior to faith, so that one who has not made this movement has not faith; for only in the infinite resignation do I become clear to myself with respect to my eternal validity, and only then can there be any question of grasping existence by virtue of faith.

Now we will let the knight of faith appear in the rôle just described. He makes exactly the same movements as the other knight, infinitely renounces claim to the love which is the content of his life, he is reconciled in pain; but then occurs the prodigy, he makes still another movement more wonderful than all, for he says, "I believe nevertheless that I shall get her, in virtue, that is, of the absurd, in virtue of the fact that with God all things are possible." [7] The absurd is not one of the factors which can be discriminated within the proper compass of the understanding: it is not identical with the improbable, the unexpected, the unforeseen. At the moment when the knight made the act of resignation, he was convinced, humanly speaking, of the impossibility. This was the result reached by the understanding, and he had sufficient energy to think it. On the other hand, in an infinite sense it was possible, namely by renouncing it; but this sort of possessing is at the same time a relinquishing, and yet there is no absurdity in this for the understanding, for the understanding continued to be in the right in affirming that in the world of the finite, where it holds sway, this was and remained an impossibility. This is quite as clear to the knight of faith, [8] so the only thing that can save him is the absurd, and this he grasps by faith. So he recognizes the impossibility, and that very instant he believes the absurd; for if, without recognizing the impossibility with all the passion of his soul and with all his heart, he should wish to imagine that he has faith, he deceives himself, and his testimony has no bearing, since he has not even reached the infinite resignation.

Faith therefore is not an aesthetic emotion but something far higher, precisely because it has resignation as its presupposition; it is not an immediate instinct of the heart, [9] but is the paradox of life and existence. So, when in spite of all difficulties a young girl still remains convinced that her wish will surely be fulfilled, this conviction is not the assurance of faith, even if she was brought up by Christian parents, and for a whole year perhaps has been catechized by the parson. She is convinced in all her childish naïveté and innocence, this conviction also ennobles her nature and imparts to her a preternatural greatness, so that like a thaumaturge she is able to conjure the finite powers of existence and make the very stones weep, while on the other hand in her flurry she may just as well run to Herod as to Pilate and move the whole world by her tears. Her conviction is very lovable, and one can learn much from her, but one thing is not to be learned from her, one does not learn the movements, for her conviction does not dare in the pain of resignation to face the impossibility.

So I can perceive that it requires strength and energy and freedom of spirit to make the infinite movements of resignation; I can also

---

[7] At the time S.K. was writing this (May 17, 1843) an entry in the *Journal* reads: "If I had had faith, I should have remained with Regina."

[8] Sc., "as it is to the knight of infinite resignation."

[9] Cf. *Journals, supra,* p. 7.

perceive that it is feasible. But the next thing astonishes me, it makes my head swim, for after having made the movement of resignation, then by virtue of the absurd to get everything, to get the wish whole and uncurtailed—that is beyond human power, it is a prodigy. But this I can perceive, that the young girl's conviction is mere levity in comparison with the firmness faith displays, nothwithstanding it has perceived the impossibility. Whenever I essay to make this movement, I turn giddy, the very instant I am admiring it absolutely a prodigious dread grips my soul—for what is it to tempt God? And yet this move-ment is the movement of faith and remains such, even though philosophy, in order to confuse the concepts, would make us believe that it has faith, and even though theology would sell out faith at a bargain price.

For the act of resignation faith is not required, for what I gain by resignation is my eternal consciousness, and this is a purely philosophical movement which I dare say I am able to make if it is re-quired, and which I can train myself to make, for whenever any finiteness would get the mastery over me, I starve myself until I can make the movement, for my eternal consciousness is my love to God, and for me this is higher than everything. For the act of resignation faith is not required, but it is needed when it is a case of acquiring the very least thing more than my eternal consciousness, for this is the paradoxical. The movements are frequently confounded, for it is said that one needs faith to renounce the claim to everything, yea, a stranger thing than this may be heard, when a man laments the loss of his faith, and when one looks at the scale to see where he is, one sees, strangely enough, that he has only reached the point where he should make the infinite movement of resignation. In resignation I make renunciation of everything; this movement I make by myself, and if I do not make it, it is because I am cowardly and effeminate and without enthusiasm and do not feel the significance of the lofty dignity which is assigned to every man, that of being his own censor, which is a far prouder title than that of Censor General to the whole Roman Republic. This movement I make by myself, and what I gain is myself in my eternal consciousness, in blissful agreement with my love for the Eternal Being. By faith I make renunciation of nothing; on the contrary, by faith I acquire everything, precisely in the sense in which it is said that he who has faith like a grain of mustard can remove mountains. A purely human courage is required to renounce the whole of the temporal to gain the eternal; but this I do gain, and to all eternity I cannot renounce it—that being a self-contradiction. But a paradox enters in, and a humble courage is required to grasp the whole of the temporal by virtue of the absurd, and this is the courage of faith. By faith Abraham did not renounce his claim upon Isaac, but by faith he got Isaac. By virtue of resignation that rich young man should have given away everything, but then when he had done that, the knight of faith should have said to him, "By virtue of the absurd thou shalt get every penny back again. Canst thou believe that?" And this speech ought by no means to have been indifferent to the aforesaid rich young man, for in case he gave away his goods because he was tired of them, his resignation was not much to boast of.

It is about the temporal, the finite, that everything turns in this case. I am able by my own strength to renounce everything, and then to find peace and repose in pain. I can stand everything—even though that horrible demon, more dreadful than death, the king of terrors, even though madness were to hold up before my eyes the motley of the fool, and I understood by its look that it was I who must put it on, I still am able to save my soul, if only it is more to me than my earthly happiness that my love to God should triumph in me. A man may still be able at the last instant to concentrate his whole soul in a single glance toward that heaven from which cometh every good gift, and his glance will be intelligible to himself and also to Him whom it seeks, as a sign that he nevertheless remained true to his love. Then he will calmly put on the motley garb. He whose soul has not this romantic enthusiasm has sold his soul, whether he got a kingdom for it or a paltry piece of silver. But by my own strength I am not able to get the least of the things which belong to finiteness, for I am constantly using my strength to renounce everything. By my own strength I am able to give up the princess, and I shall not become a grumbler, but shall find joy and repose in my pain; but by my own strength I am not able to get her again, for I am employing all my strength to be resigned. But by faith, says that marvelous knight, by faith I shall get her in virtue of the absurd.

So this movement I am unable to make. As soon as I would begin to make it, everything turns around dizzily, and I flee back to the pain of resignation. I can swim in existence, but for this mystical soaring I am too heavy. To exist in such a way that my opposition to existence is expressed as the most beautiful and assured harmony is something I cannot do. And yet it must be glorious to get the princess, that is what I say every instant, and the knight of resignation who does not say it is a deceiver, he has not had one only wish, and he has not kept the wish young by his pain. Perhaps there was one who thought it fitting enough that the wish was no longer vivid, that the barb of pain was dulled, but such a man is no knight. A free-born soul who caught himself entertaining such thoughts would despise himself and begin over again, above all he would not permit his soul to be deceived by itself. And yet it must be glorious to get the princess—and yet the knight of faith is the only happy one, the heir apparent to the finite, whereas the knight of resignation is a stranger and a foreigner. Thus to get the princess, to live with her joyfully and happily day in and day out (for it is also conceivable that the knight of resignation might get the princess, but that his soul had discerned the impossibility of their future happiness): thus to live joyfully and happily every instant by virtue of the absurd, every instant to see the sword hanging over the head of the beloved, and yet to find repose in the pain of resignation, but also joy by virtue of the absurd—this is marvelous. He who does it is great, the only great man. The thought of its stirs my soul, which never was niggardly in the admiration of greatness. . . .

PROBLEM I

IS THERE SUCH A THING AS A TELEOLOGICAL SUSPENSION OF THE ETHICAL?

THE ethical as such is the universal, it applies to everyone, and the same thing is expressed from another point of view by saying that it applies every instant. It reposes immanently in itself, it has nothing outside itself which is its *telos*,[1] but is itself *telos* for everything outside it, and when this has been incorporated by the ethical it can go no further. Conceived immediately as physical and psychical, the particular individual is the particular which has its *telos* in the universal, and its task is to express itself constantly in it, to abolish its particularity in order to become the universal. As soon as the individual would assert himself in his particularity over against the universal he sins, and only by recognizing this can he again reconcile himself with the universal. Whenever the individual after he has entered the universal feels an impulse to assert himself as the particular, he is in temptation (*Anfechtung*), and he can labor himself out of this only by abandoning himself as the particular in the universal. If this be the highest thing

[1] End or fulfillment.

that can be said of man and of his existence, then the ethical has the same character as man's eternal blessedness, which to all eternity and at every instant is his *telos,* since it would be a contradiction to say that this might be abandoned (i.e. teleologically suspended), inasmuch as this is no sooner suspended than it is forfeited. . . .

If such be the case, then Hegel is right when, in dealing with the Good and the Conscience, he characterizes man merely as the particular and regards this character as "a moral form of the evil" which is to be annulled in the teleology of the moral, so that the individual who remains in this stage is either sinning or subjected to temptation (*Anfechtung*). On the other hand, he is wrong in talking of faith, wrong in not protesting loudly and clearly against the fact that Abraham enjoys honor and glory as the father of faith, whereas he ought to be prosecuted and convicted of murder.

For faith is this paradox, that the particular is higher than the universal—yet in such a way, be it observed, that the movement repeats itself, and that consequently the individual, after having been in the universal, now as the particular isolates himself as higher than the universal. If this be not faith, then Abraham is lost, then faith has never existed in the world—because it has always existed. For if the ethical (i.e. the moral) is the highest thing, and if nothing incommensurable remains in man in any other way but as the evil (i.e. the particular which has to be expressed in the universal), then one needs no other categories than those which the Greeks possessed or which by consistent thinking can be derived from them. This fact Hegel ought not to have concealed, for after all he was acquainted with Greek thought. . . .

Faith is precisely this paradox, that the individual as the particular is higher than the universal, is justified over against it, is not subordinate but superior—yet in such a way, be it observed, that it is the particular individual who, after he has been subordinated as the particular to the universal, now through the universal becomes the individual who as the particular is superior to the universal, *inasmuch as the individual as the particular stands in an absolute relation to the absolute.* This position cannot be mediated, for all mediation comes about precisely by virtue of the universal; it is and remains to all eternity a paradox, inaccessible to thought. And yet faith is this paradox. . . .

That for the particular individual this paradox may easily be mistaken for a temptation (*Anfechtung*) is indeed true, but one ought not for this reason to conceal it. That the whole constitution of many persons may be such that this paradox repels them is indeed true, but one ought not for this reason to make faith something different in order to be able to possess it, but ought rather to admit that one does not possess it, whereas those who possess faith should take care to set up certain criteria so that one might distinguish the paradox from a temptation (*Anfechtung*).

Now the story of Abraham contains such a teleological suspension of the ethical. . . . Abraham's relation to Isaac, ethically speaking, is quite simply expressed by saying that a father shall love his son more dearly than himself. Yet within its own compass the ethical has various gradations. Let us see whether in this story there is to be found any higher expression for the ethical such as would ethically explain his conduct, ethically justify him in suspending the ethical obligation toward his son, without in this search going beyond the teleology of the ethical.

When an undertaking in which a whole nation is concerned is hindered,[2] when such an enterprise is brought to a standstill by the disfavor of heaven, when the angry deity sends a calm which mocks all efforts, when the seer performs his heavy task and proclaims that the deity demands a young maiden as a sacrifice—then will the father heroically make the sacrifice. He will magnanimously conceal his pain, even though he might wish that he were "the lowly man who dares to weep," [3] not the king who must act royally. And though solitary pain forces its way into his breast and he has only three confidants among the people, yet soon the whole nation will be cognizant of his pain, but also cognizant of his exploit, that for the welfare of the whole he was willing to sacrifice her, his daughter, the lovely young maiden. "O charming bosom! O beautiful cheeks! O bright golden hair!" (v.687). And the daughter will affect him by her tears, and the father will turn his face away, but the hero will raise the knife.—When the report of this reaches the ancestral home, then will the beautiful maidens of Greece blush with enthusiasm, and if the daughter was betrothed, her true love will not be angry but be proud of sharing in the father's deed, because the maiden belonged to him more feelingly than to the father.

[2] The Trojan War. When the Greek fleet was unable to set sail from Aulis because of an adverse wind, the seer Calchas announced that King Agamemnon had offended Artemis and that the goddess demanded his daughter, Iphigenia, as a sacrifice of expiation. (L)

[3] Euripides, *Iphigenia in Aulis*, v. 448. (L)

When the intrepid judge,[4] who saved Israel in the hour of need, in one breath binds himself and God by the same vow, then heroically the young maiden's jubilation, the beloved daughter's joy, he will turn to sorrow, and with her all Israel will lament her maiden youth; but every free-born man will understand, and every stout-hearted woman will admire Jephtha, and every maiden in Israel will wish to act as did his daughter. For what good would it do if Jephtha were victorious by reason of his vow, if he did not keep it? Would not the victory again be taken from the nation?

When a son is forgetful of his duty,[5] when the state entrusts the father with the sword of justice, when the laws require punishment at the hand of the father, then will the father heroically forget that the guilty one is his son, he will magnanimously conceal his pain, but there will not be a single one among the people, not even the son, who will not admire the father, and whenever the law of Rome is interpreted, it will be remembered that many interpreted it more learnedly, but none so gloriously as Brutus.

If, on the other hand, while a favorable wind bore the fleet on with swelling sails to its goal, Agamemnon had sent that messenger who fetched Iphigenia in order to be sacrificed; if Jephtha, without being bound by any vow which decided the fate of the nation, had said to his daughter, "Bewail now thy virginity for the space of two months, for I will sacrifice thee"; if Brutus had had a righteous son and yet would have ordered the lictors to execute him—who would have understood them? If these three men had replied to the query why they did it by saying, "It is a trial in which we are tested," would people have understood them better? ...

The difference between the tragic hero and Abraham is clearly evident. The tragic hero still remains within the ethical. He lets one expression of the ethical find its *telos* in a higher expression of the ethical; the ethical relation between father and son, or daughter and father, he reduces to a sentiment which has its dialectic in the idea of morality. Here there can be no question of a teleological suspension of the ethical.

With Abraham the situation was different. By his act he overstepped the ethical entirely and possessed a higher *telos* outside of it, in relation to which he suspended the former. For I should very much

---

[4] Jephtha. Judges 11:30–40.

[5] The son of Brutus, while his father was consul, took part in a conspiracy to restore the king Rome had expelled, and Brutus ordered him to be put to death. (L)

like to know how one would bring Abraham's act into relation with the universal, and whether it is possible to discover any connection whatever between what Abraham did and the universal—except the fact that he transgressed it. It was not for the sake of saving a people, not to maintain the idea of the state, that Abraham did this, and not in order to reconcile angry deities. If there could be a question of the deity being angry, he was angry only with Abraham, and Abraham's whole action stands in no relation to the universal; it is a purely personal undertaking. Therefore, whereas the tragic hero is great by reason of his moral virtue, Abraham is great by reason of a personal virtue. In Abraham's life there is no higher expression for the ethical than this, that the father shall love his son. Of the ethical in the sense of morality there can be no question in this instance. Insofar as the universal was present, it was indeed cryptically present in Isaac, hidden as it were in Isaac's loins, and must therefore cry out with Isaac's mouth, "Do it not! Thou art bringing everything to naught."

Why then did Abraham do it? For God's sake, and (in complete identity with this) for his own sake. He did it for God's sake because God required this proof of his faith; for his own sake he did it in order that he might furnish the proof. The unity of these two points of view is perfectly expressed by the word which has always been used to characterize this situation: it is a trial, a temptation (*Fristelse*). A temptation—but what does that mean? What ordinarily tempts a man is that which would keep him from doing his duty, but in this case the temptation is itself the ethical—which would keep him from doing God's will.

Here is evident the necessity of a new category if one would understand Abraham. Such a relationship to the deity paganism did not know. The tragic hero does not enter into any private relationship with the deity, but for him the ethical is the divine, hence the paradox implied in his situation can be mediated in the universal.

Abraham cannot be mediated, and the same thing can be expressed also by saying that he cannot talk. As soon as I talk I express the universal, and if I do not do so, no one can understand me. Therefore if Abraham would express himself in terms of the universal, he must say that his situation is a temptation (*Anfechtung*), for he has no higher expression for that universal which stands above the universal which he transgresses.

Therefore, though Abraham arouses my admiration, he at the same time appalls me. He who denies himself and sacrifices himself for duty gives up the finite in order to grasp the infinite, and that man is secure enough. The tragic hero gives up the certain for the still more certain, and the eye of the beholder rests upon him confidently. But he who gives up the universal in order to grasp something still higher which is not the universal—what is he doing? Is it possible that this can be anything else but a temptation (*Anfechtung*)? And if it be possible, but the individual was mistaken—what can save him? He suffers all the pain of the tragic hero, he brings to naught his joy in the world, he renounces everything—and perhaps at the same instant debars himself from the sublime joy which to him was so precious that he would purchase it at any price. Him the beholder cannot understand nor let his eye rest confidently upon him. . . .

The story of Abraham contains therefore a teleological suspension of the ethical. As the individual he became higher than the universal: this is the paradox which does not permit of mediation. It is just as inexplicable how he got into it as it is inexplicable how he remained in it. If such is not the position of Abraham, then he is not even a tragic hero but a murderer. To want to continue to call him the father of faith, to talk of this to people who do not concern themselves with anything but words, is thoughtless. A man can become a tragic hero by his own powers—but not a knight of faith. When a man enters upon the way, in a certain sense the hard way of the tragic hero, many will be able to give him counsel; to him who follows the narrow way of faith no one can give counsel, him no one can understand. Faith is a miracle, and yet no man is excluded from it; for that in which all human life is unified is passion, and faith is a passion.

REPETITION: AN ESSAY IN
EXPERIMENTAL PSYCHOLOGY

BY CONSTANTINE CONSTANTIUS (1843)

TRANSLATED BY WALTER LOWRIE

If you wish to be and remain enthusiastic, then draw the silk curtains of facetiousness (irony's), and so hide your enthusiasm.

The first form of "the interesting" is to love change; the other is to desire the repetition, but in self-contentment and with no pain attached to it.—THE JOURNALS

WHEN S.K. gave up Regina and fled to Berlin, he acted as sincerely as possible; yet the sincerest of human actions are not always wholly sincere, for one must reckon with those obscure forces which lie below the surface of consciousness. So it proved in S.K.'s case: he had renounced the thought of marriage with Regina—and yet, in the depths of his soul, he still hoped to be able to marry her—still hoped for the possibility of "a repetition." This category, suggested to him by his own personal experience, became the subject of what is possibly his most attractive book from a purely literary point of view.

Not only did the category of "repetition" come from his own experience, but the very "plot" of the book as well. (We may almost speak of a "plot" in this case, for *Repetition* comes the closest of S.K.'s works to being a novel in the generally accepted sense.) The "young man" who is the hero of the work undergoes an experience very much like S.K.'s: he falls in love with a girl, but finds it impossible to realize the union because of his melancholy, retrospective nature. The story is told under a symbolic pseudonym, by one Constantine Constantius who is the "young man's" friend and confidant:

"As he paced back and forth across the floor he repeated again and again a verse of Poul Møller's:

> To my arm-chair there comes a dream
> From the springtime of youth,
> A longing intense
> For thee, thou sun amongst women!

"His eye filled with a tear, he flung himself down on a chair and repeated the verse again and again. Upon me this scene made a harrowing impression. Great God! thought I, such a melancholy has never before presented itself in my practice. . . . He was in love, deeply and sincerely in love, that was evident—and yet at once, on one of the first days of his engagement, he was capable of recollecting his love. Substantially he was through with the whole relationship. Before he begins he has taken such a terrible stride that he has leapt over the whole of life. Though the girl dies tomorrow, it will produce no essential change, he will again fling himself upon a chair, again his eye will fill with a tear, he will again repeat the words of the poet. What a strange dialectic! He longs for the girl, he has to restrain himself by force from hanging around her the whole day, and yet at the very first instant he has become an old man with respect to the whole relationship. . . . That he would become unhappy was clear enough, and that the girl too would become unhappy was no less clear. . . ." (pp. 11-12).

Constantine's prophecy is fulfilled and the young man languishes daily. At last heroic measures are suggested—more heroic than S.K. himself took, though of essentially the same kind: the young man was to pretend that he had a mistress. Just when everything is ready, the young man disappears. "I never saw him again. He did not have the strength to carry out the plan. His soul lacked the elasticity of irony. . . ." (p. 27). But after some time

Constantine begins receiving letters from the young man, which contain profound reflections upon his experience and upon the subject of repetition in general. He still hopes for the repetition—still hopes, like Job, to "receive everything double." At last he gets news (as S.K. did) that his beloved is married; and therewith he receives the repetition and becomes a poet:

"I am again myself. . . . The discord in my nature is resolved, I am again unified. . . . The snares in which I was entangled have been hewn asunder, the magic spell which bewitched me so that I could not return to myself has now been broken. . . . It is over, my yawl is afloat. . . . I belong to the idea. When that beckons me I follow, when it appoints a tryst I await it day and night, . . . when the idea calls I forsake everything. . . .

"Hail to feminine magnanimity! Long life to the high flight of thought, to moral danger in the service of the idea! Hail to the danger of battle! Hail to the solemn exultation of victory! Hail to the dance in the vortex of the infinite! Hail to the breaking wave which covers me in the abyss! Hail to the breaking wave which hurls me up above the stars!" (pp. 144-146).

On a somewhat more mundane level is the humorous interlude in which Constantine tells of his attempt to secure a repetition of certain exquisite moments which he had once experienced in Berlin. Whereas the "young man" was at least on the border of the religious, Constantine himself is an aesthete, and his attempt suffers the fate of all repetition pursued on an aesthetic basis: it fails just because it is an *attempt* and because it is *pursued*. But in the meantime Constantine has given vent to his love of the theater in its lighter form and drawn a picture which is at once romantic and ironical.

Repetition was actually written during S.K.'s second visit to Berlin, in the spring of 1843, and some details of the interlude have a basis of fact: e.g. S.K. really went back to his old lodgings and found his landlord married. Kierkegaard's irony is always at its best when it is directed against himself. This is preeminently the case in the passage near the end of the interlude (pp. 151–152) in which S.K. seems to be satirizing his own experience of conversion, the most sacred moment of his life. In view of this passage he certainly cannot, like the hero of *Repetition*, be accused of lacking "elasticity."

CONSTANTINE CONSTANTIUS REVISITS BERLIN

As for the significance which repetition has in a given case, much can be said without incurring the charge of repetition. When in his time Professor Ussing[1] made an address before the 28th of May Association

[1] A prominent member of the society of political liberals which celebrated annually the establishment on May 28, 1831, of the new constitution of the Danish parliament. He incurred S. K.'s displeasure for some of his liberal views. (L)

and something in it met with disapprobation, what then did the professor do? Being at that period always resolute and *gewaltig,* he pounded on the table and said, "I repeat it." So on that occasion his opinion was that what he had said gained by repetition. A few years ago I heard a parson deliver on two successive Sundays exactly the same discourse. If he had been of the opinion of the professor, as he ascended the pulpit on the second occasion he would have pounded the desk and said, "I repeat what I said last Sunday." This he did not do, and he gave no hint of it. He was not of Professor Ussing's opinion—and who knows if the professor himself be still of the opinion that it was an advantage to his discourse to be repeated again? At a court reception when the Queen had told a story, and all the courtiers had laughed, including a deaf minister, who then arose and craved permission to tell his story—and told the same one—the question is, what was his view of the significance of repetition? When a school-teacher says in class, "I repeat that Jaspersen must sit still," and the same Jaspersen gets a bad mark for repeated disturbance, the significance of repetition is exactly the opposite.

However, I will dwell no longer upon such examples but will proceed to tell a little about the voyage of discovery I undertook in order to investigate the possibility and the significance of repetition. Without letting anybody know about it (lest all the gossip might render me inept for the experiment and create a disgust for repetition), I went by steamer to Stralsund, and there took a seat in a diligence for Berlin. Among the learned there are various opinions as to which seat in a diligence is the most comfortable. My *Ansicht*[2] is that it is misery for the whole crowd. On my previous journey I had the end seat inside the carriage near the front (some consider this a great prize), and then for thirty-six hours was so shaken together with my nearest neighbors, all too near, that upon reaching Hamburg I had not merely lost my mind but lost my legs too. We six persons who sat inside the carriage were kneaded into one body, and I had a lively sense of what had happened to the people of Mol,[3] who after they had been sitting together for a long time could not distinguish their own legs. In order at least to be a member of a smaller body I chose a seat in the coupé. It was a change. Nevertheless everything was repeated. The postilion blew his horn, I closed my eyes, resigned myself to despair and

[2] Viewpoint.
[3] The inhabitants of a small island east of Jutland were proverbial in Copenhagen for their naïve simplicity. (L)

thought, as I am accustomed to do on such occasions, "God knows whether thou wilt ever reach Berlin, and in that case whether thou wilt ever become a man again, capable of emancipating thyself in the individuality of isolation, or whether thou wilt retain the memory that thou art a member of a greater body." [4]

I arrived in Berlin after all, and hastened at once to my old lodging in order to convince myself how far a repetition might be possible. I can assure every sympathetic reader that on my first visit I succeeded in getting one of the most agreeable apartments in Berlin, and this I can now affirm with the more confidence because I have seen many. Gendarmes Square is surely the most beautiful in Berlin. The theater and the two churches make a fine appearance, especially as viewed from a window by moonlight. The recollection of it contributed much to hasten my steps. One ascends a flight of stairs in a house illuminated by gas, one opens a small door, one stands in the vestibule. On the left is a glass door leading to a cabinet. One goes straight ahead, one finds oneself in an antechamber. Beyond this are two rooms entirely alike and furnished entirely alike, with the effect of seeing one room doubled in a mirror. The inner room is tastefully lighted. A branch candle-stick stands on the writing table, beside which stands a handsome arm-chair covered with red velvet. The first room is not illuminated. Here the pale light of the room is blended with the stronger illumination from the inner room. One sits down on a chair by the window, one looks out upon the great square, one sees the shadows of pedestrians hasten along the walls. Everything is transformed into a theatrical decoration. A dreamy reality looms up in the background of the soul. One feels a desire to throw on a cloak and slink quietly along the walls with a searching glance. One does not do it, one merely sees oneself doing it in a renewed youth. One has smoked one's cigar, one retires to the inner room and begins to work. Midnight is past. One extinguishes the candles, one lights a small night lamp. The moonlight triumphs unalloyed. A single shadow appears still darker, a single footstep takes a long time to disappear. The cloudless vault of heaven seems sad and meditative, as though the end of the world were past and heaven, undisturbed, were concerned only with itself. One goes out again into the antechamber, into the vestibule, into that little cabinet, one goes to sleep—if one is of that fortunate number that can sleep.

But, alas, here no repetition was possible. My host, materialist that

[4] A satirical reference to Hegel's doctrine of the State.

he was, *hatte sich verändret*,[5] in the pregnant sense in which the Germans use this word, and as it is used in some quarters of Copenhagen, if I am correctly informed, in the sense of getting married. I wanted to wish him good fortune; but as I have not sufficient command of the German language to be able to turn a sharp corner, nor had promptly at my disposition the phrases appropriate to such an occasion, I confined myself to pantomimic motions. I laid my hand upon my heart and looked at him, while tender sympathy was legibly depicted upon my countenance. He pressed my hand. After we had thus come to an understanding with one another he proceeded to prove the aesthetic validity of marriage.[6] In this he was extraordinarily successful —just as he was formerly in proving the perfection of the bachelor life. When I am talking German I am the most compliant person in the world.

My former host was eager to serve me, and I was eager to lodge with him; so I took one chamber and the vestibule. When I came home the first evening and had lit the candles, I thought to myself, "Alas, alack, is this repetition?" I was in a sadly depressed mood, or if you prefer to say so, I was in a mood precisely appropriate to the day; for fate had strangely contrived that I arrive in Berlin on the first day of Lent, a day of universal fasting and penitence. It is true they did not cast dust in one's eye, with the words *Memento, o homo, quod cines est et in cinerem rivertaris,*[7] but nevertheless the whole city was one cloud of dust. I thought at first that it was all arranged by the government, but later I was convinced that the wind had made itself responsible for this and without respect of persons was following its whim or its evil habit; for in Berlin at least every other day is Ash Wednesday. But the dust has little relevance to my subject. This discovery had nothing to do with "repetition," for on my previous visit I had not observed this phenomenon, presumably because it was winter.

When one has got comfortably and snugly settled in one's dwelling, when one has thus a fixed point from which to dart out, a safe hiding-place where one can retire to devour one's prey in solitude (something I prize in particular, because like those beasts of prey I cannot eat when anybody is looking on)—then one makes oneself acquainted with the sights of the city. If one is a traveler *ex professo,* a globe-trotter who

---

[5] Had changed his way of life. (Lit., "had changed himself.")

[6] Judge William's thesis in the second part of *Either/Or.*

[7] "Remember, O man, what is dust, and that to dust thou shalt return"—the words intoned at the imposition of ashes in the Catholic church on Ash Wednesday.

travels on the scent of everything others have scented out, or in order to write the names of the principal sights in his diary, or his own name in the register of guests, then one engages a *Lohndiener* [8] and buys *Das ganze Berlin* for 4 *Groschen*. By my method one remains an impartial observer whose declaration ought to be taken on faith in every police protocol. On the other hand, if one is traveling without any pressing pretext, one may do as one pleases, see once in a while something which others have not seen, overlook the important things, and get a casual impression which has significance only for oneself. Such a carefree vagabond generally has not much to recount to others, and if he does it he readily runs the risk of impairing the good opinion good people have formed of his virtuousness and morality. If a man had journeyed abroad for a long time and had never been *auf der Eisenbahn,* ought he not to be expelled from all good society? What if a man had been in London and had never taken a ride in the Tunnel! [9] What if a man were to come to Rome, fall in love with a small corner of the town which offered him inexhaustible material for delight, and were to leave Rome without having seen one single sight!

Berlin has three theaters. What is presented at the Opera House in the way of operas and ballets is said to be *grossartig;* [10] what is presented at the Dramatic Theater is supposed to be for instruction and culture, not merely for pleasure.[11] About that I do not know. But I know that in Berlin there is a theater called Königstäter Theater. The official tourists visit it rather rarely, although (and this also is significant) somewhat more frequently than the sociable places of refection on more retired streets where a Dane can refresh his memory of Lars Mathiesen and Kehlet.[12] When I arrived in Stralsund and read in the newspaper that "Der Talisman" [13] was to be performed in that theater I was at once in good humor. The recollection of it awakened in my soul, and the first time I saw it I felt as though this first impression merely evoked in my soul a recollection which pointed far back in time.

Surely there is no young man with any imagination who has not at one time been captivated by the enchantment of the theater, and desired

[8] Servant engaged by the day.

[9] Railroads were new, and the tunnel under the Thames was opened only on May 25, 1843. (L)

[10] Grand, magnificent.

[11] "Not for pleasure only" was inscribed over the stage of the Royal Theatre in Copenhagen.

[12] Two well known restaurants in Copenhagen. (L)

[13] A musical comedy by Nestroy, first given in 1843. (L)

to be himself carried away into the midst of that fictitious reality in order to see and hear himself as an *alter ego,* to disperse himself among the innumerable possibilities which diverge from himself, and yet in such a way that every diversity is in turn a single self. . . . Although in the individual life this inclination vanishes in time, yet it is reproduced in a riper age when the soul has seriously collected itself. Yes, although the art of the theater is perhaps not serious enough for the individual, he may perhaps have pleasure in turning back occasionally to that first state and rehearsing it in sentiment. He wishes now to be affected comically, and to be himself in a comically productive relation to the theatrical performance. Therefore, though neither tragedy nor comedy can please him, precisely because of their perfection, he turns to the farce.[14]

The same phenomenon recurs also in other spheres. One sometimes sees a modern individual, sated with the strong meat of reality, who remains unaffected by a painting executed with artistic skill. On the other hand he may be moved at seeing a Nürnberg print in color, such a picture as not long ago was commonly to be found in the shops. There one sees a landscape which depicts a country scene in general. This abstraction is one which cannot be represented artistically. The effect therefore has to be attained by indirection, that is, by depicting a concrete subject casually selected. And yet I would ask every man whether from such a landscape he does not get the impression of a country scene in general, and whether this category is not left over from the days of childhood. From the days of childhood when one had such prodigious categories that now one is almost made dizzy by them, when from a piece of paper one cut out a man and a woman, which were man and woman in general, and that in a stricter sense than Adam and Eve were. A landscape painter, whether he strives to produce an effect by a faithful rendering of the subject, or by a more ideal reproduction, perhaps leaves the individual cold, but such a picture as I have in mind produces an indescribable effect for the fact that one does not know whether to laugh or cry, and because the whole effect depends upon the mood of the beholder. There is surely no person who has not passed through a period when no wealth of language, no passion of exclamation was sufficient for him, when no expression, no gesticulation satisfied, when nothing contented him except to break out with the strangest leaps and somersaults. Perhaps the same individual learned to dance, perhaps he often saw ballets and admired the art of the dancer,

[14] The *Posse* was a kind of farce which became popular in Berlin about 1840. (L)

perhaps there came a time when the ballet no longer affected him, and yet he had moments when he could retire to his room, give himself up entirely to his impulse, and feel an indescribably humoristic relief in standing upon one leg in a picturesque attitude, or in consigning the whole world to death and the devil, and accomplishing it all by a leap head over heels.

At the Königstäter Theater they give farces, and of course the audience is exceedingly diversified. Anyone who desires to make a pathological study of laughter at different social levels and as it is affected by diversity of temperament ought not to miss the opportunity afforded by the performance of a farce. The jubilation and clangor of the amphitheater and second gallery is something quite different from the applause of a cultivated and critical public; it is a steady accompaniment, without which the farce could not be performed at all. The action generally takes place in the lower spheres of society, therefore the gallery and the second tier promptly recognize themselves, and their shouts and bravos do not express an aesthetic appreciation of the individual actors, but rather a purely lyrical explosion of their sense of contentment; they are not in the least conscious of being an audience, but want to take part in what is going on down in the street, or wherever the scene is laid. However, since this is impossible because of the distance, they behave like children who are merely permitted to see from a window a row in the street. The first tier of boxes and the *parterre* are also convulsed by laughter, although this is essentially different from the national yells of the Cimbro-Teutonic race, and even within this select sphere there are infinite nuances in the quality of the laughter, far more than at the performance of the best vaudeville. . . .

Every attempt at an aesthetic definition which might claim universal validity founders upon the farce, which is by no means capable of producing a uniformity of mood in the more cultured part of the audience. For since the effect depends in great part upon the spontaneous creative activity of the spectator, the single individual asserts himself to an unusual degree, and in his own enjoyment is emancipated from the aesthetic obligation to admire, laugh, be touched, etc., according to the prescription of tradition. To view a farce is for a person of culture like playing the lottery, except that one is spared the annoyance of winning money. But such uncertainty is not what theater-goers generally want; hence they neglect the farce, or look down upon it loftily, which is all the worse for them. The real theatrical public has in general a certain narrow-minded seriousness; it wants (or at least imagines that it wants) to be ennobled and educated at the theater, it wants to have had (or at least to imagine that it has had) a rare aesthetic enjoyment; it would like to be able, as soon as it has read the posters, to know in advance how the thing is going to turn out this evening. Such an accord between promise and performance is impossible in the case of the farce; for the same farce may make many different impressions, and it may happen strangely enough that it has the least effect when it is best acted. . . . One may be thrown into the most unexpected moods at seeing a farce, and therefore one never can know with assurance whether he has behaved in the theater as a worthy member of society and has laughed or wept at the appropriate place. One cannot admire as a conscientious spectator the fine characterization which is to be expected in a drama, for all the characters in the farce are sketched on the abstract scale of "the general." The situation, the action, the lines are all on this scale. One can therefore quite as well be moved to sadness as convulsed by laughter. Irony is ineffectual in the farce, everything is naïve, and therefore the spectator as a single individual must be spontaneously active; for the *naïveté* of the farce is so illusory that it is impossible for a cultivated person to be naïve in his attitude toward it. But in his spontaneous reaction to the farce consists in great part the entertainment of the individual, and he must venture to enjoy it without looking to the right or to the left or to the newspapers to find a guarantee that he really has been entertained.

On the other hand, for the cultivated person who at the same time is free and easy enough to entertain himself independently, and has enough self-confidence to know by himself, without seeking the testimony of others, whether he has been entertained or not, the farce will have perhaps a very special significance, for the fact that it will affect his spirit in various ways, now by the spaciousness of the abstraction, now by the introduction of a palpable reality. But of course he will not bring with him a ready-made mood and let everything produce its effect in relation to that, but he will have cultivated his spirit to perfection and will keep himself in the state where not one single mood is present, but the possibility of all.

At the Königstäter Theater they present farces, and to my mind excellent ones. . . . To be able to perform a farce with complete success the troupe must be composed in a special way. It must possess two (or at the most three) actors who have decided talent, or rather, creative genius. They must be the children of caprice, intoxicated with laughter, dancing for sheer humor and merriment. Although at other times, even a moment earlier, they are entirely like other people, yet the very instant they hear the bell of the stage manager they become transformed, and like the noble Arabian steed begin to puff and snort, their distended nostrils witnessing to the chafing spirit within them, wanting to be off, wanting to disport themselves wildly. They are not so much reflective artists who have made a study of laughter as they are lyrical geniuses who plunge into the abyss of laughter and then let its volcanic force cast them up upon the stage. They have therefore hardly calculated what they will do, but let the instant and the natural force of laughter be responsible for everything. They have courage to do what the ordinary man dares to do only when he is alone, what the crazy man does in the presence of all, what the genius knows how to do with the authority of genius. They know that their exuberant mirth has no bounds, that the capital they possess of the comic is inexhaustible and almost every instant a surprise even to them; they know that they are capable of keeping the laughter going the whole evening, without more effort than it costs me to scribble this on paper.

When a theater possesses two geniuses of this sort it has enough for a farce, three is the greatest number admissible, for by more geniuses the effect is weakened, just as a man may die of hypertrophy. The other members of the troupe do not need to be talented, it is not even advantageous that they should be. Nor do the other members need to be engaged with an eye to the canons of beauty, they had better be assembled haphazard. . . . If an exception is to be made with respect to any of the subordinate actors, this must be in favor of the lady-love. Of course she must not by any means be a finished actress, yet in making the choice one ought to see to it that she is attractive, that her whole appearance in the rôle is charming and pleasant, that she is agreeable to look upon, agreeable, let us say, to have around.

The troupe at the Königstäter Theater is pretty much what I would desire. If I were to make any objection, it would apply to the subordinate actors, for against Beckmann [15] and Grobecker I have not a word of complaint. Beckmann is the perfection of a comic genius, who lyrically runs wild in the comic and distinguishes himself not by characterization but by effervescence of spirit. He is not great in the artistically commensurable, but admirable in the individual incommen·surable. He has no need of the support of team-play, of scenery and arrangement; precisely because he is in form he brings everything with

[15] A favorite Berlin actor (d. 1866). (L)

him, at the same time that he is in an ecstasy of wantonness he paints the scenery for himself as well as any painter could. What Baggesen says of Sara Nickels, that she rushes upon the stage with a country landscape behind her, applies in a good sense to Beckmann, only he is able to come walking. In the artistic theater properly so called one seldom sees an actor who can really walk and stand. I have seen, however, one single instance, but what Beckmann is capable of I have never before beheld. He not only can walk but he can *come walking*. This ability to "come walking" is a very different thing, and by this stroke of genius Beckmann improvises the scenic environment. He not only can represent a wandering apprentice lad, he can come walking like him, and in such a way that one sees the whole thing: through the dust of the highway one espies a smiling village, hears its subdued din, sees the footpath which winds yonder down to the pond where it turns off at the smithy—when one sees Beckmann come walking with his little bundle on his back, his walking-stick in his hand, carefree and indefatigable. He is capable of coming on the stage with the street-urchins following him—whom one does not see. Even Dr. Ryge [16] in "King Solomon and George the Hatter" could not produce this effect. Indeed Herr Beckmann is a pure economy for a theater, for when it possesses him it has no need of street-urchins or painted scenery. However, this young apprentice is no characterization; for that the figure is too hastily sketched in its truly masterly contours, it is an incognito in which dwells the mad demon of laughter, which soon disengages itself and carries the whole thing off with unbridled mirth. In this respect Beckmann's dancing is incomparable. He has sung his couplet, now the dance begins. What Beckmann dares to do is perilous; for presumably he does not think himself competent in the strictest sense to produce an effect by his dancing attitudes. He is now beside himself. The madness of laughter within him can no longer be contained either in mimicry or in *réplique*; only to take himself like Münchhausen by the nape of the neck and abandon himself to crazy caprioles is consonant with his mood. The ordinary man, as I have said, may very well recognize what assuagement is to be found in this, but it requires indisputable genius to do it on the stage, it requires the authority of genius, otherwise it is pitiable.

Every burlesque actor must have a voice which is audible from behind the scenes, so that he can thus prepare the way for himself. Beckmann has a capital voice, which of course does not mean the same

[16] A Danish actor who played in a vaudeville of this title by J. L. Heiberg.

thing as a good vocal organ. Grobecker's voice is more strident, but one word from him behind the scenes produces the same effect as three flourishes of the trumpets on the festival of Dyrehavsbakken,[17] it predisposes one to laughter. In this respect I give him the preference even over Beckmann. Beckmann's fundamental superiority consists in a certain indomitable common sense in his wantonness, and it is through this he attains to frenzy. Grosbeck, on the other hand, sometimes rises to frenzy through sentimentality and a languishing mood. So it is I remember seeing him play in a farce the part of a steward who, by reason of his devotion to his noble masters and by virtue of his faith in the importance of festal preparations for embellishing their life, is engrossed with the thought of celebrating their lordships' arrival by a rustic fete. Everything is in readiness. Grosbeck has chosen to represent Mercury. He has not altered his costume as steward, he has merely attached wings to his feet and put a helmet on his head, he assumes a picturesque attitude upon one leg, and begins his address to their lordships. Grosbeck is not so great a lyrical artist as Beckmann, nevertheless he too is on good lyrical terms with laughter. He has a certain tendency toward correctness, and in this respect his acting is often masterly, especially in dry comedy, but he is not such a fermenting ingredient in the farce as is Beckmann. A genius he is nevertheless, and a genius for farce.

One enters the Königstäter Theater. One takes one's seat in the first tier of boxes; for here there are relatively few people, and when one is to see a farce one must be seated at one's ease, without feeling in the remotest way embarrassed by the solemn pretense of art which causes many to let themselves be jammed into a theater to see a play as if it were a question of their eternal salvation.[18] The air in this theater is also fairly pure, not contaminated by the sweat of an audience moved by sensibility to art, or by the finer emanations of art connoisseurs. In the first tier of boxes one can be fairly sure of getting a box by oneself. If that is not the case, I recommend to the reader (in order that he may at least get some profitable knowledge from what I write) the choice of boxes 5 and 6 on the left. There one finds at the very back a seat in a corner which is calculated for only one person, where one is incomparably well off. One sits there alone in one's box, and from this position the theater appears empty. The orchestra plays an overture, the

---

[17] An annual fair in a forest near Copenhagen.

[18] S.K. says in another place, "People nowadays go to church to be entertained and to the theatre to be edified." (L).

music resounds in the hall rather uncannily for the reason that the theater is so empty. One has not gone to the theater as a tourist, or as an aesthetic spirit, or as a critic, but if possible as though it were a matter of no importance, and one is content with being well and comfortably installed, almost as well as in one's own room. The orchestra has finished, the curtain already rises a little, then begins that other orchestra which does not obey the conductor's baton but follows an inner impulse, that other orchestra, the voice of nature in the gallery, which already has sensed Beckmann behind the stage. I generally sat far back in the box and therefore could not see the second row of boxes and the gallery, which like a visor projected beyond my head. All the more marvellous was the effect of this din. Wherever I was able to see, there was empty space for the most part, the vastness of the theater was transformed into the belly of the sea monster in which Jonah sat, the noise in the gallery was like a movement of the monster's viscera. From the moment the gallery has begun its music no other accompaniment is necessary, Beckmann inspires it, and it him.

. . . Thus it was I lay back in my loge, cast aside like the clothing of a bather, flung beside the stream of laughter and merriment and jubilation which foamed past me incessantly. I could see nothing but the vast expanse of the theater, hear nothing but the din in the midst of which I dwelt. Only now and then did I raise myself, look at Beckmann and laugh so heartily that for very fatigue I sank down again beside the foaming stream. This in itself was blissful, and yet I sensed the lack of something. Then in the desert which I beheld about me I discovered a figure which gladdened me more than the sight of Friday gladdened the heart of Robinson. In a box directly opposite me was a young girl, seated in the third row, half hidden by an older lady who sat in the first row. The young girl evidently was not in the theater in order to be seen—as in fact in this theater one is in a great measure dispensed from the sight of these disgusting feminine exhibitions. She sat in the third row, her dress was simple and plain, almost a house dress. She was not wrapped in sable and marten but was enveloped in a big cloak, and projecting from its folds her head was graciously bowed, as the topmost bell of the lily-of-the-valley is bowed above the great enveloping leaves. When I had looked at Beckmann and let the laughter convulse my whole body, when I had sunk back in fatigue and suffered myself to be carried away by the stream of shouting and merriment, and when I stepped out of this bath and returned to myself, then my eyes sought her, and the sight of her refreshed my whole being by its friendly mildness. And when in the farce itself a more pathetic mood cropped up, then I looked at her, and her nature bestowed upon me resignation to bear the pathos, for through it all she sat with perfect self-repose, with her quiet smile of childlike wonder.

Like me she came there every evening. Sometimes I fell to thinking what could have brought her, but these thoughts too remained merely sentiments which were like feelers after her, so for an instant it seemed to me as if she might be a girl who had suffered much and now wrapped herself closely in her shawl and would have nothing more to do with the world, until the expression of her face convinced me that she was a happy child who hugged herself in her cloak in order to enjoy herself thoroughly. She did not suspect that she was seen, and still less that my eye was watching over her; this would have been a sin too against her, and the worse for me; for there is an innocence, an unconsciousness, which even the purest thought may embarrass. One does not oneself discover such a thing, but when one's good genius confides to one where such a primitive soul of retirement lies hidden, then let him not offend it or grieve its genius. If she had felt merely a presentiment of my mute gladness, half fallen in love with her, all would have been spoiled, not to be made good again even by her whole love. . . .

"The Talisman" was to be performed at the Königstäter Theater. The memory of it awoke in my soul, it all stood as vividly before me as when I left the theater the last time. I hastened to the theater. There was no box to be had for me alone, not even in those numbered 5 and 6 on the left. I had to go to the right. There I encountered a society which didn't know definitely whether it should enjoy itself or be bored. Such a company one can definitely regard as boring. There were hardly any empty boxes. The young girl was not to be seen, or else she was there and I could not recognize her because she was in company. Beckmann was unable to make me laugh. I held out for half an hour and then left the theater. "There is no such thing as repetition," I thought. This made a profound impression upon me. I am not so very young, nor altogether unacquainted with life, and already long before I came to Berlin the last time I had weaned myself from the habit of counting upon uncertainties. Nevertheless I still believed that the enjoyment I once had in that theater ought to be of a more durable kind. . . . The comical is after all the least one can demand—cannot even that be repeated?

With these thoughts in my mind I went home. My writing-table was in the accustomed place. The velvet armchair still existed. But when I saw it I was so exasperated that I was near breaking it to bits—all the more because everybody in the house had gone to bed, and there was no one to take it away. What is the good of a velvet armchair when the rest of the environment doesn't correspond with it? It is as if a man were to walk naked wearing a cocked hat. When I had gone to bed without having had a single rational thought, it was so light in the room that I constantly saw the velvet armchair, whether awake or in my dreams, so when I got up next morning I carried into effect my resolution and had it thrown into a storeroom.

My home had become cheerless, precisely because it was the reverse of a repetition, my mind was unfruitful, my troubled imagination was engaged in transmuting into the delights of Tantalus the memory of how richly the thoughts presented themselves on the former occasion, and this rank weed of memory strangled every thought at birth.

I went out to the coffeehouse, where on the previous visit I went every day to enjoy the drink which according to the words of the poet,[19] if it is "pure and warm and strong and not abused," can be placed alongside that with which the poet compares it, namely "friendship." I insist at least upon good coffee. Perhaps the coffee was just as good as before, one might almost suppose so, but I didn't like it. The sun blazed hotly upon the window of the shop, the place was stuffy, pretty much like the air in a casserole, fit to stew in. A draft like a small trade-wind penetrated everywhere and forbade me to think of any repetition, even if an opportunity had presented itself.

That evening I went to the restaurant where I used to go on my former visit, and where, presumably by force of habit, the food agreed with me. When I went there every evening I was acquainted with it most accurately; I knew how the early guests when they were on the point of leaving greeted the fraternity they parted from, whether they put on their hats in the inner room, or in the last room, or only when they opened the door, or not till they were outside. Nothing escaped my observation. Like Proserpine[20] I plucked a hair from every head, even the bald ones.—It was always the same, the same jokes, the same courtesies, the same expressions of comradeship; the locality in all respects the same, in short, "the same in the same."[21] Solomon says that "the contentions of a wife are like a continual dropping," which would

---

[19] The German poet Ewald inscribed verses to this effect on his coffee urn. (L)
[20] *Aeneid*, IV, 697. (L)
[21] Socrates always said "the same thing in the same way." (L)

apply to this still-life. Dreadful thought! Here a repetition was possible!

The next night I was at the Königstäter Theater. The only thing repeated was the impossibility of repetition. In Unter den Linden the dust was insupportable, and every attempt to press in among the people and wash off the dust with a human bath was discouraging in the highest degree. However I turned and twisted, it was in vain. The little *danseuse* who had formerly enchanted me by her grace, which consisted so to say in a leap, had taken the leap. The blind man outside the Brandenburger Thor, my harpist (for I was surely the only one who was concerned about him) was wearing a coat of mixed gray, instead of light green which corresponded with my sad longing, for it made him look like a weeping willow. He was lost for me and won for the universal human. The beadle's much admired nose had turned pale. Professor A. A. wore a new pair of trousers which imparted to him an almost military air. . . .

When this experience had been repeated for several days I became so exasperated, so tired of repetition, that I resolved to make my way home again. My discovery was of no importance, and yet it was a strange one, for I discovered that there is no such thing as repetition, and I had convinced myself of this by trying in every possible way to get it repeated.

My hope was set upon my home. Justinus Kerner [22] tells somewhere of a man who was so tired of his home that he had his horse saddled in order to ride forth into the wide world. When he had gone a little distance his horse threw him. This turn of events was decisive for him, for when he turned to mount his horse his eye lit again upon the home he wished to leave, and he looked, and behold! it was so beautiful that he at once turned back. In my home I could reckon with tolerable certainty upon finding everything ready for repetition. I have always had a great distrust of upheavals, indeed I go so far that for this reason I even hate any sort of cleaning, and above all household scrubbing. So I had left the severest instructions to have my conservative principles maintained even in my absence. But what happens! My faithful servant held a different opinion. He reckoned that if he commenced the commotion soon after my departure, it surely would have ceased before my return, and he was surely man enough to put back everything punctually in its place. I arrive, I ring the doorbell, my servant opens. That

---

[22] A German poet (1786–1862); but this story has not been identified as his. Lowrie maintains that it comes from an Icelandic saga.

was a momentous moment. My servant became as white as a corpse, and through the half-opened door I saw the most dreadful sight: everything was turned upside down. I was petrified. My servant in his consternation did not know what to do, his evil conscience smote him, and he slammed the door in my face. That was too much, my distress had reached its climax, I might expect the worst, to be taken for a ghost. like Commerzienrat Grünmeyer.[23] I perceived that there is no such thing as repetition, and my earlier view of life triumphed. . . .

The older one grows and the more understanding of life one acquires, and taste for the agreeable and ability to relish it, in short, the more competent one becomes, the less one is content. Content—entirely and absolutely and in every way content—one never becomes, and to be tolerably content is not worth the trouble, so it is better to be entirely discontented. Everyone who has thoroughly considered the matter will agree with me that it is never granted to a man in his whole life, even for so much as half an hour, to be absolutely content in all imaginable ways. That for this more is required than having food and clothing, I surely do not need to say.

Once I was very close to it.[24] I got up in the morning feeling uncommonly well. This sense of well-being increased out of proportion to all analogy during the forenoon. Precisely at one o'clock I was at the highest peak and surmised the dizzy maximum which is not indicated on any scale of well-being, not even on the poetical thermometer. The body had lost all its earthly heaviness, it was as though I had no body, just for the reason that every function enjoyed its completest satisfaction, every nerve tingled with delight on its own account and on account of the whole, while every pulsation, as a disquietude in the organism, only suggested and reported the sensuous delight of the instant. My gait became a glide, not like the flight of a bird that cleaves the air and leaves the earth behind, but like the billows of the wind over a field of grain, like the yearning bliss of the cradling waves of the sea, like the dreamy gliding of the clouds. My very being was transparent, like the depths of the sea, like the self-contented silence of the night, like the quiet monologue of midday. Every feeling of my soul composed itself to rest with melodious resonance. Every thought proffered itself freely, every thought proffered itself with festal gladness and solemnity, the silliest conceit not less than the richest idea. Every impression was

[23] In J. L. Heiberg's *Kjoge Haskors,* Scene 46. (L)

[24] Lowrie believes that in this passage S.K. is "parodying his own experience of conversion," the "indescribable joy" of May 19, 1838. (*Supra*, p. 10.)

surmised before it arrived and was awakened within me. The whole of existence seemed to be as it were in love with me, and everything vibrated in preordained *rapport* with my being. In me all was ominous, and everything was enigmatically transfigured in my microcosmic bliss, which was able to transform into its own likeness all things, even the observations which were most disagreeable and tiresome, even disgusting sights and the most fatal collisions. When precisely at one o'clock I was at the highest peak, where I surmised the ultimate attainment, something suddenly began to chafe one of my eyes, whether it was an eye-lash, a mote, a bit of dust, I do not know; but this I know, that in that selfsame instant I toppled down almost into the abyss of despair—a thing which everyone will understand who has been so high up as I was, and when he was at that point has been engaged with the generic question how nearly absolute contentment can be attained. Since that time I have given up every hope of ever feeling myself content absolutely and in all ways, have given up the hope I once cherished, not indeed of being absolutely content at all times, but at least at particular instants, even if these units of instants were not more numerous than, as Shakespeare says,[25] "a tapster's arithmetic was capable of summing up."

I had got so far as to entertain this modest hope before I learned to know that young man.[26] As soon as I asked myself, or somebody raised a question, about perfect contentment, though it be but for half an hour, I always "renounced" the play. Then it was that time and again I conceived the idea of repetition and grew enthusiastic about it—thereby becoming again a victim of my zeal for principles. For I am thoroughly convinced that, if I had not taken that journey for the express purpose of assuring myself of the possibility of repetition, I should have diverted myself immensely on finding everything the same. . . .

[25] *Troilus and Cressida,* Act 1, Sc. 2. (L)
[26] The hero of the serious part of *Repetition.*

PHILOSOPHICAL FRAGMENTS, OR A FRAGMENT OF PHILOSOPHY

BY JOHANNES CLIMACUS
RESPONSIBLE FOR PUBLICATION:
S. KIERKEGAARD (1844)

TRANSLATED BY DAVID F. SWENSON

The idea of philosophy is mediation; Christianity's is the paradox.

If ever there should be any question of such a thing, Danish philosophy would differ from German philosophy in this: that it would not begin from nothing, or without assumptions, or explain everything through mediation; on the contrary, it would begin with the proposition there are many things in heaven and earth which no philosopher has explained.

It is the duty of the human understanding to understand that there are things which it cannot understand, and what those things are. . . . The paradox is not a concession but a category, an ontological definition which expresses the relation between an existing cognitive spirit and eternal truth.—THE JOURNALS

WITH this work we enter the period of S.K.'s intellectual maturity, the period to be climaxed two years later by the great *Unscientific Postscript*, for which the *Fragments* do little more than set the stage.

This stage-setting, however, is important. It is important to get clearly in mind the question S.K. was trying to answer, before we see how he answered it in the *Postscript*. As Reinhold Niebuhr has said, there is nothing so "foolish" as the answer to a question that is not asked. The *Fragments* ask S.K.'s question—the question which he regarded as the *sine qua non* for the survival of Christianity—without attempting to answer it.

This question appears on the title page of the book: "Is an historical point of departure possible for an eternal consciousness; how can such a point of departure have any other than a mere historical interest; is it possible to base an eternal happiness upon historical knowledge?" These questions reduce to the simpler one with which Johannes Climacus begins his "Propositio": "How far does the Truth admit of being learned?" That is to say, how far is the Truth (ultimate truth, not merely the truth of this or that) outside oneself to begin with so that in being learned, it has to be, so to speak, injected into one's consciousness from without? Or is it rather that in coming to know something, we merely come into full possession of what was latent in us all along—merely bring into consciousness what was in our "subconscious," or in other words merely realize our true selves? This latter was the assumption of Socrates, who in all of his philosophizing regarded himself not as one who had certain truths to communicate to others, but rather as one only a little less ignorant than they, whose mission was simply that of a midwife—i.e. to help others become conscious of themselves and bring to birth what they already bore within themselves. This has also been the assumption, explicit or implicit, of all Idealistic philosophy from Socrates and Plato to the present day.

Now, says Kierkegaard, let us assume for a moment, merely as an "experiment of thought," that this *immanent* point of view (i.e. the truth as within ourselves) is not correct. Truth would then have to be brought to us from the outside; for mankind (on this second assumption) is not in the truth or the truth in him. He is rather in error—not merely in error in the sense that he is ignorant of many things (this even the opposite assumption will admit), but actively in error—not advancing toward the Light "with feeble steps and slow," but running away from it as fast as his legs will carry him. On this premise mankind would require a teacher, not in the Socratic sense of one who helps him come to a realization of himself, but a Teacher who himself is in possession of that which mankind does not possess. The minute we make clear to ourselves this possibility, we see that it is in fact the assumption which Christianity makes in its twin doctrines of original sin and of salvation through the coming into history of the God-man, Jesus Christ. He is the Teacher, because He is not in error like ourselves. Johannes proceeds to dramatize this possibility in the beautiful story of the King and the Humble Maiden, a parable of the Incarnation; but he does not commit himself to it. Like Johannes de Silentio in *Fear and Trembling*, he remains on the outside, an admirer of those who can bear to make this assumption, a much less comfortable one than that of immanence; but he himself does not see his way clear to making it, does not become a "disciple."

This is not, he hastens to point out, because it is any harder for the "disciple at second hand" (i.e. the individual living 2000 years after Christ) to apprehend the Truth than it is for "the contemporary disciple"; it is rather that both contemporary and noncontemporary face the same essential difficulty in believing—viz. the fact that the Truth in which they are asked to believe is "the absolute Paradox," the paradox of God in time. If one is to believe this paradox, God Himself must give him the condition for doing so by giving him "a new organ" of apprehension—that of Faith.

A PROJECT OF THOUGHT

A

How far does the Truth admit of being learned? With this question let us begin. It was a Socratic question, or became such in consquence of the parallel Socratic question with respect to virtue, since virtue was again determined as insight. (*Protagoras, Gorgias, Meno, Euthydemus.*) In so far as the Truth is conceived as something to be learned, its non-existence is evidently presupposed, so that in proposing to learn it one makes it the object of an inquiry. Here we are confronted with the difficulty to which Socrates calls attention in the *Meno* (80, near the end) and there characterizes as a "pugnacious proposition": one cannot seek for what he knows, and it seems equally impossible for him to seek for what he does not know. For what a man knows he cannot seek, since he knows it; and what he does not know he cannot seek, since he does not even know for what to seek. Socrates thinks the difficulty through in the doctrine of Recollection, by which all learning and inquiry is interpreted as a kind of remembering: one who is ignorant needs only a reminder to help him come to himself in the consciousness of what he knows. Thus the Truth is not introduced into the individual from without, but was within him all the time. This thought receives further development at the hands of Socrates, and it ultimately becomes the point of concentration for the pathos of the Greek consciousness, since it serves as a proof for the immortality of the soul; but with a backward reference, it is important to note, and hence as proof for the soul's preexistence.

In the light of this idea it becomes apparent with what wonderful consistency Socrates remained true to himself, through his manner of life giving artistic expression to what he had understood. He entered into the role of midwife and sustained it throughout; not because his thought "had no positive content,"[1] but because he perceived that this relation is the highest that one human being can sustain to another. And in this surely Socrates was everlastingly right; for even if a divine point of departure is ever given, between man and man this is the true relationship, provided we reflect upon the absolute and refuse to dally with the accidental, from the heart renouncing the understanding of the half-truths which seem the delight of men and the secret of the System.[2] Socrates was a midwife subjected to a divine

---

[1] Such is the criticism commonly passed upon Socrates in our age, which boasts of its positivity much as if a polytheist were to speak with scorn of the negativity of a monotheist; for the polytheist has many gods, the monotheist only one. So our philosophers have many thoughts, all valid to a certain extent; Socrates had only one, which was absolute. (K)

[2] Hegel's philosophy, in contrast to which S.K. took delight in stressing the *fragmentariness* of his own thought. The present work is a mere "fragment of philosophy," *Either/Or* was a "fragment of life."

examination; his work was in fulfillment of a divine mission (Plato's *Apology*), though he seemed to men in general a most singular creature (*Theaetetus*, 149); it was in accordance with a divine principle, as Socrates also understood it, that he was by God forbidden to beget (*Theaetetus*, 150); for between man and man the maieutic relationship is the highest, and begetting belongs to God alone.

From the standpoint of the Socratic thought every point of departure in time is *eo ipso* accidental, an occasion, a vanishing moment. The teacher himself is no more than this; and if he offers himself and his instruction on any other basis, he does not give but takes away, and is not even the other's friend, much less his teacher. Herein lies the profundity of the Socratic thought and the noble humanity he so thoroughly expressed, which refused to enter into a false and vain fellowship with clever heads, but felt an equal kinship with a tanner; whence he soon "came to the conclusion that the study of Physics was not man's proper business, and therefore began to philosophize about moral matters in the workshops and in the market-place" (Diogenes Laertius, II, v, 21), but philosophized with equal absoluteness everywhere. With slipshod thoughts, with higgling and haggling, maintaining a little here and conceding a little there, as if the individual might to a certain extent owe something to another, but then again to a certain extent not; with loose words that explain everything except what this "to a certain extent" means—with such makeshifts it is not possible to advance beyond Socrates, nor will one reach the concept of a Revelation, but merely remain within the sphere of idle chatter. In the Socratic view each individual is his own center, and the entire world centers in him, because his self-knowledge is a knowledge of God. It was thus Socrates understood himself, and thus he thought that everyone must understand himself, in the light of this understanding interpreting his relationship to each individual with equal humility and with equal pride. He had the courage and self-possession to be sufficient unto himself, but also in his relations to his fellowmen to be merely an occasion, even when dealing with the meanest capacity. How rare is such magnanimity! How rare in a time like ours, when the parson is something more than the clerk, when almost every second person is an authority, while all these distinctions and all these many authorities are mediated in a common madness, a *commune naufragium*. For while no human being was ever truly an authority for another, or ever helped anyone by posing as such, or was ever able to take his client with him in truth, there is another sort of success that may by such methods be won; for it has never yet been known to fail that one fool, when he goes astray, takes several others with him.

With this understanding of what it means to learn the Truth, the fact that I have been instructed by Socrates or by Prodicus or by a servant-girl can concern me only historically; or insofar as I am a Plato in sentimental enthusiasm, it may concern me poetically. . . . Nor can it interest me otherwise than historically that Socrates' or Prodicus' doctrine was this or that; for the Truth in which I rest was within me, and came to light through myself, and not even Socrates could have given it to me, as little as the driver can pull the load for the horses, though he may help them by applying the lash. My relation to Socrates or Prodicus cannot concern me with respect to my eternal happiness, for this is given me retrogressively through my possession of the Truth, which I had from the beginning without knowing it. If I imagine myself meeting Socrates or Prodicus or the servant-girl in another life, then here again neither of them could be more to me than an occasion, which Socrates fearlessly expressed by saying that even in the lower world he proposed merely to ask questions; for the underlying principle of all questioning is that the one who is asked must have the Truth in himself, and be able to acquire it by himself. The temporal point of departure is nothing; for as soon as I discover that I have known the Truth from eternity without being aware of it, the same instant this moment of occasion is hidden in the eternal, and so incorporated with it that I cannot even find it, so to speak, even if I sought it; because in my eternal consciousness there is neither here nor there, but only an *ubique et nusquam*.[3]

B

Now if things are to be otherwise, the moment in time must have a decisive significance, so that I will never be able to forget it either in time or eternity; because the eternal, which hitherto did not exist, came into being in this moment. Under this presupposition let us now proceed to consider the consequences for the problem of how far it is possible to acquire a knowledge of the Truth.

(a) THE ANTECEDENT STATE

We begin with the Socratic difficulty about seeking the Truth, which seems equally impossible whether we have it or do not have it. The Socratic thought really abolishes this disjunction, since it ap-

[3] "Everywhere and nowhere."

pears that at bottom every human being is in possession of the **Truth.** This was Socrates' explanation; we have seen what follows from it with respect to the moment. Now if the latter is to have decisive significance, the seeker must be destitute of the Truth up to the very moment of his learning it; he cannot even have possessed it in the form of ignorance, for in that case the moment becomes merely occasional. What is more, he cannot even be described as a seeker. . . . He must therefore be characterized as beyond the pale of the Truth, not approaching it like a proselyte, but departing from it; or as being in Error. He is then in a state of Error. But how is he now to be reminded, or what will it profit him to be reminded of what he has not known, and consequently cannot recall?

(b) THE TEACHER

If the Teacher serves as an occasion by means of which the learner is reminded, he cannot help the learner to recall that he really knows the Truth; for the learner is in a state of Error. What the Teacher can give him occasion to remember is, that he is in Error. But in this consciousness the learner is excluded from the Truth even more decisively than before, when he lived in ignorance of his Error. In this manner the Teacher thrusts the learner away from him, precisely by serving as a reminder; only that the learner, in thus being thrust back upon himself, does not discover that he knew the Truth already, but discovers his Error; with respect to which act of consciousness the Socratic principle holds, that the Teacher is merely an occasion, whoever he may be, even if he is a God. For my own Error is something I can discover only by myself, since it is only when I have discovered it that it is discovered, even if the whole world knew of it before. (Under the presupposition we have adopted concerning the moment, this remains the only analogy to the Socratic order of things.)

. . . Now if the learner is to acquire the Truth, the Teacher must bring it to him; and not only so, but he must also give him the condition necessary for understanding it. For if the learner were in his own person the condition for understanding the Truth, he need only recall it. The condition for understanding the Truth is like the capacity to inquire for it: the condition contains the conditioned, and the question implies the answer. (Unless this is so, the moment must be understood in the Socratic sense.)

But one who gives the learner not only the Truth, but also the condition for understanding it, is more than teacher. All instruction depends upon the presence, in the last analysis, of the requisite condition; if this is lacking, no teacher can do anything. For otherwise he would find it necessary not only to transform the learner, but to re-create him before beginning to teach him. But this is something that no human being can do; if it is to be done, it must be done by God himself.

Insofar as the learner exists he is already created, and hence God must have endowed him with the condition for understanding the Truth. For otherwise his earlier existence must have been merely brutish, and the Teacher who gave him the Truth and with it the condition was the original creator of his human nature. But insofar as the moment is to have decisive significance (and unless we assume this we remain at the Socratic standpoint) the learner is destitute of this condition, and must therefore have been deprived of it. This deprivation cannot have been due to an act of God (which would be a contradiction), nor to an accident (for it would be a contradiction to assume that the lower could overcome the higher); it must therefore be due to himself. If he could have lost the condition in such a way that the loss was not due to himself, and if he could remain in the state of deprivation without his own responsibility, it would follow that his earlier possession of the condition was accidental merely. But this is a contradiction, since the condition for understanding the Truth is an essential condition. Error is then not only outside the Truth, but polemic in its attitude toward it; which is expressed by saying that the learner has himself forfeited the condition, and is engaged in forfeiting it.

The Teacher is then God himself, who in acting as an occasion prompts the learner to recall that he is in Error, and that by reason of his own guilt. But this state, the being in Error by reason of one's own guilt, what shall we call it? Let us call it *Sin*.

The Teacher is God, and he gives the learner the requisite condition and the Truth. What shall we call such a Teacher? for we are surely agreed that we have already far transcended the ordinary functions of a teacher. Insofar as the learner is in Error, but in consequence of his own act (and in no other way can he possibly be in this state, as we have shown above), he might seem to be free; for to be what one is by one's own act is freedom. And yet he is in reality unfree and bound and exiled; for to be free from the Truth is to be exiled from the Truth, and to be exiled by one's own self is to be bound. But since he is bound by himself, may he not loose his bonds and set himself free?

For whatever binds me, the same should be able to set me free when it wills; and since this power is here his own self, he should be able to liberate himself. But first at any rate he must will it. Suppose him now to be so profoundly impressed by what the Teacher gave him occasion to remember (and this must not be omitted from the reckoning): suppose that he wills his freedom. In that case, i.e., if by willing to be free he could by himself become free, the fact that he had been bound would become a state of the past, tracelessly vanishing in the moment of liberation; the moment would not be charged with decisive significance. He was not aware that he had bound himself, and now he had freed himself.[4] Thus interpreted, the moment receives no decisive significance, and yet this was the hypothesis we proposed to ourselves in the beginning. By the terms of our hypothesis, therefore, he will not be able to set himself free.—And so it is in very truth; for

[4] Let us take plenty of time to consider the point, since there is no pressing need for haste. . . . Let us talk about this a little in the Greek manner. Suppose a child had been presented with a little sum of money, and could buy with it either a good book, for example, or a toy, both at the same price. If he buys the toy, can he then buy the book for the same money? Surely not, since the money is already spent. But perhaps he may go to the bookseller and ask him to make an exchange, letting him have the book in return for the toy. Will not the bookseller say: My dear child, your toy is not worth anything; it is true that when you still had the money you could have bought the book instead of the toy, but a toy is a peculiar kind of thing, for once it is bought it loses all value. Would not the child think that this was very strange? And so there was also a time when man could have bought either freedom or bondage at the same price, this price being the soul's free choice and commitment in the choice. He chose bondage; but if he now comes forward with a proposal for an exchange, would not God reply: Undoubtedly there was a time when you could have bought whichever you pleased, but bondage is a very strange sort of thing; when it is bought it has absolutely no value, although the price paid for it was originally the same. Would not such an individual think this very strange? Again, suppose two opposing armies drawn up in the field, and that a knight arrives whom both armies invite to fight on their side; he makes his choice, is vanquished and taken prisoner. As prisoner he is brought before the victor, to whom he foolishly presumes to offer his services on the same terms as were extended to him before the battle. Would not the victor say to him: My friend, you are now my prisoner: there was indeed a time when you could have chosen differently, but now everything is changed. Was this not strange enough? Yet if it were not so, if the moment had no decisive significance, the child must at bottom have bought the book, merely imagining in his ignorance and misunderstanding that he had bought the toy; the captive knight must really have fought on the other side, the facts having been obscured by the fog, so that at bottom he had fought on the side of the leader whose prisoner he now imagined himself to be.—"The vicious and the virtuous have not indeed power over their moral actions; but at first they had the power to become either the one or the other, just as one who throws a stone has power over it until he has thrown it, but not afterwards." (Aristotle). Otherwise throwing would be an illusion; the thrower would keep the stone in his hand in spite of all his throwing; it would be like the "flying arrow" of the skeptics, which did not fly. (K)

he forges the chains of his bondage with the strength of his freedom, since he exists in it without compulsion; and thus his bonds grow strong, and all his powers unite to make him the slave of sin.

What now shall we call such a Teacher, one who restores the lost condition and gives the learner the Truth? Let us call him *Saviour*, for he saves the learner from his bondage and from himself; let us call him *Redeemer*, for he redeems the learner from the captivity into which he had plunged himself, and no captivity is so terrible and so impossible to break, as that in which the individual keeps himself. And still we have not said all that is necessary; for by his self-imposed bondage the learner has brought upon himself a burden of guilt, and when the Teacher gives him the condition and the Truth he constitutes himself an *Atonement,* taking away the wrath impending upon that of which the learner has made himself guilty.

Such a Teacher the learner will never be able to forget. For the moment he forgets him he sinks back again into himself, just as one who, while in original possession of the condition, forgot that God exists, and thereby sank into bondage. If they should happen to meet in another life, the Teacher would again be able to give the condition to anyone who had not yet received it; but to one who had once received the condition he would stand in a different relation. The condition was a trust, for which the recipient would always be required to render an account. But what shall we call such a Teacher? A teacher may determine whether the pupil makes progress or not, but he cannot judge him; for he ought to have Socratic insight enough to perceive that he cannot give him what is essential. This Teacher is thus not so much teacher as *Judge.* Even when the learner has most completely appropriated the condition, and most profoundly apprehended the Truth, he cannot forget this Teacher or let him vanish Socratically. . . .

And now the moment. Such a moment has a peculiar character. It is brief and temporal indeed, like every moment; it is transient as all moments are; it is past, like every moment in the next moment. And yet it is decisive, and filled with the eternal. Such a moment ought to have a distinctive name; let us call it the *Fullness of Time.*

(c) THE DISCIPLE

When the disciple is in a state of Error (and otherwise we return to Socrates) but is none the less a human being, and now receives the condition and the Truth, he does not become a human being for the first time, since he was a man already. But he becomes another man; not in the frivolous sense of becoming another individual of the same quality as before, but in the sense of becoming a man of a different quality, or as we may call him: *a new creature.*

Insofar as he was in Error he was constantly in the act of departing from the Truth. In consequence of receiving the condition in the moment, the course of his life has been given an opposite direction, so that he is now turned about. Let us call this change *Conversion,* even though this word be one not hitherto used; but that is precisely a reason for choosing it, in order namely to avoid confusion, for it is as if expressly coined for the change we have in mind.

Insofar as the learner was in Error by reason of his own guilt, this conversion cannot take place without being taken up in his consciousness, or without his becoming aware that his former state was a consequence of his guilt. With this consciousness he will then take leave of his former state. But what leave-taking is without a sense of sadness? The sadness in this case, however, is on account of his having so long remained in his former state. Let us call such grief *Repentance;* for what is repentance but a kind of leave-taking, looking backward indeed, but yet in such a way as precisely to quicken the steps toward that which lies before?

Insofar as the learner was in Error, and now receives the Truth and with it the condition for understanding it, a change takes place within him like the change from non-being to being. But this transition from non-being to being is the transition we call birth. Now one who exists cannot be born; nevertheless, the disciple is born. Let us call this transition the *new birth,* in consequence of which the disciple enters the world quite as at the first birth, an individual human being knowing nothing as yet about the world into which he is born, whether it is inhabited, whether there are other human beings in it besides himself; for while it is indeed possible to be baptized *en masse,* it is not possible to be born anew *en masse.* Just as one who has begotten himself by the aid of the Socratic midwifery now forgets everything else in the world, and in a deeper sense owes no man anything, so the disciple who is born anew owes nothing to any man, but everything to his divine Teacher. And just as the former forgets the world in his discovery of himself, so the latter forgets himself in the discovery of his Teacher.

Hence if the *Moment* is to have decisive significance—and if not we speak Socratically whatever we may say, even if through not even understanding ourselves we imagine that we have advanced far be-

yond that sage of the simple mind—if the Moment has decisive significance the breach is made, and man cannot return. He will take no
pleasure in remembering what Recollection brings to his mind; still less
will he be able in his own strength to bring God anew over to his side.

But is the hypothesis here expounded thinkable? . . . Before we
reply, let us ask ourselves from whom we may expect an answer to
our question. This thing of being born, is it thinkable? Certainly, why
not? But for whom is it thinkable, for one who is born, or for one who is
not born? This latter supposition is an absurdity which could never
have entered anyone's head. . . . When one who has experienced birth
thinks of himself as born, he conceives this transition from non-being
to being. The same principle must also hold in the case of the new
birth. Or is the difficulty increased by the fact that the non-being which
precedes the new birth contains more being than the non-being which
preceded the first birth? But who then may be expected to think the
new birth? Surely the man who has himself been born anew, since it
would be absurd to imagine that one not so born should think it. Would
it not be the height of the ridiculous for such an individual to entertain
this notion?

There you have my project. But I think I hear someone say: "This
is the most ridiculous of all projects; or rather, you are of all projectors
of hypotheses the most ridiculous. For even when a man propounds
something nonsensical, it may still remain true that it is he who has
propounded it; but you behave like a lazzarone who takes money for
exhibiting premises open to everybody's inspection; you are like the
man who collected a fee for exhibiting a ram in the afternoon, which
in the forenoon could be seen gratis, grazing in the open field."—
"Perhaps it is so; I hide my head in shame. But assuming that I am
as ridiculous as you say, let me try to make amends by proposing a
new hypothesis. Everybody knows that gunpowder was invented
centuries ago, and in so far it would be ridiculous of me to pretend to
be the inventor; but would it be equally ridiculous of me to assume
that somebody was the inventor? Now I am going to be so polite as to
assume that you are the author of my project; greater politeness than
this you can scarcely ask. Or if you deny this, will you also deny that
someone is the author, that is to say, some human being? In that case
I am as near to being the author as any other human being. So that
your anger is not vented upon me because I appropriated something

that belongs to another human being, but because I appropriated something of which no human being is the rightful owner; and hence your anger is by no means appeased when I deceitfully ascribe the authorship to you. Is it not strange that there should be something such in existence, in relation to which everyone who knows it knows also that he has not invented it, this pass-me-by not stopping or capable of being stopped even if we approached all men in turn? This strange fact deeply impresses me, and casts over me a spell; for it constitutes a test of the hypothesis, and proves its truth. It would certainly be absurd to expect of a man that he should of his own accord discover that he did not exist. But this is precisely the transition of the new birth, from non-being to being. That he may come to understand it afterwards can make no difference; for because a man knows how to use gunpowder and can resolve it into its contituent elements, it does not follow that he has invented it. Be then angry with me and with whoever else pretends to the authorship of this thought; but that is no reason why you should be angry with the thought itself."

GOD AS TEACHER AND SAVIOUR: AN ESSAY OF THE IMAGINATION

... Much is heard in the world about unhappy love, and we all know what this means: the lovers are prevented from realizing their union, the causes being many and various. There exists another kind of unhappy love, the theme of our present discourse, for which there is no perfect earthly parallel, though by dint of speaking foolishly a little while we may make shift to conceive it through an earthly figure. The unhappiness of this love does not come from the inability of the lovers to realize their union, but from their inability to understand one another. This grief is infinitely more profound than that of which men commonly speak, since it strikes at the very heart of love, and wounds for an eternity; not like that other misfortune which touches only the temporal and the external, and which for the magnanimous is as a sort of jest over the inability of the lovers to realize their union here in time. This infinitely deeper grief is essentially the prerogative of the superior, since only he likewise understands the misunderstanding; in reality it belongs to God alone, and no human relationship can afford a valid analogy. Nevertheless, we shall here suggest such an analogy, in order to quicken the mind to an apprehension of the divine.

Suppose there was a king who loved a humble maiden. But the reader has perhaps already lost his patience, seeing that our beginning sounds like a fairy tale and is not in the least systematic.[1] So the very learned Polos found it tiresome that Socrates aways talked about meat and drink and doctors, and similar unworthy trifles, which Polos deemed beneath him *(Gorgias)*. But did not the Socratic manner of speech have at least one advantage, in that he himself and all others were from childhood equipped with the necessary prerequisites for understanding it? And would it not be desirable if I could confine the terms of my argument to meat and drink, and did not need to bring in kings, whose thoughts are not always like those of other men, if they are indeed kingly. But perhaps I may be pardoned the extravagance, seeing that I am only a poet, proceeding now to unfold the carpet of my discourse (recalling the beautiful saying of Themistocles), lest its workmanship be concealed by the compactness of its folding.

Suppose then a king who loved a humble maiden. The heart of the king was not polluted by the wisdom that is loudly enough proclaimed; he knew nothing of the difficulties that the understanding discovers in order to ensnare the heart, which keep the poets so busy and make their magic formulas necessary. It was easy to realize his purpose. Every statesman feared his wrath and dared not breathe a word of displeasure; every foreign state trembled before his power and dared not omit sending ambassadors with congratulations for the nuptials; no courtier groveling in the dust dared wound him, lest his own head be crushed. Then let the harp be tuned, let the songs of the poets begin to sound, and let all be festive while love celebrates its triumph. For love is exultant when it unites equals, but it is triumphant when it makes that which was unequal equal in love.—Then there awoke in the heart of the king an anxious thought; who but a king who thinks kingly thoughts would have dreamed of it! He spoke to no one about his anxiety; for if he had, each courtier would doubtless have said: "Your majesty is about to confer a favor upon the maiden, for which she can never be sufficiently grateful her whole life long." This speech would have moved the king to wrath, so that he would have commanded the execution of the courtier for high treason against the beloved, and thus he would in still another way have found his grief increased. So he wrestled with his troubled thoughts alone. Would she be happy in the life at his side? Would she be able to summon confidence enough never

---

[1] Again Hegel is the object of S.K.'s irony.

to remember what the king wished only to forget, that he was king and she had been a humble maiden? For if this memory were to waken in her soul, and like a favored lover sometimes steal her thoughts away from the king, luring her reflections into the seclusion of a secret grief; or if this memory sometimes passed through her soul like the shadow of death over the grave: where would then be the glory of their love? Then she would have been happier had she remained in her obscurity, loved by an equal, content in her humble cottage; but confident in her love, and cheerful early and late. What a rich abundance of grief is here laid bare, like ripened grain bent under the weight of its fruitfulness, merely waiting the time of the harvest, when the thought of the king will thresh out all its seed of sorrow! For even if the maiden would be content to become as nothing, this could not satisfy the king, precisely because he loved her, and because it was harder for him to be her benefactor than to lose her. And suppose she could not even understand him? For while we are thus speaking foolishly of human relationships, we may suppose a difference of mind between them such as to render an understanding impossible. What a depth of grief slumbers in this unhappy love . . . !

But if the *Moment* is to have decisive significance (and if not we return to Socrates even if we think to advance beyond him), the learner is in Error, and that by reason of his own guilt. And yet he is the object of God's love, and God desires to teach him, and is concerned to bring him to equality with himself. If this equality cannot be established, God's love becomes unhappy and his teaching meaningless, since they cannot understand one another. Men sometimes think that this might be a matter of indifference to God, since he does not stand in need of the learner. But in this we forget—or rather, alas! we prove how far we are from understanding him; we forget that God loves the learner. And just as that kingly grief of which we have spoken can be found only in a kingly soul, and is not even named in the language of the multitude of men, so the entire human language is so selfish that it refuses even to suspect the existence of such a grief. But for that reason God has reserved it to himself, this unfathomable grief: to know that he may repel the learner, that he does not need him, that the learner has brought destruction upon himself by his own guilt, that he can leave the learner to his fate; to know also how wellnigh impossible it is to keep the learner's courage and confidence alive, without which the purposed understanding and equality will fail, and the love become unhappy. The man who cannot feel at least some faint intimation of this grief is a paltry soul of base coinage, bearing neither the image of Caesar nor the image of God.

Our problem is now before us. . . . The poet's task will be to find a solution, some point of union, where love's understanding may be realized in truth, God's anxiety be set at rest, his sorrow banished. For the divine love is that unfathomable love which cannot rest content with that which the beloved might in his folly prize as happiness.

A

The union might be brought about by an elevation of the learner. God would then take him up unto himself, transfigure him, fill his cup with millennial joys (for a thousand years are as one day in his sight), and let the learner forget the misunderstanding in tumultuous joy. Alas, the learner might perhaps be greatly inclined to prize such happiness as this. How wonderful suddenly to find his fortune made, like the humble maiden, because the eye of God happened to rest upon him! And how wonderful also to be his helper in taking all this in vain, deceived by his own heart! Even the noble king could perceive the difficulty of such a method, for he was not without insight into the human heart, and understood that the maiden was at bottom deceived; and no one is so terribly deceived as he who does not himself suspect it, but is as if enchanted by a change in the outward habiliments of his existence.

The union might be brought about by God showing himself to the learner and receiving his worship, causing him to forget himself over the divine apparition. Thus the king might have shown himself to the humble maiden in all the pomp of his power, causing the sun of his presence to rise over her cottage, shedding a glory over the scene, and making her forget herself in worshipful admiration. Alas, and this might have satisfied the maiden, but it could not satisfy the king, who desired not his own glorification but hers. It was this that made his grief so hard to bear, his grief that she could not understand him; but it would have been still harder for him to deceive her. And merely to give his love for her an imperfect expression was in his eyes a deception, even though no one understood him and reproaches sought to mortify his soul.

Not in this manner, then, can their love be made happy, except perhaps in appearance, i.e. in the learner's and the maiden's eyes, but not in the Teacher's and the king's, whom no delusion can satisfy. Thus

God takes pleasure in arraying the lily in a garb more glorious than that of Solomon; but if there could be any thought of an understanding here, would it not be a sorry delusion of the lily's, if when it looked upon its fine raiment it thought that it was on account of the raiment that God loved it? Instead of standing dauntless in the field, sporting with the wind, carefree as the gust that blows, would it not under the influence of such a thought languish and droop, not daring to lift up its head? It was God's solicitude to prevent this, for the lily's shoot is tender and easily broken. But if the Moment is to have decisive significance, how unspeakable will be God's anxiety! There once lived a people who had a profound understanding of the divine; this people thought that no man could see God and live.—Who grasps this contradiction of sorrow: not to reveal oneself is the death of love, to reveal oneself is the death of the beloved! The minds of men so often yearn for might and power, and their thoughts are constantly being drawn to such things, as if by their attainment all mysteries would be resolved. Hence they do not even dream that there is sorrow in heaven as well as joy, the deep grief of having to deny the learner what he yearns for with all his heart, of having to deny him precisely because he is the beloved.

B

... Since we found that the union could not be brought about by an elevation, it must be attempted by a descent. Let the learner be x. In this x we must include the lowliest; for if even Socrates refused to establish a false fellowship with the clever, how can we suppose that God would make a distinction! In order that the union may be brought about, God must therefore become the equal of such a one, and so he will appear in the likeness of the humblest. But the humblest is one who must serve others, and God will therefore appear in the form of a *servant*. But this servant-form is no mere outer garment, like the king's beggar-cloak, which therefore flutters loosely about him and betrays the king; it is not like the filmy summer-cloak of Socrates, which though woven of nothing yet both conceals and reveals. It is his true form and figure. For this is the unfathomable nature of love, that it desires equality with the beloved, not in jest merely, but in earnest and truth. And it is the omnipotence of the love which is so resolved that it is able to accomplish its purpose, which neither Socrates nor the king could do. . . .

Behold where he stands—God! Where? There; do you not see him? He is God; and yet he has not a resting-place for his head, and he dares not lean on any man lest he cause him to be offended. He is God; and yet he picks his steps more carefully than if angels guided them, not to prevent his foot from stumbling against a stone, but lest he trample human beings in the dust, in that they are offended in him. He is God; and yet his eye surveys mankind with anxious care, for the tender shoots of an individual life may be crushed as easily as a blade of grass. How wonderful a life, all sorrow and all love: to yearn to express the equality of love and yet to be misunderstood; to apprehend the danger that all men may be destroyed, and yet only so to be able really to save a single soul; his own life filled with sorrow, while each hour of the day is taken up with the troubles of the learner who confides in him! This is God as he stands upon the earth, like unto the humblest by the power of his omnipotent love. He knows that the learner is in Error—what if he should misunderstand, and droop, and lose his confidence! To sustain the heavens and the earth by the fiat of his omnipotent word, so that if this word were withdrawn for the fraction of a second the universe would be plunged into chaos—how light a task compared with bearing the burden that mankind may take offense, when one has been constrained by love to become its saviour!

But the servant-form was no mere outer garment, and therefore God must suffer all things, endure all things, make experience of all things. He must suffer hunger in the desert, he must thirst in the time of his agony, he must be forsaken in death, absolutely like the humblest—behold the man! His suffering is not that of his death, but his entire life is a story of suffering; and it is love that suffers, the love which gives all is itself in want. What wonderful self-denial! for though the learner be one of the lowliest, he nevertheless asks him anxiously: Do you now really love me? For he knows where the danger threatens, and yet he also knows that every easier way would involve a deception, even though the learner might not understand it.

Every other form of revelation would be a deception in the eyes of love; for either the learner would first have to be changed, and the fact concealed from him that this was necessary (but love does not alter the beloved, it alters itself); or there would be permitted to prevail a frivolous ignorance of the fact that the entire relationship was a delusion. (This was the error of paganism.) Every other form of revelation would be a deception from the standpoint of the divine love.

And if my eyes were more filled with tears than those of a repentant woman, and if each tear were more precious than a pardoned woman's many tears; if I could find a place more humble than the place at his feet, and if I could sit there more humbly than a woman whose heart's sole choice was this one thing needful; if I loved him more sincerely than the most loyal of his servants, eager to shed the last drop of his life-blood in his service; if I had found greater favor in his eyes than the purest among women—nevertheless, if I asked him to alter his purpose, to reveal himself differently, to be more lenient with himself, he would doubtless look at me and say: Man, what have I to do with thee? Get thee hence, for thou art Satan, though thou knowest it not! Or if he once or twice stretched forth his hand in command, and it happened, and I then meant to understand him better or love him more, I would doubtless see him weep also over me, and hear him say: To think that you could prove so faithless, and so wound my love! Is it then only the omnipotent wonder-worker that you love, and not him who humbled himself to become your equal?

But the servant-form was no mere outer garment; hence God must yield his spirit in death and again leave the earth. And if my grief were deeper than the sorrow of a mother when her heart is pierced by the sword, and if my danger were more terrible than the danger of a believer when his faith fails him, and if my misery were more pitiful than his who crucifies his hope and has nothing left but the cross— nevertheless, if I begged him to save his life and stay upon the earth, it would only be to see him sorrowful unto death, and stricken with grief also for my sake, because this suffering was for my profit, and now I had added to his sorrow the burden that I could not understand him. O bitter cup! More bitter than wormwood is the bitterness of death for a mortal, how bitter then for an immortal! O bitter refreshment, more bitter than aloes, to be refreshed by the misunderstanding of the beloved! O solace in affliction to suffer as one who is guilty, what solace then to suffer as one who is innocent!

Such will be our poet's picture. . . . Now if someone were to say: "This poem of yours is the most wretched piece of plagiarism ever perpetrated, for it is neither more nor less than what every child knows," I suppose I must blush with shame to hear myself called a liar. But why the most wretched? Every poet who steals, steals from some other poet, and insofar we are all equally wretched; indeed, my own theft is perhaps less harmful, since it is more readily discovered. If I were to be so polite as to ascribe the authorship to you who now condemn me, you would perhaps again be angry. Is there then no poet, although there is a poem? This would surely be strange, as strange as flute-playing without a flute-player. Or is this poem perhaps like a proverb, for which no author can be assigned, because it is as if it owed its existence to humanity at large; was this perhaps the reason you called my theft the most wretched, because I did not steal from any individual man but robbed the human race, and arrogantly, although I am only an individual man, aye even a wretched thief, pretended to be mankind? If this then is the case, and I went about to all men in turn, and all knew the poem, but each one also knew that he was not the author of it, can I then conclude: mankind must be the author? Would not this be a strange conclusion? For if mankind were the author of this poem, this would have to be expressed by considering every individual equally close to the authorship. Does it not seem to you that this is a difficult case in which we have become involved, though the whole matter appeared to be so easily disposed of in the beginning, by your short and angry word about its being the most wretched plagiarism, and my shame in having to hear it?

So then perhaps it is no poem, or at any rate not one for which any human being is responsible, nor yet mankind; ah, now I understand you, it was for this reason you called my procedure the most wretched act of plagiarism, because I did not steal from any individual, nor from the race, but from God; or as it were stole God away, and though I am only an individual man, aye even a wretched thief, blasphemously pretended to be God. Now I understand you fully, dear friend, and recognize the justice of your resentment. But then my soul is filled with new wonder—even more, with the spirit of worship; for it would surely have been strange had this poem been a human production. It is not impossible that it might occur to man to imagine himself the equal of God, or to imagine God the equal of man, but not to imagine that God would make himself into the likeness of man; for if God gave no sign, how could it enter into the mind of man that the blessed God should need him? This would be a most stupid thought, or rather, so stupid a thought could never have entered into his mind; though when God has seen fit to entrust him with it, he exclaims in worship: This thought did not arise in my own heart! and finds it a most miraculously beautiful thought. And is it not altogether miraculous, and does not this word come as a happy omen to my lips; for as I have just said, and as you yourself involuntarily exclaim, we stand here before the *Miracle*. And as we both now stand before the miracle, whose solemn silence cannot be perturbed by human wrangling over mine and thine, whose awe-inspiring speech infinitely subdues all human strife about mine and thine, forgive me, I pray, the strange delusion that I was the author of this poem. It was a delusion, and the poem is so different from every human poem as not to be a poem at all, but the *Miracle*.

STAGES ON LIFE'S WAY: STUDIES BY SUNDRY PERSONS

COLLECTED, FORWARDED TO THE PRESS AND PUBLISHED BY HILARIUS BOOKBINDER (1845)

TRANSLATED BY WALTER LOWRIE

. . . I am, as it were, a spy in the service of the highest. The police also use spies. They do not always pick out men whose lives have been the purest and best, quite the contrary: they are cunning, crafty offenders, whose cunning the police use, while they coerce them through the consciousness of their *vita ante acta*. Alas, thus does God use sinners.

I believe that my task lies precisely in always being able to produce what the vanity and worldliness of the world longs for and considers the highest of all things . . . in always being able, but not always willing. The world is so weak that, when it thinks that a man who serves Christianity is one who is aesthetically incapable, they look down upon religion.—THE JOURNALS

ON April 30, 1845—little more than two years after *Either/Or* and some ten months after the *Fragments* and *The Concept of Dread*—appeared the sixth and last of Kierkegaard's "aesthetic" writings, a large work which he called *Stages on Life's Way*, consisting of "studies by sundry persons." The work is similar to *Either/Or* in that it delineates different "spheres of existence"; but whereas *Either/Or* dealt only with the aesthetic and the ethical spheres (the religious being merely hinted at in the concluding Sermon), the *Stages* set before us three realms, "an aesthetic, an ethical, and the religious, not abstract . . . but concrete in the existential factors: pleasure—perdition; action—victory; suffering. . . . The trouble with *Either/Or* was that it concluded ethically. In the *Stages* the situation has been clarified and the religious is given its rights" (Johannes Climacus in the *Unscientific Postscript*).

The reader of the *Stages* may feel that the religious is given even more than its rights, for "Quidam's Diary" takes up almost two-thirds of the book. This diary, entitled "Guilty/Not Guilty: a Passion Narrative," is in essence the story of S.K.'s unhappy love. It is followed by a lengthy "Epistle to the Reader" from one "Frater Taciturnus," a series of reflections on the Diary and its religious significance. Subtle as both the Diary and the Epistle are in psychological detail, the good Frater is probably justified when in his Conclusion he expresses doubt as to whether he has any readers left. In the Diary itself the Kierkegaardian introspection reaches its zenith, and unless sustained by an overwhelming interest in S.K.'s love affair (a brief account of which has already been provided [1]), the reader of this book would probably find Quidam's diary suffering by comparison with the one in *Either/Or*.

Justly the most famous part of the *Stages* is "The Banquet" or opening scene, which has been compared to Plato's *Symposium* and which, as a depiction of "the aesthetic moment" deliberately raised to its highest terms, is unexcelled in the world's literature. From this scene I have selected the opening and closing portions, omitting the speeches on love, which again seem longwinded and over-elaborate, though as portraits of the somewhat exotic speakers (the "young man"; Constantine Constantius, the author of *Repetition*; Victor Eremita; the "ladies' tailor"; and Johannes the Seducer, whose acquaintance we have made in *Either/Or*) they are more than admirable. After the speeches have been made, the banqueters ride out into the country in the early morning freshness and unexpectedly come upon Judge William and his wife in their garden, enjoying breakfast in conjugal felicity. This leads over to the second part, "Various Observations about Marriage, in Reply to Objections," by "A Married Man" (i.e. Judge William), in which the thoughts of the first letter in the second part of *Either/Or* [2] are extended and clarified.

The story of the Banquet is told by "William Afham" (i.e. "by him"); presumably it harks back to an actual banquet staged by Kierkegaard in his university days, when he travelled the "path to perdition" with what seemed the greatest of ease. Be it noted, however, that the diabolical quality of the scene does not consist in any of the "actual facts" connected with it. Even later in life Kierkegaard was anything but an ascetic. The "aesthetic" side of his personality may be gathered from the testimony of his secretary, Israel Levin:

". . . We had soup every day—tremendously strong—fish and some melon, and with it a glass of fine sherry—then the coffee was brought in in two silver coffee pots . . . then he opened the cupboard where he had at least fifty cups and saucers, though only one of each kind (he also had an incredible number of canes)—and said: Now! which will you have? . . . the coffee was tremendously strong—he ruined himself with it—it was excellent—

[1] *Supra,* pp. 14–18. [2] *Supra,* pp. 80–97.

Minni supplied the beans at an exorbitant price—the sugar was from Sundorph, and he paid his bills exactly on the first of every month—his life cost him amazing sums.

"The drives into North Zealand all had to go at a tremendous tempo: the 'air-bath' did him good—the carriage arrived punctually and he himself was always exasperatingly punctual—and off we went—we arrived at Fredensborg—the driver hurried into the inn and simply said 'Magisteren'—everything was set in motion—Kierkegaard went in and simply said in his weak voice: Good morning—and then went out into the woods—when we came back we had soup and chicken or duck—then K. took ten Rd. and said: Here, my little girl, be good enough to pay everything—and home again in a single go. The driver smiled because he got Rd. 5 tip—On these tours he could be charm itself, so captivating, and overflowing with wit, feelings and thoughts."

More attractive still is the picture furnished by one of S.K.'s nieces, Henriette Lund, in her description of a party given by "Uncle Soren" for herself and her cousins: "As we went in Uncle Soren gave my cousin and myself a bouquet of lily of the valley, which was something of a rarity at that time of year, and thereupon handed round beautiful presents to everyone. We had hardly finished admiring the different things before 'Anders,' Uncle Soren's trusted servant, the familiar messenger of many a lovely surprise at Christmas time and on birthdays, announced that the carriage was at the door. Where were we off to? That no one was to know until we reached the different halts, which had all been fixed beforehand, and we were shown the more unusual sights of the town. . . . On our return we played 'lottery' for different things, mainly books, and then came the evening meal consisting of *Smorrebrod,* a marzipan cake with a particularly wonderful sugar top decorated with flowers, and champagne. Uncle Soren was the most attentive, indefatigable host, and Anders just as quick in serving. But as children in those days were not as spoilt as they are now, and wine was a rarity, and champagne even for grownups was only seen on the table on great occasions, father and mother were not at all pleased with such treatment, just as they found all the arrangements for that evening rather exaggerated. I heard remarks such as 'spoiling the children,' accompanied by some indirect reference or other to the 'fantastic man.'"

None of this was at variance with S.K.'s philosophy, for his mature judgment was that the aesthetic has not to be superseded, but "dethroned"—i.e. that it must cease to be the end or motivating power of one's existence. "We need, in fact, to be warned not to regard the three stages as a prescribed curriculum which one must pass through in advancing from youth to age. Such is not S.K.'s meaning. . . . Neither does he represent that one stage must be definitely left behind before a man enters upon the next. . . . There is (almost) no definite delimitation of the spheres, and in 'existence' they overlap. . . . The logical delimitation . . . is confounded by the movement in which each individual is involved, the *direction* of this movement is the prime consideration, and this is aptly indicated by the word 'stages'. 'There are many ways which lead to the same truth, and each man takes his own.'" (Lowrie's Introduction to the *Stages,* p. 9; S.K. in the first of the *Three Discourses* which accompanied the *Stages*.)

IN VINO VERITAS: A RECOLLECTION

SUBSEQUENTLY RELATED BY WILLIAM AFHAM [1]

IT was about ten o'clock in the evening of one of the last days of July when the participators assembled for that banquet. I have forgotten the day of the month and even the year; such things are the concern of memory, not of recollection. The only thing that properly concerns recollection is mood and what pertains to mood; and just as a generous wine gains by passing over the line because the watery particles evaporate, so too does recollection gain by losing the watery particles of memory—yet by this the recollection no more becomes a mere fancy than does the generous wine.

The men who participated in the banquet were five in number: Johannes, nicknamed the Seducer, Victor Eremita, Constantine Constantius,[2] and two more, whose names I cannot precisely say I have forgotten, but whose names I never learned to know. It was as though these two possessed no proper name, for they were constantly indicated by an epithet. One was called the "young man."[3] He was certainly not over twenty-some years of age, slenderly built and graceful, with a decidedly dark complexion. The expression of his face was thoughtful, but even more pleasing was his amiable and attractive bearing which gave evidence of a purity of soul in perfect harmony with the almost womanly and vegetative softness and transparence of his whole figure. But this outward beauty one would be inclined to forget, or to keep it merely *in mente,* when contemplating a youth who, being brought up—or, to employ a more tender expression, coddled up—exclusively by thought,

---

[1] The name means literally "by him"—i.e. the one who arranged and paid for the Banquet.

[2] The author of *The Seducer's Diary,* the editor of *Either/Or,* and the author of *Repetition* respectively.

[3] The main character in *Repetition.*

nourished by the content of his own soul, had had nothing to do with the world, had neither been aroused and inflamed, nor rendered disturbed and uneasy. Like a sleep-walker he had within himself the law of his behavior, and his amiable, kindly attitude was not concerned with others, but merely reflected the fundamental disposition of his soul. The other was called the "Ladies' Tailor," that being his occupation. Of him it was impossible to get an integral impression. He was dressed in the very latest fashion, curled and perfumed and odorous of *eau de Cologne.* At some moments he did not lack an air of solid assurance, but the next moment he assumed in his gait a certain dancing air of festiveness, a certain hovering motion which was definitely limited, however, by the robustness of his figure. Even when he was most malicious in his speech, his voice constantly had something of the ingratiating tone of the shop-keeper, the sweetishness of gallantry, which I am sure was highly distasteful to him and only gratified his spirit of defiance. When I think of him now I understand him better than when I saw him alight from the carriage and found myself unable to suppress a laugh. Some contrariety, however, is still left unresolved. He has enchanted and bewitched himself, by the sorcery of his will he has transformed himself into a figure almost foolish, but with it he is not entirely content, and hence reflection now and then peeks out.[4]

When I think of it now, it seems to me almost absurd that five such men should be able to arrange a banquet. Presumably nothing would have come of it if Constantine had not been one of the party. At a coffee-house where they sometimes met in a private room the matter had once been broached, but the proposal had completely fallen through when the question was raised as to who should take the lead. The young man declared himself unqualified, the Ladies' Tailor had no time. Victor Eremita excused himself, not indeed by saying that he had married a wife or that he had bought a yoke of oxen and must go to prove them,[5] yet even though he was ready to make an exception and come, he would decline the honor of taking the lead, being able to "show just cause why. . . ." Johannes regarded this as the right word spoken in good

---

[4] We must suppose that the three named characters are not described for the reason that Johannes the Seducer was sufficiently known from his "Diary" in *Either/Or,* and that Victor Eremita, as the reputed author of the last part of the *Stages,* and Constantine Constantius, who is one of the two principal figures in this part, sufficiently reveal themselves in the sequel. But the same might be said of the "young man," who is contrasted with Constantine in the *Repetition.* Evidently S.K. had a special fondness for the "young man," who represents that side of his own character which he considered the best or the most amiable. (L)

[5] Luke 14: 19.

season, for to his mind there was one only able to serve a banquet, and
that was the magic cloth which spreads itself and serves the dinner when
one merely utters the word, "Spread!" It was not always, he said, the
most correct thing to enjoy a young girl in haste, but a banquet he could
not wait for, and generally he was tired of it a long while in advance.
However, if this were to be taken seriously, he proposed one condition,
that it should be so arranged as to be accomplished all of a sudden. To
this all were agreed. The surroundings should be fashioned anew, and
everything subsequently destroyed, indeed one might well be pleased on
rising from the table to hear the preparations for destruction. Nothing
should remain over; "not so much," said the Ladies' Tailor, "as there
remains of a gown when it is made over into a hat"; "nothing at all
should remain," said Johannes, "for nothing is more unpleasant than a
piece of sentimentality, and nothing is more disgusting than to know
that somewhere or other there is an external setting which directly and
impertinently gives itself out to be a reality."

When the conversation had thus become animated, Victor Eremita
suddenly arose, struck an attitude beside the table, making a gesture of
the hand like one in command, stretching out his arm like one who lifts
a goblet, and as though flourishing the goblet, he said: "With this goblet,
the fragrance of which already befuddles my senses, the cooling heat of
which already inflames my blood, I hail you, dear pot-companions, and
bid you welcome; and with the same goblet I drink to your health after
eating, being assured that everyone is sufficiently sated merely by the
talk about the banquet, for the good Lord satisfies the stomach before
the eye is satisfied,[6] but imagination acts inversely." Thereupon he
thrust his hand into his pocket, brought out a cigar-case, took out of it
a cigar and began to smoke.

When Constantine Constantius protested against his highhandedness
in thus transforming the projected banquet into a sheer illusion, Victor
declared that he did not in the least believe it could be carried out, and
in any case a mistake had been made in talking about it in advance. "To
be good, a thing must be all at once, for 'at once' is the most divine of all
categories and deserves to be honored as in the Latin language is the
word *ex templo*,[7] because it is the starting-point of the divine in life, so
that what does not occur at once is of the evil." However, he did not
care to dispute about it; if the others were inclined to speak or act differ-

---

[6] Cf. Eccles. 1:8. (L)

[7] Might be interpreted, "from the temple," but it means "on the spot," or "at
once." (L)

ently, he would not say a word; if they wanted him to develop his views further, they must give him leave to make a set speech, for to occasion a discussion he regarded as ungracious.

Accordingly the permission was granted, and as the others exhorted him to begin "at once," he spoke as follows: "A banquet in and for itself [8] is a difficult business, for even though it be arranged with all possible taste and talent, there is still something else essential to it, namely, luck. By this I do not mean what the anxious housewife might be most likely to think about, but something else which no one can absolutely make sure of: a happy concord of moods and of the subordinate features of the banquet, that fine ethereal touch upon the chords, that inward music which one cannot bespeak in advance from the town band. . . . Habit and thoughtlessness are the only fathers and godfathers of most banquets, and it is due to a lack of critical sense that the absence of idea is not noticed. For the first thing, there ought never to be women present at a banquet. . . . Since at a banquet the essential business is to eat and drink, woman ought not to be included in the company, for she cannot acquit herself properly, and if she does, it is exceedingly unaesthetic. Where a woman is present, the business of eating and drinking ought to be reduced to insignificant proportions. At the very most the eating and drinking must be a little feminine occupation just to give the hands something to do. In the country more especially such a small repast (which may even be appointed at another hour than that of the important meals) may be extremely charming and, if so, this is always attributable to the other sex. To do as the English do and let the other sex retire before the real drinking begins is neither one thing nor the other, for every constructive plan ought to be a whole, and the very way I seat myself at the table and take hold of the knife and fork stands in relation to the totality. So too a political banquet is unaesthetic because of its ambiguity. . . .

"I require now the richest abundance of everything that can be thought of. Even though not everything is actually present, the possibility of it, which is more seductive than the sight, must be immediately at hand, hovering over the table. From banqueting off matches, or, like the Dutch, off a loaf of sugar which all lick by turns, I beg to be excused. My requirement, on the other hand, is difficult to satisfy, for the meal itself must be calculated to awaken and incite that inexpressible desire which every worthy member of the party

[8] S.K.'s way of poking fun at what he regarded as Kantian jargon about "the thing-in-itself." (L)

brings with him. I require that the fruitfulness of the earth shall be at our service, as though everything were sprouting the very instant when appetite desires it. I require a more exuberant abundance of wine than Mephistopheles procured by boring holes in the table.[9] I require an illumination more voluptuous than that of the gnomes when they heave up the mountain upon pillars and dance in a sea of flame. I require what most excites the senses, I require that delicious refreshment of perfumes which is more glorious than anything in the Arabian Nights. I require a coolness which voluptuously kindles desire, and then appeases the desire already satisfied. I require the ceaseless animation of a fountain. If Maecenas could not sleep without hearing the splash of a fountain, I cannot eat without it. Do not misunderstand me: I can eat stockfish without it, but I cannot eat at a banquet without it; I can drink water without it, but I cannot drink wine at a banquet without it. I require a staff of servants, well chosen and good-looking, as though I were seated at the table of the gods; I require chamber-music, strong and subdued, and I require that at every instant it shall be an accompaniment to me; and as for you, my friends, the requirements I make in this respect are incredible. Behold! By reason of all these requirements, which are just as many reasons against it, I hold that banquet is a *pium desiderium,* and, regarding it in this light, I am so far from being inclined to talk about a repetition, that I assume the thing cannot be achieved in the first instance."

The only one who had taken no real part in this conversation or in defeating the banquet was Constantine Constantius. But for him the whole thing would have ended in mere talk. He had reached a different conclusion and believed that, if one were to take the others with a trump, the idea might well be realized. Then some time elapsed and both the banquet and the talk about it were forgotten, when suddenly, one day, the participants received from Constantine a card of invitation to a banquet that very same night. As the password for the occasion he fixed upon *In vino veritas,* because, though speeches were to be allowed as well as conversation, no speeches might be made except *in vino,* and no truths were to be heard except such as are *in vino,* when wine vindicates the truth and the truth vindicates the wine.

The place chosen was in a wooded region a few miles from Copenhagen. The hall where they were to eat was newly decorated and rendered entirely unrecognizable. A small room separated from the hall by a corridor was arranged for the orchestra. Shutters and curtains were

[9] Faust 1, 2257 ff.

disposed at every window, and behind them the sashes were thrown open. Constantine had it in mind that, driving thither in the dusk of the evening, they might get an inkling of what was coming. Even though one knows that one is driving to a banquet, and imagination endeavors for an instant to deal with the voluptuous thought, the impression made by natural surroundings is so powerful that it must prevail. That this might occur was Constantine's only fear; for while there is no power which knows so well how to beautify all things as does imagination, neither is there any power which can so profoundly disturb everything when it fails one upon coming into contact with real life. Driving on a summer evening does not deflect imagination from luxurious thoughts, but has exactly the contrary effect. Even though one may not see or hear it, imagination spontaneously constructs a picture of the evening's longing for cosiness, thus one sees men and maidens making their way home from labor in the field, hears the hurried clatter of the hay wagon, and interprets the faraway lowing from the meadows as longing. Thus it is the summer evening elicits an idyllic mood, refreshes even the aspiring mind by its quietude, induces even the fleeting fancy to abide with autochthonous nostalgia upon the earth as the place from which it came, teaches the insatiable mind to be satisfied with little, making a man content, for in the evening hours time is standing still and eternity is lingering.

So the invited guests arrived in the evening, for Constantine had come out somewhat earlier. Victor Eremita, who was dwelling in the country not far off, came on horseback, the others in a carriage; and just as their carriage drew up, a Holstein wagon swung through the gate, bearing a jolly crew of four mechanics, who were entertained in the common-room, to be ready to act at the decisive moment as a demolition corps—just as in the theater, for an opposite reason, the firemen are on hand to extinguish a fire at once.

So long as one is a child one has sufficient imagination, though it were for an hour in the dark room, to keep one's soul on tiptoe, on the tiptoe of expectation; but when one is older, imagination easily has the effect of making one tired of the Christmas tree before one has a chance to see it.

The folding doors are thrown open; the effect of the radiant illumination, of the coolness which encountered them, of the infatuating fragrance of perfume, of the elegance of the table-arrangement, overwhelmed for an instant the guests who were on the point of entering the room, and when at the same moment strains from the ballet of *Don Giovanni* reached them from the orchestra, they were transfixed and for an instant stood still as if in reverence before an invisible spirit which encompassed them, like a man whom admiration has awakened and who has risen to his feet to admire.

Who is there that knows the happy instant, who has comprehended the delight of it and has not sensed that dread lest something might suddenly occur, the most insignificant thing, yet with power to disturb it all! Who has held in his hand the magic lamp and yet has not felt that swooning of delight at the thought that one only needs to wish? Who has held in his hand that which beckons and has not learned to keep his wrist supple so as to let it go at once?

Thus they stood close to one another. Only Victor stood somewhat apart, absorbed in his own thoughts; a shudder passed through him, he almost trembled; then, collecting himself, he saluted the prognostication in these words: "Ye secret, festive, seductive strains which tore me from the cloistered seclusion of my tranquil youth and beguiled me by a sense of loss, like a recollection, most terrible, as if Elvira had not been seduced at all but only desired to be! Immortal Mozart, to whom I owe all! But no, not yet do I owe thee all; but when I have become an old man, if ever I do, or when I am ten years older than now, if ever I come to that, or when I shall die, for of this at least I am certain, then I will say, Immortal Mozart, to whom I owe all! Then the admiration which is the first and only one I have known I will suffer to break out with all its might, suffer it to slay me, as it often has threatened to do. Then I have set my house in order, then I have remembered my beloved, then I have confessed my love, then I have completely verified the fact that I owe thee all, then I belong to thee no more, no more belong to this world, but only to the solemn thought of death!"

Just then the orchestra played that invitation in which pleasure exults most prodigiously, storming the very heavens as it soars triumphantly above Elvira's sorrowful words of thanksgiving; and then with a quick apostrophe Johannes repeated the words, *"Viva la liberta"*—*"Et veritas,"* adjoined the young man; "But above all," said Constantine, interrupting them, "above all *in vino,"* thereupon taking his seat at the table and inviting the others to do likewise.

How easy it is to give a banquet, and yet Constantine has affirmed that he would never again take the risk! How easy it is to admire, and yet Victor has affirmed that he will never again give word to his admiration, because a discomfiture is more dreadful than to be invalided in war! How easy it is to desire when one has a wishing-rod, and it is sometimes more dreadful than to perish from want.

They took their seats at the table. That same instant the little group was launched half-way out upon the endless ocean of enjoyment, as though with a single bound. Everyone had all his thought, all his desire, set upon the banquet, his soul freely afloat for the enjoyment which was proffered overflowingly and with which the soul overflowed. The practised driver is recognized by the fact that he knows how to let the champing team start with a single bound, and how to hold them evenly together; the well-trained steed is recognized by the fact that by a single leap he rises with absolute decision. If one or another of the guests was perhaps not quite on a par, Constantine proved himself a good host.

So then they dined. Soon conversation had woven its beautiful garland about the guests, so they sat there crowned with it. At one moment the conversation seemed to be in love with the food, then with the wine, then again with itself; at one moment it was as though it was on the point of signifying something, then again it meant nothing at all. Now a fanciful notion came to development, that gorgeous fancy which blooms but once, that tender fancy which straightway closes its petals; then there was heard an outburst from a banqueter, "These truffles are superb!" then a shout to the host, "But this Château Margaux!" Now the music was drowned by the noise, now it was heard again. For one instant the company of servants stood still *in pause* at the important moment when a new course was to be served or a new wine was ordered by the name of its vintage; and then they were all busy again. Now silence intervened for a second, then the reanimating spirit of the music descended upon the guests. Now an individual with an audacious thought threw himself in front of the other talkers, and they all followed him as their leader, almost forgetful of the food, and the music followed in the rear as it follows an exulting host; then in turn there was heard only the tinkling of glasses and the clinking of plates, and the work of eating proceeded in silence, supported only by the music, which joyously took the lead and again recalled conversation.—So they dined.

How poor a thing is language compared with the unmeaning yet significant combination of clangorous sounds in a battle or at a banquet, which not even a theatrical rendering can reproduce, and for which language possesses but a few words! Yet how rich is language in the service of the wish, compared with its use for the description of reality!

Only once did Constantine abandon the role of omnipresence in which his presence was hardly noticed. At the very beginning he got them to sing one of the old drinking-songs, "to recall the pleasant times when men and women banqueted together." The effect of this proposal was sheer burlesque, as perhaps Constantine intended; but that spirit almost got the upper hand, for the Ladies' Tailor wanted them to sing "The Night I Get into the Bridal Bed, falderi, faldera." After a few courses had been served, Constantine proposed that the banquet should be concluded by every man making a speech, with the precaution, however, that the speakers be not permitted to flutter around too indefinitely. Accordingly, he made two conditions: first, that there were to be no speeches till after the meal; second, that no one might speak until he had drunk so much that he could perceive the power of the wine or was in that state in which one says much which in other conditions one would rather not say—without implying that the coherence of the speech or the thought needed to be interrupted constantly by hiccups.[10] Hence before speaking, everyone should solemnly declare that he was in this state. It would not be possible to prescribe the precise quantity of wine required, seeing that the saturation point might be so different. Against this Johannes made a formal protest. He never could get drunk, and when he had reached a certain point he became more and more sober the more he drank. Victor Eremita was of the opinion that the experimental reflection involved in watching how drunk one got would prevent one from getting drunk. If one were to get drunk, it must be accomplished by "immediacy." Then there was divers talk about the diverse effect of wine upon consciousness, noting in particular that in the case of very reflective individuals the consumption of a great deal of wine might be expressed, not by any strange impetus but, on the contrary, by cool discretion. As for the content of the speeches, Constantine proposed that they should deal with love, or with the relationship between man and woman. No love-experiences, however, might be told, though such affairs might perfectly well lie at the basis of the particular view one maintained.

The conditions were accepted. All the just and reasonable demands a host makes upon his guests were fulfilled: they ate and "they drank and they drank largely," as the Hebrew tongue expresses it—which being translated means that "they made merry."

The dessert was served. If Victor had not yet found his requirement

[10] Alluding to the situation in which Aristophanes found himself in Plato's *Symposium.* (L)

fulfilled of hearing the splash of a fountain (which, fortunately for him, he had forgotten again since that conversation), at least champagne now sparkled abundantly. The clock struck twelve. Then Constantine enjoined silence, drank to the young man with these words, *"Quod felix sit faustumque,"*[11] and bade him speak first.

.　　.　　.　　.　　.　　.　　.　　.　　.

They rose from the table. Only a hint from Constantine was needed; the participants understood among themselves with military punctuality when it was time for "Right about! Face!" With the invisible wand of command, which in his hand was as elastic as a wishing-rod, Constantine touched them once again, in order by a fleeting reminiscence to recall the banquet and the mood of sheer enjoyment which had been in a measure suppressed by the reasoning processes of the speakers; and in order that, as in the phenomenon of resonance, the tone of festivity which had vanished might return again to the guests for the brief instant of an echo, he gave the parting salute with a full glass, he emptied it, he flung it against the door in the wall behind him. The others followed his example and performed this symbolic act with the solemnity of initiates. The pleasure of breaking off was thus given its rights, this imperial pleasure which, though briefer than any other, is yet emancipating as no other is. With a libation every enjoyment of the table ought to begin, but this oblation wherewith one flings the glass away into annihilation and oblivion and tears oneself passionately away from every remembrance as if one were in mortal danger, this libation is made to the gods of the underworld. One *breaks* off, and it requires strength to do it, greater strength than to cut a knot with the sword, because the difficulty of the knot bestows passion, but the strength required for breaking off one must bestow upon oneself. In a certain outward sense the result is the same, but in an artistic respect there is a heaven-wide difference whether one leaves off (comes to an end) or breaks off by an act of freedom, whether it is an accident or a passionate decision, whether it is all over like the ballad of the schoolmaster when there is no more of it, or is brought to an end by the imperial sword-stroke of pleasure, whether it is a triviality everybody has experienced, or that mystery which escapes the majority.

It was a symbolic act of Constantine's when he threw away the goblet, and in another sense this throw was a decisive blow, for at the last

[11] The formula with which the Romans would often introduce a speaker: "Whatever is happy and of good omen."

blow the doors were thrown open and one saw, like him who has presumptuously knocked at the portal of death and sees when it is opened the puissance of annihilation—so one saw that crew of destruction prepared to lay everything waste—a memento which in a second changed the participants into fugitives from that place, and in the same second transformed, as it were, the whole environment into a ruin.

A carriage stood ready at the door. At Constantine's invitation they took their places and drove away in good spirits, for that tableau of destruction in the background had imparted a new elasticity to their souls.

A mile from the starting-place the carriage halted. Here Constantine took leave of them as host, informing them that there were five carriages at their service, so that each might follow his own inclination, drive whither he would, alone, or, if he would, in company, and with whomsoever he would. So it is that a rocket by the force of powder rises as a single shoot, stands for an instant still, collected as one entity, then disperses to all the winds.

While the horses were being hitched, the nocturnal guests strolled a little way along the road. The fresh morning air purified their hot blood by its coolness, to the refreshment of which they abandoned themselves completely; whereas upon me their figures and the groups they formed made a fantastic impression. For that the morning sun shines upon field and meadow and upon every creature which at night found rest and strength to arise jubilant with the sun—with this we have a sympathetic and wholesome understanding; but a nocturnal party beheld by morning illumination, in the midst of a smiling rustic environment, makes an almost uncanny impression. One begins to think of ghosts which are surprised by the dawn of day, of elves which cannot find the crevice through which they are accustomed to vanish because it is visible only in the dark, of unfortunates for whom the difference between day and night has become obliterated by the monotony of their suffering.

A footpath led them through a bit of field to a hedged garden, behind which a modest country house betrayed itself in the distance. At the end of the garden next the field there was an arbor formed by trees. Noticing that there was someone in the arbor, they all became curious, and with the searching look of observers the besiegers closed in around this friendly hiding-place, looking as tense as the emissaries of the police when they are bent on outwitting somebody. Like emissaries of the police—well, I must confess that their outward appearance made possible the confusion that the emissaries of the police might be seeking them. Each had taken up his position to peek in, when Victor drew back a step and said to his neighbor, "Why, my God! it's Judge William and his wife!"

They were surprised—I do not mean the two whom the foliage concealed, that happy pair, too much absorbed in domestic pleasures to be observers, too confident of their security to believe themselves the object of anyone's attention, except that of the morning sun which peeked in upon them with delight, while a gentle breeze rocked the boughs above them, and while the rural peace, like everything else around them, protected this little arbor. The happy married couple were not surprised and noticed nothing. That they were married people was clear enough, it was to be seen at a glance, alas, when one stands in a relation of consanguinity with an observer.[12] Although nothing, nothing in the wide world, nothing evident, nothing hiddenly evident, nothing hidden, has any notion of wanting to disturb the happiness of two lovers, nevertheless when they are sitting alongside of one another they do not feel themselves thus secure; blissful they are, and yet it is as though there were some power that wished to separate them, so closely do they cling to one another, and yet it is as though there were an enemy at hand against whom they must protect themselves, and yet it is as though they never could be sufficiently assured. It is not thus with married people, and was not thus with that married couple in the arbor. How long they had been married it was not possible, however, to determine precisely. The way the wife busied herself with the tea-table did seem to indicate the assurance acquired by long practice, and yet she showed an almost childish eagerness in this occupation, as if she were a recently wedded woman in that intermediate state where she does not yet know definitely whether marriage is play or earnest, whether being a housewife is a business or a game or a pastime. Perhaps she may have been married for a considerable time, but did not as a rule preside at the tea-table, perhaps she did so only here in the country, or perhaps she did it only that morning, which may possibly have had a special significance for them. Who can decide? All reckoning is to a certain extent futile when it has to do with one who possesses originality of soul, for this prevents time from leaving its mark. When the sun shines in all its summer splendor, one thinks at once that it must be to celebrate some solemn occasion or other (it cannot surely shine thus for daily use), or that this is the first time it shines so brightly, or at least one of the first times. . . . So

[12] S.K. himself, being a constant and acute observer, frequently remarks upon this trait, and even likens himself to a detective. (L)

thinks he who sees it only once, or sees it for the first time—and it was the first time I had seen the Judge's wife. . . .

So then our amiable housewife was occupied: she poured boiling water into two tea cups (presumably to warm them thoroughly), she emptied that out, set the cup on a tray, poured in the tea, served the condiments, so all was ready—was this play or earnest? In case someone is not ordinarily a tea-lover, he ought to have sat in the Judge's place, for at that moment this drink seemed to me most inviting, and only the inviting look of the kind lady herself seemed more inviting.

Presumably she had not had time to talk until this moment; now she broke the silence, and as she passed the tea she said, "Be quick now, dear, drink while the tea is hot; after all, the morning air is rather cool, and so the least thing I can do is to be a little careful of you." "The least?" rejoined the Judge laconically. "Well, or the most, or the only thing." The Judge looked at her inquiringly, and while she was helping herself she continued, "You interrupted me yesterday when I was about to say this, but I have thought it over again, many a time I have thought it over, and especially now—you know well enough what has suggested it to me—anyway it is certainly true that if you hadn't married you would have become a much greater person in the world." With the cup still on the tray the Judge sipped the first mouthful with obvious delight and felt refreshed—or was it perhaps joy in the lovely woman? I believe it was that, but she seemed only to rejoice that it tasted so good to him. Then he put the cup on the table beside him, took out a cigar and said, "May I light it at your samovar?" "With all my heart," she replied, taking a glowing coal with the teaspoon and handing it to him. He lit his cigar and put his arm about her waist while she leaned against his shoulder, he turned his head the other way to blow out the smoke, then his eyes rested upon her with all the devotion a look can express; he smiled, but this smile of joy had a little ingredient of sad irony; finally he said, "Do you really believe that, my girl?" "Believe what?" said she. He was silent again, the smile predominated, yet his voice was perfectly serious when he said, "Then I forgive your former foolishness, since you yourself have forgotten it so quickly, for you speak like one of the foolish women—what sort of a great person would I have become in the world?" His wife seemed for an instant embarrassed by this rejoinder, but she promptly collected herself and elaborated her point with feminine eloquence. The Judge looked straight ahead of him, he did not interrupt her, but as she went on he began to thrum on the table with the fingers of his right hand, he hummed a tune, the words of the ballad were momentarily audible; just as the woven pattern in a piece of damask in one aspect is visible and again disappears, so did the words fade again into the humming of the ballad's tune: "Her husband went out to the forest and cut him the cudgels white." After this melodramatic address, i.e. the wife's explanation of her cause accompanied by the humming of the Judge, the dialogue began again. "You still are unaware," he said, "that the Danish law permits a man to beat his wife, the only trouble is that it doesn't specify on what occasions it is permissible." His wife smiled at the threat and continued, "But why can't I ever get you to be serious when I speak of this? You don't understand me. Believe me, I mean it honestly, it seems to me a very pretty thought. Of course, if you were not my husband, I shouldn't dare to think it, but here now I have thought it, for your sake and for my sake, so please be serious, for my sake, and answer me honestly." "No, you can't get me to be serious, and no serious answer do you get. I must either laugh at you and make you forget it, as I have done before, or else thrash you, or you must stop talking about it, or I must find some other way of keeping you silent. You see it's a joke, and that is why there are so many expedients possible." He arose, pressed a kiss upon her forehead, put her arm in his and they disappeared in a heavily wooded path which led away from the arbor.

The arbor remained empty, there was nothing more to be done here, the corps of occupation retreated without any booty. None of them seemed pleased with this result; however, the others [13] contented themselves with some malicious remarks. They turned back, but missed Victor. He had rounded the corner, skirted the garden and reached the rural edifice. Here the door of a garden-room stood open on the side of the lawn, and a window facing the street was open also. Presumably he had seen something which attracted his attention. He entered the door, and just as he was leaping out through the window he encountered the others who had been searching for him. Triumphantly he holds up a packet of papers and shouts, "A manuscript written by the Judge! If I have published the other one, [14] it is no more than my duty to publish this too." He thrust it into his pocket, or rather he meant to stick it into his pocket, but when he had bent his arm and already had the hand and the manuscript half-way in his pocket, I stole it from him.

[13] I.e. *not* the sympathetic reporter of this scene. (L)

[14] Victor Eremita appears on the title page of *Either/Or* as the pseudonymous editor, who therefore was responsible for the publication of the letters of Judge William which constitute the second half of that book. (L)

But who then am I? Let nobody ask. If it has not occurred to any-body to ask, I am relieved, for then I am over the worst of it. Besides, I am not worth asking about, for I am the most insignificant of all things, it makes me quite bashful to have people ask about me. I am "pure being"[15] and therefore almost less than nothing. I am the pure being which is the accompaniment of everything yet never observable, because I am constantly *aufgehoben*.[16] I am like the line above which is written the task for the pupil to reckon out, and below it the answer— who cares about the line? I myself am not capable of doing anything whatever,[17] for even the idea of stealing the manuscript from Victor was not my own whim, but even this whim of "borrowing" the manuscript, as the thieves say, was borrowed from Victor. And now in publishing the manuscript I again am nothing whatever, for the manuscript was written by the Judge, and I, as editor, am in my nothingness only a nemesis upon Victor, who surely meant to get his revenge by publish-ing it.

[15] Here we have a satire upon Hegel which might apply as well to Kant. (L)

[16] A term of Hegel's which has been the despair of translators. Literally it means "raised" or "taken up," but to render precisely its philosophical significance, we should have to say, "cancelled as a separate entity while preserved as part of a larger whole."

[17] The Lutheran dogma of the total impotence of man was frequently the subject of S.K.'s reflection. He takes it seriously; but cf. a passage in the *Efterskrift*, pp. 450–474, where the comical aspect is also made the subject of reflection. But "to be nothing, less than nothing" was his own poignant experience in religious conversion. (L)

CONCLUDING UNSCIENTIFIC POSTSCRIPT TO THE "PHILOSOPHICAL FRAGMENTS"

AN EXISTENTIAL CONTRIBUTION BY
JOHANNES CLIMACUS

RESPONSIBLE FOR PUBLICATION:
S. KIERKEGAARD (1846)

TRANSLATED BY DAVID F. SWENSON, LILLIAN MARVIN SWENSON,
AND WALTER LOWRIE

What an extraordinary change takes place when one first learns the rules for the indicative and the subjunctive, when for the first time the fact that everything depends upon how a thing is thought first enters the consciousness, when, in consequence, thought in its absoluteness replaces an apparent reality. (1837)

. . . It was intelligence and nothing else that had to be opposed. Presumably that is why I, who had the job, was armed with an immense intelligence. (1854)

—THE JOURNALS

"ONE DAY a man, Kierkegaard, was deeply dissatisfied with the ideas of Hegel. Hegel had shown that the truth is the whole, be it in art, in science, in history, and that beyond the particular wholes there is the absolute whole which contains everything. But Kierkegaard said: 'I am no part of a whole, I am not integrated, not included. To put me in this whole you imagine is to negate me. . . .' Another idea of Kierkegaard's was that the rationalistic scheme of Hegel destroyed possibility, and our actions are only understandable in a world where possibility exists. Individuality as separated from society, from reason . . . , and possibility as distinct from reality, were vindicated by Kierkegaard."

These words from a recent article by the greatest French interpreter of Kierkegaard,[1] give something of the spirit of S.K.'s most monumental work, the *Concluding Unscientific Postcript*. Published just one hundred years ago, this book was nothing less than a declaration of independence, not only from the reigning Hegelianism of S.K.'s time and locality, but also from the whole tradition of rationalistic, "systematic" thought which, with one or two significant interruptions, had held the stage in Europe for at least two centuries. Although not without precedent in the writings of Pascal, Hamann, and F. H. Jacobi, the *Postscript* marks a definite turning point in the history

[1] Jean Wahl. See Bibliography, III: 32.

of philosophy—one that we can see clearly enough today, but which was not even dimly recognized during S.K.'s lifetime.

Throughout the *Postcript* Hegel and his cohorts are attacked with every weapon in S.K.'s armory—with dialectics, with rhetoric, and with humor ranging from subtle satire to downright ridicule. This latter he regarded as a legitimate mode of attack because Hegel, he maintained, was essentially a *comic* figure—like all persons who unwittingly contradict themselves, i.e. who automatically refute what they *say* by what they *do* and *are*. This does not mean that S.K. was without admiration for Hegel's intellect and for his peculiar accomplishment. In one place he makes the shrewd remark that if Hegel had constructed his whole systematic edifice, just as he did, and then at the end appended a footnote saying that the whole thing, after all, was only a "thought-experiment," he would have been the greatest thinker who ever lived; as it is he is "merely comic."

It will be remembered that in the *Philosophical Fragments* Johannes Climacus had conducted a thought-experiment, the upshot of which had been the delineation of another possibility than the Socratic one of discovering the truth within ourselves. At the end of the *Fragments* Johannes promised, in a later work, to invest this second possibility with its "historical costume." This historical costume, however, is provided by the one word, "Christianity." The question then arises, Is Christianity true? This problem—"the *objective* problem concerning the truth of Christianity"—is dealt with in the First Part of the *Postcript* under two main headings, "The Historical Point of View" and "The Speculative Point of View." Briefly, Kierkegaard shows that neither historically (via the Scriptures or the testimony of the Church) nor speculatively (via Hegel's philosophy or any other systematic, intellectual approach) can we have objective knowledge of Christianity's truth— or of its untruth. The conclusion of this first part is strictly agnostic; but along the way S.K. has brought out several interesting points in opposition to Hegel—e.g. that "a logical system is possible, but an existential system is impossible."

All this time we have been looking for truth in the object of apprehension —the "what" of thought; suppose now that we look for it in the "how," i.e. in the subject's relationship to what he thinks. The minute we do this we see that there is a kind of relationship of which we may say with absolute certainty that the individual who is in this relationship to an object is "in the truth," even though the object to which he is so related may turn out to be an untruth. If a man, knowing no better, worships an idol, but does it with absolute sincerity and the whole "passion" of his being, he is nearer the truth than the enlightened individual who has a correct knowledge of God, but holds this knowledge at second-hand and remains unmoved by it. With this ethical, personal kind of truth in mind, Kierkegaard boldly proclaims his thesis: Truth is subjectivity.

As Th. Haecker points out, it is important to realize that Kierkegaard is not denying the usual definition of truth as a correspondence between thought and reality. "Kierkegaard's conception of subjectivity and truth sets a totally different problem to European philosophy than is propounded by subjectivism and individualism, which lead to skepticism and agnosticism. . . . The question is really whether the separation of the intellect from all else in man is not a special characteristic of European philosophy, whether it comes half so naturally to the Slavs as to us, while it seems that it is by no means natural to the Oriental. . . . European philosophy . . . proceeds from the world through the person, who is but an empty relative point, back to the world; it goes from the objects, things, sensations . . . , passing as quickly as possible over the subject, the self, the individual, back to the objects, things, and sensations. . . . Kierkegaard does not follow this age-old development, because he aims at something higher. He wishes to reverse the order and the procedure for both philosophy and thought. He wishes to go from the person over the things to the person, and not from the things over the person to the things. . . ." (*Søren Kierkegaard,* pp. 25-27.)

Having defined the truth as subjectivity, the *Postscript* proceeds on its leisurely course, the main direction of which, however, is quite clear: since truth lies in the "how" of the subject's relationship, *the fullest truth attainable by human beings will be that relationship in which the subjective element—the passion with which one holds to an object—reaches its highest intensity.* Johannes Climacus does not put it in just this way; he puts it in terms of "how to become a Christian," which is alike the problem of the *Postscript* and of S.K.'s whole career as an author; and in the Conclusion (pp. 252–258) he gives us a very clear summary of the four possible answers to this question. With answers (1) and (3)—the answers of Protestant and Catholic orthodoxy, generally speaking—he has almost no sympathy. Answer (2) is much better; it represents the religion of immanence, "religiousness A," of which his own *Edifying Discourses* were and continued to be an example. All that it lacks is "the Paradox" of the Word made flesh, the central doctrine of Christianity. This doctrine by its very nature raises the passion of faith to its highest pitch, because to the human understanding it is absurd and repels the believer. This thought will be further developed in *Training in Christianity.*

Besides this Conclusion, our selections from the *Postscript* comprise the whimsical description of how Johannes Climacus became a writer; the section showing why an existential system is impossible; part of the important chapter, "Truth is Subjectivity"; a few passages dealing with "The Subjective Thinker"; and finally a long passage (though not nearly as long as in the original) which S.K. calls "an edifying Divertissement" and which is at once an exquisite satire on the average Church sermon and the average churchgoer, and a serious attempt to show how the truly religious man will apply his faith to the trivial problems of everyday life—e.g. whether one should or should not go for an outing in the Deer Park. The poor man reaches the Deer Park in the end, but it takes S.K. so long to tell how he does it, that "a novelist would have had space to recount the highly interesting events of ten years, with great scenes and tense situations and assignations and clandestine childbirths"! The passage is important, among other things, as illustrating S.K.'s attitude toward Catholic monasticism; but I hereby plead guilty to having chosen it partly for its entertainment value. It is one of the passages that prove S.K. right when he described himself as "essentially a humorist," with a bent toward the religious. Later on his humor took a more caustic and perhaps less attractive turn.

HOW JOHANNES CLIMACUS BECAME AN AUTHOR

It is now about four years since I got the notion of wanting to try my hand as an author. I remember it quite clearly; it was on a Sunday, yes, that's it, a Sunday afternoon. As usual I was sitting out-of-doors at the café in the Frederiksberg Garden, that wonderful garden which for the child was fairyland, where the King dwelt with his Queen, that delightful garden which afforded the youth happy diversion in the merriment of the populace, that friendly garden where now for the man of riper years there is such a homely feeling of sad exaltation above the world and all that is of the world, where even the invidious glory of royal dignity is what it is now out there—a queen's remembrance of her deceased lord.[1] There I sat as usual and smoked my cigar. . . .

I had been a student for ten years. Although never lazy, all my activity nevertheless was like a glittering inactivity, a kind of occupation for which I still have a strong predilection, and perhaps even a little talent. I read much, spent the rest of the day idling and thinking, or thinking and idling, but that was all it came to; the earliest sproutings of my productivity barely sufficed for my daily use and were consumed in their first greening. An inexplicable and overwhelming might constantly held me back, by strength as well as by artifice. This might was my indolence. It is not like the vehement aspiration of love, nor like the strong incentive of enthusiasm, it is rather like a housekeeper who holds one back, and with whom one is very well off, so well off that it never occurs to one to get married. This much is sure: though with the com-

[1] Referring to the widow of Frederik VI, who continued to reside there a great part of the year. (L)

forts of life I am not on the whole unacquainted, of all, indolence is the most comfortable.

So there I sat and smoked my cigar until I lapsed into reverie. Among other thoughts I remember this: "You are now," I said to myself, "on the way to becoming an old man, without being anything, and without really undertaking to do anything. On the other hand, wherever you look about you, in literature and in life, you see the celebrated names and figures, the precious and much heralded men who are coming into prominence and are much talked about, the many benefactors of the age who know how to benefit mankind by making life easier and easier, some by railways, others by omnibuses and steamboats, others by telegraph, others by easily apprehended compendiums and short recitals of everything worth knowing, and finally the true benefactors of the age who by virtue of thought make spiritual existence systematically easier and easier, and yet more and more significant. And what are you doing?"

Here my self-communion was interrupted, for my cigar was burned out and a new one had to be lit. So I smoked again, and then suddenly there flashed through my mind this thought: "You must do something, but inasmuch as with your limited capacities it will be impossible to make anything easier than it has become, you must, with the same humanitarian enthusiasm as the others, undertake to make something harder." This notion pleased me immensely, and at the same time it flattered me to think that I, like the rest of them, would be loved and esteemed by the whole community. For when all combine in every way to make everything easier and easier, there remains only one possible danger, namely, that the easiness might become so great that it would be too great; then only one want is left, though not yet a felt want—that people will want difficulty. Out of love for mankind, and out of despair at my embarrassing situation, seeing that I had accomplished nothing and was unable to make anything easier than it had already been made, and moved by a genuine interest in those who make everything easy, I conceived it my task to create difficulties everywhere. I was struck also by the strange reflection that, after all, I might have to thank my indolence for the fact that this task became mine. For far from having found it, as Aladdin did the lamp, I must rather suppose that my indolence, by hindering me from intervening at an opportune time to make things easy, had forced upon me the only task that was left. . . .

THESES ATTRIBUTABLE TO LESSING

LESSING HAS SAID THAT, IF GOD HELD ALL TRUTH IN HIS RIGHT HAND, AND IN
HIS LEFT HAND HELD THE LIFELONG PURSUIT OF IT, HE WOULD CHOOSE THE
LEFT HAND

LESSING's words are: *"Wenn Gott in seiner Rechten alle Wahrheit, und
in seiner Linken den einzigen immer regenden Trieb nach Wahrheit,
obschon mit dem Zusatze mich immer und ewig zu irren, verschlossen
hielte, und spräche zu mir: wähle! Ich fiele ihm mit Demuth in seine
Linke und sagte: Vater, gieb! die reine Wahrheit ist ja doch nur für
dich allein!"* [1] When Lessing wrote these words the System was presumably
not finished; alas! and now Lessing is dead. Were he living in
these times, now that the System is almost finished, or at least under
construction, and will be finished by next Sunday—believe me, Lessing
would have stretched out both his hands to lay hold of it. He would not
have had the leisure, nor the manners, nor the exuberance, thus in jest
as if to play odd and even with God, and in earnest to choose the left
hand. But then, the System also has more to offer than God had in both
hands; this very moment it has more, to say nothing of next Sunday,
when it is quite certain to be finished. . . .

Here first an assurance respecting my own humble person. I shall
be as willing as the next man to fall down in worship before the System, if only I can manage to set eyes on it. Hitherto I have had no
success; and though I have young legs, I am almost weary from running
back and forth between Herod and Pilate. Once or twice I have been
on the verge of bending the knee. But at the last moment, when I
already had my handkerchief spread on the ground, to avoid soiling
my trousers, and I made a trusting appeal to one of the initiated who
stood by: "Tell me now sincerely, is it entirely finished; for if so I
will kneel down before it, even at the risk of ruining a pair of trousers
(for on account of the heavy traffic to and from the system, the road has
become quite muddy),"—I always received the same answer: "No, it is
not yet quite finished." And so there was another postponement—of
the System, and of my homage.

System and finality are pretty much one and the same, so much so
that if the system is not finished, there is no system. . . . A system which

---

[1] "If God held all truth concealed in his right hand, and in his left hand the persistent striving for the truth, and while warning me against eternal error, should say:
Choose! I should humbly bow before his left hand, and say: "Father, give thy gift;
the pure truth is for thee alone." Lessing, *Werke*, Vol. x, p. 53.

is not quite finished is an hypothesis; while on the other hand to speak of a half-finished system is nonsense. . . . A persistent striving to realize a system is, on the other hand, still a striving; and a striving, aye, a persistent striving, is precisely what Lessing talks about. And surely not a striving for nothing! On the contrary, Lessing speaks of a striving for truth, and he uses a remarkable phrase about it: *den einzigen immer regenden Trieb.* This word *einzig* [2] can scarcely be understood otherwise than as equivalent to infinite, in the same sense as that having one thought and one thought only is higher than having many thoughts. So it seems that these two, Lessing and the systematist, both talk about a persistent striving; only that Lessing is stupid or honest enough to call it a persistent striving, while the systematist is clever or dishonest enough to call it the System. . . .

Let us then proceed, but let us not try to deceive one another. I, Johannes Climacus, am a human being, neither more nor less; and I assume that anyone I may have the honor to talk with is also a human being. If he presumes to be speculative philosophy in the abstract, pure speculative thought, I must renounce the effort to speak with him; for in that case he instantly vanishes from my sight, and from the feeble sight of every mortal.

And so we shall here posit and expound two theses: (A) *a logical system is possible;* (B) *an existential system is impossible.*

A. *A logical system is possible.*

(α) In the construction of a logical system, it is necessary first and foremost to take care not to include in it anything which is subject to an existential dialectic, anything which is, only because it *exists* or has existed, and not simply because it *is.* From this it follows quite simply that Hegel's unparalleled discovery, the subject of so unparalleled an admiration, namely, the introduction of movement into logic, is a sheer confusion of logical science; to say nothing of the absence, on every other page, of even so much as an effort on Hegel's part to persuade the reader that it is there. And surely it is strange to make movement fundamental in a sphere where movement is unthinkable; and to make movement explain logic, when as a matter of fact logic cannot explain movement. . . .

Nothing must then be incorporated in a logical system that has any relation to existence, that is not indifferent to existence. The infinite

[2] Single, individual.

preponderance which the logical as the objective has over all thinking is again limited by the fact that seen subjectively it is an hypothesis, precisely because it is indifferent to existence in the sense of actuality. This double aspect of the logical distinguishes it from the mathematical, which has no relationship at all either to or from existence, but simply has objectivity—not objectivity and the hypothetical together. . . .

(β) The System, so it is said, begins with the immediate,[3] and hence without any presuppositions, and hence absolutely; the beginning of the System is an absolute beginning. This is quite correct, and has also been sufficiently admired. But before making a beginning with the System, why is it that the second, equally, aye, precisely equally important question has not been raised, taken understandingly to heart, and had its clear implications respected: *How does the System begin with the immediate? That is to say, does it begin with it immediately?* The answer to this question must be an unconditional negative. If the System is presumed to come after existence, by which a confusion with an existential system may be occasioned, then the System is of course *ex post facto,* and so does not begin immediately with the immediacy with which existence began; although in another sense it may be said that existence did not begin with the immediate, since the immediate never is as such, but is transcended as soon as it is. The System's beginning which begins with the immediate *is thus itself reached by means of a process of reflection.*

Here is the difficulty. For unless, in disingenuousness or in thoughtlessness or in breathless haste to get the System finished, we let this one thought slip away from us, it is, in all its simplicity, sufficient to decide that no existential system is possible; and that no logical system may boast of an absolute beginning, since such a beginning, like pure being, is a pure chimera.

Since it is impossible to begin immediately with the immediate, which would be to think as by accident or miracle, and therefore not to think, and it is necessary to reach the beginning through a process of reflection, let us quite simply ask. . . . How do I put an end to the reflection which was set up in order to reach the beginning here in question? Reflection has the remarkable property of being infinite. But to say that it is infinite is equivalent, in any case, to saying that it cannot be stopped by itself; because in attempting to stop itself it must use

[3] That which is not "mediated" by any process of thought or reflection—i.e. what modern epistemology calls "the given." S.K.'s thesis is that immediacy does not exist as such.

itself, and is thus stopped in the same way that a disease is cured when it is allowed to choose its own treatment, which is to say that it waxes and thrives. But perhaps the infinity thus characterizing reflection is the bad infinite (*das schlechte Unendlichkeit*)? In that case we shall naturally soon have finished with our process of reflection, for the bad infinite is supposed to be something so contemptible that it must at all odds be renounced, the sooner the better. But may I not ask in this connection, if it is permitted to offer a question, How does it happen that Hegel himself and all Hegelians, who are otherwise supposed to be dialecticians, become angry at this point, angry as Dutchmen? Or is "bad" a logical determination? From whence does such a predicate find its way into logic? How does it happen that derision, and contempt, and measures of intimidation, are pressed into service as legitimate means of getting forward in logic, so that the consent of the reader is secured for an absolute beginning, because he is afraid of what acquaintances and neighbors will think of him if he does not agree to its validity?

Is not "bad" an ethical category? What is the implication involved in speaking of a bad infinite? The implication is that I hold some person responsible for refusing to end the infinite reflective process. And this means, does it not, that I require him to do something? But as a genuinely speculative philosopher I assume, on the contrary, that reflection ends itself. If that is the case, why do I make any demand upon the thinker? And what is it that I require of him? I ask him for a resolve. And in so doing I do well, for in no other way can the process of reflection be halted. But a philosopher is never justified, on the other hand, in playing tricks on people, asserting one moment that the reflective process halts itself and comes to an end in an absolute beginning; and the next moment proceeding to mock a man whose only fault is that he is stupid enough to believe the first assertion, mocking him so as to help him to arrive in this manner at an absolute beginning, which hence seems to be achieved in two different ways. But if a resolution of the will is required to end the preliminary process of reflection, the presuppositionless character of the System is renounced. Only when reflection comes to a halt can a beginning be made, and reflection can be halted only by something else, and this something else is something quite different from the logical, being a resolution of the will. Only when the beginning, which puts an end to the process of reflection, is a radical breach of such a nature that the absolute beginning breaks through the continued infinite reflection, then only is the beginning without presuppositions.[4] But when the breach is effected by breaking off the process of reflection arbitrarily, so as to make a beginning possible, then the beginning so made cannot be absolute; for it has come into being through a μετάβασις εἰς ἄλλο γένος.[5]

When a beginning with the immediate is arrived at by means of a preliminary reflection, the term "immediate" must evidently mean something else than it usually does. Hegelian logicians have quite rightly perceived this, and they therefore define this "immediate," with which logic begins, as the most abstract content remaining after an exhaustive reflection. To this definition there can be no objection, but it is certainly objectionable not to respect the implications of what is thus asserted; for this definition says indirectly that there is no absolute beginning. "How so," I think I hear someone say, "when we have abstracted from everything, is there then not, etc., etc.?" Aye, to be sure—*when* we have abstracted from everything. Why can we not remember to be human beings? This act of abstraction, like the preceding act of reflection, is infinite. How then does it come to an end? . . . Let us try an experiment in thought. Suppose the infinite act of abstraction to be *in actu*. However, the beginning is not identical with the act of abstraction, but comes afterwards. With what do I begin, now that I have abstracted from everything? Ah, here an Hegelian will perhaps fall on my breast, overcome by deep emotion, blissfully stammering the answer: *with nothing*. And it is indeed true, as the system says, that it begins with nothing. Very well, but now I must offer my second question: *How* do I begin with nothing? Unless in fact the infinite act of abstraction is one of those tricks of legerdemain which may readily be performed two at a time; if, on the contrary, it is the most strenuous of all acts of thought, what then? Why then of course, all my strength is required to hold it fast. If I let slip any part of my strength, I no longer abstract from everything. And if under such circumstances I make a beginning, I do not begin with nothing; precisely because I did not abstract from everything when I began. That is to say, if it is at all possible for a human being to abstract from everything in his thinking, it is at any rate impossible for him to do more, since if this act does not transcend human power, it absolutely exhausts it. To grow weary of the act of abstracting, and thus to arrive at a begin-

---

[4] This is the position S.K. is ready to defend—the Christian philosophy, according to which the "absolute beginning" was made in time nineteen and a half centuries ago—and continues to be made in the lives of individuals.

[5] Change into another kind.

ning, is an explanation of the sort valid only for costermongers, who do not take a little discrepancy so seriously. . . .

What if, instead of talking or dreaming about an absolute beginning, we talked about a leap. To be content with a "mostly," an "as good as," a "you could almost say that," a "when you sleep on it until tomorrow, you can easily say that," suffices merely to betray a kinship with Trop,[6] who, little by little, reached the point of assuming that almost having passed his examinations was the same as having passed them. We all laugh at this; but when philosophers reason in the same manner, in the kingdom of the truth and in the sanctuary of science, then it is good philosophy, genuine speculative philosophy. Lessing was no speculative philosopher; hence he assumed the opposite, namely, that an infinitesimal difference makes the chasm infinitely wide, because it is the presence of the leap itself that makes the chasm infinitely wide. . . .

(γ) In order to throw some light on the nature of logic, it might be desirable to orient oneself psychologically in the state of mind of anyone who thinks the logical—so as to determine what kind of a dying away from the self is involved, and how far the imagination plays a rôle in this connection. . . . A philosopher has gradually come to be so fantastic a being that scarcely the most extravagant fancy has ever invented anything so fabulous. In general, how does the empirical ego stand related to the pure ego, the I-am-I? Anyone who is ambitious to become a philosopher would naturally like to have a little information on this point, and above all, cannot wish to become ridiculous by being transformed, *ein zwei drei kokolorum,* into speculative philosophy in the abstract. If the logical thinker **is** at the same time human enough not to forget that he is an existing individual, even if he completes the system, all the fantasticalness and charlatanry will gradually disappear. Granted that it would require an eminent logical talent to reconstruct Hegel's *Logic,* it needs only sound common sense in one who once enthusiastically believed in the great achievement that Hegel professed, and proved his enthusiasm by believing it, and his enthusiasm for Hegel by believing it of him—it needs only sound common sense for such a one to see that Hegel has in many places dealt indefensibly, not with costermongers, who never believe the half of what a man says, but with enthusiastic youth who believed him. Even if such a youth has not been exceptionally gifted, when he has had enthusiasm enough to despair of himself in the moment of difficulty, rather than give up Hegel—if such a youth ever comes to himself, he has a right to demand

[6] In Heiberg's comedy, *The Reviewer and the Beast,* Scene 2. (L)

this Nemesis, that laughter should destroy in Hegel what laughter has a just claim upon.[7] And such a youth has honored Hegel more highly than many a follower, who in deceptive asides sometimes makes Hegel everything, and sometimes a mere triviality.

B. *An existential system is impossible.*

An existential system cannot be formulated. Does this mean that no such system exists? By no means; nor is this implied in our assertion. Existence itself is a system—for God; but it cannot be a system for any existing spirit. System and finality correspond to one another, but existence is precisely the opposite of finality. It may be seen, from a purely abstract point of view, that system and existence are incapable of being thought together; because in order to think existence at all, systematic thought must think it as abrogated, and hence as not existing. Existence separates and holds the various moments of existence discretely apart; systematic thought consists of the finality which brings them together.

In reality we are likely to encounter a deception, an illusion. This was dealt with in the *Fragments,* and to this treatment I must here refer. It will be found in the Interlude, in the discussion of the question whether the past is more necessary than the future. Whenever a particular existence has been relegated to the past, it is complete, has acquired finality, and is in so far subject to a systematic apprehension. Quite right—but for whom is it so subject? Anyone who is himself an existing individual cannot gain this finality outside existence which corresponds to the eternity into which the past has entered. If a good-natured thinker is so absent-minded as to forget that he is an existing individual, still, absent-mindedness and speculation are not precisely the same thing. On the contrary, the fact that the thinker is an existing individual signifies that existence imposes its own requirement upon him. And if he is a great individual, it may signify that his own contemporary existence may, when it comes to be past, have the validity of finality for the systematic thinker. But who is this systematic thinker? Aye, it is he who is outside of existence and yet in existence, who is in his eternity forever complete, and yet includes all existence within himself—it is God. Why the deception? Because the world has stood now for six thousand years, does not existence have the same claim upon the existing individual as always? And this claim is, not that he should be a contemplative spirit in imagination, but an existing spirit in reality. All understanding comes after the fact. Now, while the existing individual undoubtedly comes after the preceding six thousand years, if we as-

[7] I.e. the fact that his practice contradicts his theory.

sume that he spends his life in arriving at a systematic understanding of these, the strangely ironical consequence would follow, that he could have no understanding of himself in his existence, because he had no existence, and thus had nothing which required to be understood afterwards. Such a thinker would either have to be God, or a fantastic *quodlibet*. Everyone doubtless perceives the immorality of such a situation, and doubtless also perceives that it is quite in order, as another author [8] has said respecting the Hegelian system, that we owe to Hegel the completion of the System, the Absolute System—without the inclusion of an Ethics. Let us smile if we will at the ethico-religious extravaganzas of the Middle Ages in asceticism and the like; but let us above all not forget that the speculative low-comedy licentiousness of assuming to be an I-am-I—and nevertheless, *qua* human being, often so Philistine a character that no man of enthusiasm could endure to live such a life—is equally ridiculous.

Respecting the impossibility of an existential system, let us then ask quite simply, as a Greek youth might have asked his teacher (and if the superlative wisdom can explain everything, but cannot answer a simple question, it is clear that the world is out of joint): "Who is to write or complete such a system?" Surely a human being; unless we propose again to begin using the strange mode of speech which assumes that a human being becomes speculative philosophy in the abstract, or becomes the identity of subject and object. So then, a human being—and surely a living human being, i.e. an existing individual. Or if the speculative thought which brings the system to light is the joint effort of different thinkers—in what last concluding thought does this fellowship finally realize itself, how does it reach the light of day? Surely through some human being? And how are the individual participants related to the joint effort, what are the categories which mediate between the individual and the world-process, and who is it again who strings them all together on the systematic thread? Is he a human being, or is he speculative philosophy in the abstract? But if he is a human being, then he is also an existing individual. Two ways, in general, are open for an existing individual: *Either* he can do his utmost to forget that he is an existing individual, by which he becomes a comic figure, since existence has the remarkable trait of compelling an existing individual to exist whether he wills it or not. (The comical contradiction in willing to be what one is not, as when a man wills to be a bird, is not more comical than the contradiction of not willing to be what one is, as *in casu* an

[8] Frater Taciturnus in the *Stages*. (L)

existing individual; just as the language finds it comical that a man forgets his name, which does not so much mean forgetting a designation, as it means forgetting the distinctive essence of one's being.) *Or* he can concentrate his entire energy upon the fact that he is an existing individual. It is from this side, in the first instance, that objection must be made to modern philosophy; not that it has a mistaken presupposition, but that it has a comical presupposition, occasioned by its having forgotten, in a sort of world-historical absent-mindedness, what it means to be a human being. Not indeed, what it means to be a human being in general; for this is the sort of thing that one might even induce a speculative philosopher to agree to; but what it means that you and I and he are human beings, each one for himself.

The existing individual who concentrates all his attention upon the circumstance that *he* is an existing individual will welcome these words of Lessing about a persistent striving, as a beautiful saying. To be sure, it did not win for its author an immortal fame, because it is very simple; but every thoughtful individual must needs confirm its truth. The existing individual who forgets that he is an existing individual will become more and more absent-minded; and as people sometimes embody the fruits of their leisure moments in books, so we may venture to expect as the fruit of his absent-mindedness the expected existential system—well, perhaps not all of us, but only those who are almost as absent-minded as he is. While the Hegelian philosophy goes on and becomes an existential system in sheer distraction of mind, and what is more, is finished—without having an Ethics (where existence properly belongs)—the more simple philosophy which is propounded by an existing individual for existing individuals, will more especially emphasize the ethical.

As soon as it is remembered that philosophizing does not consist in addressing fantastic beings in fantastic language, but that those to whom the philosopher addresses himself are human beings; so that we have not to determine fantastically *in abstracto* whether a persistent striving is something lower than the systematic finality, or *vice versa,* but that the question is what existing human beings, insofar as they are existing beings, must needs be content with: then it will be evident that the ideal of a persistent striving is the only view of life that does not carry with it an inevitable disillusionment. Even if a man has attained to the highest, the repetition by which life receives content (if one is to escape retrogression or avoid becoming fantastic) will again constitute a persistent striving; because here again finality is moved further on, and postponed.

It is with this view of life as it is with the Platonic interpretation of love as a want; and the principle that not only he is in want who desires something he does not have, but also he who desires the continued possession of what he has. In a speculative-fantastic sense we have a positive finality in the System, and in an aesthetic-fantastic sense we have one in the fifth act of the drama. But this sort of finality is valid only for fantastic beings.

Persistent striving is the ethical life view of the existing subject. This striving must not be understood metaphysically; nor indeed is there any individual who exists metaphysically. One might set up an opposition between finality and the persistent striving after truth; but this would be a misunderstanding in the metaphysical sphere. In the ethical sense, on the contrary, the persistent striving represents the consciousness of being an existing individual: the constant learning is the expression for this incessant realization, in no moment complete as long as the subject is in existence; the subject is aware of this fact, and hence is not deceived. But Greek philosophy always had a relation to Ethics. Hence it was not imagined that the principle of always being a learner was a great discovery, or the enthusiastic enterprise of a particular distinguished individual; for it was neither more nor less than the realization that a human being is an existing individual, which it constitutes no great merit to be aware of, but which it is thoughtless to forget.

So-called pantheistic systems have often been characterized and challenged by the assertion that they abrogate the distinction between good and evil, and destroy freedom. Perhaps one would express oneself quite as definitely if one said that every such system fantastically dissipates the concept *existence*. But we ought to say this not merely of pantheistic systems; it would be more to the point to show that every system must be pantheistic precisely on account of its finality. Existence must be revoked in the eternal before the system can round itself out; there must be no existing remainder, not even such a little minikin as the existing Herr Professor who writes the system. But this is not the way in which the problem is usually dealt with. No, pantheistic systems are attacked, partly in tumultuous aphorisms which again and again promise a new system; and partly by way of scraping together something supposed to be a system, and inserting in it a special paragraph in which it is laid down that the concept *existence,* or actuality, is intended to be especially emphasized. That such a paragraph is a mockery of the entire system, that instead of being a paragraph in a system it is an absolute protest against the system, makes no difference to busy systematists. If the concept of existence is really to be stressed, this cannot be given a direct expression as a paragraph in a system; all direct oaths and devil-take-me's only make the didactic awkwardness more and more ridiculous. An actual emphasis on existence must be expressed in an essential form; in view of the elusiveness of existence, such a form will have to be an indirect form, namely, the absence of a system.[9] But this again must not degenerate into an asseverating formula, for the indirect character of the expression will constantly demand rejuvenation in the form. In the case of committee reports, it may be quite in order to incorporate in the report a dissenting opinion; but an existential system which includes the dissenting opinion as a paragraph in its own logical structure is a curious monstrosity. What wonder that the System continues to stand its ground as a going concern. In general, objections are haughtily ignored; if a particular objection seems to attract a little attention, the systematic entrepreneurs engage a copyist to copy off the objection, which thereupon is incorporated in the System; and when the book is bound, the System is complete.

The systematic Idea is the identity of subject and object, the unity of thought and being. Existence, on the other hand, is their separation.[10] It does not by any means follow that existence is thoughtless; but it has brought about, and brings about, a separation between subject and object, thought and being. In the objective sense, thought is understood as being pure thought; this corresponds in an equally abstract-objective sense to its object, which object is therefore the thought itself, and the truth becomes the correspondence of thought with itself. This objective thought has no relation to the existing subject; and while we are always confronted with the difficult question of how the existing subject slips into this objectivity, where subjectivity is merely pure abstract subjectivity (which again is an objective determination, not signifying any existing human being), it is certain that the existing subjectivity tends more and more to evaporate. And finally, if it is possible for a human being to become anything of the sort, and the whole thing is not something of which at most he becomes aware through the imagination, he becomes the pure abstract conscious participation in and knowledge of this pure relationship between thought and being, this pure identity,

---

[9] The titles of S.K.'s more distinctly philosophical works (this and the *Fragments*) give expression to this form.

[10] With such precision do these two sentences state the difference between Idealism and Existentialism that they might be taken as a charter of the latter movement.

aye, this tautology, because this being which is ascribed to the thinker does not signify that he *is,* but only that he is engaged in thinking.

The existing subject, on the other hand, is engaged in existing, which is indeed the case with every human being. Let us therefore not deal unjustly with the objective tendency, by calling it an ungodly and pantheistic self-deification; but let us rather view it as an essay in the comical. For the notion that from now on until the end of the world nothing could be said except what proposed a further improvement in an almost completed system, is merely a systematic consequence for systematists.

By beginning at once to use ethical categories in criticism of the objective tendency, one does it an injustice, and fails to make contact with it, because one has nothing in common with what is under attack. But by remaining in the metaphysical sphere one is enabled to use the comical, which also lies in the metaphysical, so as to bring such a transfigured professor to book. If a dancer could leap very high, we should admire him. But if he tried to give the impression that he could fly, let laughter single him out for suitable punishment, even though it might be true that he could leap as high as any dancer ever had done. Leaping is the accomplishment of a being essentially earthly, one who respects the earth's gravitational force, since the leaping is only momentary. But flying carries a suggestion of being emancipated from telluric conditions, a privilege reserved for winged creatures, and perhaps also shared by the inhabitants of the moon—and there perhaps the System will first find its true readers.

Being an individual man is a thing that has been abolished, and every speculative philosopher confuses himself with humanity at large, whereby he becomes something infinitely great—and at the same time nothing at all. He confounds himself with humanity in sheer distraction of mind, just as the opposition press uses the royal "we," and sailors say: "devil take me!" But when a man has indulged in oaths for a long time, he returns at last to the simple utterance, because all swearing is self-nugatory; and when one discovers that every street urchin can say "we," one perceives that it means a little more, after all, to be a particular individual. And when one finds that every basement-dweller can play the game of being humanity, one learns at last that being purely and simply a human being is a more significant thing than playing the society game in this fashion. And one thing more. When a basement-dweller plays this game everyone thinks it ridiculous; and yet it is equally ridiculous for the greatest man in the world to do it. And one may very well permit oneself to laugh at him for this, while still entertaining a just and proper respect for his talents and his learning and so forth.

THE TASK OF BECOMING SUBJECTIVE

OBJECTIVELY[1] we consider only the matter at issue, subjectively we have regard to the subject and his subjectivity; and behold, precisely this subjectivity is the matter at issue. This must constantly be borne in mind, namely, that the subjective problem is not something about an objective issue, but is the subjectivity itself. For since the problem in question poses a decision, and since all decisiveness, as shown above, inheres in subjectivity, it is essential that every trace of an objective issue should be eliminated. If any such trace remains, it is at once a sign that the subject seeks to shirk something of the pain and crisis of the decision; that is, he seeks to make the problem to some degree objective. If the Introduction still awaits the appearance of another work before bringing the matter up for judgment, if the System still lacks a paragraph, if the speaker has still another argument up his sleeve, it follows that the decision is postponed. Hence we do not here raise the question of the truth of Christianity in the sense that when this has been determined, the subject is assumed ready and willing to accept it. No, the question is as to the mode of the subject's acceptance; and it must be regarded as an illusion rooted in the demoralization which remains ignorant of the subjective nature of the decision, or as an evasion springing from the disingenuousness which seeks to shirk the decision by an objective mode of approach, wherein there can in all eternity be no decision, to assume that the transition from something objective to the subjective acceptance is a direct transition, following upon the objective deliberation as a matter of course. On the contrary, the subjective acceptance is precisely the decisive factor; and an objective acceptance of Christianity is paganism or thoughtlessness.

Christianity proposes to endow the individual with an eternal happiness, a good which is not distributed wholesale, but only to one individual at a time. Though Christianity assumes that there inheres in the subjectivity of the individual, as being the potentiality of the appropriation of this good, the possibility for its acceptance, it does not assume that the subjectivity is immediately ready for such acceptance or even that it has, without further ado, a real conception of the significance of such a good. The development or transformation of the individual's

---

[1] Part One has dealt with "the *objective* problem concerning the truth of Christianity," from the standpoint of (a) historical objectivity and (b) speculative objectivity.

subjectivity, its infinite concentration in itself over against the conception of an eternal happiness, that highest good of the infinite—this
constitutes the developed potentiality of the primary potentiality which
subjectivity as such presents. In this way Christianity protests every form
of objectivity; it desires that the subject should be infinitely concerned
about himself. It is subjectivity that Christianity is concerned with, and
it is only in subjectivity that its truth exists, if it exists at all; objectively,
Christianity has absolutely no existence. If its truth happens to be in only
a single subject, it exists in him alone; and there is greater Christian joy
in heaven over this one individual than over universal history and the
System, which as objective entities are incommensurable with that which
is Christian.

It is commonly assumed that no art or skill is required in order to be
subjective. To be sure, every human being is a bit of a subject, in a sense.
But now to strive to become what one already is: who would take the
pains to waste his time on such a task, involving the greatest imaginable
degree of resignation? Quite so. But for this very reason alone it is a very
difficult task, the most difficult of all tasks in fact, precisely because every
human being has a strong natural bent and passion to become something more and different. And so it is with all such apparently insignificant tasks: precisely their seeming insignificance makes them infinitely
difficult. In such cases the task itself is not directly alluring, so as to support the aspiring individual; instead it works against him, and it needs
an infinite effort on his part merely to discover that his task lies here,
that this is his task—an effort from which he is otherwise relieved. To
think about the simple things of life, about what the plain man also
knows after a fashion, is extremely forbidding; for the differential distinction attainable even through the utmost possible exertion is by no
means obvious to the sensual man. No indeed, thinking about the high-
falutin is very much more attractive and glorious.

When one overlooks this little distinction, humoristic from the
Socratic standpoint and infinitely anxious from the Christian, between
being something like a subject so-called, and being a subject, or becoming one, or being what one is through having become what one is: then
it becomes wisdom, the admired wisdom of our own age, that it is the
task of the subject increasingly to divest himself of his subjectivity in
order to become more and more objective. It is easy to see what this
wisdom understands by being a subject of a sort. It understands by it
quite rightly the accidental, the angular, the selfish, the eccentric, and
so forth, all of which every human being can have enough of. Nor does

Christianity deny that such things should be gotten rid of; it has never been a friend of loutishness. But the difference is, that philosophy teaches that the way is to become objective, while Christianity teaches that the way is to become subjective, i.e. to become a subject in truth. Lest this should seem a mere dispute about words, let me say that Christianity wishes to intensify passion to its highest pitch; but passion is subjectivity, and does not exist objectively.

In a curiously indirect and satirical manner it is often enough inculcated, though men refuse to heed the instruction, that the guidance of philosophy in this matter is misguidance. While we are all subjects of a sort, and labor to become objective, in which endeavor many succeed bestially enough, poesy goes about anxiously seeking its subject matter. In spite of our all being subjects, poesy must be content with a very sparing selection of subjects it can use; and yet it is precisely subjects that poesy must have. Why then does it not take the very first that comes to hand from among our estimable circle? Alas, he will not do; and if his only ambition is to become objective, he will never do. This would actually seem to signify that there might after all be something quite special about being a subject. Why have a few become immortal as enthusiastic lovers, a few as high-minded heroes, and so forth, if all men in every generation are such as a matter of course, merely by virtue of being subjects in the immediate sense? And yet, being a lover, a hero, and so forth, is precisely a prerogative of subjectivity; for one does not become a hero or a lover objectively. And now the clergy! Why does the religious address repeatedly return to the revered remembrance of a select circle of devout men and women, why does the clergyman not take the very first that comes to hand from our esteemed circle, and make him our pattern: are we not all subjects of a sort? And yet devoutness inheres in subjectivity, and no one ever becomes devout objectively.

Love is a determination of subjectivity, and yet real lovers are very rare. We do indeed say, just as when we speak of everyone being a subject of a sort: There went a pair of lovers, there goes another pair; last Sunday the banns were published for sixteen couples; there are in Storm Street a couple of lovers who cannot live peaceably together. But when poesy explains love in terms of its own lofty and festive conception, the honored name which it brings forward to exemplify the ideal sometimes carries us several centuries back in time; while the speech of daily life strikes us as humorously as funeral sermons generally do according to which every moment sees the burial of a hero. Is this merely a *chicane* on the part of poesy, which is otherwise a friendly power, seeking to console us by uplifting our spirits in the contemplation of what is excellent? And what sort of excellence? Why, to be sure, the excellence of subjectivity. So then it would seem that there must be something distinguished about being subjective.

Faith is the highest passion in the sphere of human subjectivity. But take note merely of what the clergy say, concerning how rarely it is found in the community of believers. For this phrase, the community of believers, is used in about the same manner as being subjects of a sort. Now pause a moment, and do not be so ironical as to ask further how rare perhaps faith is among the clergy! But this complaint, is it merely a cunning device on the part of the clergy, who have consecrated their lives to the care of our souls, by uplifting us in the spirit of devotion, while the soul's longing goes out to the transfigured ones—but to which transfigured ones? Why, to be sure, to those who proved that they had faith. But faith inheres in subjectivity, and so there must after all be something distinguished about subjectivity.

The objective tendency, which proposes to make everyone an observer, and in its maximum to transform him into so objective an observer that he becomes almost a ghost, scarcely to be distinguished from the tremendous spirit of the historical past—this tendency naturally refuses to know or listen to anything except what stands in relation to itself. If one is so fortunate as to be of service within the given presupposition, by contributing one or another item of information concerning a tribe perhaps hitherto unknown, which is to be provided with a flag and given a place in the paragraph parade; if one is competent within the given presupposition to assign China [2] a place different from the one it has hitherto occupied in the systematic procession—in that case one is made welcome. But everything else is divinity-school prattle. For it is regarded as a settled thing that the objective tendency toward intellectual contemplation is, in the newer linguistic usage, the *ethical* answer to the question of what I *ethically* have to do; and the task assigned to the contemplative nineteenth century is world history.

THE SUBJECTIVE TRUTH: INWARDNESS
TRUTH IS SUBJECTIVITY

WHEN *the question of truth is raised in an objective manner, reflection is directed objectively to the truth, as an object to which the knower*

[2] A reference to Hegel's *Philosophy of History*, which begins with a description of China and Persia. (S)

is related. Reflection is not focused upon the relationship, however, but upon the question of whether it is the truth to which the knower is related. If only the object to which he is related is the truth, the subject is accounted to be in the truth. When the question of the truth is raised subjectively, reflection is directed subjectively to the nature of the individual's relationship: if only the mode of this relationship is in the truth, the individual is in the truth, even if he should happen to be thus related to what is not true.[1] Let us take as an example the knowledge of God. Objectively, reflection is directed to the problem of whether this object is the true God; subjectively, reflection is directed to the question whether the individual is related to a something *in such a manner* that his relationship is in truth a God-relationship. On which side is the truth now to be found? Ah, may we not here resort to a mediation, and say: It is on neither side, but in the mediation of both? Excellently well said, provided we might have it explained how an existing individual manages to be in a state of mediation. For to be in a state of mediation is to be finished, while to exist is to become. Nor can an existing individual be in two places at the same time—he cannot be an identity of subject and object. When he is nearest to being in two places at the same time he is in passion; but passion is merely momentary, and passion is also the highest expression of subjectivity.

The existing individual who chooses to pursue the objective way enters upon the entire approximation-process by which it is proposed to bring God to light objectively. But this is in all eternity impossible, because God is a subject, and therefore exists only for subjectivity in inwardness. The existing individual who chooses the subjective way apprehends instantly the entire dialectical difficulty involved in having to use some time, perhaps a long time, in finding God objectively; and he feels this dialectical difficulty in all its painfulness, because he must use God at that very moment, since every moment is wasted in which he does not have God[2] That very instant he has God, not by virtue of any objective deliberation but by virtue of the infinite passion of in-

---

[1] The reader will observe that the question here is about essential truth, or about the truth which is essentially related to existence, and that it is precisely for the sake of clarifying it as inwardness or as subjectivity that this contrast is drawn. (K)

[2] In this manner God certainly becomes a postulate, but not in the otiose manner in which this word is commonly understood. It becomes clear rather that the only way in which an existing individual comes into relation with God is when the dialectical contradiction brings his passion to the point of despair, and helps him to embrace God with the "category of despair" (faith). Then the postulate is so far from being arbitrary that it is precisely a life-necessity. It is then not so much that God is a postulate as that the existing individual's postulation of God is a necessity. (K)

wardness. The objective inquirer, on the other hand, is not embarrassed by such dialectical difficulties as are involved in devoting an entire period of investigation to finding God—since it is possible that the inquirer may die tomorrow; and if he lives he can scarcely regard God as something to be taken along if convenient, since God is precisely that which one takes *a tout prix,* which in the understanding of passion constitutes the true inward relationship to God.

It is at this point, so difficult dialectically, that the way swings off for everyone who knows what it means to think, and to think existentially; which is something very different from sitting at a desk like a fantastical being and writing about what one has never done, something very different from writing *de omnibus dubitandum,* and at the same time being as existentially credulous as the most sensuous of men. Here is where the way swings off, and the change is marked by the fact that, while objective knowledge rambles comfortably on by way of the long road of approximation without being impelled by the urge of passion, subjective knowledge counts every delay a deadly peril, and the decision so infinitely important and so instantly pressing that it is as if the opportunity had already passed unutilized.

Now when the problem is to reckon up on which side there is most truth, whether on the side of one who seeks the true God objectively, and pursues the approximate truth of the God-idea; or on the side of one who, driven by the infinite passion of his need of God, feels an infinite concern for his own relationship to God in truth (and to be at one and the same time on both sides equally is, as we have noted, not possible for an existing individual, but is merely the happy delusion of an imaginary I-am-I): the answer cannot be in doubt for anyone who has not been demoralized with the aid of science. If one who lives in the midst of Christianity goes up to the house of God, the house of the true God, with the true conception of God in his knowledge, and prays, but prays in a false spirit; and one who lives in an idolatrous community prays with the entire passion of the infinite, although his eyes rest upon the image of an idol: where is there most truth? The one prays in truth to God though he worships an idol; the other prays falsely to the true God, and hence worships in fact an idol.

When one man investigates objectively the problem of immortality, and another embraces an uncertainty with the passion of the infinite: where is there most truth, and who has the greater certainty? The one has entered upon a never-ending approximation, for the certainty of immortality lies precisely in the subjectivity of the individual; the other is immortal, and fights for his immortality by struggling with the uncertainty. Let us consider Socrates. Nowadays everyone dabbles in a few proofs; some have several such proofs, others fewer. But Socrates! He puts the question objectively in a problematic manner: *if* there is an immortality. Must he therefore be accounted a doubter in comparison with one of our modern thinkers with the three proofs? By no means. On this "if" he risks his entire life, he has the courage to meet death, and he has with the passion of the infinite so determined the pattern of his life that it must be found acceptable—*if* there is an immortality. Can any better proof be given for the immortality of the soul? But those who have the three proofs do not at all determine their lives in conformity therewith; if there is an immortality, it must feel disgust over their manner of life: can any better refutation be given of the three proofs? The "bit" of uncertainty that Socrates had helped him, because he himself contributed the passion of the infinite; the three proofs that the others have do not profit them at all, because they are and remain dead to spirit and enthusiasm, and their three proofs, in lieu of proving anything else, prove just this. A young girl may enjoy all the sweetness of love on the basis of what is merely a weak hope; but she is beloved, because she rests everything on this weak hope; but many a wedded matron more than once subjected to the strongest expressions of love has in so far indeed had proofs, but strangely enough has not enjoyed *quod erat demonstrandum*. The Socratic ignorance, which Socrates held fast with the entire passion of his inwardness, was thus an expression for the principle that the eternal truth is related to an existing individual, and that this truth must therefore be a paradox for him as long as he exists; and yet it is possible that there was more truth in the Socratic ignorance as it was in him, than in the entire objective truth of the System, which flirts with what the times demand and accommodates itself to *Privatdocents*.

The objective accent falls on WHAT is said, the subjective accent on HOW it is said. This distinction holds even in the aesthetic realm, and receives definite expression in the principle that what is in itself true may in the mouth of such and such a person become untrue. In these times this distinction is particularly worthy of notice for, if we wish to express in a single sentence the difference between ancient times and our own, we should doubtless have to say: "In ancient times only an individual here and there knew the truth; now all know it, but the inwardness of its appropriation stands in an inverse relationship to the extent of its dissemination. Aesthetically the contradiction that truth becomes untruth in this or that person's mouth is best construed comically. In the ethico-religious sphere, the accent is again on the "how." But this is not to be understood as referring to demeanor, expression, delivery, or the like; rather it refers to the relationship sustained by the existing individual, in his own existence, to the content of his utterance. Objectively the interest is focused merely on the thought-content, subjectively on the inwardness. At its maximum this inward "how" is the passion of the infinite, and the passion of the infinite is the truth. But the passion of the infinite is precisely subjectivity, and thus subjectivity becomes the truth. Objectively there is no infinite decision, and hence it is objectively in order to annul the difference between good and evil, together with the principle of contradiction, and therewith also the infinite difference between the true and the false. Only in subjectivity is there decision, to seek objectivity is to be in error. It is the passion of the infinite that is the decisive factor and not its content, for its content is precisely itself. In this manner subjectivity and the subjective "how" constitute the truth.

But the "how" which is thus subjectively accentuated, precisely because the subject is an existing individual, is also subject to a dialectic with respect to time. In the passionate moment of decision, where the road swings away from objective knowledge, it seems as if the infinite decision were thereby realized. But in the same moment the existing individual finds himself in the temporal order, and the subjective "how" is transformed into a striving, a striving which receives indeed its impulse and a repeated renewal from the decisive passion of the infinite, but is nevertheless a striving.

When subjectivity is the truth, the conceptual determination of the truth must include an expression for the antithesis to objectivity, a memento of the fork in the road where the way swings off; this expression will also indicate the tension of the subjective inwardness. Here is such a definition of truth: *An objective uncertainty held fast in an appropriation-process of the most passionate inwardness is the truth, the highest truth attainable for an existing individual*. At the point where the way swings off (and where this is cannot be specified objectively, since it is a matter of subjectivity), there objective knowledge is placed in abeyance. Thus the subject merely has, objectively, the uncertainty; but it is this which precisely increases the tension of that infinite passion which constitutes his inwardness. The truth is precisely the venture which chooses an objective uncertainty with the passion of the infinite. I contemplate nature in the hope of finding God, and I see omnipotence and wisdom; but I also see much else that disturbs my mind and excites anxiety. The sum of all this is an objective uncertainty. But it is for this very reason that the inwardness becomes as intense as it is, for it embraces this objective uncertainty with the entire passion of the infinite. In the case of a mathematical proposition the objectivity is given, but for this reason the truth of such a proposition is also an indifferent truth.

But the above definition of truth is an equivalent expression for faith. Without risk there is no faith. Faith is precisely the contradiction between the infinite passion of the individual's inwardness and the objective uncertainty. If I am capable of grasping God objectively, I do not believe, but precisely because I cannot do this I must believe. If I wish to preserve myself in faith I must constantly be intent upon holding fast the objective uncertainty, so that in the objective uncertainty I am out "upon the seventy thousand fathoms of water," and yet believe.

In the principle that subjectivity, inwardness, is the truth, there is comprehended the Socratic wisdom, whose everlasting merit it was to have become aware of the essential significance of existence, of the fact that the knower is an existing individual. For this reason Socrates was in the truth by virtue of his ignorance, in the highest sense in which this was possible within paganism. To attain to an understanding of this, to comprehend that the misfortune of speculative philosophy is again and again to have forgotten that the knower is an existing individual, is in our objective age difficult enough. "But to have made an advance upon Socrates, without even having understood what he understood, is at any rate not Socratic." Compare the "Moral" of the *Fragments*.[3]

Let us now start from this point and, as was attempted in the *Fragments,* seek a determination of thought which will really carry us further. I have nothing here to do with the question of whether this proposed thought-determination is true or not, since I am merely experimenting; but it must at any rate be clearly manifest that the Socratic thought is understood within the new proposal, so that at least I do not come out behind Socrates.

When subjectivity, inwardness, is the truth, the truth objectively defined becomes a paradox; and the fact that the truth is objectively a paradox shows in its turn that subjectivity is the truth. For the objective situation is repellent; and the expression for the objective repulsion constitutes the tension and the measure of the corresponding inward-

[3] English edition, p. 93.

ness. The paradoxical character of the truth is its objective uncertainty; this uncertainty is an expression for the passionate inwardness, and this passion is precisely the truth. So far the Socratic principle. The eternal and essential truth, the truth which has an essential relationship to an existing individual because it pertains essentially to existence (all other knowledge being from the Socratic point of view accidental, its scope and degree a matter of indifference), is a paradox. But the eternal essential truth is by no means in itself a paradox; it becomes paradoxical by virtue of its relationship to an existing individual. The Socratic ignorance is the expression for the objective uncertainty; the inwardness of the existing individual is the truth. To anticipate here what will be developed later, let me make the following remark: the Socratic ignorance is an analogue to the category of the absurd, only that there is still less of objective certainty in the repellent effect that the absurd exercises. It is certain only that it is absurd, and precisely on that account it incites to an infinitely greater tension in the corresponding inwardness. The Socratic inwardness in existing is an analogue to faith; only that the inwardness of faith, corresponding as it does, not to the repulsion of the Socratic ignorance, but to the repulsion exerted by the absurd, is infinitely more profound.

Socratically the eternal essential truth is by no means in its own nature paradoxical, but only in its relationship to an existing individual. This finds expression in another Socratic proposition, namely, that all knowledge is recollection. This proposition is not for Socrates a cue to the speculative enterprise, and hence he does not follow it up; essentially it becomes a Platonic principle. Here the way swings off: Socrates essentially accentuates existence, while Plato forgets this and loses himself in speculation. Socrates' infinite merit is to have been an *existing* thinker, not a speculative philosopher who forgets what it means to exist. For Socrates therefore the principle that all knowledge is recollection has at the moment of his leave-taking, and as the constantly rejected possibility of engaging in speculation, the following two-fold significance: (1) that the knower is essentially *integer,* and that with respect to the knowledge of the eternal truth he is confronted with no other difficulty than the circumstance that he exists; which difficulty, however, is so essential and decisive for him that it means that existing, the process of transformation to inwardness in and by existing, the deepening in and through existing, is the truth; (2) that existence in time does not have any decisive significance, because the possibility of taking oneself back into eternity through recollection is always there, though this possibility is constantly nullified by the fact that the deepening in existence utilizes the time, not for speculation, but for the transformation to inwardness in existing.

The infinite merit of the Socratic position was precisely to accentuate the fact that the knower is an existing individual, and that the task of existing is his essential task. Making an advance upon Socrates by failing to understand this is quite a mediocre achievement. This Socratic principle we must therefore bear in mind, and then inquire whether the formula may not be so altered as really to make an advance beyond the Socratic position.

Subjectivity, inwardness, has been posited as the truth; can any expression for the truth be found which has a still *higher degree of inwardness?* Aye, there is such an expression, provided the principle that subjectivity or inwardness is the truth begins by positing the opposite principle: that subjectivity is untruth. Let us not be overhasty. Speculative philosophy also says that subjectivity is untruth, but says it exactly conversely, by saying that objectivity is the truth. Speculative philosophy determines subjectivity negatively as tending toward objectivity. This second determination of ours, however, places a hindrance in its own way while proposing to begin, which precisely makes the inwardness far more intensive. Socratically speaking, subjectivity is untruth if it refuses to understand that subjectivity is truth, but, for example, desires to become objective. Here, on the other hand, subjectivity, in beginning upon the task of becoming the truth through a subjectifying process, is in the difficulty that it is already untruth. Thus the labor of the task is thrust backward, backward, that is, in inwardness. So far is it from being the case that the way tends in the direction of objectivity, that the beginning merely lies still deeper in subjectivity.

But the subject cannot be untruth eternally, or eternally be presupposed as having been untruth; it must have been brought to this condition in time, or here become untruth in time. The Socratic paradox consisted in the fact that the eternal truth was related to an existing individual, but now existence has stamped itself upon the existing individual a second time. There has taken place so essential an alteration in him that he cannot now possibly take himself back Socratically into the eternal by way of recollection. To do this is to speculate; to be able to do this, but to reject the possibility by apprehending the task of life as a realization of inwardness in existing, is the Socratic position. But now the difficulty is that what followed Socrates on his way as a rejected possibility has become an impossibility. If engaging in speculation was a dubious merit, even from the point of view of the Socratic, it is now neither more nor less than confusion.

The paradox emerges when the eternal truth and existence are placed in juxtaposition with one another; each time the fact of existence is realized, the paradox becomes more clearly evident. Viewed Socratically the knower was simply an existing individual, but now the existing individual bears the stamp of having been essentially altered by existence.

Let us now call the untruth of the individual *Sin*. Viewed eternally he cannot be in sin, nor can he be eternally presupposed as having been in sin. By coming into existence therefore (for the beginning was that subjectivity is untruth) he becomes a sinner. He is not born as a sinner in the sense that he is presupposed as being a sinner before he is born, but he is born in sin and as a sinner. This we might call *Original Sin*. But if existence has in this manner acquired a power over him, he is prevented from taking himself back into the eternal by way of recollection. If it was paradoxical to posit the eternal truth in relationship to an existing individual, it is now absolutely paradoxical to posit it in relationship to such an individual as we have here defined. But the more difficult it is made for him to take himself out of existence by way of recollection, the more profound is the inwardness that his existence may have in existence; and when it is made impossible for him, when he is held so fast in existence that the back door of recollection is forever closed to him, then his inwardness will be the most profound possible. But let us never forget that the Socratic merit was to stress the fact that the knower is an existing individual; for the more difficult the matter becomes, the greater the temptation to hasten along the easy road of speculation, away from fearful dangers and crucial decisions, to the winning of renown and honors and prosperity, and so forth. If even Socrates understood the dubiety of taking himself speculatively out of existence back into the eternal, although no other difficulty confronted the existing individual except that he existed, and that existing was his essential task: now it is impossible. Forward he must, backward he cannot go.

Subjectivity is the truth. By virtue of the relationship subsisting between the eternal, essential truth and the existing individual, the paradox came into being. Let us now go further, let us suppose that the eternal essential truth is itself a paradox. How does the paradox come into being? By putting the eternal essential truth into juxtaposition with existence. Hence when we posit such a conjunction within the truth itself, the truth becomes a paradox. The eternal truth has come into being in time: this is the paradox. If, in accordance with the determinations just posited, the subject is prevented by sin from taking himself back into the eternal, now he need not trouble himself about this; for now the eternal essential truth is not behind him but in front of him, through its being in existence or having existed, so that, if the individual does not existentially and in existence lay hold of the truth, he will never lay hold of it.

Existence can never be more sharply accentuated than by means of these determinations. The evasion by which speculative philosophy attempts to recollect itself out of existence has been made impossible. Here the only question is about understanding this impossibility; every speculative attempt which insists upon being speculative shows *eo ipso* that it has not been understood. The individual may thrust all this away from him, and take refuge in speculation; but it is impossible first to accept it, and then to wish to revoke it by means of speculation, since it is definitely calculated to prevent speculation.

When the eternal truth is related to an existing individual, it becomes a paradox. The paradox repels in the inwardness of the existing individual, through the objective uncertainty and the corresponding Socratic ignorance. But since the paradox is not in the first instance itself paradoxical (but only in its relationship to the existing individual), it does not repel with a sufficient intensive inwardness. For without risk there is no faith, and the greater the risk, the greater the faith; the more objective security, the less inwardness (for inwardness is precisely subjectivity), and the less objective security, the more profound the possible inwardness. When the paradox is paradoxical in itself, it repels the individual by virtue of its absurdity, and the corresponding passion of inwardness is faith. But subjectivity, inwardness, is the truth; for otherwise we have forgotten what the merit of the Socratic position is. But there can be no stronger expression for inwardness than when the retreat out of existence into the eternal by way of recollection is impossible: when, with truth confronting the individual as a paradox, gripped in the anguish and pain of sin, facing the tremendous risk of the objective insecurity, the individual believes. But without risk no faith, not even the Socratic form of faith, much less the form of which we here speak.

When Socrates believed that there was a God, he held fast to the objective uncertainty with the whole passion of his inwardness, and it is precisely in this contradiction and in this risk, that faith is rooted. Now it is otherwise. Instead of the objective uncertainty, there is here a certainty, namely, that objectively it is absurd; and this absurdity, held fast in the passion of inwardness, is faith. The Socratic ignorance is like a witty jest in comparison with the earnestness of facing the absurd; and the Socratic existential inwardness is like Greek light-mindedness in comparison with the grave strenuosity of faith.

What now is the absurd? The absurd is—that the eternal truth has come into being in time, that God has come into being, has been born, has grown up, and so forth, has come into being precisely like any other individual human being, quite indistinguishable from other individuals. For every assumption of immediate recognizability is pre-Socratic paganism, and from the Jewish point of view, idolatry; and every determination of what really makes an advance beyond the Socratic must essentially bear the stamp of having a relationship to God's having come into being; for faith *sensu strictissimo,* as was developed in the *Fragments,*[4] refers to becoming. When Socrates believed that there was a God, he saw very well that where the way swings off there is also an objective way of approximation, for example, by the contemplation of nature and human history, and so forth. His merit was precisely to shun this way, where the quantitative siren song enchants the mind and deceives the existing individual.

In relation to the absurd, the objective approximation-process is like the comedy, *Misunderstanding upon Misunderstanding,*[5] which is generally played by *Privatdocents* and speculative philosophers. The absurd is precisely by its objective repulsion the measure of the intensity of faith in inwardness. Suppose a man who wishes to acquire faith; let the comedy begin. He wishes to have faith, but he wishes also to safeguard himself by means of an objective inquiry and its approximation-process. What happens? With the help of the approximation-process the absurd becomes something different: it becomes probable, it becomes increasingly probable, it becomes extremely and emphatically probable. Now he is ready to believe it, and he ventures to claim for himself that he does not believe as shoemakers and tailors and sin.ple folk believe, but only after long deliberation. Now he is ready to believe it; and lo, now it has become precisely impossible to believe it. Anything that is almost probable, or probable, or extremely and emphatically probable, is something he can almost know, or as good as know,

[4] English edition, pp. 68–70.
[5] The title of a comedy by Overskou.

or extremely and emphatically almost *know*—but it is impossible to *believe*. For the absurd is the object of faith, and the only object that can be believed.

Or suppose a man who says that he has faith, but desires to make his faith clear to himself, so as to understand himself in his faith. Now the comedy begins again. The object of faith becomes almost probable, as good as probable, extremely and emphatically probable. He has completed his investigations, and he ventures to claim for himself that he does not believe as shoemakers and tailors and other simple folk believe, but that he has also understood himself in his believing. Strange understanding! On the contrary, he has in fact learned something else about faith than when he believed; and he has learned that he no longer believes, since he almost knows, or as good as knows, or extremely and emphatically almost knows.

Insofar as the absurd comprehends within itself the factor of becoming, one way of approximation will be that which confuses the absurd fact of such a becoming (which is the object of faith) with a simple historical fact, and hence seeks historical certainty for that which is absurd precisely because it involves the contradiction that something which can become historical only in direct opposition to all human reason has become historical. It is this contradiction which constitutes the absurd, which can only be believed. If historical certainty with respect to it is assumed, the certainty attained is merely that the something which is thus assumed as certain is not the thing in question. A witness can testify that he has believed it, and hence that, so far from being an historical certainty, it is directly contrary to his own reason; but such a witness thrusts the individual away in precisely the same sense that the absurd itself does. And a witness who does not so repel is *eo ipso* a deceiver, or a man who talks about something quite different, and can help only to obtain certainty about something quite different. A hundred thousand individual witnesses, who are individual witnesses just on account of the peculiar character of their testimony (that they have believed the absurd) cannot *en masse* become anything else, so as to make the absurd less absurd—why should they? Because a hundred thousand human beings have separately, each one for himself, believed that it was absurd? On the contrary, these hundred thousand witnesses again exercise a repellent influence in nearly the same way that the absurd itself exercises it.

But this I need not here expound in greater detail. In the *Fragments* (especially where the distinction between the disciple at first-hand and at second-hand is shown to be illusory),[6] and in the first part of this book, I have already carefully enough expounded the thesis that all approximation is useless, since on the contrary it behooves us to get rid of introductory observations, guarantees of security, proofs from consequences, and the whole mob of public pawnbrokers and guarantors, so as to permit the absurd to stand out in all its clarity—in order that the individual may believe, if he wills it; I merely say that it must be extremely strenuous so to believe.

If speculative philosophy wishes to take cognizance of this and say, as always, that there is no paradox when the matter is viewed eternally, · divinely, theocentrically—then I admit that I am not in a position to determine whether the speculative philosopher is right, for I am only a poor existing human being, not competent to contemplate the eternal either eternally or divinely or theocentrically, but compelled to content myself with existing. So much is certain, however, that speculative philosophy carries everything back, back past the Socratic position, which at least comprehended that for an existing individual existence is essential; to say nothing of the failure of speculative philosophy to take time to grasp what it means to be so critically *situated* in existence as the existing individual in the experiment. . . .

Christianity has declared itself to be the eternal essential truth which has come into being in time. It has proclaimed itself as the *Paradox,* and it has required of the individual the inwardness of faith in relation to that which is an offense [7] to the Jews and a folly to the Greeks—and an absurdity to the understanding. It is impossible to express more strongly the fact that subjectivity is truth and that objectivity merely repels, even by virtue of the absurd. And indeed it would seem very strange that Christianity should have come into the world just to receive an explanation; as if it had been somewhat bewildered about itself, and hence had entered the world to consult that wise man, the speculative philosopher, who can help by furnishing the explanation. It is impossible to express with more intensive inwardness the principle that subjectivity is truth, than when subjectivity is in the first instance untruth, and yet subjectivity is the truth. . . .

The immediate relationship to God is paganism, and only after the breach has taken place can there be any question of a true God-relationship. But just this breach is the first act of inwardness in the direction

[6] English edition, pp. 77 ff.
[7] "The offense" was to be the subject of Kierkegaard's last great book, the *Training in Christianity*.

of determining the truth as inwardness. Nature is, indeed, the work of God, but only the handiwork is directly present, not God. Is not this to behave, in His relationship to the individual, like an illusive author who nowhere sets down his result in large type, or gives it to the reader beforehand in a preface? And why is God illusive? Precisely because He is the truth, and by being illusive desires to keep men from error. The observer does not attain a result immediately, but must himself take pains to find it, and thereby the direct relationship is broken. But this breach is precisely the act of self-activity, the irruption of inwardness, the first determination of the truth as inwardness.

Or is not God so unnoticeable, so secretly present in His works, that a man might very well live his entire life, be married, become known and respected as citizen, father, and captain of the hunt, without ever having discovered God in His works, and without ever having received any impression of the infinitude of the ethical, because he helped himself out with what constitutes an analogy to the speculative confusion of the ethical with the historical process, because he helped himself out by having recourse to the customs and traditions prevailing in the town where he happened to live? As a mother admonishes her child when it sets off for a party: "Now be sure to behave yourself, and do as you see the other well-behaved children do"—so he might manage to live by conducting himself as he sees others do. He would never do anything first, and he would never have any opinion which he did not first know that others had; for this "others" would be for him the first. Upon extraordinary occasions he would behave as when at a banquet a dish is served, and one does not know how it should be eaten: he would spy around until he saw how the others did it, and so forth. Such a man might perhaps know many things, perhaps even know the System by rote; he might be an inhabitant of a Christian country, and bow his head whenever the name of God was mentioned; he would perhaps also see God in nature when in company with others who saw God; he would be a pleasant society man—and yet he would have been deceived by the direct nature of his relationship to the truth, to the ethical, and to God.

If one were to delineate such a man experimentally, he would be a satire upon the human. It is really the God-relationship that makes a man a man, and yet he would be lacking this. No one would hesitate, however, to regard him as a real man (for the absence of inwardness is not directly apparent); in reality he would constitute a sort of marionette, very deceptively imitating everything externally human—even to the extent of having children by his wife. At the end of his life, one would have to say that one thing had escaped him: his consciousness had taken no note of God. If God could have permitted a direct relationship, he would doubtless have taken notice. If God, for example, had taken on the figure of a very rare and tremendously large green bird, with a red beak, sitting in a tree on the mound, and perhaps even whistling in an unheard of manner—then the society man would have been able to get his eyes open, and for the first time in his life would be first.

All paganism consists in this, that God is related to man directly, as the extraordinary is to the astonished observer. But the spiritual relationship to God in the truth, i.e. in inwardness, is conditioned by a prior irruption of inwardness, which corresponds to the divine elusiveness that God has absolutely nothing obvious about Him, that God is so far from being obvious, that He is invisible. It cannot immediately occur to anyone that He exists, although His invisibility is again His omnipresence. But a ubiquitous person is one who is seen everywhere, like a policeman, for example: how deceptive then, that an omnipresent being should be recognizable precisely by being invisible, only and alone recognizable by this trait, since his visibility would annul his omnipresence. The relationship between invisibility and omnipresence is like the relation between mystery and revelation. The mystery is the expression for the fact that the revelation is a revelation in the stricter sense, so that the mystery is the only trait by which it is known; for otherwise a revelation would be something very like a policeman's ubiquitousness.

If God were to reveal Himself in human form and grant a direct relationship by giving Himself, for example, the figure of a man six yards tall, then our hypothetical society man and captain of the hunt would doubtless have his attention aroused. But the spiritual relationship to God in truth, when God refuses to deceive, requires just that there be nothing remarkable about the figure, so that the society man would have to say: "There is nothing whatever to see." When God has nothing obviously remarkable about Him, the society man is perhaps deceived by not having his attention at all aroused. But this is not God's fault, and the actuality of such a deception is at the same time the constant possibility of the truth. But if God has anything obviously remarkable, He deceives men because they have their attention called to what is untrue, and this direction of attention is at the same time the impossibility of the truth. In paganism the direct relationship is idolatry; in Christianity, everyone knows that God cannot so reveal Himself. But this knowledge is by no means inwardness, and in Christianity it may well happen to one who knows everything by rote that he is left altogether "without God in the world," [8] in a sense impossible in paganism, which did however have the untrue relationship of idolatry. Idolatry is indeed a sorry substitute, but that the item *God* should be entirely omitted is still worse.

Not even God, then, enters into a direct relationship with derivative spirits. And this is the miracle of creation, not the creation of something which is nothing over against the Creator, but the creation of something which is something, and which in true worship of God can use this something in order by its true self to become nothing before God. Much less can one human being sustain such a direct relationship to another *in the truth*. Nature, the totality of created things, is the work of God. And yet God is not there; but within the individual man there is a potentiality (man is potentially spirit) which is awakened in inwardness to become a God-relationship, and then it becomes possible to see God everywhere. The sensuous distinctions of the great, the astonishing, the shrieking superlatives of a southern people, constitute a retreat to idolatry, in comparison with the spiritual relationship of inwardness. Is this not as if an author wrote one hundred and sixty-six folio volumes, and a reader read and read, just as people look and look at nature, but did not discover that the meaning of this tremendous literature lay in himself; for astonishment over the many volumes, and the number of lines to a page, which is like the astonishment over the vastness of nature and the countless forms of animal life, is not the true understanding.

A direct relationship between one spiritual being and another, with respect to the essential truth, is unthinkable. If such a relationship is assumed, it means that one of the parties has ceased to be spirit. This is something that many a genius omits from consideration, both when he helps people into the truth *en masse,* and when he is complaisant enough to think that acclamation, willingness to listen, the affixing of signatures, and so forth, is identical with the acceptance of the truth. Equally as important as the truth, and if one of the two is to be emphasized, still more important, is the manner in which the truth is accepted. It would help very little if one persuaded millions of men to accept the truth, if precisely by the method of their acceptance they were transferred into error. Hence it is that all complaisance, all per-

[8] Ephesians 2:12.

suasiveness, all bargaining, all direct attraction by means of one's own person, reference to one's suffering so much for the cause, one's weeping over humanity, one's enthusiasm—all this is sheer misunderstanding, a false note in relation to the truth, by which, in proportion to one's ability, one may help a job-lot of human beings to get an illusion of truth.

THE SUBJECTIVE THINKER

ETHICALLY regarded, reality is higher than possibility. The ethical proposes to do away with the disinterestedness of the possible by making existence the infinite interest. It therefore opposes every confusing attempt, like that of proposing ethically to *contemplate* humanity and the world. Such ethical contemplation is impossible since there is only one kind of ethical contemplation, namely, self-contemplation. Ethics closes immediately about the individual, and demands that he exist ethically; it does not make a parade of millions or of generations of men; it does not take humanity in the lump any more than the police arrest humanity at large. The ethical is concerned with particular human beings, and with each and every one of them by himself. If God knows how many hairs there are on a man's head, the ethical knows how many human beings there are; and its enumeration is not in the interest of a total sum, but for the sake of each individual. The ethical requirement is imposed upon each individual, and when it judges, it judges each individual by himself; only a tyrant or an impotent man is content to decimate. The ethical lays hold of each individual and demands that he refrain from all contemplation, especially of humanity and the world; for the ethical, as being the internal, cannot be observed by an outsider. It can be realized only by the individual subject, who alone can know what it is that moves within him. This ethical reality is the only reality which does not become a mere possibility through being known, and which cannot be known merely by being thought; for it is the individual's own reality. Before it became a reality it was known by him in the form of a conceived reality, and hence as a possibility. But in the case of another person's reality he could have no knowledge about it until he conceived it in coming to know it, which means that he transformed it from a reality into a possibility.

With respect to every reality external to myself, I can get hold of it only through thinking it. In order to get hold of it really, I should have to be able to make myself into the other, the acting individual, and make the foreign reality my own reality, which is impossible.[1] For if I make the foreign reality my own, this does not mean that I become the other through knowing his reality, but it means that I acquire a new reality, which belongs to me as opposed to him.

When I think something which I propose to do but have not yet done, the content of this conception, no matter how exact it may be, if it be ever so much entitled to be called a *conceived reality,* is a possibility. Conversely, when I think about something that another has done, and so conceive a reality, I lift this given reality out of the real and set it over into the possible; for a *conceived reality* is a possibility, and is higher than reality from the standpoint of thought, but not from the standpoint of reality. This also implies that there is no immediate relationship, ethically, between subject and subject. When I understand another person, his reality is for me a possibility, and in its aspect of possibility this conceived reality is related to me precisely as the thought of something I have not done is related to the doing of it. . . .

In connection with the aesthetic and the intellectual, to ask whether this or that is real, whether it really has happened, is a misunderstanding. So to ask betrays a failure to conceive the aesthetic and the intellectual ideality as a possibility, and forgets that to determine a scale of values for the aesthetic and the intellectual in this manner is like ranking sensation higher than thought. Ethically it is correct to put the question: "Is it real?" But it is important to note that this holds true only when the individual subject asks this question ethically of himself, and concerning his own reality. He can apprehend the ethical reality of another only by thinking it, and hence as a possibility.

The Scriptures teach: "Judge not, that ye be not judged." This is expressed in the form of a warning, an admonition, but it is at the same time an impossibility. One human being cannot judge another ethically, because he cannot understand him except as a possibility. When therefore anyone attempts to judge another, the expression for his impotence is that he merely judges himself.

The mode of apprehension of the truth is precisely the truth. It is therefore untrue to answer a question in a medium in which the question cannot arise. So for example, to explain reality within the medium

[1] This is where S.K. would be challenged by a monistic Idealism.

of the possible, or to distinguish between possibility and reality within possibility. By not asking about reality aesthetically and intellectually, but only ethically, and again only in the direction of one's own ethical reality, each individual will be ethically isolated. Irony and hypocrisy as opposite forms,—both expressing the contradiction that the internal is not the external, irony by seeming to be bad, hypocrisy by seeming to be good—emphasize the principle . . . that reality and deceit are equally possible, and that deceit can clothe itself in the same appearance as reality. Only the individual himself can know which is which. It is unethical even to ask at all about another person's ethical inwardness, insofar as such inquiry constitutes a diversion of attention. But if the question is asked nevertheless, the difficulty remains that I can lay hold of the other's reality only by conceiving it, and hence by translating it into a possibility; and in this sphere the possibility of a deception is equally conceivable. This is profitable preliminary training for an ethical mode of existence: to learn that the individual stands alone.

It is a misunderstanding to be concerned about reality from the aesthetic [2] or intellectual point of view. And to be concerned ethically about another's reality is also a misunderstanding, since the only question of reality that is ethically pertinent is the question of one's own reality. Here we may clearly note the difference that exists between faith *sensu strictissimo* on the one hand . . . and the ethical on the other. To ask with infinite interest about a reality which is not one's own is to wish to believe and expresses a paradoxical relationship to the paradoxical. Aesthetically it is impossible to raise such a question except in thoughtlessness, since possibility is aesthetically higher than reality. Nor is it possible to raise such a question intellectually, since intellectually possibility is higher than reality. Nor is it possible to raise it ethically, because the individual ethically is solely and alone infinitely interested in his own reality. The analogy between faith and the ethical is found in the infinite interest, which suffices to distinguish the believer absolutely from an aesthetician or a thinker. But the believer differs from the ethicist in being infinitely interested in the reality of another (in the fact, for example, that God has existed in time).

The aesthetic and intellectual principle is that no reality is thought or understood until its *esse* [3] has been resolved into its *posse*.[3] The ethical

[2] A view of art seems here to be implied which was considerably ahead of its time.
[3] Reality—possibility.

principle is that no possibility is understood until each *posse* has really become an *esse*. An aesthetic and intellectual scrutiny protests every *esse* which is not a *posse*; the ethical scrutiny condemns every *posse* which is not an *esse*, but this refers only to a *posse* in the individual himself, since the ethical has nothing to do with the possibilities of other individuals. In our own age everything is mixed up together: the aesthetic is treated ethically, faith is dealt with intellectually, and so forth. Philosophy has answered every question; but no adequate consideration has been given the question concerning what sphere it is within which each question finds its answer. This creates a greater confusion in the world of the spirit than when in the civic life an ecclesiastical question, let us say, is handled by the bridge commission.

Is the real then the same as the external? By no means. Aesthetically and intellectually it is usual and proper to stress the principle that the external is merely a deception for one who does not grasp the ideality involved. . . . What then is the real? It is the ideality. But aesthetically and intellectually the ideality is the possible (the translation from *esse ad posse*). Ethically the ideality is the real within the individual himself. The real is an inwardness that is infinitely interested in existing; this is exemplified in the ethical individual.

When I understand a thinker, and just in the same degree that I understand him, his reality (that he exists as an individual man; that he has *actually* understood something in this way; or that he has himself *actually* realized it, and so on) is a matter of complete indifference. Aesthetic and speculative thought is quite justified in insisting on this point, and it is important not to lose sight of it. But this does not suffice for a defense of pure thought as a medium of communication between man and man. Because the reality of the teacher is properly indifferent to me as his pupil, and my reality conversely to him, it does not by any means follow that the teacher is justified in being indifferent to his own reality. His communication should bear the stamp of this consciousness, but not directly, since the ethical reality of an individual is not directly communicable (such a direct relationship is exemplified in the para-doxical relation of a believer to the object of his faith), and cannot be understood immediately, but must be understood indirectly through indirect signs.

When the different spheres are not decisively distinguished from one another, confusion reigns everywhere. When people are curious about a thinker's reality and find it interesting to know something about it, and so forth, this interest is intellectually reprehensible. The maximum of attainment in the sphere of the intellectual is to become altogether indifferent to the thinker's reality. But by being muddle-headed in the intellectual sphere, one acquires a certain resemblance to a believer. A believer is one who is infinitely interested in another's reality. This is a decisive criterion for faith, and the interest in question is not just a little curiosity, but an absolute dependence upon faith's object.

The object of faith is the reality of another, and the relationship is one of infinite interest. The object of faith is not a doctrine, for then the relationship would be intellectual, and it would be of importance not to botch it, but to realize the maximum intellectual relationship. The object of faith is not a teacher with a doctrine; for when a teacher has a doctrine, the doctrine is *eo ipso* more important than the teacher, and the relationship is again intellectual, and it again becomes important not to botch it, but to realize the maximum intellectual relationship. The object of faith is the reality of the teacher, that the teacher really exists. The answer of faith is therefore unconditionally yes or no. For the answer of faith is not concerned as to whether a doctrine is true or not, nor with respect to a teacher, whether his teaching is true or not; it is the answer to a question concerning a fact: "Do you or do you not suppose that he has really existed?" And the answer, it must be noted, is with infinite passion. In the case of a human being, it is thoughtless to lay so great and infinite a stress on the question whether he has existed or not. If the object of faith is a human being, therefore, the whole proposal is the vagary of a stupid person, who has not even understood the spirit of the intellectual and the aesthetic. The object of faith is hence the reality of the God-man in the sense of his existence. But existence involves first and foremost particularity, and this is why thought must abstract from existence, because the particular cannot be thought, but only the universal. The object of faith is thus God's reality in existence as a particular individual, the fact that God has existed as an individual human being.

Christianity is no doctrine concerning the unity of the divine and the human, or concerning the identity of subject and object; [4] nor is it any other of the logical transcriptions of Christianity. If Christianity were a doctrine, the relationship to it would not be one of faith, for only an intellectual type of relationship can correspond to a doctrine.

---

[4] S.K., of course, is thinking of Hegelianism; but compare "the Perennial Philosophy" and other gnostic interpretations of Christianity in our own day.

Christianity is therefore not a doctrine, but the fact that God has existed.

The realm of faith is thus not a class for numskulls in the sphere of the intellectual, or an asylum for the feeble-minded. Faith constitutes a sphere all by itself, and every misunderstanding of Christianity may at once be recognized by its transforming it into a doctrine, transferring it to the sphere of the intellectual. The maximum of attainment within the sphere of the intellectual, namely, to become completely indifferent as to the reality of the teacher, is in the sphere of faith at the opposite end of the scale. The maximum of attainment within the sphere of faith is to become infinitely interested in the reality of the teacher. . . .

God does not think, He creates; God does not exist, He is eternal. Man thinks and exists, and existence separates thought and being, holding them apart from one another in succession. . . .

Subjectivity is truth, subjectivity is reality.

N.B. *Necessity* must be dealt with by itself. The fact that modern speculative thought has imported necessity into the historical process has caused much confusion; the categories of possibility, of actuality, and of necessity have all been compromised. In the *Philosophical Fragments* [5] I have sought to indicate this briefly.

THE RELIGIOUS TASK:
AN EDIFYING DIVERTISSEMENT

. . . And now what does the task look like in daily life? For I always have my favorite theme *in mente*. Is everything quite in order with the urge which our theocentric nineteenth century feels to advance beyond Christianity, to speculate, to carry the evolution further, to fashion a new religion, or to abolish Christianity? As for my own humble person, the reader will please remember that it is I who find the matter and the task so extremely difficult, which would seem to indicate that I have not successfully realized it, I who do not even profess to be a Christian; but please note that this is not to be taken in the sense that I have ceased to be a Christian in consequence of having gone further. Still, it is always something to have called attention to the difficulty, even if this is done, as here, only in an edifying *divertissement,* brought

[5] Pages 60 ff. in the English edition.

forward with the aid of a spy whom I send out among men on week days, and with the additional assistance of a few dilettantes who are made to play a role against their wills.

Last Sunday the clergyman said: "You must not depend upon the world, and not upon men, and not upon yourself, but only and alone upon God; for a human being can of himself do nothing." And we all understood it, myself included; for the ethical and the ethico-religious are so very easy to understand, but on the other hand so very difficult to do. A child can understand it, the most simple-minded individual can understand it quite as it is said, that we can do absolutely nothing, that we must renounce everything, forsake everything. On Sunday it is understood with such fearful ease (aye, fearful; for this ease leads often enough the same way as the good resolutions) *in abstracto,* and on Monday it is so very difficult to understand that it concerns this little particular within the relative and concrete existence in which the individual has his daily life, where the mighty man is tempted to forget humility, and the humble person is tempted to confound humility before God with a relative deference toward his superiors; and yet this particular something is a sheer trifle in comparison with everything. Aye, even when the clergyman complains that no one acts in accordance with his admonition, this is again so fearfully easy to understand; but the next day this understanding has become so difficult that the person himself contributes through this particular, through this little insignificance, his own share of the guilt. Then the clergyman added: "This is a fact we ought always to remember." And we all understood it; for *always* is a glorious word which says everything at once, and is so fearfully easy to understand; but it is on the other hand the most difficult thing in the world to do something always, and on Monday afternoon at four o'clock it is extremely difficult to understand this *always* merely for the space of half an hour. Even in the clergyman's discourse there was a hint of something which indirectly called attention to this difficulty; for there were a few matters so described as to indicate that he himself scarcely did it always; aye, that he had scarcely done it in each one of the few moments in which he meditated on his sermon; moreover, that he scarcely did it in every part of the brief address.

Now today it is Monday, and the spy has abundant time to go out and seek contact with men; for the clergyman makes speeches for them, but the observer converses with them. So then he strikes up a conversation with a man, and the talk finally veers around to the subject that the spy wants to bring up. He says: "That is all quite true, but there is still something that you cannot do; you cannot build a palace with four wings and marble floors." The other answers: "No, you are quite right about that; how should I be able to do that when my income is just about enough for my necessities, perhaps permitting me to save a little each year, but I certainly have no capital for building palaces, and besides I do not understand the builder's trade." So then it appears that this man does not have the power. The spy leaves him, and next has the honor to meet a man of great importance; he flatters his vanity, and finally the conversation turns to the matter of the palace: "But a palace with four wings and marble floors will surely be too much for you to manage." "What," says the other, "you surely forget that I have already accomplished this, that my great residence in Palace Square is precisely the structure you describe." So this man turned out to have the power, and the spy bows himself out of his presence, heaping congratulations upon the mighty man. In going away the spy now meets a third man, to whom he recounts the conversation he has just had with the two others, and this man exclaims: "Aye, the destinies allotted to men in this world are strange indeed, their capabilities vary exceedingly, one man is able to do so much and another so very little; and yet every human being would be able to accomplish something if he would learn from experience and the available knowledge of the world to remain within the sphere of his own limitations." The differences then are noteworthy; but is it not still more noteworthy that three different speeches about the differences say one and the same thing, and say that all men are equally endowed with capacity for accomplishment? Number one is unable to do this or that because he does not have the money, which means that he has the power essentially; number two can do it, he is essentially endowed with the power, and this fact reveals itself accidentally through his having the money; number three is even able by virtue of his shrewdness to do without some of the conditions and still have the power—what a mighty man would he not be if he possessed the conditions!

But last Sunday, that is to say yesterday, the clergyman said that a human being can do absolutely nothing of himself, and we all understood it. When the clergyman says it in church we all understand it, and if a man tries to express it existentially during the six days of the week so that people notice it, it is not long before we all understand—that he is crazy. Even the most religious man will have occasion to catch himself a dozen times a day entertaining the delusion that he can at least do something. But when the clergyman says that a man can do absolutely nothing, we all understand it with such fearful ease. . . .

So it goes. In the six days of the week we can all do something, the king more than his minister; the witty journalist says: "I will show this man or that what I can do," that is, make him appear ridiculous; the policeman says to the man in the shabby jacket: "Perhaps you do not know what I can do to you," namely, arrest him; the cook says to the poor woman who comes on Saturdays: "You may have forgotten what I can do," namely, persuade the mistress not to give her any longer the week's left-overs. We can all do something, and the king smiles at the minister's power, and the minister laughs at the journalist's power, and the journalist laughs at the policeman's, and the policeman at the man in the shabby jacket, and the shabby man at the Saturday woman —and on Sunday we all go to church (with the exception of the cook, who never has time because there are always dinner guests on Sunday at his Honor's) and hear from the lips of the clergyman that a man can do absolutely nothing of himself— that is, if we are so fortunate as not to be listening to a speculative preacher. Yet, one moment: we have arrived at church; with the assistance of a very authoritative usher (for the usher is especially formidable on Sundays, and indicates with a silent glance at so-and-so what he can do) we are severally assigned to our seats with reference to our particular position in society. The clergyman enters the pulpit—but at the very last moment there is a very influential man who has come late, and the usher must now exercise his authority. Then the preacher begins, and we all now understand from our different positions and standpoints what the clergyman says from his lofty standpoint, namely, that a man can do nothing of himself. On Monday the clergyman himself is a very influential man, that we must all acknowledge, except those who are more influential. But one of the two must surely be a jest: either what the clergyman says is a jest, a kind of social game, to consider once in a while that a man can do nothing at all; or the clergyman is right, after all, in saying that a human being should always remember this—and we others, including the clergyman and myself too, are wrong when we so wretchedly interpret the word *always,* although a man has thirty, forty, or fifty years for the perfecting of himself in this art, so that every day is a day of preparation, but also a day of testing.

Today it is Tuesday, and the spy is paying a visit to a man who has under construction a large building just outside the town; he again leads the conversation around to touch upon what a man can do, and upon his respected host's ability to do things. But this man replies, not without a certain solemnity: "A man can do absolutely nothing of himself, and it is only with God's help that I have accumulated this great fortune, and with God's help that I . . ." Here the solemn stillness of the conversation is broken in upon by a loud noise outside the house. The man excuses himself and rushes out; he leaves the door half open, and our spy, whose ears are sharp, now hears to his great astonishment blow upon blow to the accompaniment of these words: "I will show you what I can do to you." The spy can scarcely restrain his laughter—well, the spy, too, is a human being, who may at any moment be tempted by the delusion that he can do something, as now, for example, to think that it was he who had caught the mighty man in his ludicrousness.

But if a man proposes to himself every day to bear in mind and existentially to hold fast what the clergyman says on Sunday, understanding this as the earnestness of life, and therewith again understanding all his ability and inability as a jest: does this mean that he will undertake nothing at all, because everything is empty and vain? Ah, no, for then precisely he will have no occasion to appreciate the jest, since the contradiction will not arise which brings it into juxtaposition with the earnestness of life: there is no contradiction in the thought that everything is vanity in the eyes of a creature of vanity. Sloth, inactivity, the affectation of superiority over against the finite—this is poor jesting, or rather is no jest at all. But to shorten one's hours of sleep and buy up the hours of the day and not to spare oneself, and then to understand that the whole is a jest: aye, that is earnestness. And religiously the positive is always recognizable by the negative: the earnestness by the jest that it is a religious earnestness, not the immediate earnestness, the stupid official importance of a counsellor, the stupid self-importance of a journalist with reference to the age, an "awakened" individual's stupid importance before God, as if God could not create a million men of genius if He were in any way embarrassed. To hold the fate of many human beings in one's hand, to transform the world, and then constantly to understand that this is a jest: aye, that is earnestness indeed! But in order that this should be possible all finite passions must be atrophied, all selfishness outrooted, both the selfishness which wants to have everything, and the selfishness which proudly turns its back on everything. But just herein sticks the difficulty, and here arises the suffering in the dying away from self; and while it is the specific criterion of the ethical that it is so easy to understand in its abstract expression, it is correspondingly difficult to understand *in concreto*.

We ought always to bear in mind that a human being can do nothing of himself, says the clergyman; hence also when one proposes to take an outing in the Deer Park [1] he ought to remind himself of this, as for example, that he cannot enjoy himself; and that the illusion that he surely is able to enjoy himself at the Deer Park, since he feels such a strong desire for it, is the temptation of his immediacy; and that the illusion that he surely can take this outing since he can easily afford it, is the temptation of his immediacy. Now today happens to be Wednesday, and a Wednesday in the Deer Park season; let us then again send the spy out among men.

But perhaps one or another religious individual is of the opinion that it is not seemly for him to take an outing of this kind. If this is the case, then I must by virtue of the qualitative dialectic demand respect for the cloister, for mere dabbling will get us nowhere. If the religious man is to be in any way peculiar in his behavior outwardly, then the cloister is the only energetic expression therefor; the rest is mere bungling. But our age has advanced beyond the Middle Ages in religiosity; what then did the religiosity of the Middle Ages express? That there was something in the finite world which could not be thought together with or existentially held together with the thought of God. The passionate expression for this was to break with the finite. If the religiosity of our age is more advanced, it follows that it can hold fast existentially to the thought of God in connection with the frailest expression of the finite, as for example with the enjoyment of an outing in the Deer Park; unless indeed the advanced character of our religiosity is betokened by its having retreated to childish forms of religiosity, in comparison with which the youthful enthusiasm of the Middle Ages is a glory.

It is a childish form of religiosity, for example, once a week to seek permission from God, as it were, to indulge one's pleasure the whole of the following week, and so again the next Sunday to ask permission for the next week by going to church, and hearing the clergyman say that we should always bear in mind that a man can do absolutely nothing. . . . The religiosity which is to be an advance upon the medieval must find an expression in its devout reflections for the principle that the religious man will and must exist in the same categories on Monday, and will on Monday actually so exist. The Middle Ages were praise-

---

[1] An extensive park including a great tract of wild woodland north of Copenhagen. (L)

worthy in that they were earnestly concerned about this problem; but then they arrived at the conclusion that it could be done only in the cloister. The religiosity of our age goes further: on Sunday the clergyman says that we must always bear in mind the fact that we can do nothing of ourselves; but for the rest we must be just like other men, we must not enter the cloister, we can take our outings in the Deer Park. . . .

Now the spy goes forth. He will doubtless come upon a man who cannot take an outing in the Deer Park because he has no money. . . . If the spy were to give him the money and say, "Nevertheless, you cannot do it," he would probably think him mad, or assume that there must be some undisclosed obstacle, that perhaps the money was counterfeit, or that perhaps the city gates were closed and the tollgates likewise. In short, out of politeness, and in order not immediately to reward the spy's benevolence by declaring him mad, he would doubtless attempt a number of acute guesses; and when all these failed in consequence of the spy's assertion that there was nothing of that kind in the way of his going, he would regard him as mad, thank him for the gift—and proceed to go out to the Deer Park. And the same man would understand the clergyman next Sunday very well when he preaches about a man's inability to do anything of himself, and that we always ought to bear this in mind. Herein precisely lies the jest, namely, that he can well understand the clergyman; for if there were a single human being so simple-minded that he could not understand the task that the clergyman essentially has set forth, who could then endure to live?

So the spy meets another man, who says: "To take an outing in the Deer Park when one can well afford it, and one's engagements permit it, when one takes wife and children and even the servants along, and returns home at a decent time, is an innocent form of enjoyment. And one ought to partake of the innocent pleasures of life, and not retire like a coward into a monastery, which is tantamount to fleeing the danger."

The spy answers: "But did you not say in the beginning of our conversation that you heard the clergyman say last Sunday that a man can do absolutely nothing of himself, and that we ought always to bear this in mind; and did you not say that you understood it?"

"Yes."

"Then you must have forgotten what it is we are talking about. When you say that such an outing is an innocent pleasure, this is the opposite of a guilty pleasure; but this contrast belongs to morals or ethics. The clergyman, on the other hand, spoke of your relation to God. Because it is ethically permissible to take an outing in the Deer Park it does not follow that it is religiously permissible; and, in any case, it is just this you have to prove, according to the clergyman, by thinking it together with the thought of God. And this not in general terms merely, for you are not a clergyman who has to preach on this theme, though you and many others seem in daily life to confuse yourselves with the parson, so that it is clear that it cannot be the most difficult of tasks to be a clergyman. A clergyman speaks in general terms about the innocent pleasures of life, but you have to express existentially what the clergyman says. Hence you are not called upon today to deliver a little lecture on the innocent joys of life, in view of your proposing to yourself an outing in the Deer Park, for that is the business of a speaker. But you are to consider, in view of the fact that you propose today, Wednesday, the fourth of July, to take an outing in the Deer Park with wife, children, and servants, what the clergyman said last Sunday, namely, that a man can of himself do nothing, and that he should always bear this in mind. It was about how you manage to realize this task that I wished for some information from you, for if I had desired a kind of lecture I should have addressed myself to the clergyman."

"How absurd," the man replies, "to demand more of me than of the clergyman. I find it quite in order for the clergyman to preach in this manner, it is for this he receives a salary from the State; and as far as my own pastor is concerned, the Reverend Mr. Michaelsen, I shall always be ready to testify that he preaches the genuine evangelical doctrine, and that is why I attend the church where he preaches. For I am no heretic, who wants to have the articles of faith altered; even if it might seem doubtful, according to what you say, whether I am really a believer, it is certain all the same that I am a true orthodox believer, one who abominates the Baptists. But it never occurs to me to bring such trifles as an outing in the Deer Park into connection with the thought of God; moreover, that seems to me to be an affront to God, and I know also that it does not occur to any single one of my many acquaintances to do it."

"And so you doubtless find it in order, just as you approve of the clergyman's preaching in this manner, that he also preaches about no one doing as he says!"

"What nonsense!" the man replies, "Of course I find it in order for such a man of God to speak in that fashion on Sundays and at funerals and weddings; it is no longer than two weeks ago that I publicly thanked him in the newspaper for the glorious unsolicited address he delivered, and which I shall *never* forget."

"Say, rather, which you will *always* remember; for this expression connects itself more closely with the subject of our conversation, namely, that we ought *always* to bear in mind that a man can do nothing of himself. But let us discontinue this conversation, for we evidently do not understand one another, and I see no hope of eliciting from you the information I sought, about how you manage to do what the clergyman says; but I willingly concede you an unmistakable talent for preaching. However, you can do me one service if you will: give me the assurance in writing, and if possible get me similar attestations from your many acquaintances, that it never occurs to you or to them to bring the thought of God into connection with anything like taking an outing in the Deer Park." . . .

So much for the spy, who must now be left to shift for himself; and back to the dictum of the clergyman, that a man can do nothing of himself, and that we should always bear this in mind—therefore, even when we propose to take an outing in the Deer Park. Many readers have presumably long since grown weary of this process of concretion, which never ends, and which nevertheless says nothing at all in comparison with the summary statement that we can do absolutely nothing, and that we should always bear this in mind. But so it is, the ethical and the ethico-religious is in its abstract generality so quickly said and so fearfully easy to understand; in the concreteness of the daily life, however, the discourse which attempts to deal with it is so slow, and the execution of it so very difficult. Nowadays a clergyman scarcely dares to speak in church on the subject of taking an outing in the Deer Park, or even so much as mention the words: so difficult is the task, merely in a religious address to bring a pleasure outing and the thought of God together.

But on the other hand, we are all able to do it in practice. Where then do the difficult tasks arise? In the living-room and on the Shore Road leading to the Deer Park. Nowadays, although preaching against the cloister, the religious address observes the most rigid monastic abstinence, and keeps itself at a distance from reality quite as much as the cloister, thereby adequately revealing in an indirect way that everyday life is really carried on in connection with all the most petty trifles or that the religious does not assimilate the daily life to itself. It is in this fashion that we make an advance upon the Middle Ages. But in such a situation the religious individual is compelled by the qualitative dialectic to demand the cloister. If we are not to preach the cloister, and if our religiosity is to be an advance upon the medieval, let the clergyman be so good as to talk about the simplest of things, and let him abstain from the eternal truths *in abstracto.* . . .

When the religious speaker, in explaining that a man can do nothing of himself, sets something wholly particular in relation to this principle, he gives the auditor occasion to secure a profound insight into his own inmost heart, helps him to penetrate the delusions and illusions, so as to lay aside at least for a moment the bourgeois, small-town sugar-coating in which he otherwise goes wrapped. Essentially, the religious orator operates by referring finally to the absolute relationship, that a man can do nothing of himself; but he makes the transition by means of the particulars which he brings into connection with it. If he confines himself merely to saying, *nothing, always, never, everything*—it might easily happen that the whole issues in nothing; but if he forgets himself and the fundamental absolute, *nothing, always, never, everything*—then he transforms the temple, if not into a den of robbers, at least into a stock exchange.

If then no one else can be found willing to bring together in exposition the absoluteness of the religious and the particularities of life, which togetherness is in existence precisely the ground and significance of the religious suffering, then I propose to myself the task, though I am neither a religious orator, nor myself a religious individual, but merely a humoristic experimenting psychologist. . . .

What the conception of God or an eternal happiness is to effect in the individual is, that he transform his entire existence in relation thereto, and this transformation is a process of dying away from the immediate. This is slowly brought about, but finally he will feel himself confined within the absolute conception of God; for the absolute conception of God does not consist in having such a conception *en passant,* but consists in having the absolute conception at every moment. This is the check on his immediacy, the death verdict which announces its annihilation. Like the bird which flits carefree here and there, when it is imprisoned; like the fish which fearlessly cleaves the waters and makes its way among the enchanted regions of the deep, when it lies out of its element on the dry ground—so the religious individual is confined; for absoluteness is not directly the element of a finite creature. And as one who is sick and cannot move because he feels pain everywhere, and as one who is sick and cannot keep from moving as long as he lives, although he feels pain everywhere—so the religious individual lies fettered in the finite with the absolute conception of God present to him in human frailty. Neither the bird in its cage, nor the fish on the shore, nor the invalid on his sickbed, nor the prisoner in the narrowest cell, is so confined as he who is imprisoned in the conception of God; for just as God is omnipresent, so the imprisoning conception is also everywhere and in every moment. Aye, just as it must be terrible for one who is thought to be dead while he still lives, and has the power of sensation, and can hear what those present say about him, but is unable in any way to express that he is still alive, so also for the religious individual is the suffering of his annihilation a fearful thing, when he has the absolute conception present with him in his nothingness, but no mutuality. If it has happened, and if it is poetically true so to conceive it, that merely a great and comprehensive plan laid down in the human mind and there held fast has crushed the frail vessel; if it has happened that a young woman, as a consequence of being loved by one who is the object of her admiration, has been annihilated in the suffering of her good fortune—what wonder then that the Jews assumed that to see God was to die, and the pagans thought that the God-relationship was the precursor of madness![2] Even though it be true that the conception of God is the absolute help, it is also the only help which is absolutely capable of revealing to man his own helplessness. The religious man lies in the finite like a helpless child; he desires absolutely to hold fast to the conception, and precisely this annihilates him; he desires to do all and, while he summons his will to the task, his impotence begins, since for a finite being there is always a meanwhile; he desires to do all, to express this religious absoluteness, but he cannot make this finite commensurable for that purpose.

Is there anyone who wishes to laugh? If ever the position of the stars in the firmament has portended something fearful, then the position of the categories in this situation portends something other than laughter and jesting. Try now the proposal to take a pleasure outing in the Deer Park. You will shudder, you will seek some excuse, it will seem to you that there are higher ends for which a man can live. Just so. And so you will turn away. But there is always a meanwhile—and meanwhile the impotence returns. You will say to yourself: "little by little." But there, where for the first time, the first beginning of this "little by little" revealed itself as a transition from the absolute, there is

[2] This has in view the argument in Plato's *Phaedrus,* p. 22. (S)

just the place where the fearfulness is. Novelistically, to let a year intervene is naturally only to make a fool of myself religiously and of the religious individual.

The religious individual has lost the relativity of the immediate, its diversions, its pastimes—precisely its pastimes; the absolute consciousness of God consumes him like the burning heat of the summer sun when it will not go down, like the burning heat of the summer sun when it will not abate. But then he is sick; a refreshing sleep will strengthen him, and sleep is an innocent pastime. Aye, let one who has never had any intercourse except with sleeping partners find it in his sleepy order to go to bed; but one who has merely gone about with a great plan in his head, for him the cry of the watchman is indeed a sad reminder, and the approach of sleep more saddening than the coming of death; for the sleep of death is only a moment and a momentary check, but sleep is a long delay.

Then let him begin some task. Perhaps taking the first that comes to hand? No, let a nimble-fingered tradesman of the finite always have something at hand to putter with; one who merely stands in a relationship to his beloved through the thought of love knows something different: when the will to do everything still does not seem enough, and the exertion involved in willing all generates lassitude and weakness, and he again stands at the beginning. But then he must come to himself, seek to understand himself. Perhaps express himself in words? If one who believes that to speak is to let one's tongue run on unchecked can boast that he was never at a loss for an expression, that he never in vain sought for the right word—then one who merely lost his power to speak in admiration of human greatness doubtless learned that at least in such a moment he needed no admonition to keep his tongue in check. And he that never went weeping to bed, weeping not because he could not sleep, but because he dared not remain longer awake; and he that never endured to the end the suffering of the impotence felt when making a beginning; and he that never was struck dumb, he at least should never take it upon himself to talk about the religious sphere, but remain where he belongs—in the sleeping chamber, in the shop, in the tittle-tattle of the street. Nevertheless, how relative must that be which permits a man to experience such things, how relative in comparison with the religious individual's absolute relationship to the absolute!

A man can do nothing of himself, this he should always bear in mind. The religious individual is in this situation—he is thus among other things also unable to take an outing in the Deer Park, and why? Because he is in his own estimation better than other men? *Absit,*[3] this is the superior pose of the cloister. No, it is because he really is a religious individual, not a fantastic clergyman who talks about "always," or a fantastic listener who understands "always—and nothing." It is because he understands hour by hour that he can do nothing. In his sickly condition, the religious individual is unable to bring the God-idea together with such an accidental finitude as the taking of a pleasure outing in the Deer Park. He feels the pain of this, and it is surely a deeper expression for his impotence that he understands it in relation to something so insignificant, than the use of the pretentious expression, *nothing*, which, when nothing more is said, may readily become unmeaning. The difficulty is not that he cannot do it, humanly speaking, but the difficulty is first and foremost to understand that he cannot do it, and do away with the illusion, since he should always bear in mind that he can do nothing of himself—he is over this difficulty, and now there remains the second difficulty: with God to be able to do it.

The more critical an enterprise, a resolution, an event, the easier it is, precisely because it is more direct and natural, to bring the God-idea into relation with it—the easier it is: that is to say, this ease has its ground in the fact that one can be so easily self-deceived through resting in a delusion. In romances and novels one may frequently see at the great crises, either the entire novelistic personnel picturesquely grouped and kneeling in prayer, or the principal character kneeling by himself. However, the respected authors and authoresses are naïve enough to betray, indirectly by the content and form of the prayer, and by the attitude of the petitioner, that their heroes and heroines cannot have prayed many times before in their lives, and that although the scene is laid in the year 1844, in a Christian country, and the persons are Christians, and both the romance and the novel have set themselves the task of describing men as they actually are, even a little better. With great inwardness the hero of the novel brings the God-idea into connection with this extremely important event—but from the religious point of view the inwardness of the prayer is not measured by its momentary impetuosity, but by its persistence.[4] The more insignificant, on the other hand, anything is, the more difficult it is to bring the God-idea into relation with it; and yet it is precisely here that we have the

[3] "Not so!"

[4] Cf. Judge William's argument in *Either/Or: supra.* pp. 88–91.

touchstone of the God-relationship. In making a great decision, in the publication of a work which will presumably transform the world, in time of earthquakes, at golden-wedding festivities, in perils of the sea, and in connection with a clandestine birth, the name of God is perhaps used quite as often by way of ejaculation as religiously. One must not, therefore, let oneself be deceived by the fact that a clergyman ignores the petty events of life, concentrating his eloquence and gesticulation on great scenes; and then at most, half-abashed and as tribute to decency, adds at the close of the discourse that one should also show in daily life the same faith, the same hope, and the same courage; instead of planning his discourse conversely, as befits religious discourse, namely, with reference to the small events, the ordinary humdrum activities of life, and then at most adding a few words of warning against the illusion which may so easily be the foundation of that religiosity which manifests itself only on special days, for this is aestheticism, and aesthetically the invocation of God is neither more nor less than the loudest of ejaculations: God's manifestation of himself in great events is a theatrical tableau.

We left the religious individual in the crisis of his sickness, but this sickness is not unto death. We shall now permit him to be strengthened by precisely the same concept that annihilated him, the conception of God. I use again a foreshortened perspective, because the chief interest of my task has not yet begun; and I do not dwell upon how the ethical (which is always somewhat distant from the absolute God-relationship) must enter in regulatively and take command. Nevertheless, I shall ask the reader to pause at this point for one or two remarks. First and foremost, that in each generation there are doubtless not many who even get so far as to exhaust the suffering connected with the beginning of the absolute God-relationship; and next, that a beginning in the medium of existence is far from being something that is decided once for all; for it is only on paper that one finishes the first state, and then has nothing further to do with it. The absolute decision in the medium of existence is and remains merely an approximation, though this must not be understood comparatively, in relation to the more or less of others, for then the individual will have lost his ideality. This is because the eternal aims from above at the existing individual, who by existing is in process of movement, and thus at the moment when the eternal strikes he is already a little moment away. The beginning of an absolute decision in the medium of existence is the last thing in the world that can be characterized, once for all, as something left behind; for the existing individual is not an abstract X, who passes through something and then goes on further, if I may so express myself, undigested through life. The existing individual becomes concrete in his experience, and in going on he still has his experience with him, and hence may at any moment lose it; he has it with him not as something one has in a pocket, but his having it constitutes a definite something by which he is himself specifically determined, so that by losing it he loses his own specific determination. As a consequence of having made a decision in existence, the existing individual has attained a more specific determination of what he is; if he lays it aside, then it is not he who has lost something; he does not have himself while happening to have lost something, but he has lost himself and must now begin from the beginning.

The religious individual has thus got over his illness, though tomorrow perhaps it may return as a result of a little carelessness. He strengthens himself perhaps by means of the edifying consideration that God who made man must Himself know best all the many things that may seem impossible to bring into connection with the thought of God, all this earthly distress, all the confusion in which he may be involved, and the necessity of diversion, of rest, as well as of the night's sleep.

It follows of itself that we do not here have reference to that indulgence which is proclaimed in the world, where one man comforts himself by appealing to another, where men console themselves mutually and leave God out of account. Every human being is gloriously constituted, but what ruins so many is, among other things, also this wretched tittle-tattle between man and man about that which should be suffered and matured in silence, this confession before men instead of before God, this hearty communication between this man and that about what ought to be secret and exist only before God in secrecy, this impatient craving for intermediary consolation. No, in suffering the pain of his annihilation, the religious individual has learned that human indulgence profits nothing, and therefore refuses to listen to anything from that side; but he exists before God and exhausts the suffering of being human and at the same time existing before God. Therefore it cannot comfort him to know what the human crowd knows, man with man, what men know who have a shopkeeper's notion of what it means to be a man, and a facile gossipy notion at seventeenth hand of what it means to exist before God. From God he must derive his consolation, lest his entire religiosity be reduced to a rumor. That is not to say that he is to discover new truths, etc.; no, he is merely to keep a watch over himself lest the craving for gossip and the lust for preaching should prevent him from experiencing what thousands upon thousands have experienced before him. If it be true even of love, that only then does a love experience become ennobling when it teaches a man to keep his feeling within himself, how much more is this true about the religious! ...

But one ingredient in the lowliness of a human being is that he is temporal, and cannot endure to lead uninterruptedly the life of the eternal in time. And if his life is in time, then it is *eo ipso* piecemeal; and if it is piecemeal, it is mingled with distractions; and in the diversion the human being is absent from his God-relationship, or present in it, yet not as in the strong moment.

Men say it is a hardship when lovers are separated; should not then such separation be a heavy thing for the religious individual to bear, and is it less heavy because it is a diversion rather than a toilsome task that separates them, when the necessity for diversion is precisely the most unequivocal indication of his lowliness? For our religious individual is not so situated that the clergyman needs to admonish him to seek God; rather he is so strongly stirred that there must be diversion for him if he is not to perish. Here is the place where the monastic movement becomes tempting. Would it not become possible through superhuman exertion to approach nearer to God, to preserve the relationship without interruption, without sleep if possible! We say in another connection that love has power to make the lovers equal.[5] Aye, and this is quite true with reference to a love-relationship between two human beings, because they stand essentially on the same level, and the differences between them are accidental. Between God and man, however, there exists an absolute difference, and hence this direct equality is a presumptuous and dizzy thought, though this constitutes no comparative human indulgence from the utmost exertion. But since there is this absolute difference between God and man, how does the principle of equality in love express itself? By means of the absolute difference. And what is the form of this absolute difference? Humility. What sort of humility? The humility that frankly admits its human lowliness with humble cheerfulness before God, trusting that God knows all this better than man himself. The monastic movement is an attempt to be superhuman, an enthusiastic, perhaps even a devout attempt to resemble God. But herein lies the profound suffering of true religiosity, the deep-

<hr>

[5] See the *Fragments: supra*, pp. 165–170.

est thinkable, namely to stand related to God in an absolutely decisive manner, and to be unable to find any decisive external expression for this (for a happy love between human beings expresses itself externally in the union of the lovers). This inability is rooted in the necessary relativity of the most decisive external expression, in its being both too much and too little; it is too much because it involves a certain presumptuousness over against other men, and it is too little because it is after all a worldly expression.

There are thus two ways disclosed to deliberation: the way of humble diversion and the way of desperate exertion, the way to the Deer Park and the way to the cloister. To the Deer Park? Oh, yes, let me mention only this, though I might just as well name much else that comes under the same classification. A fool will doubtless laugh at this thought, and a priggish religious individual will feel offended, and both will serve as proof that the thought has its validity. But why mention such a thing as an outing in the Deer Park? It is much more elegant to talk on Sunday in very indeterminate and vague Sunday-decorous expressions about these innocent pleasures—and then on week-days to talk about them in commonplace terms. Of course it is more elegant, and I can suspect the degree of embitterment which will be aroused in the breast of a fastidious man by the very word 'Deer Park' in this connection; because in this connection it serves perhaps as an indirect reminder of the sense in which the religiosity of our time is more advanced than the medieval, and because it is unpleasant to have the religious by means of such a word brought so near home, instead of glimpsing it from afar, as when saying *nothing, everything, always, never, daily watchfulness.*

Our religious individual chooses the way to the Deer Park, and why? Because he does not dare to choose the way to the cloister. And why does he not dare? Because it is too high-flown. So then he takes the outing. "But he does not enjoy himself," someone will say. Oh yes, he certainly does. And why does he enjoy himself? Because it is the humblest expression for his God-relationship to admit his humanity, and because it is human to enjoy oneself. If a woman can succeed in wholly transforming herself merely that she may please her husband, why should not the religious individual in his relation to God succeed in enjoying himself, when this is the humblest expression for the God-relationship? ...

Up to this point I have kept my exposition still somewhat abstract, and shall now refer to my problem as if it were an occurrence of today, for today is Wednesday in the Deer Park season, and our religious individual is to take a pleasure outing, while I experimentally observe his psychological condition. It is easy enough to talk about it, to do it is something else. And yet, in a certain sense talking about it may not be quite so easy; I understand very well the risk I take, that I risk the loss of my little bit of reputation as an author, since everyone will find it extremely tiresome. It is still the same Wednesday in the Deer Park season, the whole thing is about taking an outing there, and yet so many pages have already been filled that a novelist would have had space to recount the highly interesting events of ten years, with great scenes and tense situations and assignations and clandestine childbirths; aye, so many pages have been used that half of them would have been enough for a clergyman to have finished up both time and eternity and death and the resurrection, *all* and *always* and *never* and *nothing,* and that in such a manner that one would have enough from one such sermon for the whole of life.

It is, accordingly, a Wednesday in the Deer Park season. The religious individual has understood himself in the general consideration of the significance of necessary diversion, but it does not by any means follow that diversion is necessary precisely today. Here lies the difficulty of the process of concretion, which remains as long as the religious individual is in the medium of existence, when he has to bring the general principle into connection with this particular moment on this particular day, with these particular moods and states of mind, and under these particular circumstances. When life is understood in this manner, the vain quantitative differences between human beings vanish, for the "how" of a man's inwardness determines the significance, not the quantitative "what."

Our religious individual happens to be an independent and well-to-do man who keeps a carriage and horses, and has in so far both time and means at his disposal for an outing in the Deer Park every day if he so desires. In this manner our experiment shapes up most effectively, for, as was said above, the religious address ought to be sufficiently ironical to make men more than usually fortunate in external circumstances, merely in order that the religious may thus more clearly show itself. A man who has only one Wednesday free during the park season has perhaps not so many difficulties in getting away. But this ease, and the difficulty that he cannot get away on the other days, also makes it possible that the religious factor does not become the determinant in his motivation. It is with this as it is with seriousness. Many a man believes himself to be serious because he has a wife and children and burden-some engagements. But it does not follow from this that he has religious seriousness; his seriousness might also be moroseness and surliness. When religious seriousness is to be depicted, it therefore shows itself best in outwardly privileged circumstances, for here it cannot so easily be confused with something else.

Our individual will then first make sure that it is not a momentary craving, a whim of his immediacy, that determines him; he wishes to be conscious of the fact that he actually needs the diversion, and trusts that God doubtless also knows it. This is not the impudent self-assur-ance of an "awakened" individual [6] over against God, as in general such an aesthetic coxcomb may be recognized by the fact that he has once for all secured his letter of credit from God. But though he is conscious of this, and that his search for diversion is not the craving of his immediacy, since he would more than gladly do without, nevertheless his concern of mind about this will arouse distrust of himself, the thought that perhaps he might be able to do without it a little longer. But on this point also he is conscious that as long ago as last Sunday he felt this need of diversion without giving way to the impulse, in order to prove from which side the impulse came; for he is convinced that God will not leave him in the lurch but help him to find the right, where the boundary between what is indolence and that which is due to finite limitations is so difficult to find. But at the same moment when, concerned, he would if possible dispense with the diversion so as to stick it out another day, almost at the same moment there awakes in him the human irritability which keenly feels the sting of being so dependent, of so constantly having to understand that a man can do nothing of himself. And this irritability is defiant and impatient; it is almost ready to enter into a dubious conspiracy with the concern, for the concern would relinquish the distraction from enthusiasm but the defiance from pride. And this irritability is sophistical; it tries to make him think that the God-relationship is vitiated when it is applied to such insignificant matters, and that it reveals itself in its truth only in the greater crises. And this irritability is proud; for although the religious individual has more than once convinced himself that yielding to the need for diversion is the humblest expression for the God-relation-ship, it is always seductive to understand what is perhaps not to be done in the same moment, seductive to understand something in the strong

---

[6] The followers of Grandtvig, the "Danish Carlyle," were often the object of S.K.'s satire—as was Grandtvig himself. (L)

moment of enthusiasm when the work prospers under his hands, seductive in comparison with understanding it precisely when it is to be done in connection with a definite particularity.

But this *Anfechtung* [7] vanishes again, for the religious individual is silent, and whoever is silent before God doubtless learns to yield, but also learns that this is blessed. Had our religious individual had a gossipy friend at hand he would have reached the Deer Park easily enough, for it is a small matter when one has a carriage and horses and sufficient means, and is talkative—but in that case he would not have been our religious individual, and our religious individual also reaches the Deer Park. Now then, the resolution is made to seek diversion, and in the same moment the task is altered. If little by little the thought steals into his soul that it was a mistake, then he takes refuge in an ethical principle to defend himself against it; for over against a resolution taken after conscientious deliberation, a fugitive thought must not be permitted to play the role of master. He disarms this thought ethically, in order not again to be driven back into the highest relationship, whereby the significance of the diversion resolved upon would be nullified. Thus the movement of the mind is not here, as when the clergyman preaches, in a direction toward the God-relationship; but the God-relationship itself bids the religious individual to withdraw from it temporarily; it is, as it were, an agreement entered into between God's solicitude and man's self-defense. The ethical principle in question is quite simply this, that if a mistake has to be made, it is worse to become a fickle-minded waverer than resolutely to carry out what has been decided upon; for a habit of vacillation is the absolute ruin of every spiritual relationship.

We all await some great event, in order that we may have occasion to show in action what brave fellows we are; and when a crown prince takes up the reins of government in the mightiest European kingdom, taking over the responsibility for the destinies of millions, then there is occasion to conceive a resolution and to act *sensu eminenti*. Undeniably! But this is the profundity, and also the ironical feature of existence, that it is fully as possible to act *sensu eminenti* when the actor is an absolutely common man, and the enterprise is to take an outing in the Deer Park. For the highest thing that His imperial Highness can do is to make a resolution before God. The accent lies on this: before God; the many millions are only an illusion. But even the humblest man can conceive a resolution before God, and a man who is really so religious that he is able before God to resolve to take an outing

[7] Temptation.

in the Deer Park need not be put to shame when standing by the side of any imperial highness.

So much for the religious suffering, which is a dying away from immediacy; let this be sufficient. I myself feel most keenly how poor a showing it makes to prosecute inquiries in regard to such an everyday affair, one that everybody down to the simplest servant-girl and soldier-boy is completely familiar with; how imprudent it is to admit the presence of difficulties, thus betraying one's inability to raise oneself even a little above the intellectual horizon of the lower classes; how near at hand is the satire, that after having devoted one's time and industry over a series of years one realizes in the end no further advance than is involved in arriving at what the most stupid human being knows—alas, instead of in the same period of time and with the same industry, perhaps to have been able to produce something about China, Persia,[8] or even astronomy. There are perhaps not ten people who have the patience to read what I have expounded above, and scarcely one man in the kingdom who would take the trouble to compose anything like it; which last, however, in one way consoles me, for if everybody can do it, if the work is mere routine, contract-writing by the sheet, then it becomes precisely my merit to have done what all can do (this is the humiliating feature of it for the weak human heart), but which no one else cares to do. Well, then, no one cares to expound it—but existentially to express it, to do it? To be sure, there is one advantage that action has over description, namely, that what needs a long time to relate may be done so quickly—if one can. But before the individual has acquired this skill, what about the trouble involved in learning? Well, I merely say that I cannot do it; but since the secret consists precisely in the hidden inwardness of religiosity, it is possible that they can all do it—at least there is no one who notices anything in their manner or behavior.

If, on the other hand, someone shrinks back in fear from facing the tremendous strenuousity of living in this manner (and how strenuous it is I can perceive sufficiently from the fact that even I who merely sit and experiment with it, and thus essentially keep myself outside, feel the strenuousness of this labor), well, I do not say anything to contradict him, though I admire the enterprise of inwardness which religiosity has embarked upon, admire it as the greatest of miraculous actions, but also frankly admit that I should not succeed in doing it: in passing from and with the highest conception of God and an eternal happiness to

[8] Cf. footnote, p. 210.

arrive at enjoying myself in the Deer Park. Miraculous it is, so I consider it; and I do not talk about it for the sake of making life still more troublesome for poor people, if it was my business to do so, far from it, since it is already troublesome enough for them; or for the sake of vexing any human being by making life more difficult for him, insofar as it is already sufficiently difficult, God forbid! On the contrary, I hope to render a service to the cultured classes, either by eulogizing the secret inwardness of their religiosity (for the point is that no one should notice anything, and there is no one who does) or else by making the matter, if possible, so difficult that it could meet their requirements, since in their going further they have left so many difficulties behind. For if anyone shrinks back in fear from facing the tremendous exertion involved in living thus, I find it still more fearful that there are those who even go further and, moreover, go further by passing over to speculative philosophy and world-history—that I find more fearful still. Yet what am I saying—everything that has the characteristic of going further is known by its being *not only this, but also* something more; that, then, is something I find more fearful still and also something more: fearfully stupid.

CONCLUSION: WHAT IT IS TO BECOME A CHRISTIAN

OBJECTIVELY, becoming or being a Christian is defined as follows:

1. A Christian is one who accepts the doctrine of Christianity. But if it is the *what* of this doctrine which in the last resort decides whether one is a Christian, attention is instantly turned outward, with the intent of learning down to the last detail what then the doctrine of Christianity is, because this 'what' is to decide, not merely what Christianity is, but whether I am a Christian. That same instant begins the erudite, the anxious, the timorous contradictory effort of approximation. Approximation may be protracted indefinitely, and with that the decision whereby one becomes a Christian is relegated to oblivion.

This incongruity has been remedied by the assumption that everyone in Christendom is a Christian, that we are all of us what one in a way calls Christians. With this assumption things go better with the objective theories. We are all Christians. The Bible-theory has now to investigate quite objectively what Christianity is (and yet we are in fact Christians, and the objective information is assumed to make us Christians, the objective information which we who are Christians shall now for the first time learn to know—for if we are not Christians, the road here taken will never lead us to become such). The Church theory assumes that we are Christians, but now we have to be assured in a purely objective way what Christianity is, in order that we may defend ourselves against the Turk and the Russian and the Roman yoke, and gallantly fight out the battle of Christianity so that we may make our age, as it were, a bridge to the peerless future which already is glimpsed. This is sheer aesthetics. Christianity is an existence-communication, the task is to become a Christian and continue to be one, and the most dangerous of all illusions is to be so sure of being one that one has to defend the whole of Christendom against the Turk—instead of being alert to defend our own faith against the illusion about the Turk.

2. One says, No, not every acceptance of the Christian doctrine makes one a Christian; what it principally depends upon is appropriation, that one appropriates and holds fast this doctrine quite differently from anything else, that one is ready to live in it and to die in it, to venture one's life for it, etc.

This seems as if it were something. However, the category "quite differently" is a mediocre category, and the whole formula, which makes an attempt to define more subjectively what it is to be a Christian, is neither one thing nor the other; in a way it avoids the difficulty involved in the distraction and deceit of approximation, but it lacks categorical definition. The pathos of approximation which is talked of here is that of immanence; one can just as well say that an enthusiastic lover is so related to his love: he holds fast to it and appropriates it quite differently from anything else, he is ready to live in it and die in it, he will venture everything for it. To this extent there is no difference between a lover and a Christian with respect to inwardness, and one must again recur to the *what,* which is the doctrine—and with that we again come under No. *1.*

The pathos of appropriation needs to be so defined that it cannot be confused with any other pathos. The more subjective interpretation is right in insisting that it is appropriation which decides the matter, but it is wrong in its definition of appropriation, which does not distinguish if from every other immediate pathos.

Neither is this distinction made when one defines appropriation as faith, but at once imparts to faith headway and direction toward reaching an understanding, so that faith becomes a provisional function whereby one holds what essentially is to be an object for understanding, a provisional function wherewith poor people and stupid men have to be content, whereas *Privatdocents* and clever heads go further. The mark of being a Christian (i.e. faith) is appropriated, but in such a way that it is not specifically different from other intellectual appropriation where a preliminary assumption serves as a provisional function looking forward to understanding. Faith is not in this case the specific mark of the relationship to Christianity, and again it will be the *what* of faith which decides whether one is a Christian or not. But therewith the thing is again brought back under No. *1*.

That is to say, the appropriation by which a Christian is a Christian must be so specific that it cannot be confused with anything else.

3. One defines the thing of becoming and being a Christian, not objectively by the *what* of the doctrine, nor subjectively by appropriation, not by what has gone on in the individual, but by what the individual has undergone: that he was baptized. Though one adjoins to baptism the assumption of a confession of faith, nothing decisive will be gained, but the definition will waver between accentuating the *what* (the path of approximation) and talking indefinitely about acceptance and acceptance and appropriation, etc., without any specific determination.

If being baptized is to be the definition, attention will instantly turn outward toward the reflection, whether I have really been baptized. Then begins the approximation with respect to a historical fact.

If, on the other hand, one were to say that he did indeed receive the Spirit in baptism and by the witness it bears together with his spirit, he knows that he was baptized—then the inference is inverted, he argues from the witness of the Spirit within him to the fact that he was baptized, not from the fact of being baptized to the possession of the Spirit. But if the inference is to be drawn in this way, baptism is quite rightly not regarded as the mark of the Christian, but inwardness is, and so here in turn there is needed a specific definition of inwardness and appropriation whereby the witness of the Spirit in the individual is distinguished from all other (universally defined) activity of spirit in man.

It is noteworthy moreover that the orthodoxy which especially has made baptism the decisive mark is continually complaining that among the baptized there are so few Christians, that almost all, except for an immortal little band, are spiritless baptized pagans—which seems to indicate that baptism cannot be the decisive factor with respect to becoming a Christian, not even according to the latter view of those who in the first form insist upon it as decisive with respect to becoming a Christian.

Subjectively, what it is to become a Christian is defined thus:

The decision lies in the subject. The appropriation is the paradoxical inwardness which is specifically different from all other inwardness. The thing of being a Christian is not determined by the *what* of Christianity but by the *how* of the Christian. This *how* can only correspond with one thing, the absolute paradox. There is therefore no vague talk to the effect that being a Christian is to accept, and to accept, and to accept quite differently, to appropriate, to believe, to appropriate by faith quite differently (all of them purely rhetorical and fictitious definitions); but *to believe* is specifically different from all other appropriation and inwardness. *Faith is the objective uncertainty along with the repulsion of the absurd held fast in the passion of inwardness, which precisely is inwardness potentiated to the highest degree.* This formula fits only the believer, no one else, not a lover, not an enthusiast, not a thinker, but simply and solely the believer who is related to the absolute paradox.

Faith therefore cannot be any sort of provisional function. He who, from the vantage point of a higher knowledge, would know his faith as a factor resolved in a higher idea has *eo ipso* ceased to believe. Faith *must* not *rest content* with unintelligibility; for precisely the relation to or the repulsion from the unintelligible, the absurd, is the expression for the passion of faith.

This definition of what it is to be a Christian prevents the erudite or anxious deliberation of approximation from enticing the individual into byways, so that he becomes erudite instead of becoming a Christian, and in most cases a smatterer instead of becoming a Christian; for the decision lies in the subject. But inwardness has again found its specific mark whereby it is differentiated from all other inwardness and is not disposed of by the chatty category "quite differently," which fits the case of every passion at the moment of passion.

The psychologist generally regards it as a sure sign that a man is beginning to give up a passion when he wishes to treat the object of it objectively. Passion and reflection are generally exclusive of one another. Becoming objective in this way is always retrogression, for passion is man's perdition, but it is his exaltation as well. In case dialectic and reflection are not used to intensify passion, it is a retrogression to become objective; and even he who is lost through passion has not lost so much as he who lost passion, for the former had the possibility.

Thus it is that people in our age have wanted to become objective with relation to Christianity; the passion by which every man is a

Christian has become too small a thing for them, and by becoming objective we all of us have the prospect of becoming a *Privatdocent....*

Because people in our age and in the Christendom of our time do not appear to be sufficiently aware of the dialectic of inward appropriation, or of the fact that the "how" of the individual is an expression just as precise and more decisive for what he has than is the "what" to which he appeals—for this very reason there crop up the strangest and (if one is in the humor and has time for it) the most laughable confusions, more comic than even the confusions of paganism, because in them there was not so much at stake, and because the contradictions were not so strident. . . .

An orthodox champion fights in defense of Christianity with the most frightful passion, he protests with the sweat of his brow and with the most concerned demeanor that he accepts Christianity pure and simple, that he will live and die in it—and he forgets that such acceptance is an all too general expression for the relation to Christianity. He does everything in Jesus' name and uses Christ's name on every occasion as a sure sign that he is a Christian and is called to fight in defense of Christendom in our age—and he has no inkling of the little ironical secret that a man, merely by describing the "how" of his inwardness, can show indirectly that he is a Christian without mentioning God's name.[1] A man becomes converted New Year's Eve precisely at six o'clock. With that he is fully prepared. Fantastically decked out with the fact of conversion, he now must run out and proclaim Christianity—in a Christian land. Well, of course, even though we are all baptized, every man may well need to become a Christian in another sense. But here is the distinction: there is no lack of information in a Christian land, something else is lacking, and this is a something which the one man cannot directly communicate to the other. And in such fantastic categories would a converted man work for Christianity; and yet he proves (just in proportion as he is the more busy in spreading and spreading) that he himself is not a Christian. For to be a Christian is something so

[1] In relation to love (by which I would illustrate again the same thing) it does not hold good in the same sense that a man merely by defining his "how" indicates what or whom it is he loves. All lovers have the "how" of love in common, the particular person must supply the name of his beloved. But with respect to believing (*sensu strictissimo*) it holds good that this "how" is appropriate only to one as its object. If anybody would say, "Yes, but then one can also learn the 'how' of faith by rote and patter"; to this one must reply that it cannot be done, for he who declares it directly contradicts himself, because the content of the assertion must constantly be reduplicated in the form of expression, and the isolation contained in the definition must reduplicate itself in the form. (K)

deeply reflected that it does not admit of the aesthetical dialectic which allows one man to be for others something he is not for himself. On the other hand, a scoffer attacks Christianity and at the same time expounds it so reliably that it is a pleasure to read him, and one who is in perplexity about finding it distinctly set forth may almost have recourse to him.[2]

All ironical observations depend upon paying attention to the "how," whereas the gentleman with whom the ironist has the honor to converse is attentive only to the "what." A man protests loudly and solemnly, "This is my opinion." However, he does not confine himself to delivering this formula verbatim, he explains himself further, he ventures to vary the expressions. Yes, for it is not so easy to vary as one thinks it is. More than one student would have got *laudabilis* for style if he had not varied his expressions, and a great multitude of men possess the talent which Socrates so much admired in Polos: they never say the same thing—about the same. The ironist then is on the watch, he of course is not looking out for what is printed in large letters or for that which by the speaker's diction betrays itself as a formula (our gentleman's "what"), but he is looking out for a little subordinate clause which escapes the gentleman's haughty attention, a little beckoning predicate, etc., and now he beholds with astonishment (glad of the variation—*in variatione voluptas*) that the gentleman *has not* that opinion—not that he is a hypocrite, God forbid! that is too serious a matter for an ironist—but that the good man has concentrated his force in bawling it out instead of possessing it within him. To that extent the gentleman may be right in asserting that he has that opinion which with all his vital force he persuades himself he has, he may do everything for it in the quality of talebearer, he may risk his life for it, in very much troubled times he may carry the thing so far as to lose his life for this opinion—with that, how the deuce can I doubt that the man had this opinion; and yet there may have been living contemporaneously with him an ironist who, even in the hour when the unfortunate gentleman is executed, cannot resist laughing, because he knows by the circumstantial evidence he has gathered that the man had never been clear about the thing himself. Laughable it is, nor is it disheartening that such a thing can occur; for he who with quiet introspection is honest before God and concerned for himself, the Deity saves from being in error, though he be never so simple; him the Deity leads by

[2] S.K. may have been thinking of Feuerbach; we can hardly help thinking of Nietzsche.

the suffering of inwardness to the truth. But meddlesomeness and noise are signs of error, signs of an abnormal condition, like wind in the stomach, and this thing of stumbling by chance upon getting executed in a tumultuous turn of affairs is not the sort of suffering which essentially characterizes inwardness.

It is said to have chanced in England that a man was attacked on the highway by a robber who had made himself unrecognizable by wearing a big wig. He falls upon the traveler, seizes him by the throat and shouts, "Your purse!" He gets the purse and keeps it, but the wig he throws away. A poor man comes along the same road, puts it on and arrives at the next town where the traveler had already denounced the crime, he is arrested, is recognized by the traveler, who takes his oath that he is the man. By chance, the robber is present in the court-room, sees the misunderstanding, turns to the judge and says, "It seems to me that the traveler has regard rather to the wig than to the man," and he asks permission to make a trial. He puts on the wig, seizes the traveler by the throat, crying, "Your purse!"—and the traveler recognizes the robber and offers to swear to it—the only trouble is that already he has taken an oath.

So it is, in one way or another, with every man who has a "what" and is not attentive to the "how": he swears, he takes his oath, he runs errands, he ventures life and blood, he is executed—all on account of the wig.

THE PRESENT AGE: A LITERARY REVIEW

BY S. KIERKEGAARD (1846)

TRANSLATED BY ALEXANDER DRU

After the individual has given up every effort to find himself outside himself in existence, in relation to his surroundings, and when after that shipwreck he turns toward the highest things, the absolute, coming after such emptiness, bursts upon him not only in all its fullness, but in the responsibility which he feels.

Had I to carve an inscription on my grave I would ask for none other than "the individual."—THE JOURNALS

SHORTLY after the appearance of the *Postscript,* Kierkegaard published a very lengthy review of a now forgotten novel, *The Two Ages.* The novel, like many a preacher's text, was little more than a peg on which S.K. proceeded to hang his own ideas about the essential difference between "antiquity" and the modern era. By the latter S.K. means primarily his own century, in which he say the "leveling" tendency and the rule of "the public" as predominant; in contrast to a society dominated by *individuals* (those who precisely are *not* "like everybody else"). In the passage here presented, however, he makes a threefold division: antiquity, dominated by the principle of *leadership;* Christendom, of which the ruling idea is *representation;* and the present age, which "tends towards *equality.*"

It can hardly be maintained that Kierkegaard's sympathies were democratic. Unlike Thomas Mann, he remained an "unpolitical man" to the end of his life, in the sense that the value of individuality was for him supreme and could neither be enhanced, nor on the other hand impaired, by any change of social organization. Thus in the important conclusion to his article he makes it clear that "the development" (toward numerical equality) "is, in spite of everything, a progress"; not, however, for the reason the social up-lifters consider it such, but on the contrary because it renders the plight of the individual more desperate. When the leveling process is completed, "then the time has come for work to begin, for every individual must work for himself, each for himself. No longer can the individual, as in former times, turn to the great for help when he grows confused. That is past; he is either lost in the dizziness of unending abstraction, or saved forever in the reality of religion."

The chief organ of the public is the *press,* which by its very nature appeals to humanity's lowest common denominator. (Cf. p. 265.) At the time of writing *The Present Age* Kierkegaard's judgment of the Press was not the most objective imaginable, for the impudent *Corsair* had just launched against him its campaign of ridicule. Cartoons played up S.K.'s physical peculiarities and idiosyncrasies, which were many. Everybody in Copenhagen read the *Corsair,* and S.K. became a household word; small boys hooted at him and followed him in the streets, when he tried to take his beloved walks. The "common people," whom S.K. (like many other professing aristocrats) sincerely loved and with whom he had been accustomed to mingle freely, were alienated from him and began treating him as an amiable lunatic. In view of all this, some of his priceless remarks about journalism (See pp. 430–431) become all the more understandable; but his attitude toward both Press and Public antedates the *Corsair* episode and was only strengthened thereby.

The relation between Kierkegaard and latter day chroniclers of social decay such as Oswald Spengler, Ortega y Gasset, and Denis de Rougemont cannot be discussed here; but unquestionably he was one of the first to call attention to the concrete danger of newspapers—and to foreshadow many other points of modern social diagnosis. What is not quite so clear, from the passage here reproduced, is the deeper psychological setting of S.K.'s ideas.

"Our age is essentially one of understanding and *reflection*, without passion, momentarily bursting into enthusiasm and shrewdly relapsing into repose." By "reflection" Kierkegaard means not the exercise of our intellectual faculties as such, but rather the tendency to feel one's reality as "reflected" in something external to oneself—and specifically not in another person (this would be love or religion), but in some collective organization. It is important to bear this in mind, for "reflection" is the principal category of *The Present Age,* just as—with the ambivalence typical of all Kierkegaard's categories—it was also the salient mark of his own attitude and personality.

THE INDIVIDUAL AND
"THE PUBLIC"

THE dialectic of antiquity tended towards *leadership* (the great individual and the masses—the free man and the slaves); so far the dialectic of Christendom tends toward *representation* (the majority sees itself in its representative and is set free by the consciousness that it is the majority which is represented, in a sort of self-consciousness); the dialectic of the present age tends toward *equality,* and its most logical —though mistaken—fulfillment is leveling, as the negative relationship of the particular units to one another.

It must be obvious to everyone that the profound significance of the leveling process lies in the fact that it means the predominance of the category "generation" over the category "individuality." In antiquity the total number of the individuals was there to express, as it were, the value of the outstanding individual. . . . The individual in the masses had no importance whatsoever; the outstanding individual signified them all. The present age tends toward a mathematical equality in which it takes so and so many to make one individual. Formerly the outstanding individual could allow himself everything and the individual in the masses nothing at all. Now everyone knows that so and so many make an individual, and quite consistently people add themselves together (it is called joining together, but that is only a polite euphemism) for the most trivial purposes. Simply in order to put a passing whim into practice a few people add themselves together, and the thing is done—then they dare do it. For that reason not even a pre-eminently gifted man can free himself from reflection,[1] because he very soon becomes conscious of himself as a fractional part in some quite

[1] I.e. from viewing himself as *reflected* in a collective entity of some sort.

trivial matter, and so fails to achieve the infinite freedom of religion.

The fact that several people united together have the courage to meet death does not nowadays mean that each, individually, has the courage, for even more than death the individual fears the judgment and protest of reflection upon his wishing to risk something on his own. The individual no longer belongs to God, to himself, to his beloved, to his art or to his science; he is conscious of belonging in all things to an abstraction to which he is subjected by reflection, just as a serf belongs to an estate. That is why people band together in cases where it is an absolute contradiction to be more than one. The apotheosis of the positive principle of association is nowadays the devouring and demoralizing principle which in the slavery of reflection makes even virtues into *vitia splendida*. There is no other reason for this than that eternal responsibility and the religious singling out of the individual before God is ignored. When corruption sets in at that point, people seek consolation in company, and so reflection catches the individual for life. And those who do not realize even the beginning of this crisis are engulfed without further ado in the reflective relationship.

The leveling process is not the action of an individual, but the work of reflection in the hands of an abstract power. It is therefore possible to calculate the law governing it in the same way that one calculates the diagonal in a parallelogram of forces. The individual who levels down is himself engulfed in the process, . . . and while he seems to know selfishly what he is doing, one can only say of people *en masse* that they know not what they do; for just as collective enthusiasm produces a surplus which does not come from the individual, there is also a surplus in this case. A demon is called up over whom no individual has any power, and though the very abstraction of leveling gives the individual a momentary, selfish kind of enjoyment, he is at the same time signing the warrant for his own doom. Enthusiasm *may* end in disaster, but leveling is *eo ipso* the destruction of the individual. No age, and therefore not the present age, can bring the skepticism of that process to a stop, for as soon as it tries to stop it, the law of the leveling process is again called into action. It can therefore only be stopped by the individual's attaining the religious courage which springs from his individual religious isolation.

I was once the witness of a street fight in which three men most shamefully set upon a fourth. The crowd stood and watched them with indignation; expressions of disgust began to enliven the scene; then several of the onlookers set on one of the three assailants and knocked him down and beat him. The avengers had, in fact, applied precisely the same rules as the offenders. . . . I went up to one of the avengers and tried by argument to explain to him how illogical his behavior was; but it seemed quite impossible for him to discuss the question: he could only repeat that such a rascal richly deserved to have three people against him. The humor of the situation would have been even more apparent to someone who had not seen the beginning of the brawl and so simply heard one man saying of another (who was alone) that he was three against one, and heard the remark just when the very reverse was the case—when they were three to one against him. In the first place it was humorous because of the contradiction which it involved, as when the policeman told a man standing in the street "to kindly disperse." Secondly it had all the humor of self-contradiction. But what I learned from it was that I had better give up all hope of putting a stop to that skepticism, lest it should turn upon me.

No single individual (I mean no outstanding individual—in the sense of leadership and conceived according to the dialectical category "fate") will be able to arrest the abstract process of leveling, for it is negatively something higher, and the age of chivalry is gone. No society or association can arrest that abstract power, simply because an association is itself in the service of the leveling process. Not even the individuality of the different nationalities can arrest it, for on a higher plane the abstract process of leveling is a negative representation of *humanity pure and unalloyed*. The abstract leveling process, that self-combustion of the human race, produced by the friction which arises when the individual ceases to exist as singled out by religion, is bound to continue, like a trade wind, and consume everything. But through it each individual for himself may receive once more a religious education and, in the highest sense, be helped by the *examen rigorosum* of the leveling process to an essentially religious attitude. For the younger men who, however strongly they personally may cling to what they admire as eminent, realize from the beginning that the leveling process is evil in both the selfish individual and in the selfish generation, but that it can also, if they desire it honestly and before God, become the starting-point for the highest life—for them it will indeed be an education to live in the age of leveling. Their age will, in the very highest sense, develop them religiously and at the same time educate them aesthetically and intellectually, because in this way the comic will receive its absolute expression. The highest form of the comic arises precisely when the individual comes directly under the infinite abstraction of "pure humanity," without any of those intermediary qualifications which temper the humor of man's position and strengthen its pathos, without any of the concrete particulars of organization which the leveling process destroys. But that again is only another expression of the fact that man's only salvation lies in the reality of religion for each individual.

And it will add fuel to their enthusiasm to understand that it is in fact through error that the individual is given access to the highest, if he courageously desires it. But the leveling process will have to continue and must be completed, just as scandal had to come into the world, though woe to them by whom it comes.

It has often been said that a reformation should begin with each man reforming himself. That, however, is not what actually happened, for the Reformation produced a hero who paid God high enough for his position as hero. By joining up with him directly people buy cheap, indeed at bargain prices, what he had paid for so dearly; but they do not buy the highest of all things. The abstract principle of leveling, on the contrary, like the biting east wind, has no personal relation to any individual, but has only an abstract relationship which is the same for everyone. There no hero suffers for others, or helps them; the task-master of all alike is the leveling process, which itself takes on their education. And the man who learns most from the leveling and himself becomes greatest does not become an outstanding man or a hero— that would only impede the leveling process, which is rigidly consistent to the end; he himself prevents that from happening because he has understood the meaning of leveling: he becomes a man and nothing else, in the complete equalitarian sense. That is the idea of religion. But, under those conditions, the equalitarian order is severe and the profit is seemingly very small; seemingly, for unless the individual learns in the reality of religion and before God to be content with himself, and learns, instead of dominating others, to dominate himself, content as priest to be his own audience, and as author his own reader— if he will not learn to be satisfied with that as the highest, because it is the expression of the equality of all men before God and of our likeness to others, then he will not escape from reflection. It may be that for one deceptive moment it will seem to him, in relation to his gifts, as though he were leveling, but in the end he will sink down beneath the leveling process. There is no good calling upon a Holger Danske or a Martin Luther; their day is over, and at bottom it is only the individual's laziness which makes a man long to have them back, a worldly impatience which prefers to buy something cheap, second-hand, rather than to buy the highest of all things very dear and first-hand. It is worse than useless to found society after society, because negatively speaking there is something above them, even though the short-sighted member of the society cannot see it.

The principle of individuality in its *immediate* and beautiful formation symbolizes the generation in the outstanding and eminent individual; it groups subordinate individualities around the representative. This principle of individuality, in its *eternal* truth, uses the abstraction and equality of the generation to level down, and in that way co-operates in developing the individual religiously into a real man. For the leveling process is as powerful where temporary things are concerned as it is impotent where eternal things are concerned. Reflection is a snare in which one is caught but, once the "leap" of enthusiasm has been taken, the relation is a different one and it becomes a noose which drags one into eternity. Reflection is and remains the hardest creditor in existence; hitherto it has cunningly bought up all the possible views of life, but it cannot buy the essentially religious and eternal view of life; on the other hand, it can tempt people astray with its dazzling brilliance and dishearten them by reminding them of all the past. But, by leaping into the depths, one learns to help oneself, learns to love others as much as oneself, even though one is accused of arrogance and pride—because one will not accept help—or of selfishness, because one will not cunningly deceive people by helping them, i.e. by helping them to escape their highest destiny. . . .

Throughout many changes the tendency in modern times has remained a leveling one. These changes themselves have not, however, all of them been leveling, for they are none of them abstract enough, each having a certain concrete reality. To some extent it is true that the leveling process goes on when one great man attacks another, so that both are weakened, or when one is neutralized by the other, or when an association of people, in themselves weak, grow stronger than the eminent. Leveling can also be accomplished by one particular caste, e.g. the clergy, the bourgeois, the peasants, or by the people themselves. But all that is only the first movement of an abstract power within the concreteness of individuality.

In order that everything should be reduced to the same level it is first of all necessary to procure a phantom, a spirit, a monstrous abstraction, an all-embracing something which is nothing, a mirage—and that phantom is *the public*. It is only in an age which is without passion, yet reflective, that such a phantom can develop itself with the help of the Press which itself becomes an abstraction. In times of passion and tumult and enthusiasm, even when a people desire to realize a fruitless idea and lay waste and destroy everything—even then there is no such thing as a public. There are parties and they are concrete. The Press, in times such as those, takes on a concrete character according to the division of parties. But just as sedentary professional people are the first to take up any fantastic illusion which comes their way, so a passionless, sedentary, reflective age, in which only the Press exhibits a vague sort of life, fosters this phantom. The public is, in fact, the real leveling-master rather than the actual leveler, for whenever leveling is only approximately accomplished it is done by something, but the public is a monstrous nothing. The public is a concept which could not have occurred in antiquity because the people *en masse in corpore* took part in any situation which arose and were responsible for the actions of the individual, and, moreover, the individual was personally present and had to submit at once to applause or disapproval for his decision. Only when the sense of association in society is no longer strong enough to give life to concrete realities is the Press able to create that abstraction, "the public," consisting of unreal individuals who never are and never can be united in an actual situation or organization—and yet are held together as a whole.

The public is a host, more numerous than all the peoples together, but it is a body which can never be reviewed; it cannot even be represented, because it is an abstraction. Nevertheless, when the age is reflective and passionless and destroys everything concrete, the public becomes everything and is supposed to include everything. And that again shows how the individual is thrown back upon himself.

The real moment in time and the real situation of being simultaneous with real people, each of whom is something—that is what helps to sustain the individual. But the existence of a public produces neither a situation nor simultaneity. The individual reader of the Press is not the public, and even though little by little a number of individuals or even all of them should read it, the simultaneity is lacking. Years might be spent gathering the public together, and still it would not be there. This abstraction, which the individuals so illogically form, quite rightly repulses the individual instead of coming to his help. The man who has no opinion of an event at the actual moment accepts the opinion of the majority or, if he is quarrelsome, of the minority. But it must be remembered that both majority and minority are real people, and that is why the individual is assisted by adhering to them. A public, on the contrary, is an abstraction. To adopt the opinion of this or that man means that one knows that they will be subjected to the same dangers as oneself, that they will go astray with one if the opinion goes astray. But to adopt the same opinion as the public is a deceptive consolation, because the public is only there *in abstracto*. Whilst, therefore, no majority has ever been so certain of being right and victorious as the public, that is not much consolation to the individual, for a public is a phantom which forbids all personal contact. And if a man adopts public opinion today and is hissed tomorrow, he is hissed by the public.

A generation, a people, an assembly of the people, a meeting, or a man are responsible for what they are and can be made ashamed if they are inconstant and unfaithful; but a public remains a public. A people, an assembly or a man can change to such an extent that one may say: they are no longer the same; a public on the other hand can become the very opposite and still be the same—a public. But it is precisely by means of this abstraction and this abstract discipline that the individual will be formed (insofar as the individual is not already formed by his inner life), if he does not succumb in the process: taught to be content, in the highest religious sense, with himself and his relation to God, to be at one with himself instead of being in agreement with a public which destroys everything that is relative, concrete and particular in life; educated to find peace within himself and with God, instead of counting hands; and the absolute difference between the modern world and antiquity will be: that the totality is not concrete and is therefore unable to support the individual, or to educate him as the concrete should (though without developing him absolutely), but is an abstraction which by its abstract equality repels him and thus helps him to be educated absolutely—unless he succumbs in the process. The *taedium vitae* so constant in antiquity was due to the fact that the outstanding individual was what others *could not be*; the inspiration of modern times will be that any man who finds himself, religiously speaking, has only achieved what *everyone can achieve*.

A public is neither a nation, nor a generation, nor a community, nor a society, nor these particular men, for all these are only what they are through the concrete. No single person who belongs to the public makes a real commitment; for some hours of the day, perhaps, he belongs to the public—at moments when he is nothing else, since when he really is what he is, he does not form part of the public. Made up of such individuals, of individuals at the moments when they are nothing, a public is a kind of gigantic something, an abstract and deserted void which is everything and nothing. But on this basis anyone can arrogate to himself a public, and just as the Roman Church chimerically extended its frontiers by appointing bishops *in partibus infidelium,* so a public is something which everyone can claim, and even a drunken sailor exhibiting a "peep-show" has dialectically absolutely the same right to a public as the greatest man; he has just as logical a right to put all those many noughts *in front* of his single number.

A public is everything and nothing, the most dangerous of all powers and the most insignificant: one can speak to a whole nation in the name of the public and still the public will be less than a single real man, however unimportant. The qualification "public" is produced by the deceptive juggling of an age of reflection, which makes it appear flattering to the individual, who in this way can arrogate to himself this monster in comparison with which concrete realities seem poor. The public is the fairy story of an age of understanding, which in imagination makes the individual into something even greater than a king above his people; but the public is also a gruesome abstraction through which the individual will receive his religious formation—or sink.

. . . More and more individuals, owing to their bloodless indolence, will aspire to be nothing at all—in order to become the public, that abstract whole formed in the most ludicrous way, by all participants becoming a third party (an onlooker). This indolent mass which understands nothing and does nothing itself, this gallery, is on the look-out for distraction and soon abandons itself to the idea that everything that anyone does is done in order to give it (the public) something to gossip about. That indolent mass sits with its legs crossed wearing an air of superiority, and anyone who tries to work, whether king, official, school teacher or the better type of journalist, the poet or the artist, has to struggle to drag the public along with it, while the public thinks in its own superior way that it is the horse.

If I tried to imagine the public as a particular person . . . I should perhaps think of one of the Roman emperors, a large well-fed figure, suffering from boredom, looking only for the sensual intoxication of laughter, since the divine gift of wit is not earthly enough. And so for a change he wanders about, indolent rather than bad, but with a negative desire to dominate. Everyone who has read the classical authors knows how many things a Caesar could try out in order to kill time. In the same way the public keeps a dog to amuse it. That dog is literary scum.[2] If there is some one superior to the rest, perhaps even a great man, the dog is set on him and the fun begins. The dog goes for him, snapping and tearing at his coat-tails, allowing itself every possible ill-mannered familiarity—until the public tires, and says it may stop. That is an example of how the public levels. Their betters and superiors in strength are mishandled—and the dog remains a dog which even the public despises. The leveling is therefore done by a third party; a non-existent public leveling with the help of a third party which in its insignificance is less than nothing, being already more than leveled. And so the public is unrepentant, for it was after all not the public that acted, but the dog; just as one says to children—the cat's mother did it. The public is unrepentant—it was not really belittling anyone; it just wanted a little amusement. . . .

The public is unrepentant, for it is not they who own the dog—they only subscribe. They neither set the dog on anyone, nor whistle it off—directly. If asked, they would answer: the dog is not mine, it has no master. And if the dog had to be killed, they would say: it was really a good thing that bad-tempered dog was put away, everyone wanted it killed—even the subscribers.

Perhaps someone, familiarizing himself with such a case, and inclined to fix his attention upon the outstanding individual who suffered at the hands of the public, may be of the opinion that such an ordeal is a great misfortune. I cannot at all agree with such an opinion, for any-one who really wishes to be helped to attain the highest is in fact benefited by undergoing such a misfortune, and must rather desire it, even though people may be led to revolt. The really terrible thing is the thought of the many lives that are or easily may be wasted. I will not even mention those who are lost, or at any rate led completely astray—those who play the part of the dog for money—but the many who are helpless, thoughtless and sensual, who live superior lazy lives and never receive any deeper impression of existence than this mean-ingless grin, and all those bad people who are led into further tempta-tion because in their stupidity they even become self-important by com-miserating with the one who is attacked, without even understanding that in such a position the person attacked is always the stronger, with-out understanding that in this case the terrible and ironical truth applies: Weep not over him, but over yourselves.[3]

That is the leveling process at its lowest, for it always equates itself

2 E.g. *The Corsair.*
3 Luke 23: 28.

to the divisor by means of which everyone is reduced to a common denominator. Eternal life is also a sort of leveling, and yet that is not so, because the unity is that everyone should really and essentially be a man in a religious sense. . . .

And so when the generation, which itself desired to level and to be emancipated, to destroy authority and at the same time itself, has, through the skepticism of the principle "association," started the hopeless forest fire of abstraction; when as a result of leveling with this skepticism, the generation has rid itself of the individual and of everything organic and concrete, and put in its place "humanity" and the numerical equality of man and man; when the generation has, for a moment, delighted in this unlimited panorama of abstract infinity, unrelieved by even the smallest eminence, undisturbed by even the slightest interest, a sea of desert: then the time has come for work to begin, for every individual must work for himself, each for himself. No longer can the individual, as in former times, turn to the great for help when he grows confused. That is past; he is either lost in the dizziness of unending abstraction or saved forever in the reality of religion. . . .

For the development is, in spite of everything, a progress, because all the individuals who are saved will receive the specific weight of religion, its essence at first hand, from God himself. Then it will be said: "Behold, all is in readiness: see how the cruelty of abstraction makes the true form of worldliness only too evident, the abyss of eternity opens before you, the sharp scythe of the leveler makes it possible for every one individually to leap over the blade—and behold, it is God who waits. Leap, then, into the arms of God."

PURITY OF HEART
EDIFYING DISCOURSES IN
VARIOUS SPIRITS

BY S. KIERKEGAARD (1847)

TRANSLATED BY DOUGLAS V. STEERE

. . . "Mary chose the better part."

What is the better part? It is God, and consequently everything, but it is called the better part because it must be chosen; one does not receive everything as everything, that is not how one begins: one begins by choosing the better part, which is, nevertheless, everything.—THE JOURNALS

FROM the day of the publication of *Either/Or,* Kierkegaard continued to put out, in addition to his large-scale pseudonymous works, modest collections of "discourses" on Biblical texts; and these latter were issued under his own name. This meant that he assumed responsibility for them in a sense different from the pseudonymous writings—that they were "direct communications," not indirect. Whereas the pseudonyms, even Johannes Climacus, represent but parts or aspects of Kierkegaard, these discourses represented the whole man; they say what "the heart" told him must be uttered, in contrast to what his mind prompted him to say by way of distinction, clarification, and illustration of the various modes of human existence and of man's relation to the Divine. This does not mean that the pseudonymous works were products of mere cogitation; it means only that in the final anlysis Kierkegaard could still step away from them and view them as but partial and limited expressions of what he himself believed most passionately—and what he would communicate to men, if this were his last or only chance at communication. In the works signed with his own name S.K. is speaking to "the solitary individual"; he speaks eloquently, using all the devices of rhetoric just as a great preacher does, to drive his point home; and he speaks directly. His object is frankly persuasion. He himself recommended that these discourses be read aloud.

Whether in spite of all this or because of it, the discourses contain as much food for thought, including highly "theoretical" thought, as any of S.K.'s more pretentious works. *Purity of Heart* is a striking example of this, for it suggests a theory of value as well as a religious psychology in line with the "self-integration" school of present-day psychoanalysis. (We shall observe an even stronger foreshadowing of "depth psychology" in *The Sickness unto Death*.) Yet the purpose of the discourse is purely practical. Relentlessly Kierkegaard shows up the excuses and evasions of the human heart confronted with the privilege of loving God above all else and with the task of expressing this love in every moment of one's life. These are the "Barriers to Willing One Thing," of which the passage here presented discusses the first: "Variety and Great Moments Are Not One Thing." "The oneness of pleasure is a snare and a delusion," and only he can be said to will one thing who truly wills the Good. This assault on "the aesthetic way of life" proceeds from a higher vantage-point than anything Judge William has said, and just for this reason it is a great deal more effective.

Like many of the discourses, *Purity of Heart* was written for an "occasion" —the "Feast of Confession." At a time when many churches are restoring the confessional element in their services, if not the practice of auricular confession itself, it has a peculiar relevance. The whole discourse (of which this passage is but a small part) is decidedly worthwhile. (The English translation, like that of *The Works of Love,* has the benefit of an excellent introduction by Professor Douglas V. Steere, of Haverford College.)

BARRIERS TO WILLING ONE THING: VARIETY AND GREAT MOMENTS ARE NOT ONE THING

So let us, then, upon the occasion of a Feast of Confession, speak about this sentence: PURITY OF HEART IS TO WILL ONE THING, as we base our meditation on the Apostle James' words in his Epistle, Chapter 4, verse 8:

"Draw nigh to God and he will draw nigh to you. Cleanse your hands, ye sinners; and purify your hearts, ye double-minded." For only the pure in heart can see God, and therefore draw nigh to Him; and only by God drawing nigh to them can they maintain this purity. And he who in truth wills only one thing can will only the Good, and he who only wills one thing when he wills the Good can only will the Good in truth. . . .

IF IT IS TO BE POSSIBLE THAT A MAN CAN WILL ONLY ONE THING
THEN HE MUST WILL THE GOOD.

To will only one thing: but will this not inevitably become a long-drawn-out talk? If one should consider this matter properly must he not first consider, one by one, each goal in life that a man could conceivably set up for himself, mentioning separately all of the many things that a man might will? And not only this; since each of these considerations readily becomes too abstract in character, is he not obliged as the next step to attempt to will, one after the other, each of these goals in order to find out what is the single thing he is to will, if it is a matter of willing only one thing? Yes, if someone should begin in this fashion, then he would never come to an end. Or more accurately, how could he ever arrive at the end, since at the outset he took the wrong way and then continued to go on further and further along this false way? It is only by a painful route that this way leads to the Good, namely, when the wanderer turns around and goes back. For as the Good is only a single thing, so all ways lead to the Good, even the false ones—when the repentant one follows the same way back. Oh Thou, the unfathomable trustworthiness of the Good! Wherever a man may be in the world, whichever road he travels, when he wills one thing he is on a road that leads him to Thee! Here such a far-flung enumeration would only work harm. Instead of wasting many moments on naming the vast multitude of goals or squandering life's costly years in personal experiments upon them, can the talk do as life ought to do—with a commendable brevity stick to the point?

In a certain sense nothing can be spoken of so briefly as the Good, when it is well described. For the Good without condition and without qualification, without preface and without compromise, is absolutely the only thing that a man may and should will, and is only one thing. Oh blessed brevity, oh blessed simplicity, that seizes swiftly what cleverness, tired out in the service of vanity, may grasp but slowly! That which a simple soul, in the happy impulse of a pious heart, feels no need of understanding in an elaborate way, since he simply seizes the Good immediately, is grasped by the clever one only at the cost of much time and much grief. The way this one thing is willed is not such that one man wills one thing but that which he wills is not the Good; another wills one thing nor is what he wills the Good; a third wills one thing and what he wills *is* the Good. No, it is not done in that way. The person who wills one thing that is not the Good, he does not truly will one thing. It is a delusion, an illusion, a deception, a self-deception that he wills only one thing. For in his innermost being he is, he is bound to be, double-minded. Therefore the Apostle says, "Purify your hearts ye double-minded," that is, purify your hearts of double-mindedness; in other words, let your heart in truth will only one thing, for therein is the heart's purity.

And again it is of this same purity of heart that the Apostle is speaking when he says, "If someone lacks wisdom, then let him pray . . . but in faith, not like a double-minded man" (James 1:5, 6, 8). For purity of heart is the very wisdom that is acquired through prayer. A man of prayer does not pore over learned books, for he is the wise man "whose eyes are opened"—when he kneels down (Numbers 24:16).

In a word, then, there is a man whose mind remains piously ignorant of the multitude of things, for the Good is one thing. The more difficult part of the talk is directed to the man whose mind in its double-mindedness has made the doubtful acquaintance of the multitude of things, and of knowledge. If it is certain that a man in truth wills one thing, then he wills the Good, for this alone can be willed in this manner. But both of these assertions speak of identical things, or they speak of different things. The one assertion plainly designates the name of the Good, declaring it to be that one thing. The other assertion cunningly conceals this name. It appears almost as if it spoke of something else. But just on that account it forces its way searchingly into a man's innermost being. And no matter how much he may protest, or defy, or boast that he wills only one thing, it searches him through and through in order to show the double-mindedness in him if the one thing he wills is not the Good.

For in truth there was a man on earth who seemed to will only one thing. It was unnecessary for him to insist upon it. Even if he had been silent about it, there were witnesses enough against him who testified how inhumanly he steeled his mind, how nothing touched him, neither tenderness, nor innocence, nor misery; how his blinded soul had eyes for nothing, and how the senses in him had only eyes for the one thing that he willed. And yet it was certainly a delusion, a terrible delusion, that he willed one thing. For pleasure and honor and riches and power and all that this world has to offer only appear to be one thing. It is not, nor does it remain one thing, while everything else is in change or while he himself is in change. It is not in all circumstances the same. On the contrary, it is subject to continual alteration. Hence even if this man named but one thing, whether it be pleasure or honor or riches, actually he did not will one thing. Neither can he be said to will one thing when that one thing which he wills is not in itself one—is in itself a multitude of things, a dispersion, the toy of changeableness, and the prey of corruption! In the time of pleasure see how he longed for one gratification after another. Variety was his watchword. Is variety, then, to will one thing that shall ever remain the same? On the contrary, it is to will one thing that must never be the same. It is to will a multitude of things. And a person who wills in this fashion is not only double-minded but is at odds with himself. For such a man wills first one thing and then immediately wills the opposite, because the oneness of pleasure is a snare and a delusion. It is the diversity of pleasures that he wills. So when the man of whom we are speaking had gratified himself up to the point of disgust, he became weary and sated. Even if he still desired one thing—what was it that he desired? He desired new pleasures; his enfeebled soul raged so that no ingenuity was sufficient to discover something new—something new! It was change he cried out for as pleasure served him, change! change! And it was change that he cried out for as he came to pleasure's limit, as his servants were worn out—change! change!

Now it is to be understood that there are also changes in life that can prove to a man whether he wills one thing. There is the change of the perishable nature when the sensual man must step aside, when dancing and the tumult of the whirling senses are over, when all becomes soberly quiet. That is the change of death. If, for once, the perishable nature should seem to forget to close in, if it should seem as if the sensual one has succeeded in slipping by—death does not forget. The sensual one will not slip past death, who has dominion over what belongs to the earth and who will change into nothing the one thing which the sensual person desires.

And last of all there is the change of eternity, which changes all. Then only the Good remains and it remains the blessed possession of the man who has willed only one thing. But that rich man whom no misery could touch, that rich man who even in eternity to his own damnation must continue to will one thing, ask him now whether he really wills one thing. So, too, with honor and riches and power. For in the time of strength as he aspired to honor, did he really discover some limit, or was that not simply the striver's restless passion to climb higher and higher? Did he find some rest amid his sleeplessness in which he sought to capture honor and to hold it fast? Did he find some refreshment in the cold fire of his passion? And if he really won honor's highest prize, then is earthly honor in itself one thing? Or in its diversity when the thousands and thousands braid the wreath, is honor to be likened to the gorgeous carpet of the field—created by a single hand? No, like worldly contempt, worldly honor is a whirlpool, a play of confused forces, an illusory moment in the flux of opinions. It is a sense-deception, as when a swarm of insects at a distance seem to the eye like one body; a sense deception, as when the noise of the many at a distance seems to the ear like a single voice.

Even if honor were unanimous it would still be meaningless, and the more so, the more thousands that create the unanimity. And the greater the multitude that created unanimity, the sooner will it show itself to be meaningless. And indeed it was this unanimity of the thousands that he desired. It was not the approbation of the good men; they are soon counted. No, it was rather the approbation of the thousands. Is, then, this desire for counting, is this to will one thing? To count and count until it suffices, to count and count until a mistake is made—is this to will one thing? Whoever, therefore, wills this honor or fears this contempt, whether or not he is said to will one thing in his innermost being, is not merely double-minded but thousand-minded, and at variance with himself. So is his life when he must grovel—in order to attain honor; when he must flatter his enemies—in order to attain honor; when he must woo the favor of those he despises—in order to attain honor; when he must betray the one whom he respects—in order to attain honor. For to attain honor means to despise oneself after one has attained the pinnacle of honor—and yet to tremble before any change. Change, yes, where does change rage more unchecked than here? What desertion is more swift and sudden, like a mistake in foolery, like a hit by a blind man, when the seeker for honor has not even time to take off the garb of honor before insult seizes him in it? Change, the final change, the absolute certainty among the range of unpredictables: no matter how loud the thunder of honor may sound over his grave, even if it could be heard over the whole earth, there is one who cannot hear it—the dead man, he who died with honor, the single thing he had desired. But also in dying he lost the honor, for it remains outside, it marches home again, it dies away like an echo. Change, the true change, when eternity exists—I should like to know if honor's crown reaches the much-honored one there! And yet eternity is more just than the earth and the world; for in eternity there is a crown of honor laid aside for each of those that have in truth willed only one thing. So also with riches and power and the world that passes away and the lust thereof. The one who has willed any of them, even if he only willed one thing, must, to his own agony, continue to will it when it has passed, and learned by the agony of contradiction that it is not one thing. But the one who in truth willed one thing and therefore willed the Good, even if he be sacrificed for it, why should he not go on willing the same in eternity, the same thing that he was willing to die for? Why should he not will the same, when it has triumphed in eternity?

To will one thing, therefore, cannot mean to will that which only appears to be one thing. The fact is that the worldly goal is not one thing in its essence, because it is unreal. Its so-called unity is actually nothing but emptiness which is hidden beneath the manyness. In the short-lived moment of delusion the worldly goal is therefore a multitude of things and thus not one thing. So far is it from a state of being and remaining one thing, that in the next moment it changes into its opposite. Carried to its extreme limit, what is pleasure other than disgust? What is earthly honor at its dizzy pinnacle other than contempt for existence? What are riches, the highest superabundance of riches, other than poverty? For no matter how much all the earth's gold hidden in covetousness may amount to, is it not infinitely less than the smallest mite hidden in the contentment of the poor! What is worldly omnipotence other than dependence? What slave in chains is as unfree as a tyrant! No, the worldly goal is not one thing. Diverse as it is, in life it is changed into its opposite, in death into nothing, in eternity into damnation—for the one who has willed this goal. Only the Good is one thing in its essence and the same in each of its expressions. Take love as an illustration. The one who truly loves does not love once and for all. Nor does he use a part of his love, and then again another part. For to change it into small coins is not to use it rightly. No, he loves with all of his love. It is wholly present in each expression. He continues to give it away as a whole, and yet he keeps it intact as a whole, in his heart. Wonderful riches! When the miser has gathered all the world's gold in sordidness—then he has become poor. When the lover gives away his whole love, he keeps it entire—in the purity of the heart. Shall a man in truth will one thing, then this one thing that he wills must be such that it remains unaltered in all changes, so that by willing it he can win immutability. If it changes continually, then he himself becomes changeable, double-minded, and unstable. And this continual change is nothing else than impurity.

Now, willing one thing does not mean to commit the grave mistake of a brazen, unholy enthusiasm, namely to will the big, no matter whether it be good or bad. Also, one who wills in this fashion, no matter how desperately he does it, is indeed double-minded. Is not despair simply double-mindedness? For what is despairing other than to have two wills? For whether the weakling despairs over not being able to wrench himself away from the bad, or whether the brazen one despairs over not being able to tear himself completely away from the Good [1]—they are both double-minded, they both have two wills. Neither

---

[1] The theme of *The Sickness unto Death* is here foreshadowed.

of them honestly wills one thing, however desperately they may seem to will it. Whether it was a woman, whom desire brought to desperation, or whether it was a man who despaired in defiance; whether a man despaired because he got his will or despaired because he did not get his will: each one in despairing has two wills, one that he fruitlessly tries wholly to follow and one that he fruitlessly tries wholly to avoid. In this fashion has God, better than any king, insured himself against every rebellion. For it has indeed happened that a king has been dethroned by a rebellion. But each rebel against God, in the last instance, is himself reduced to despair. Despair is the limit—"here and no further!" Despair is the limit. Here are met the cowardly, timorous ill-temper of self-love, and the proud defiant presumption of the mind —here they are met in equal impotence.

Only too soon personal experience and the experience of others teaches how far most men's lives are from being what a man's life ought to be. All have great moments. They see themselves in the magic mirror of possibility which hope holds before them while the wish flatters them. But they swiftly forget this sight in the daily round of things. Or perhaps they talk enthusiastic words, "for the tongue is a little member and boasteth great things." [2] But talk takes the name of enthusiasm in vain by proclaiming loudly from the house-top what it should work out in silence, And in the midst of the trivial details of life these enthusiastic words are quickly forgotten. It is forgotten that such a thing was said of this man. It is forgotten that it was he himself who said it. Now and then, perhaps, memory wakens with horror, and remorse seems to promise new strength. But alas, this too lasts only for a good-sized moment. All of them have intentions, plans, resolutions for life, yes, for eternity. But the intention soon loses its youthful strength and fades away. The resolution is not firmly grounded and is unable to withstand opposition. It totters before circumstances and is altered by them. Memory, too, has a way of failing, until by common practice and habit they learn to draw sympathy from one another. If some one proclaims the slender comfort that excuses yield, instead of realizing how treacherous is such sympathy, they finally come to regard it as edifying, because it encourages and strengthens indolence. Now there are men who find it edifying that the demand to will one thing be asserted in all its sublimity, in all its severity, so that it may press its claim into the innermost fastness of the soul. Others find it edifying that a wretched compromise should be made between God, the claim, and the language

[2] James 3:5.

used. There are men who find it edifying if only someone will challenge them. But there are also the sleepy souls who regard it as not only pleasing, but even edifying, to be lulled to sleep.[3]

This is indeed a lamentable fact; but there is a wisdom which is not from above but is earthly and fleshly and devilish. It has discovered this common human weakness and indolence; it wants to be helpful. It perceives that all depends upon the will and so it proclaims loudly, "Unless it wills one thing, a man's life is sure to become one of wretched mediocrity, of pitiful misery. He must will one thing regardless of whether it be good or bad. He must will one thing, for therein lies a man's greatness." Yet it is not difficult to see through this powerful error.[4] As to the working out of salvation, the holy Scripture teaches that sin is the corruption of man. Salvation, therefore, lies only in the purity with which a man wills the Good. That very earthly and devilish cleverness distorts this into a temptation to perdition: weakness is a man's misfortune; strength the sole salvation: "When the unclean spirit is gone out of a man, he walketh through dry and empty places but finds no rest. Then he turns back again and now he brings with him" that unclean cleverness, the wisdom of the desert and the empty places, that unclean cleverness—that now drives out the spirit of indolence and of mediocrity "so that the last stage becomes worse than the first."[5] How shall one describe the nature of such a man? It is said of a singer that by overscreeching he can crack his voice. In like fashion, such a man's nature, by overscreeching itself and the voice of conscience, has cracked. It is said of a man who stands dizzily upon a high place that all things run together before his eyes. Such a man has made himself giddy in the infinite, where those things which are forever separate run together into one thing, so that only the vast remains.

It is this dryness and emptiness that always gives birth to giddiness. But no matter how desperately such a man may seem to will one thing, he is double-minded. If he, the self-willed one, had his way then there would be only this one thing; he would be the only one that was not double-minded, he the only one that had cast off every chain, he the only one that was free. But the slave of sin is not yet free; nor has he cast off the chain, "because he scoffs at it." He is in bonds, and therefore double-minded, and for once he may not have his own way. There

[3] At the time this was written S.K. was coming to feel that the Church, all too often, served merely to "lull men to sleep."

[4] S.K. here refutes the Nietzschean perversion of his thesis—and with it those who seek to identify him with modern forms of irrationalism.

[5] Matthew 12:43–45.

is a power that binds him. He cannot tear himself loose from it. Nay, he cannot even wholly will it. For this power, too, is denied him. If you, my listener, should see such a man, although it is unlikely, for without a doubt weakness and mediocrity are the more common; if you should meet him in what he himself would call a weak moment but which, alas, you would have to call a better moment; if you should meet him when he had found no rest in the desert, when the giddiness passes away for a moment and he feels an agonizing longing for the Good; if you should meet him when, shaken in his innermost being, and not without sadness, he was thinking of that man of single purpose who even in all his frailty still wills the Good: then you would discover that he had two wills, and you would discover his painful double-mindedness.

Desperate as he was, he thought: lost is lost. But he could not help turning around once more in his longing for the Good. How terribly embittered he had become against this very longing, a longing which reveals that, just as a man in all his defiance has not power enough wholly to loose himself from the Good, because it is the stronger, so he has not even the power wholly to will it.

Perhaps you may even have heard that desperate one say, "Some good went down with me." When a man meets his death by drowning, as he sinks, without being quite dead he comes to the surface again. At last a bubble comes out of his mouth. When this has happened, then he sinks, dead. That bubble was the last breath, the last supply of air that could make him lighter than the sea. So with that remark. In that remark the last hope of salvation expired. In that remark he gave himself up. . . .

Alas, it is horrible to see a man rush toward his own destruction. It is horrible to see him dance on the rim of the abyss without any intimation of it. But this clarity about himself and about his own destruction is even more horrible. It is horrible to see a man seek comfort by hurling himself into the whirlpool of despair. But this coolness is still more horrible: that, in the anxiety of death, a man should not cry out for help, "I am going under, save me"; but that he should quietly choose to be a witness to his own destruction! Oh, most extreme vanity, not to wish to draw man's eyes to himself by beauty, by riches, by ability, by power, by honor, but to wish to get his attention by his own destruction, by choosing to say of himself what at most pity in all sadness may venture to say of such a person at his grave, "Yet, some good went down with him." Oh, horrible doubleness of mind in a man's destruction, to wish to draw a sort of advantage out of the fact that the Good remains the only thing that a man has not willed. For now the other will become apparent to him, Good in the presence of perdition, an attempt to be exceptional by means of his own destruction.

To will one thing cannot, then, mean to will what in its essence is not one thing, but only seems to be so by means of a horrible falsehood. Only through a lie is it one thing. Now just as he that only wills this one thing is a liar, so he that conjures up this one thing is the father of lies. That dryness and emptiness is not in truth one thing, but is in truth nothing at all. And it is destruction for the man that only wills that one. If, on the contrary, a man should in truth will only one thing, then this thing must, in the truth of its innermost being, be one thing. It must, by an eternal separation, cut off the heterogeneous from itself in order that it may in truth continue to be one and the same thing and thereby fashion that man who only wills one thing into conformity with itself.

In truth to will one thing, then, can only mean to will the Good, because every other object is not a unity; and the will that only wills that object, therefore, must become double-minded. For as the coveted object is, so becomes the coveter. Or would it be possible that a man by willing the evil could will one thing, provided that it was possible for a man so to harden himself as to will nothing but the evil? Is not this evil, like evil persons, in disagreement with itself, divided against itself? Take one such man, separate him from society, shut him up in solitary confinement. Is he not at odds with himself there, just as a poor union between persons of his sort is an association that is ridden with dissension? But a good man, even if he lived in an out-of-the-way corner of the world and never saw any human being, would be at one with himself and at one with all about him because he wills one thing, and because that one thing is the Good. *Each one who in truth would will one thing must be led to will the Good,* even though now and then it happens that a man begins by willing one thing that is not in its deepest sense the Good although it may be something quite innocent; and then, little by little, he is changed really in truth to will one thing by willing the Good. Love, from time to time, has in this way helped a man along the right path. Faithfully he only willed one thing, his love. For it, he would live and die. For it, he would sacrifice all and in it alone he would have his eternal reward. Yet the act of being in love is still not in the deepest sense the Good. But it may possibly become for him a helpful educator, who will finally lead him by the possession of his beloved one or perhaps by her loss, in truth to will one thing and to will the Good. In this fashion a man is educated by many means; and true love is also an education toward the Good.

Perhaps there was a man whose enthusiasm reached out toward a definite endeavor. In his enthusiasm he desired only one thing. He would live and die for that endeavor. He would sacrifice all for that in which alone he would have his happiness, for love and enthusiasm are not satisfied with a divided heart. Yet his endeavor was perhaps still not in the deepest sense the Good. Thus enthusiasm became for him a teacher, whom he outgrew, but to whom also he owed much. For, as it is said, all ways lead to the Good, when a man in truth only wills one thing. And where there is some truth in the fact that he wills one thing, this is all for the best. But there is danger that the lover and the enthusiast may swerve out of the true course and aim perhaps for the impressive instead of being led to the Good. The Good is also in truth the impressive, but the impressive is not always the Good. And one can bid for a woman's favor by willing something when it is merely impressive. This can flatter the girl's pride and she can repay it with her adoration. But God in heaven is not as a young girl's folly. He does not reward the impressive with admiration. The reward of the good man is to be allowed to worship in truth.

WORKS OF LOVE

BY S. KIERKEGAARD (1847)

TRANSLATED BY LILLIAN MARVIN SWENSON

The highest of all is not to understand the highest but to act upon it.

. . . To the Christian love is the works of love. To say that love is a feeling or anything of the kind is an unchristian conception of love. That is the aesthetic definition and therefore fits the erotic and everything of that nature. But to the Christian love is the works of love. Christ's love was not an inner feeling, a full heart and what not, it was the work of love which was his life.—THE JOURNALS

RELIGIOUSLY speaking, one of the striking features of S.K.'s career is the way in which he came to react against some of the basic emphases of Protestantism. In the "Deer Park" passage of the *Postcript* we have already seen him expressing sympathy for Catholic monasticism as against the modern religiosity which makes "inwardness" the excuse for neglecting to express one's faith in any external actions. This feeling grew upon him, the more he observed the mediocrity and "worldliness" of the Danish State Church of his time (a worldliness timid enough compared to Catholicism in certain phases of its history), until the final outburst of his indignation against "Christendom" in the last year of his life.

Naturally this has been seized upon by Catholics as proving that S.K. might have found his way into the true Church, had he lived a few years longer. This is perhaps a fruitless subject of debate. It can be argued that Kierkegaard's way of thinking was fundamentally and irrevocably Protestant, and that what he did was not to set aside any of the great Protestant principles, but rather to correct the one-sidedness incident upon the exclusive and exaggerated emphasis on these principles *apart from others equally important*. This, of course, is in line with the "dialectical" tenor of his mind in general. It is also in line with his dynamic view of truth, as that which is *tending toward* unity or completeness, rather than as something formed or complete in itself. The truth of a proposition, for Kierkegaard, is not a thing that can be asserted once for all; it is relative to the intention of the asserter and depends ultimately upon what the proposition is asserted *against*.

Thus the doctrine of Justification by Faith, as asserted by Luther in the sixteenth century against the Catholic theories of merit and the Catholic practice of indulgences, was true; but in the nineteenth or twentieth century, this doctrine may represent a wrong, because largely superfluous, emphasis. As one writer on Kierkegaard puts it: "Nobody who omits doing good works nowadays does so in order not to be tempted to become self-righteous; he omits it because it is easier." [1] From the very beginning S.K., while acknowledging the truth of Justification by Faith as directed against "work-righteousness" and the assumption that one can earn his salvation, had seen that the temper of the times ("especially in Protestantism and more especially in Denmark") required the proclamation of a complementary truth—a bringing to the fore of the practical, ethical side of Christianity, not by any means to the exclusion or minimizing of its dogmatic aspect, but to the exclusion of that barren orthodoxy which would make mere intellectual belief the primary act of Christian faith. The highly practical Epistle of James, which Luther called "an epistle of straw," was and remained S.K.'s favorite scripture.

The works of Christianity, however, are works of a peculiar kind—"works of love," works springing from love and motivated by love; love not in the sense of inclination or emotion—not "preferential love"—but love in the sense of the duty to love all men everywhere. This "duty to love" is a paradox, as Kierkegaard points out; it is one of Christianity's "hard sayings" which are

---

[1] Philip Merlan, "Toward the Understanding of Kierkegaard," *The Journal of Religion*, April 1943, p. 79.

foolishness to the natural man, but especially to poets and romanticists, for whom preferential love is always the highest. The idea of the "neighbor"— the man who is "nearest" at hand, the man who most needs our love here and now—is, as Kierkegaard says, a very unpoetic conception. Nevertheless it is Christianity, and that apart from such universalism there is no hope of curing the world's ills should be even clearer to us than to Kierkegaard.

The *Works of Love* may be said to leave the door wide open for the "social gospel"; Kierkegaard the expounder of Christian ethics herein proving himself more enlightened (though no more penetrating) than Kierkegaard the social philosopher of *The Present Age*, who may be accused of having rationalized his inherent conservatism as a privileged member of capitalist society. Certainly a section like the one on "Love Covers a Multitude of Sins" presents what may at first seem to be a different Kierkegaard from the one usually visible; yet it is the same man who wrote so illuminatingly of dread, despair, "the sickness unto death"—who, of all men, had no illusions about human nature—and who here recommends the way of pure love, the way of the "lover" who ignores and overlooks evil as far as is humanly possible, "finds an extenuating explanation" for it wherever it cannot be overlooked, and by the practice of forgiveness actually banishes it from existence. Nothing is more Kierkegaardian than this poetic but closely reasoned analysis of *caritas* and its operation. Nothing is more Kierkegaardian (to mention but one detail) than the opening paragraph bristling with abstractions, which immediately become clearer and clearer as S.K. descends to the level of human experience and begins to give examples.

Even after reading this section one may still question the applicability of pure love in a world actually as full of evil as we and S.K. know it to be. Are there not situations under which the absolute ethical ideal must be tempered by prudential considerations and prudential action, so that—as in the case of at least some wars—we find ourselves in the position of being compelled to do evil that good may result? Kierkegaard knew this dilemma from experience, but he does not discuss it in just these terms. We know, for example, that he was no pacifist; but his only escape from pacifism would seem to be via the dubious distinction between individual and social morality. Otherwise, must not the man who is really in earnest about *The Works of Love* go on extenuating and forgiving the actions of a Hitler indefinitely?

"Love Covers a Multitude of Sins" should in any case be read in conjunction with another and equally moving discourse on the same text, one of those intended "for the Communion on Friday," wherein it is shown how Christ's love covers over the believer's sin, making it impossible for Divine Justice to "discover" any trace of guilt. (See pp. 418–426.) The two passages belong together, as S.K. himself recognized—the ethical emphasis being thus balanced by a dogmatic one.

The *Works of Love* is a big book and contains the following divisions: *First Part:* I. Love's hidden life and the discovery of it by its fruits. II. (A) *Thou *shalt* love. (B) Thou shalt love thy *neighbor*. (C) *Thou* shalt love thy neighbor. III. (A) Love is the fulfillment of the Law. Rom. 13:10. (B) Love is a matter of conscience. 1 Tim. 1:5. IV. Our duty to love the men we see. 1 Jn. 4:20. V. Our duty to remain in love's debt to one another. Rom. 8:8. *Second Part:* I. Love edifieth. 1 Cor. 8:1. II. Love believeth all things—and yet is never deceived. 1 Cor. 13:7. III. Love hopeth all things—and yet is never put to shame. 1. Cor. 13:7. IV. Love seeketh not her own. 1 Cor. 13:5. V. *Love covereth a multitude of sins. 1 Pet. 4:8. VI. Love abideth. 1 Cor. 13:13. VII. Compassion is a work of love, even if it can give nothing and is unable to do anything. VIII. The victory of forgiveness through love, which wins the defeated. IX. It is a work of love to remember the deceased. X. It is a work of love to sing the praise of love. (The two sections here reproduced are designated by *.)

THOU *SHALT* LOVE

But the second commandment is like unto it: Thou shalt love thy neighbor as thyself.—MATTHEW 22:39.

EVERY speech, especially a portion of a speech, usually presupposes something from which it proceeds. He who desires to make the speech or the assertion a subject of reflection does well, therefore, to look first for this presupposition, in order to start from it. So there is also a presupposition contained in the text we read, which although it comes last is nevertheless the starting point. Therefore when we are told: "Thou shalt love thy neighbor as thyself," then this statement contains *the presupposition that every man loves himself.* Consequently Christianity presupposes this, since Christianity, unlike those ambitious thinkers,[1] by no means begins without presuppositions, or with a flattering assumption.

And would we dare to deny that what Christianity presupposes is true? But, on the other hand, could anyone so misunderstand Christianity as to believe it was its intention to teach that which worldly wisdom unanimously (alas, and yet divisively) teaches, that everyone loves himself best? Could anyone misunderstand this, as if it were the intention of Christianity to hold self-love in honor? On the contrary, it is its intention to strip us of our selfishness. This selfishness consists in lov-

---

[1] The Hegelians.

ing one's self; but if one must love his neighbor as himself, then the commandment opens the lock of self-love as with a picklock, and the man with it. If the commandment about loving one's neighbor were expressed in some other way than by the use of this little phrase, "as thyself," which is at once so easy to use and yet has the tension of eternity, then the commandment would not be able thus to master the self-love. This "as thyself" does not vacillate in its aim, and so it enters with the condeming inflexibility of eternity into the most secret hiding place, where a man loves himself. It does not leave self-love the least excuse, the least loophole open. How strange! Long and shrewd speeches might be made about how a man ought to love his neighbor; and then, after all the speeches had been heard, self-love could still hit upon an excuse and find a way of escape, because the subject had not been absolutely exhausted; all alternatives had not been canvassed; because something had been forgotten, or not accurately and bindingly enough expressed and described.

But this "as thyself"! Certainly no wrestler can get so tight a clinch upon his opponent as that with which this commandment embraces the selfishness which cannot stir from its place. Truly, when selfishness has striven with this word, which yet is so easy to understand that no one should break his head on it, then it must perceive that it has been striving with the stronger power. As Jacob limped after he had wrestled with God, so shall the selfishness be broken when it has striven with this word which, however, does not wish to teach a man that he ought not to love himself but, on the contrary, simply wishes to teach him the proper kind of self-love. How strange! What struggle is so protracted, so terrible, so complicated, as the battle of self-love in its own defense? —and yet Christianity decides everything with a single blow. The whole is swift as a handspring, everything is decided, like the eternal decision of the resurrection, "in a moment, in the twinkling of an eye": Christianity presupposes that a man loves himself, and merely adds to this the word about loving your neighbor "as yourself." And yet there lies the difference of eternity between the first and the last.

But would this really be the highest form of love? Would it not be possible to love a man *better than one's self?* We hear such talk now and then, the expression of a poet's enthusiasm. Could it perhaps be true that it was because Christianity was not able to soar so high, presumably also because it addresses itself to simple, commonplace men, that it wretchedly continues to stress the requirement of loving one's neighbor "as one's self"? Could that be why, instead of basing its demand on that object of ambitious love which poets celebrate, a "beloved," a "friend," it bases it on the apparently very unpoetical "neighbor"? For certainly no poet has ever sung about loving one's neighbor, any more than he has sung about loving him "as one's self." Could this perhaps be the case? Or should we, as we make a concession to the love which the poet *sings* as compared with the love *commanded,* humbly praise the circumspection of Christianity and its understanding of life, because it holds itself to earth more soberly and more enduringly, perhaps with the same import as that of the proverb which says: "Love me little, love me long"?

Be this far from us! Christianity knows a better answer to the question of what love is and about loving than does any poet. Precisely therefore it knows too that which escapes the attention of many poets, that the love they praise is secretly self-love, and that this explains its intoxicated expression about loving another man better than one's self. Earthly love is still not the eternal love; it is the beautiful fantasy of the infinite, its highest expression is mysterious foolishness. That is why it tries its hand at an even more fantastic expression, the "loving a man more than God." And this foolishness pleases the poet beyond all measure, it is delicious in his ears, it inspires him to sing. Alas, Christianity teaches that this is blasphemy.

And what is true of love is also true of friendship, insofar as this too is a consequence of partiality—of loving this one man above all others, of loving him as distinct from all others. Therefore the objects of both love and friendship bear the nomenclature of this partiality, "the beloved," "the friend," who is loved above all the rest of the world. On the contrary, the Christian teaching is to love the neighbor, to love the whole race, all men, even one's enemy, and to make no exception, either of partiality or of dislike.

There is only One whom a man may with the truth of the eternal love better than himself, that is God. Therefore it does not say, "Thou shalt love God as thyself," but it says, "Thou shalt love the Lord thy God with all thy heart and with all thy soul and with all thy mind." A man must love God in *unconditional obedience* and love Him in *adoration.* It would be ungodliness if any man dared to love himself in this way, or dared to love another man in this way, or dared to permit another man to love him in this way. If your beloved or your friend begged you for something which you, because you honestly loved him, had anxiously considered would be injurious to him: then a responsibility would rest upon you if you showed your love by acquiescing in his wish, instead of showing it by denying him its fulfillment. But God you must love in unconditional obedience even if that which He demands of you may seem injurious to you, moreover injurious to His own interests. For God's wisdom is incomparable with respect to your own, and God's providence is not obliged to be responsible for your cleverness. You have only to obey in love. A man, on the contrary, you must only —yet, no, this is the highest—you must love a man as yourself; if you can better perceive his best than he can, then you will not be able to excuse yourself by the fact that the harmful thing was his own wish, was what he himself asked for. If this were not the case, then there might quite rightly be something said about loving another man better than yourself; for this love would consist in: despite your own conviction that it would be harmful to him, *obediently* doing it because he asked it, or *adoringly,* because he wished it. But this you simply have no right to do; you are responsible if you do it, just as the other is responsible if he should misuse his relationship to you in this way.

Consequently—"as thyself." If the most cunning deceiver who has ever lived . . . in order, if possible, to have the right to use many words and to become long-winded, for then he would soon triumph—if this deceiver were to persist year out and year in inquiring "temptingly" of the "royal law," "How shall I love my neighbor?"—then will the laconic commandment unchanged continue to repeat the brief phrase, "as thyself." And if any deceiver deceived himself all his life by all sorts of difficulties concerning this matter, then will eternity only reprove him with the brief words of the commandment, "as thyself." Verily, no one will be able to escape the commandment; if its "as thyself" presses as hard on life as possible, so again "neighbor" is a category which in its offensiveness is as perilous to self-love as possible. That it is impossible to escape from these two categories, self-love itself readily perceives. The only escape is the one the Pharisee in his time attempted in order to justify himself: to make it doubtful who his neighbor was—in order to get him out of the way.

Who then is one's neighbor? The word is evidently derived from "nearest," so the neighbor is the one who is nearer you than all others, although not in the preferential sense; for to love the one who is preferentially nearer one than all others is self-love—"Do not even the heathen the same?" The neighbor, then, is nearer to you than all others. But is he also nearer to you than you are to yourself? No, not so; but he is, or should be, equally near. The concept "neighbor" is really a reduplication of your own self; the "neighbor" is what philosophers would call the "other," the touchstone for testing what is selfish in self-love. Insofar, for the sake of the thought, it is not even necessary that the neighbor should exist. If a man lived on a desert island, if he developed his mind in harmony with the commandment, then by renouncing self-love he could be said to love his neighbor.

"Neighbor" is itself a multitude, for "neighbor" implies "all men," and yet in another sense one man is enough to enable you to obey the commandment. In a selfish sense it is an impossibility consciously to be two in being a self; self-love demands that it be one. Nor are three needed, for if there are two, that is, if there is one other human being whom, in the Christian sense, you love "as yourself," or in whom you love the "neighbor," then you love all men. But what the selfish definitely cannot tolerate is duplication, and the words of the commandment, "as thyself," are exactly a duplication. One who is burning with love can never, because of or by virtue of this burning, endure the reduplication which here would mean the relinquishing of love, if the object of the love required it. Consequently the lover does not love the beloved "as himself," for he is a claimant; but this "as thyself" precisely involves a claim upon him—and yet, alas, the lover still believes that he loves the other man better than himself.

"Neighbor" presses as closely as possible upon the selfishness in life. If there are only two men, the other man is the neighbor; if there are millions, each one of these is the neighbor, who is again closer to one than "the friend" and "the beloved," insofar as those, the objects of preferential love, gradually become analogous to the self-love in one. We are ordinarily conscious that the neighbor exists and that he is close at hand when we believe that we have rights with regard to him, that we may claim something from him. If someone with this idea asks: Who is my neighbor? then will Christ's answer to the Pharisee be a reply only in a very peculiar sense, for in the answer the question is first really transformed into its opposite, whereby it is intimated how a man ought to ask. After having related the parable of the good Samaritan, Christ says to the Pharisees, "Which of these three do you think was neighbor to him who fell among thieves?" And the Pharisees answer "rightly," "The one who showed mercy to him." That is, by recognizing your duty to him you readily discover who your neighbor is. The answer of the Pharisees is implicit in Christ's question, which by its form compelled the Pharisee to answer as he did. He to whom I have an obligation is my neighbor, and when I fulfill my obligation I show that I am his neighbor. Christ does not talk about knowing one's neighbor, but about one's self being a neighbor, about proving one's self a neighbor, as the Samaritan proved himself one by his compassion. For by his compassion he did not prove that the man attacked was his neighbor, but that he was the neighbor of the one who was assaulted. The Levite and the priest were in a closer sense the neighbors of the victim, but these refused to recognize that fact; the Samaritan, on the contrary, who through prejudice might have misunderstood, still rightly understood that he was the neighbor of the man who had fallen among thieves. To choose a beloved, to find a friend, those are indeed complicated tasks, but a neighbor is easy to know, easy to find, if we will only —recognize our duty.

This was the commandment, "Thou shalt love thy neighbor as thyself," but when the commandment is rightly understood it also says the converse, *"Thou shalt love thyself in the right way."* If anyone, there-fore, will not learn from Christianity to love *himself* in the right way, then neither can he love his neighbor; he may perhaps, as we say, "for life and death" cling to one or several other human beings, but this is by no means loving one's neighbor. To love one's self in the right way and to love one's neighbor are absolutely analogous concepts, are at bottom one and the same. When the "as thyself" of the commandment has taken from you the selfishness which Christianity, sad to say, must presuppose as existing in every human being, then you have rightly learned to love yourself. Hence the law is: "You shall love yourself as you love your neighbor when you love him as yourself."

Whoever has some knowledge of men will certainly admit that as he has often wished to be able to influence men to give up their self-love, so he has also often wished that it were possible to teach them to love themselves. When the busy man wastes his time and energy on vain and unimportant projects, is this not because he has not rightly learned to love himself? When the frivolous man abandons himself, almost as a mere nothing, to the folly of the moment, is not this because he does not rightly understand how to love himself? When the melancholy man wishes to be done with life, even with himself, is this not because he will not learn strictly and earnestly to love himself? When a man, because the world or another man faithlessly betrayed him, yields himself up to despair, how was he to blame (for we are not here speaking of innocent suffering), except for not having loved himself in the right way? When a man in self-torment thinks to do God a service by torturing himself, what is his sin except this, of not willing to love himself in the right way? Ah, and when a man presumptuously lays his hand upon himself, does not his sin precisely consist in not loving himself in the way in which a man *ought* to love himself? Oh, there is so much said in the world about treachery and faithlessness, and, God help us! this is unfortunately only too true, but still let us never forget that the most dangerous traitor of all is the one every man has in his own breast. This treachery, whether it consists in a man's selfishly loving himself, or in the fact that he selfishly does not wish to love himself in the right way, this treachery is certainly a mystery because there is no outcry about it, as is usual in cases of treachery and faithlessness. But is it not therefore all the more important that we should repeatedly be reminded about the Christian teaching: that a man should love his neighbor as himself, that is, as he ought to love himself?

The commandment about love to one's neighbor uses one and the same word, "as thyself," about this love and about the love for one's self—and now the introduction to this discourse pauses at that which it desires to make the subject of our consideration. That by which the commandment about love to one's neighbor and about love to one's self become synonymous is not only this "as thyself," but even more that word, "Thou shalt." It is about this that we wish to speak: for this is precisely the criterion of the Christian love and its characteristic, that it contains the apparent contradiction, *that loving is a duty.*

Thou *shalt* love: this is consequently the word of the "royal law." And truly, my hearer, if you are able to form any conception of the world as it was before these words were uttered, or if you strive to understand yourself, and pay some attention to the lives and state of mind of those who, although they call themselves Christian, still really live under the categories of paganism—you will then humbly admit, with the wonder of faith, that with respect to this Christian word, as with all Christian expressions, such a commandment has not originated in any human heart. But now since this commandment has been in force through eighteen hundred years of Christianity, and before that time in Judaism; now since everyone has been brought up in it, and from the spiritual point of view is like a child brought up in the home of well-to-do parents, who quite naturally forgets that his daily bread is a gift; now since the Christian religion has many times been rejected by those who were brought up in it, because they preferred all kinds of novelties, just as wholesome food is refused by a person who has never been hungry, in favor of sweets; now since the Christian religion is everywhere presupposed, presupposed as known, as given, as indicated—in order to go further: now it is certainly asserted as a matter of course by everyone; and yet, alas, how seldom is it considered, how seldom perhaps does a Christian earnestly and with a thankful heart dwell upon the idea of what his condition might have been if Christianity had not come into the world! What courage was not needed in order to say for the first time, "Thou shalt love," or rather, what divine authority was not needed in order by this word to reverse the ideas and concepts of the natural man! For there at the border-line where human language pauses and courage weakens, there the revelation breaks forth with divine primitiveness and proclaims what is not difficult to understand in the sense of requiring depth of understanding or human parallels, but which nevertheless does not originate in any human heart. It is not really difficult to understand when it has been said, and it only wishes to be understood in order to be obeyed; but it does not originate in any human heart.

Let us consider a pagan who has not been spoiled by having thoughtlessly learned to repeat the Christian commandments by rote, or spoiled by imagining that he is a Christian, and this commandment, "Thou *shalt* love," will not only astonish him, but it will shock him, it will offend him. Just because of this, that commandment of love, which is the Christian recognition that "all things are become new," applies again here. . . . Love also existed in heathendom; but the idea that love is a duty is an everlasting innovation—and everything has become new. What a difference between the play of the emotions and impulses and inclinations and passions, in short, that play of the forces of immediacy, that glory celebrated in poetry, in smiles or in tears, in wishing or in need—what a difference between that and eternity, the earnestness of the commandment in spirit and in truth, in sincerity and self-denial!

But human ingratitude! Oh, what a short memory it has! Because the supreme good is offered to everyone, one regards it as nothing, perceives nothing in it, to say nothing of really evaluating its precious quality, as if the highest really lost something through the fact that everyone has or may have the same. If a family possesses one or another costly treasure which is closely associated with a definite event, then the parents tell their children about it from generation to generation, and their children in turn tell their children how this came about. But because Christianity has for so many centuries been the possession of the whole race, must therefore all talk about what an eternal change took place in the world because of its coming, cease? Is not every generation equally near to this, that is, equally bound to make it explicit? Is the change less remarkable because it happened eighteen hundred years ago? ... This is surely the most distressing and the most impious kind of deception, to allow one's self through ingratitude to be defrauded of the highest good which one believes one possesses—and, alas, to find that one does not possess it. For what, indeed, is the highest possession, what is the possession of everything, if I never get the right impression of my possession of it, and of what it is that I possess! Because, according to the Scriptures, he who has worldly goods should be as one who does not have them, I wonder if this is also right with respect to the supreme good: to have it and still be as one who does not have it. I wonder if that is right, yet no, let us not be deceived by the question, as if it would be possible to have the supreme good in this way. Let us realize that this is truly an impossibility. The earthly goods are of no consequence, and therefore the Scriptures teach that when they are possessed they should be possessed as the unimportant; but the supreme good cannot and must not be possessed as the unimportant. Earthly goods are an external reality, therefore one can own them even while being as one who does not own them; but spiritual goods exist only inwardly, exist only in *being possessed,* and therefore one cannot, if one really possesses them, be as one who does not possess them; on the contrary, if one is such, then one simply does not possess them. If someone believes that he has faith and yet is indifferent to his possession, neither cold nor warm, then he can be sure that he does not have faith. If someone believes that he is a Christian and yet is indifferent to the fact that he is, then he truly is not a Christian. What would we think about a man who protested that he was in love, and also stated that it was a matter of indifference to him?

So therefore let us not forget, as little now as on any other occasion when we speak about Christianity, let us not forget its beginning, that is, that it did not originate in any human heart; let us not forget to mention it along with the origin of faith, which never, when it is present in a man, believes because others have believed, but because *this* man, too, has been gripped by that which has gripped countless multitudes before him, but not therefore less primitively. For a tool that a handworker uses becomes blunted through years of use, a spring loses its elasticity and is weakened; but that which has the elasticity of eternity retains it through the ages absolutely unchanged. When a dynamometer has been used a long time, at last even a weak man can pass the test; but the dynamometer of eternity, on which every man must be tested as to whether he has faith or not, remains through all the ages absolutely unchanged.

When Christ said "Beware of men," I wonder if that warning did not imply this: "Beware lest through men, that is, through perpetual comparison with other men, through habit and externalities, you allow yourself to be defrauded of the supreme good." For the artfulness of a deceiver is not so dangerous, one more easily perceives it; but to hold the supreme good in a sort of common fellowship, in the indolence of habit, moreover in the indolence of a habit which even wishes to posit the race instead of the individual, wishes to make the race the receiver, and the individual a participant as a matter of course by virtue of his belonging to the race—this is truly the terrible thing. Certainly the highest must not be mere plunder; you must not have it for yourself in a selfish sense, for what you have for yourself alone is never the highest good; but even if you, in the most profound sense of the word, have the highest in common with everyone else (and this is precisely what makes it the highest, that you can have it in common with all others), you must still have it for yourself in such a way that you keep it, not only when everyone else has it, but so that you retain it even if all others renounce it. . . .

But the primitiveness of faith is related to the beginning of Christianity. Extravagant descriptions of heathendom, its errors, its characteristics, are by no means needed; the signs of the Christlike are contained in Christianity itself. Make an experiment: forget for a moment Christian love, consider what you know about other love, recall what you read in the poets, what you yourself can discover, and then say whether it ever occurred to you to conceive this: Thou *shalt* love. Be honest, or, that this may not embarrass you, I shall honestly confess that many, many times in my life it has awakened all my astonishment of wonder, that it has sometimes seemed to me as if love lost everything by this comparison, although it gains everything. Be honest, confess that this is perhaps the case with many people, that when they read the poets' glowing descriptions of love or friendship, these seem to them something far higher than the humble: "Thou *shalt* love."

"Thou shalt love." *Only when it is a duty to love, only then is love everlastingly secure against every change; everlastingly emancipated in blessed independence; everlastingly happy, assured against despair.*

However glad, however happy, however indescribably confident the love of impulse and inclination, the immediate love as such, can be, it still feels, even in its most beautiful moment, a need to bind itself if possible even more closely. Therefore the two take an oath; they take an oath of loyalty or friendship to each other; and when we speak most solemnly, we do not say about the two, "They love one another"; we say, "They swore fidelity to each other," or "They took an oath of friendship to each other." But by what does this love swear? . . . It is the poet who exacts a promise from the two, the poet who unites the two, the poet who dictates an oath to the two and lets them take it; in short, it is the poet who is the priest. Does this love then swear by something that is higher than itself? No, it does not. This is what exactly constitutes the beautiful, the moving, the mysterious, the poetical misunderstanding, that the two do not themselves discover it; and precisely because of this, the poet is their only, their beloved confidant, because neither does he discover it.

When this love takes an oath, it really gives itself that significance by which it swears; it is the love itself which casts a glamour over that by which it swears, so it consequently not only does not swear by anything higher, but it really swears by something lower than itself. So indescribably rich is this love in its loving misunderstanding; for just because it is itself an infinite wealth, a limitless trustworthiness, it happens that when it wishes to take an oath it swears by something lower, but it does not even discover this. That is why it again happens that this oath, which certainly should be and which also honestly believes itself to be supremely serious, is still the most charming jest. And neither does that mysterious friend, the poet, whose perfect confidence is this love's supreme understanding, understand it. Still it is certainly easy to understand, that if one will swear in truth, then one must swear by something higher; only God in heaven is truly in a position to swear by Himself. However, the poet cannot understand this, that is, the individual who is a poet can understand it, but he cannot understand it insofar as he is poet, since "the poet" cannot understand it. . . .

So this love takes an oath, and then the two add to the oath that they will love each other "forever." If this is not added, then the poet does not unite the two; he turns indifferently away from such a temporal love, or he turns mockingly against it, whereas he forever belongs to that eternal love. There are then really two unions, first, the two who will love each other forever, and then the poet who will forever belong to those two. And in that the poet is right, that if two men will not love each other forever, then their love is not worth talking about, and certainly not forth celebrating in verse. On the other hand, the poet does not notice the misunderstanding that the two swear *by their love* to love each other forever, instead of swearing their love to each other by *eternity*. Eternity is the higher; if one wishes to take an oath, then must one swear by the higher, but if one will swear by the eternal, then one swears by the *duty of loving*. Alas, but that favorite of lovers, the poet! Even more seldom than the two true lovers is he himself the lover for whom he longs, even if he is a marvel of lovableness. He is like the affectionate child, he cannot endure hearing this "shalt"; as soon as it is said to him, he either becomes impatient, or he bursts into tears.

Hence, this immediate love contains the eternal in the form of a beautiful fantasy, but it is not consciously grounded on the eternal, and therefore it can be *changed*. Even if it does not change, it still retains the possibility of change, for it depends on good fortune. But if what is true of fortune is true about happiness, which if we think of the eternal cannot be considered without sadness, it is like saying with a shudder: "Happiness *is,* when it *has been*." That is, as long as it existed, or was existing, a change was possible; only when it is past can one say that it existed. "Call no man happy as long as he is living"; as long as he is living his fortune may change; only when he is dead, and happiness had not forsaken him while he lived, can one know that he—had been happy. What merely exists, what has suffered no change, always has the possibility of change outside itself. Change is always possible; even at the last moment it may come, and not until life is finished can one say: "The change did not come"—or perhaps it did come. That which has suffered no change certainly has *continuance,* but it does not have *immutability*. Insofar as it has continuance it exists, but insofar as it has gained immutability through change, it cannot become contemporaneous with itself, and then it is either happily unconscious of this disproportion, or it is inclined to sadness. For the eternal is the only thing which can be and become and continue contemporaneously with every age. On the other hand, temporal existence is divisive in itself, and the present cannot be contemporaneous with the future, or the future with the past, or the past with the present. As to that which by undergoing change gained immutability, one cannot merely say, when it has existed, "It existed," but one can say, "It has existed while it existed." Just this is what affords the security, and it is an entirely different relation from that of happiness. When love has undergone the change of eternity through having become duty, then it has gained immutability, and it follows as a matter of course that it exists. It is not a matter of course that what exists at this moment also exists the next moment, but it is a matter of course that the immutable exists.

We say that something has stood the test, and we praise it when it has met the test. But we are still talking about the imperfect, for the immutability of the immutable *will* not and *can* not become apparent by undergoing a test—for it is immutable, and only the perishable can give itself the appearance of immutability by meeting a test. That is why it would never occur to anyone to say about sterling silver that it will stand the test of years, because it is sterling silver. So too with love. The love which merely has continuance, however happy, however blissful, however confident, however poetic it is, must still stand the testing of the years; but the love which underwent the change of eternity through becoming duty, won immutability; it is sterling.

Is this love which underwent the change of eternity therefore less practicable, less useful in life? Is sterling silver less useful? Surely not; but language involuntarily and thought consciously honors sterling silver in a characteristic way, for one merely says of this that "one uses it." There is simply nothing said about testing it; one does not insult it by wishing to test it, for one knows already that sterling silver stands the test. Therefore if one uses a less reliable product, then one is compelled to be more tactless and to speak less simply; one is compelled to speak almost ambiguously, to say two things, that "one uses it and while he uses it, he is also testing it," for it is always possible that it might change.

Consequently *only when love is a duty, only then is love eternally secure.* This security of eternity drives out all anxiety and makes love perfect, perfectly secure. For in that love which only has continuance, however confident it is, there is still an anxiety, an anxiety about the possibility of change. It does not itself understand, as little as does the poet, that it is anxiety; for the anxiety is hidden, and there is only the burning desire for the expression of love, which is just the admission that anxiety lies at the bottom. How otherwise does it happen that the immediate love is so inclined to, moreover so enamored with, the idea of putting love to the test? This is just because love has not, through becoming duty, in the deepest sense undergone the "test." Hence this which the poet would call sweet unrest wishes more and more rashly to make the test. The lover would test the beloved, friend would test the friend; the testing no doubt is based on love, but this violently burning desire to test, this wishful craving to put love to the test, nevertheless testifies that the love itself is unconsciously insecure. Here again is a mysterious misunderstanding in the immediate love and in the explanations of the poet. The lover and the poet think that this desire to test love is simply an expression for how certain it is. But is this really true? It is true that one does not care to test what is unimportant; but from that it does not follow that wishing to test the beloved expresses confidence. The two love each other, they love each other forever, they are so certain of this that they—put it to the test. Is this the highest certainty? Is not the relation here precisely what it is when love takes an oath and yet swears by what is lower than love? So here the highest expression of the lovers for the constancy of their love is an expression of the fact that it merely has existence, for one tests that which merely has existence, one puts it to the test.

But when it is a duty to love, there no test is needed and the insulting stupidity of wishing to test is superfluous; since love is higher than any proof, it has already more than met the test, in the same sense that faith "more than conquers." The very fact of testing always presupposes a possibility; it is still always possible that that which is tested may not meet the test. Hence if someone wished to test whether he has faith, or tried to get faith, then this would really mean that he will hinder himself in acquiring faith; he will become a victim of the restless craving where faith is never won, for "thou *shalt* believe." If a believer were to implore God to put his faith to the test, then this is not an indication of the believer's having faith to an extraordinary degree (to think that is a poetic misunderstanding, as it is also a misunderstanding to have faith to an "extraordinary" degree, since the ordinary degree of faith is the highest), but it indicates that he does not quite have faith, for "thou *shalt* believe." There is no higher assurance, and the repose of eternity is never found anywhere but in this "shalt." However attractive it may be, "testing" is a disquieting thought, and it is anxiety which would make you imagine that the testing constitutes a higher assurance; for the idea of testing is in itself ingenious and inexhaustible, just as human wisdom has never been able to reckon all the chances, while, on the contrary, as earnestness so excellently says, "Faith has taken all chances into account." And if one *must,* then it is eternally decided; and if you are willing to understand that you *must* love, then is your love eternally secure.

And love is also through this "shalt" eternally secure *against every change.* For the love which merely has continuance can be changed, it can be changed *in itself,* and it can be changed *from itself.*

The immediate love can be changed in itself, it can be changed into its opposite, into *hate*. Hate is a love which has become its opposite, a love which has perished. At bottom love burns constantly, but the flame is that of hate; only when the love is burnt out is the flame of hate also quenched. As it is said about the tongue, that "out of the same mouth proceedeth both blessing and cursing," so we must also say that it is the same love which loves and hates; but just because it is the same love, precisely therefore it is not in the eternal sense the true love, which *remains the same and unchanged,* while that immediate love, if *it is changed,* at bottom is still *the same.* The true love, which underwent the change of the eternal by becoming duty, is never changed; it is simple, it loves—and never hates, never hates—the beloved. It might seem as if the immediate love were the stronger because it can do two things, because it can *both* love *and* hate; it might seem as if it had a quite different power over its object when it says, "If you will not love me, then I will hate you": still this is only an illusion. For is the changeable really a stronger power than the unchangeable? And who is the stronger, the one who says, "If you will not love me, then I will hate you," or the one who says, "Even if you hate me I shall continue to love you"? Moreover, it is certainly terrifying and terrible that love should be changed into hate; but I wonder for whom it is really terrible: is it not for the one to whom it happened that his love was changed to hate?

The immediate love can undergo a change; it can spontaneously become *jealousy,* can change from the greatest happiness into the greatest agony. So dangerous is the heat of this immediate love ... that this heat can easily become a sickness. The immediate love is like fermentation, which is so called just because it has still undergone no change, and therefore has not yet separated out from itself the poison which at the same time furnishes the heat of the fermentation. If love sets itself on fire through this poison, instead of separating it out, then comes jealousy; and, alas! the word itself indicates a desire to become sick, a sickness of desire [*Iver*—desire, *Sygdom*—sickness; hence *Iversyge,* desire-sickness, or jealousy]. The jealous person does not hate the object of love, far from it, but he tortures himself with the fire of reciprocated love, which sanctifyingly ought to purify his love. The jealous lover intercepts, almost imploringly, every ray of love from the beloved, but he focuses all these rays upon his own love through the burning-glass of his jealousy, and he is slowly consumed. On the other hand, the love which underwent the change of eternity through becoming duty knows no jealousy;

it loves, not only as it is loved, but *it loves.* Jealousy loves as it is loved; in jealous agony about whether it is loved, it is as jealous for its own love, whether it may not be disproportionate to the other's indifference, as it is jealous for the expression of the other's love; anxiously tortured in its self-occupation, it neither dares to believe the beloved absolutely nor to resign itself absolutely, lest it give too much, and therefore it is always burning itself, as one burns himself on that which is not hot—except to the anxious touch. It is comparable to spontaneous combustion. It might seem as if there would be quite a different kind of fire in the immediate love, since it can become jealousy; but, alas, this fire is just the appalling thing about it. It might seem as if jealousy held its object fast in quite a different way when it watches over it with a hundred eyes, while simple love has, as it were, but a single eye for its love. But I wonder if dispersion is stronger than unity, I wonder if a heart wrenched asunder is stronger than one perfect and undivided. I wonder if a perpetually grasping anxiety holds its object closer than the united forces of simplicity! And how does that simple love assure itself against jealousy? I wonder if it is not by virtue of the fact that it does not love in a comparative way. It does not begin by immediately loving perferentially; it loves. Therefore it can never love morbidly in a comparative way; it loves.

The immediate love can be changed *from itself,* it can be changed by the years, as is so often seen. Then love loses its ardor, its gladness, its desire, its primitiveness, the freshness of its life; like the river which sprang out of the rock when it later on spreads out in the sluggishness of stagnant water, so love is weakened by the lukewarmness and indifference of habit. Alas, perhaps of all enemies force of habit is the most crafty, and above all it is crafty enough never to let itself be seen, for one who sees the habit is saved from habit. Habit is not like other enemies which one sees and against which one strives to defend himself; the struggle is really with one's self in getting to see it. In its cunning it is like that familiar beast of prey, the vampire bat, which stealthily falls upon its sleeping victim; while it sucks his blood, its gently moving wings waft the coolness over him and make his slumber even more refreshing. Such is habit—or it is even worse; for that animal seeks its prey among the sleeping, but it has no means of soothing the waking to sleep. Habit, on the contrary, has this power; it creeps soporifically upon a man, and when he has fallen asleep, then it sucks his blood, whilst it wafts the coolness over him and makes his sleep even more delicious.

So the immediate love can be changed from itself and become un-recognizable—whereas hate and jealousy are still perceptible in the love. So a man himself sometimes notices, as when a dream floats by and is forgotten, that habit has changed him; then he wishes to make good again, but he does not know where he can go to buy new oil to enkindle his love. Then he becomes despondent, irritated, bored by himself, bored by his love, bored by the wretchedness of things as they are, bored by the fact that he cannot change them; alas, for he had not paid attention in time to the change of eternity, and now he has even lost the power to endure the healing.

Oh, we sometimes see with sorrow the impoverishment of a man who once lived in affluence, and yet how much more distressing than this change it is to see love changed into something almost abhorrent! If, on the contrary, love has undergone the change of eternity by becoming duty, then it does not know the force of habit, then habit can never get power over it. As it is said of the eternal life, that there is neither sighing nor weeping, so we might add that there is also no habit; and thereby we truly are not saying anything less excellent. If you wish to save your soul or your love from the perfidy of habit: men believe that there are many ways of keeping themselves awake and safe, but truly there is but one—eternity's "shalt." Let the thunder of a hundred cannon three times a day remind you to resist the thraldom of habit; keep, as did that mighty Eastern emperor, a slave who daily reminds you, keep a hundred; have a friend who reminds you every time he sees you, have a wife who reminds you early and late in love: but watch yourself lest this too becomes a habit! For you can become accustomed to the thunder of a hundred cannon, so that you can sit at table and hear the most insignificant remark more clearly than the roar of the hundred cannon you are in the habit of hearing. And you can become accustomed to having a hundred slaves remind you every day, so that you no longer listen, because through habit you have developed an ear wherewith you hear and yet do not hear. No, only the "thou shalt" of eternity—and the listening ear which will hear this "thou shalt"—can save you from the thraldom of habit. Habit is the most distressing change, and on the other hand, one can accustom one's self to every change; only the eternal, and consequently that which underwent the change of eternity through becoming duty, is the unchangeable, but the unchangeable can never become habit. However firmly a habit is fixed, it never becomes unchangeable, even if a man remains incorrigible; for habit is constantly that which *should be changed;* the unchangeable, on the contrary, is that which neither *can* nor *should* be changed. But the eternal never becomes old and never becomes habit.

Only when it is a duty to love, only then is love everlastingly free in blessed independence. But is, then, that immediate love not free; does not the lover enjoy freedom in his love? And, on the other hand, could it be the intention of the discourse to recommend the desolate independence of self-love, which became independent because it did not have the courage to bind itself, and hence became dependent on its cowardice; the desolate independence which vacillates because it found no place of refuge, and is like "the one who wanders hither and thither, an armed brigand, who puts up wherever evening finds him"; the desolate independence which independently will not endure fetters—at least not visible ones? Oh, far from it; on the contrary, we have in the preceding discourse reminded you that the expression for the greatest wealth is to have a need; and this is also the true expression of freedom, that it is a need in the free. He in whom love is a necessity certainly feels free in his love; and just the one who feels himself so dependent on his love that he would lose everything in losing the beloved, just he is independent. Yet on one condition, that he does not confuse love with the possession of the beloved.

If one were to say, "Either love or die," and thereby mean that a life without love was not worth living, then we should admit that he was absolutely right. But if by this he meant possessing the beloved, and consequently meant, either possess the beloved or die, either gain this friend or die, then we must say that such a love is dependent in a false sense. When love does not make the same demands upon itself that it makes on the object of its love, while it is still dependent on that love, then it is dependent in a false sense: the law of its existence lies outside itself, and hence it is dependent in the corruptible, earthly, temporal sense. But the love which underwent the change of eternity by becoming duty, and loves because it *must* love, it is independent: it has the law of its existence in the relation of love itself to the eternal. This love can never become dependent in a false sense, for the only one it is dependent upon is duty, and duty is the only emancipating power. Immediate love makes a man free one moment, and in the next moment dependent. It is like a man's coming into existence: by existing, by becoming a "self," he becomes free, but in the next moment he is dependent on this self. Duty, on the other hand, makes a man dependent and at the same time eternally independent. "Only the law can give freedom." Alas, we often think that freedom exists, and that it is the law which restricts freedom. However, it is just the other way: without law freedom simply does not exist, and it is the law which gives freedom. We think, too, that it is the law which makes distinctions, because where there is no law there are no distinctions. Still it is the other way: when it is the law which makes the distinction, then it is exactly the law which makes everyone equal before the law.

Thus this "shalt" sets love free in blessed independence: such a love stands and falls not by some accidental circumstance of its object, it stands and falls by the law of eternity—but then it never falls; such a love does not depend upon this or that, it depends only on—the one liberating force, consequently it is eternally independent. There is nothing comparable to this independence. Sometimes the world praises the proud independence which believes it feels no need of being loved, although it also thinks that it "needs other men, not to be loved by them, but in order to love, in order to have someone to love." Oh, how false is this independence! It feels no *need* to be loved, and yet it *needs* someone to love; consequently it needs another man—in order to be able to satisfy its proud self-esteem. Is not this as when vanity believes that it can dispense with the world, and yet needs the world, that is, it needs that the world should become conscious of the fact that its vanity does not need the world! But the love which underwent the change of eternity by becoming duty certainly feels a need of being loved, and this need together with this "shalt" is therefore an eternally harmonious concord; but it can do without this love, if so it *must* be, while it still continues to love: is this not independence? This independence is dependent only on love itself through the "shalt" of eternity; it is not dependent on anything else, and therefore it is not dependent on love's object as soon as this appears to be something else. However, this does not indicate that the independent love then ceased, transformed itself into a proud self-satisfaction, that is, into dependence. No, love abides, it is independence. The unchangeableness is the true independence: every change, be it the swoon of weakness or the arrogance of pride, the sighing or the self-satisfied, is dependence. If one man, when another man says to him, "I can no longer love you," proudly answers, "Then I can also stop loving you," is this independence? Alas, it is only dependence, for the fact as to whether he will continue to love or not depends on whether the other will love. But the one who answers, "Then I will still continue to love you," his love is everlastingly free in blessed independence. He does not say it proudly—dependent on his pride; no, he says it humbly, humbling himself under the "shalt" of eternity, and just for that reason he is independent.

Only when it is a duty to love, only then is love everlastingly secured again despair. Immediate love can become unhappy, can come to despair. Again, it might seem an expression for the strength of love, that it has the energy of despair, but this is only an appearance; for the energy of despair, however much it is recommended, is still impotence, its highest possibility is just its own destruction. Still, the fact that the immediate love can reach despair shows that it is despairing, that even when it is happy it loves with the energy of despair—loves another man "better than himself, better than God." About despair it must be said: only he can despair who is desperate. When immediate love despairs over unhappiness, then it merely becomes evident that it was— desperate, that in its happiness it had also been desperate. Despair consists in laying hold on an individual with infinite passion; for unless one is desperate, one can lay hold only on the eternal with infinite passion. Immediate love *is* thus desperate; but when it becomes happy, as we say, it is hidden from it that it is desperate; when it becomes unhappy it becomes evident that it—was desperate. On the other hand, the love which underwent the change of eternity by becoming duty can never despair, just because it *is* not desperate. Despair is, namely, not something which may happen to a man, an event like fortune and misfortune. Despair is a disproportion in his inmost being [2]—so far down, so deep, that neither fate nor events can encroach upon it, but can only reveal the fact that the disproportion—was there. Therefore there is only one assurance against despair: to undergo the change of eternity by the "shalt" of duty; anyone who has not understood this change *is* desperate; fortune and prosperity may conceal it; misfortune and adversity, on the contrary, do not, as he thinks, make him desperate, but they reveal the fact that he—was desperate. Insofar as we speak otherwise, it is because we frivolously confuse the highest concepts. That which really makes a man despair is not misfortune, but it is the fact that he lacks the eternal; despair is to lack the eternal; despair consists in not having undergone the change of eternity by duty's "shalt." Consequently despair is not the loss of the beloved, that is, misfortune, pain, suffering; but despair is the lack of the eternal.

How then is the love enjoined by the commandment assured against despair? Quite simply, through the commandment, through this, "Thou shalt love." It consists first and foremost in the fact that you must not

[2] A theme treated at greater length in *The Sickness unto Death, infra,* pp. 341–344.

love in such a way that the loss of the beloved would reveal the fact that you were desperate—that is, that you simply must not love despairingly. Does this mean that it is forbidden to love? By no means; that would indeed be a strange speech, if the commandment which says "Thou shalt love," should by its command forbid one to love. Hence the commandment merely forbids loving in a way which is not commanded; essentially the commandment does not forbid but commands that thou shalt love. Hence the commandment of love does not assure against despair by means of weak, lukewarm grounds of comfort, that one must not take things too seriously, and all that. And truly is such a wretched wisdom, which "has ceased to sorrow," any less despairing than the despair of the lover—is it not rather an even worse form of despair! No, the commandment of love forbids despair—by commanding one to love. Who would have the courage to say this except eternity? Who is prepared to speak this "shalt" except eternity who, at the very moment when love would despair over its unhappiness, commands it to love? Where can this commandment arise except in eternity? For when it becomes impossible to possess the beloved in the temporal existence, then eternity says, "Thou shalt love"—that is, eternity saves love from despairing just by making it eternal. Suppose it is death which separates the two—when the one left would sink in despair: where then can he find help? Temporal consolation is an even more distressing kind of despair; but then eternity helps. When it says, "Thou shalt love," then in saying that it says, "Thy love hath an everlasting validity." But it does not say this consolingly, for that would not help; it says it commandingly, just because there is something wrong. And when eternity says, "Thou shalt love," then it assumes the responsibility for guaranteeing that it can be done. Oh, what is all other consolation compared with that of eternity, what is all other deep-felt sorrow against that of eternity! If one would speak more gently and say, "Take comfort," then the sorrowing would have objections ready; but . . . out of solicitude for the sorrowful, it commands, "Thou shalt love."

Wonderful consolation! Wonderful compassion! For, humanly speaking, it is indeed the strangest thing, almost like mockery, to say to the despairing that he *ought* to do that which would be his sole wish, but the impossibility of which reduces him to despair. Is there any other proof needed that the commandment of love is of divine origin? If you have tried it, or if you do try it, go to such a sorrowing one at the very moment when the loss of the beloved threatens to overwhelm him, and see then what you can find to say; confess that you wish to console him; the only thing it will *not* occur to you to say is, "Thou shalt love." And on the other hand, see if this does not, as soon as it is said, almost embitter the sorrowing, because it seems the most unsuitable thing to say on this occasion. Oh, but you who had the bitter experience, you who at the hard moment found human consolation empty and annoying —without consolation; you who with terror discovered that not even the admonition of the eternal could keep you from sinking down: you learned to love this "shalt" which saves from despair! What you perhaps have often verified in minor situations—that true edification is, strictly speaking, that which taught you in the most profound sense: that only this "shalt" forever happily saves from despair. Eternally happy—aye, for only that one is saved from despair who is *eternally* saved from despair. The love which underwent the change of eternity by becoming duty is not exempt from unhappiness, but it is saved from despair, in fortune and misfortune equally saved from despair.

Lo, passion excites, earthly wisdom cools, but neither this heat nor this coolness, nor the blending of the heat and coolness is the pure air of the eternal. There is in this heat something ardent, and in this coolness something sharp, and in the blending of the two something indefinite, or an unconscious deceitfulness, as in the hazardous season of spring. But this "Thou *shalt* love" takes away all the unsoundness and preserves the soundness of eternity. Thus it is everywhere: this "shalt" of eternity is the saving, the purifying, the ennobling. Sit with one who is in deep sorrow; you may soothe for a moment if you have the ability to give expression to the passion of despair as not even the sorrowing is able to do; but it is still false comfort. It may for a moment tempt refreshingly, if you have the wisdom and the experience to afford a temporary outlook where the sorrowing sees none; but it is still false comfort. On the other hand, this "Thou shalt sorrow" is both true and beautiful. I have no right to harden my heart against the pain of life, for I *must* sorrow; but neither have I the right to despair, for I *must* sorrow; and yet neither have I the right to cease to sorrow, for I *must* sorrow. So also with love. You have no right to harden yourself against this emotion, for thou *shalt* love; but neither have you the right to love despairingly, for thou *shalt* love; and just as little have you the right to corrupt this feeling in you, for thou *shalt* love. You must preserve the love and you must preserve yourself, and in preserving yourself preserve your love. There where the purely human would rush forth, the commandment retards; there where the purely human would lose courage, the commandment strengthens; there where the purely human would become weary and prudent, the commandment enkindles and gives wisdom. The commandment consumes and burns up the unsoundness in your love, but through the commandment you will again be able to enkindle it when humanly speaking it would cease. There where you think yourself easily able to advise, there you must take the commandment for counsel; there where you despairingly would direct yourself, there you must take the commandment for your counselor; but there where you do not know how to advise, there will the commandment give counsel, so that all is well.

LOVE COVERETH A MULTITUDE OF SINS

THE temporal has three times, and therefore it never really absolutely exists, or absolutely exists in any one of them. The eternal *is*. A temporal object can have many different attributes, and in a certain sense can be said to have them all at one time, insofar as it is what it is in these definite attributes. But *duplication in itself* never has a temporal object; as the temporal disappears in time, so too it only exists in its attributes. On the contrary, when the eternal is present in a man then this eternal so *reduplicates itself* in him that every moment it is present in him, it is present in a twofold manner: in an outward direction, and in an inward direction back into itself; but in such a way that this is one and the same thing, for otherwise it is not duplication. The eternal is not merely in its own attributes, but is in itself in its attributes; it not only has attributes, but is in itself when it has attributes.

So now with love. What love does, that it is; what it is, that it does— and at one and the same time: at the very moment it goes out of itself (the direction outward) it is in itself (the direction inward); and at the very moment it is in itself, it thereby goes out of itself—so that this outgoing and this return, this return and this outgoing, are simultaneously one and the same.

When we say that "Love gives fearlessness," we mean by that, that the lover by his very nature makes others fearless; wherever love is present, it spreads fearlessness; one freely approaches the lover, for he drives out fear. Whereas the suspicious man frightens everyone away from him, whereas the cunning and the crafty spread fear and painful unrest about them, whereas the presence of the tyrant oppresses like the heavy pressure of sultry air—love gives fearlessness. But when we say that "love gives fearlessness," we also say at the same time something else, that the lover has fearlessness, just as it is said that love gives boldness on the day of judgment, that is, it makes the lover fearless in the judgment.

When we say, "Love saves from death," it is precisely a duplication of the thought: the lover saves another man from death, and he saves, either in absolutely the same or yet in another sense, himself from death; he does it at one and the same time, it is one and the same thing; he does not save the other at one moment and himself the next, but at the very moment that he saves the other, he saves himself from death. Only love never thinks about the latter, about saving himself, about himself acquiring fearlessness; the lover in his love thinks only about giving fearlessness and saving another from death. Yet the lover is not therefore forgotten. No, the one who lovingly forgets himself, forgets his own suffering to consider another's, forgets all his own wretchedness in order to think of another's misery, forgets what he himself loses in order lovingly to consider another's loss, forgets his own advantage in order lovingly to look at another's: truly such a one is not forgotten. There is One who considers him: God in heaven; or love considers him. God is love, and when a man from love forgets himself, how then could God forget him! No, while the lover forgets himself and thinks of the other man, God thinks of the lover. The self-lover is busy, he shrieks and shouts, and stands for his rights in order to make certain of not being forgotten—and yet he is forgotten; but the lover who forgets himself, he is remembered by love. There is One who thinks of him, and thereby it comes to pass that the lover gets what he gives.

Look at the duplication: what the lover does, that he is, or he becomes that; what he gives, that he has, or he gets it—wonderful as that "out of the eater came forth meat." Still, perhaps someone says, "It is not so wonderful that the lover has what he gives, that is always the case; what one does not have, one cannot give." Oh, well, but is it then always the case that one *keeps* what one gives, or that one *gets* that which one gives to another; that just by giving one gets, and gets exactly the same one gives, so that the thing given and the thing received are one and the same? Ordinarily this is not the case, but, on the contrary, what I give the other gets—not that I myself get that which I give to another.

So love is always duplicated in itself. This holds true, too, when it is said that love covers a multitude of sins.

In the Scriptures we read that which is "love's" own word, that many sins were forgiven to the one who loved much—because the love in him conceals the multitude of sins. However, we shall not speak about that[1] at this time. In this little essay we are constantly discussing the works of love, consequently we are looking at love directed outward. With this meaning in mind, we shall now speak about:

Love Covereth a Multitude of Sins.

Love covers a multitude of sins. For it does not discover the sins; but the fact that it does not discover what still must exist, insofar as they can be discovered—that is hiding them.

The concept "multiplicity" is in itself indefinite. Thus we speak about all the multiplicity of creation, yet this same word signifies something very different, depending on who is speaking. A man who has spent his entire life in an out-of-the way place, and has therefore acquired little taste for studying nature: how little does he know, and yet he speaks about the multiplicity of creation! A naturalist, however, who has traveled around the world, who has been almost everywhere, both above and beneath the surface of the earth, who has seen the much that he has seen; who has by the use of the telescope sometimes discovered otherwise invisible stars, sometimes by the use of the microscope has discovered otherwise invisible insects: what an astonishing variety he knows, yet he uses the same word, "the multiplicity of creation." And further: while the naturalist rejoices at what he succeeded in seeing, he readily admits that there is no limit to discoveries, since there is no limit to the invention of instruments used in making these discoveries. Consequently the multiplicity of creation, with new instruments constantly being invented, becomes greater and greater, and can always appear to increase—while it still, all things considered, is comprehended in the phrase, "multiplicity of creation." The same holds true about the multitude of sins, in that the word may signify very different things, depending on who the speaker is.

Consequently one *discovers* that the multitude of sins is constantly increasing; that is, through their discovery it constantly seems to be increasing, naturally also by the help of the discoveries one makes about

---

[1] S.K. had treated the verse from this angle in the *Three Edifying Discourses* of 1843. (See Vol. I of the English edition of the *Discourses,* published by the Augsburg Press.)

how cunningly, how suspiciously one acts in order to make discoveries. He who *makes no discoveries* consequently hides the multitude of sins, for to him the multitude is less.

But discovery is something praiseworthy, something admirable, even if this admiration is sometimes forced to bring the heterogeneous together in a strange way; for one admires the naturalist who discovers a bird, but one also admires the dog that discovered purple. Still, we shall let this pass for what it is worth, but it is certain that the world admires and praises discoveries. And on the other hand, one who makes no discoveries, or as good as none, is rated very low. We readily say about someone, in order to brand as an eccentric one who is wrapped up in his own thoughts, "He really does not discover anything." And if we wish to designate one as being especially limited and stupid, we say, "He will certainly never invent gunpowder!"—which certainly is not necessary in our time, since it has already been invented; so it would be an even more questionable matter if someone in our time were to think that he was the one who invented it. Oh, but the fact of having made some discovery is so admired by the world that one cannot forget the enviable lot—of the one who discovered gunpowder!

Of course, it is easy to see that the lover who discovers nothing looks very mediocre in the eyes of the world. For even in regard to evil, in regard to sin and the multiplicity of sin, one discovers that there is the smooth, cunning, obtrusive, perhaps half-corrupt observer, who really can make discoveries: that is highly regarded in the world. Even the youth, the very moment that he steps out into life (for he would certainly object to having the world call him a fool) is most willing to disclose how he knows and has discovered evil. Even a woman in her earliest youth (for she would then object to having the world call her a little goose, or a rustic innocent) will readily disclose that she is vain of being a judge of character, naturally in the direction of evil. Moreover, it is incredible how the world has changed in comparison with olden times: then there were some few who knew themselves; now all men are judges of character. And this is the curious thing: if someone had discovered how fundamentally humane almost every man is, he would scarcely dare to make his discovery known for fear of being laughed at; perhaps he might even fear that the community would feel insulted at the idea. On the other hand, if someone pretends that he has discovered how fundamentally paltry every man is, how envious, how selfish, how faithless, what abominations can dwell secretly in even the purest, that is, in the one who is regarded by fools and geese and rustic innocents as the purest: then he knows vaingloriously that he is welcome, that the world is longing to hear the results of his observations, his research, his stories. Thus have sin and evil acquired a greater power over men than one ordinarily imagines: it is so silly to be good, so intellectually stupid to believe the good, so provincial to betray ignorance, or that one is not an initiate—an initiate into the most intimate mysteries of sin.

Here we see very clearly how evil and sin in a great measure are the consequence of a vainglorious comparison of one's self with the world and with other men. For one can be quite certain that the same men, just because they vaingloriously fear the judgment of the world, strive in their intercourse with others to be agreeable and interesting by betraying a sophisticated knowledge of evil. One can be quite certain that those same men, when they are alone in quiet meditation, where they do not need to be ashamed of the good, hold a very different view. But in intercourse with others, in society, when one is with many or at least a few, and hence where the company affords a comparison, a comparison-relation, of which vanity cannot possibly remain unconscious— then each one tempts the other to disclose what he has discovered.

Yet even the absolutely worldly-minded man sometimes makes an exception, sometimes judges a little more leniently the one who discovers nothing. Suppose that two shrewd men of affairs had some decision to make to which they did not wish to have witnesses, but they were unable to arrange it otherwise, so that their conference must take place in a room where a third party was present—this third party, as they knew, was very much in love, happy in the first days of love: is it not true that one of the businessmen might say to the other, "Well, it doesn't matter if he is present, he won't hear anything." They would say it with a smile, and by this smile they would pay tribute to their own astuteness; but they would still have a kind of respect for the lover who discovers nothing.

And now the lover! For whether the world laughs at him, whether it ridicules him, whether it pities him, or whatever the world says about him, it is certain that concerning the multitude of sins, he *discovers* nothing, not even this laughter, this ridicule, this pity; he *discovers* nothing, and he sees but very little. He discovers nothing; we here make a difference between discovering as a conscious act, as a deliberate attempt to find out something, and the involuntary seeing or hearing something. He discovers nothing. And yet, whether one laughs at him or not, whether or not one ridicules him: fundamentally one has an inward respect for him, because engrossed in his love he discovers nothing.

The lover discovers nothing, hence he conceals the multitude of sins which would be exposed through the discovery. The life of the lover is an expression of the apostolic precept of being a child in malice. That which the world really admires as shrewdness is an understanding of evil; wisdom is essentially the understanding of the good. The lover has no understanding of evil and does not wish to have; he is and remains, he wishes to be and to continue to be, in this respect, a child. Place a child in a den of thieves, but the child must not remain there so long that it becomes itself perverted, hence let it remain there only a very short time; then let it come home and tell of all its experiences: you will see that the child, who (like every child) is a good observer and has an excellent memory, will tell everything with the utmost detail, yet in such a way that in a sense the most important things are omitted, so that one who did not know that the child had been among bandits would least suspect it from the child's narrative. What is it then which the child omits? What is it that the child did not discover? It is the evil. And yet the child's description of what it saw and heard is absolutely accurate. What is it then the child lacks? What is it that so frequently makes a child's narration the most profound mockery of its elders? It is the sense of evil, and that the child lacks the sense of evil, so that the child finds no pleasure in wishing to understand it. Herein the lover resembles the child. But as a basis of all *understanding* there must first and foremost be an *understanding* between the one who will understand and the thing which shall be understood. Therefore, too, the understanding of evil (however much it wishes to delude itself and others into thinking that it can preserve its purity, that it has a pure understanding of evil) is still in *understanding* with the evil; if this understanding did not exist, if the intelligent man did not take pleasure in understanding it, then he would abominate the understanding of it, would prefer not to understand it. Even if this sense of evil indicates nothing else, it is still a dangerous curiosity about evil; or it is a cunning search for an excuse for its own fault in spreading evil by the aid of knowledge; or it is the false reckoning which exaggerates a man's feeling of importance by the help of his knowledge about another man's corruption.

But let one set a strict guard upon himself; for if out of curiosity one offers evil the little finger, it soon takes the whole hand. And it is most dangerous of all to have ready a stock of excuses; and to become better, or to seem to be better, through comparison with the badness of others, is to become better in a bad way. However, if even this understanding discovers the multitude of sins, what discoveries must not the even more confidential understanding, which is really in a covenant with evil, be able to make! As the jaundiced see everything as yellow, so such a man discovers, as he sinks deeper and deeper, an increasing manifold of sin about him. His eye is alert and trained, not for the understanding of truth, hence for untruth; consequently his sight is prejudiced more and more so that, increasingly defiled, he sees evil in everything, impurity even in what is purest—and this sight (Oh terrible thought!) is still to him a kind of consolation, for it is important to him to discover as boundless a multitude as possible. At last there are no limits to his discovery; for now he discovers sin even where he himself knows that there is none; he discovers it by the help of backbiting, slander, the fabrication of lies, in which he has trained himself so long that he at last believes it. Such a man has verily discovered the multitude of sins!

But the lover discovers nothing. There is something so infinitely solemn and yet also so childlike, something which recalls a childish game, when the lover by discovering nothing at all hides the multitude of sins; something that recalls a childish game, for that is the way we play with a child. We play that we cannot see the child who is standing in front of us, or the child plays that it cannot see us, and this the child finds indescribably amusing. The childlikeness here is that the lover, as in the game, with his eyes wide open, cannot see what is happening just in front of him; the solemnity consists in the fact that it is the evil which he cannot see. We all know that orientals honor a demented person, but this lover, who is worthy of honor, is, as it were, a demented person. We all know that in the old times they made, and rightly, a great distinction between the two kinds of madness: one was a distressing sickness, and one bemoaned such a misfortune; the other was called a divine madness. If we may for once be excused for using the pagan word "divine," it is a divine kind of madness lovingly not to be able to see the evil which lies just in front of one. Truly it is necessary in these clever times which have so much understanding of evil that we should make some effort to learn to honor this madness; for unfortunately it is all too frequent in these times that such a lover, who has a great understanding of the good but does not wish to understand the evil, is looked upon as a madman.

Imagine, to mention the supreme example, imagine Christ at the moment when He was silent before the Counsel: imagine the infuriated mob, imagine the group of dignitaries—and then imagine how many a glance they directed towards Him, their eyes upon Him, only waiting for Him to look at them so that their glance might convey their mockery, their contempt, their pity, their insults, to the accused! But He discovered nothing, lovingly He concealed the multitude of their sins. Imagine how many an abusive epithet, how many insults, how many taunts were shouted at Him—and each participant was so terribly insistent that his voice should be heard, so that, above all, it might not seem that he had been so indescribably stupid as to have missed the opportunity, as not to have been there participating in common with everyone else, hence as the true instrument of public opinion, in insulting, in injuring, in mistreating an innocent man! But He discovered nothing; lovingly He hid the multitude of their sins—by discovering nothing.

And He is the pattern: from Him the lover has learned, when he discovers nothing and thereby hides the multitude of sins; when like a worthy disciple, "forsaken, hated, bearing his cross," he walks between mockery and pity, between insults and lamentations, and yet lovingly discovers nothing—in truth more wonderful than when the three men walked unscathed in the fiery furnace. Still, ridicule and insults really do no harm, if the one insulted does not harm himself by *discovering* them, that is, by becoming resentful. For if he is resentful he discovers the multitude of sins. If you really wish to illustrate more clearly how the lover, by discovering nothing, hides the multitude of sins, then sometime do away with love. Imagine that the lover had a wife who loved him. Therefore, just because she loved him, she would discover how many sinned against him; she would, affronted, with resentment in her soul, discover every mocking glance; with bruised heart she would hear the insults—whereas he, the lover, would discover nothing. And when the lover, insofar as he could not avoid seeing and hearing some things, would still have the excuse ready for the aggressor, that he himself was at fault: then his wife would not be able to discover any fault in him, but only the more, how many had sinned against him. Do you see now, as you consider what his wife and with truth discovered—do you see how true it is that the lover who discovers nothing hides a multitude of sins? Imagine this applied to all the relationships of life, and you will admit that the lover really hides a multitude of sins.

Love covers a multitude of sins; for what it cannot avoid seeing or hearing, it hides by keeping silent, by a lenient explanation, by forgiveness.

Through *silence* it hides the multitude of sins.

It is sometimes the case that two lovers wish to keep their relationship secret. Suppose now that at the moment they confessed their love for each other and promised each other secrecy, there happened quite accidentally to be a third party present, but this intruder was an honest and kindly man who could be relied on, and that he pledged them his silence: would not the love of the two be concealed and continue to be so? But this is the way the lover behaves when he inadvertently, quite accidentally, never because he had tried to, becomes cognizant of a man's sin, of his fault, of how he had offended, or how he had been overtaken in a fault: the lover keeps silent, and hides a multitude of sins.

Say not that "the multitude of sins still remains equally great whether one keeps silent or tells about them, since the silence certainly does not take them away merely because no one mentions them"; rather answer the question: "Does not the one who discloses his neighbor's faults and sins increase the multitude of sins?" Even if it be true that the multitude of sins remains equally great whether I keep silent about them or not, when I keep silent, I am still doing my part to conceal them. And, furthermore, do we not say that rumor really increases them? We mean thereby that rumor makes the guilt greater than it actually is. Still, I am not thinking of this now. It is in quite a different sense that we may say that the rumor which tells of the neighbor's fault increases the multitude of sins. Let one not take too thoughtlessly the knowledge of a neighbor's faults, as if it were quite proper if it was once decided that what was said was true. Truly not every witness as to what is true concerning a neighbor's faults is therefore without guilt; and just through being made a witness to a neighbor's fault one may easily himself become guilty. So rumor grows, i.e. the one who tells of his neighbor's fault increases the multitude of sins. The fact that men through rumor, through village gossip, are accustomed inquisitively, frivolously, enviously, maliciously perhaps, to learn of their neighbor's faults—that debases men. It would certainly be desirable if men once more learned how to be silent. But if there must be talk, and consequently inquisitive and frivolous talk, then let it be about stuff and nonsense—the neighbor's fault is and ought to be too serious a matter; inquisitively, frivolously, enviously, to talk about that is, therefore, a sign of depravity. But he who, by telling of his neighbor's faults, helps to pervert men, he increases the multitude of sins.

It is unfortunately only too certain that every man has a strong propensity for seeing his neighbor's faults, and perhaps for making them even greater in telling about them. If there were nothing more to this (alas, but there is) than, to use the mildest expression possible, a kind of nervousness which makes one so weak in this temptation, in this excitement of being able to tell something bad about one's neighbor, in securing for a moment the breathless attention of everyone by the help of such an interesting story! But that which is already pernicious enough as a nervous desire which cannot keep silent is sometimes in a man a horrible, devilish passion developed on the most terrible scale. . . .

Oh, there are criminals whom the world does not call criminals, whom it rewards and almost honors—and yet, yet would I rather . . . enter into eternity with three repented-of murders on my conscience than as a worn-out slanderer with this horrible, interminable burden of offense, which had been accumulating year after year, which had been spreading itself to an almost inconceivable degree, which had laid men in the grave, embittered the most intimate relationships, injured the most innocent compassion, defiled youth, led astray and perverted both old and young in short, extended itself on a scale which even the most vivid imagination can form no conception of—this horrible burden of offense, which I still had never found time to begin to repent of, because the time must be used in committing new offenses, and because the infinitude of the offenses had secured me wealth, influence, everything but esteem, and, above all, an enjoyable life!

We still make a difference, with respect to incendiarism, whether the one who sets fire to a house knows that it is occupied by a number of people, or that it is vacant: but through scandal to set, as it were, a whole community on fire, that is not even regarded as a crime. We still quarantine against the plague—but that plague which is worse than the oriental pestilence, slander, which perverts the soul and mind, that we open our house to, we pay money in order to be defiled, we greet as a welcome guest that which brings defilement!

Say, then, whether it is not true, that the lover by keeping silent about his neighbor's faults hides a multitude of sins, when you consider how by telling them, one increases them.

By an extenuating explanation, the lover hides the multitude of sins.

There is always an explanation for something being what it is. The fact or the facts underlie the situation, but the explanation swings the balance. Every event, every word, every act, in short everything, may be explained in many ways; as someone has falsely said that clothes make the man, so one can truly say that the explanation makes the object of the explanation into what it is. As regards another man's words, deeds, modes of thought, and so on, there is no such certainty, so that to accept them really indicates choosing. The interpretation, the explanation is therefore, just because a different explanation is possible, a choice. But if there is a choice, then it constantly lies in my power, if I am the lover, to choose the most extenuating explanation. If, then, this milder or more extenuating explanation explains what others frivolously, overhastily, hardheartedly, enviously, maliciously, in short unlovingly, as a matter of course, explain as guilt—if the extenuating explanation explains this in another way, then it takes away now one fault, now another, and thus makes the multitude of sins less, or conceals it.

Oh, if men would rightly understand what a beautiful use they could make of their imagination, their acuteness, their ingenuity, their ability to co-ordinate by using it in every possible way to discover an extenuating explanation: then would they increasingly taste one of the most beautiful joys in life; it could become to them a passionate pleasure and need, which would cause them to forget everything else.

Do we not see this in other relationships, how (to mention this one instance) the hunter with every year becomes more and more passionately devoted to the chase? We do not commend his choice, but we are not speaking about that, we are speaking only about how with every passing year, he devotes himself more and more passionately to this occupation. And why does he do this? Because with every year his experience increases, he becomes more and more resourceful, he overcomes more and more difficulties, so he, the old, experienced hunter, now knows trails no one else knows, knows how to track the game where no one else is able to, now has signs that no one else understands how to make use of, now has discovered a more ingenious method of setting traps, so that he is fairly certain of always succeeding in having a good hunt, even when everyone else is unsuccessful.

We regard it as a burdensome, yet in another respect a satisfying and fascinating occupation, to be the servants of justice who track down guilt and crime. We are astonished at such knowledge of the human heart, at their knowledge of all, even the most sophistical excuses and inventions: how they can remember from year to year all, even the most trivial circumstances, just in order, if possible, to secure a clue; at how, if they only glance at the circumstances, they can, as it were, adjure them so they will provide the proof against the guilty; how nothing is too humble to attract their attention, insofar as it might contribute to enlightening their understanding of crime. We admire him when such an officer of justice, by bearing with what he calls a really hardened and thoroughgoing hypocrite, still succeeds in wresting away his disguise and making his guilt evident. Ought it not to be just as satisfying, just as fascinating, by bearing with what one calls an occasional unseemly conduct, to discover that it was really something quite different, something well-intentioned! Let the judge be appointed by the state, let the officers of justice work to discover guilt and crime; the rest of us are neither called on to be the judge nor the officer of justice, but on the contrary we are called by God to love, hence by the help of the extenuating explanation, to cover the multitude of sins.

Imagine such a lover, equipped by nature with the most glorious capacities, which every judge must envy him, but all these capacities employed with a zeal and an endeavor which would do honor to a judge, in the service of love, in order to train himself in the art, in order to practice the art, the art of interpretation, which by the help of an extenuating explanation conceals the multitude of sins! Imagine his rich, his blessed experience, considered in its noblest sense: what a knowledge he has of the human heart; how many noteworthy and touching incidents he has seen, in which, no matter how complicated they seemed, he still succeeded in discovering the good, or even the better, because he had for a long, long time held his judgment in suspense, until quite definitely a little circumstance came to light which led him to a clue; how by swiftly and boldly centering his whole attention on a quite different aspect of the matter, he had had the good fortune to discover what he was looking for; how, by thoroughly exploring the man's life-relationships, by obtaining the most meticulous enlightenment about his condition, he finally triumphed in his explanation! Hence, he "came upon the trail," "he had the good fortune to find what he sought," "he triumphed in his explanation"—alas, is it not strange that whenever these words are read outside of their context almost every man involuntarily connects them with the uncovering of a crime: we are all so much more apt to think about discovering evil than about discovering good. So the state appoints the judges and the civil officers for the purpose of discovering and punishing the evil. As to the rest, we form associations for the praiseworthy purpose of relieving the poor, educating the orphans, and lifting up the fallen: but, in addition to these worthy undertakings, to get by means of the extenuating explanation only a little power, even if it were very little, over the multitude of sins—for this purpose no association has been created!

How the lover by means of extenuating explanation hides the multitude of sins, we do not care to pursue further at this time, since in the two preceding reflections [2] we have considered that love believes all things and hopes all things. But lovingly to believe all things and lovingly to hope all things are the two principal expedients which love, that lenient interpreter, uses for the extenuating explanation which hides a multitude of sins.

Through forgiveness love covers a multitude of sins.

Silence really takes nothing away from the multitude of notorious sins. The extenuating explanation takes away some from the multitude by showing that this or that was not really sin; forgiveness takes away that which still cannot be denied as being sin. So love strives in every way to hide the multitude of sins; but forgiveness is the most outstanding way.

In one of the preceding chapters we were reminded of the expression "multiplicity of creation"; let us again employ it for the purpose of illustration. When we say that the philosopher *discovers* a multitude of things, while in comparison with him, the ignorant, who also speak about the multiplicity of creation, certainly know very little: then, consequently, the ignorant do not know that this and that exists, but it exists for all that; it is not taken away by nature because of their ignorance; it is only that in their ignorance it does not exist for them. It is different concerning the relation of forgiveness of sins to the multitude of sins; forgiveness takes the forgiven sins away.

This is a wonderful thought, hence also the thought of faith; for faith always lays hold on that which is not seen. I *believe* that the visible has come into existence from that which is not seen; I see the world, but the invisible I do not see, I believe it. So there is also in "forgiveness—and sin" a relation of faith, which one more rarely notices. What here is the invisible? The invisible is, that forgiveness takes away that which still exists: the invisible is, that that which is seen yet still is not seen; for when it is seen it is evidently invisible so that it is not seen. The lover sees the sin he forgives, but he believes that forgiveness takes it away. Since this cannot be seen, then the sin can be seen; and, on the other hand, if the sin could not be seen, then neither could it be forgiven. As one, therefore, through faith *believes the invisible in* the

[2] Part II, Chaps. 2 and 3.

visible, so the lover through forgiveness *believes* the visible *away*. Both premises are true. Blessed the believer, he believes what he cannot see; blessed the lover, he believes that away which he still can see.

Who can believe this? The lover. But why is forgiveness so rare? Is it not because faith in the power of forgiveness is so little and so rare? Even a better man who is by no means inclined to bear malice or spite, and far from being unforgiving, is often heard to say: "I could readily forgive him, but I don't see how that can help." Oh, it is not seen! Still, if you have ever yourself needed forgiveness, then you know what forgiveness can do: why do you speak with so little experience or with such unkindness about forgiveness? For there is something really unkind in saying: "I do not see how my forgiveness can help him." We are not saying that as if a man should become self-important through having it in his power to be able to forgive another man, far from it. This would also be unkindness; truly there is one way to forgive which perceptibly increases the guilt instead of diminishing it. Only love has—I know it seems like jesting, but let us speak thus—only love has ability enough through its forgiveness to take the sin away. When I am oppressed by the thought of forgiveness (the fact that I am slow to forgive, or when the being able to forgive makes me feel self-important), then no miracle takes place. But when love forgives, the miracle of faith takes place (and since every miracle is one of faith, what wonder, therefore, that, along with faith, miracles too are abolished!): so that which is seen, yet through being forgiven is not seen.

It is erased, it is forgiven and forgotten, or, as the Scriptures say about what God forgives, it is hidden behind His back. But that which is forgotten, one is not ignorant of, for one is only ignorant of that which one does not know and never has known; what one has forgotten, that one has known. Forgetting is in this highest sense not the opposite of remembering but of hoping; for hoping is to give existence in reflection; forgetting is in reflection to take existence from that which still exists, to erase it. The Scriptures teach that faith lays hold on things not seen, but they also say that faith is the substance of things hoped for; which means that that which is hoped for is, as it were, the unseen, that which does not exist, that to which, on the contrary, hope through reflection gives existence. Forgetting, when God does it in relation to sin, is the opposite of creating; for creating is bringing forth from nothing; forgetting is resolving back into nothing. What is hidden before my eyes, that I have never seen; but what is hidden behind my back, that I have seen. And just in this way does the lover forgive: he forgives, he forgets, he erases the sin; affectionately he turns toward the one he forgives; but when he turns toward him he cannot see what is lying behind his back. That it is impossible to see what lies behind one's back is easy to understand, as also that this expression is rightly the invention of love; but on the other hand, it is perhaps then difficult to become the lover who by the aid of forgiveness puts the other's fault behind his own back. It is generally easy for men to place the guilt, even of a murder, upon another man's conscience; but by the aid of forgiveness to put his guilt behind his own back, that is difficult. However, not for the lover; for he hides the multitude of sins.

Do not say, "The multitude of sins remains equally great, whether the sin is forgiven or not, since forgiveness neither takes from nor adds to." Rather answer the question: "Does not the one who unlovingly refuses his forgiveness increase the multitude of sins, not only by the fact that this, his unforgivingness, becomes one sin more, which nevertheless is true and ought then to be taken into account?" Still, we shall not emphasize this at this time. But is there not a secret relationship between sin and forgiveness? When a sin is not forgiven, it demands punishment; it cries to men or to God for punishment; but when a sin cries for punishment, then it looks quite different, far greater than when the same sin is forgiven. Is this only an optical illusion? No, it is actually so. It is, to use a rather imperfect figure, not an optical illusion that a sore which has looked dreadful, after the doctor has drained and treated it looks far less dreadful, although it is, nevertheless, the same sore. What does the one who refuses forgiveness do? He increases the sin, he makes it seem greater. And next, forgiveness takes the life from the sin; but denying forgiveness nourishes the sin. Therefore, even if no new sin appears, if the same old sin still persists, the multitude of sins is really increased. When a sin persists, a new sin really comes, for sin increases through sin; the fact that sin persists is really a new sin. And this new sin you might have prevented by lovingly forgiving, by taking away the old sin, as the lover does who hides a multitude of sins.

Love covers a multitude of sins; for love prevents the sin from coming into existence, strangles it at birth.

Even though with respect to one or another undertaking, a work one wishes to accomplish, one has everything in readiness: one must still wait for one thing, the occasion. So, too, with sin: when it is in a man it waits for an occasion to manifest itself.

The occasion can be very diversified. The Scripture says that sin takes occasion by the commandment or by the prohibition. Just the fact that something is commanded or prohibited becomes then the occasion; not as if the occasion brought forth sin, for the occasion never produces anything. The occasion is like a middleman, a broker, only helpful in the turnover; it occasions only that which has already been brought about, that which in another sense already existed, namely, as possibility. The commandment, the prohibition, tempts, just because it wishes to constrain the evil, and now if sin takes occasion it *takes* that, because the prohibition *is* the occasion. Thus the occasion is, as it were, nothing—a swift something which walks between sin and the prohibition; in a certain sense it belongs to both, while in another sense it is as if it did not exist, although again nothing which is actually existent ever came into existence without an occasion.

The commandment, the prohibition, is the occasion. In an even more distressing sense is sin in others the occasion which produces sin in everyone who comes in contact with it. Oh, how often has not an unconsidered, a thoughtless, casually dropped word, been sufficient to furnish an occasion for sin! How frequently has not a frivolous glance caused the multitude of sins to become greater! To say nothing of when a man lives under daily circumstances where he sees and hears nothing but sin and ungodliness: what a rich occasion for the sin in him, how easy the transition between this, the giving occasion and the taking occasion! When the sin in a man is encompassed by sin, is it not as if it were in its own element? Nourished by the perpetual occasion, it thrives and grows (if one may be allowed to speak of thriving in connection with evil); it becomes more and more malignant; it takes on a more and more definite form (if one may speak about gaining form in connection with evil, since evil is a lie and a deception, hence without form).[3] It consolidates itself more and more, even though its life is hovering over the abyss, hence without a foothold.

Still, everything which is occasion contributes, insofar as the occasion to sin is taken advantage of, to increase the multitude of sins.

But there is one environment which absolutely does not give and is not an occasion for sin: that is love. When a man's sin is encompassed by love, then it is outside its own element; it is like a beleaguered city

---

[3] Quoted out of context, this could almost be used as evidence that S.K. was a Christian Scientist! Rather, it shows that he would have accepted for whatever it is worth the Scholastic definition of evil as *non-being*. Cf. Th. Haecker, *Soren Kierkegaard,* pp. 24–25.

whose every connection with its own people is cut off; it is like a man who has been addicted to drink: when placed upon a scanty ration he loses his strength, vainly waiting an occasion to become intoxicated. It is certainly true, it is possible (for what cannot a depraved man divert to his own depravity!) that sin can make love the occasion for resentment, can rage against it. However, sin cannot in the long run hold out with love; such advantage as it has is generally at the beginning, just as when the drunkard in the first days before the medical treatment has had the necessary time to make its effects felt, rages with the strength of his impotence. And next, if there were really a man such that even love must give up—no, love never does that; but a man who, continually without love, took occasion to sin—just because there is one incorrigible, it does not necessarily follow that there are not many who are healed. So it continues to be exactly and absolutely true that love does cover a multitude of sins.

Oh, the magistrate must often devise very ingenious means to hold a criminal prisoner, and a physician often employs great ingenuity in formulating coercive methods for restraining a demented person: in connection with sin there is no environment so coercive, but also no coercive environment so saving as love. How often was not the wrath that smoldered within a man only awaiting an occasion; how often was it not stifled because love gave it no occasion! How often did not the evil passion which ... sat on watch, spying for an occasion, perish; how often did it not perish at birth because love gave it no occasion, and lovingly watched to see that no occasion should be given! How often did it not free its soul from that resentment, which was so assured of and so prepared, moreover so set upon being able to find ever new occasions to be resentful of the world, of God, of everything; how often did it not find alleviation in a milder mood because love gave no occasion at all for resentment! How often this conceited and defiant mood, which, believing itself injured and misunderstood, therefore took occasion to become even more conceited in its desire for a new occasion to prove that it was right, melted away; how often it again died down, because love so soothing, so mildly discutient, simply gave no occasion to the sick conceit! How often did it not go back to what it had contemplated, just to see if it might not succeed in finding an occasion which would justify it, and how often it returned because love simply gave no occasion for finding an excuse—for the evil! Oh, how many crimes have been prevented, how many evil purposes defeated, how many desperate resolutions consigned to oblivion, how many sinful thoughts halted on the way to becoming deeds, how many rash words repressed in time, because love gave no occasion!

Woe to the man by whom the offense cometh; blessed the lover who by refusing to furnish the occasion covers a multitude of sins!

THE POINT OF VIEW
FOR MY WORK AS AN AUTHOR

BY S. KIERKEGAARD (1848)

TRANSLATED BY WALTER LOWRIE

There are some purely human lives in which religion comes first. They are those who from the beginning have suffered and are cut off from the universal by some particular suffering, to whom the enjoyment of life is denied and who therefore must either become purely demoniacal—or else essentially religious.

The majority of men are subjective toward themselves and objective toward all others, terribly objective sometimes—but the real task is to be objective toward oneself and subjective toward all others.

. . . What our age needs is education. And so this is what happened: God chose a man who also needed to be educated, and educated him *privatissime,* so that he might be able to teach others from his own experience.—THE JOURNALS

THE FULL title of this little book, which is of the utmost importance for understanding Kierkegaard's work as a whole, reads: "The Point of View for my Work as an Author. A Direct Communication: A Report to History." It is indeed as direct as anyone could desire; above all it brings to light a unity of purpose running through the highly diverse literature which S.K. had already produced and which he was to go on producing (though in somewhat abated volume) until his death seven years later.

He could not bring himself to publish this intensely personal document during his lifetime; instead, he wrote a sort of laconic abridgment of it, which did appear. The objections to publishing *The Point of View* were in some measure those which made him hesitant about publishing everything written during that "tremendously fruitful" year, 1848—viz. the fact that he was running out of money and was seriously thinking of obtaining a position on the theological faculty at the University. Not only was the publishing of his books expensive, but the works of 1848 contained things that would offend Church dignitaries and thus jeopardize his chance of gaining a position. This dilemma, recorded and discussed in many passages of the *Journals,* was an excruciating one for him; but he resolved it at last by "not abating the price, not giving in"—by "venturing far out" onto the waters of truth. The other works of 1848 (*The Sickness unto Death, Training in Christianity,* and one or two smaller ones) were published, but not *The Point of View.*

S.K. had another reason for withholding this book: he doubted "whether anybody has a right to let people know how good he is." In a manner of speaking *The Point of View* does just that unless we pay special heed to the eloquent last paragraph, in which the author's whole work is characterized as "his own education in Christianity," which "he could not ascribe to any man, least of all . . . to himself; if he were to ascribe it to anyone, it would be to Governance, to whom it was in fact ascribed, day after day and year after year, by the author, who historically died of a mortal disease, but poetically died of longing for eternity, where he would have nothing to do save uninterruptedly to give thanks to God."

THE POINT OF VIEW
FOR MY WORK AS AN AUTHOR

PART ONE

A

THE AMBIGUITY OR DUPLICITY IN THE WHOLE AUTHORSHIP:[1] AS TO
WHETHER THE AUTHOR IS AN AESTHETIC OR A RELIGIOUS AUTHOR

It remains . . . to be shown that there is such a duplicity from first to last. This is not an instance of the common case where the assumed duplicity is discovered by some one else and the person concerned is obliged to prove that it *does not exist.* Not that at all, but quite the contrary. In case the reader should not be sufficiently observant of the duplicity, it is the business of the author to make as evident as possible the fact that it is there. That is to say, the duplicity, the ambiguity, is a

---

[1] In order that the titles of the books may be readily available, they are given here. First group (aesthetic work): *Either/Or; Fear and Trembling; Repetition; The Concept of Dread; Prefaces; Philosophical Fragments; Stages on Life's Road*—along with eighteen edifying discourses which were published successively. Second group: *Concluding Unscientific Postscript.* Third group (religious works): *Edifying Discourses in Divers Spirits; The Works of Love; Christian Discourses*—along with a little aesthetic article, *The Crisis and a Crisis in the Life of an Actress.* (K)

conscious one, something the author knows more about than anybody else; it is the essential dialectical distinction of the whole authorship, and has therefore a deeper reason.

But is this a fact, is there such a pervading duplicity? May one not explain the phenomenon in another way, by supposing that there is an author who first was an aesthetic author, and then in the course of years *changed* and became a religious author? I will not dwell upon the consideration that, if this were the case, the author would not have written such a book as the present one, and surely would hardly have undertaken to give a survey of the whole work—least of all would he have chosen the moment which coincides with the republication of his first book. Neither will I dwell upon the fact that it would be strange if such a change were to be accomplished in the course of only a few years. In other instances where an author originally aesthetic becomes a religious author it is usual for many years to elapse, so that the hypothesis which explains the change by pointing to the fact that he has actually become considerably older does not lack plausibility. But this I will not dwell upon; for though it might seem strange and almost inexplicable, though it might prompt one to seek and find some other explanation, nevertheless it would not be absolutely impossible for such a change to occur in the space of only three years. I will show rather that it is impossible to explain the phenomenon in this way. For when one looks closer it will be seen that nothing like three years elapsed before the change occurred, but that the change is simultaneous with the beginning—that is, the duplicity dates from the very start. For the *Two Edifying Discourses* are contemporaneous with *Either/Or*. The duplicity in the deeper sense, that is, in the sense of the authorship as a whole, is not at all what was a subject of comment in its time, viz. the contrast between the two parts of *Either/Or*. No, the duplicity is discovered by comparing *Either/Or* and the *Two Edifying Discourses*.

The religious is present from the beginning. Conversely, the aesthetic is present again at the last moment. After two years, during which religious works only were published, there follows a little aesthetic article.[2] Hence assurance was provided both first and last against an interpretation of the phenomenon which supposes an aesthetic author who with the lapse of time has changed and become a religious author. Just as the *Two Edifying Discourses* came out between two and three months after *Either/Or*, so this little aesthetic article came out between

---

[2] *The Crisis and a Crisis in the Life of an Actress*, in *The Fatherland* for July 1848. (K) This has not been translated into English.

two and three months after the purely religious writings of the two years. The *Two Edifying Discourses* and the little article correspond to one another conversely and prove conversely that the duplicity is present both first and last. Although *Either/Or* attracted all the attention, and nobody noticed the *Two Edifying Discourses*, this book betokened, nevertheless, that the edifying was precisely what must come to the fore, that the author was a religious author, who for this reason has never written anything aesthetic, but has employed pseudonyms for all the aesthetic works, whereas the *Two Edifying Discourses* were by Magister Kierkegaard. Conversely, although the purely edifying works produced during the two years have possibly attracted the notice of others, no one, perhaps, in a deeper sense, has remarked upon the significance of the little article, which indicates that now the whole dialectical structure of the authorship is completed. The little article serves as a testimony in the confrontation of witnesses, in order to make it impossible at the end (as the *Two Edifying Discourses* did at the beginning) to explain the phenomenon by supposing that there was an author who first was an aesthetic author and later *changed* and became subsequently a religious author—for he was a religious author from the beginning, and was aesthetically productive even at the last moment.

The first group of writings represents aesthetic productivity, the last group is exclusively religious: between them, as the turning-point, lies the *Concluding Postscript*. This work concerns itself with and sets "the Problem," which is the problem of the whole authorship: how to become a Christian. So it takes cognizance of the pseudonymous work, and of the eighteen edifying discourses as well, showing that all of this serves to illuminate the Problem—without, however, affirming that this was the aim of the foregoing production, which indeed could not have been affirmed by a pseudonym, a third person, incapable of knowing anything about the aim of a work which was not his own. The *Concluding Postscript* is not an aesthetic work, but neither is it in the strictest sense religious. Hence it is by a pseudonym, though I add my name as editor—a thing I did not do in the case of any purely aesthetic work. This is a hint for him who is concerned about such things and has a flair for them. Then came the two years during which nothing but religious works came out, all bearing my name. The period of the pseudonyms was past, the religious author had developed himself out of the aesthetic disguise—and then, as a testimony and as a precaution, came the little aesthetic article by a pseudonym, *Inter et Inter*. This is calculated to make one conscious all at once of the authorship as a whole. As I have remarked, it reminds one inversely of the *Two Edifying Discourses.*

B

THE EXPLANATION

That the Author is and was a Religious Author

It might seem that a mere protestation to this effect on the part of the author himself would be more than enough; for surely he knows best what is meant. For my part, however, I have little confidence in protestations with respect to literary productions and am inclined to take an objective view of my own works. If as a third person, in the role of a reader, I cannot substantiate the fact that what I affirm is so, and that it could not but be so, it would not occur to me to wish to win a cause which I regard as lost. If I were to begin *qua* author to protest, I might easily bring to confusion the whole work, which from first to last is dialectical.

So I cannot make any protestation—not at least before I have gone about in another way to make the explanation so evident that a protestation of the sort here contemplated would be entirely superfluous. When that has been accomplished, a protestation might be *permissible* as a lyrical satisfaction to me, in case I were to feel an impulse to make it, and it might be *required* as a religious duty. For *qua* man I may be justified in protesting, and it may be my religious duty to make a protestation. But this must not be confounded with authorship: *qua* author it does not avail much that I protest *qua* man that I have intended this or that. But everybody will admit that when one is able to show with respect to a phenomenon that it cannot be explained in any other way, and that in this particular way it can be explained in every detail, or that the explanation fits at every point, then this explanation is substantiated as evidently as it is ever possible to establish the correctness of an explanation. . . .

Let the attempt be made. Let us try to explain the whole of this literary production on the assumption that it was written by an aesthetic author. It is easy to perceive that from the beginning it is incongruous with this explanation, which breaks down when it encounters the *Two Edifying Discourses.* If, on the contrary, one will experiment with the assumption that it is a religious author, one will perceive that, step by step, the assumption corresponds at every point. The only thing that remains inexplicable is how it could occur to a religious author to employ aesthetics in such a way. That is to say, we are confronted again by the ambiguity or the dialectical reduplication. Only the difference now is that the assumption of his being a religious author will have taken firm hold, and it remains only to explain the ambiguity. How far it may be possible for a third person to do this I do not venture to determine; but the explanation is that contained in the Second Part of this little book.[3]

Here only one thing more—a thing which, as I have said, may be a lyrical satisfaction to me *qua* man, and *qua* man is my religious duty: namely, a direct protestation that the author is and was a religious author. When I began *Either/Or* (of which, be it said parenthetically, there existed beforehand literally only about a page, viz. a few Diapsalmata, whereas the whole book was written in the space of eleven months, and the Second Part first) I was potentially as deeply under the influence of religion as ever I have been. I was so deeply shaken that I understood perfectly well that I could not possibly succeed in striking the comforting and secure *via media* in which most people pass their lives: I had either to cast myself into perdition and sensuality, or to choose the religious absolutely as the only thing—either the world in a measure that would be dreadful, or the cloister. That it was the second I would and must choose was at bottom already determined: the eccentricity of the first movement was merely the expression for the intensity of the second; it expressed the fact that I had become thoroughly aware how impossible it would be for me to be religious only up to a certain point. Here is the place of *Either/Or*. It was a poetical catharsis, which does not, however, go farther than the ethical. Personally, I was very far from wishing to summon the course of existence to return comfortingly to the situation of marriage for my sake, who religiously was already in the cloister—a thought which lies concealed in the pseudonym *Victor—Eremita*.

Such is the situation; strictly speaking, *Either/Or* was written in a monastery, and I can assure the reader ... that the author of *Either/Or* devoted a definite time every day, regularly and with monastic precision, to reading for his own sake edifying books, and that in fear and in much trembling he reflected upon his responsibility. Among other things, he reflected especially (how wonderful!) upon "The Diary of the Seducer." And then what occurred? The book had an immense success—especially (how wonderful!) "The Diary of the Seducer." The

[3] *Infra*, pp. 330–335.

world opened its arms in an extraordinary way to the admired author, whom all this, however, did not "seduce"—for he was an eternity too old for that.

Then followed *Two Edifying Discourses*—things of the most vital importance often seem insignificant. The big work, *Either/Or,* which was "much read and more discussed"—and then the *Two Edifying Discourses,* dedicated to my deceased father, published on my birthday (May 5th), "a little flower hidden in the great forest, not sought out either for its beauty, or for its scent, or because it was nourishing." [4] No one took serious notice of the two discourses or concerned himself about them. Indeed I remember even that one of my acquaintances came to me with the complaint that in good faith he had gone and bought the book with the notion that, since it was by me, it must be something witty and clever. I remember, too, that I promised him that if he wished, he should get his money back. I held out *Either/Or* to the world in my left hand, and in my right the *Two Edifying Discourses;* but all, or as good as all, grasped with their right what I held in my left.

I had made up my mind before God what I should do: I staked my case on the *Two Edifying Discourses;* but I understood perfectly that only very few understood them. And here for the first time comes in the category "that *individual* whom with joy and gratitude I call *my* reader," a stereotyped formula which was repeated in the Preface to every collection of *Edifying Discourses.* No one can justly lay it to my charge that I have changed, that perhaps at a later moment, perhaps for the reason that I was not in the good graces of the public, I judged differently about this matter than I had before. No. If ever I stood in the good graces of the public, it was two or three months after the publication of *Either/Or.* And this very situation, which to many perhaps would be a temptation, I regarded as the one favorable moment for doing what I had to do to assert my position, and I employed it in the service of the truth to introduce my category "the individual"—it was then that I broke with the public not out of pride and arrogance, &c. (and certainly not because at that moment the public was unfavorable to me, since on the contrary it was entirely favorable), but because I was conscious of being a religious author and as such was concerned with "the individual" ("the individual"—in contrast to "the public"), a thought in which is contained an entire philosophy of life and of the world.

[4] Cf. the Preface to the *Two Edifying Discourses* of 1843. (K)

From now on, that is, as early as the publication of *Fear and Trembling,* the serious observer who himself disposes of religious presuppositions, the serious observer to whom it is possible to make oneself intelligible at a distance, and to whom one can talk in silence (cf. the pseudonym Johannes—*de silentio*) was in a position to discern that this, after all, was a very singular sort of aesthetic production. And this was justly emphasized by the most reverend signature Kts., which delighted me greatly.[5]

PART TWO

The Whole Work of Authorship construed from the point of view that the author is a religious author

CHAPTER I

A. THE AESTHETIC WORKS

Why the beginning of the work was aesthetic, or what
this signifies, understood in relation to the whole [6]

§ I

That "Christendom" is a prodigious illusion.

EVERYONE with some capacity for observation, who seriously considers what is called Christendom, or the conditions in a so-called Christian country, must surely be assailed by profound misgivings. What does it mean that all these thousands and thousands call themselves Christians as a matter of course? These many, many men, of whom the greater part, so far as one can judge, live in categories quite foreign to Christianity! Anyone can convince himself of it by the simplest observation. People who perhaps never once enter a church, never think about God, never mention His name except in oaths! People upon whom it has never dawned that they might have any obligation to God, people who either regard it as a maximum to be guiltless of transgressing the criminal law, or do not count even this quite necessary! Yet all these

---

[5] "Kts." was the signature which Bishop Mynster, the Primate of Denmark, commonly attached to his critical articles in the press. (L)

[6] Once and for all I must earnestly beg the kind reader always to bear *in mente* that the thought behind the whole work is: what it means to become a Christian. (K)

people, even those who assert that no God exists, are all of them Christians, call themselves Christians, are recognized as Christians by the State, are buried as Christians by the Church, are certified as Christians for eternity!

That at the bottom of this there must be a tremendous confusion, a frightful illusion, there surely can be no doubt. But to stir up such a question! Yes, I know the objections well. For there are those who understand what I mean, but would say with a good-natured slap on the back, "My dear fellow, you are still rather young to want to embark on such an undertaking, an undertaking which, if it is to have any success at all, will require at least half a score of well-trained missionaries; an undertaking which means neither more nor less than proposing to reintroduce Christianity—into Christendom. No, my dear fellow, let us be men; such an undertaking is beyond your powers and mine. It is just as madly ambitious as wanting to reform the "crowd," with which no sensible person wants to mix. To start such a thing is certain ruin." Perhaps; but though ruin were certain, it is certain also that no one has learned this objection from Christianity; for when Christianity came into the world it was still more definitely "certain ruin" to start such a thing—and yet it was started. And it is certain, too, that no one learned this objection from Socrates; for he mixed with the "crowd" and wanted to reform it.

This is roughly how the case stands. Once in a while a parson causes a little hubbub from the pulpit, about there being something wrong somewhere with all these numerous Christians—but all those *to* whom he is speaking are Christians, and those he speaks *about* are not present. This is most appropriately described as a feigned emotion. Once in a while there appears a religious enthusiast: he storms against Christendom, he vociferates and makes a loud noise, denouncing almost all as not being Christians—and accomplishes nothing. He takes no heed of the fact that an illusion is not an easy thing to dispel. Supposing now it is a fact that most people, when they call themselves Christians, are under an illusion—how do they defend themselves against an enthusiast? First and foremost, they do not bother about him at all, they do not so much as look at his book, they immediately lay it aside, *ad acta;* or, if he employs the living word, they go round by another street and do not hear him. As the next step, they spirit him out of the way by carefully defining the whole concept, and settle themselves securely in their illusion; they make him a fanatic, his Christianity an exaggeration—in the end he remains the only one, or one of the few, who is not seriously a Christian (for exaggeration is surely a lack of seriousness), whereas the others are all serious Christians.

No, an illusion can never be destroyed directly, and only by indirect means can it be radically removed. If it is an illusion that all are Christians—and if there is anything to be done about it, it must be done indirectly, not by one who vociferously proclaims himself an extraordinary Christian, but by one who, better instructed, is ready to declare that he is not a Christian at all.[7] That is, one must approach from behind the person who is under an illusion. Instead of wishing to have the advantage of being oneself that rare thing, a Christian, one must let the prospective captive enjoy the advantage of being the Christian, and for one's own part have resignation enough to be the one who is far behind him—otherwise one will certainly not get the man out of his illusion, a thing which is difficult enough in any case.

If then, according to our assumption, the greater number of people in Christendom only imagine themselves to be Christians, in what categories do they live? They live in aesthetic, or at the most, in aesthetic-ethical categories.

Supposing then that a religious writer has become profoundly attentive to this illusion, Christendom, and has resolved to attack it with all the might at his disposal (with God's aid, be it noted)—what then is he to do? First and foremost, no impatience. If he becomes impatient, he will rush headlong against it and accomplish nothing. A direct attack only strengthens a person in his illusion, and at the same time embitters him. There is nothing that requires such gentle handling as an illusion, if one wishes to dispel it. If anything prompts the prospective captive to set his will in opposition, all is lost. And this is what a direct attack achieves, and it implies moreover the presumption of requiring a man to make to another person, or in his presence, an admission which he can make most profitably to himself privately. This is what is achieved by the indirect method which, loving and serving the truth, arranges everything dialectically for the prospective captive, and then shyly withdraws (for love is always shy), so as not to witness the admission which he makes to himself alone before God—that he has lived hitherto in an illusion.

The religious writer must, therefore, first get into touch with men. That is, he must begin with aesthetic achievement. This is earnest-

[7] One may recall the *Concluding Unscientific Postscript,* the author of which, Johannes Climacus, declares expressly that he himself is not a Christian. (K)

money. The more brilliant the achievement, the better for him. Moreover he must be sure of himself, or (and this is the one and only security) he must relate himself to God in fear and trembling, lest the event most opposite to his intentions should come to pass, and instead of setting the others in motion, the others acquire power over him, so that he ends by being bogged in the aesthetic. Therefore he must have everything in readiness, though without impatience, with a view to bringing forward the religious promptly, as soon as he perceives that he has his readers with him, so that with the momentum gained by devotion to the aesthetic they rush headlong into contact with the religious.

It is important that religion should not be introduced either too soon or too late. If too long a time elapses, the illusion gains ground that the aesthetic writer has become older and hence religious. If it comes too soon, the effect is not violent enough.

Assuming that there is a prodigious illusion in the case of these many men who call themselves Christians and are regarded as Christians, the way of encountering it which is here suggested involves no condemnation or denunciation. It is a truly Christian invention, which cannot be employed without fear and trembling, or without real self-denial. The one who is disposed to help bears all the responsibility and makes all the effort. But for that reason such a line of action possesses intrinsic value. Generally speaking, a method has value only in relation to the result attained. Some one condemns and denounces, vociferates and makes a great noise—all this has no intrinsic value, though one counts upon accomplishing much by it. It is otherwise with the line of action here contemplated. Suppose that a man had dedicated himself to the use of it, suppose that he used it his whole life long—and suppose that he accomplished nothing: he has nevertheless by no means lived in vain, for his life was true self-denial.

§ 2

That if real success is to attend the effort to bring a man to a definite position, one must first of all take pains to find HIM where he is and begin there.

This is the secret of the art of helping others. Anyone who has not mastered this is himself deluded when he proposes to help others. In order to help another effectively I must understand more than he—

yet first of all surely I must understand what he understands. If I do not know that, my greater understanding will be of no help to him. If, however, I am disposed to plume myself on my greater understanding, it is because I am vain or proud, so that at bottom, instead of benefiting him, I want to be admired. But all true effort to help begins with self-humiliation: the helper must first humble himself under him he would help, and therewith must understand that to help does not mean to be a sovereign but to be a servant, that to help does not mean to be ambitious but to be patient, that to help means to endure for the time being the imputation that one is in the wrong and does not understand what the other understands.

Take the case of a man who is passionately angry, and let us assume that he is really in the wrong. Unless you can begin with him by making it seem as if it were he that had to instruct you, and unless you can do it in such a way that the angry man, who was too impatient to listen to a word of yours, is glad to discover in you a complaisant and attentive listener—if you cannot do that, you cannot help him at all. Or take the case of a lover who has been unhappy in love, and suppose that the way he yields to his passion is really unreasonable, impious, unchristian. In case you cannot begin with him in such a way that he finds genuine relief in talking to you about his suffering and is able to enrich his mind with the poetical interpretations you suggest for it, notwithstanding you have no share in this passion and want to free him from it—if you cannot do that, then you cannot help him at all; he shuts himself away from you, he retires within himself—and then you only prate to him. Perhaps by the power of your personality you may be able to coerce him to acknowledge that he is at fault. Ah! my dear, the next moment he steals away by a hidden path for a rendezvous with his hidden passion, for which he longs all the more ardently, and is almost fearful lest it might have lost something of its seductive warmth; for now by your behavior you have helped him to fall in love all over again, in love now with his unhappy passion itself—and you only prate to him!

So it is with respect to what it means to become a Christian—assuming that the many who call themselves Christians are under an illusion. Denounce the magical charm of aesthetics—well, there have indeed been times when you might have succeeded in coercing people. But with what result? With the result that privately, with secret passion, they love that magic. No, let it come out. And remember, serious and stern as you are, that if you cannot humble yourself, you are not genuinely serious. Be the amazed listener who sits and hears what the other finds the more delight in telling you because you listen with amazement. But above all do not forget one thing, the purpose you have in mind, the fact that it is the religious you must bring forward. If you are capable of it, present the aesthetic with all its fascinating magic, enthrall if possible the other man, present it with the sort of passion which exactly suits him, merrily for the merry, in a minor key for the melancholy, wittily for the witty, &c. But above all do not forget one thing, the purpose you have to bring forward—the religious. By all means do this, and fear not to do it; for truly it cannot be done without fear and trembling.

If you can do that, if you can find exactly the place where the other is and begin there, you may perhaps have the luck to lead him to the place where you are.

For to be a teacher does not mean simply to affirm that such a thing is so, or to deliver a lecture, &c. No, to be a teacher in the right sense is to be a learner. Instruction begins when you, the teacher, learn from the learner, put yourself in his place so that you may understand what he understands and in the way he understands it, in case you have not understood it before. Or if you have understood it before, you allow him to subject you to an examination so that he may be sure you know your part. This is the introduction. Then the beginning can be made in another sense. . . .

So then the religious writer, whose all-absorbing thought is how one is to become a Christian, starts off rightly in Christendom as an aesthetic writer. For a moment let it remain undetermined whether Christendom is a monstrous illusion, whether it is a vain conceit for the many to call themselves Christians; let the opposite rather be assumed. Well then, this beginning is a superfluity, counting upon a situation which does not exist—yet it does no harm. The harm is much greater, or rather the only harm is, when one who is not a Christian pretends to be one. On the other hand, when one who is a Christian gives the impression that he is not, the harm is not great. Assuming that all are Christians, this deception can at the most confirm them more and more in being such. . . .

Thus it is that the whole literary activity turns upon the problem of becoming a Christian in Christendom; and this is the expression of the share Governance had in the authorship, that it is the author himself who has been educated, yet with consciousness of this from the very first.

EPILOGUE

. . . And now—now I am no longer interesting. That the problem of becoming a Christian, that this *really* should be the fundamental thought in my whole activity as an author—how tiresome! And this thing of *The Seducer's Diary,* this tremendously witty production! Why, it seems now that even this belonged to the plan! If anyone asks me in a purely aesthetic interest what my judgment is about the aesthetic production, I will not make any attempt to conceal the fact that I know perfectly well what has been accomplished, but I will add that for me even the aesthetic value of the accomplishment consists in a deeper sense in the indication it furnishes of how momentous the decision to become a Christian is. In the sphere of immediacy it is a perfectly *straightforward* thing to become a Christian; but the truth and inwardness of the reflective expression for becoming a Christian is measured by the value of the thing which reflection is bound to reject. For one does not become a Christian by means of reflection, but to become a Christian in reflection means that there is another thing to be rejected; one does not reflect oneself into being a Christian, but out of another thing in order to become a Christian; and this is more especially the case in Christendom, where one must reflect oneself out of the semblance of being a Christian. The nature of the other thing decides how deep, how significant, the movement of reflection is. What precisely characterizes the nature of the reflection is the fact that from a distance, and from how great a distance, one reaches the point of becoming a Christian. The reflection is defined by the difficulty, which is greater just in proportion to the value of the thing left behind.

Thus it is, as I believe, that I have rendered a service to the cause of Christianity while I myself have been educated by the process. He who was regarded with astonishment as about the shrewdest of fellows (and this was attained with *Either/Or*), he to whom the place of "the interesting man" was willingly conceded (and this was attained with *Either/Or*)—precisely he, as it turned out, was engaged in the service of Christianity, had consecrated [8] himself to this from the very instant

[8] The consecration, insofar as it dated from an earlier time, consisted in the resolution before God that, even if I were never to attain the goal of becoming a Christian, I would employ all my time and diligence to getting it made clear at least what Christianity is and where the confusions in Christendom lie—a labor for which I had prepared myself substantially from my earliest youth. Humanly speaking, that was surely a magnanimous undertaking. But Christianity is a power far too great to be willing as a matter of course to make use of a man's magnanimous resolution (which

he began that pseudonymous activity: he, personally and as an author, was striving to bring out this simple thing about becoming a Christian. The movement is not from the simple to the interesting, but from the interesting to the simple, the thing of becoming a Christian, which is the place where the *Concluding Postscript* comes in, the "turning point," as I have called it, of the whole authorship, which states the "Problem" and at the same time, by indirect attack and Socratic dialectic, inflicts upon the System a mortal wound—from behind, fighting the System and Speculation in order to show that "the way" is not from the simple to the System and Speculation, but from the System and Speculation back again to the simple thing of becoming a Christian, fighting for this cause and vigorously slashing through to find the way back.

So we have not to do here with a one-time aesthetic author who subsequently turns away from the world and the world's wisdom; he may rightly be said to have had from the earliest time quite exceptional predispositions for becoming a Christian, but they were all dialectical. Nor does he feel at this instant any impulse to go further than becoming a Christian. With his conception of this task, and with the consciousness he has how far he is from being perfect, he feels only an impulse to go further in becoming a Christian. . . .

CONCLUSION

I HAVE nothing further to say, but in conclusion I will let another speak, my poet, who when he comes will assign me a place among those who have suffered for the sake of an idea, and he will say:

"The martyrdom this author suffered may be briefly described thus: He suffered from being a genius in a provincial town. The standard he applied in relation to talents, industry, disinterestedness, devotedness, definition of thought, &c., was on the average far too great for his contemporaries; it raised the price on them too terribly, and reduced their price too terribly; it almost made it seem as if the provincial town and the majority in it did not possess *dominium absolutum,* but that there was a God in existence. So for a while, at the first, people entertained one another mutually with voluble discussions about how under the sun he

in my case was for the most part an expression of my relationship to my father), wherefore Christianity or Governance took the liberty of so arranging my subsequent life that there could be no misunderstanding (as indeed there was not from the beginning) as to whether it was I that stood in need of Christianity, or Christianity that stood in need of me. (K) got such extraordinary talents, why he should have independent means and at the same time be able to be so industrious—that they disputed about for so long a time (while at the same time they took offense at one or another singularity in his mode of living, which, however, was not singular but very singularly calculated to serve the purpose of his life)—so long they disputed, that in the end it came to this: It is his pride, everything can be explained by his pride. Thereupon they went further, from disputation to action. Since it is his pride, they said, every insidious opposition, every insolence toward him or maltreatment of him is not only permissible but is a duty to God—it is his pride that should be punished. O priceless market town! How inestimable thou art when attired in thy comical dressing-gown and in the way of becoming holy, when abandonment to every disgusting inclination of envy, rudeness, and vulgarity becomes an expression of the worship of God! But how about his pride? Did the pride consist in the great talents? That would be like reproaching the golden sparrow by saying that it was its pride or because of its pride that it wears its golden finery. Or was it his diligence, &c? If a child who had been very strictly brought up were to study in a class together with others, would it not be strange to say that his diligence, &c., was pride, even if it were the case that the others could not keep up with him? But such a case seldom occurs, for then the child is moved up to a higher class. But, unfortunately, for one who is in many ways developed for eternity's class there exists only one class, that of the temporal order, where perhaps he must remain a long while.

"This was the martyrdom. . . . But in eternity it consoles him that he has suffered this, that he had exposed himself voluntarily to it, that he had not bolstered up his cause by any illusion, did not hide behind any illusion, but with God-fearing shrewdness transmuted his sufferings into a treasure for eternity: the memory of sufferings endured, and of fidelity to himself and to his first love, beside whom he has loved only them that have suffered in this world. Humble as he is, he will not with shame of face advance to meet those glorious ones who enjoy their reward in eternity—not with shame of face, as he would have approached them had his earthly life expressed the conviction that their life must have been either a casual happening, or a falsehood, or a proof of immaturity, since he by serving the truth had gained great honor and reputation, had everywhere encountered spiritual affinity and understanding, whereas they on the contrary encountered almost everywhere bestiality and misunderstanding.

"Yet it is true that he found also here on earth what he sought. He himself was 'that individual,' if no one else was, and he became that more and more. It was the cause of Christianity he served, his life from childhood on being marvelously fitted for such a service. Thus he carried to completion the work of reflection, the task of translating completely into terms of reflection what Christianity is, what it means to become a Christian. His purity of heart was to will only one thing. What his contemporaries complained of during his lifetime, that he would not abate the price, would not give in—this very thing is the eulogy pronounced upon him by after ages, that he did not abate the price, did not give in. But the grand enterprise he undertook did not infatuate him. Whereas as author he had dialectically a survey of the whole, he understood Christianly that the whole signified his own education in Christianity. The dialectical structure he brought to completion, of which the several parts are whole works, he could not ascribe to any man, least of all would he ascribe it to himself; if he were to ascribe it to anyone, it would be to Governance, to whom it was in fact ascribed, day after day and year after year, by the author, who historically died of a mortal disease, but poetically died of longing for eternity, where uninterruptedly he would have nothing else to do but to thank God."

THE SICKNESS UNTO DEATH

BY ANTI-CLIMACUS

EDITED BY S. KIERKEGAARD (1849)

TRANSLATED BY WALTER LOWRIE

. . . The consciousness of sin is the *conditio sine qua non* of Christianity.

CHRISTMAS DAY

Unto you is born this day a Saviour—and yet it was night when he was born.
That is an eternal illustration: it must be night—and becomes day in the middle of the night when the Saviour is born.—THE JOURNALS

THE YEAR 1848 S.K. described in his Journal as "incomparably the richest and most fruitful year I have experienced as an author." According to Lowrie it was "in fact the zenith of his productivity," the works written in this year (though not published until later) being representative of Kierkegaard in his intellectual and spiritual maturity.

The Sickness unto Death, the first of these works to be published, takes high rank among S.K.'s books, although its author complains of one "difficulty" connected with it: that it is "too dialectical to permit of the employment of rhetoric, . . . of moving effect." Many readers, however, will find this rigorous treatment of the "despair" which pervades all human life—this "anatomy of melancholy"—more impressive than any rhetoric. Personally I have found it so, and it is my favorite of all of S.K.'s works; I have therefore permitted myself the luxury of quoting from it more extensively, in proportion to its length, than from any of the other books; the sections reproduced amounting to almost one-third of the whole and to about three-fifths of Part One, with its masterly analysis of the different gradations of despair.

The reader has been spared some of the bleaker stretches of S.K.'s dialectic—for example the notorious opening passage, which may be quoted here for the edification of all:

"Man is spirit. But what is spirit? Spirit is the self. But what is the self? The self is a relation which relates itself to its own self, or it is that in the relation which accounts for it that the relation relates itself to its own self; the self is not the relation but consists in the fact that the relation relates itself to its own self. Man is a synthesis of the infinite and the finite, of the temporal and the eternal, of freedom and necessity, in short it is a synthesis. A synthesis is a relation between two factors. So regarded, man is not yet a self."

Here we have S.K., almost with tongue in cheek, expressing himself with great precision in the terminology of that Hegelianism which he hated above all else. Manipulating the jargon with great ease, he gives us a definition of "spirit" or "selfhood" which, after all, is a just and adequate one—but whose sting lies in the little concluding sentence: "So regarded, man is not yet a self." This dramatic letdown (which made a friend of mine want to send the whole passage to the *New Yorker's* "Words of One Syllable" department) brings out exactly the difference between S.K. and the Idealist philosophers, whose definition of man he can adopt in principle, but upon which he immediately throws a different light by insisting that man is actually not at all what he is in principle—that his *existence* is not only at variance with his ideal nature, but really its polar opposite. Man is not a unity, but a disunity; he is not his true self, which means that he is not a *self* at all. *The Sickness unto Death* is an investigation of this corruption in human nature, which of course is what the Church calls *sin,* but which Kierkegaard, in accordance with the "psychological" viewpoint here adopted, chooses to call *despair.*

That the choice is by no means arbitrary, the whole development of modern clinical psychology attests. In view of the remarkable passage, "Despair is 'the Sickness unto Death,'" it is clear that Kierkegaard understood the "death instinct" fifty years before Freud. Indeed, the whole murky realm of the subconscious is here opened up in so illuminating a fashion as to prove Kierkegaard one of the fathers of "depth psychology," even though his interest in this realm is always a religious and more specifically a Christian one. This is shown by the pseudonym which he adopts—"Anti-Climacus," meaning that while Johannes Climacus *described* Christianity without recommending it or even conceding that it was possible as a way of life, the author of the *Sickness* definitely commits himself to it as the only cure for the mortal disease which infects every soul, whether that soul is aware of it or not. Every individual—whether by "not willing to be himself," or by "willing despairingly to be himself," or by remaining "despairingly unconscious of having a Self and an eternal Self"— has in reality willed to "tear his self away from the Power which constituted it." This is sin; and its opposite is not virtue, but *faith*:

"By relating itself to its own self and by willing to be itself, the self is grounded transparently in the Power which constituted it. . . ." The Christian heroism . . . is to venture wholly to be oneself, as an individual man, this definite individual man, alone before the face of God, alone in this tremendous exertion and this tremendous responsibility. . . ." (pp. 216; 4).

DESPAIR IS "THE SICKNESS UNTO DEATH"

THE concept of the sickness unto death must be understood in a peculiar sense. Literally it means a sickness the end and outcome of which is death. Thus one speaks of a mortal sickness as synonymous with a sickness unto death. In this sense despair cannot be called the sickness unto death. For in the Christian understanding of it, death itself is a transition unto life. In view of this, there is from the Christian standpoint no earthly, bodily sickness unto death. For death is doubtless the last phase of the sickness, but death is not the last thing. If in the strictest sense we are to speak of a sickness unto death, it must be one in which the last thing is death, and death the last thing. And this precisely is despair.

Yet in another and still more definite sense despair is the sickness unto death. It is indeed very far from being true that, literally understood, one dies of this sickness, or that this sickness ends with bodily death. On the contrary, the torment of despair is precisely this: not to be able to die. So it has much in common with the situation of the moribund when he lies and struggles with death, and cannot die. So to be sick *unto* death is, not to be able to die—yet not as though there were hope of life; no, the hopelessness in this case is that even the last hope, death, is not available. When death is the greatest danger, one hopes for life; but when one becomes acquainted with an even more dreadful danger, one hopes for death. So when the danger is so great that death has become one's hope, despair is the disconsolateness of not being able to die.

It is in this last sense that despair is the sickness unto death, this agonizing contradiction, this sickness in the self, everlastingly to die, to die and yet not to die, to die the death. For dying means that it is all over, but dying the death means to live to experience death; and if for a single instant this experience is possible, it is tantamount to experiencing it forever. If one might die of despair as one dies of a sickness, then the eternal in him, the self, must be capable of dying in the same sense that the body dies of sickness. But this is an impossibility; the dying of despair transforms itself constantly into a living. The despairing man cannot die; no more than "the dagger can slay thoughts" can despair consume the eternal thing, the self, which is the ground of despair, whose worm dieth not, and whose fire is not quenched. Yet despair is precisely *self*-consuming, but it is an impotent self-consumption which is not able to do what it wills; and this impotence is a new form of self-consumption, in which again, however, the despairer is not able to do what he wills, namely, to consume himself. This is despair raised to a higher potency, or it is the law for the potentiation. This is the hot incitement, or the cold fire in despair, the gnawing canker whose movement is constantly inward, deeper and deeper, in impotent self-consumption. The fact that despair does not consume him is so far from being any comfort to the despairing man that it is precisely the opposite, this comfort is precisely the torment, it is precisely this that keeps the gnawing pain alive and keeps life in the pain. This precisely is the reason why he despairs—not to say despaired—because he cannot consume himself, cannot get rid of himself, cannot become nothing. This is the potentiated formula for despair, the rising of the fever in the sickness of the self.

A despairing man is in despair over *something*. So it seems for an instant, but only for an instant; that same instant the true despair manifests itself, or despair manifests itself in its true character. For in the fact that he despaired of *something,* he really despaired of himself, and now would be rid of himself. Thus when the ambitious man whose watchword was "Either Caesar or nothing" does not become Caesar, he is in despair thereat. But this signifies something else, namely, that precisely because he did not become Caesar he now cannot endure to be himself. So properly he is not in despair over the fact that he did not become Caesar, but he is in despair over himself for the fact that he did not become Caesar. This self which, had he become Caesar, would have been to him a sheer delight (though in another sense equally in despair), this self is now absolutely intolerable to him. In a profounder sense it is not the fact that he did not become Caesar which is intolerable to him, but the self which did not become Caesar is the thing that is intolerable; or, more correctly, what is intolerable to him is that he cannot get rid of himself. If he had become Caesar he would have been rid of himself in desperation, but now that he did not become Caesar he cannot in desperation get rid of himself. Essentially he is equally in despair in either case, for he does not possess himself, he is not himself. By becoming Caesar he would not after all have become himself but have got rid of himself, and by not becoming Caesar he falls into despair over the fact that he cannot get rid of himself. Hence it is a superficial view (which presumably has never seen a person in despair, not even one's own self) when it is said of a man in despair, "He is consuming himself." For precisely this it is he despairs of, and to his torment it is precisely this he cannot do, since by despair fire has entered into something that cannot burn, or cannot burn up, that is, into the self.

So to despair over something is not yet properly despair. It is the beginning, or it is as when the physician says of a sickness that it has not yet declared itself. The next step is the declared despair, despair over oneself. A young girl is in despair over love, and so she despairs over her lover, because he died, or because he was unfaithful to her. This is not a declared despair; no, she is in despair over herself. This self of hers, which, if it had become "his" beloved, she would have been rid of in the most blissful way, or would have lost—this self is now a torment to her when it has to be a self without "him"; this self which would have been to her her riches (though in another sense equally in despair) has now become to her a loathsome void, since "he" is dead, or it has become to her an abhorrence, since it reminds her of the fact that she was betrayed. Try it now, say to such a girl, "Thou art consuming thyself," and thou shalt hear her reply, "Oh, no, the torment is precisely this, that I cannot do it."

. . . A despairing man wants despairingly to be himself. But if he despairingly wants to be himself, he will not want to get rid of himself. Yes, so it seems; but if one inspects more closely, one perceives that after all the contradiction is the same. That self which he despairingly wills to be is a self which he is not (for to will to be that self which one truly is is indeed the opposite of despair); what he really wills is to tear his self away from the Power which constituted it. But notwithstanding all his despair, this he is unable to do; notwithstanding all the efforts of despair, that Power is the stronger, and it compels him to be the self he does not will to be. But for all that he wills to be rid of himself, to be rid of the self which he is, in order to be the self he himself has chanced to choose. To be *self* as he wills to be would be his delight (though in another sense it would be equally despair), but to be compelled to be *self* as he does not will to be is his torment, namely, that he cannot get rid of himself.

Socrates proved the immortality of the soul from the fact that the sickness of the soul (sin) does not consume it as sickness of the body consumes the body. So also we can demonstrate the eternal in man from the fact that despair cannot consume his self, that this precisely is the torment of contradiction in despair. If there were nothing eternal in a man, he could not despair; but if despair could consume his self, there would still be no despair.

Thus it is that despair, this sickness in the self, is the sickness unto death. The despairing man is mortally ill. In an entirely different sense than can appropriately be said of any disease, we may say that the sickness has attacked the noblest part; and yet the man cannot die. Death is not the last phase of the sickness, but death is continually the last. To be delivered from the sickness of death is an impossibility, for the sickness and its torment—and death—consist in not being able to die.

This is the situation in despair. And however thoroughly it eludes the attention of the despairer, and however thoroughly the despairer may succeed (as in the case of that kind of despair which is characterized by unawareness of being in despair) in losing himself entirely, and losing himself in such a way that it is not noticed in the least—eternity nevertheless will make it manifest that his situation was despair, and it will so nail him to himself that the torment nevertheless remains that he cannot get rid of himself, and it becomes manifest that he was deluded in thinking that he succeeded. And thus it is eternity must act, because to have a self, to be a self, is the greatest concession made to man, but at the same time it is eternity's demand upon him.

FORMS OF DESPAIR

With every increase in the degree of consciousness, and in proportion to that increase, the intensity of despair increases: the more consciousness, the more intense the despair. This is everywhere to be seen, most clearly in the maximum and minimum of despair. The devil's despair is the most intense despair, for the devil is sheer spirit, and therefore absolute consciousness and transparency; in the devil there is no obscurity which might serve as a mitigating excuse, his despair is therefore absolute defiance. This is the maximum of despair. The minimum of despair is a state which (as one might humanly be tempted to express it) by reason of a sort of innocence does not even know that there is such a thing as despair. So when consciousness is at its minimum the despair is least; it is almost as if it were a dialectical problem whether one is justified in calling such a state despair.

(a) *The Despair which is Unconscious that it is Despair, or the Despairing Unconsciousness of having a Self and an Eternal Self*

. . . It is far from being the case that men in general regard relationship to the truth, the fact of standing in relationship to the truth, as the highest good, and it is very far from being the case that they Socratically regard being under a delusion as the greatest misfortune; for their sensuous nature is generally predominant over their intellectuality. So when a man is supposed to be happy, he imagines that he is happy (whereas viewed in the light of the truth he is unhappy), and in this case he is generally very far from wishing to be torn away from that delusion. On the contrary, he becomes furious, he regards the man who does this as his most spiteful enemy, he considers it an insult, something near to murder, in the sense that one speaks of killing joy. What is the reason for this? The reason is that the sensuous nature and the psycho-sensuous completely dominate him; the reason is that he lives in the sensuous categories agreeable/disagreeable, and says goodbye to truth etc.; the reason is that he is too sensuous to have the courage to venture to be spirit or to endure it. However vain and conceited men may be, they have nevertheless for the most part a very lowly conception of themselves, that is to say, they have no conception of being spirit, the absolute of all that a man can be. . . . In case one were to think of a house, consisting of cellar, ground-floor and *premier étage,* so tenanted, or rather so arranged, that it was planned for a distinction of rank between the dwellers on the several floors; and in case one were to make a comparison between such a house and what it is to be a man—then unfortunately this is the sorry and ludicrous condition of the majority of men, that in their own house they prefer to live in the cellar. The soulish-bodily synthesis in every man is planned with a view to being spirit, such as the building; but the man prefers to dwell in the cellar, that is, in the determinants of sensuousness. And not only does he prefer to dwell in the cellar; no, he loves that to such a degree that he becomes furious if anyone would propose to him to occupy the *bel étage* which stands empty at his disposition—for in fact he is dwelling in his own house.

No, to be in error or delusion is (quite unsocratically) the thing they fear the least. One may behold amazing examples which illustrate this fact on a prodigious scale. A thinker erects an immense building, a system, a system which embraces the whole of existence and world-history, etc.—and if we contemplate his personal life, we discover to our astonishment this terrible and ludicrous fact, that he himself personally does not live in this immense high-vaulted palace, but in a barn alongside of it, or in a dog kennel, or at the most in the porter's lodge. If one were to take the liberty of calling his attention to this by a single word, he would be offended. For he has no fear of being under a delusion, if only he can get the system completed—by means of the delusion.

So then, the fact that the man in despair is unaware that his condition is despair has nothing to do with the case, he is in despair all the same. If despair is bewilderment (*forvildelse*), then the fact that one is unconscious of it is the additional aggravation of being at the same time under a delusion (*Vildfarelse*). Unconsciousness of despair is like unconsciousness of dread (cf. *The Concept of Dread*, by Vigilius Haufniensis): the dread characteristic of spiritlessness is recognizable precisely by the spiritless sense of security; but nevertheless dread is at the bottom of it, and when the enchantment of illusion is broken, when existence begins to totter, then too does despair manifest itself as that which was at the bottom.

The despairing man who is unconscious of being in despair is, in comparison with him who is conscious of it, merely a negative step further from the truth and from salvation. Despair itself is a negativity, unconsciousness of it is a new negativity. But to reach truth one must pierce through every negativity. For here applies what the fairy tale recounts about a certain enchantment: the piece of music must be played through backwards; otherwise the enchantment is not broken.[1] However, it is only in one sense, in a purely dialectical sense, that he who is unconscious of despair is further away from truth and salvation than the man who is conscious of his despair and yet remains in it. For in another sense, an ethical-dialectic sense, the despairing man who consciously remains in despair is further from salvation, since his despair is more intense. But unawareness is so far from removing despair, or of transforming despair into non-despair, that, on the contrary, it may be the most dangerous form of despair. By unconsciousness the despairing man is in a way secured (but to his own destruction) against becoming aware—that is, he is securely in the power of despair.

In unconsciousness of being in despair a man is farthest from being conscious of himself as spirit. But precisely the thing of not being conscious of oneself as spirit is despair, which is spiritlessness—whether the condition be that of complete deadness, a merely vegetative life, or a life of higher potency the secret of which is nevertheless despair. In the latter instance the man is like the sufferer from consumption: he feels well, considers himself in the best of health, seems perhaps to others to be in florid health, precisely when the sickness is most dangerous.

This form of despair (i.e. unconsciousness of it) is the commonest in the world—yes, in what people call the world, or, to define it more exactly, what Christianity calls "the world," i.e. paganism and the natural man in Christendom. Paganism as it historically was and is, and paganism within Christendom, is precisely this sort of despair: it is despair but does not know it. It is true that a distinction is made also in paganism, as well as by the natural man, between being in despair and not being in despair; that is to say, people talk of despair as if only certain particular individuals were in despair. But this distinction is just as deceitful as that which paganism and the natural man make between sexual love and self-love, as though this love were not essentially self-love.[2] Further, however, than this deceitful distinction it was impossible for paganism, including the natural man, to go; for the specific character of this despair is precisely that it is unconscious of being despair.

From this we can easily perceive that the *aesthetic* concept of spiritlessness by no means furnishes the scale for judging what is despair and what is not—which moreover is a matter of course; for since it is

[1] Cf. note, p. 97.
[2] Cf. *The Works of Love, supra,* p. 286.

unable to define what spirit truly is, how could the aesthetical make answer to a question which does not exist for it at all? It would also be a prodigious stupidity to deny that pagan nations *en masse,* as well as individual pagans, have performed amazing exploits which have prompted and will prompt the enthusiasm of poets; to deny that paganism exhibits examples of achievement which aesthetically cannot be sufficiently admired. It would also be foolish to deny that in paganism lives have been led which were rich in aesthetic enjoyment, and that the natural man can lead such a life, utilizing every advantage offered with the most perfect good taste, even letting art and learning enhance, embellish, ennoble the enjoyment. No, it is not the aesthetic definition of spiritlessness which furnishes the scale for judging what is despair and what is not; the definition which must be used is the ethico-religious: either spirit/or the negative lack of spirit, spiritlessness.

Every human existence which is not conscious of itself as spirit, or conscious of itself before God as spirit, every human existence which is not thus grounded transparently in God but obscurely reposes or terminates in some abstract universality (state, nation, etc.), or which, in obscurity about itself, takes its faculties merely as active powers, without in a deeper sense being conscious whence it has them, which regards itself as an inexplicable something which is to be understood *per se*—every such existence, whatever it accomplishes, though it be the most amazing exploit, whatever it explains, though it were the whole of existence, however intensely it enjoys life aesthetically—every such existence is after all despair. It was this the old theologians meant when they talked about the virtues of the pagans being splendid vices. They meant that the most inward experience of the pagan was despair, that the pagan was not conscious of himself before God as spirit. Hence it came about . . . that the pagans judged self-slaughter so lightly, yea, even praised it,[3] notwithstanding that for the spirit it is the most decisive sin, that to break out of existence in this way is rebellion against God. The pagan lacked the spirit's definition of the self, therefore he expressed such a judgment of *self*-slaughter; and this the same pagan did who with moral severity condemned theft, unchastity, etc. He lacked the point of view for regarding self-slaughter, he lacked the God-relationship and the self. From a purely pagan point of view self-slaughter is a thing indifferent, a thing every man

[3] This applies to the Stoics, but Plato, like S.K., regarded suicide as rebellion against God. (L)

may do if he likes, because it concerns nobody else. If from a pagan point of view one were to warn against self-slaughter, it must be by a long detour, by showing that it was breach of duty toward one's fellow men. The point in self-slaughter, that it is a crime against God, entirely escapes the pagan. One cannot say, therefore, that the self-slaughter was despair, which would be a thoughtless *hysteron proteron*; one must say that the fact that the pagan judged self-slaughter as he did was despair.

Nevertheless there is and remains a distinction, and a qualitative one, between paganism in the narrowest sense, and paganism within Christendom. The distinction (as Vigilius Haufniensis has pointed out in relation to dread) is this, that paganism, though to be sure it lacks spirit, is definitely oriented in the direction of spirit, whereas paganism within Christendom lacks spirit with a direction away from it, or by apostacy, and hence in the strictest sense is spiritlessness.

(b) *The Despair which is Conscious of being Despair, as also it is Conscious of being a Self wherein there is after all something Eternal, and then is either in despair at not willing to be itself, or in despair at willing to be itself.*

A distinction, of course, must be made as to whether he who is conscious of his despair has the true conception of what despair is. Thus a man may be right, according to the conception he has, in asserting that he is in despair, it may be true that he is in despair, and yet this is not to say that he has the true conception of despair. It may be that one who contemplated this man's life in the light of the true conception would say, "You are far more in despair than you are aware, the despair lies far deeper." So with the pagan (to recall the foregoing instance), when in comparison with others he considered himself in despair, he doubtless was right in thinking that he was in despair, but he was wrong in thinking that the others were not; that is to say, he had not the true conception of despair.

So then, for conscious despair there is requisite on the one hand the true conception of what despair is. On the other hand, clearness is requisite about oneself—insofar, that is to say, as clearness and despair are compatible. How far complete clarity about oneself, as to whether one is in despair, may be united with being in despair, whether this knowledge and self-knowledge might not avail precisely to tear a man out of his despair, to make him so terrified about himself that he would cease to be in despair—these questions we shall not decide here, we shall not even attempt to do so, since later we shall find a place for this whole investigation. But without pursuing the thought to this extremest point, we here merely call attention to the fact that, although the degree of consciousness as to what despair is may be very various, so also may be the degree of consciousness touching one's own condition, the consciousness that it is despair. Real life is far too multifarious to be portrayed by merely exhibiting such abstract contrasts as that between a despair which is completely unconscious, and one which is completely conscious of being such. Most frequently, no doubt, the condition of the despairing man, though characterized by multiform nuances, is that of a half obscurity about his own condition. He himself knows well enough in a way up to a certain point that he is in despair, he notices it in himself, as one notices in oneself that one is going about with an illness as yet unpronounced, but he will not quite admit what illness it is. At one moment it has almost become clear to him that he is in despair; but then at another moment it appears to him after all as though his indisposition might have another ground, as though it were the consequence of something external, something outside himself, and that if this were to be changed, he would not be in despair. Or perhaps by diversions, or in other ways, e.g. by work and busy occupations as means of distraction, he seeks by his own effort to preserve an obscurity about his condition, yet again in such a way that it does not become quite clear to him that he does it for this reason, that he does what he does in order to bring about obscurity. Or perhaps he even is conscious that he labors thus in order to sink the soul into obscurity, does this with a certain acuteness and shrew calculation, with psychological insight, but is not in a deeper sense clearly conscious of what he does, of how despairingly he labors, etc. For in fact there is in all obscurity a dialectical interplay of knowledge and will, and in interpreting a man one may err, either by emphasizing knowledge merely, or merely the will.

But, as was pointed out above, the degree of consciousness potentiates despair. In the same degree that a man has a truer conception of despair while still remaining in it, and in the same degree that he is more conscious of being in despair, in that same degree is his despair more intense. He who with the consciousness that suicide is despair, and to that extent with the true conception of what despair is, then commits suicide —that man has a more intense despair than the man who commits suicide without having the true conception that suicide is despair; conversely, the less true his conception of suicide is, the less intense his despair. On the other hand, the clearer consciousness of himself (self-consciousness) a man has in committing suicide, the more intense is his despair, in comparison with that of the man whose soul, compared with his, is in a confused and obscure condition.

In what follows I shall go on to examine the two forms of conscious despair, in such a way as to display at the same time a heightening of the consciousness of what despair is, and of the consciousness of the fact that one's own condition is despair—or, what is the same thing and the decisive thing, a heightening of the consciousness of the self. But the opposite of being in despair is believing; hence we may perceive the justification for what was stated above as the formula which describes a condition in which no despair at all exists, for the same formula is also the formula for believing: by relating itself to its own self, and by willing to be itself, the self is grounded transparently in the Power which constituted it.

(1) In despair at not willing to be oneself, the despair of weakness.

When this form of despair is called the despair of weakness, there is already contained in this a reflection upon the second form (2), in despair at willing to be oneself. So the contrast here is only relative. No despair is entirely without defiance: in fact defiance is implied in the very expression, "not to will to be." On the other hand, even the extremest defiance of despair is after all never without some weakness. The difference is therefore only relative. The one form is, so to speak, the despair of womanliness, the other of manliness.

(i) *Despair over the earthly or over something earthly.* This is pure immediacy, or else an immediacy which contains a quantitative reflection. Here there is no infinite consciousness of the self, of what despair is or of the fact that the condition is one of despair; the despair is passive, succumbing to the pressure of the outward circumstance, it by no means comes from within as action. It is, if I may say so, by an innocent misuse of language, a play upon words, as when children play at being soldiers, that in the language of immediacy such words as the *self* and *despair* occur.

The *immediate* man (insofar as immediacy is to be found without any reflection) is merely soulishly determined, his self or he himself is a something included along with "the other" in the compass of the temporal and the worldly, and it has only an illusory appearance of possessing in it something eternal. Thus the self coheres immediately with "the other," wishing, desiring, enjoying, etc., but passively; even in desiring, the self is in the dative case, like the child when it say "me" for I. Its dialectic is: the agreeable and the disagreeable; its concepts are: good fortune, misfortune, fate.

Now then there *happens,* befalls (falls upon) this immediate self something which brings it to despair; in no other way can this come about, since the self has no reflection in itself. That which brings it to despair must come from without, and the despair is merely passive. That wherein immediacy has its being, or (supposing that after all it has a little bit of reflection in itself) that part thereof to which it especially clings, a man is deprived of by "a stroke of fate," in short he becomes, as he calls it, unfortunate, that is, the immediacy in him receives such a shock that it cannot recover itself—he despairs. Or (to mention a case which is more rarely to be seen in real life, but which dialectically is entirely correct) this despair of immediacy occurs through what the immediate man calls an all-too-great good fortune; for it is a fact that immediacy as such is prodigiously fragile, and every *quid nimis* which demands of it reflection brings it to despair.

So then he despairs, that is to say, by a strangely preposterous attitude and a complete mystification with regard to himself, he calls this despair. But to despair is to lose the eternal—and of this he does not speak, does not dream. The loss of the earthly as such is not the cause of despair, and yet it is of this he speaks, and he calls it despairing. What he says is in a certain sense true, only it is not true in the sense in which he understands it; he stands with his face inverted, and what he says must be understood inversely: he stands and points at that which is not a cause of despair, and he declares that he is in despair, and nevertheless it is quite true that despair is going on behind him without his knowing it. It is as if one were to stand with one's back toward the City Hall and the Court House, and pointing straight before him were to say, "There is the City Hall and the Court House." The man is right, there it is—if he turns around. It is not true, he is not in despair, and yet he is right when he says it. But he calls himself "in despair," he regards himself as dead, as a shadow of himself. But dead he is not; there is, if you will, *life* in the characterization. In case everything suddenly changes, everything in the outward circumstances, and the wish is fulfilled, then life enters into him again, immediacy rises again, and he begins to live as fit as a fiddle. But this is the only way immediacy knows how to fight, the one thing it knows how to do: to despair and swoon—and yet it knows what despair is less than anything else. It despairs and swoons, and thereupon it lies quite still as if it were dead, like the childish play of "lying dead"; immediacy is like certain lower animals which have no other weapon or means of defense but to lie quite still and pretend they are dead.

Meanwhile time passes. If outward help comes, then life returns to the despairer, he begins where he left off; he had no self, and a self he did not become, but he continues to live on with only the quality of immediacy. If outward help does not come, then in real life something else commonly occurs. Life comes back into him after all, but "he never will be himself again," so he says. He now acquires some little understanding of life, he learns to imitate the other men, noting how they manage to live, and so he too lives after a sort. In Christendom he too is a Christian, goes to church every Sunday, hears and understands the parson, yea, they understand one another; he dies; the parson introduces him into eternity for the price of $10—but a self he was not, and a self he did not become.

This form of despair is: in despair at not willing to be oneself; or still lower, in despair at not willing to be a self; or lowest of all, in despair at willing to be another than himself. Properly speaking, immediacy has no self, it does not recognize itself, so neither can it recognize itself again; it terminates therefore preferably in the romantic. When immediacy despairs it possesses not even enough self to wish or to dream that it had become what it did not become. The immediate man helps himself in a different way: he wishes to be another. Of this one may easily convince oneself by observing immediate men. At the moment of despair no wish is so natural to them as the wish that they had become or might become another. In any case one can never forebear to smile at such a despairer, who, humanly speaking, although he is in despair, is so very innocent. Usually such a despairer is infinitely comic. Think of a self (and next to God there is nothing so eternal as a self), and then that this self gets the notion of asking whether it might not let itself become or be made into another than itself. And yet such a despairer, whose only wish is this most crazy of all transformations, loves to think that this change might be accomplished as easily as changing a coat. For the immediate man does not recognize his self, he recognizes himself only by his dress, he recognizes (and here again appears the infinitely comic trait)—he recognizes that he has a self only by externals. There is no more ludicrous confusion, for a self is just infinitely different from externals. When then the whole of existence has been altered for the immediate man and he has fallen into despair, he goes a step further, he thinks thus, this has become his wish: "What if I were to become another, were to get myself a new self?" Yes, but if he did become another, I wonder if he would recognize himself again! It is related of a peasant who came cleanly shaven to the Capital, and had made so much money that he could buy himself a pair of shoes and stockings and still had enough left over to get drunk on—it is related that as he was trying in his drunken state to find his way home, he lay down in the middle of the highway and fell asleep. Then along came a wagon, and the driver shouted to him to move or he would run over his legs. Then the drunken peasant awoke, looked at his legs, and since by reason of the shoes and stockings he didn't recognize them, he said to the driver, "Drive on, they are not my legs." So in the case of the immediate man, when he is in despair it is impossible to represent him truly without a touch of the comic. . . .

When immediacy is assumed to have self-reflection, despair is somewhat modified: there is somewhat more consciousness of the self, and therewith in turn of what despair is and of the fact that one's condition is despair; there is some sense in it when such a man talks of being in despair; but the despair is essentially that of weakness, a passive experience. Its form is, in despair at not wanting to be oneself.

The progress in this case, compared with pure immediacy, is at once evident in the fact that the despair does not always come about by reason of a blow, by something that happens, but may be occasioned by the mere reflection within oneself, so that in this case despair is not a purely passive defeat by outward circumstances, but to a certain degree is self-activity, action. Here there is in fact a certain degree of self-reflection, and so a certain degree of observation of oneself. With this certain degree of self-reflection begins the act of discrimination whereby the self becomes aware of itself as something essentially different from the environment, from externalities and their effect upon it. But this is only to a certain degree. Now when the self with a certain degree of self-reflection wills to accept itself, it stumbles perhaps upon one difficulty or another in the composition of the self. For as no human body is perfection, so neither is any self. This difficulty, be it what it may, frightens the man away shudderingly. Or something happens to him which causes within him a breach with immediacy deeper than he has made by reflection. Or his imagination discovers a possibility which, if it were to come to pass, would likewise become a breach with immediacy.

So he despairs. His despair is that of weakness, a passive suffering of the self, in contrast to the despair of self-assertion; but, by the aid of relative self-reflection which he has, he makes an effort (which again distinguished him from the purely immediate man) to defend his self. He understands that the thing of letting the self go is a pretty serious business after all, he is not so apoplectically muddled by the blow as the immediate man is, he understands by the aid of reflection that there is much he may lose without losing the self; he makes admissions, is capable of doing so—and why? Because to a certain degree he has dissociated his self from external circumstances, because he has an obscure conception that there may even be something eternal in the self. But in vain he struggles thus; the difficulty he stumbled against demands a breach with immediacy as a whole, and for that he has not sufficient self-reflection or ethical reflection; he has no consciousness of a self which is gained by the infinite abstraction from everything outward, this naked, abstract self (in contrast to the clothed self of immediacy) which is the first form of the infinite self and the forward impulse in the whole process whereby a self infinitely accepts its actual self with all its difficulties and advantages.

So then he despairs, and his despair is: not willing to be himself. On the other hand, it strikes him as ridiculous to want to be another; he maintains the relationship to his self—to that extent reflection has identified him with the self. He then is in just such a situation with regard to the self as a man may be with regard to his dwelling-place. The comic feature is that a self certainly does not stand in such a casual relation to itself as does a man to his dwelling-place. A man finds his dwelling-place distasteful, either because the chimney smokes, or for any other reason whatsoever; so he leaves it, but he does not move out, he does not engage a new dwelling, he continues to regard the old one as his habitation; he reckons that the offense will pass away. So it is with the despairer. As long as the difficulty lasts he does not dare to come to himself (as the common phrase expresses it with singular pregnancy), he does not want to be himself—but that surely will pass by, perhaps things will change, the dark possibility will surely be forgotten. So meanwhile he comes to himself only once in a while, as it were on a visit, to see whether the change has not occurred, and so soon as it has occurred he moves home again, "is again himself," so he says. However, this only means that he begins again where he left off; he was to a certain degree a self of a sort, and he became nothing more.

But if no change occurs, he helps himself in another way. He swings away entirely from the inward direction which is the path he ought to have followed in order to become truly a self. The whole problem of the self in a deeper sense becomes a sort of blind door in the background of his soul, behind which there is nothing. He accepts what in his language he calls his self, that is to say, whatever abilities, talents, etc. may have been given him; all this he accepts, yet with the outward direction toward what is called life, the real, the active life; he treats with great precaution the bit of self-reflection which he has in himself, he is afraid that this thing in the background might again emerge. So little by little he succeeds in forgetting it; in the course of years he finds it almost ludicrous, especially when he is in good company with other capable and active men who have a sense and capacity for real life. *Charmant!* He has now, as they say in romances, been happily married for a number of years, is an active and enterprising man, a father and a citizen, perhaps even a great man; at home in his own house the servants speak of him as "him"; in the city he is among the *honoratiores;* his bearing suggests "respect of persons," or that he is to be respected as a person; to all appearance he is to be regarded as a person. In Christendom he is a Christian (quite in the the same sense in which in paganism he would have been a pagan, and in England an Englishman), one of the cultured Christians. The question of immortality has been often in his mind, more than once he has asked the parson whether there really was such an immortality, whether one would really recognize oneself again—which indeed must have for him a very singular interest, since he has no self.

It is impossible to represent truly this sort of despair without a certain admixture of satire. The comical thing is that he will talk about having been in despair; the dreadful thing is that after having, as he thinks, overcome despair, he is then precisely in despair. It is infinitely comic that at the bottom of the practical wisdom which is so much extolled in the world, at the bottom of all the devilish lot of good counsel and wise saws and "wait and see" and "put up with one's fate" and "write in the book of forgetfulness"—that at the bottom of all this, ideally understood, lies complete stupidity as to where the danger really is and what the danger really is. But again this ethical stupidity is the dreadful thing.

Despair over the earthly or over something earthly is the commonest sort of despair, especially in the second form of immediacy with a quantitative reflection. The more thoroughly reflected the despair is, the more rarely it occurs in the world. But this proves that most men have not become very deep even in despair; it by no means proves, however, that they are not in despair. There are very few men who live even passably in the category of spirit; yea, there are not many even who so much as make an attempt at this life, and most of those who do so, shy away. They have not learned to fear, they have not learned what "must" means, regardless, infinitely regardless of what it may be that comes to pass. Therefore they cannot endure what even to them seems a contradiction, and which as reflected from the world around them appears much more glaring, that to be concerned for one's own soul and to want to be spirit is a waste of time, yes, an inexcusable waste of time, which ought if possible to be punishable by law, and at all events is punished by contempt and ridicule as a sort of treason against men, as a froward madness which crazily fills up time with nothing. Then there is a period in their lives (alas, their best period) when they begin after all to take the inward direction. They get about as far as the first difficulties, there they veer away; it seems to them as though this road were leading to a disconsolate desert—*und rings umher liegt schöne grüne Weide.*[4] So they are off, and soon they forget that best period of theirs; and, alas, they forget it as though it were a bit of childishness. At the same time they are Christians, tranquilized by the parson with regard to their salvation.

This despair, as I have said, is the commonest, it is so common that only thereby can one explain the rather common opinion . . . that despair is something belonging to youth, which appears only in youthful years, but is not to be found in the settled man who has come to the age of maturity and the years of wisdom. This is a desperate error, or rather a desperate mistake, which overlooks (yes, and . . . what it overlooks is pretty nearly the best thing that can be said of a man, since far worse often occurs)—it overlooks the fact that the majority of men do never really manage in their whole life to be more than they were in childhood and youth, namely, immediacy with the addition of a little dose of self-reflection. No, despair verily is not something which appears only in the young, something out of which one grows as a matter of course—"as one grows out of illusion." But neither is illusion something one grows out of, though people are foolish enough to think so.

[4] *Faust,* I, 1479. (L)

On the contrary, one encounters grown men and women and aged persons who have as much childish illusion as any youth. People overlook the fact that illusion has essentially two forms: that of hope, and that of recollection. But just because the older person is under illusion, he has also an entirely onesided conception of what illusion is, thinking that it is only the illusion of hope. And this is natural. The older man is not plagued by the illusion of hope, but he is, on the other hand, by the whimsical idea of looking down at the illusion of youth from a supposedly superior standpoint which is free from illusion. The youth is under illusion, he hopes for the extraordinary from life and from himself. By way of compensation one often finds in an older man illusion with respect to the recollections of his youth. An elderly woman who has now supposedly given up all illusions is often found to be as fantastic in her illusion as any young girl, with respect to how she remembers herself as a girl, how happy she once was, how beautiful, etc. This *fuimus* [5] which is so often heard from old people is fully as great an illusion as the futuristic illusion of the youth. They both are lying or poetizing.

But far more desperate than this is the mistake that despair belongs only to youth. In the main it is a great folly, and precisely a lack of sense as to what spirit is, and moreover it is failure to appreciate that man is spirit, not merely an animal, when one supposes that it might be such an easy matter to acquire faith and wisdom, which come with the years as a matter of course, like teeth and a beard and such like. No, whatever it may be that a man as a matter of course comes to, and whatever it may be that comes to a man as a matter of course—one thing it is not, namely, faith and wisdom. But the thing is this: with the years man does not, spiritually understood, come to anything; on the other hand, it is very easy with the years to go from something. And with the years one perhaps goes from the bit of passion, feeling, imagination, the bit of inwardness which one had, and goes as a matter of course (for such things go as a matter of course) under triviality's definition of the understanding of life. This prearranged condition, which true enough has come about with the years, he now in despair regards as a good, he readily assures himself (and in a certain satirical sense there is nothing more sure) that now it never could occur to him to despair—no, he has assured himself against this, yet he *is* in despair, spiritually in despair. Why, I wonder, did Socrates love youths—unless it was because he knew men!

[5] *Aeneid* II, 325. (L)

And if it does not so happen that a man with the years sinks into the most trivial kind of despair, from this it does not by any means follow that despair may belong only to youth. If a man really develops with the years, if he ripens into essential consciousness of the self, he may perhaps despair in a higher form. And if he does not essentially develop with the years, neither does he sink into sheer triviality, that is to say, if he remains pretty much a young man, a youth although he is mature, a father and gray-haired, retaining therefore something of the good traits of youth—then indeed he will be exposed also to the possibility of despairing as a youth over the earthly or over something earthly.

So a difference there may well be between the despair of an older man and of a youth, but no essential difference, only a fortuitous one. The youth despairs over the future, as a present tense *in futuro;* there is something in the future he is not willing to accept, hence he is not willing to be himself. The older man despairs over the past, as a present *in praeterito,* which refuses to become more and more past— for so desperate he is not that he succeeds entirely in forgetting it. This past is perhaps something even which repentance should have taken in hand. But if repentance were to emerge, one would first have to despair completely, to despair out and out, and then the spirit-life might break through from the very bottom. But desperate as he is, he dare not let the thing come to such a pass. So there he remains standing, time goes on—unless he succeeds, still more desperately, by the help of forgetfulness, in healing it, so that instead of becoming a penitent he becomes his own accomplice. But such despair, whether it be of the youth or of the man, is essentially the same: it does not reach any metamorphosis in which the consciousness of the eternal in the self breaks through, so that the battle might begin which either potentiates despair to a higher power, or leads to faith.

But is there no essential difference between the two expressions hitherto used as identical: to despair over the earthly (the determinant of totality), and to despair over something earthly (the particular)? Indeed there is. When with infinite passion the self by means of imagination despairs over something earthly, this infinite passion transforms this particular, this something, into the earthly *in toto,* that is to say, the determinant of totality inheres in and belongs to the despairer. The very nature of the earthly and temporal is to fall apart into discrete particulars. It is impossible actually to lose or be deprived of all that is earthly, for the determinant of totality is a thought-determinant. So the self first increases infinitely the actual loss, and then it despairs over the earthly *in toto*. But as soon as this distinction (between despairing over the earthly and over something earthly) is essentially affirmed, there is also an essential advance made in the consciousness of the self. This formula, "to be in despair over the earthly," is a dialectic first expression for the next form of despair.

(ii) *Despair about the eternal or over oneself.* Despair over the earthly or over something earthly is really despair also about the eternal and over oneself, insofar as it is despair, for this is the formula for all despair.[6] But the despairer, as he was depicted in the foregoing, did not observe what was happening behind him, so to speak; he thinks he is in despair over something earthly and constantly talks about what he is in despair over, and yet he is in despair about the eternal; for the fact that he ascribes such great value to the earthly, or, to carry the thought further, that he ascribes to something earthly such great value, or that he first transforms something earthly into everything earthly, and then ascribes to the earthly such great value, is precisely to despair about the eternal.

This despair represents quite an advance. If the former was the despair *of weakness,* this is *despair over his weakness,* although it still remains as to its nature under the category "despair of weakness," as distinguished from defiance in the next section. So there is only a relative difference. This difference consists in the fact that the foregoing form has the consciousness of *weakness* as its final consciousness, whereas in this case consciousness does not come to a stop here, but potentiates itself to a new consciousness, a *consciousness* of its weakness. The despairer understands that it is weakness to take the earthly so much to heart, that it is weakness to despair. But then, instead of veer-

[6] Therefore it is linguistically correct to say, "in despair *over* the earthly" (the occasion), and "*about* the eternal," but "*over*" oneself," because this is again another expression for the occasion of despair, which in its concept is always *about* the eternal, whereas that *over* which one despairs may be of the most various sorts. One despairs *over* that which fixes one in despair, over one's misfortune, for example, over the earthly, over the loss of one's fortune; but *about* that which, rightly understood, releases one from despair, therefore about the eternal, about one's salvation, about one's own power, etc. In relation to the self one employs both words: to despair *over* and *about* oneself, because the self is doubly dialectic. And herein consists the obscurity, especially in all lower forms of despair, and in almost all despairers, that with such passionate clearness a man sees and knows *over* what he is in despair, but *about* what it is escapes his notice. The condition requisite for healing is always this *about*-face, and from a purely philosophical point of view it might be a subtle question whether it is possible for one to be in despair with full consciousness of what it is *about* which one despairs. (K)

ing sharply away from despair to faith, humbling himself before God for his weakness, he is more deeply absorbed in despair and despairs over his weakness. Therewith the whole point of view is inverted, he becomes now more clearly conscious of his despair: recognizing that he is in despair about the eternal, he despairs over himself that he could be weak enough to ascribe to the earthly such great importance, which now becomes his despairing expression for the fact that he has lost the eternal and himself.

Here is the scale of ascent. First, in consciousness of himself: for to despair about the eternal is impossible without having a conception about the self, that there is something eternal in it, or that it has had something eternal in it. And if a man is to despair over himself, he must indeed be conscious also of having a self; that, however, is the thing over which he despairs—not over the earthly or over something earthly, but over himself. Moreover, there is in this case a greater consciousness of what despair is; for despair is precisely to have lost the eternal and oneself. As a matter of course there is greater consciousness of the fact that one's condition is that of despair. Furthermore, despair in this case is not merely passive suffering, but action. For when the earthly is taken away from the self and a man despairs, it is as if despair came from without, though it comes nevertheless always from the self, in-direct-directly from the self, as counter-pressure (reaction), differing in this respect from defiance, which comes directly from the self. Finally, there is here again . . . a further advance. For just because this despair is more intense, salvation is in a certain sense nearer. Such a despair will hardly forget, it is too deep; but despair is held open every instant, and there is thus the possibility of salvation.

For all that, this despair is to be referred to the formula: in despair at not willing to be oneself. Just as a father disinherits a son, so the self is not willing to recognize itself after it has been so weak. In its despair it cannot forget this weakness, it hates itself in a way, it will not humble itself in faith under its weakness in order to gain itself again; no, in its despair it will not hear of itself, so to speak, will not know anything about itself. But there can be no question of being helped by for-getfulness, no question of slipping by the aid of forgetfulness under the determinant of selflessness, and so being a man and a Christian like other men and Christians; no, for this the self is too much a self. As it often was the case with the father who disinherited his son, that the outward fact was of little avail to him, he did not by this get free of his son, at least his thought did not; as is often the case with th lover's curse upon the hated one (i.e. the loved one), that it does not help much, it almost imprisons him the more—so it is in the case of the despairing self with relation to itself.

This despair is one quality deeper than the foregoing and is a sort which rarely is met with in the world. That blind door behind which there was nothing is in this case a real door, a door carefully locked, to be sure, and behind it sits as it were the self and watches itself employed in filling up time with not willing to be itself, and yet is self enough to love itself. This is what is called *introversion*. And from now on we shall be dealing with introversion, which is the direct opposite of immediacy and has a great contempt for it, in the sphere of thought more especially.

But does there then in the realm of reality exist no such self? Has he fled outside of reality to the desert, to the cloister, to the mad-house? Is he not a real man, clothed like others, or like others clad in the customary outer-garments? Yes, certainly there is! Why not? But with respect to this thing of the self he initiates no one, not a soul, he feels no urge to do this, or he has learned to suppress it. Hear how he talks about it.[7] "After all it's only the purely immediate men—who so far as spirit is concerned are about at the same point as the child in the first period of earliest infancy when, with a thoroughly endearing nonchalance, it lets everything out—it's the purely immediate men who can't retain anything. It is this sort of immediacy which often with great pretentiousness proclaims itself 'truth,' that one is 'a true man and just like people generally are'—which is just as true as it is untrue that a grown man, as soon as he feels a corporal need, at once yields to it. Every self which is even a little bit reflective has surely a notion of what it is to repress the self." And our despairer is introverted enough to be able to keep every intruder (that is, every man) at a distance from the topic of the self, whereas outwardly he is completely "a real man." He is a university man, husband and father, an uncommonly competent civil functionary even, a respectable father, very gentle to his wife and carefulness itself with respect to his children. And a Christian? Well, yes, he is that too after a sort; however, he preferably avoids talking on the subject, although he willingly observes and with a melancholy joy that his wife for her edification engages in devotions. He very seldom goes to church, because it seems to him that most parsons really don't know what they are talking about. He makes an exception in

[7] It is S.K. himself talking in the days of his despair—e.g. through the mouth of the "young friend" of Judge William in the second part of *Either/Or*. (L)

the case of one particular priest, of whom he concedes that he knows what he is talking about, but he doesn't want to hear him for another reason, because he has a fear that this might lead him too far.

On the other hand, he often feels a need of solitude, which for him is a vital necessity—sometimes like breathing, at other times like sleeping. The fact that he feels this vital necessity more than other men is also a sign that he has a deeper nature. Generally the need of solitude is a sign that there is spirit in a man after all, and it is a measure for what spirit there is. The purely twaddling inhuman and too-human men are to such a degree without feeling for the need of solitude that, like a certain species of social birds (the so-called love birds), they promptly die if for an instant they have to be alone. As the little child must be put to sleep by a lullaby, so these men need the tranquilizing hum of society before they are able to eat, drink, sleep, pray, fall in love, etc. But in ancient times as well as in the Middle Ages people were aware of the need of solitude and had respect for what it signifies. In the constant sociability of our age people shudder at solitude to such a degree that they know no other use to put it to but (oh, admirable epigram!) as a punishment for criminals. But after all it is a fact that in our age it is a crime to have spirit, so it is natural that such people, the lovers of solitude, are included in the same class with criminals.

The introverted despairer thus lives on *horis succesivis,* through hours which, though they are not lived for eternity, have nevertheless something to do with the eternal, being employed about the relationship of one's self to itself—but he really gets no further than this. So when this is done, when the need for solitude is satisfied, he goes outside as it were—even when he goes in or converses with wife and children. That which as a husband makes him so gentle and as a father so careful, is, apart from his good-nature and his sense of duty, the admission he has made to himself in his most inward reserve concerning his weakness.

If it were possible for anyone to be privy to his introversion and were to say to him, "This is in fact pride, thou art proud of thyself," he would hardly be likely to admit it to another. When he was alone with himself he would likely admit that there was something in it; but the passionateness with which his self had pictured his weakness would quickly make him believe again that it could not possibly be pride, for it was in fact precisely over his weakness he was in despair— just as if it were not pride which attached such prodigious weight to weakness, just as if it were not because he wanted to be proud of himself that he could not endure this consciousness of weakness.—If one were to say to him, "This is a strange complication, a strange sort of knot; for the whole misfortune consists in the way thought is twined; otherwise the direction is quite normal, it is just this path you must travel through the despair of the self to faith. It is true enough about the weakness, but it is not over this you must despair; the self must be broken in order to become a self, so cease to despair over it." If one were to talk to him thus, he would perhaps understand it in a dispassionate moment, but soon passion would again see falsely, and so again he takes the wrong turn into despair.

As I have said, such despair is rather rare. If it does not stay at that point, merely marking time, and if on the other hand there does not occur a radical change in the despairer so that he gets on the right path to faith, then such despair will either potentiate itself to a higher form and continue to be introversion, or else break through to the outside and demolish the outward disguise under which the despairing man has been living in his incognito. In the latter case such a despairer will then plunge into life, perhaps into the distractions of great undertakings, he will become a restless spirit which leaves only too clear a trace of its actual presence, a restless spirit which wants to forget, and inasmuch as the noise within is so loud, stronger means are needed, though of a different sort than those which Richard III employs in order not to hear his mother's curses.[8] Or he will seek forgetfulness in sensuality, perhaps in debauchery; in desperation he wants to return to immediacy, but constantly with consciousness of the self, which he does not want to have. In the first case, when despair is potentiated it becomes defiance, and it now becomes manifest how much truth there was in this notion of weakness, it becomes manifest how dialectically correct it is to say that the first expression of defiance is precisely despair over one's weakness.

However, let us in conclusion take another little look at the introvert who in his introversion marks time on the spot. If this introversion is absolutely maintained, *omnibus numeris absoluta,* then suicide will be the danger nearest to him. The common run of men have of course no presentiment of what such an introvert is capable of bearing; if they were to come to know it, they would be astonished. If on the other hand he talks to someone, if to one single man he opens his heart, he is in all probability strained to so high a tension, or so much let down,

[8] Shakespeare's *Richard III,* Act IV, Scene 4. He ordered trumpets to be blown. (L)

that suicide does not result from introversion. Such an introvert, with one person privy to his thought, is a whole tone milder than the absolute case. He probably will shun suicide. It may happen, however, that he falls into despair just for the fact that he has opened his heart to another; it may be that he thinks it would have been infinitely preferable to maintain silence rather than have anyone privy to his secret. There are examples of introverts who are brought to despair precisely because they have acquired a confidant. So after all suicide may be the consequence. Poetically the catastrophe (assuming *poetice* that the protagonist was e.g. a king or emperor) might be fashioned in such a way that the hero had the confidant put to death. One could imagine such a demoniacal tyrant who felt the need of talking to a fellow man about his torment, and in this way consumed successively a whole lot of men; for to be his confidant was certain death.—It would be the task for a poet to represent this agonizing self-contradiction in a demoniac man who is not able to get along without a confidant, and not able to have a confidant,[9] and then resolving it in such a way as this.

(2) The despair of willing despairingly
to be oneself—defiance.

As it was shown that one might call the despair dealt with in section 1 the despair of weakness, so one might call the despair now to be considered the despair of manliness. In connection with the kind just described it may be called: despair viewed under the determinant of spirit. Thus manliness belongs more precisely under the determinant of spirit, and womanliness is a lower synthesis.

The despair described in section 1 (ii) was despair over one's weakness: the despairer does not want to be himself. But if one goes a single dialectical step further, if despair thus becomes conscious of the reason why it does not want to be itself, then the case is altered, then defiance is present, for then it is precisely because of this that a man is despairingly determined to be himself.

First comes despair over the earthly or something earthly, then despair over oneself about the eternal. Then comes defiance, which really is despair by the aid of the eternal, the despairing abuse of the eternal in the self to the point of being despairingly determined to be oneself. But just because it is despair by the aid of the eternal it lies in a sense very close to the true, and just because it lies very close to the true

[9] S.K. was precisely such a person.

it is infinitely remote. The despair which is the passageway to faith is also by the aid of the eternal: by the aid of the eternal the self has courage to lose itself in order to gain itself. Here on the contrary it is not willing to begin by losing itself, but wills to be itself.

In this form of despair there is now a mounting consciousness of the self, and hence greater consciousness of what despair is and of the fact that one's condition is that of despair. Here despair is conscious of itself as a deed, it does not come from without as a suffering under the pressure of circumstances, it comes directly from the self. And so after all defiance is a new qualification added to despair over one's weakness.

In order to will in despair to be oneself there must be consciousness of the infinite self. This infinite self, however, is really only the abstractest form, the abstractest possibility of the self, and it is this self the man despairingly wills to be, detaching the self from every relation to the Power which posited it, or detaching it from the conception that there is such a Power in existence. By the aid of this infinite form the self despairingly wills to dispose of itself or to create itself, to make itself the self it wills to be, distinguishing in the concrete self what it will and what it will not accept. The man's concrete self, or his concretion, has in fact necessity and limitations, it is this perfectly definite thing, with these faculties, dispositions, etc. But by the aid of the infinite form, the negative self, he wills first to undertake to refashion the whole thing, in order to get out of it in this way a self such as he wants to have, produced by the aid of the infinite form of the negative self—and it is thus he wills to be himself. That is to say, he is not willing to begin with the beginning, but with "in the beginning." [10] He is not willing to attire himself in himself, nor to see his task in the self given him; by the aid of being the infinite form he wills to construct it himself. [11]

If one would have a common name for this despair, one might call it Stoicism—yet without thinking only of this philosophic sect. And to illuminate this sort of despair more sharply one would do well to distinguish between the active and the passive self, showing how the self is related to itself when it is active, and how it is related to itself in suffering when it is passive, and showing that the formula constantly is: in despair to will to be oneself.

If the despairing *self* is *active,* it really is related to itself only as experimenting with whatsoever it be that it undertakes, however great

[10] Genesis 1:1.
[11] Compare Faust's effort to achieve a universal experience.

it may be, however astonishing, however persistently carried out. It acknowledges no power over it, hence in the last resort it lacks seriousness and is able only to conjure up a show of seriousness when the self bestows upon its experiments the utmost attention. Like the fire which Prometheus stole from the gods, so does this mean to steal from God the thought which is seriousness, that God is regarding one, instead of which the despairing self is content with regarding itself, and by that it is supposed to bestow upon its undertakings infinite interest and importance, whereas it is precisely this which makes them mere experiments. For though this self were to go so far in despair that it becomes an experimental god, no derived self can by regarding itself give itself more than it is: it nevertheless remains from first to last the self, by self-duplication it becomes neither more nor less than the self. Hence the self, in its despairing effort to will to be itself, labors itself into the direct opposite, it becomes really no self. In the whole dialectic within which it acts there is nothing firm; what the self is does not for an instant stand firm, that is, eternally firm. The negative form of the self exercises quite as much the power of loosing as of binding, every instant it can quite arbitrarily begin all over again, and however far a thought may be pursued, the whole action is within a hypothesis.[12] It is so far from being true that the self succeeds more and more in becoming itself, that in fact it merely becomes more and more manifest that it is a hypothetical self. The self is its own lord and master, so it is said, its own lord, and precisely this is despair, but so also is what it regards as its pleasure and enjoyment. However, by closer inspection one easily ascertains that this ruler is a king without a country, he rules really over nothing; his condition, his dominion, is subjected to the dialectic that every instant revolution is legitimate. For in the last resort this depends arbitrarily upon the self.

So the despairing self is constantly building nothing but castles in the air, it fights only in the air. All these experimented virtues make a brilliant showing; for an instant they are enchanting, like an oriental poem: such self-control, such firmness, such ataraxia, etc., border almost on the fabulous. Yes, they do, to be sure; and also at the bottom of it all there is nothing. The self wants to enjoy the entire satisfaction of making itself into itself, of developing itself, of being itself; it wants to have the honor of this poetical, this masterly plan according to which it has understood itself. And yet in the last resort it is a riddle how it understands itself; just at the instant when it seems to be nearest to

---

[12] Cf. Judge William's argument against the secular view of marriage: *supra*, pp. 84–85.

having the fabric finished, it can arbitrarily resolve the whole thing into nothing.

If the despairing self is a *passive* sufferer, we have still the same formula: in despair at willing to be oneself. Perhaps such an experimenting self which in despair wills to be itself, at the moment when it is making a preliminary exploration of its concrete self, stumbles upon one or another hardship of the sort that the Christian would call a cross, a fundamental defect, it matters not what. The negative self, the infinite form of the self, will perhaps cast this clean away, pretend that it does not exist, want to know nothing about it. But this does not succeed, its virtuosity in experimenting does not extend so far, nor does its virtuosity in abstraction; like Prometheus, the infinite, negative self feels that it is nailed to this servitude. So then it is a passively suffering self. How then does the despair which despairingly wills to be itself display itself in this case?

Note that in the foregoing the form of despair was represented which is in despair over the earthly or over something earthly, so understood that at bottom this is and also shows itself to be despair about the eternal, i.e. despair which wills not to let itself be comforted by the eternal, which rates the earthly so high that the eternal can be of no comfort. But this too is a form of despair: not to be willing to hope that an earthly distress, a temporal cross, might be removed. This is what the despair which wills desperately to be itself is not willing to hope. It has convinced itself that this thorn in the flesh [13] gnaws so profoundly that he cannot abstract it—no matter whether this is actually so, or whether his passion makes it true for him,[14] and so he is willing

[13] This word is enough to make the reader who knows S.K. alert to the fact that he is dealing here with his most intimate experience, which he often described mysteriously by this term. (L)

[14] From this standpoint, it is well to note here, one will see also that much which is embellished by the name of resignation is a kind of despair, that of willing despairingly to be one's abstract self, of willing despairingly to be satisfied with the eternal and thereby be able to defy or ignore suffering in the earthly and temporal sphere. The dialectic of resignation is commonly this: to will to be one's eternal self, and then, with respect to something positive wherein the self suffers, not to will to be oneself, contenting oneself with the thought that after all this will disappear in eternity, thinking itself therefore justified in not accepting it in time, so that, although suffering under it, the self will not make to it the concession that it properly belongs to the self, that is, it will not humble itself under it in faith. Resignation regarded as despair is essentially different from the form, "in despair at not willing to be oneself," for it wills desperately to be itself—with exception, however, of one particular, with respect to which it wills despairingly not to be itself. (K)

to accept it as it were eternally. So he is offended by it,[15] or rather from it he takes occasion to be offended at the whole of existence; in spite of it he would be himself, not despitefully be himself without it (for that is to abstract from it, and that he cannot do, or that would be a movement in the direction of resignation); no, in spite of or in defiance of the whole of existence he wills to be himself with it, to take it along, almost defying his torment. For to hope in the possibility of help, not to speak of help by virtue of the absurd, that for God all things are possible —no, that he will not do. And as for seeking help from any other —no, that he will not do for all the world; rather than seek help he would prefer to be himself—with all the tortures of hell, if so it must be.

And of a truth it is not quite so true after all when people say that "it is a matter of course that a sufferer would be so glad to be helped, if only somebody would help him"—this is far from being the case, even though the opposite case is not always so desperate as this. The situation is this. A sufferer has one or more ways in which he would be glad to be helped. If he is helped thus, he is willing to be helped. But when in a deeper sense it becomes seriousness with this thing of needing help, especially from a higher or from the highest source—this humiliation of having to accept help unconditionally and in any way, the humiliation of becoming nothing in the hand of the Helper for whom all things are possible, or merely the necessity of deferring to another man, of having to give up being oneself so long as one is seeking help—ah, there are doubtless many sufferings, even protracted and agonizing sufferings, at which the self does not wince to this extent, and which therefore at bottom it prefers to retain and to be itself.

But the more consciousness there is in such a sufferer who in despair is determined to be himself, all the more does despair too potentiate itself and become demoniac. The genesis of this is commonly as follows. A self which in despair is determined to be itself winces at one pain or another which simply cannot be taken away or separated from its concrete self. Precisely upon this torment the man directs his whole passion, which at last becomes a demoniac rage. Even if at this point God in heaven and all his angels were to offer to help him out of it —no, now he doesn't want it, now it is too late, he once would have given everything to be rid of this torment but was made to wait, now

---

[15] The "offense" of Christianity was to be the theme of S.K.'s next great book, the *Training in Christianity*.

that's all past, now he would rather rage against everything, he, the one man in the whole of existence who is the most unjustly treated, to whom it is especially important to have his torment at hand, important that no one should take it from him—for thus he can convince himself that he is in the right. This at last becomes so firmly fixed in his head that for a very peculiar reason he is afraid of eternity —for the reason, namely, that it might rid him of his (demoniacally understood) infinite advantage over other men, his (demoniacally understood) justification for being what he is. It is himself he wills to be; he began with the infinite abstraction of the self, and now at last he has become so concrete that it would be an impossibility to be eternal in that sense, and yet he wills in despair to be himself. Ah, demoniac madness! He rages most of all at the thought that eternity might get it into its head to take his misery from him!

This sort of despair is seldom seen in the world, such figures generally are met with only in the works of poets, that is to say, of real poets, who always lend their characters this "demoniac" ideality (taking this word in the purely Greek sense). Nevertheless such a despairer is to be met with also in real life. What then is the corresponding outward mark? Well, there is no "corresponding" mark, for in fact a corresponding outward expression, corresponding to close reserve, is a contradiction in terms; for if it is corresponding, it is then of course revealing. But outwardness is the entirely indifferent factor in this case where introversion, or what one might call inwardness with a jammed lock, is so much the predominant factor. The lowest form of despair, where there really was no inwardness, or at all events none worth talking about, the lowest forms of despair one might represent by describing or by saying something about the outward traits of the despairer. But the more despair becomes spiritual, and the more inwardness becomes a peculiar world for itself in introversion, all the more is the self alert with demoniac shrewdness to keep despair shut up in close reserve, and all the more intent therefore to set the outward appearance at the level of indifference, to make it as unrevealing and indifferent as possible. As according to the report of superstition the troll disappears through a crack which no one can perceive, so it is for the despairer all the more important to dwell in an exterior semblance, behind which it ordinarily would never occur to anyone to look for it. This hiddenness is precisely something spiritual and is one of the safety-devices for assuring oneself of having as it were behind reality an enclosure, a world unto itself locking all else out, a world where the despairing self is employed as tirelessly as Tantalus in willing to be itself.

We began in section 1 (ii) with the lowest form of despair, which in despair does not will to be itself. The demoniac despair is the most potentiated form of the despair which despairingly wills to be itself. This despair does not will to be itself with Stoic doting upon itself, nor with self-deification, willing in this way, doubtless mendaciously, yet in a certain sense in terms of its perfection; no, with hatred for existence it wills to be itself, to be itself in terms of its misery; it does not even in defiance or defiantly will to be itself, but to be itself in spite; it does not even will in defiance to tear itself free from the Power which posited it; it wills to obtrude upon this Power in spite, to hold on to it out of malice. And that is natural, a malignant objection must above all take care to hold on to that against which it is an objection. Revolting against the whole of existence, it thinks it has hold of a proof against it, against its goodness. This proof the despairer thinks he himself is, and that is what he wills to be, therefore he wills to be himself, himself with his torment, in order with this torment to protest against the whole of existence. Whereas the weak despairer will not hear about what comfort eternity has for him, so neither will such a despairer hear about it, but for a different reason, namely, because this comfort would be the destruction of him as an objection against the whole of existence. It is (to describe it figuratively) as if an author were to make a slip of the pen, and that this clerical error became conscious of being such—perhaps it was no error but in a far higher sense was an essential constituent in the whole exposition—it is then as if this clerical error would revolt against the author, out of hatred for him were to forbid him to correct it, and were to say, "No, I will not be erased, I will stand as a witness against thee, that thou art a very poor writer."

TRAINING IN CHRISTIANITY

BY ANTI-CLIMACUS. EDITED BY

S. KIERKEGAARD (1850)

TRANSLATED BY WALTER LOWRIE

ALL—NOTHING

God creates everything out of nothing—and everything which God is to use He first reduces to nothing.

What is true of the relation between two men is not true of the relation of man to God: that the longer they live together and the better they get to know each other, the closer do they come to one another. The very opposite is true in relation to God: the longer one lives with Him, the more infinite He becomes—and the smaller one becomes oneself. Alas, as a child it seemed as though God and man could play together. Alas, in youth one dreamed that if one really tried with all the passion of a man in love . . . the relationship might yet be brought into being. Alas, as a man one discovers how infinite God is, and the infinite distance. This is the education.—THE JOURNALS

WHICH of Kierkegaard's works is the "greatest" may be regarded as a question both futile and un-Kierkegaardian; but if we ask which was his own favorite, the answer is *Training in Christianity*. The reason for this is simple. The whole problem of S.K.'s authorship, as we have seen, "turns on the question of what it means to be a Christian—in Christendom"; and it is in the *Training* that we find this question definitively answered.

The answer takes the form of a single concept—*contemporaneousness with Christ*. Introduced at once in the Invocation, this theme runs through the entire work. To be a Christian is not to hold a certain view about Who Christ was (though Kierkegaard holds this view to be correct and inescapable); nor is it to believe in Christianity as the greatest force for good in the history of the world (though Kierkegaard would agree that it has been all of that); Christianity is: to become contemporary with Christ in His suffering and humiliation, to be and act as the Apostles did when they followed Christ as the Holy One in spite of the world's rejection of Him, in spite of the social and intellectual stigma involved in doing so. This contemporaneousness is the polar opposite of what S.K. briefly refers to as "the 1800 years" or "the upshot," i.e. the historical results of Christ's existence. And his point is that when anyone embraces Christianity, either consciously or subconsciously for the sake of these "glorious results," his state of mind has literally no relation to the Apostles' save that of being precisely the opposite! The one believes because of externalities of one sort or another; the "contemporary" believes in spite of the external, in spite of appearances, in spite of what it may cost him in physical or mental anguish. Although the *object* of belief in the two cases may seem to be the same, we see that the *quality* is entirely different; and we have learned from the *Postscript* that "truth is subjectivity."

Contemporaneousness, as Kierkegaard proceeds to show, involves the possibility of *the offense*; it involves the possibility that Christ and His teaching not only do not appeal to one, but that one is positively offended by them for one or another reason. The idea of "the offense" is a generalization but also an intensification of "the paradox" which we encountered in the *Postscript*. "The paradox" may be defined as the offense in the realm of the intellect; and "the offense" is that which repels a man at the very center of his being, whether it acts as a stumbling-block to his intellect, his aesthetic nature, his herd instincts, his prudential commonsense, or any other aspect of his "immediacy." Thus Kierkegaard summons up the reactions of several different types of men (the minister, the philosopher, the statesman, the cautious agnostic, the "sententious *bourgeois*," etc.) to the claims of Christ, as if they had been actual contemporaries of His. All reject Him because all are offended at Him in one way or another. But "blessed is he whosoever is not offended in Me."

Between the two extremes of being offended and never having so much as the possibility of being offended (because one accepts Christianity as "the natural thing," because it's the "thing to do," or because of "the 1800 years" with their "glorious results") lies Christianity, which is the possibility and even the actuality of the offense—and the subsequent, deliberate, and resolute refusal to be offended. Of the two extremes the latter is by far the worst, and the latter is the situation of "Christendom," a "Christian world," where "all are Christians" as a matter of course. He who is truly offended at Christ may sometime cease to be offended; but he who does not know the meaning of the offense lacks the possibility of ever putting himself in the state of mind wherein that which is potentially offensive is embraced in spite of its offensiveness. Kierkegaard's quarrel with modern Christianity was just that it took away the possibility of the offense, by concentrating on "the 1800 years" and "the upshot" and "the glorious results" rather than on becoming a contemporary of Christ in His suffering and humiliation. Thus Lowrie is right in pointing out that the essential elements of "The Attack on 'Christendom'" are all present here in the *Training,* written almost seven years before S.K. began his series of pamphlets against the State Church. Bishop Mynster indeed was astute enough to see what dynamite lay hidden in the *Training,* and rebuked S.K. in an interview recorded in the *Journals*. It was the beginning of estrangement between the two men, and of course it broke up the plan S.K. had been entertaining of getting a position on the theological faculty of the University. His decision to "venture far out" and publish the *Training,* when he knew it would have this effect, required no little courage and some two years of reflection.

It may be asked why *Training in Christianity* is by "Anti-Climacus" and not by "S. Kierkegaard," seeing that it is so definite a statement of S.K.'s own position. The line between these two authors is indeed a shadowy one, and S.K. actually went to the printer's at the last moment to have Anti-Climacus removed from the title-page, but it was too late. The name "Anti-Climacus" expresses opposition to Johannes Climacus's viewpoint of "mere description." This does not mean that Anti-Climacus gives himself out to be a Christian in the ideal sense—which is the sense here insisted upon; but it means that with all his shortcomings he embraces Christianity as the Way and the Truth.

The heart of *Training in Christianity* is really Part II, with its "Thoughts which determine the meaning of the Offense properly so-called"; but Part I is a necessary prelude and is more effective by itself, so I have chosen to use it here, together with the first of the seven "Christian Reflections" of Part III. This discourse on the text of John 12:32 ("And I, if I be lifted up from the earth, will draw all unto Myself") is from an aesthetic point of view one of the most thrilling things S.K. ever wrote, the repetition of phrases like "on high" and "the Lord Jesus Christ" producing an effect of great exaltation, especially at the end, where the motif "on high" recurs as though transposed into a triumphant major chord. The bringing out of these effects in English is a high tribute to the translator, Dr. Walter Lowrie.

"COME HITHER, ALL YE THAT LABOR AND ARE HEAVY LADEN, I WILL GIVE YOU REST"

FOR REVIVAL AND INCREASE OF INWARDNESS
BY ANTI-CLIMACUS

EDITOR'S PREFACE
[i.e. S.K.'s]

IN this little book, which originated in the year 1848, the requirement for being a Christian is strained by the pseudonym to the highest pitch of ideality.

Yet indeed the requirement ought to be uttered, plainly set forth, and heard. There must be no abatement of the requirement, not to speak of the suppression of it—instead of making admission and acknowledgment on one's own behalf.[1]

---

[1] The admission, namely, that one, alas, is not fulfilling the requirement. This is the "admission" S.K. was from this time on constantly urging the Church to make through

The requirement must be heard; and I understand what is said as addressed solely to me [2]—that I might learn not only to take refuge in "grace," but to take refuge in such a way as to make use of "grace."

INVOCATION

IT is eighteen hundred years and more since Jesus Christ walked here on earth. But this is not an event like other events which, only when they are bygone, pass over into history, and then as events long bygone, pass over into forgetfulness. No, His presence here on earth never becomes a bygone event, and never becomes more and more bygone— in case faith is to be found on earth. And if not, then indeed at that very instant it is a long, long time since He lived. But so long as there is a believer, such a one must, in order to become such, have been, and as a believer must continue to be, just as contemporary with His presence on earth as were those [first] contemporaries.[3] This contemporaneousness is the condition of faith, and more closely defined, it *is* faith.

O Lord Jesus Christ, would that we also might be contemporary with Thee, see Thee in Thy true form and in the actual environment in which Thou didst walk here on earth; not in the form in which an empty and meaningless tradition, or a thoughtless and superstitious, or a gossipy historical tradition, has deformed Thee; for it is not in the form of abasement the believer sees Thee, and it cannot possibly be in the form of glory, in which no man has yet seen Thee. Would that we might see Thee as Thou art and wast and wilt be until Thy return in glory, see Thee as the sign of offense and the object of faith, the lowly man, and yet the Saviour and Redeemer of the race, who out of love came to earth in order to seek the lost, in order to suffer and to die; and yet sorely troubled as Thou wast, alas, at every step Thou didst take

its chief bishop, the acknowledgment that it was not a fair exponent of Christianity, but a compromise with worldliness. This would at least be "honesty," and that, he thought, was the only way to justify the Church so long as it remains as it is. On his own behalf he made this admission again and again, not only privately in his journals, but publicly in his Works, that he was not yet truly a Christian but only in process of becoming one. (L)

[2] One will be more irritated than edified by the pungent reflections of this book if one will not take S.K. at his word when he affirms that he regards them as addressed primarily to himself, does not recognize how poignantly they wounded him, and does not know how salutary his wounds proved to be at the last. (L)

[3] Contemporaneousness with Christ is from this time forth an emphatic and persistent theme of S.K.'s. (L)

upon earth, every time Thou didst stretch out Thy hand to perform signs and wonders, and every time, without moving a hand, Thou didst suffer defenselessly the opposition of men—again and again Thou wast constrained to repeat: Blessed is he whosoever is not offended in Me. Would that we might see Thee thus, and then that for all this we might not be offended in Thee.

THE INVITATION

Come hither to me, all ye that labor and are heavy laden,
I will give you rest

OH! Wonderful, wonderful! That the one who has help to give is the one who says, Come hither! What love is this! There is love in the act of a man who is able to help and does help him who begs for help. But for one to offer help! and to offer it to all! Yes, and precisely to all such as can do nothing to help in return! To offer it—no, to shout it out, as if the Helper were the one who needed help, as if in fact He who is able and willing to help all was Himself in a sense a needy one, in that He feels an urge, and consequently need to help, need of the sufferer in order to help him!

I

"COME hither!"—There is nothing wonderful in the fact that when one is in danger and in need of help, perhaps of speedy, instant help, he shouts, "Come hither!" Neither it is wonderful that a quack shouts out, "Come hither! I heal all diseases." Ah, in the instance of the quack there is only too much truth in the falsehood that the physician has need of the sick man. "Come hither, all ye that can pay for healing at an exorbitant price—or at least for physic. Here is medicine for everybody . . . who can pay. Come hither, come hither!"

But commonly it is understood that one who is able to help must be sought out; and when one has found him, it may be difficult to gain access to him, one must perhaps implore him for a long time; and when one has implored him for a long time, he may perhaps at last be moved. That is, he sets a high value upon himself. And when sometimes he declines to receive any pay, or magnanimously relinquishes claim to it, this merely expresses the value he attaches to himself. He, on the other hand, who made the great self-surrender here surrenders himself anew.

He Himself it is who seeks them that stand in need to help; it is He Himself who goes about and, calling them, almost beseeching them, says, "Come hither!" He, the only one who is able to help, and to help with the one thing needful, to save from the sickness which in the truest sense is mortal, does not wait for people to come to Him, but He comes of His own accord, uncalled for—for He indeed it is that calls them, that offers help—and what help! That simple wise man, too, of ancient times [1] was just as infinitely right as the majority who do the opposite are wrong, in that he did not set a high value upon himself or his instruction, though it is true that, in another sense, he thereby gave expression with a noble pride to the incommensurability of the pay. But he was not so deeply concerned through love to men that he begged anyone to come to him. And he behaved as he did—shall I say, in spite of the fact, or because?—he was not altogether certain what his help really amounted to. For the more certain one is that his help is the only help, just so much more reason he has, humanly speaking, to make it dear; and the less certain he is, so much the more reason he has to offer with great alacrity such help as he disposes of, for the sake of accomplishing something at least. But He who calls Himself the Saviour, and knows Himself to be such, says with deep concern, "Come hither."

"Come hither *all* ye!"—Wonderful! For that one who perhaps is impotent to give help to a single soul—that he with lusty lungs should invite all is not so wonderful, human nature being what it is. But when one is perfectly certain that he can help; when one is willing, moreover, to devote oneself entirely to this cause and to make every sacrifice, it is usual, at least, to reserve the liberty of selecting the objects of one's care. However willing a person may be, still it is not everyone he would help, he would not sacrifice himself to that extent. But He, the only one who can truly help, the only one who can truly help all, and so the only one who truly can invite all, He stipulates no condition at all. This word which was as though coined for him from the foundation of the world, he accordingly utters: "Come hither all." O, human self-sacrifice! even at thy fairest and noblest, when we admire thee most, there still is one act of sacrifice beyond thee, the sacrifice of every determinant of one's own ego, so that in the willingness to help there is not the least prejudice of partiality. What loving-kindness, thus to set no price upon oneself, entirely to forget oneself, to forget that it is he who helps, entirely

---

[1] Socrates, who took no fees for the instruction he imparted. (L)

blind to the question who it is one helps, seeing with infinite clearness only that it is a sufferer, whoever he may be; thus to will unconditionally to help all—alas, in this respect so different from us all!

"Come hither *to* me!"—Wonderful! For human compassion does indeed do something for them that labor and are heavy laden. One feeds the hungry, clothes the naked, gives alms, builds charitable institutions, and, if the compassion is more heartfelt, one also visits them that labor and are heavy laden. But to invite them to come to us, that is a thing that cannot be done; it would involve a change in all our household and manner of life. It is not possible while one is living in abundance, or at least in joy and gladness, to live and dwell together in the same house, in a common life in daily intercourse, with the poor and wretched, with them that labor and are heavy laden. In order to be able to invite them thus one must live entirely in the same way, as poor as the poorest, as slightly regarded as the lowliest man of the people, familiar with life's sorrow and anguish, sharing completely the same conditions as they whom one invites to one's home, namely they that labor and are heavy laden. If a man will invite the sufferer to come to him, he must either alter his condition in likeness to the sufferer's, or the sufferer's in likeness to his own. Otherwise the difference will be all the more glaring by reason of the contrast. And if a man will invite all sufferers to come to him (for with a single individual one can make an exception and alter his condition), it can be done in only one way, by altering one's own condition in likeness to theirs, if originally it was not adapted to this end, as was the case with Him who says, "Come hither to me, all ye that labor and are heavy laden." This He said, and they that lived with Him beheld, and lo! there is not the very least thing in His life which contradicts it. With the silent and veracious eloquence of deeds His life expresses, even if He had never given utterance to these words, "Come hither to me, all ye that labor and are heavy laden." He is true to His word, He is what He says, and in this sense also He is the Word.

"*All ye that labor and are heavy laden.*"—Wonderful! The only thing He is concerned about is that there might be a single one of those that labor and are heavy laden who failed to hear the invitation. As for the danger that too many might come, He had no fear of it. Oh, where heart-room is, there house-room always is to be found. But where was there ever heart-room if not in His heart? How the individual will understand the invitation He leaves to the individual himself. His conscience is clear: He has invited all them that labor and are heavy laden.

But what then is it to labor and to be heavy laden? Why does He not explain it more precisely, so that one may know exactly who it is He means? Why is He so laconic? O, thou petty man, He is so laconic in order not to be petty; thou illiberal man, He is so laconic in order not to be illiberal; it is the part of love (for "love" is toward all) to prevent that there be a single person who is thrown into alarm by pondering whether he also is among the invited. And he who might require a closer definition—would he not be a self-loving person, reckoning that this ought especially to take care of his case and apply to him, without considering that the more of such closer and closer definitions there were, just so much the more inevitable that there must be individuals for whom it became more and more indefinite whether they are the invited. O man, why doth thine eye look only to its own?

Why is it evil because He is good? The invitation to all throws open the Inviter's arms, and there He stands, an everlasting picture.[2] As soon as the closer definition is introduced, which perhaps might help the individual to another sort of certainty, the Inviter has a different aspect, and there passes over Him as it were a fleeting shadow of change.

"I will give thee rest."—Wonderful! For these words, "Come hither to me," must thus be understood to mean, abide with me, I am that rest, or, to abide with me is rest. So it is not as in other instances, when the helper who says, "Come hither," must thereupon say, "Go hence again," declaring to each individual severally where the help he needs is to be found, where there grows the pain-quenching herb which can heal him, or where the tranquil place is where he can cease from labor, or where is that happier region of the world where one is not heavy laden. No, He who opens His arms and invites all—oh, in case all, all they that labor and are heavy laden were to come to Him, He would embrace them in His arms and say, "Abide with Me, for in abiding with Me there is rest." The Helper is the help. Oh, wonderful! He who invites all and would help all has a way of treating the sick just as if it were

[2] Here (as also in one of his *Edifying Discourses* which he delivered within sight of it) S.K. is presumably thinking of Thorwaldsen's famous representation of Christ, the statue with outspread arms which was placed over the altar of the cathedral in Copenhagen, where Bishop Mynster commonly preached and S.K. always went to hear him. (L)

intended for each several one, as if each patient He deals with were the only one. Commonly a physician must divide himself among his many patients who, however many they are, are very far from being all. He prescribes the medicine, tells what is to be done, how it is to be used— and then he departs to another patient. Or else, in case the patient has come to see him, he lets him depart. The physician cannot remain sitting all the day long beside one patient, still less can he have all his sick people in his own home and yet sit all the day long beside one patient—without neglecting the others. Hence in this case the helper and the help are not one and the same thing. The patient retains beside him all the day long the help which the physician prescribes, so as to use it constantly; whereas the physician sees him only now and then, and only now and then does he see the physician. But when the Helper is the help, He must remain with the patient all the day long, or the patient with Him. Oh, wonderful! that it is this very Helper who invites all!

II

Come hither, all ye that labor and are heavy laden,
I will give you rest

WHAT prodigious multiplicity, what almost boundless diversity, amongst the people invited! For a man, even a mere man, can well enough attempt to conceive of some of the individual differences; but the Inviter must invite all, yet every one severally as an individual.

So the invitation fares forth, along frequented roads and along the solitary paths, along the most solitary, aye, where there is a path so solitary that only one knows it, one single person, or no one at all, so that there is only one footprint, that of the luckless man who fled along that path with his misery, no other indication whatsoever, and no indication that in following that path one might return again. Even there the invitation penetrates, finding its own way back easily and surely— most easily when it bears the fugitive back with it to the Inviter. Come hither, all ye—and thou, and thou . . . and thou, too, most solitary of all fugitives!

Thus the invitation fares forth, and wherever there is a parting of the ways it stops and calls aloud. Like the trumpet-call of the warrior which turns to all four quarters of the world, so the invitation resounds wherever there is a parting of the ways—and with no uncertain sound (for who then would come?) but with the unequivocal sureness of eternity.

It halts at the crossways, where suffering temporal and earthly has planted its cross, and there it calls aloud. Come hither, all ye poor and miserable, ye who in poverty must toil to ensure for yourselves not a carefree but a toilsome future. Oh, bitter contradiction—to have to toil to *attain* what one groans under, what one *flees* from!—Ye who are despised and disdained, about whose existence none is concerned, not a single one, not even so much as for the beasts, which have a higher value!—Ye sick, lame, deaf, blind, crippled, come hither!—Ye bed-ridden, yea, come ye also hither! For the invitation makes bold to bid the bedridden: come!—Ye lepers! For the invitation abolishes every barrier of difference in order to bring all together. It proposes to make amends for the inequalities chargeable to the difference which allots one a place as a ruler over millions, possessing all the favors of fortune, and relegates another to the desert. And why? (Oh, the cruelty of it!) Because (oh, cruel human logic!), *because* he is miserable, indescribably miserable; consequently for this further reason, because he craves help, or at least compassion; and consequently for this further reason, because human compassion is a paltry invention, cruel where the need of com-passion is most evident, and compassionate only where in a true sense it is not compassion!—Ye sick at heart, ye who only through pain learn to know that a man has a heart in a sense quite different from the heart of a beast, and learn what it means to suffer in that part, learn how it is that the physician may be right in declaring that one's heart is sound while nevertheless he is heart-sick. Ye whom unfaithfulness deceived, and then human sympathy (for human sympathy is seldom in delay) made a target for mockery. All ye who have been discrim-inated against, wronged, offended, and ill-used; all ye noble ones who (as everybody can tell you) deservedly reap the reward of ingratitude. For why were ye foolish enough to be noble, why stupid enough to be kindly, disinterested, and faithful? All ye victims of cunning and deceit and backbiting and envy, whom baseness singled out and cowardice left in the lurch, whether ye be sacrificed in remote and lonely places whither ye have crept away to die, or whether ye be trampled under foot by the thronging human crowd where no one inquires what right ye have on your side, no one inquires what wrong ye suffer, or where the smart of your suffering is, or how ye smart under it, while the throng, replete with animal health, tramples you in the dust [3]—come hither!

The invitation stands at the parting of the ways where death separates life and life. Come hither, all ye sorrowful, all ye that travail in vain and are sore troubled! For it is true that there is rest in the grave; but to sit beside a grave, to stand by a grave, or to visit a grave, all that is not yet to lie in the grave; and to scan again and again the production of one's own pen, which one knows by heart, the inscription which one placed there oneself and which the man himself can best understand, telling who lies buried there—that, alas, is not to lie buried there oneself. In the grave there is rest, but *beside* the grave there is no rest—the meaning of it is: hitherto and no farther . . . then one can go home. But often as you return to *that* grave, day after day, whether in thought or on foot—one gets no farther, not one step from the spot; and this is very exhausting, far from expressing rest. Come ye therefore hither, here is the path along which one goes farther, here is rest beside the grave, rest from the pain of loss, or rest in the pain of loss—with Him who eternally reunites the separated, more firmly than nature unites parents and children, children and parents (alas, they were parted), more inwardly than the priest unites husband and wife (alas, separation occurred), more indissolubly than the bond of friendship unites friend with friend (alas, that was dissolved). Separation everywhere forced its way between, bringing sorrow and unrest; but here is rest!—Come hither, ye whose abodes were assigned to you among the tombs, ye who are accounted dead to human society, yet not missed and not mourned—not buried, although dead, that is, belonging neither to life nor to death; ye, alas, to whom human society cruelly closed its doors, and yet for whom no grave mercifully opened —come ye then hither: here is rest and here is life!

The invitation halts at the parting of the ways where the path of sin deviates from the hedged road of innocence.—Oh, come hither, ye are so near to Him; a single step on the other path, and ye are so endlessly far from Him. It may well be, perhaps, that ye have not felt as yet the need of rest, and hardly understand what it means; yet follow nevertheless the invitation, so that the Inviter might save you *from* a state which only with great difficulty and peril ye might be saved *out of,* so that as the saved ye might abide with Him who is the Saviour of all

---

[3] S.K. says in the Journal that he was being "trampled to death by geese"—thinking of the popular ridicule he was exposed to as a consequence of the cartoons in the *Corsair.* He shuddered at the sheer "animal health" of the "louts" who derided him. (L)

men including the innocent. For if it were possible that somewhere there might be found innocence entirely unsullied, why should it not also require a saviour who could preserve it safe from the evil one?— The invitation halts at the parting of the ways where the path of sin veers more deeply into sin. Come hither, all ye that have strayed and lost your way, whatever your error and sin may have been, whether it be one which in human eyes was more pardonable and yet perhaps more dreadful, or one more dreadful in human eyes and yet perhaps more pardonable, one which was revealed here on earth, or one which is concealed here yet known in heaven—did ye find forgiveness here on earth and yet no rest in your inward mind, or found ye no forgiveness because ye sought it not, or sought it in vain—oh, turn about and come hither, here is rest!—The invitation halts at the parting of the ways where the path of sin again veers, for the last time, and is lost to view— in perdition. Oh, turn about, turn about, come hither! Shrink not at the difficulty of the journey back,[4] however hard it be; fear not the toilsome path of conversion, however laboriously it leads to salvation, whereas sin with winged speed, with ever-increasing velocity, leads onward . . . or downward, so easily, with such indescribable ease, as easily indeed as when a horse, relieved entirely of the strain of pulling, cannot with all his might bring the wagon to a halt which thrusts him over into the abyss. Be not in despair at every relapse, which the God of patience possesses patience enough to forgive and which a sinner might well have patience enough to be humbled under. Nay, fear nothing and despair not. He who says, "Come hither," is with you on your way; from Him come help and forgiveness in the path of conversion which leads to Him; and with Him there is rest.

Come hither all, all, all of you, with Him is rest, and He makes no difficulties, He does but one thing, He opens his arms. He will not first (as righteous people do, alas, even when they are willing to help)—He will not first ask thee, "Art thou not after all to blame for thy misfortune? Hast thou in fact no cause for self-reproach?" It is so easy, so human, to judge after the outward appearance, after the result—when a person is a cripple, or deformed, or has an unprepossessing appearance, to judge that *ergo* he is a bad man; when a person fares badly in

---

[4] S.K., during his own laborious return from "the path of perdition," remarked that one was compelled to tread backwards the whole way one had gone, and he remembered a fairy tale which recounted that deliverance from an enchantment wrought by a piece of music was possible only when one was able to play it backwards without an error. (L.) Cf. *supra*, pp. 97 and 346.

the world so that he is brought to ruin or goes downhill, then to judge that *ergo* he is a vicious man. Oh, it is such an exquisite invention of cruel pleasure to enhance the consciousness of one's own righteousness in contrast with a sufferer, by explaining that his suffering is God's condign punishment, so that one hardly even . . . dares to help him; or by challenging him with that condemning question which flatters one's own righteousness in the very act of helping him. But he will put no such questions to thee, He will not be thy benefactor in so cruel a fashion. If thou thyself art conscious of being a sinner, he will not inquire of thee about it, the bruised reed He will not further break, but he will raise thee up if thou wilt attach thyself to Him. He will not single thee out by contrast, holding thee apart from Him, so that thy sin will seem still more dreadful; He will grant thee a hiding-place within Him, and once hidden in Him He will hide thy sins. For He is the friend of sinners: When it is a question of a sinner He does not merely stand still, open His arms and say, "Come hither"; no, he stands there and waits, as the father of the lost son waited, rather He does not stand and wait, he goes forth to seek, as the shepherd sought the lost sheep, as the woman sought the lost coin. He goes—yet no, he has gone, but infinitely farther than any shepherd or any woman, He went, in sooth, the infinitely long way from being God to becoming man, and that way He went in search of sinners.

III

Come hither to me, all ye that labor and are heavy laden,
I will give you rest

"COME *hither!*" For He assumes that they that labor and are heavy laden feel the burden all too heavy, the labor heavy, and now stand in perplexity, heaving sighs—one glancing around searchingly to see if no help is to be found, another with eyes bent down upon the ground because he descried no comfort, a third gazing upward as though from heaven it still must come, but all of them seeking. Therefore He says, "Come hither." Him who has ceased to seek and to sorrow He does not invite.—"*Come hither!*" For He, the Inviter, knows it as a sign of true suffering that one goes apart to brood alone in disconsolate silence, lacking the courage to confide in anyone, not to say the confidence to hope for help. Alas, that demoniac was not the only person possessed by a dumb spirit.[5] Suffering which does not begin by making the sufferer dumb does not amount to much—no more than love which does not make the lover silent. Sufferers whose tongues run easily over the story of their sufferings neither labor nor are heavy laden. Lo! for this reason the Inviter dare not wait till they that labor and are heavy laden come to Him of their own accord: He Himself lovingly summons them. All His willingness to help would perhaps be no help at all if He did not utter this word and thereby take the first step. For in this summons, "Come unto me," it is He in fact who comes to them. Oh, human compassion! Perhaps it may sometimes indicate praiseworthy self-restraint, perhaps also sometimes a genuine and heart-felt sympathy, when thou refrainest from questioning a man who, as may be surmised, is constantly brooding over a hidden suffering; yet how often it may be only worldly wisdom, which has no desire to learn to know too much. Oh, human compassion, how often was it merely curiosity, not compassion, which prompted thee to venture to penetrate a sufferer's secret! And what a burden didst thou feel it to be—almost a punishment upon thy curiosity—when he followed thine invitation and came to thee! But He who utters this saving word, "Come hither," was not deceived in Himself when He uttered the word, neither will He deceive thee when thou comest to Him to find rest by casting thy burden upon Him. He follows the prompting of His heart in uttering it, and His heart accompanies [follows] the word—follow then thou the word, and it will accompany [follow] thee back to His heart. It is a matter of course [*selvfølge*]; the one thing follows the other—oh, that thou wouldst follow the invitation.[6]—*"Come hither!"* For He assumes that they that labor and are heavy laden are so tired and exhausted, in a state of swoon, that they have forgotten again, as in a stupor, that there is comfort; or, alas, He knows that it is only too true that there is no comfort and help unless it is sought in Him; and so He has to call them to "come hither."

"Come hither!" For it is characteristic of every society that it possesses a token or a sign of some sort by which one who is a member can be recognized. When a young girl is adorned in a certain manner, one knows that she is on her way to a ball. Come hither, all ye that labor and are heavy laden.—*"Come hither!"* Thou dost not need to

---

[5] Mk. 9: 17, 25. (L)

[6] In brackets I have sought to indicate that there is a play on words: "follow," with its two meanings and its derivative. (L)

wear a distinctive outward and visible mark . . . come also with anointed head and a face newly washed, if only thou dost inwardly labor and art heavy laden.

"Come hither!" Oh, stand not still, considering the matter. Consider rather, oh, consider that for every instant thou standest still after hearing the invitation, thou wilt in the next instant hear its call fainter and fainter, and thus be withdrawing to a distance though thou be standing at the same spot.—*"Come hither!"* Oh, however tired and weary thou art with thy labor, or with the long, long quest in search of help and salvation, although it seem to thee as if thou couldst not follow one step farther or hold out a moment longer without sinking to the ground— oh, but this one step more, and here is rest! *"Come hither!"* Ah, if there were only one so wretched that he could not come—a sigh is enough, to sigh for Him is also to come hither.

THE OBSTACLE

Come hither unto me, all ye that labor and are heavy laden,
I will give you rest.

Halt now! But what is there to impose a halt? That which in a single instant infinitely alters everything—so that in reality, instead of getting a sight, as one might expect, of an interminable throng of such as labor and are heavy laden following the invitation, you behold in fact a sight which is exactly the opposite: an interminable throng of men who turn backward in flight and shudder, until in the scramble to get away they trample one another under foot; so that if from the result one were to infer what had been said, one must conclude that the words were, *"Procul, o procul este profani,"*[1] rather than, "Come hither." [The halt is imposed, finally,] by something infinitely more important and infinitely more decisive: by the INVITER. Not as though He were not the man to do what He says, or not God to keep the promise He has made—no, in a sense very different from that.

[IN the sense, namely,] that the Inviter is and insists upon being the definite historical person He was 1,800 years ago, and that as this definite person, living under the conditions He then lived under, He

---

[1] Far away—be far away—ye profane.

uttered those words of invitation.—He is not, and for nobody is He willing to be, one about whom we have learned to know something merely from history[2] (i.e. world-history, secular history, in contrast to sacred history), for from history we can learn to know nothing about Him, because there is absolutely nothing that can be "known" about Him.—He declines to be judged in a human way by the consequences of His life, that is to say, He is and would be the sign of offense[3] and the object of faith. To judge Him by the consequences of His life is mere mockery of God; for, seeing that He is God, His life (the life which he actually lived in time) is infinitely more important than all the consequences of it in the course of history.

a

Who spoke these words of invitation?

The Inviter. Who is the Inviter? Jesus Christ. Which Jesus Christ? The Jesus Christ who sits in glory at the right hand of the Father? No. From the seat of His glory he has not spoken one word. Therefore it is Jesus Christ in His humiliation, in the state of humiliation, who spoke these words.

Is then Jesus Christ not always the same? Yes, He is the same yesterday and today, the same that 1,800 years ago humbled Himself and took upon Him the form of a servant, the Jesus Christ who uttered these words of invitation. In His coming again in glory He is again the same Jesus Christ, but this has not yet occurred.

Is He, then, not now in glory? Yes indeed; this the Christian *believes.* But it was in the state of humiliation He uttered these words; from the seat of His glory He has not uttered them. And about His coming again in glory nothing can be known; in the strictest sense, it can only be believed. But one cannot have become a Christian without having already come to Him in His estate of humiliation—without having come to Him, who is the sign of offense and the object of faith. In no other wise does He exist on earth, for it was only thus that He existed. That He shall come in glory is to be expected, but it can be expected and believed only by one who has attached himself and continues to hold fast to Him as He actually existed.

[2] In this paragraph, as in an overture, the principal themes of the whole work are suggested. (L)

[3] The "offense" of Christianity has already been considered in the *Fragments,* e.g. Chap. iii, Appendix. (L)

Jesus Christ is the same; but He lived 1,800 years ago in His humiliation and first becomes changed [for us] with His coming again. As yet He has not returned, so He remains still the lowly one about whom it is believed that He shall return in glory. What He said and taught, every word He has spoken, becomes *eo ipso* untrue when we make it appear as if it were Christ in glory who says it. No, *He* maintains silence, it is the *lowly one* who speaks. The interval (between His humiliation and His coming again in glory), which at this moment is about 1,800 years and may possibly be protracted to many times 1,800—this interval, rather, all that this interval makes of Him, secular history and Church history, with all the worldly information they furnish about Christ, about who Christ was, and consequently about who uttered these words, is a thing completely indifferent, neither here nor there, which merely distorts Him, and thereby renders these words of invitation untrue.

For it is untruth if I imaginatively ascribe to a man words which he never uttered, affirming that *he* said them. But it is also untruth if I imaginatively represent him as essentially different from what he was when he spake certain words. I say, "essentially different," for a falsehood which has to do only with some accidental trait does not make it untrue that he said the thing.—And so, when God is pleased to walk here on earth in a strict incognito such as only an almighty being can assume, an incognito impenetrable to the most intimate observation, when it pleases Him to come in the lowly form of a servant, to all appearance like any other man (and why He does it, with what purpose, He surely knows best; but whatever the reason or purpose may be, they testify that the incognito has some essential significance), when it pleases Him to come in this lowly form to teach men—and then somebody repeats exactly the words He uttered, but makes it appear as if it was God who said them, the thing becomes untrue, for it is untrue that He uttered these words.

b

Can one learn from history [4] anything about Christ?

No. Why not? Because one can "know" nothing at all about "Christ"; He is the paradox, the object of faith, existing only for faith. But all historical communication is communication of "knowledge,"

[4] By "history" is to be understood throughout profane history, world history, history as ordinarily understood, in contrast to sacred history. (K)

hence from history one can learn nothing about Christ. For if one learns little or much about Him, or anything at all, He [who is thus known] is not He who in truth He is, i.e. one learns to know nothing about Him, or one learns to know something incorrect about Him, one is deceived. History makes out Christ to be another than He truly is, and so one learns to know a lot about—Christ? No, not about Christ, for about Him nothing can be known, He can only be believed.

c

Can one prove from history that Christ was God?

Let me first put another question: Is it possible to conceive of a more foolish contradiction than that of wanting to PROVE (no matter for the present purpose whether it be from history or from anything else in the wide world one wants to *prove* it) that a definite individual man is God? That an individual man is God, declares himself to be God, is indeed the "offense" κατ᾽ ἐξοχήν.[5] But what is the offense, the offensive thing? What is at variance with (human) reason. And such a thing as that one would attempt to prove! To "prove" is to demonstrate something to be the rational reality it is. Can one demonstrate that to be a rational reality which is at variance with reason? Surely not, unless one would contradict oneself. One can "prove" only that it is at variance with reason. The proofs which Scripture presents for Christ's divinity —His miracles, His Resurrection from the dead, His Ascension into heaven—are therefore only for faith, that is, they are not "proofs," they have no intention of proving that all this agrees perfectly with reason; on the contrary they would prove that it conflicts with reason and therefore is an object of faith.

But to return to the proofs from history. Is it not 1,800 years since Christ lived, is not His name proclaimed and believed on throughout the whole world, has not His doctrine (Christianity) changed the face of the world, triumphantly permeated all relationships—and in this way has not history abundantly, and more than abundantly, established who He was, namely, that He was God? No, history has not established that, either abundantly or more than abundantly; that is something which history in all eternity cannot establish. So far, however, as the first assertion is concerned, it is sure enough that His name is pro-

---

[5] *Par excellence.*

claimed in all the world—whether it is believed on I will not decide. It is sure enough that Christianity has changed the face of the world, triumphantly permeated all relationships—so triumphantly that all now say that they are Christians.

But what does that prove? At the most it might prove that Jesus Christ was a great man, perhaps the greatest of all; but that He was . . . God—nay, stop there. The conclusion shall by God's help never be drawn.

If, in order to lead up to this conclusion, one begins with the assumption that Jesus Christ was a man, and then considers the history of the 1,800 years [6] (the consequences of His life), one may conclude, with an ascending superlative scale: great, greater, greatest, exceedingly and astonishingly the greatest man that ever lived.—If on the contrary one begins with the assumption (the assumption of faith) that He was God, one has thereby canceled, annulled, the 1,800 years as having nothing to do with the case, proving nothing *pro* nor *contra,* inasmuch as the certitude of faith is something infinitely higher.—And it is in one or the other of these ways one must begin. If one begins in the latter way, everything is as it should be.

If one begins in the first way, one cannot, without being guilty at one point or another of a μετάβασίς εἰς ἄλλο γένος,[7] arrive suddenly by an inference at the new quality . . . God; as if the consequence or consequences of . . . a man's life might suddenly furnish the proof that this man was God. If this could be done, then one might answer the following query: What consequences must there be, how great the effects produced, how many centuries must elapse, in order to establish a proof from the consequences of a man's life (this being the assumption) that he was God? Whether perhaps it might be said that in the year 300 Christ was not yet completely proved to be God, something approaching that having been attained, namely, that He was already a little more than the exceedingly, astonishingly greatest man that ever lived, but there still was need of several centuries more? If such be the case, the further consequence presumably follows, that they who lived in the year 300 did not regard Christ as God, and still less they who lived in the first century, whereas on the other hand the certitude that He is God increases regularly with each century, so in our time, the

---

[6] The argument from the 1,800 years was demolished already in the *Postscript* (e.g. Part 1, chap. 1, § 3) and S.K. returned to the assault in *The Instant*. (L)

[7] Transition to another *kind.*

nineteenth century, it is greater than it has ever been before, a certitude in comparison with which the first centuries seem barely to have glimpsed His divinity. One may make answer to this or leave it alone—it makes no essential difference.

What can this mean? Is it possible that by contemplating the consequences of something as they unfold themselves more and more one might by a simple inference from them produce another quality different from that contained in the assumption? Is it not a sign of insanity (supposing man in general to be sane) that the first proposition (the assumption with which one starts out) is so far astray about what is what that it errs to the extent of a whole quality? And when one begins with this error, how shall one at any subsequent point be able to perceive the mistake and apprehend that one is dealing with another and an infinitely different quality? The print of a foot along a path is obviously a consequence of the fact that some creature has gone that way. I may now go on to suppose erroneously that it was, for example, a bird, but on closer inspection, pursuing the track farther, I convince myself that it must have been another sort of animal. Very well. But here we are far from having an infinite qualitative alteration. But can I, by a closer inspection of such a track, or by following it farther, reach at one point or another the conclusion: *ergo* it was a spirit that passed this way? A spirit which leaves no trace behind it! Just so it is with this thing of concluding from the consequences of an (assumed) human existence that *ergo* it was God. Do God and man resemble one another to such a degree, is there so slight a difference between them, that I (supposing I am not crazy) can begin with the assumption that Christ was a man? And, on the other hand, has not Christ Himself said that He was God? If God and man resemble one another to that degree, if they have that degree of kinship, and thus essentially are included in the same quality, the conclusion, *"ergo* it was God," is nevertheless humbug; for if God is nothing else but that, then God doesn't exist at all. But if God exists, and consequently is distinguished by an infinite difference of quality from all that it means to be a man, then neither can I nor anybody else, by beginning with the assumption that He was a man, arrive in all eternity at the conclusion, "therefore it was God." Everyone who has the least dialectical training can easily perceive that the whole argument about consequences is incommensurable with the decision of the question whether it is God, and that this decisive question is presented to man in an entirely different form: whether he will believe that He is what He said He was; or whether he will not believe.

. . . This ought to be enough to throw a spike into the gears of that argument from the consequences of Christ's life: *ergo* He was God. But faith, in the province of its jurisdiction, raises a still more essential protest against every attempt to approach Christ by the help of what one happens to know of Him through history and the information history has preserved about the consequences of His life. Faith's contention is that this whole attempt is—*blasphemy*. Faith's contention is that the one and only proof which unbelief allowed to stand when it demolished all the other proofs of the truth of Christianity, the proof which unbelief itself discovered (yes, the situation is curiously complicated), which unbelief discovered, and discovered as a proof of the truth of Christianity (mighty good! Unbelief discovers proofs in defense of Christianity!), the proof which Christendom has since made so much ado about, the proof of the 1,800 years—faith's contention is that this is—*blasphemy*.

In the case of a *man* it may justly enough be said that the consequences of his life are more important than his life. When a person then seeks to find out who Christ was, and essays to draw a logical conclusion from the consequences of His life—he makes Him out *eo ipso* to be a man, a man who like other men has to pass his examination in history. . . .

"History," says faith, "has nothing whatever to do with Christ. As applying to Him, we have only sacred history (qualitatively different from history in general), which recounts the story of His life under the conditions of His humiliation, and reports moreover that He himself said that He was God. He is the paradox, which history can never digest or convert into a common syllogism. In His humiliation He is the same as in His exaltation—but the 1,800 years (or if there were 18,000 of them) have nothing whatever to do with the case. The brilliant consequences in world-history which well nigh convince even a professor of history that He was God—these brilliant consequences are surely not His return in glory! But this is really about what they mean by it: it appears here again that they make out Christ to be a man whose return in glory can be nothing more than the consequences of His life in history—whereas Christ's return in glory is something entirely different, something that is believed. He humbled Himself and was swaddled in rags—He will come again in glory. But the brilliant consequences (especially upon closer inspection) turn out to be a shabby sort of glory, at all events entirely incongruous, about which faith never speaks when it speaks of His glory. . . .

. . . Strange! and they want above all things to make use of history to prove that Christ was God.

d

Are the consequences of Christ's life more important than His life?

No, by no means, quite the contrary—if this were so, Christ was merely a man.

There is surely nothing noteworthy in the fact that a man lived; millions upon millions of them of course have lived. If this fact is to become noteworthy, the man's life must acquire some noteworthy distinction, which means that with respect to a man's life noteworthiness emerges only in the second instance. It is not noteworthy that he lived, but his life exhibited one or another noteworthy trait. Among such traits may be included what he accomplished, the consequences of his life.

But the fact that God lived here on earth as an individual man is infinitely noteworthy. Even if it had no consequences whatsoever, the fact is the same, it remains just as noteworthy, infinitely noteworthy, infinitely more noteworthy than all consequences. Make the attempt of introducing here the noteworthy distinction in the second instance, and you will readily perceive the foolishness of it. How could it be noteworthy that God's life had noteworthy consequences? To talk in such a way is to twaddle.

No, the fact that God lived is the infinitely noteworthy, the in-and-for-itself noteworthy. Assume that Christ's life had no consequences—to say then that His life was not noteworthy would be blasphemy. For it is noteworthy all the same; and if anything need be said about noteworthiness in the second instance, this would be: the noteworthy fact that His life had no consequences. If on the contrary someone says that Christ's life is noteworthy because of the consequences, this again is blasphemy, for this life is in-and-for-itself noteworthy.

No emphasis falls upon the fact that a man lived, but infinite is the emphasis which falls upon the fact that God lived. God alone can attach to Himself such great weight that the fact that He lived and has lived is infinitely more important than all the consequences which are registered in history.

e

A comparison between Christ and a man who in his lifetime suffered the same opposition from his age that Christ suffered

Let us think of a man,[8] one of those glorious figures who was unjustly treated by his own age but afterwards was reinstated in his rights by history, which, by means of the consequences of his life, made it evident who he was. . . . He lives among his contemporaries, but he is not understood, not recognized for what he is, he is misunderstood, then derided, persecuted, and finally put to death as a malefactor. But the consequences of his life make it manifest who he was; history which records these consequences does him justice, he now is acclaimed century after century as a great and noble man, his humiliation being as good as forgotten. It was due to the blindness of his age that it did not recognize him for what he was, it was due to the impiety of that generation that they scorned and derided him and finally put him to death. But let that now be forgotten; it was only after his death that he really became what he was, through the consequences of his life, which were indeed more important than his life.

Should the same be true also of Christ? It was indeed a blindness, an impiety on the part of that generation—but let that now be forgotten, history has now reinstated Him in His right, we now know from history who Jesus Christ was, we now do Him justice.

Oh, impious heedlessness, which reduces sacred history to profane history, Christ to a mere man! Can one then from history learn to know anything about Christ? (Cf. above under § *b*.) By no manner of means. Jesus Christ is the object of faith; one must either believe on Him or be offended. For to "know" signifies exactly that the reference is not to Him. It is true enough that history furnishes knowledge in abundance, but knowledge demolishes Jesus Christ.

Again, oh, impious heedlessness! if anyone were to have the presumption to say of Christ's humiliation, Let us now forget all that has to do with His humiliation. Yet surely Christ's humiliation was not something which merely happened to Him (even though it was the sin of that generation that they crucified Him), something which happened to Him and perhaps would not have happened to Him in a better age. Christ Himself willed to be the humiliated and lowly one. Humiliation (the fact that it pleased God to be the lowly man) is

[8] S.K. is thinking especially of Socrates.

therefore something He Himself has joined together, something He wills to have knit together, a dialectical knot which no one shall presume to untie, which indeed no one can untie before He Himself has untied it by coming again in glory. With Him it is not as with a man who by the injustice of his age was not permitted to be himself or to be accounted for what he was, whereas history made this manifest; for Christ Himself willed to be the humble man, this is just what He would be accounted. Hence history must not incommode itself to do Him justice, nor must we with impious heedlessness fancy presumptuously that we know as a matter of course who He was. For no one *knows* that, and he who *believes* it must be contemporary with Him in His humiliation. When God chooses to let Himself be born in lowly station, when He who holds all possibilities in His hand clothes Himself in the form of a servant, when He goes about defenseless and lets men do with Him as they will, He surely must know well what He does and why He does it; it is He nevertheless who has men in His power, not men who have power over Him—so let not history pretend to be such a wiseacre as to explain who He was.

Finally, oh, blasphemy! if anyone presume to say that the persecution Christ suffered expresses something accidental. Because a man is persecuted by his age, it does not follow that he has a right to say that this would have happened to him in any age. So far forth there may be something in it when posterity says, Let now all that be forgot which he suffered unjustly while he lived. Very different is the case with Jesus Christ! It is not He that, after letting Himself be born, and making His appearance in Judea, has presented Himself for an examination in history; it is He that is the Examiner, His life is the examination, and that not alone for the race and generation, but for the whole race. Woe to the generation that dared to say, Let now all the injustice He suffered be forgotten, history has now made manifest who He was and reinstated Him in His rights.

By assuming that history is capable of doing this we put Christ's humiliation in an accidental relation to Him, i.e. we make Him out to be a man, a distinguished man to whom this happened through the impiety of his age, a thing which for his part he was very far from wishing, for he would fain (that is human) have been something great in the world—whereas on the contrary Christ freely willed to be the lowly one, and though His purpose in this was to deliver man, yet He also would express what "the truth" had to suffer in every generation and what it must always suffer. But if such is His royal will, and if only

at His return will He show Himself in glory, and if He has not yet
returned; and if no generation can contemplate without the compunc-
tion of repentance what that generation did to Him, with a sense of
guilty participation—then woe to him who presumes to take His lowliness from Him, or to let it be forgot what injustice He suffered, decking
Him fabulously in the human glory of the historical consequences,
which is neither the one thing nor the other.

f

The misfortune of Christendom

But this precisely is now the misfortune of Christendom, as for
many, many years it has been, that Christ is neither the one thing nor
the other, neither what He was when He lived on earth, nor what (as
is believed) He shall be at His return, but one about whom in an illicit
way, through history, people have learned to know something to the
effect that He was somebody or another of considerable consequence.
In an unpermissible and unlawful way people have become *knowing*
about Christ, for the only permissible way is to be *believing*. People
have mutually confirmed one another in the notion that by the aid of
the upshot of Christ's life and the 1,800 years (the consequences) they
have become acquainted with the answer to the problem. By degrees,
as this came to be accounted wisdom, all pith and vigor was distilled
out of Christianity; the tension of the paradox was relaxed, one became
a Christian without noticing it, and without in the least noticing the
possibility of offense. One took possession of Christ's doctrine, turned
it about and pared it down, while He of course remained surety for its
truth, He whose life had such stupendous results in history. All became
as simple as thrusting a foot into the stocking. And quite naturally,
because in that way Christianity became paganism. In Christianity
there is perpetual Sunday twaddle about Christianity's glorious and
priceless truths, its sweet consolation; but it is only too evident that
Christ lived 1,800 years ago. The Sign of Offense and the object of
Faith has become the most romantic of all fabulous figures, a divine
Uncle George.[9] One does not know what it is to be offended, still less

---

[9] The name S.K. employs is "Godmand," alluding to Uncle Franz Godmand, a
benevolent figure in a German story for children which was translated into Danish. I
allude to the wise and versatile tutor in Abbott's *Rollo Books*. But though this perhaps is
the nearest analogy in English (more properly American) literature, alas, I know that
nowadays the reading even of our children is so various that literary allusions no longer
allude. (L)

what it is to worship. What one especially praises in Christ is precisely what one would be most embittered by if one were contemporary with it, whereas now one is quite secure in reliance upon the upshot; and in reliance upon this proof from history, that He quite certainly was the great one, one draws the conclusion: *Ergo* that was the right thing. This is to say, That is the right, the noble, the sublime, the true thing, if it was He that did it; this is the same as to say that one does not trouble oneself to learn to know in a deeper sense what it was He did, still less to try, according to one's slender ability, by God's help to imitate Him in doing the thing that is right and noble and sublime and true. For what that is one does not apprehend and may therefore in the situation of today form a judgment diametrically opposite to the truth. One is content to admire and praise, and may be (as was said of a scrupulous translator who rendered an author word for word and therefore made no meaning) "too conscientious," perhaps also too cowardly and too feeble of heart really to wish to understand.

Christendom has done away with Christianity, without being quite aware of it. The consequence is that, if anything is to be done, one must try again to introduce Christianity into Christendom.[10]

THE INVITER

THE Inviter, therefore, is Jesus Christ in His humiliation, and He it was who uttered these words of invitation. It was not from His glory that He uttered them. If such had been the case, Christianity is paganism and Christ is in vain—wherefore this supposition is not true. But supposing the case were such that He who sits in glory were disposed to utter this word, "Come hither," as though it were an unambiguous invitation to rush straight into the arms of glory—what wonder then if a crowd were to come rushing up! But they who run in that fashion are on a wild-goose chase, vainly fancying that they *know* who Christ is. But that no one *knows*, and in order to believe, one must begin with the humiliation.

The Inviter who utters these words, consequently He whose words these are (whereas in the mouth of another these same words would be a falsehood), is the humiliated Jesus Christ, the lowly man, born of a despised maiden, His father a carpenter, His kindred people of the

---

[10] As Lowrie points out, we have here already the theme of the pamphleteering attack on "Christendom" five years later.

lowest class, the lowly man who at the same time (like pouring oil upon fire) declared that He was God. . . . It is this lowly man, living in poverty, with twelve poor fellows as His disciples who were drawn from the simplest classes of society, who for a while was singled out as an object of curiosity, but later was to be found only in company with sinners, publicans, lepers, and madmen; for it might cost a man honor, life, and property, or at any rate expulsion from the synagogue (for this punishment we know was imposed), if he merely suffered himself to be helped by Him. Come now hither, all ye that labor and are heavy laden! Oh, my friend, though thou wert deaf and blind and lame and leprous, &c., though thou wert to unite (a thing never before seen or heard of) all human wretchedness in thy wretchedness, and though He stood ready to help thee by a miracle—it yet is possible that thou (for this is only human) wouldst fear more than all these sufferings the suffering imposed for letting oneself be helped by Him, the punishment of being banished from the society of other men, of being scorned and scoffed at day in and day out, of losing, perhaps, life itself. It would be human (only too human) if thou wert to say within thyself: No, I thank you; I had rather continue to be deaf, and dumb, and blind, &c., than to be helped in such a way. . . .

Now examine thyself—for that thou hast a right to do. On the other hand, thou hast properly no right, without self-examination, to let thyself be deluded by "the others," or to delude thyself into the belief that thou art a Christian—therefore examine thyself. Suppose that thou wert contemporary with Him! True enough, He said—ah, it was *He* that said it—that He was God! Many a madman has done the same—and His whole generation was of the opinion that He "blasphemed." That, indeed, was the reason for the punishment imposed upon those who let themselves be helped by Him. On the part of the established order and of public opinion it was god-fearing care for souls, lest anyone be led astray. They persecuted Him thus out of godly fear. Therefore before a man resolves to let himself be helped he must consider that he has not only to expect the opposition of men, but consider this too, that even if thou couldst bear all the consequences of such a step, consider this too, that human punishment is God's punishment upon the blasphemer— the Inviter!

Now come hither, all ye that labor and are heavy laden!

Here obviously there is no call for haste. There is a brief halt which might appropriately be turned to account by going round by another street. And if thou, supposing that thou wert contemporary, wilt not sneak away thus by another street, or in present-day Christendom wilt not be one of the sham Christians—then truly there is occasion for a tremendous halt, for a halt which is the condition for the very existence of faith: thou art brought to a halt by the possibility of the offense.

. . . It is Jesus Christ in His humiliation, a lowly man, born of a despised virgin, his father a carpenter. But for all that, He makes His appearance under circumstances which are bound to fix very special attention upon Him. The little nation in which He appears—God's chosen people, as it calls itself—looks forward to an Expected One who will usher in a golden age for His land and nation. It is true that the form in which He appears upon the scene was as different as possibly could be from what most people expected. On the other hand, it corresponded better to the ancient prophecy with which the nation might be supposed to be acquainted. Thus He makes His appearance. A precursor had drawn attention to Him, and He too fixes attention upon Himself by signs and wonders which are talked about in the whole land—and He is the hero of the hour, a countless multitude surrounds Him wherever He goes or stops. The sensation he awakens is prodigious, all eyes are turned toward Him, everything that can walk, yea, what can only crawl, must see this wonder—and all must have a judgment about Him, form an opinion, so that the professional purveyors of opinions and judgments are well nigh driven to bankruptcy because the demands are so pressing and the contradictions so glaring. Yet He, the miracle worker, continues to be the lowly man who literally has nowhere to lay His head.—And let us not forget that in the situation of contemporaneousness signs and wonders have quite a different elasticity for repelling and attracting than has the vapid affair (still more vapid when the parsons, as they are accustomed to do, serve the thing up as a warmed-over dish) of dealing with signs and wonders of . . . 1,800 years ago. Signs and wonders in the situation of contemporaneousness are an exasperatingly impertinent thing, a thing which in a highly embarrassing way pretty nearly compels one to have an opinion, and which, if one is not in the humor to believe, may produce the utmost degree of exasperation at the misfortune of being contemporary with them, since they make life all too strenuous, and all the more so the more intelligent, educated, and cultured one is. It is an exceedingly delicate matter to find oneself obliged to give assent to signs and wonders performed by a contemporary. When one has Him at a distance, and when the upshot of His life helps one to entertain such a conceit, it is easy enough to fancy somehow that one believes.

So then the multitude is carried away by Him, follows Him jubilantly, beholds signs and wonders—not only such as He performs but such as He does not perform—exulting in the hope that the golden age will commence when He becomes King. But the crowd seldom can render a reason for its opinions; it thinks one thing today, another tomorrow. For this cause wise and prudent men are not in haste to adopt the opinions of the crowd. Let us see now what the judgment of the wise and prudent is as soon as the first impression of surprise and astonishment is past.

The wise and prudent man might say: "Even assuming that this person is, as he gives himself out to be, the Extraordinary (for all the talk of his being God I cannot but regard as an exaggeration, for which I should be quite ready to excuse and forgive him if I really could regard him as the Extraordinary, for I am not inclined to quarrel about words),[1] assuming (though about this I have my doubts or at all events suspend my judgment) that the things he does are actually miracles, is it not then an inexplicable riddle that this same man can be so ignorant, so shallow, so totally unacquainted with human nature, so weak, so good-naturedly vain, or whatever one might prefer to call it, as to behave in such a way, almost forcing his benefits upon people! Instead of holding people at a distance with a proud and lordly mien, keeping them in the deepest subjection, and receiving their worship on the rare occasions when he permits himself to be seen, that is to say, being instead approachable to all, or, more properly expressed, himself approaching all, consorting with all, almost as if to be the Extraordinary meant to be the servant of all, as if to be the Extraordinary, as he himself says he is, meant to be anxious whether people will derive profit from him or not—in short, as if to be the Extraordinary were to be the most anxiously troubled of all men. On the whole, it is inexplicable to me what he wants, what his purpose is, what he is striving for, what he desires to accomplish, what the meaning of it all is. In many an individual utterance of his he discloses, I cannot deny, so deep an insight into human nature that presumably he must know what I, with half my shrewdness, can tell him in advance, that in such a fashion nobody can get on in the world—unless it might be that, despising worldly

---

[1] In this connection it is amusing to recall the first sentence of Renan's *Life of Jesus.* It is as if that great man had stepped inadvertently into a trap S.K. had long before laid to trip him up. (L)

prudence, a man simple-heartedly aims at becoming a fool, or perhaps carries his simple-heartedness so far that he prefers to be put to death—but then a man is crazy, if that's what he wants. Having, as I said, a knowledge of human nature, he presumably knows that what one has to do is to deceive people and at the same time make one's deceit appear a benefaction to the whole race. In this way one stands to reap every advantage, including that which yields the most precious enjoyment of all, that of being called by one's contemporaries the benefactor of the human race—and when one is in the grave, a fig for what posterity may say. But to make such renunciation, not to take the least account of himself, almost begging people to accept these benefactions—no, as for joining him, such a thing could never enter my mind. And as a matter of fact he extends no invitation to me, for he invites only those who labor and are heavy laden. . . .

Or—"So many hasty judgments are expressed by people who understand nothing—and deify him, and so many harsh judgments by those who perhaps misunderstand him, that for my part I shall not give anyone occasion to charge me with a hasty judgment; I keep perfectly cool and calm, and what is more, I am conscious of being as indulgent and moderate as possible. Suppose it is true (which I concede, however, only up to a certain point) that even the understanding is not unimpressed by this man—what judgment then must I pass upon him? My judgment is that at the outset I can form no judgment about him. I do not mean with respect to the fact that he says he is God, for about that I can never to all eternity form any judgment at all. No, I mean an opinion about him regarded as a man. Only the upshot of his life can determine whether he is the Extraordinary, or whether, deceived by his imagination, he has applied, not only to himself but to mankind in general, a standard far too high for men. With the best will in the world I can do no more for him than this; even if he were my only friend or my own son, I could not judge him more indulgently or to any other effect. But hence it follows that I cannot on sufficient grounds reach any opinion about him. For to have an opinion I must first see the upshot of his life, even up to the very end. That is to say, he must be dead. Then I can (but still only perhaps) have an opinion about him; and this being assumed, it is still only in a non-natural sense an opinion about him, for then in fact he is no more. It follows as a matter of course that I cannot possibly join myself to him as long as he lives. The *authority* with which he is said to teach cannot have for me decisive significance, for it is easy to see that it moves in a circle, appealing to the very fact he has to prove, which in turn can only be proved by the upshot, insofar as it does not derive from the fixed idea of his that he is God; for if it is *therefore* he possesses authority, because he is God, the rejoinder is—*if*. This much, however, I can concede to him, that if I could fancy myself living in a later generation, and if then the upshot of his life, the consequences of it in history, were to make it evident that he was the Extraordinary—then it might not be altogether impossible that I might come very near to being his disciple."

A clergyman might say—"For an impostor and seducer of the people there is really something uncommonly honest about him, and for this reason he can hardly be so absolutely dangerous as he appears to be. He appears now to be so dangerous while the storm lasts, appears so dangerous because of his immense popularity, until the storm has passed over and the people—yes, precisely these people—overthrow him. It is honesty that while desiring to make himself out to be the Expected One, he resembles this figure as little as he does—the sort of honesty one can detect in a person who would issue false bank-notes, and makes them so badly that everyone who has any intelligence can easily detect the fraud.—True enough, we all look forward to an Expected One; but that it is God in His own person that should come is the expectation of no reasonable man, and every religious soul shudders at the blasphemy this person is guilty of. Nevertheless, we all look forward to an Expected One, in this we are all agreed. But the regiment of this world does not move forward tumultuously by leaps, the world development is (as the word itself implies) *evolutionary,* not *revolutionary.* The veritable Expected One will therefore appear totally different; He will come as the most glorious flower and the highest unfolding of the established order. Thus it is that the veritable Expected One will come; and He will act in a totally different way, He will recognize the established order as an authority, He will summon all the clergy to a council, lay before this body a report of what He has accomplished along with His credentials —and then, if by ballot He obtains a majority vote, He will be acclaimed as the extraordinary man He is, as the Expected One.

"But in this man's course of action there is an ambiguity. He is far too much the judge. It is as if he would be the judge which condemns the established order, and yet at the same time the Expected One. If it is not the former he wishes to be, to what purpose then his absolute isolation from the established order, his aloofness from everything that has to do with it! If he does not wish to be the judge, then to what

purpose his fantastic flight outside reality and into the society of ignorant peasantry, to what purpose his proud contempt for all the intelligence and efficiency of the established order, and his resolution to begin
entirely afresh and anew by the help of . . . fishermen and artisans!
His whole mode of existence is aptly typified by the fact that he is an
illegitimate child. If he wishes to be merely the Expected One, to what
purpose his warning about putting a new piece of cloth upon an old
garment? This is the watchword of every revolution, for it implies not
merely the will to ignore the established order, but the will to do away
with it—instead of joining forces with the establishment and as a
reformer bettering it, or as the Expected One raising it to its highest
potency. There is an ambiguity, and it is not feasible to be at once the
judge and the Expected One. And this ambiguity must result in his
downfall, which I have already calculated in advance. The catastrophe
of the judge is rightly imagined by the dramatists as a violent death;
but the thing looked forward to with hopeful expectation cannot possibly be downfall, and so he is *eo ipso* not the Expected One, that is to
say, not him whom the established order expects in order to deify him.
The people do not yet perceive this ambiguity; they regard him as the
Expected One, which the established order cannot possibly do, and the
people can, the formless and fickle crowd, because they are at the
farthest remove from being anything that can be called established. But
as soon as the ambiguity is made manifest, it will be his downfall. Why,
his precursor was a far more definitely defined figure. He was one
thing only: the judge. But how confusing and bewildering to want to
be both things at once, and what an extremity of confusion it is to
recognize his precursor as the one who was to act as judge, which precisely means, of course, to make the established order receptive for the
Expected One and to put it entirely in condition to receive him, and
then to want to be himself the Expected One who follows close after
the judge—and yet still not be willing to join hands with the established order!"

And the philosopher might say—"Such dreadful, or rather, insane
vanity. For an individual man to want to be God is something hitherto
unheard of. Never before has there been seen such an example of pure
subjectivity and sheer negation carried to the utmost excess. He has no
doctrine, no system, no fundamental knowledge; it is merely by detached aphoristic utterances, some bits of sententious wisdom, constantly
repeated with variations, that he succeeds in dazzling the masses, for

whom also he performs signs and wonders, so that they, instead of learning something and receiving instruction, come to believe in him, who continues in the most odious manner possible to force his subjectivity upon people. There is absolutely nothing *objective* or *positive*[2] in him or in what he says. So far as this goes, one might say that he does not need to be brought to destruction, for philosophically considered he is already destroyed, perishableness being the very essence of subjectivity.[3] One may concede that his is a remarkable subjectivity, and that regarded as a teacher (be it as it may with his other signs and wonders) he continually repeats the miracle of the five small loaves: by the aid of a little lyric and a few aphorisms he sets the whole land in commotion. But even if one would overlook the madness revealed in the fact that *he* thinks himself to be God, it is an incomprehensible mistake, disclosing surely a lack of philosophic culture, to suppose that God could anyhow reveal Himself in the form of a single individual. The race, the universal, the totality, is God; but surely the race is not any single individual. In general it is characteristic of subjectivity that the individual desires to be something of importance. But this you can understand. Insanity is evinced by the fact that the individual desires to be God. If this insane thing were possible, that an individual was God, then logically one must worship this individual. A greater philosophical bestiality cannot be conceived."

The statesman might say—"That at the moment this man is a power cannot be denied—leaving out of account, of course, the conceit he has that he is God. One can afford to ignore once for all a private hobby like that, which need not be reckoned with practically and concerns nobody else, least of all the statesman. A statesman is interested only in what power a man possesses, and, as has already been said, at this moment he is a power to be reckoned with. But what he wants, what he is heading for, it is not easy to make out. If this is shrewdness, it must be of an entirely new and peculiar order, not unlike what commonly is called madness. He has conspicuously strong points, but he seems to annul them instead of making use of them. He expends his forces, but gets nothing in return for *himself*. I regard him as a phenomenon with which—as with every phenomenon—one does best not to ally oneself, since it is always impossible to calculate on him or on the catastrophe which confronts him. It is possible that he may become king—that is at least possible. But it is not impossible, or rather it is

[2] Two of the watchwords of Hegelianism.
[3] Cf. Hegel's *Logic*, Part III (1st ed. of *Works,* v, p. 32 f.) (L)

equally possible, that he may end on the scaffold. What is lacking in his whole effort is seriousness.[4] With a vast spread of wing he hovers, merely hovers; he makes no end fast,[5] makes no businesslike reckoning —he hovers. Would he fight for national interests, or is it a communistic revolution he aims after, is it a republic he wants or a kingdom, which party will he join or which oppose, will he try to stand well with all parties, or will he struggle against them all? Get into touch with him? No, that is the very last thing I should want to do. I do even more than avoid him; I keep perfectly still, make as if I did not exist; for it is impossible to reckon how he might intervene to confound one, if one were to take in hand the least thing, or how things might get tangled up in his hands. The man is dangerous, in a certain sense he is tremendously dangerous; but I calculate to catch him, just by doing nothing. For he must be overthrown—and the surest way is to let him do it himself, by stumbling over himself. At this moment at least I have not the power to overthrow him, and I know of no one who has. To undertake the least thing against him now would be merely to get oneself crushed. No, a steady negative resistance is the thing. To do nothing! then presumably he will involve himself in the enormous consequences he drags after him, he will finally trip on his own train —and fall."

Or the solid citizen might express an opinion which in his own family would be received as a verdict.—"No, let us be men.[6] Everything is good in moderation; too little and too much spoils all. And according to a French proverb, which I heard from a traveling salesman, every energy exerted to excess collapses—and as for this man, his downfall is obviously a sure thing. So I have seriously taken my son to task, warning and admonishing him that he should not drift into evil ways and join himself to that person. And why should he? Because all are running after him. Yes, but who are these 'all'? Idle and unstable people, street loungers and vagabonds, who find it easy to run. But not very many who have their own houses and are well-to-do, and none of the wise and respected people after whom I always set my clock, not

[4] S.K. found it both irksome and ridiculous that this complaint was commonly made against him. (L)

[5] The necessity of knotting the end of the thread in sewing was a favorite analogy of S.K.'s. He looked forward to his own martyrdom as a way of "fastening the end." (L)

[6] Strangely enough, S.K. ascribes to the sententious *bourgeois* an exclamation which he himself in his youth seems to have used only too often—to judge by the parody of him which Hans Christian Andersen cruelly perpetrated in *The Lucky Galoshes,* where S.K. is the parrot which, with its rasping voice, has nothing to say but, "Let us be men." (L)

a one of them, neither Councillor Brown, nor Congressman Jones, nor the wealthy broker Robinson—nay, nay, these people know what's what. And if we look at the clergy, who surely must understand such matters best—they thank him kindly. This is what Pastor Green said yesterday evening at the club: 'That life will have a terrible ending.' And he is a chap who doesn't only know how to preach. One should not hear him on Sundays in church, but on Mondays at the club—I only wish I had half his knowledge of the world. He said quite rightly and as from his very heart, 'it is only idle and unstable people that run after him.' And why do they run after him? Because he is able to perform some miracles. But who knows whether they really are miracles, or whether he can confer the same power upon his disciples? In any case a miracle is a very uncertain thing, whereas certainty is certainty. Every serious father who has grown-up children must be truly concerned lest his sons be seduced and carried away to throw in their lot with him and with the desperate men who follow him, desperate men who have nothing to lose. And even these men—how does he help them? One must be mad to want to be helped in that fashion. It is true, even with regard to the poorest beggars, that he helps them out of the frying-pan into the fire, helps them into a new misery which the beggar could have avoided by remaining what he was, a mere beggar."

And the mocker—not one who is despised by all for his malice, but one who is admired by all for his wit and liked for his good nature—the mocker might say—"After all, that is a priceless idea, which must eventually inure to the advantage of all of us—that an individual man, just like the rest of us, says that he is God. If that is not to confer a benefit upon men, I do not know what benevolence and beneficence or beneficence and benevolence can mean. Granted that the criterion of being God is (I declare, who in all the world could hit upon such an idea! How true it is that such a thing never entered into the heart of man!)[7] that it is just to look like all the rest of us, neither more nor less —hence we are all gods. *Quod erat demonstrandum.* Three cheers for him, the discoverer of this invention so extraordinarily helpful to men! Tomorrow I shall proclaim that I, the undersigned, am God—and the discoverer at least cannot deny it without contradicting himself. All cats are gray in the dark—and if to be God is to look like all the rest, then it is dark, and we are all—or what was I about to say? we are all and every one of us God, and no one will have ground to be invidious

_____

[7] An ironical quotation from *Philosophical Fragments, supra,* pp. 170–172.

of another. This is the most ludicrous thing imaginable; contradiction, which always is at the bottom of the comic, is here evident in the highest degree—but the credit for it is not mine, it belongs only and solely and exclusively to the discoverer of the fact that a man just like the rest of us, only not by any means so well dressed as the average, hence a shabbily dressed person who most nearly (at least more nearly than under the rubric God) comes under the attention of the Supervisor of the poor—that he is God. It is a pity, however, for the poor Supervisor of the poor, who with this general advancement of the human race will be out of a job."

Oh, my friend, I know well what I am doing, and my soul is eternally assured of the rightness of what I do. Imagine thyself, therefore, contemporary with Him, the Inviter. Imagine that thou wast a sufferer—but reflect to what thou dost expose thyself by becoming His disciple, by following Him. Thou dost expose thyself to the loss of almost everything accounted precious in the eyes of people who are prudent, sensible, and held in esteem. He, the Inviter, requires of thee that thou give up everything, let all go—but the common sense which is contemporary with thee in thy generation will not easily let thee go, its verdict is that to join Him is madness. And cruel mockery will taunt thee. Whereas it almost spares Him out of pity, it accounts it a madder thing than the maddest to become His disciple. "For," says common sense, "a fanatic is a fanatic. Bad enough. But seriously to—become his disciple is the greatest possible madness. There is only one possible way of being madder than a madman: it is the higher madness of attaching oneself in all seriousness to a madman, regarding him as a wise man."

Oh, say not that this whole treatment is an exaggeration. Thou knowest indeed (yet perhaps thou art not yet thoroughly sensible of it) that among all the men who were respected, enlightened, and wise, though some may have conversed with Him out of curiosity, yet there was only one, one single man, who seriously sought Him out, and he came to Him—by night. And thou knowest well that by night one treads forbidden paths, night is chosen as the time to go to a place one would not be seen frequenting. Think what a disparaging opinion of the Inviter this implies—to visit Him was a disgrace, something no respectable person, no man of honor, could openly do—no more than to go to . . . yet, no, I would not go on with what follows this "no more than!"

Come *now* hither *to me,* all ye that labor and are heavy laden, I will give you rest!

CHRISTIANITY AS THE ABSOLUTE:
CONTEMPORANEOUSNESS WITH CHRIST

With this invitation to all them "that labor and are heavy laden" Christianity did not come into the world (as the parsons snivelingly and falsely introduce it) as an admirable example of the gentle art of consolation—but as *the absolute.* It is out of love God wills it so, but also it is *God* who wills it, and He wills what He will. He will not suffer Himself to be transformed by men and be a nice . . . human God: He will transform men, and that He wills out of love. He will have nothing to do with man's pert inquiry about why and why did Christianity come into the world: it is and shall be the absolute. Therefore everything men have hit upon relatively to explain the why and the wherefore is falsehood. Perhaps they have hit upon an explanation out of a humane compassion of a sort, which thinks that one might chaffer about the price—for God presumably does not understand men, His requirements are exorbitant, and so the parsons must be on hand to chaffer. Perhaps they hit upon an explanation in order to stand well with men and get some advantage out of preaching Christianity; for when it is toned down to the merely human, to what has "entered into the heart of man," then naturally people will think well of it, and quite naturally also of the amiable orator who can make Christianity so gentle a thing—if the Apostles had been able to do that, people would also have thought well of the Apostles. But all this is falsehood, it is misrepresentation of Christianity, which is the absolute. But what, then, is the use of Christianity? It is, then, merely a plague to us! Ah, yes, that too can be said: relatively understood, the absolute is the greatest plague. In all moments of laxness, sluggishness, dullness, when the sensuous nature of man predominates, Christianity seems madness, since it is incommensurable with any finite wherefore. What is the use of it, then? The answer is: Hold thy peace! It is the absolute! And so it *must* be represented, viz. in such a way as to make it appear madness in the eyes of the sensuous man. And hence it is true, so true . . . when the wise and prudent man in the situation of contemporaneousness condemns Christ by saying, "He is literally nothing"—most certainly true, for He is the absolute. Christianity came into the world as the absolute—not for consolation, humanly understood; on the contrary, it speaks again and again of the sufferings which a Christian must endure, or which a man must endure to become and to be a Christian, sufferings he can well avoid merely by refraining from becoming a Christian.

There is an endless yawning difference between God and man, and hence, in the situation of contemporaneousness, to become a Christian (to be transformed into likeness with God) proved to be an even greater torment and misery and pain than the greatest human torment, and hence also a crime in the eyes of one's neighbors. And so it will always prove when becoming a Christian in truth comes to mean to become contemporary with Christ. And if becoming a Christian does not come to mean this, then all the talk about becoming a Christian is nonsense and self-deception and conceit, in part even blasphemy and sin against the Second Commandment of the Law and sin against the Holy Ghost.

For in relation to the absolute there is only one tense: the present. For him who is not contemporary with the absolute—for him it has no existence. And as Christ is the absolute, it is easy to see that with respect to Him there is only one situation: that of contemporaneousness. The five, the seven, the fifteen, the eighteen hundred years are neither here nor there; they do not change Him, neither do they in any wise reveal who He was, for who He is is revealed only to faith.

Christ is (if I may express it so seriously) not a comedian, not at all a merely historical person, since as the Paradox He is an extremely unhistorical person. But this is the difference between poetry and reality: contemporaneousness. The difference between poetry and history is clearly this, that history is what really occurred, whereas poetry is the possible, the imaginary, the poetized. But what really occurred (the past) is not (except in a special sense, i.e. in contrast with poetry) the real. It lacks the determinant which is the determinant of truth (as inwardness)[1] and of all religiousness, the FOR THEE. The past is not reality—for me: only the contemporary is reality for me. What thou dost live contemporaneous with is reality—for thee. And thus every man can be contemporary only with the age in which he lives—and then with one thing more: with Christ's life on earth; for Christ's life on earth, sacred history, stands for itself alone outside history.

History you can read and hear about as referring to the past. Here, if you like, you can form your judgments according to the upshot. But Christ's life on earth is not a past event; in its time 1,800 years ago it

---

[1] S.K. here alludes to the conception of truth as subjective which he maintained in the *Postscript,* especially in Part II, 2nd section, chap. 2. (L)

did not wait, nor does it wait now, for any assistance from the upshot. An historical Christianity is galimatias and unchristian confusion; for what true Christians there are in each generation are contemporary with Christ, having nothing to do with Christians of former generations, but everything to do with the contemporary Christ. His earthly life accompanies the race and accompanies every generation in particular, as the eternal history; His earthly life possesses the eternal contemporaneousness. And all the professional lecturing on Christianity (which lecturing has its stalking-blind and stronghold in the notion that Christianity is something past, and in the history of the 1,800 years) transforms it into the most unchristian of heresies, a fact which everyone will perceive (and therefore give up lecturing) if only he will try to imagine the generation contemporary with Christ . . . delivering lectures—but indeed every generation (of believers) is contemporary.

If thou canst not prevail upon thyself to become a Christian in the situation of contemporaneousness with Him, or if He in the situation of contemporaneousness cannot move thee and draw thee to Himself—then thou wilt never become a Christian. Thou mayest honor, praise, thank, and reward with all worldly goods him who maketh thee believe thou nevertheless art a Christian—but he deceiveth thee. Thou mightest count thyself fortunate if thou wert not contemporary with anyone who dared to say this; thou canst become exasperated to frenzy at the torture, like the sting of the "gadfly," [2] of being contemporary with one who says it. In the first case thou art deceived; in the second, thou hast at least heard the truth.

If thou canst not endure contemporaneousness, canst not endure this sight in reality, if thou couldst not go out in the street and perceive that it is God in this horrible procession, and that this is thy case wert thou to fall down and worship Him—then thou art not *essentially* a Christian. What thou hast to do then is unconditionally to admit this to thyself, so that above all thou mayest preserve humility and fear and trembling with relation to what it means in truth to be a Christian. For that is the way thou must take to learn and to get training in fleeing to grace in such a wise that thou dost not take it in vain. Do not, for God's sake, repair to anyone to be "set at ease." For sure enough it was said, "Blessed are the eyes which see the things that ye see," [3] which saying the parsons make much ado about . . . just as if this was not said solely

---

[2] Alluding to the passage in Plato's *Apology* where Socrates says of himself that, like the gadfly on the horse, he is allotted to the Athenians to keep them alert. (L)

[3] Luke 10: 23.

and only about the contemporaries who had become believers. If the glory had been directly visible, so that everybody as a matter of course could see it, then it is false that Christ humbled Himself and took upon Him the form of a servant; it is superfluous to give warning against being offended, for how in the world could anybody be offended by glory attired in glory! And how in the world can it be explained that with Christ it fared as it did, that not everybody rushed up to see what was directly to be seen! No, there was 'nothing about Him for the eye, no glamour that we should look upon Him, no outward appearance that we should desire Him';[4] directly there was nothing to be seen but a lowly man, who, by signs and wonders and by affirming that He was God, continually posited the possibility of offense. A lowly man who thus expressed (1) what God understands by compassion (and the very fact of being the lowly and poor man when a man will be the compassionate one is included in this); and (2) what God understands by man's misery, which in both cases is utterly different from what man's understanding is, and which in every generation until the end of time everyone for his own part must learn from the beginning, beginning always at the same point as every other man who is contemporary with Christ, practising it in the situation of contemporaneousness. Human hot-headedness and unruliness naturally are of no help at all. In how far a man may succeed essentially in becoming a Christian, no one can tell him. But dread and fear and despair are of no avail. Candor before God is the first and last. Candidly to admit to oneself where one is, with candor before God holding the task in view—however slowly it goes, though one only creeps forward—yet one thing a man has, he is in the right position (facing forward), not misled and deceived by the trick of poetizing Christ, so that instead of being God He becomes that languishing compassion which men themselves have invented, so that Christianity instead of drawing men to heavenly places is impeded on its way and becomes the merely human.

THE MORAL

AND what does all this mean? It means that everyone for himself, in quiet inwardness before God, shall humble himself before what it means in the strictest sense to be a Christian, admit candidly before God how it stands with him, so that he might yet accept the grace

[4] Isa. 53: 2 (S.K.'s version).

which is offered to everyone who is imperfect, that is, to everyone. And then no further; then for the rest let him attend to his work, be glad in it, love his wife, be glad in her, bring up his children with joyfulness, love his fellow men, rejoice in life. If anything further is required of him, God will surely let him understand, and in such case will also help him further; for the terrible language of the Law is so terrifying because it seems as if it were left to man to hold fast to Christ by his own power, whereas in the language of love it is Christ that holds him fast. So if anything further is required of him, God will surely let him understand; but this is required of everyone, that before God he shall candidly humble himself in view of the requirements of ideality. And therefore these should be heard again and again in their infinite significance. To be a Christian has become a thing of naught, mere tomfoolery, something which everyone is as a matter of course, something one slips into more easily than into the most insignificant trick of dexterity.

"But if the Christian life is something so terrible and frightful, how in the world can a person get the idea of accepting it?" Quite simply, and, if you want that too, quite in a Lutheran way: only the consciousness of sin can force one into this dreadful situation—the power on the other side being grace. And in that very instant the Christian life transforms itself and is sheer gentleness, grace, loving-kindness, and compassion. Looked at from any other point of view Christianity is and must be a sort of madness or the greatest horror. Only through the consciousness of sin is there entrance to it, and the wish to enter in by any other way is the crime of *lèse-majesté* against Christianity.

But sin, the fact that thou and I are sinners (as individuals) people have abolished, or they have illicitly abated it, both with respect to life (the domestic, the civic, the ecclesiastical life) and to learning, which has invented the *doctrine* of sin in general. As a compensation they have wanted to help men into Christianity and keep them in it by means of all that about world-history, all that about the gentleness of this teaching, its exalted and profound character, &c., all of which Luther would have called bosh, and which is blasphemy, since it is impudence to wish to fraternize with God and Christ.

Only the consciousness of sin is the expression of absolute respect, and just for this reason, i.e. because Christianity requires absolute respect, it must and will display itself as madness or horror, in order that the qualitative infinite emphasis may fall upon the fact that only consciousness of sin is the way of entrance, is the vision which, by being absolute respect, can see the gentleness, loving-kindness, and compassion of Christianity.

The simple man who humbly confesses himself to be a sinner—himself personally (the individual)—does not at all need to become aware of all the difficulties which emerge when one is neither simple nor humble. But when this is lacking, this humble consciousness of being personally a sinner (the individual)—yea, if such a one possessed all human wisdom and shrewdness along with all human talents, it would profit him little. Christianity shall in a degree corresponding to his superiority erect itself against him and transform itself into madness and terror, until he learns either to give up Christianity, or else by the help of what is very far remote from scientific propaedeutic, apologetic, &c., that is, by the help of the torments of a contrite heart (just in proportion to *his* need of it) learns to enter by the narrow way, through the consciousness of sin, into Christianity.

FROM ON HIGH
HE WILL DRAW ALL UNTO HIMSELF

CHRISTIAN EXPOSITIONS BY ANTI-CLIMACUS

I[1]

O LORD JESUS CHRIST, there is so much to drag us back: empty pursuits, trivial pleasures, unworthy cares. There is so much to frighten us away: a pride too cowardly to submit to being helped, cowardly apprehensiveness which evades danger to its own destruction, anguish for sin which shuns holy cleansing as disease shuns medicine. But Thou art stronger

[1] "This discourse was delivered by Magister Kierkegaard in the Church of Our Lady on Friday, Sept. 1st, 1848. Since it is this which furnished me with the title [to Part III], I have printed it here with his consent." . . . The above note is by Anti-Climacus; but I would call attention to the fact that it was four and a half months earlier, on April 18th, that this title was suggested to S.K. in the same church where this discourse was delivered, and that he then proposed to write "seven discourses," which are evidently the "seven reflections" comprised in Part III. In this case, therefore, as in the case of *Either/Or,* the last part of the book was written before the first, and the reader will perceive that the themes so "mildly" presented here were later more definitely thought out and more strongly presented—with the emphasis of constant repetition which was justified as well as occasioned by men's dullness of hearing.—It needs to be observed that in Denmark the people were accustomed to communicate on Fridays, and that all of S.K.'s "discourses on Fridays," if not actually delivered before the Holy Communion, were written in view of such an occasion—"at the foot of the altar." (L)

than these, so draw Thou us now more strongly to Thee. We call Thee our Saviour and Redeemer, since Thou didst come to earth to redeem us from the servitude under which we were bound or had bound ourselves, and to save the lost. This is Thy work, which Thou didst complete, and which Thou wilt continue to complete unto the end of the world; for since Thou Thyself hast said it, therefore Thou wilt do it—lifted up from the earth Thou wilt draw all unto Thee.

John 12: 32. AND I, IF I BE LIFTED UP FROM THE EARTH, WILL, DRAW ALL UNTO MYSELF

From on high He will draw all unto Himself.

Devout hearer, if a man's life is not to be led unworthily, like that of the beast which never erects its head, if it is not to be frittered away, being emptily employed with what while it lasts is vanity and when it is past is nothingness, or busily employed with what makes a noise indeed at the moment but has no echo in eternity—if a man's life is not to be dozed away in inactivity or wasted in bustling movement, there must be something higher which draws it. Now this "something higher" may be something very various; but if it is to be truly capable of drawing, and at every instant, it must not itself be subject to "variableness or the shadow of turning," but must have passed triumphantly through every change and become transfigured like the transfigured life of a dead man.[2] And now, as there is only one name that is named among the living, the Lord Jesus Christ, so also there is only one dead man who yet lives, the Lord Jesus Christ. He from *on high* will draw all unto Himself. See, therefore, how rightly oriented is the Christian life, directed toward that which is above, toward Him who from on high will draw Christians unto Himself—in case the Christians remember Him, and he who does not is surely no Christian. And thou, my hearer, thou to whom this discourse is addressed, thou art come here today in *remembrance* of Him.

It follows as a matter of course that if He is to be able from on high to draw Christians unto Himself, there is much that has to be forgotten, much that has to be looked away from, much that has to be died from. How can this be done? Oh, in case thou, in deep distress, perhaps in distress for thy future, thy life's happiness, hast ever heartily wished to forget something: a disappointed expectation, a shattered

[2] Doubtless S.K. was thinking of his father's life as it was transfigured for him.

hope, a bitter and embittering memory; or in case thou, in anxiety, alas, for thy soul's salvation, hast wished still more heartily to forget something: anguish at some sin which constantly confronts thee, a terrifying thought which will not leave thee—then thou hast surely experienced how empty is the advice the world gives when it says, "Try to forget it!" That indeed is only a hollow mockery, if it is anything at all. No, if there is something thou art fain to forget, try to get something else to remember, and then it will succeed. Therefore if Christianity requires Christians to forget something, and in a certain sense to forget everything, to forget the multifarious, it also recommends the means: to remember something else, to remember one thing, the Lord Jesus Christ. Therefore in case thou art aware that the world's pleasures enthrall thee and thou art fain to forget, in case thou art aware that earthly anxieties distress thee so that thou art fain to forget, in case thou art aware that the bustle of life carries thee away as the current carries the swimmer, and thou art fain to forget, in case the dread of temptation overpowers thee and thou art heartily fain to forget—then remember Him, the Lord Jesus Christ, and it will succeed. If indeed it might be possible for thee—as now today thou eatest bread and drinkest wine in remembrance of Him—if it might be possible for thee to have Him in remembrance every day as thy constant thought in everything thou undertakest to do—with this thou wouldst also have forgotten everything that ought to be forgotten, thou wouldst be as forgetful as a feeble old man with regard to everything that ought to be forgotten, as oblivious to it all as one who in a foreign land has forgotten his mother tongue and babbles without meaning, as oblivious as the absent-minded—thou wouldst be completely drawn to the heights with Him who from on high will draw all unto Himself.

From on high He will draw all unto Himself.
From on high—for here upon earth He went about in lowliness, in the lowly form of a servant, in poverty and wretchedness, in suffering. This indeed was Christianity, not that a rich man makes the poor rich, but that the poorest of all makes all men rich, both the rich and the poor. And this indeed was Christianity, not that it is the happy man who comforts the afflicted, but that it is He who of all men is the most afflicted.—He will draw all to Himself—*draw* them to Himself, for He would *entice* no one. To draw to Himself truly, means in *one* sense to repel men. In thy nature and in mine and in that of every man there

is something He would do away with; with respect to all this He repels men. Lowliness and humiliation are the stone of stumbling, the possibility of offense, and thou art situated between His humiliation which lies behind, and the exaltation—this is the reason why it is said that He draws to Himself. To entice is an untrue way of drawing to Himself; but He would entice no one; humiliation belongs to Him just as essentially as exaltation. In case there was one who could love Him only in His exaltation—such a man's vision is confused, he knows not Christ, neither loves Him at all, but takes Him in vain. Christ was the truth [in His humiliation] and is the truth. If then one can love Him only in His exaltation, what does that signify? It signifies that he can love the truth . . . only when it has conquered, when it is in possession of and surrounded by power and honor and glory. But while it was in conflict it was foolishness, to the Jews a stumbling-block, to the Greeks a foolish thing. So long as it was scorned, ridiculed, and (as the Scripture says) spat upon, he desired to hold himself aloof from it. Thus he desired to keep the truth from him, but this in fact means precisely to be in untruth. It is as essential for "the truth" to suffer in this world as to triumph in another world, the world of truth—and Christ Jesus is the same in His humiliation as in His exaltation. But, on the other hand, in case one could feel himself drawn to Christ and able to love Him only in His humiliation, in case such a man would refuse to hear anything about this exaltation when power and honor and glory are His—in case (oh, pitiable perversity!), with the impatience of an unstable mind, tired (as he would express it) of Christendom's triumphant boast of "seeing good days," he longs only for the spectacle of horror, to be with Him when He was scorned and persecuted—such a man's vision also is confused, he knows not Christ, neither loves Him at all. For melancholy is no closer to Christianity than light mindedness,[3] both are equally worldly, equally remote from Christianity, both equally in need of conversion.

My hearer, thou to whom my discourse is addressed, thou who today art come in His remembrance, our Lord Jesus Christ's, art come hither as drawn by Him who from on high will draw all unto Himself. But it is precisely on this day thou art reminded of His humiliation, His suffering and death, so that it is He that draws thee to Him. Though He is raised up on high, He has not forgotten thee—and thou

---

[3] *Tungsind/Letsind*—literally, heavy-minded/light-minded. Here S.K. evidently condemns his own melancholy, which in its darkest periods disposed him to a gloomy and "perverse" view of Christianity. (L)

art not forgetful of His humiliation, dost love Him in His humiliation, but at the same time dost love His glorious revelation.

From on high He will draw all unto Himself.

It is now eighteen centuries since He left the earth and ascended up on high. Since that time the form of the world has undergone more than one change, thrones have been erected and overthrown, great names have cropped up and been forgotten; and on a smallar scale, in thy daily life, changes regularly occur, the sun rises and sets, the wind shifts in its courses, now something new is sought out and soon is forgotten again, and again something new—and from Him, in a certain sense, we hear nothing. And yet He has said that from on high He will draw all unto Himself. So also on high He is not resting, but He works hitherto, employed and concerned with drawing all unto Himself. Amazing! Thus thou beholdest in nature all about thee the many forces stirring; but the power which supports all thou dost not behold, thou seest not God's almightiness—and yet it is fully certain that He also works, that a single instant without Him, and the world is nothing. So likewise He is invisible on high, yet everywhere present, employed in drawing all unto Himself—while in this world, alas, there is worldly talk about everything else but Him, as though He did not exist. He employs the most various things as the way and the means of drawing unto Himself—but this we cannot dwell upon here, least of all today, when a period unusually short is prescribed for the address, because the sacred action predominates and the Communion is our divine service. But though the means He employs are so many, all ways come together at one point, the consciousness of sin—through this passes "the way" by which He draws a man, the repentant sinner, to Himself.

My hearer, thou to whom my discourse is addressed, thou who to-day art come hither in remembrance of Him to partake of a holy feast, the Lord's Supper—today thou didst go first to confession before coming to the altar. From on high He hath drawn thee to Himself, but it was through the consciousness of sin. For He will not entice all to Himself, He will draw all to Himself.

From on high He will draw all unto Himself.

My hearer, thou to whom my discourse is addressed! Today He is indeed with thee, as though He were come nearer, as though He were touching the earth. He is present at the altar where thou seekest Him; He is present—but only in order to draw thee from on high unto Himself. For because thou dost feel thyself drawn to Him, and therefore art come hither today, it does not necessarily follow that thou mayest venture to conceive that He has already drawn thee entirely to Himself. "Lord, increase my faith." He who made that prayer was not an unbeliever but a believer; and so it is also with this prayer, "Lord, draw me entirely to Thee"; for he who rightly makes this prayer must already feel himself drawn. Ah, and is it not true that precisely today, and precisely because thou dost feel thyself drawn, thou wilt today be ready to admit how much is still lacking, how far thou art from being drawn entirely to Him—drawn up on high, far from all the base and the earthly which hold thee back? Ah, it is not I, my hearer, nor any other man, that says this to thee, or might presume to say it. No, every man has enough to do with saying this to himself. I do not know, my hearer, who thou art, how far He has perhaps already drawn thee to Himself, how far perhaps thou art advanced beyond me and many another in the way of being a Christian—but God grant that this day, whoever thou art, and whereuntosoever thou hast attained, thou who art come hither today to partake of the holy feast of the Lord's Supper —that this day may be to thee truly blessed; God grant that at this sacred moment thou mayest thyself be entirely drawn to Him and be sensible of His presence. He is there—He from whom in a sense thou dost separate when thou departest from the altar, but who nevertheless will not forget thee if thou dost not forget Him; yea, will not forget thee even when, alas, thou dost sometimes forget Him, who from on high continues to draw thee unto Himself, until the last blessed end when thou shalt be by Him and with Him on high.

TWO DISCOURSES
AT THE COMMUNION ON FRIDAYS
BY S. KIERKEGAARD (1851)
TRANSLATED BY WALTER LOWRIE

When the thought of God does not remind him of his sin but that it is forgiven, and the past is no longer the memory of how much he did wrong, but of how much he was forgiven—then man rests in the forgiveness of sins.—THE JOURNALS

LITTLE need be said about this brief discourse save that it forms a complement to the treatment of the same text in *The Works of Love* (see pp. 306–323), as S.K. himself points out. The subject here is "the divine initiative," whereas there it was the human response; but in dealing with each side Kierkegaard always has in mind the other and the relation between the two—thus bridging the gulf between orthodoxy and "modernism."

As Lowrie says, "one must feel a grateful sense of relief in passing from the more trenchant and closely reasoned works to the Discourses, which were really as well as ostensibly addressed to simple Christians." The two discourses of which this is the second were written to accompany *For Self-Examination* (as they do in the English edition). They are dedicated "to one unnamed, whose name shall some day be named" (i.e. Regina) "along with the whole of the authorship from the very beginning." Some lines from the Preface are equally significant:

"A gradually progressing work as a writer which had its beginning in *Either/Or* seeks here its definite point of rest at the foot of the altar, where the author, who personally knows best his imperfection and guilt, does not by any means call himself a witness for the truth, but only a peculiar sort of poet and thinker who, 'without authority,' has nothing new to bring, but would read the fundamental document of the individual, humane existence-relationship, the old, well-known, from the fathers handed down—would read it through yet once again, if possible in a more heartfelt way. . . .

"Turning now to the other side, and expressing thanks for such sympathy and good will as have been shown me, I could wish that I might present these works (as I now take the liberty of doing) and commend them to the nation whose language I am proud to have the honor of writing, feeling for it a filial devotion and an almost womanly tenderness, yet comforting myself also with the thought that it will not be disgraced by the fact that I have used it."

PRAYER

O Lord Jesus Christ, the birds have their nests, the foxes their holes, and Thou didst not have whereon to lay Thy head, homeless wast Thou upon earth—and yet a hiding-place, the only one, where a sinner could flee. And so today Thou art still the hiding-place; where the sinner flees to Thee, hides himself in Thee, is hidden in Thee—then he is eternally defended, then "love" hides the multitude of sins.

I PETER 4: 8.

LOVE SHALL HIDE THE MULTITUDE
OF SINS

This is true when it is a question of human love—and in a double sense, as we have shown in another place.[1] The loving man, he in whom

[1] *The Works of Love*, Part II, v; *supra*, pp. 306–308.

there is love, hides the multitude of sins, sees not his neighbor's fault, or, if he sees, hides it from himself and from others; love makes him blind in a sense far more beautiful than this can be said of a lover, blind to his neighbor's sins. On the other hand, the loving man, he in whom there is love, though he has his faults, his inperfections, yea, though they were a multitude of sins, yet love, the fact that there is love in him, hides the multitude of sins.

When it is a question of Christ's love, the word can be taken only in one sense; the fact that He was love did not serve to hide what imperfection there was in Him—in Him the holy One in whom there was no sin, neither was guile found in His mouth, this being inevitably so, because in Him there was only love, love in His heart and love only, in His every word, in all His work, in His whole life, in His death, until the very last. Ah, in a man love is not so perfect, and therefore, or rather nevertheless, he profits by his love: while he lovingly hides a multitude of sins, love does unto him as he unto others, it hides his sins. Thus he himself has need of the love which he shows to others, thus he profits by the love within him, which though it be directed outwardly to hide the multitude of sins, does not, however, like Christ's sacrificial love, embrace the whole world but only very few persons. Ah, though it is seldom enough a man is loving, yet "what wonder," as a man might be tempted to say, "what wonder a man endeavors to be loving, seeing that he himself is in need of love, and to that extent is really looking after his own interest by being loving." But Christ was not in need of love. Suppose that He had not been love, suppose that unlovingly He would only be what He was, the holy One, suppose that instead of saving the world and hiding the multitude of sins He had come into the world to judge the world in holy wrath—imagine this in order to conceive the more vividly that precisely to Him it applies in a singular sense that His love covered the multitude of sins, that *this* is "love," that (as the Scripture says) only one is good, namely, God, and that thus He was the only one who in love hid the multitude of sins, not of some individuals but of the whole world.

Let us then in the brief moment prescribed speak about this word: *Love* (Christ's love) *hides the multitude of sins.*

And is it not true that thou hast felt the need, and today especially, of a love which is able to hide sins, to hide thy sins? For this reason it is thou art come today to the Lord's altar. For though it is only too true, as Luther says, that every man has a preacher with him, who eats with him, drinks with him, wakes with him, sleeps with him, is always with him wheresoever he may be, whatsoever he has in hand, a preacher called flesh and blood, lusts and passions, custom and inclination—yet it also is certain that every man has a confidant who is privy to his inmost thoughts, namely conscience. A man may succeed in hiding his sins from the world, he may perhaps rejoice foolishly in his success, or perhaps with a little more truthfulness he may acknowledge to himself that this is a pitful weakness and cowardice, that he does not possess the courage to reveal himself—but a man cannot hide his sins from himself. That is impossible; for the sin which was hid absolutely even from the man himself would indeed not be sin, any more than if it were hid from God, a thing which cannot be, inasmuch as a man so soon as he is conscious of himself, and in everything in which he is conscious of himself, is also conscious of God, and God of him. And for this reason conscience is so mighty and so precise in its reckoning, so ever-present and so incorruptible, because this privy confidant which follows man everywhere is in league with God, this preacher which is with man when he wakes and when he sleeps (ah, if only it does not make him sleepless with its sermon!), with him everywhere, in the noisy bustle of the world (ah, if only it does not with its voice transform the world's noise into stillness!), in loneliness (ah, if only it does not hinder him from feeling alone in the most solitary place!), in his daily work (ah, if only it does not estrange him from it and distract him!), in festal surroundings (ah, if only it does not make this seem to him a dismal prison!), in holy places (ah, if only it does not hold him back from going there!), this privy preacher which follows man, knowing privily what now, now at this instant, he does or leaves undone, and what long, long ago—I do not say was forgotten, for this privy confidant, having a frightful memory, takes care of that—but long, long ago was past. Man cannot escape from this confidant, any more than (according to the saying of the pagan poet [2]) he can ride away from the sorrow which sits behind him on horseback, or any more (if one would give a different turn to the comparison) than it "helps the deer to rush forward to escape the arrow lodged in its breast—the more violently it moves forward, only the more deeply does it run the arrow into it."

Today, however, thou art far indeed from wishing to make the vain attempt to flee from or avoid this privy preacher, thou hast given him leave to speak. For in the pulpit it is doubtless the parson who preaches, yet the true preacher is the confidant of thine inmost thoughts.

[2] Horace: *Odes,* iii. i, 40. (L)

The parson can only preach in general terms—but the preacher within thee is exactly the opposite: he preaches solely and alone about thee, to thee, in thee.

I would make no attempt to dismay men, being myself only too much dismayed; but whosoever thou art, even if thou art, humanly speaking, almost pure and blameless, when this privy preacher preaches before thee in thine inward man, thou also dost feel what others perhaps sense with more dismay—thou also dost feel a need to hide thyself, and though it had been told thee a thousand times, and a thousand times again, that it is impossible to find this hiding-place, thou yet art sensible of the need. Oh, would it were possible for me to flee to a desert isle where never any man had come or would come; oh, that there were a place of refuge whither I could flee far away from myself, that there were a hiding-place where I am so thoroughly hid that not even the consciousness of my sin could find me out, that there were a frontier line, which were it never so narrow, would yet be a separation between my sin and me, that on the farther side of the yawning abyss there were a spot never so small where I might stand while the consciousness of my sin must remain on the other side, that there were a pardon, a pardon which does not make me increasingly sensible of my sin, but truly takes my sin from me and the consciousness of it as well, would that there were oblivion! [3]

But such is actually the case, for love (Christ's love) hides the multitude of sins. Behold, all has become new! What in paganism was sought after and sought in vain, what under the dominance of the Law was and is a fruitless effort—that the Gospel made possible. At the altar the Saviour stretches out His arms, [4] precisely for that fugitive who would flee from the consciousness of his sin, flee from that which is worse than pursuit, namely, gnawing remorse; He stretches out His arms, He says, "Come hither," and the attitude of stretching out His arms is a way of saying, "Come hither," and of saying at the same time, "Love hides the multitude of sins." Oh, believe Him! Couldst thou think that He who savingly opens His bosom for thee might be capable of playing upon words, capable of using a meaningless phrase, capable of deceiving thee, and at this precise instant—that He could say, "Come hither," and the instant thou art come and He holds thee in

---

[3] It was only in the Easter experience of 1848 that S.K. attained—after so many years of penance!—the consciousness that his sins were "forgotten" by God as well as forgiven, and that it was his duty as well as his privilege to forget them. (L)

[4] Cf. note, p. 379.

His embrace it then might be as if thou wert entrapped, for here, just here there could be no forgetting, here ... with the Holy One! No, this thou couldst not believe, and if thou didst believe it, thou wouldst not come hither—but blessed is he who quite literally believes that love (Christ's love) hides the multitude of sins. For the loving man, yea, even the most loving, can only shut his eyes to thy sins—oh, but thine eye for them he cannot shut. A man can with loving speech and sympathy seek to mitigate thy guilt in thine eyes also, and so hide it as it were from thee, or at least up to a certain point almost, as it were, hide it from thee—ah, but really to hide it from thee, literally to hide it from thee, so that it is hidden like what is hidden in the depths of the sea and which no one any more shall behold, hidden as when what was red as blood becomes whiter than snow,[5] so hidden that sin is transformed to purity and thou canst dare to believe thyself justified and pure—that is something only one can do, the Lord Jesus Christ, who hides the multitude of sins. A man has no authority, he cannot command thee to believe and merely by commanding help thee to believe. But authority is required even if it be to teach, and what authority must that be (greater even than the authority which bade the troubled waves be still)—what authority is required to bid the despairing man, the man who in the tortures of repentance cannot and dare not forget, the contrite sinner who cannot and dare not cease to gaze upon his guilt, what authority is requisite to shut his eyes, and what authority to bid him open the eyes of faith so that he can see purity where he saw guilt and sin! This divine authority is possessed only by Him, Jesus Christ, whose love hides the multitude of sins.

He hides them quite literally. When a man places himself in front of another and covers him entirely with his body so that no one at all can get a sight of him who is hidden behind—so it is that Jesus Christ covers with His *holy body* thy sin. Though justice were to rage, what more can it want? For satisfaction has indeed been made. Though the repentance within thee be so contrite that it thinks it a duty to aid external justice to discover thy guilt—satisfaction indeed has been made, a satisfaction, a vicarious satisfaction which covers thy sin entirely and makes it impossible to see it, impossible for justice, and therewith impossible for the repentance within thee or for thyself to see it, for repentance loses the sense of sight when justice to which it makes appeal says, "I can see nothing."

He hides them quite literally. As when the hen concerned for her

[5] Cf. Isaiah 1: 18.

brood gathers her chickens under her wing at the instant of danger, covering them completely and ready to give her life rather than deprive them of this shelter which makes it impossible for the enemy's eye to discover them—precisely thus does He hide thy sin. Precisely thus; for He too is concerned, infinitely concerned in love, ready to give His life rather than deprive thee of thy secure shelter under His love. Ready to give His life—yet, no, it was just for this He gave His life, to assure thee of shelter under His love. Therefore not just like the hen, concerned indeed in the same way, but infinitely more concerned than the hen when she hides her chickens; but otherwise unlike, for He hides by His death. Oh, eternally secure; oh, blessedly reassuring hiding-place! There is still one danger for the chickens; although hidden, they are constantly in danger: when the mother has done her utmost, when out of love she has given her life, then are they deprived of their shelter. But He on the contrary—true enough, if with His life He had covered thy sin, there would be possibility of the danger that He might be deprived of His life, and thou of thy shelter. It is quite different when with His death He covers thy sin. He would be ready (if such a thing were needful, if all had not been done decisively once for all)—He would be ready to give His life again to procure for thee a shelter by His death, rather than that thou shouldst be deprived of the shelter. It is to be taken quite literally: He covers over thy sin just by covering it with His death. Death may dispose of a living man, but a dead man cannot possibly be thus disposed of, and so it is impossible that thou mightest be deprived of thy shelter. Infinite love! They talk about works of love, and many such works can be enumerated. But when they say "the work of love," then there is only one work, yea, only one work, and thou knowest at once (strange as it may seem) precisely about whom they are speaking, about Him, Jesus Christ, about His atoning death, about Him who hides the multitude of sins.

This is preached at the altar; for what is preached from the pulpit is essentially His life, but at the altar, His death. He died once for the sins of the whole world, and for thy sins; His death is not repeated, but *this* is repeated: that He died also for thee,[6] for thee who dost receive the pledge that He died also for thee, this is repeated at the altar where He gives *Himself* to thee for a shelter. Oh, sure hiding-place for sinners! Oh, blessed hiding-place!—especially if one has first learned what it

<hr>

[6] "Also for me" expressed S.K.'s joyful experience at his first conversion in 1838— just after he had registered in his Journal the Hegelian reflection that "Christ died for all," not for the single individual. (L)

means when conscience accuses, and the Law condemns, and justice pursues with punishment, and then, when wearied unto despair, to find repose in the one shelter that is to be found! A man, even the most loving man, can at the most give thee extenuation and excuse, leaving it to thee to make what use of them thou art able; but himself he cannot give thee. That only Jesus Christ can do; He gives thee Himself as a shelter; it is not some comforting thought He gives thee, it is not a doctrine He communicates to thee; no, He gives thee Himself. As the night spreads concealment over everything, so did He give up His life and became a covering behind which lies a sinful world which He has saved. Through this covering justice does not break as the sun's rays break through colored glass, merely softened by refraction; no, it impotently breaks against this covering, is reflected from it and does not pass through it. He gave Himself as a covering for the whole world, for thee as well, and for me.

Therefore Thou, my Lord and Saviour, Thou whose love covers and hides the multitude of sins, when I am thoroughly sensible of my sin and of the multitude of my sins, when before the justice of heaven only wrath is pronounced upon me and upon my life, when on earth there is only *one* man whom to escape I would flee were it to the end of the world, and that man myself—then I will not commence the vain attempt which leads only to despair or to madness, but at once I will flee unto Thee, and Thou wilt not deny me the shelter which Thou lovingly hast offered unto all; Thou wilt screen me from the eye of justice, save me from this man and from the memory with which he plagues me; Thou wilt help me, as I become a transformed, another, a better man, to dare to abide in my shelter, forgotten by Justice and by that man I abhor.

My hearer, today thou art come to seek the love which hides the multitude of sins, seeking it at the altar. From the minister of the Church thou hast received assurance of the gracious pardon of thy sins; at the altar thou dost receive the pledge of it. Oh, not this only; for thou dost not merely receive this pledge as thou mightest receive from a man a pledge that he has such-and-such a feeling for thee or purpose toward thee; no, thou dost receive the pledge as a pledge that thou dost receive Him: in receiving the pledge thou dost receive Christ Himself, in and with the sensible sign He gives Himself to thee as a covering for thy sins. As He is the truth, thou dost not learn to know from Him what the truth is, to be left then to thine own devices, but thou dost remain in the truth only by remaining in Him; as He is the way, thou dost not learn from Him to know which way thou shalt go, and then being left to thine own devices canst go thine own way, but only by remaining in Him canst thou remain in the way; as He is life, thou dost not from Him have life given thee, and then canst shift for thyself, but only by remaining in Him hast thou life: so it is also that He is the covering; only by remaining in Him, only by living into Him, art thou in hiding, is there a cover over the multitude of thy sins. Hence the Lord's Supper is called Communion with Him; it is not merely in remembrance of Him, not merely a pledge that thou hast communion with Him, but it is the communion, the communion which thou shalt endeavor to maintain in thy daily life by more and more living thyself out of thyself and living thyself into Him, into His love who hides the multitude of sins.

THE JOURNALS (1850–1854)

THE NIGHT OF THE ABSOLUTE

Man has a natural dread of walking in the dark—what wonder then that he has a dread of the absolute, of which it is true that no night and "no deepest gloom is half so dark" as this gloom and this night, where all relative ends (the common milestones and sign-posts), where all relative considerations (the lanterns which are normally a help to us), where even the tenderest and sincerest feelings of devotion—are quenched ... for otherwise it is not unconditionally the absolute.—THE JOURNALS

FOR over three years (September 1851 to December 1854) Kierkegaard published nothing whatsoever. One reason was that he had very little money left; another was that he did not want to publish what he still had to say to the world while the venerable Bishop Mynster was still alive. The thoughts of these three years are recorded in the *Journals* and are increasingly polemical in tone—"loading the gun," as Lowrie says, for the attack on "Christendom."

I have here grouped together a few Journal passages, all except one or two dating from this period of suspended literary activity. Several of them ("Science," "The Daily Press," "Ludicrous," and the Note to "A Sad Reflection") are priceless enough as aphorisms, and they demonstrate S.K.'s dexterity in this field. Just as he could take an unconscionably long time to say a thing, when he wanted to, so he could perform the most striking feats of concentration. (For the extreme in this direction, see the passages "Short and Sharp" in the *Attack*.)

Many of S.K.'s violent dislikes are represented here: science, freedom in the negative sense, the newspapers, "dons," parsons and professors. The editor of this volume recalls with some embarrassment hearing "A Sad Reflection" read as a fitting introduction to his lecture on Kierkegaard! What S.K. will think of my latest offense I know only too well—unless the other world has softened him.

PRAYER

LORD JESUS CHRIST! A whole life long didst thou suffer that I too might be saved, and yet thy suffering is not yet at an end; but this too wilt thou endure, saving and redeeming me, this patient suffering of having to do with me, I who so often go astray from the right path, or even when I remained on the straight path stumbled along it or crept so slowly along the right path. Infinite patience, suffering of infinite patience. How many times have I not been impatient, wished to give up and forsake everything, wished to take the terribly easy way out, despair: but thou didst not lose patience. Oh, I cannot say what thy chosen servant says: that he filled up that which is behind of the afflictions of Christ in his flesh; no, I can only say that I increased thy sufferings, added new ones to those which thou didst once suffer in order to save me.

. . . What a curious, yet profound turn of phrase which makes it possible to say: in this case there is no question of a *choice*—I choose this and this. To continue: Christianity says to a man: you shall choose the one essential thing but in such a way that there is no question of a choice—if you drivel on any longer then you do not in fact choose the one essential thing; like the Kingdom of God it must be chosen *first*.

So there is consequently something in regard to which there may not be, and in thought cannot be, a choice and nevertheless it is a choice. Consequently, the very fact that in this case there is no *choice* expresses the tremendous passion or intensity with which it must be *chosen*. Could there be a clearer expression of the fact that the liberty of choice is only a qualified form of freedom? . . . However astonishing it may seem, one is therefore obliged to say that only "fear and trembling," only constraint, can help a man to freedom. Because "fear and trembling" and compulsion can master him in such a way that there is no longer any question of choice—and then one chooses the right thing. At the hour of death most people choose the right thing.

Now how are the sciences to help? Simply not at all, in no way whatsoever. They reduce everything to calm and objective observation

—with the result that freedom is an inexplicable something. Scientifically Spinoza is the only one who is consistent.

. . . Freedom really only *exists* because the same instant it (freedom of choice) exists it rushes with infinite speed to bind itself unconditionally by choosing resignation, in the choice of which it is true that there is no question of a choice. . . . But alas, man is not so purely spirit. It seems to him that since the choice is left to him he can take time and *first of all* think the matter over *seriously*. What a miserable anti-climax. "Seriousness" simply means to choose God at once and "first." In that way man is left juggling with a phantom: freedom of choice—with the question whether he does or does not possess it, etc. And it even becomes scientific. He does not notice that he has thus suffered the loss of his freedom. For a time perhaps he delights in the thought of freedom until it changes again, and he becomes doubtful whether he is free or not. Then he loses his freedom of choice. He confuses everything by his faulty tactics (militarily speaking). By directing his mind toward "freedom of choice" instead of choosing, he loses both freedom and freedom of choice. Nor can he ever recover it by the use of thought alone. If he is to recover his freedom it can only be through an intensified "fear and trembling" brought forth by the thought of having lost it.

The most tremendous thing which has been granted to man is: the choice, freedom. And if you desire to save it and preserve it there is only one way: in the very same second unconditionally and in complete resignation to give it back to God, and yourself with it. If the sight of what is granted to you tempts you, and if you give way to the temptation and look with egoistic desire upon the freedom of choice, then you lose your freedom. And your punishment is: to go on in a kind of confusion priding yourself on having—freedom of choice, but woe upon you, that is your judgment: You have freedom of choice, you say, and still you have not chosen God. Then you will grow ill, freedom of choice will become your *idée fixe,* till at last you will be like the rich man who imagines that he is poor, and will die of want: you sigh that you have lost your freedom of choice—and your fault is only that you do not grieve deeply enough or you would find it again. . . .

FREEDOM OF CONSCIENCE, FREEDOM OF BELIEF

Ideally speaking it may be perfectly true that every man should be given freedom of conscience and freedom of belief, etc.

But what then; where are the men who are spiritually strong enough to be able to use that freedom, who are really capable of standing absolutely alone, alone with God?

That is what is untrue, demagogical, and mealy-mouthed in all that talk about everyone being such a devil of a fellow—if only there were neither law nor constraint. . . . Remove all constraint, which is precisely what a man needs and particularly therefore in matters of great concern (and logically always more, the loftier the matter)—and the mass of mankind will either cease to be anything at all, or fall into the hands of parties, etc.

. . . The apostles, Luther and so on, were what they were simply owing to there being every possible obstacle and constraint against them—but they overcame them. Had the constraint not been there we should never have been able to see that they were what they were.

Now everyone wants to do away with all constraint, so as to play the apostle—which is like doing away with cannon, powder, and bayonet and then wanting to be a very brave soldier. In order that it should really and truly be the *conscience* alone which decides (and not a belch, a slothful idea, a caprice, confused thoughts or a foolish imitation), for that very reason is it necessary to have opposition and constraint. The qualification "conscience" is so inward that it requires the very finest filters in order to discover it. But if it is found, if it really is conscience, conscience alone, then your regulations be blowed—I should only laugh at them. . . .

The man who can really stand alone in the world, only taking counsel from his conscience—that man is a hero. . . .

Marg. Add. One ought then to say: we are weak, afraid and have neither the courage nor the strength—we want the constraint removed. That would be sense. But in the lying thieves' slang of the day it is called: fighting for freedom of conscience.

THE MOST BLESSED CONSOLATION, THE ETERNALLY CERTAIN
PROOF THAT I AM LOVED BY GOD

This is the syllogism. Love (true love, not self-love which only loves the remarkable, the brilliant and consequently really loves itself) stands in inverse ratio to the greatness and excellence of the object. And so if I am of infinitely, infinitely little importance, if in my wretchedness I feel myself to be the most miserable of all: then it is eternally, eternally certain that God loves me.

Christ says: not a sparrow shall fall to earth unless it be at his will. Oh, I bid lower still, to God I am less than a sparrow—that God loves me becomes more certain still, the syllogism more solid still in its conclusion.

It might seem to the Emperor of Russia that God could overlook him, God has so much to attend to and the Emperor of Russia is so great. But not a sparrow—for God is love, and love is in inverse ratio to the greatness and excellence of the object.

You feel lost in the world in your suffering, no one cares for you, alas, and you conclude, neither does God care for me. You fool! you traducer, to speak thus of God. No, if there were anyone of whom it were literally true that he was of all the most neglected—he is the one whom God loves. Or if he were not quite the most neglected, if he still had a little human consolation—and that were taken from him: in the very same moment it would be more certain still that God loves him.

SCIENCE

. . . That a man should simply and profoundly say that he cannot understand how consciousness comes into existence—is perfectly natural. But that a man should glue his eye to a microscope and stare and stare and stare—and still not be able to see how it happens—is ridiculous, and it is particularly ridiculous when it is supposed to be serious. . . . If the natural sciences had been developed in Socrates's day as they are now, all the sophists would have been scientists. One would have hung a microscope outside his shop in order to attract custom, and then would have had a sign painted saying: "Learn and see through a giant microscope how a man thinks" (and on reading the advertisement Socrates would have said: "that is how men who do not think behave"). An excellent subject for an Aristophanes, particularly if he let Socrates look through a microscope. (1846)

THE DAILY PRESS

The demoralization which comes from the press can be seen from this fact: There are not ten men in every generation who, socratically, are afraid of having a wrong opinion; but there are thousands and millions who are more frightened of standing alone, even with an opinion which is quite right, than of anything else. But when something is in the papers, it is *eo ipso* certain that there is always a good number of people having that opinion or about to express it.

Indeed, if the press were to hang a sign out like every other trade, it would have to read: Here men are demoralized in the shortest possible time on the largest possible scale for the smallest possible price.

What we need is a Pythagorean silence. There is a far greater need for total-abstaining societies which would not read newspapers than for ones which do not drink alcohol. (1847)

When truth conquers with the help of 10,000 yelling men—even supposing that that which is victorious is a truth: with the form and manner of the victory a far greater untruth is victorious.

The lowest depth to which people can sink before God is defined by the word "Journalist." . . . If I were a father and had a daughter who was seduced, I should not despair over her; I would hope for her salvation. But if I had a son who became a journalist, and continued to be one for five years, I would give him up. . . .

GENIUS—TALENT

Talent is to be ranked according to the sensation it produces; Genius according to the opposition it arouses (religious character according to the scandal it gives). Talent adapts itself immediately and directly; Genius does not adapt itself to the given circumstances. Talent warms up what is given (to take a metaphor from cooking) and sees to its appearance; Genius brings something new. . . .

RELIGIOUS SUFFERING

. . . Dons and parsons live by presenting the sufferings of others, and that is regarded as religious, uncommonly deep religion even; for the religion of the congregation is nothing but hearing this presented. As a religion, *charmante,* just about as genuine as tea made from a bit of paper which once lay in a drawer beside another bit of paper which had once been used to wrap up a few dried tea-leaves from which tea had already been made three times.

A SAD REFLECTION

In one of the Psalms it is said of the rich man that he heaps up treasures with great toil "and knoweth not who shall inherit them." So I shall leave behind me, intellectually speaking, a capital by no means insignificant—and alas, I know full well who will be my heir. It is that figure so exceedingly distasteful to me, he that till now has inherited all that is best and will continue to do so: the Docent, the Professor.

Yet this also is a necessary part of my suffering—to know this and then go calmly on with my endeavor, which brings me toil and trouble and the profit of which, in one sense, the Professor will inherit. "In one sense"—for in another sense I take it with me.

Note. And even if the "Professor" should chance to read this, it will not give him pause, will not cause his conscience to smite him; no, this too will be made the subject of a lecture. And again this observation, if the Professor should chance to read it, will not give him pause; no, this too will be made the subject of a lecture. For longer even than the tapeworm which recently was extracted from a woman . . . even longer is the Professor, and the man in whom the Professor is lodged cannot be rid of this by any human power, only God can do it, if the man himself is willing.

. . . Catholicism has a conception of the Christian ideal: to become nothing in this world. Protestantism is worldliness from beginning to end.

LUDICROUS

A man's whole life is worldliness, all his thought and effort from morning till night, his waking and his dreaming.

At the same time, *naturally,* he is a Christian, for doesn't he live in Christendom!—and in his quality as a Christian he is "a stranger and a pilgrim" in the world.

This is just as ludicrous as when the savages adorn themselves with a single piece of European clothing—for example, the savage who comes on board stark naked except for the epaulets of a general on his shoulders.

THE TAME GEESE

A REVIVALISTIC MEDITATION

Suppose it was so that the geese could talk—then they had so arranged it that they also could have their religious worship, their divine service.

Every Sunday they came together, and one of the ganders preached.

The essential content of the sermon was: what a lofty destiny the geese had, what a high goal the Creator (and every time this word was mentioned the geese curtsied and the ganders bowed the head) had set before the geese; by the aid of wings they could fly away to distant regions, blessed climes, where properly they were at home, for here they were only strangers.

So it was every Sunday. And as soon as the assembly broke up each waddled home to his own affairs. And then the next Sunday again to divine worship and then again home—and that was the end of it, they throve and were well-liking, became plump and delicate—and then were eaten on Martinmas Eve—and that was the end of it.

That was the end of it. For though the discourse sounded so lofty on Sunday, the geese on Monday were ready to recount to one another what befell a goose that had wanted to make serious use of the wings the Creator had given him, designed for the high goal that was proposed to him—what befell him, what a terrible death he encountered. This the geese could talk about knowingly among themselves. But, naturally, to speak about it on Sundays was unseemly; for, said they, it would then become evident that our divine worship is really only making a fool of God and of ourselves.

Among the geese there were, however, some individuals which seemed suffering and grew thin. About them it was currently said among the geese: There you see what it leads to when flying is taken seriously. For because their hearts are occupied with the thought of wanting to fly, therefore they become thin, do not thrive, do not have the grace of God as we have who therefore become plump and delicate.

And so the next Sunday they went again to divine worship, and the old gander preached about the high goal the Creator (here again the geese curtsied and the ganders bowed the head) had set before the geese, whereto the wings were designed.

So with the divine worship of Christendom. Man also has wings, he has imagination. . . .

THE ATTACK UPON
"CHRISTENDOM" (1854–1855)

TRANSLATED BY WALTER LOWRIE

Most people believe that the Christian commandments are intentionally a little too severe—like putting the clock on half an hour to make sure of not being late in the morning. (1837)

. . . The most terrible fight is not when there is one opinion against another, the most terrible is when two men say the same thing—and fight about the interpretation, and this interpretation involves a difference of quality.—THE JOURNALS

ALREADY we have had occasion to remark that the external events of Kierkegaard's life were incommensurable with the results they produced. In no case is this more evident than in the incident which provoked the last phase of his authorship, the sharp and even brutal attack on the established religion of his native land. Bishop Mynster, the primate of all Denmark, died on January 30, 1854; and a few days afterward Professor Martensen (who afterward succeeded to the bishopric) preached a sermon in the Court church in which the late Bishop was eulogized as "a genuine witness to the Truth," a member of "that holy line which like a great chain stretches back to the Apostles." Lesser men than Mynster have certainly received more fulsome praise; but to S.K., who heard Martensen's sermon, it was not only grossly untrue, but a dangerous and abominable untruth.

S.K.'s reaction becomes harder to understand when we realize that Bishop Mynster was no worldly ecclesiastic, but a wise and able administrator, and a man of some intellectual power and spiritual discernment, whose sermons S.K. had listened to with profit. Moreover, he was a man who had greatly influenced S.K.'s father. It was not that Kierkegaard despised the Bishop; on the contrary, he had a very high regard for him—within limits. But it was just these limits which to S.K. were all-important. In the upright Bishop Mynster there was something lacking—something which S.K. regarded as the very essence of a "witness to the Truth," a successor to the Apostles.

This something may be described as the upholding of the Christian *ideal* of life, with consequent humility in the recognition of how utterly we have failed to live up to this ideal. Reading parts of the *Attack*, one may get the impression that Kierkegaard was a perfectionist, but nothing could be farther from the truth—unless by "perfectionism" one means holding forth the *ideal* in all its purity and severity. This Kierkegaard insisted upon; he would not have the Christian law of love and self-denial watered down to a comfortable code of *bourgeois* ethics. But he did not assume the possibility of fulfilling this law completely; least of all did he assume that he himself had fulfilled it. Over and over again he insists that all he wants from the Church is an *admission* of its mediocrity—in order that it might then "take refuge in Grace" and receive strength for making a step or two, at least, in the right direction. But this admission the Church steadily refused to make.

Strictly speaking, however, we may say that "S.K.'s criticism was not directed against the Church as such, but against 'Christendom,' the established order of things in a presumably 'Christian land' and 'a Christian world'" (Lowrie). Part of his polemic—the part dealing with "the King's functionaries," i.e. the evils of Establishment—is inapplicable to America today and many of these passages have been omitted from the following selections. But as Lowrie says, it is surprising how much *is* applicable today and how much is applicable with even greater point than in S.K.'s Denmark.

In an article on Kierkegaard a few years ago I made the remark that in his assault on established Christianity S.K. for once became "undialectical," seeing only one side of the question and magnifying that side out of its true proportion. This was rather a fatuous observation, since exaggeration and one-sidedness are of the very nature of satire. A deathbed conversation between S.K. and Pastor Boisen has been recorded, in which the latter objected that the "attack" "did not correspond with reality, it was more severe"; to which S.K. replied, "So it must be; otherwise it does not help." Thus "the corrective," itself one-sided, has the sacrificial function of restoring the general balance.

As satire *The Attack* is magnificent even when it is most offensive, as in the section (not reproduced here) in which "the priests" are shown to be cannibals, or in the one entitled "Confirmation and the Wedding." Here we have not merely a protest against the routinized practice of these sacraments, but a "transvaluation of values" with respect to the institutions themselves. S.K. sees only too clearly how Protestantism has glossed over the New Testament ideal of celibacy set forth by St. Paul, and he sees how the Catholic-Lutheran formalism reduces conversion to a pretty ceremony gone through "before one is dry behind the ears." I hope that many will be as shocked as I am at this and other passages; for S.K.'s object was precisely to shock—into reflection, repentance, and action.

Whatever one may think of this ultimate phase of S.K.'s authorship, it cannot be denied that he spent himself to the utmost. Nine months after the first article [1] was published, he fell sick on the street while carrying home from the bank the very last of his considerable inheritance. Taken to the hospital, he died two months later of a malady vaguely diagnosed. He went without the Sacrament at the last, because he would not receive it from a

---

[1] S.K.'s invective was published partly in the form of articles in *The Fatherland* and partly in a series of pamphlets entitled *The Instant*. "The Attack upon 'Christendom'" is merely the title of the English edition which gathers all this material together.

priest—only from a layman. The pamphlets had created a furor, and a riot almost took place at the funeral. A group of University students formed a guard of honor, and order was preserved by the tactfulness of S.K.'s brother Peter, who preached the funeral sermon. Even so, there was a last-minute outburst at the grave from one of S.K.'s sympathizers, who inveighed against the hypocrisy of the Church in appropriating this man who had denounced it, and insisted on reading from the Apocalypse the passage about the church of the Laodiceans. "No doubt it was very shocking," says Lowrie; "but S.K. was at peace, and I cannot think that his peace would be disturbed by knowing that the fire he had kindled continued to burn." [2]

FEAST OF THE ANNUNCIATION

O THOU, whosoever thou art under whose eye this falls—when I read in the New Testament the life of our Lord Jesus Christ here on earth, and see what he meant by being a Christian—and when I reflect that now we are Christians by the millions, just as many Christians as we are men, that from generation to generation Christians by the millions are handed over for inspection by eternity—frightful! For that there is something wrong with this, nothing can be more certain. Say for thyself what good it does—even if it were ever so pious and well-meant!—what good it does to wish (lovingly?) to confirm thee in the vain conceit that thou art a Christian, or to wish to alter the definition of what it is to be a Christian, in order presumably that thou mayest more securely enjoy this life; what good it does thee, or rather is not this precisely to do thee harm, since it is to help thee to let the temporal life go by unused in a Christian sense—until thou art standing in eternity where thou art not a Christian, in case thou wast not one, and where it is impossible to become a Christian? Thou who readest this, say to thyself: Was I not in the right, and am I not, in saying that first and foremost everything must be done to make it perfectly definite what is required in the New Testament for being a Christian; that first and foremost everything must be done in order that at least we might become attentive?

THE RELIGIOUS SITUATION

IN the New Testament the situation is this: the speaker, our Lord Jesus Christ, Himself absolutely expressing opposition, stands in a world which in turn absolutely expresses opposition to Him and to His teach-

[2] *Kierkegaard*, p. 587.

ing. When of the individual Christ requires faith, then (and with this we have a sharper definition of what He understands by faith), then by reason of the situation this is not feasible without coming into a relationship with the surrounding world which perhaps involves mortal danger; when Christ says, "Confess me before the world," "Follow me," or when He says, "Come unto me," etc., etc., then, by reason of the situation which furnishes the more express understanding, the consequences will always be exposure to danger, perhaps to mortal danger. On the other hand, where all are Christians, the situation is this: to call oneself a Christian is the means whereby one secures oneself against all sorts of inconveniences and discomforts, and the means whereby one secures worldly goods, comforts, profit, etc., etc. But we make as if nothing had happened, we declaim about believing ("He who knows best, that is our priest" [1]), about confessing Christ before the world, about following Him, etc., etc.; and orthodoxy flourishes in the land, no heresy, no schism, orthodoxy everywhere, the orthodoxy which consists in playing the game of Christianity.

. . . We are what is called a "Christian" nation—but in such a sense that not a single one of us is in the character of the Christianity of the New Testament, any more than I am, who again and again have repeated, and do now repeat, that I am only a poet. The illusion of a Christian nation is due doubtless to the power which number exercises over the imagination. I have not the least doubt that every single individual in the nation will be honest enough with God and with himself to say in solitary conversation, "If I must be candid, I do not deny that I am not a Christian in the New Testament sense; if I must be honest, I do not deny that my life cannot be called an effort in the direction of what the New Testament calls Christianity, in the direction of denying myself, renouncing the world, dying from it, etc.; rather the earthly and the temporal become more and more important to me with every year I live." I have not the least doubt that everyone will, with respect to ten of his acquaintances, let us say, be able to hold fast to the view that they are not Christians in the New Testament sense, and that their lives are not even an effort in the direction of becoming so. But when there are 100,000, one becomes confused.

They tell a ludicrous story about an innkeeper, a story moreover which is related incidentally by one of my pseudonyms,[2] but I would

---

[1] A Danish jingle which every child knew. (L)
[2] Vigilius Haufuiensis in *The Concept of Dread*. (L)

use it again because it has always seemed to me to have a profound meaning. It is said that he sold his beer by the bottle for a cent less than he paid for it; and when a certain man said to him, "How does that balance the account? That means to spend money," he replied, "No, my friend, it's the big number that does it"—big number, that also in our time is the almighty power. When one has laughed at this story, one would do well to take to heart the lesson which warns against the power which number exercises over the imagination. For there can be no doubt that this innkeeper knew very well that one bottle of beer which he sold for 3 cents meant a loss of 1 cent when it cost him 4 cents. Also with regard to ten bottles the innkeeper will be able to hold fast that it is a loss. But 100,000 bottles! Here the big number stirs the imagination, the round number runs away with it, and the innkeeper becomes dazed—it's a profit, says he, for the big number does it. So also with the calculation which arrives at a Christian nation by adding up units which are not Christian, getting the result by means of the notion that the big number does it. For true Christianity this is the most dangerous of all illusions, and at the same time it is of all illusions precisely the one to which every man is prone; for number (the high number, when it gets up to 100,000, into the millions) tallies precisely with the imagination. But Christianly of course the calculation is wrong, and a Christian nation composed of units which honestly admit that they are not Christians, *item* honestly admit that their life cannot in any sense be called an effort in the direction of what the New Testament understands by Christianity—such a Christian nation is an impossibility. On the other hand, a knave could not wish to find a better hiding-place than behind such phrases as "the nation is Christian," "the people are making a Christian endeavor," since it is almost as difficult to come to close quarters with such phrases as it would be if one were to say, "N. N. is a Christian, N. N. is engaged in Christian endeavor."

But inasmuch as Christianity is spirit, the sobriety of spirit, the honesty of eternity, there is of course nothing which to its detective eye is so suspicious as are all fantastic entities: Christian states, Christian lands, a Christian people, and (how marvelous!) a Christian world. And even if there were something true in this talk about Christian peoples and states—but, mind you, only when all mediating definitions, all divergencies from the Christianity of the New Testament, are honestly and honorably pointed out and kept in evidence—yet it is certain that at this point a monstrous criminal offense has been perpetrated, yea, everything this world has hitherto seen in the way of criminal affairs is a mere bagatelle in comparison with this crime, which has been carried on from generation to generation throughout long ages, eluding human justice, but has not yet got beyond the arm of divine justice.

WHAT DO I WANT?

March 1855.   S. Kierkegaard.

QUITE simply: I want honesty. I am not, as well-intentioned people [1] represent (for I can pay no attention to the interpretations of me that are advanced by exasperation and rage and impotence and twaddle), I am not a Christian severity as opposed to a Christian leniency.

By no means. I am neither leniency nor severity: I am—a human honesty.

The leniency which is the common Christianity in the land I want to place alongside of the New Testament in order to see how these two are related to one another.

Then, if it appears, if I or another can prove, that it can be maintained face to face with the New Testament, then with the greatest joy I will agree to it.

But one thing I will not do, not for anything in the world. I will not by suppression, or by performing tricks, try to produce the impression that the ordinary Christianity in the land and the Christianity of the New Testament are alike.

Behold, this it is I do not want. And why not? Well, because I want honesty. Or, if you wish me to talk in another way—well then, it is because I believe that, if possibly even the very extremest softening down of Christianity may hold good in the judgment of eternity, it is impossible that it should hold good when even artful tricks are employed to gloss over the difference between the Christianity of the New Testament and this softened form. What I mean is this: If a man is known for his graciousness—very well then, let me venture to ask him to forgive me all my debt; but even though his grace were divine grace, this is too much to ask, if I will not even be truthful about how great the debt is.

And this in my opinion is the falsification of which official Christianity is guilty: it does not frankly and unreservedly make known the

---

[1] Professor Nielsen, who had defended him. (L)

Christian requirement—perhaps because it is afraid people would shudder to see at what a distance from it we are living, without being able to claim that in the remotest way our life might be called an effort in the direction of fulfilling the requirement. Or (merely to take one example of what is everywhere present in the New Testament): when Christ requires us to save our life eternally (and that surely is what we propose to attain as Christians) and to hate our own life in this world, is there then a single one among us whose life in the remotest degree could be called even the weakest effort in this direction? And perhaps there are thousands of "Christians" in the land who are not so much as aware of this requirement. So then we "Christians" are living, and are loving our life, just in the ordinary human sense. If then by "grace" God will nevertheless regard us as Christians, one thing at least must be required: that we, being precisely aware of the requirement, have a true conception of how infinitely great is the grace that is shown us. "Grace" cannot possibly stretch so far, one thing it must never be used for, it must never be used to suppress or to diminish the requirement; for in that case "grace" would turn Christianity upside down.

Or, to take an example of another kind: A teacher is paid, let us say, several thousand. If then we suppress the Christian standard and apply the ordinary human rule, that it is a matter of course a man should receive a wage for his labor, a wage sufficient to support a family, and a considerable wage to enable him to enjoy the consideration due to a government official—then a few thousand a year is certainly not much. On the other hand, as soon as the Christian requirement of poverty is brought to bear, family is a luxury and several thousand is very high pay. I do not say this in order to deprive such an official of a single shilling, if I were able to; on the contrary, if he desired it, and I were able, he might well have double as many thousands: but I say that the suppression of the Christian requirement changes the point of view for all his wages. Honesty to Christianity demands that one call to mind the Christian requirement of poverty, which is not a capricious whim of Christianity, but is because only in poverty can it be truly served, and the more thousands a teacher of Christianity has by way of wages, the less he can serve Christianity. On the other hand, it is not honest to suppress the requirement or to perform artful tricks to produce the impression that this sort of business career is simply the Christianity of the New Testament. No—let us take money, but for God's sake not the next thing: let us not wish to gloss over the Christian requirement, so that by suppression or by falsification we may bring about an appearance of decorum which is in the very highest degree demoralizing and is a sly death-blow to Christianity.

Therefore I want honesty; but till now the Established Church has not been willing of its own accord to go in for that sort of honesty, and neither has it been willing to let itself be influenced by me. That does not make me, however, a leniency or a severity; no, I am and remain quite simply a human honesty.

THE COMFORTABLE—AND THE CONCERN
FOR AN ETERNAL BLESSEDNESS

[April 11.]

IT is these two things—one might almost be tempted to say, what the deuce have these two things to do with one another?—and yet it is these two things that official Christianity, or the State by the aid of official Christianity, has jumbled together, and done it as calmly as when, at a party where the host wants to include everybody, he jumbles many toasts in one.

It seems that the reasoning of the State must have been as follows. Among the many various things which man needs on a civilized plane and which the State tries to provide for its citizens as cheaply and comfortably as possible—among these very various things, like public security, water, illumination, roads, bridge-building, etc., etc., there is also—an eternal blessedness in the hereafter, a requirement which the State ought also to satisfy (how generous of it!), and that in as cheap and comfortable a way as possible. Of course it will cost money, for without money one gets nothing in this world, not even a certificate of eternal blessedness in the other world; no, without money one gets nothing in this world. Yet all the same, what the State does, to the great advantage of the individual, is that one gets it from the State at a cheaper price than if the individual were to make some private arrangement, moreover it is more secure, and finally it is comfortable in a degree that only can be provided on a big scale. . . .

Far be it from me to speak disparagingly of the comfortable! Let it be applied wherever it can be applied, in relation to everything which is in such a sense a thing that this thing can be possessed irrespective of the way in which it is possessed, so that one can have it either in this way or in the other; for when such is the case, the convenient and comfortable way is undeniably to be preferred. Take water for example:

water is a thing which can be procured in the difficult way of fetching it up from the pump, but it can also be procured in the convenient way of high pressure; naturally I prefer the more convenient way.

But the eternal is not a thing which can be had regardless of the way in which it is acquired; no, the eternal is not really a thing, but is the way in which it is acquired. The eternal is acquired in *one* way, and the eternal is different from everything else precisely for the fact that it can be acquired only in one single way; conversely, what can be acquired in only one way is the eternal—it is acquired only in one way, in the difficult way which Christ indicated by the words: "Narrow is the gate and straitened the way that leadeth unto life, and few are they that find it."

That was bad news! The comfortable—precisely the thing in which our age excels—absolutely cannot be applied with respect to an eternal blessedness. When, for example, the thing you are required to do is to walk, it is no use at all to make the most astonishing inventions in the way of the easiest carriages and to want to convey yourself in these when the task prescribed to you was—walking. And if the eternal is the way in which it is acquired, it doesn't do any good to want to alter this way, however admirably, in the direction of comfort; for the eternal is acquired only in the difficult way, is not acquired indifferently both in the easy and the difficult way, but is the way in which it is acquired, and this way is the difficult one. . . .

A EULOGY UPON THE HUMAN RACE
OR
A PROOF THAT THE NEW TESTAMENT IS NO LONGER TRUTH

In the New Testament the Saviour of the world, our Lord Jesus Christ, represents the situation thus: The way that leadeth unto life is straitened, the gate narrow—few be they that find it!

—Now, on the contrary, to speak only of Denmark, we are all Christians, the way is as broad as it possibly can be, the broadest in Denmark, since it is the way in which we all are walking, besides being in all respects as convenient, as comfortable as possible; and the gate is as wide as it possibly can be, wider surely a gate cannot be than that through which we all are going *en masse*.

Ergo the New Testament is no longer truth.

All honor to the human race! But Thou, O Saviour of the world, Thou didst entertain too lowly a notion of the human race, failing to foresee the sublime heights to which, perfectible as it is, it can attain by an effort steadily pursued!

To that degree therefore the New Testament is no longer truth: the way the broadest, the gate the widest, and all of us Christians. Yea, I venture to go a step further—it inspires me with enthusiasm, for this, you must remember, is a eulogy upon the human race—I venture to maintain that, on the average, the Jews who dwell among us are to a certain degree Christians, Christians like all the others—to that degree we are all Christians, in that degree is the New Testament no longer truth. . . . I venture to go a step further, without expressing, however, any definite opinion, seeing that in this respect I lack precise information, and hence submit to persons well informed, the specialists, the question whether among the domestic animals, the nobler ones, the horse, the dog, the cow, there might not be visible some Christian token. That is not unlikely. Just think what it means to live in a Christian state, a Christian nation, where everything is Christian, and we are all Christians, where, however a man twists and turns, he sees nothing but Christianity and Christendom, the truth and witnesses to the truth—it is not unlikely that this may have an influence upon the nobler domestic animals, and thereby in turn upon that which, according to the judgment of both the veterinary and the priest, is the most important thing, namely, the progeny. Jacob's cunning device is well known, how in order to get speckled lambs he laid speckled rods in the watering troughs, so that the ewes saw nothing but speckles and therefore gave birth to speckled lambs. It is not unlikely—although I do not presume to have any definite opinion, as I am not a specialist, and therefore would rather submit the question to a committee composed, for example, of veterinaries and priests—it is not unlikely that it will end with domestic animals in "Christendom" bringing into the world a Christian progeny.

I am almost dizzy at the thought; but then, on the greatest possible scale—to the honor of the human race—will the New Testament be no longer truth.

Thou Saviour of the world, Thou didst anxiously exclaim, "When I come again, shall I find faith on the earth?" and then didst bow Thy head in death; Thou surely didst not have the least idea that in such a measure Thine expectations would be surpassed, that the human race in such a pretty and touching way would make the New Testament untruth and Thine importance almost doubtful. For can such good beings truthfully be said to need, or ever to have needed, a saviour?

MEDICAL DIAGNOSIS

A MAN becomes thinner and thinner day by day; he is wasting away. What can the matter be? He does not suffer want. "No, certainly not," says the physician, "it doesn't come from that, it comes precisely from eating, from the fact that he eats out of season, eats without being hungry, uses stimulants to arouse a little bit of appetite, and in that way he ruins his digestion, fades away as if he were suffering want."

So it is religiously. The most fatal thing of all is to satisfy a want which is not yet felt, so that without waiting till the want is present, one anticipates it, likely also uses stimulants to bring about something which is supposed to be a want, and then satisfies it. And this is shocking! And yet this is what they do in the religious sphere, whereby they really are cheating men out of what constitutes the significance of life, and helping people to waste life.

For this is the aim of the whole machinery of the State Church, which under the form of care for men's souls cheats them out of the highest thing in life, that in them there should come into being the concern about themselves, the want, which verily a teacher or priest should find according to his mind; but now, instead of this, the want (and precisely the coming into being of this want is life's highest significance for a man) does not come into being at all, but having been satisfied long before it came into being, it is prevented from coming into being. And this is thought to be the continuation of the work which the Saviour of the human race completed, this bungling of the human race! And why? Because there are now as a matter of fact so and so many royal functionaries who, with families, have to live off this, under the name of—the cure of souls!

THE CHRISTIANITY OF THE SPIRITUAL MAN / THE CHRISTIANITY OF US MEN

THERE are two points of difference between the spiritual man and us men, to which I would especially draw attention, and thereby in turn illustrate the difference between the Christianity of the New Testament and the Christianity of "Christendom."

(1) The spiritual man differs from us men in the fact that (if I may so express it) he is so heavily built that he is able to endure a duplication in himself. In comparison with him we men are like frame walls in comparison with the foundation wall, so loosely and frailly built that we cannot endure a duplication. But the Christianity of the New Testament has to do precisely with a duplication.

The spiritual man is able to endure a duplication in himself: by his understanding he is able to hold fast to the fact that something is contrary to the understanding, and then will it nevertheless; he is able to hold fast with the understanding to the fact that something is an offense, and yet to will it nevertheless; that, humanly speaking, something makes him unhappy, and yet to will it, etc. But the New Testament is composed precisely in view of this. We men on the other hand are not able to support or endure a duplication within ourselves; our will alters our understanding. Our Christianity therefore, the Christianity of "Christendom," takes this into account: it takes away from Christianity the offense, the paradox, etc., and instead of that introduces probability, the plainly comprehensible. That is, it transforms Christianity into something entirely different from what it is in the New Testament, yea, into exactly the opposite; and this is the Christianity of "Christendom," of us men.

(2) The spiritual man differs from us men in being able to endure isolation, his rank as a spiritual man is proportionate to his strength for enduring isolation, whereas we men are constantly in need of "the others," the herd; we die, or despair, if we are not reassured by being in the herd, of the same opinion as the herd, etc.

But the Christianity of the New Testament is precisely reckoned upon and related to this isolation of the spiritual man. Christianity in the New Testament consists in loving God, in hatred to man, in hatred of oneself, and thereby of other men, hating father, mother, one's own child, wife, etc., the strongest expression for the most agonizing isolation.—And it is in view of this I say that such men, men of this quality and caliber, are not born any more.

The Christianity of us men is, to love God in agreement with other men, to love and be loved by other men, constantly the others, the herd included.

Let us take an example. In "Christendom" this is what Christianity is: a man with a woman on his arm steps up to the altar, where a smart silken priest, half educated in the poets, half in the New Testament, delivers an address half erotic, half Christian—a wedding ceremony. This is what Christianity is in "Christendom." The Christianity of the New Testament would be: in case that man were really able to love in such a way that the girl was the only one he loved and one whom he loved with the whole passion of a soul (yet such men as this are no longer to be found), then, hating himself and the loved one, to let her go in order to love God.—And it is in view of this I say that such men, men of such quality and caliber, are not born any more.

WHEN ALL ARE CHRISTIANS, CHRISTIANITY *EO IPSO* DOES NOT EXIST

WHEN once it is pointed out, this is very easily seen, and once seen it can never be forgotten.

Any determinant which applies to all cannot enter into existence but must either underlie existence or lie outside as meaningless.

Take the determinant man. We are all men. This determinant therefore does not enter into human existence, for the human race as a whole is subsumed under the generic term "man." This determinant lies before the beginning, in the sense of underlying. We are all men— and then it begins.

This is an example of a determinant which applies to all and is underlying. The other alternative was that a determinant which applies to all, or by the fact that it applies to all, is meaningless.

Assume (and let us not haggle over the fact that it is a strange assumption, we shall have the explanation), assume that we are all thieves, what the police call suspicious characters—if that's what we all are, this determinant will *eo ipso* have no effect upon the situation as a whole, we shall be living just as we are living, each will then count for what he now counts, some (suspicious characters) will be branded as thieves and robbers, i.e. within the definition that we are all suspicious characters; others (suspicious characters) will be highly esteemed, etc.; in short, everything even to the least detail will be as it is, for we are all suspicious characters, and so the concept is annulled (Hegel's *aufgehoben*); when all are that, then to be that $= 0$; this is not to say that it does not mean anything much; no, it means nothing at all.

It is exactly the same with the definition that we are all Christians.

If we are all Christians, the concept is annulled, being a Christian is something which lies before the beginning, outside—and then it begins, we live then the merely human life, exactly as in paganism; the determinant Christian cannot in any way manage to enter in, for by the fact that we all are this it is precisely put outside.

God's thought in introducing Christianity was, if I may venture to say so, to pound the table hard in front of us men. To that end He set "individual" and "race," the single person and the many, at odds, set them against one another, applied the determinant of dissension; for to be a Christian was, according to His thought, precisely the definition of dissension, that of the "individual" with the "race," with the millions, with family, with father and mother, etc.

God did it that way, *partly* out of love; for He, the God of love, wanted to be loved, but is too great a connoisseur of what love is to want to have to order men to love Him by battalions or whole nations, as the command, "One, two, three," is given at the church parade. No, the formula constantly is: the individual in opposition to the others. And *partly* He did it as the ruler, in order to keep men in check and educate them. This was His thought, even though we men might say, if we dared, that it was the most annoying caprice on the part of God to put us together in this way, or cut us off in this way from what we animals regard as the true well-being, from coalescing with the herd, everyone just like the others.

God succeeded in this, he really overawed men.

But gradually the human race came to itself and, shrewd as it is, it saw that to do away with Christianity by force was not practicable— "So let us do it by cunning," they said. "We are all Christians, and so Christianity is *eo ipso* abolished."

And that is what we now are. The whole thing is a knavish trick; these 2,000 churches, or however many there are, are, Christianly considered, a knavish trick; these 1,000 priests in velvet, silk, broadcloth, or bombazine, are a knavish trick—for the whole thing rests upon the assumption that we are all Christians, which is precisely the knavish way of doing away with Christianity. Therefore it is a very peculiar sort of euphemism too when we reassure ourselves with the thought that we all will attain blessedness, or say, "I shall become blessed, just like all the others"; for when forwarded to heaven with this address, one is not received there, does no more go to heaven than one reaches New Holland by land.

SHORT AND SHARP

IN the magnificent cathedral the Honorable and Right Reverend *Geheime-General-Ober-Hof-Prädikant*, the elect favorite of the fashionable world, appears before an elect company and preaches *with emotion* upon the text he himself elected: "God hath elected the base things of the world, and the things that are despised." And nobody laughs.

When a man has a toothache the world says, "Poor man"; when a man's wife is unfaithful to him the world says, "Poor man"; when a man is in financial embarrassment the world says, "Poor man"; when it pleased God in the form of a lowly servant to suffer in this world the world says, "Poor man"; when an Apostle with a divine commission has the honor to suffer for the truth the world says, "Poor man."—Poor world!

WHAT SAYS THE FIRE CHIEF?

THAT when in any way one has what is called a cause, something he earnestly wishes to promote—and then there are others who propose to themselves the task of counteracting it, hindering it, harming it—that he then must take measures against these enemies of his, this everyone is aware of. But not everyone is aware that there is such a thing as honest good-intention which is far more dangerous and as if especially calculated with a view to preventing the cause from becoming truly serious. . . .

So also in the case of a fire. Hardly is the cry of "Fire!" heard before a crowd of people rush to the spot, nice, cordial, sympathetic, helpful people, one has a pitcher, another a basin, the third a squirt, etc., all of them nice, cordial, sympathetic, helpful people, so eager to help put out the fire.

But what says the Fire Chief? The Fire Chief, he says—yes, generally the Fire Chief is a very pleasant and polite man; but at a fire he is what one calls coarse-mouthed—he says, or rather he bawls, "Oh, go to hell with all your pitchers and squirts." And then, when these well-meaning people are perhaps offended and require at least to be treated with respect, what then says the Fire Chief? Yes, generally the Fire Chief is a very pleasant and polite man, who knows how to show everyone the respect that is due him; but at a fire he is rather different—he says, "Where the deuce is the police force?" And when some policemen arrive he says to them, "Rid me of these damn people with their pitchers and squirts; and if they won't yield to fair words, smear them a few over the back, so that we may be free of them and get down to work."

So then at a fire the whole way of looking at things is not the same as in everyday life. Good-natured, honest, well-meaning, by which in everyday life one attains the reputation of being a good fellow, is at a fire honored with coarse words and a few over the back.

And this is quite natural. For a fire is a serious thing, and whenever things are really serious, this honest good-intention by no means suffices. No, seriousness applies an entirely different law: either/or. Either thou art the man who in this instance can seriously do something, and seriously has something to do/or, if such be not thy case, then for thee the serious thing to do is precisely to get out. If by thyself thou wilt not understand this, then let the Fire Chief thrash it into thee by means of the police, from which thou mayest derive particular benefit, and which perhaps may after all contribute to making thee a bit serious, in correspondence with the serious thing which is a fire.

But as it is at a fire, so also it is in matters of the mind. Wherever there is a cause to be promoted, an undertaking to be carried out, an idea to be introduced—one can always be sure that when he who really is the man for it, the right man, who in a higher sense has and must have command, he who has seriousness and can give to the cause the seriousness it truly has—one can always be sure that when he comes (if I may so put it) to the spot, he will find there before him a genial company of twaddlers who, under the name of seriousness, lie around and bungle things by wanting to serve the cause, promote the undertaking, introduce the idea; a company of twaddlers who of course regard the fact that the person in question will not make common cause with them (precisely indicating his seriousness) as a certain proof that he lacks seriousness. I say, when the right man comes he will find things thus. I can also give this turn to it: the fact that he is the right man is really decided by the way he understands himself in relation to this company of twaddlers. If he has a notion that it is they who are to help, and that he must strengthen himself by union with them, he *eo ipso* is not the right man. The right man sees at once, like the Fire Chief, that this company of twaddlers must get out, that their presence and effect is the most dangerous assistance the fire could have. But in matters of the mind it is not as at a fire, where the Fire Chief merely has to say to the police, "Rid me of these men."

BRIEF OBSERVATIONS

GOD / THE WORLD

IF two men were to eat nuts together, and the one liked only the shell, the other only the kernel, one may say that they match one another well. What the world rejects, casts away, despises, namely the sacrificed man, the kernel—precisely upon that God sets the greatest store, and treasures it with greater zeal than does the world that which it loves with the greatest passion.

THE SORT OF PERSON THEY CALL A CHRISTIAN

FIRST PICTURE

It is a young man—let us think of it so, reality furnishes examples in abundance—it is a young man, we can imagine him with more than ordinary ability, knowledge, interested in public events, a politician, even taking an active part as such.

As for religion, his religion is—that he has none at all. To think of God never occurs to him, any more than it does to go to church, and it is certainly not on religious grounds he eschews that; he almost fears that to read God's Word at home would make him ridiculous.

When it turns out that the situation requires him to express himself about religion and there is some danger in doing it, he gets out of the difficulty by saying, as is the truth, "I have no opinion at all, such things have never concerned me."

This same young man who feels no need of religion feels the need of being—paterfamilias. He marries, then he has a child, he is—presumptive father. And then what happens?

Well, our young man is, as they say, in hot water about this child; in the capacity of presumptive father he is compelled to have a religion. And so it turns out that he has the Evangelical Lutheran religion.

How pitiful it is to have religion in this way. As a man, he has no religion; when there might be danger connected with having even an opinion about religion, he has no religion—but in the capacity of presumptive father he has (*risum teneatis!*)[1] that religion precisely which extols the single state.

So they notify the priest, the midwife arrives with the baby, a young

[1] Do not laugh!

lady holds the infant's bonnet coquettishly, several young men who also have no religion render the presumptive father the service of having, as godfathers, the Evangelical Christian religion, and assume obligation for the Christian upbringing of the child, while a silken priest with a graceful gesture sprinkles water three times on the dear little baby and dries his hands gracefully with the towel—

And this they dare to present to God under the name of Christian baptism. Baptism—it was with this sacred ceremony the Saviour of the world was consecrated for His life's work, and after Him the disciples, men who had well reached the age of discretion and who then, dead to this life (therefore immersed three times, signifying that they were baptized into communion with Christ's death), promised to be willing to live as sacrificed men in this world of falsehood and evil.

The priests, however, these holy men, understand their business, and understand too that if (as Christianity must unconditionally require of every sensible man) it were so that only when a person has reached the age of discretion he is permitted to decide upon the religion he will have—the priests understand very well that in this way their trade would not amount to much. And therefore these holy witnesses to the truth insinuate themselves into the lying-in room, where the mother is weak after the suffering she has gone through, and the paterfamilias is—in hot water. And then under the name of baptism they have the courage to present to God a ceremony such as that which has been described, into which a little bit of truth might be brought nevertheless, if the young lady, instead of holding the little bonnet sentimentally over the baby, were satirically to hold a night cap over the presumptive father. For to have religion in that way is, spiritually considered, a pitiful comedy. A person has no religion; but by reason of family circumstances, first because the mother got into the family way, the paterfamilias in turn got into embarrassment owing to that, and then with the ceremonies connected with the sweet little baby—by reason of all this a person has—the Evangelical Lutheran religion.

SECOND PICTURE

It is a tradesman. His motto is: Every man's a thief in his business. "It is impossible," says he, "to be able to get through this world if one is not just like the other tradesmen, who all pay homage to the maxim that every man is a thief in his business."

As for religion—well, really his religion is this: Every man's a thief in his business. He also has a religion in addition to this, and his opinion is that especially every tradesman ought to have one. "A tradesman," says he, "even if he has no religion, ought never to let that be noticed, for that may readily be harmful to him by casting, possibly, suspicion upon his honesty; and preferably a tradesman ought to have the religion which prevails in the land." As to the last point, he explains that the Jews always have the reputation of cheating more than the Christians, which, as he maintains, is by no means the case; he maintains that the Christians cheat just as well as the Jews, but what injures the Jews is the fact that they do not have the religion which prevails in the land. As to the first point, namely, the profit it affords to have a religion, with a view to the countenance it gives to cheating—with regard to this he appeals to what one learns from the priests; he maintains that what helps the priests to cheat more than any other class in society is precisely the fact that they are so closely associated with religion. If such a thing could be done, he would gladly give a good shilling to obtain ordination, for that would pay brilliantly.

So two or four times a year this man puts on his best clothes—and goes to communion. Up comes a priest, a priest (like those that jump up out of a snuffbox when one touches a spring) who jumps up whenever he sees "a blue banknote." [2] And thereupon the priest celebrates the Holy Communion, from which the tradesman, or rather both tradesmen (both the priest and the honest citizen) return home to their customary way of life, only that one of them (the priest) cannot be said to return home to his customary way of life, for in fact he had never left it, but rather had been functioning as a tradesman.

And this is what one dares to offer to God under the name of the Sacrament of the Lord's Supper, the Communion in Christ's body and blood!

The Sacrament of the Lord's Supper! It was at the Last Supper that Christ, Who from eternity had been consecrated to be the Sacrifice, met for the last time before His death with His disciples, who also were consecrated to death or to the possibility of death, if they truly followed Him. Hence for all the festal solemnity it is so shudderingly true, what is said about His body and blood, about this blood-covenant which has united the Sacrifice with His few faithful—blood-witnesses, as they surely were willing to be.

And now the solemnity is this: to live before and after in complete worldliness—and then a ceremony. However, for good reasons the

[2] The $5 notes were blue. (L)

priests take care not to enlighten people about what the New Testament understands by the Lord's Supper and the obligation it imposes. Their whole business is based upon *living off* the fact that others are sacrificed; their Christianity is, *to receive sacrifices*. If it were proposed to them that they themselves should be sacrificed, they would regard it as a strange and unchristian demand, conflicting violently with the *wholesome* doctrine of the New Testament, which they would prove with such colossal learning that the span of life of no individual man would suffice for studying all this through.

CONFIRMATION AND THE WEDDING: A CHRISTIAN COMEDY—OR SOMETHING WORSE

CONSCIENCE (in so far as there can be any question of that in this connection) seems to have smitten "Christendom" with the reflection that this thing after all was too absurd, that this purely bestial nonsense wouldn't do—the notion of becoming a Christian by receiving as an infant a drop of water on the head administered by a royal functionary, the family then arranging a party, a banquet, for the occasion, to celebrate this festivity.

This won't do, thought "Christendom," there must also be an expression of the fact that the baptized individual *personally* undertakes to perform the baptismal vow.

This is the purpose of confirmation—a splendid invention, if one makes a double assumption: that divine worship is in the direction of making a fool of God; and that its principal aim is to provide an occasion for family festivities, parties, a jolly evening, and a banquet which differs in this respect from other banquets, that this banquet (what a refinement!) has "also" a religious significance.

"The tender infant," says "Christendom," "cannot personally take the baptismal vow, for which a real *person* is requisite." And so (is this genius or ingenious?) they have chosen the period from fourteen to fifteen years of age, the age of boyhood. This real person—there can be no objection, he's man enough to undertake to perform the baptismal vows made in behalf of the tender infant.

A boy of fifteen! In case it were a question of ten dollars, the father would say, "No, my boy, that can't be left to your discretion, you're not yet dry behind the ears." But as for his eternal blessedness, and when a real personality must concentrate the seriousness of personality upon what in a deeper sense could not be called seriousness, namely, that a tender infant is bound by a vow—for that the age of fifteen years is the most appropriate.

The most appropriate—ah, yes, if, as was previously remarked, divine worship is assumed to have a double aim: in a delicate way (if one can call it that) to treat God as a fool; and to give occasion for family festivities. Then it is extraordinarily appropriate, as is everything else on that occasion, including the Gospel appointed for the day, which, as everyone knows, begins thus: "When the doors were shut" [1] —and is peculiarly appropriate on a Confirmation Sunday. . . .

Confirmation then is easily seen to be far deeper nonsense than infant baptism, precisely because confirmation claims to supply what was lacking in infant baptism: a real personality which can consciously assume responsibility for a vow which has to do with the decision of an eternal blessedness. On the other hand, this nonsense is in another sense shrewd enough, ministering to the egoism of the priesthood, which understands very well that, if the decision with regard to religion is postponed to the mature age of man (the only Christian and the only sensible thing), many would perhaps have character enough not to want to be feignedly Christian. Hence the priest seeks to take possession of people in young and tender years, so that in maturer years they might have the difficulty of breaking a "sacred" obligation, imposed to be sure in boyhood, but which many perhaps may feel superstitious about breaking. Therefore the priesthood takes possession of the child, the boy, receives from him sacred vows, etc. And what the "priest," this man of God, proposes to do is surely a godly undertaking. Otherwise analogy might require that, just as there is a police ordinance prohibiting the sale of liquor to boys, so there might also be issued a prohibition against taking solemn vows concerning an eternal blessedness—from boys, a prohibition to insure that the priests, because they are perjurors, should not for this reason be allowed to work in the direction of bringing about (for their own consolation) the greatest possible *commune naufragium*, namely that the whole community should become perjured; and letting boys of fifteen take a solemn vow concerning an eternal blessedness is as though calculated to this end.

So then confirmation is in itself far deeper nonsense than infant baptism. But not to neglect anything which might contribute to make confirmation the exact opposite of that which it gives itself out to be,

[1] John 20: 19-31, the Gospel for the First Sunday after Easter, the day which in S.K.'s time was appointed for Confirmation in Copenhagen. (L)

this ceremony has been associated with all finite and civil ends, so that the significance of confirmation really is the certificate issued by the priest, without which the boy or girl in question cannot get along at all in this life.

The whole thing is a comedy—and taking this view of it, perhaps something might be done to introduce more dramatic illusion into this solemnity, as, for example, if a prohibition were published against anyone being confirmed in a jacket, *item* an ordinance that upon the floor of the church male confirmants must wear a beard, which of course could fall off at the family festivities in the evening, and perhaps be used for fun and jest. . . .

THE WEDDING

True worship of God consists quite simply in doing God's will.

But this sort of worship was never to man's taste. That which in all generations men have been busied about, that in which theological learning originated, becomes many, many disciplines, widens out to interminable prolixity, that upon which and for which thousands of priests and professors live, that which is the content of the history of "Christendom," by the study of which those who are becoming priests and professors are educated, is the contrivance of another sort of divine worship, which consists in—having one's own will, but doing it in such a way that the name of God, the invocation of God, is brought into conjunction with it, whereby man thinks he is assured against being ungodly—whereas, alas, precisely this is the most aggravated sort of ungodliness.

An example. A man is inclined to want to support himself by killing people. Now he sees from God's Word that this is not permissible, that God's will is, "Thou shalt not kill." "All right," thinks he, "but that sort of worship doesn't suit me, neither would I be an ungodly man." What does he do then? He gets hold of a priest who in God's name blesses the dagger. Yes, that's something different.

In God's Word the single state is recommended. "But," says man, "that sort of worship doesn't suit me, and I am certainly not an ungodly man either. Such an important step as marriage [which, be it noted, God advises against, and thinks that not taking this "important step" is the important thing] I surely ought not to take without assuring myself of God's blessing. [Bravo!] That is what this man of God, the priest, is for; he blesses this important step [the importance of which consists in not doing it], and so it is well pleasing to God"—and I have my will, and my will becomes worship, and the priest has his will, he has ten dollars, not earned in the humble way of brushing people's clothes or serving beer or brandy at the bar; no, he was employed in God's service, and to earn ten dollars in that way is—divine worship. (Bravissimo!)

What an abyss of nonsense and abomination! When something is displeasing to God, does it become well pleasing by the fact that (to make bad worse) a priest takes part who (to make bad worse) gets ten dollars for declaring that it is well pleasing to God?

Let us stick to the subject of the wedding. In his Word God recommends the single state. Now there is a couple that want to get married. This couple, of course, since they call themselves Christians, ought to know well what Christianity is—but let that pass. The lovers apply to— the priest; and the priest is bound by an oath upon the New Testament which recommends the single state. If then he is not a liar and a perjurer who in the basest manner earns paltry dollars, he must act as follows. At the most he can say to them with human sympathy for this human thing of being in love, "My little children, I am the last man to whom you should apply; to apply to me in such a contingency is as if one were to apply to the chief of police to inquire how one should comport oneself when stealing. My duty is to employ every means to restrain you. At the utmost I can say with the Apostle (for they are not the words of the Master), yes, if it comes to that, and you have not continency, then get together, "it is better to marry than to burn." And I know very well that you will shudder inwardly when I talk thus about what you think the most beautiful thing in life; but I must do my duty. And for this reason I said that I am the last man to whom you should apply."

In "Christendom" it is different. The priest—if only there are some he can splice together, he's the man for it. If the couple had applied to the midwives, perhaps they would not be so sure of being confirmed in the notion that their project is a thing well pleasing to God.

So they are wed, i.e. "man" has his will, but this thing of having his will is refined to being also divine worship, for God's name is brought into conjunction with it. They are wed—by the priest. Ah, the fact that the priest takes part is the reassuring thing. This man, who by an oath is bound to the New Testament, and then for ten dollars is the most complaisant man one can have to deal with—this man vouches for it that this act is true divine worship.

Christianly one must say that precisely the fact that the priest takes part is the worst thing in the whole affair. If you want to marry, seek rather to be married by a blacksmith; then it might perhaps (if one may speak thus) escape God's notice; but when a priest takes part it cannot possibly escape God's notice. Remember what was said to a man who in a tempest invoked the gods: "Don't for anything let the gods observe that you are in the party!" [2] And in the same way one might say, "Take care at all events not to have a priest take part." The others, i.e. the blacksmith and the lovers, have not taken an oath to God upon the New Testament, so (if I may speak thus) the thing goes better than when the priest intervenes with his—holy presence.

What every religion in which there is any truth aims at, and what Christianity aims at decisively, is a total transformation in a man, to wrest from him through renunciation and self-denial all that, and precisely that, to which he immediately clings, in which he immediately has his life. This sort of religion, as "man" understands it, is not what he wants. The upshot therefore is that from generation to generation there lives—how equivocal!—a highly respected class in the community, the priests. Their *métier* is to invert the whole situation, so that what man likes becomes religion, on the condition, however, of invoking God's name and paying something definite to the priests. The rest of the community, when one examines the case more closely, are seen to be egoistically interested in upholding the estimation in which the priests are held—for otherwise the falsification cannot succeed.

To become a Christian in the New Testament sense is such a radical change that, humanly speaking, one must say that it is the heaviest trial to a family that one of its members becomes a Christian. For in such a Christian the God-relationship becomes so predominant that he is not "lost" in the ordinary sense of the word; no, in a far deeper sense than dying he is lost to everything that is called family. It is of this Christ constantly speaks, both with reference to himself when he says that to be his disciple is to be his mother, brother, sister, that in no other sense has he a mother, a brother, a sister; and also when he speaks continually about the collision of hating father and mother, one's own child, etc. To become a Christian in the New Testament sense is to loosen (in the sense in which the dentist speaks of loosening the tooth from the gums), to loosen the individual out of the cohesion to which he clings with the passion of immediacy, and which clings to him with the same passion.

[2] By Diogenes Laertius (1, 86) this story is ascribed to Bios. (L)

This sort of Christianity was never—no more now, precisely no more than in the year 30—to man's taste, but was distasteful to him in his inmost heart, mortally distasteful. Therefore the upshot is that from generation to generation there lives a highly respected class in the community whose *métier* is to transform Christianity into the exact opposite.

The Christianity of the priests, by the aid of religion (which, alas, is used precisely to bring about the opposite), is directed to cementing families more and more egoistically together, and to arranging family festivities, beautiful, splendid family festivities, e.g. infant baptism and confirmation, which festivities, compared for example with excursions in the Deer Park and other family frolics, have a peculiar enchantment for the fact that they are "also" religious.

"Woe unto you," says Christ to the "lawyers" (the interpreters of Scripture), "for ye took away the key of knowledge, ye entered not in yourselves [i.e. into the kingdom of heaven, cf. Matthew 23:13], and them that were entering in ye hindered.' (Luke 11:52.)

ONE LIVES ONLY ONCE

This saying is so often heard in the world, "One lives only once; therefore I could wish to see Paris before I die, or to make a fortune as soon as possible, or in fine to become something great in the world—for one lives only once."

More rarely we encounter, but it may be encountered nevertheless, a man who has only one wish, quite definitely only one wish. "This," says he, "I could wish; oh, that my wish might be fulfilled, for alas, one lives only once."

Imagine such a man upon his deathbed. The wish was not fulfilled, but his soul clings unalterably to this wish—and now, now it is no longer possible. Then he raises himself on his bed; with the passion of despair he utters once again his wish: "Oh, despair, it is not fulfilled; despair, one lives only once!"

This seems terrible, and in truth it is, but not as he means it; for the terrible thing is not that the wish remained unfulfilled, the terrible thing is the passion with which he clings to it. His life is not wasted because his wish was not fulfilled, by no manner of means; if his life is wasted, it is because he would not give up his wish, would not learn from life anything higher than this consideration of his only wish, as though its fulfillment or non-fulfillment decided everything.

The truly terrible thing is therefore an entirely different thing, as for example if a man upon his deathbed were to discover, or upon his deathbed were to become clearly aware, of that which all his life long he had understood more obscurely but had never been willing to understand, that the fact of having suffered in the world for the truth is one of the requisites for becoming eternally blessed—and one lives only once, that once which now is for him already past! And he had it indeed in his power! And eternity cannot change, that eternity to which in dying he goes as to his future.

We men are prone by nature to regard life in this way: we consider suffering an evil which in every way we strive to avoid. And if we succeed in this, we think that when our last hour comes we have special reason for thanking God that we have been spared suffering. We think that everything depends upon slipping through life happily and well— and Christianity thinks that all that is terrible really comes from the other world, that the terrible things of this world are as child's play compared with the terrors of eternity, and that it distinctly does not depend upon slipping through this life happily and well, but upon relating oneself rightly by suffering to eternity.

One lives only once. If when death comes thy life is well spent, that is, spent so that it is related rightly to eternity—then God be praised eternally. If not, then it is irremediable—one lives only once.

One lives only once. So it is here upon earth. And while thou art living this once, the extension of which in time diminishes with every fleeting hour, the God of love is seated in heaven, fondly loving thee, too. Yes, loving. Hence He would so heartily that thou finally mightest will as He for the sake of eternity would that thou shouldst will, that thou mightest resolve to will to suffer, that is, that thou mightest resolve to will to love Him, for Him thou canst love only by suffering, or, if thou lovest Him as He would be loved, thou wilt have suffering. Remember, one lives only once. If that is let slip, if thou hast experienced no suffering, if thou hast shirked it—it is eternally irremediable. Compel thee—no, that the God of love will not do at any price. He would by that attain something altogether different from what He desires. How could it occur to love to wish to use compulsion to be loved? But Love He is, and it is out of love He wills that thou shouldst will as He wills; and in love He suffers as only infinite and almighty love can, as no man is capable of comprehending, so it is He suffers when thou dost not will as He wills.

God is love. Never was there born a man whom this thought does not overwhelm with indescribable bliss, especially when it comes close to him in the sense that "God is love" signifies "Thou art loved." The next instant, when the understanding comes, "This means to experience suffering"—frightful! "Yes, but it is out of love God wills this, it is because He would be loved; and that He would be loved by thee is the expression of His love to thee"—Well, well then! The next instant, so soon as the suffering becomes serious—frightful! "Yes, but it is out of love; thou hast no notion how He suffers, because He knows very well what pain suffering involves; yet He cannot change, for then He must become something else than love"—Well, well then! The next instant, so soon as the suffering becomes very serious—frightful!

Yet beware, beware lest time perhaps go by unprofitably in unprofitable suffering; remember, one lives only once. If this may help thee, view the case thus: be assured that God suffers more in love than thou dost suffer, though by this He cannot be changed. But above all remember, one lives only once. There is a loss which is eternally irremediable, so that—still more frightful—eternity, far from effacing the recollection of the loss, is an eternal recollection of it.

THE DIVINE JUSTICE

If ever you have paid any attention to how things go in this world, you have probably like others before you turned away from the whole thing and said to yourself mournfully, "Is this a just rule? What has become of divine justice?" Encroachment upon the property of others, thievery, fraud, in short, everything that has to do with money (the god of this world) is punished, punished severely in this world. Even what hardly can be called felony, that a poor man, it may be only by a look, implores a passerby, is punished severely—so severely are crimes punished in this "righteous" world! But the most dreadful crimes, such as taking the holy in vain, taking the truth in vain, and in such a way that the man's life is every day a continuous lie—in this situation no retributive justice is seen to interfere with him. On the contrary, he has leave to expand without hindrance, to spread his toils about a larger or smaller circle of people, perhaps a whole community, which in its adoring admiration rewards him with all earthly goods. Where then is divine justice?

To this the answer may be made: It is the divine justice precisely which in its frightful severity permits things to go on thus. It is present, all eyes, but it hides itself; precisely for the sake of being able to reveal itself wholly for what it is, it would not reveal itself prematurely; whereas when it reveals itself it is seen that it was at hand, present in even the least event. For in case the divine justice were to intervene swiftly, the really capital crimes could not wholly come into existence. The man who in weakness, infatuated by his lust, transported by his passions, but yet out of weakness, took the wrong path, the path of sin— upon him divine justice takes compassion and lets the punishment fall, the sooner the better. But the really capital criminal—remember now what it was you deplored, that justice was so mild, or did not exist at all!—him divine providence makes blind, so that to his eyes it seems delusively as if his life were pleasing to God, seems as if he had succeeded in making God blind. How frightful thou art, O divine justice!

Let no one be disturbed any more by this objection against divine justice. For precisely in order that it may be justice, it must first allow the crime to develop its entire guilt. But the really capital crime needs— mark this well!—the whole of temporality to come into existence; it *is* the capital crime, properly speaking, by being continued through a whole life. But in fact no crime can be punished before it comes into existence. So this objection falls to the ground. The point of the objection really is that God ought to punish so quickly that He ought (for that's what it means) to punish the thief before he steals. But if the crime must exist before it is punished, and if the capital crime (precisely that at which you take offense) needs a whole lifetime to come into existence, then it cannot be punished in this life: to punish it in this life would not be to punish it but to prevent it, just as it would not be punishing theft if one were to punish the thief before he stole, but it would be preventing the theft, and preventing the man from becoming a thief.

Therefore never complain when you see the dreadful crime succeed which would stir up your mind against God; do not complain, rather tremble and say, "O just God! So this man then was one of the capital criminals whose crime requires a whole life in order to come into existence, and only in eternity can be punished."

So then it is precisely severity which accounts for the fact that the capital crime is not punished in this world. Also it is perhaps sometimes due to God's care for others. That is to say, there is a difference between man and man; one man may be in a high degree superior to another. But this too is an example of superiority, to be capable of being the capital criminal. So Governance leaves him unpunished, also because it would thoroughly confuse our conceptions if we should perceive that he was a criminal. You see that the case may be far worse than you conceived it when you complained that God did not punish what you can see was a crime. From time to time there has perhaps lived a criminal on such a scale that no one, no one at all, had a presentiment of it; yea, that it was as though God, if He had punished him, would not have been able to make Himself understood by the men amongst whom this criminal lived, that by wishing to punish him in time (apart from the fact that this would have prevented the crime) God must almost throw into confusion the men amongst whom this criminal lived; and *that* in His love and care for men He could not find it in His heart to do. So then the man remains unpunished in time. Frightful!

Yea, tremble at the thought that there are crimes which need a whole lifetime to come into existence, which sometimes perhaps, out of indulgence toward us others, cannot be punished in this life. Tremble, but do not impeach God's justice. No, tremble at the thought of this (how frightful it sounds when one expresses it thus!)—this dreadful advantage of being able only to be punished in eternity. Only to be punished in eternity—O merciful God! Every criminal, every sinner who can be punished in this world can also be saved, saved for eternity! But that criminal whose distinction was that he cannot be punished in this world, also cannot be saved, cannot by being punished in time be saved for eternity; no, he can (that indeed was his advantage!) only be punished in eternity. Does it seem to you that there is reason to complain of God's justice?

TREMBLE—FOR GOD IS IN ONE SENSE SO INFINITELY EASY TO HOAX!

THE way people generally talk, if they talk about such things (but talk about such things as trembling is rapidly going out of fashion), is to give this turn to the matter: Tremble, for it is impossible to deceive God, He is the Omniscient, the Omnipotent. And that too is certainly true. Nevertheless I believe that by constantly stating the case thus one will not attain the desired end.

No: tremble—God is in one sense so infinitely easy to hoax! O my friend, He is something so infinitely exalted, and thou on the other hand art so infinitely nothing in comparison with Him, that thy sleepless effort in mortal dread throughout a whole life, aiming to please Him and to heed every hint of His, is yet infinitely too little to implore, deservedly, even for a single instant, His attention. And Him thou wouldst cheat! Therefore tremble, that is to say, watch, watch! He has a punishment which He Himself regards as the most frightful—and He is the only one who has a true conception of the infinite that He is. This punishment is: not to be willing to be conscious (as in one sense, in consequence of His exaltation, He is not) of the nothing which thou art. For an almighty being it must indeed (if one may speak thus) be the greatest exertion to have to look at a nothing, be conscious of a nothing, be concerned about a nothing. And then this nothing would hoax Him! O man, shudder, this is so infinitely easy to do!

Let me make this thought clear. Take a simple citizen—whom might one say it would be most difficult for this citizen to hoax? Would it not be precisely his equal? For this equal of his is concerned to watch out that he be not hoaxed, "I really cannot endure being hoaxed by him," etc. A superior man, a man of rank, the simple citizen will find it easier to hoax, for—after all the thing doesn't much concern the man of rank. The King still easier, for his Majesty does not concern himself at all about it. Do not misunderstand me. I evidently cannot mean that the superior man, or the King, if the thing should concern him, might not be able to see that this good citizen is hoaxing him; but he is not concerned at all about this simple citizen. Remember the tale of the fly and the stag. Thou wilt recall that the fly settled upon one of the antlers and said to the stag, "I hope I am not a burden to you." "I was not aware of your existence," was the reply. The citizen's task might reasonably be, if it were possible, by his honesty, by his uprightness, to succeed in attracting his Majesty's attention. On the other hand, it is so infinitely stupid and lacking in spirit to wish to hoax the man who is too infinitely exalted to be able to concern himself about him— it is so infinitely easy to do!

And think how infinitely exalted is God, and think of the nothing which thou art—and tremble at the thought how infinitely easy it is to hoax God! Thou dost think perhaps because thou art accustomed to address Him as "Thou," because thou hast known Him very well from childhood up, because thou art accustomed lightmindedly to mingle His name with all sorts of talk, that God is thy comrade, that thou art related to Him as one barman to another, that therefore He will at once make an outcry when He notices that thou dost wish to hoax Him, to falsify His Word, to pretend that thou dost not understand it, etc., and that if He doesn't do this, it is a proof that thou hast succeeded in hoaxing Him. O man, shudder at thy success!

Yea, in His exaltation God Himself disposes the situation in such a way that it is as easy as possible for a man, if he will, to hoax God. That is, He disposes it in such a way that those whom He loves and who love Him must suffer dreadfully in this world, so that everyone can see that they are forsaken of God. The deceivers, on the other hand, make a brilliant career, so that everyone can see that God is with them, an opinion in which they themselves are more and more confirmed.

So superior is God; so far He is from making it difficult, so infinitely easy it is to deceive Him, that He Himself even offers a prize to him who does it, rewards him with everything earthly. Tremble, O man!

THE PRIEST NOT ONLY PROVES THE TRUTH OF CHRISTIANITY, BUT
HE DISPROVES IT AT THE SAME TIME

THERE is only one relation to revealed truth: believing it.

The fact that one believes can be proved in only one way: by being willing to suffer for one's faith. And the degree of one's faith is proved only by the degree of one's willingness to suffer for one's faith.

In that way Christianity came into the world, being served by witnesses who were willing absolutely to suffer everything for their faith, and who actually had to suffer, to sacrifice life and blood for the truth.

The courage of their faith makes an impression upon the human race, leading it to the following conclusion: What is able thus to inspire men to sacrifice everything, to venture life and blood, must be truth.

This is the proof which is adduced for the truth of Christianity.

Now, on the contrary, the priest is so kind as to wish to make it a livelihood. But a livelihood is exactly the opposite of suffering, of being sacrificed, in which the proof consists: it is the opposite of proving the truth of Christianity by the fact that there have lived men who have sacrificed everything, ventured life and blood for Christianity.

Here then is the proof and the disproof at the same time! The proof of the truth of Christianity from the fact that one has ventured everything for it, is disproved, or rendered suspect, by the fact that the priest who advances this proof does exactly the opposite. By seeing the glorious ones, the witnesses to the truth, venture everything for Christianity, one is led to the conclusion: Christianity must be truth. By considering the priest one is led to the conclusion: Christianity is hardly the truth, but profit is the truth.

No, the proof that something is truth from the willingness to suffer for it can only be advanced by one who himself is willing to suffer for it. The priest's proof—proving the truth of Christianity by the fact that he takes money for it, profits by, lives off of, being steadily promoted, with a family, lives off of the fact that others have suffered—is a self-contradiction; Christianly regarded, it is fraud.

And therefore, Christianly, the priest must be stopped—in the sense in which one speaks of stopping a thief. And as people cry, "Hip, ho!" after a Jew, so, until no priest is any more to be seen, they must cry, "Stop thief! Stop him, he is stealing what belongs to the glorious ones!" What they deserved by their noble disinterestedness, and what they did not get, being rewarded by unthankfulness, persecuted and put to death, that the priest steals by appropriating their lives, by describing their sufferings, proving the truth of Christianity by the willingness of these glorious ones to suffer for it. Thus it is the priest robs the glorious ones; and then he deceives the simple-minded human multitude, which has not the ability to see through the priest's traffic and perceive that he proves the truth of Christianity and at the same time disproves it.

What wonder, then, that Christianity simply does not exist, that the notion of "Christendom" is galimatias, when those who are Christians are such in reliance upon the priest's proof, and assume that Christianity is truth in reliance upon the priest's proof: that something is truth because one is willing enough to make profit out of it, or perhaps even (by a greater refinement) to get the extra profit of protesting that he is willing to suffer. To assume the truth of Christianity in reliance upon this proof is just as nonsensical as to regard oneself as an opulent man because much money passes through one's hands which is not one's own, or because one possesses a lot of paper money issued by a bank which is insolvent.

MY TASK

THE point of view which I have to indicate again and again is of such a singular sort that in the eighteen hundred years of "Christendom" I have nothing to hold on to, nothing that is analogous, nothing that corresponds to it. So also in this respect, with regard to the eighteen hundred years, I stand literally alone.

The only analogy I have before me is Socrates. My task is a Socratic task, to revise the definition of what it is to be a Christian. For my part I do not call myself a "Christian" (thus keeping the ideal free), but I am able to make it evident that the others are that still less than I.

Thou noble simpleton of olden times, thou, the only *man* I admiringly recognize as teacher: there is but little concerning thee that has been preserved, thou amongst men the only true martyr to intellectuality, just as great *qua* character as *qua* thinker; but this little, how infinitely much it is! How I long, afar from these battalions of thinkers which "Christendom" puts into the field under the name of Christian thinkers (for after all, apart from them, there have in the course of the centuries lived in "Christendom" several quite individual teachers of real significance)—how I long, if only for half an hour, to be able to talk with thee!

It is in an abyss of sophistry that Christianity is lying—far, far worse than when the Sophists flourished in Greece. These legions of priests and Christian docents are all Sophists, living (as was said of the Sophists of old) by making those who understand nothing believe something, then treating this human-numerical factor as the criterion of what truth, what Christianity is. . . .

O Socrates, if with kettledrums and trumpets thou hadst proclaimed thyself the most knowing man, the Sophists would soon have had the better of thee. No, thou wast the ignorant man; but thou didst possess at the same time the confounded quality of being able, precisely by the aid of the fact that thou thyself wast ignorant, to make it evident that the others knew still less than thou, did not even know that they were ignorant. . . .

Nevertheless it is as I say: in the eighteen hundred years of "Christendom" there is absolutely nothing corresponding to my task, nothing analogous to it; it is the first time in "Christendom."

That I know, and I know too what it has cost, what I have suffered, which can be expressed, however, in a single word: I was never like others. Oh, in the days of youth it is of all torments the most frightful, the most intense, not to be like others, never to live a single day without being painfully reminded that one is not like others, never to be able to run with the herd, which is the delight and the joy of youth, never to be able to give oneself out expansively, always, so soon as one would make the venture, to be reminded of the fetters, the isolating peculiarity which, isolatingly to the border of despair, separates one from everything which is called human life and merriment and joy.

True, one can by a frightful effort strive to hide what at that age one understands as one's dishonor, that one is not like the others; to a certain degree this may succeed, but all the same the agony is still in the heart, and after all it succeeds only to a certain degree, so that a single incautious movement may revenge itself frightfully.

With the years, it is true, this pain diminishes more and more; for as more and more one becomes spirit, it causes no pain that one is not like others. Spirit precisely is this: not to be like others.

And so at last there comes the instant when the Power which once did thus—yea, so it seems sometimes—ill-treat one, transfigures itself and says, "Hast thou anything to complain of? Does it seem to thee that in comparison with what is done for other men I have been partial and unjust? Though—out of love—I have embittered for thee thy childhood and both thine earlier and later youth, does it seem to thee that I have duped thee by what thou didst get instead?" And to this there can only remain the answer, "No, no, Thou infinite Love"— though nevertheless the human crowd doubtless would emphatically decline with thanks to be what I have become in such an agonizing way.

For by such torture as mine a man is trained to endure to be a sacrifice; and the infinite grace which was shown and is shown to me is that I should be selected to be a sacrifice, selected to this end, and then one thing more, that I should be developed under the combined influence of omnipotence and love to be able to hold fast the truth that this is the highest degree of grace the God of love can show toward anyone, and therefore shows only to His loved ones. . . .

Thou plain man! The Christianity of the New Testament is infinitely high; but observe that it is not high in such a sense that it has to do with the difference between man and man with respect to intellectual capacity, etc. No, it is for all. Everyone, absolutely everyone, if he absolutely wills it, if he will absolutely hate himself, will absolutely put up with everything, suffer everything (and this every man can if he will)—then is this infinite height attainable to him.

Thou plain man! I have not separated my life from thine; thou knowest it, I have lived in the street, am known to all; moreover I have not attained to any importance, do not belong to any class egoism, so if I belong anywhere, I must belong to thee, thou plain man, thou who once (when one profiting by thy money¹ pretended to wish thee well), thou who once wast too willing to find me and my existence ludicrous, thou who least of all hast reason to be impatient or ungrateful for the fact that I am of your company, for which the superior people rather have reason, seeing that I have never definitely united with them but maintained a looser relationship.

Thou plain man! I do not conceal from thee the fact that, according to my notion, the thing of being a Christian is infinitely high, that at no time are there more than a few who attain it, as Christ's own life attests, if one considers the generation in which He lived, and as also His preaching indicates, if one takes it literally. Yet nevertheless it is possible for all. But one thing I adjure thee, for the sake of God in heaven and all that is holy, shun the priests, shun them, those abominable men whose livelihood it is to prevent thee from so much as becoming aware of what Christianity is, and who thereby would transform thee, befuddled by galimatias and optical illusion, into what they understand by a true Christian, a paid member of the State Church, or the National Church,² or whatever they prefer to call it. Shun them. But take heed to pay them willingly and promptly what money they should have. With those whom one despises, one on no account should have money differences, lest it might perhaps be said that it was to get out of paying them one avoided them. No, pay them double, in order that thy disagreement with them may be thoroughly clear: that what concerns them does not concern thee at all, namely, money; and on the contrary, that what does not concern them concerns thee infinitely, namely, Christianity.

¹ Goldschmidt, editor of *The Corsair.*
² "National Church" is what Grundtvig preferred to call it. (L)

THE UNCHANGEABLENESS OF GOD

AN ADDRESS BY S. KIERKEGAARD (1855)

TRANSLATED BY DAVID F. SWENSON

Severity first, that is to say the severity of the ideal, and then gentleness. . . .

This is all I have known for certain, that God is love. Even if I have been mistaken on this or that point: God is nevertheless love.—THE JOURNALS

THIS eloquent discourse, written in 1851 and delivered as a sermon in the Church of the Citadel on May 18 of that year, was not published until a few months before S.K.'s death, in the very midst of his attack on the Danish church. It may thus be regarded as "the conclusion of S.K.'s religious writing . . . introducing dramatically into the bitter conflict he was waging against conventional Christianity a purely religious note, which dated, as he remarked, from an earlier time" (Lowrie). This was in accordance with his announced principle of "severity first—then mildness"; for while the discourse interprets "God's unchangeableness" in a double sense, it concludes on the positive note. S.K. did not want his polemic to be the final word, and I have not allowed it to have that place here.

Of *The Unchangeableness of God* [1] it is true what Eduard Geismar says of the *Works of Love*—that its deeply moving quality is to be sought in "two co-operating factors" of S.K.'s being: "his great intellectual powers and his wonderful aesthetic gifts. Before he formulates and drives home his message, he permits to come to expression all the objections and gainsayings harbored by the human heart. The reader cannot conceive an objection that Kierkegaard has not already thought through and interpreted. And this gives him an extraordinary power to lead the reader to the point of reaching a decision, of forming a resolve that brings him face to face with God.

"And Kierkegaard is also the poet, having at his disposal all the impressive means that poets use to find their way to the human heart. He understands how to repeat the same thought in a variety of ways, with all the effect of a musical composition. He knows how to make the Christian ideal seem beautiful, the Christian life in the midst of all suffering so unspeakably joyful, that the reader finds an inexplicable longing aroused within him, a longing to enter in, to begin upon such a life" (*Lectures on the Religious Thought of Søren Kierkegaard*, pp. 73-74.)

The Unchangeableness of God is dedicated to S.K.'s father and is preceded by the briefest of his many prefaces:

"This address was delivered in the Church of the Citadel on the 18th of

[1] *The Unchangeableness of God,* as translated by David F. Swenson, appears in the English edition of *For Self-Examination and Judge for Yourselves!*

May, 1851. The text is the first I ever used.[2] Later I have often brought it forward; now again I return to it."

O THOU who art unchangeable, whom nothing changes! Thou who art unchangeable in love, precisely for our welfare not submitting to any change: may we too will our welfare, submitting ourselves to the discipline of Thy unchangeableness, so that we may, in unconditional obedience, find our rest and remain at rest in Thy unchangeableness. Not art Thou like a man; if he is to preserve only some degree of constancy he must not permit himself too much to be moved, nor by too many things. Thou on the contrary art moved, and moved in infinite love, by all things. Even that which we human beings call an insignificant trifle, and pass by unmoved, the need of a sparrow, even this moves Thee; and what we so often scarcely notice, a human sigh, this moves Thee, O Infinite Love! But nothing changes Thee, O Thou who art unchangeable! O Thou who in infinite love dost submit to be moved, may this our prayer also move Thee to add Thy blessing, in order that there may be wrought such a change in him who prays as to bring him into conformity with Thy unchangeable will, Thou who art unchangeable!

TEXT

The Epistle of James 1:17–21

EVERY good gift and every perfect gift is from above, coming down from the Father of lights, with whom can be no variation, neither shadow that is cast by turning. Of His own will He brought us forth by the word of truth, that we should be a kind of first-fruits of His creatures. Ye know this, my beloved brethren. But let every man be swift to hear, slow to speak, slow to wrath: for the wrath of man worketh not the righteousness of God. Wherefore putting away all filthiness and overflowing of wickedness, receive with meekness the implanted word, which is able to save your souls.

My hearer, you have listened to the reading of the text. How near at hand does it seem now to turn our thoughts in the opposite direction, to the mutability of temporal and earthly things, to the changeableness of men. How depressing and wearisome to the spirit that all things are corruptible, that men are changeable, you, my hearer, and I! How sad that the change is so often for the worse! Poor human consolation, but

[2] In the *Two Edifying Discourses* of 1843: cf. *supra*, pp. 110–116.

yet a consolation, that there is still another change to which the changeable is subject, namely that it has an end!

And yet, if we were to speak in this manner, especially in this spirit of dejection, and hence not in the spirit of an earnest consideration of corruptibility, of human inconstancy, then we would not only fail to keep close to the text, but would depart from it, aye, even alter it. For the text speaks of the opposite, of the unchangeableness of God. The spirit of the text is unmixed joy and gladness. The words of the Apostle, coming as it were from the lofty silences of the highest mountain peaks, are uplifted above the mutabilities of the earthly life; he speaks of the unchangeableness of God, and of nothing else. He speaks of a "father of light," who dwells above, with whom there is no variableness, not even the shadow of any change. He speaks of "good and perfect gifts" that come to us from above, from this father, who as the father of "lights" or light is infinitely well equipped to make sure that what comes from Him really is a good and perfect gift; and as a father He has no other ambition, nor any other thought, than invariably to send good and perfect gifts. And therefore, my beloved brethren, let every man be "swift to hear"; not swift to listen to all sorts of loose talk, but swift to direct his attention upward, from whence comes invariably only good news. Let him be "slow to speak"; for our ordinary human talk, especially in relation to these things, and especially that which comes first over our lips, serves most frequently only to make the good and perfect gifts less good and perfect. Let him be "slow to wrath"; lest when the gifts do not seem to us good and perfect we become angry, and thus cause that which was good and perfect and intended for our welfare to become by our own fault ruinous to us—this is what the wrath of man is able to accomplish, and the "wrath of man worketh not the righteousness of God." "Wherefore put aside all filthiness and overflowing of wickedness"—as when we cleanse and decorate the house and bedeck our persons, festively awaiting the visit, that we may worthily receive the good and perfect gifts. "And receive with meekness the implanted word, which is able to save your souls."

With meekness! In truth, were it not the Apostle speaking, and did we not immediately obey the injunction to be "slow to speak, slow to wrath," we might well be tempted to say: This is a very strange mode of speech; are we then altogether fools, that we need an admonition to be meek in relation to one who desires only our welfare?—it is as if it were meant to mock us, in this context to make use of the word "meekness." For suppose someone were about to strike me unjustly, and another stood by, and said admonishingly: "Try to endure this treatment with meekness"—that would be straightforward speech. But imagine the friendliest of beings, one who is love itself: he has selected a gift for me, and the gift is good and perfect, as love itself; he comes to me and proposes to bestow this gift upon me—and then another man stands by and says admonishingly: "See that you accept this treatment meekly!" And yet, so it is with us human beings. A pagan, and only a human being, the simple sage of antiquity, [1] complains that whenever he proposed to take away from a man some folly or other, and so help him to a better insight, thus bestowing a benefit upon him, he had often experienced that the other became so angry that he even wished to bite him, as the simple sage said jestingly in earnest. Ah, and what has God not had to endure these six thousand years, what does He not endure from morning until night from each of mankind's many millions—for we are sometimes most wroth when He most intends our welfare. Indeed, if we men truly understood what conduces to our welfare, and in the deepest sense truly willed our own welfare, then there would be no need to admonish us to be meek in this connection. But we human beings (and who has not verified this in his own experience) are in our relationship to God as children. And hence there is need of an admonition to be meek in connection with our reception of the good and perfect—so thoroughly is the Apostle convinced that all good and perfect gifts come from Him who is eternally unchangeable.

Different viewpoints! The merely human tendency (as paganism indeed gives evidence) is to speak less about God, and to speak almost exclusively and with sadness about the mutability of human affairs. The Apostle, on the other hand, desires only and alone to speak of God's unchangeableness. Thus so far as the Apostle is concerned. For him the thought of God's unchangeableness is one of pure and unmixed comfort, peace, joy, happiness. And this is indeed eternally true. But let us not forget that the Apostle's joy has its explanation in the fact that the Apostle is the Apostle, that he has already long since wholly yielded himself in unconditional obedience to God's unchangeableness. He does not stand at the beginning, but rather at the end of the way, the narrow but good way which he had chosen in renunciation of everything, pursuing it invariably and without a backward look, hasting toward eternity with stronger and ever stronger strides. But we on the contrary, who are still beginners, and subject to discipline, for

[1] Socrates.

us the unchangeableness of God must have also another aspect; and if we forget this, we readily run in danger of taking the lofty serenity of the Apostle in vain.

LET US THEN SPEAK, IF POSSIBLE TO THE PROMOTION BOTH OF A WHOLE-SOME FEAR AND OF A GENUINE PEACE, OF THEE, WHO ART UNCHANGEABLE, OR ABOUT THY UNCHANGEABLENESS.

God is unchangeable. In His omnipotence He created this visible world—and made Himself invisible. He clothed Himself in the visible world as in a garment; He changes it as one who shifts a garment—Himself unchanged. Thus in the world of sensible things. In the world of events He is present everywhere in every moment; in a truer sense than we can say of the most watchful human justice that it is present everywhere, God is omnipresent, though never seen by any mortal; present everywhere, in the least event as well as in the greatest, in that which can scarcely be called an event and in that which is the only event, in the death of a sparrow and in the birth of the Saviour of mankind. In each moment every actuality is a possibility in His almighty hand; He holds all in readiness, in every instant prepared to change everything: the opinions of men, their judgments, human greatness and human abasement; He changes all, Himself unchanged. When everything seems stable (for it is only in appearance that the external world is for a time unchanged, in reality it is always in flux) and in the overturn of all things, He remains equally unchanged; no change touches Him, not even the shadow of a change; in unaltered clearness He, the father of lights, remains eternally unchanged. In unaltered clearness—aye, this is precisely why He is unchanged, because He is pure clearness, a clarity which betrays no trace of dimness, and which no dimness can come near. With us men it is not so. We are not in this manner clear, and precisely for this reason we are subject to change: now something becomes clearer in us, now something is dimmed, and we are changed; now changes take place about us, and the shadow of these changes glides over us to alter us; now there falls upon us from the surroundings an altering light, while under all this we are again changed within ourselves.

This thought *is terrifying, all fear and trembling.* This aspect of it is in general perhaps less often emphasized: we complain of men and their mutability, and of the mutability of all temporal things; but God is unchangeable, this is our consolation, an entirely comforting thought —so speaks even frivolity. Aye, God is in very truth unchangeable.

But first and foremost, do you also have an understanding with God? Do you earnestly consider and sincerely strive to understand—and this is God's eternally unchangeable will for you as for every human being, that you should sincerely strive to attain this understanding—what God's will for you may be? Or do you live your life in such a fashion that this thought has never so much as entered your mind? How terrifying then that He is eternally unchangeable! For with this immutable will you must nevertheless some time, sooner or later, come into collision—this immutable will, which desired that you should consider this because it desired your welfare; this immutable will, which cannot but crush you if you come into hostile collision with it.

In the second place, you who have some degree of understanding with God, do you also have a good understanding with Him? Is your will unconditionally His will, your wishes, each one of them, His commandments, your thoughts, first and last, His thoughts? If not, how terrifying that God is unchangeable, everlastingly, eternally, unchangeable! Consider but in this connection what it means to be at odds merely with a human being. But perhaps you are the stronger, and console yourself with the thought that the other will doubtless be compelled to change his attitude. But now if he happens to be the stronger—well, perhaps you think to have more endurance. But suppose it is an entire contemporary generation with which you are at odds; and yet, in that case you will perhaps say to yourself: seventy years is no eternity. But when the will is that of one eternally unchangeable—if you are at odds with this will it means an eternity: how terrifying!

Imagine a wayfarer. He has been brought to a standstill at the foot of a mountain, tremendous, impassable. It is this mountain—no, it is not his destiny to cross it, but he has set his heart upon the crossing; for his wishes, his longings, his desires, his very soul, which has an easier mode of conveyance, are already on the other side; it only remains for him to follow. Imagine him coming to be seventy years old; but the mountain still stands there, unchanged, impassable. Let him become twice seventy years; but the mountain stands there unalterably blocking his way, unchanged, impassable. Under all this he undergoes changes, perhaps; he dies away from his longings, his wishes, his desires; he now scarcely recognizes himself. And so a new generation finds him, altered, sitting at the foot of the mountain, which still stands there, unchanged, impassable. Suppose it to have happened a thousand years ago: the altered wayfarer is long since dead, and only a legend keeps his memory alive; it is the only thing that remains— aye, and also the mountain, unchanged, impassable. And now think of Him who is eternally unchangeable, for whom a thousand years are but as one day—ah, even this is too much to say, they are for Him as an instant, as if they did not even exist—consider then, if you have in the most distant manner a will to walk a different path than that which He wills for you: how terrifying!

True enough, if your will, if my will, if the will of all these many thousands happens to be not so entirely in harmony with God's will: things nevertheless take their course as best they may in the hurly-burly of the so-called actual world; it is as if God did not pay any attention. It is rather as if a just man—if there were such a man!— contemplating this world, a world which, as the Scriptures say, is dominated by evil, must needs feel disheartened because God does not seem to make Himself felt. But do you believe on that account that God has undergone any change? Or is the fact that God does not seem to make Himself felt any the less a terrifying fact, as long as it is never-theless certain that He is eternally unchangeable? To me it does not seem so. Consider the matter, and then tell me which is the more terrible to contemplate: the picture of one who is infinitely the stronger, who grows tired of letting himself be mocked, and rises in his might to crush the refractory spirits—a sight terrible indeed, and so represented when we say that God is not mocked, pointing to the times when His annihilating punishments were visited upon the human race—but is this really the most terrifying sight? Is not this other sight still more terrifying: one infinitely powerful, who—eternally unchanged! —sits quite still and sees everything, without altering a feature, almost as if He did not exist; while all the time, as the just man must needs complain, lies achieve success and win to power, violence and wrong gain the victory, to such an extent as even to tempt a better man to think that if he hopes to accomplish anything for the good he must in part use the same means; so that it is as if God were being mocked, God the infinitely powerful, the eternally unchangeable, who none the less is neither mocked nor changed—is not this the most terrifying sight? For why, do you think, is He so quiet? Because He knows with Himself that He is eternally unchangeable. Anyone not eternally sure of Himself could not keep so still, but would rise in His strength. Only one who is eternally immutable can be in this manner so still.

He gives men time, and He can afford to give them time, since He has eternity and is eternally unchangeable. He gives time, and that with premeditation. And then there comes an accounting in eternity, where nothing is forgotten, not even a single one of the improper words that were spoken; and He is eternally unchanged. And yet, it may be also an expression for His mercy that men are thus afforded time, time for conversion and betterment. But how fearful if the time is not used for this purpose! For in that case the folly and frivolity in us would rather have Him straightway ready with His punishment, instead of thus giving men time, seeming to take no cognizance of the wrong, and yet remaining eternally unchanged.

Ask one experienced in bringing up children—and in relation to God we are all more or less as children; ask one who has had to do with transgressors—and each one of us has at least once in his life gone astray, and goes astray for a longer or a shorter time, at longer or shorter intervals: you will find him ready to confirm the observation that for the frivolous it is a great help, or rather, that it is a preventive of frivolity (and who dares wholly acquit himself of frivolity!) when the punishment follows if possible instantly upon the transgression, so that the memory of the frivolous may acquire the habit of associating the punishment immediately with the guilt. Indeed, if transgression and punishment were so bound up with one another that, as in a double-barreled shooting weapon, the pressure on a spring caused the punishment to follow instantly upon the seizure of the forbidden fruit, or immediately upon the commitment of the transgression—then I think that frivolity might take heed. But the longer the interval between guilt and punishment (which when truly understood is an expression for the gravity of the case), the greater the temptation to frivolity; as if the whole might perhaps be forgotten, or as if justice itself might alter and acquire different ideas with the passage of time, or as if at least it would be so long since the wrong was committed that it will become impossible to make an unaltered presentation of it before the bar of justice. Thus frivolity changes, and by no means for the better. It comes to feel itself secure; and when it has become secure it becomes more daring; and so the years pass, punishment is withheld, forgetfulness intervenes, and again the punishment is withheld, but new transgressions do not fail, and the old evil becomes still more malignant. And then finally all is over; death rolls down the curtain—and to all this (it was only frivolity!) there was an eternally unchangeable witness: is this also frivolity? One eternally unchangeable, and it is with this witness that you must make your reckoning. In the instant that the minute-hand of time showed seventy years, and the man died, during all that time the clock of eternity has scarcely moved perceptibly: to such a degree is everything present for the eternal, and for Him who is unchangeable.

And therefore, whoever you may be, take time to consider what I say to myself, that for God there is nothing significant and nothing insignificant, that in a certain sense the significant is for Him insignificant, and in another sense even the least significant is for Him infinitely significant. If then your will is not in harmony with His will, consider that you will never be able to evade Him. Be grateful to Him if through the use of mildness or of severity He teaches you to bring your will into agreement with His—how fearful if He makes no move to arrest your course, how fearful if in the case of any human being it comes to pass that he almost defiantly relies either upon the notion that God does not exist, or upon His having been changed, or even upon His being too great to take note of what we call trifles! For the truth is that God both exists and is eternally unchangeable; and His infinite greatness consists precisely in seeing even the least thing, and remembering even the least thing. Aye, and if you do not will as He wills, that He remembers it unchanged for an eternity!

There is thus sheer fear and trembling, for us frivolous and inconstant human beings, in this thought of God's unchangeableness. Oh, consider it well! Whether God makes Himself immediately felt or not, He is eternally unchangeable. He is eternally unchangeable, consider this, if as we say you have any matter outstanding with Him: He is unchangeable. You have perhaps promised Him something, obligated yourself in a sacred pledge—but in the course of time you have undergone a change, and now you rarely think of God—now that you have grown older, have you perhaps found more important things to think about? Or perhaps you now have different notions about God, and think that He does not concern Himself with the trifles of your life, regarding such beliefs as childishness. In any case you have just about forgotten what you promised Him; and thereupon you have proceeded to forget that you promised Him anything; and finally, you have forgotten, forgotten—aye, forgotten that He forgets nothing, since He is eternally unchangeable, forgotten that it is precisely the inverted childishness of mature years to imagine that anything is insignificant for God, or that God forgets anything, He who is eternally unchangeable!

In human relationships we so often complain of inconstancy, one party accuses the other of having changed. But even in the relationship between man and man, it is sometimes the case that the constancy of one party may come to seem like a tormenting affliction for the other. A man may, for example, have talked to another person about himself. What he said may have been merely a little childish, pardonably so. But perhaps, too, the matter was more serious than this: the poor foolish vain heart was tempted to speak in lofty tones of its enthusiasm, of the constancy of its feelings, and of its purposes in this world. The other man listened calmly; he did not even smile, or interrupt the speech; he let him speak on to the end, listened and kept silence; only he promised, as he was asked to do, not to forget what had been said. Then some time elapsed, and the first man had long since forgotten all this; only the other had not forgotten. Aye, let us suppose something still stranger: he had permitted himself to be moved inwardly by the thoughts that the first man had expressed under the influence of his mood, when he poured out, so to speak, his momentary feeling; he had in sincere endeavor shaped his life in accordance with these ideas. What torment in this unchanged remembrance by one who showed only too clearly that he had retained in his memory every last detail of what had been said in that moment!

And now consider Him, who is eternally unchangeable—and this human heart! O this human heart, what is not hidden in your secret recesses, unknown to others—and that is the least of it—but sometimes almost unknown to the individual himself! When a man has lived a few years it is almost as if it were a burial-plot, this human heart! There they lie buried in forgetfulness: promises, intentions, resolutions, entire plans and fragments of plans, and God knows what—aye, so say we men, for we rarely think about what we say; we say: there lies God knows what. And this we say half in a spirit of frivolity, and half weary of life—and it is so fearfully true that God does know what to the last detail, knows what you have forgotten, knows what for your recollection has suffered alteration, knows it all unchanged. He does not remember it merely as having happened some time ago, nay, He remembers it as if it were today. He knows whether, in connection with any of these wishes, intentions, resolutions, something so to speak was said to Him about it—and He is eternally unchanged and eternally unchangeable. Oh, if the remembrance that another human being carries about with him may seem as it were a burden to you—well, this remembrance is after all not always so entirely trustworthy, and in any case it cannot endure for an eternity: sometime I may expect to be freed from this other man and his remembrance. But an omniscient witness and an eternally unchangeable remembrance, one from which you can never free yourself, least of all in eternity: how fearful!

No, in a manner eternally unchanged, everything is for God eternally present, always equally before Him. No shadow of variation, neither that of morning nor of evening, neither that of youth or of old age, neither that of forgetfulness nor of excuse, changes Him; for Him there is no shadow. If we human beings are mere shadows, as is sometimes said, He is eternal clearness in eternal unchangeableness. If we are shadows that glide away—my soul, look well to thyself; for whether you will it or not, you go to meet eternity, to meet Him, and He is eternal clearness. Hence it is not so much that He keeps a reckoning, as that He is Himself the reckoning. It is said that we must render up an account, as if we perhaps had a long time to prepare for it, and also perhaps as if it were likely to be cluttered up with such an enormous mass of detail as to make it impossible to get the reckoning finished: O my soul, the account is every moment complete! For the unchangeable clearness of God is the reckoning, complete to the last detail, preserved by Him who is eternally unchangeable, and who has forgotten nothing of the things that I have forgotten, and who does not, as I do, remember some things otherwise than they really were.

There is thus sheer fear and trembling in this thought of the unchangeableness of God, almost as if it were far, far beyond the power of any human being to sustain a relationship to such an unchangeable power; aye, as if this thought must drive a man to such unrest and anxiety of mind as to bring him to the verge of despair.

But then it is also true that *there is rest and happiness in this thought.* It is really true that when, wearied with all this human inconstancy, this temporal and earthly mutability, and wearied also of your own inconstancy, you might wish to find a place where rest may be found for your weary head, your weary thoughts, your weary spirit, so that you might rest and find complete repose: Oh, in the unchangeableness of God there is rest! When you therefore permit this unchangeableness to serve you according to His will, for your own welfare, your eternal welfare; when you submit yourself to discipline, so that your selfish will (and it is from this that the change chiefly comes, more than from the outside) dies away, the sooner the better—and there is no help for it, you must whether willing or resisting, for think how vain it is for your will to be at odds with an eternal immutability; be therefore as the child when it profoundly feels that it has over against itself a will in relation to which nothing avails except obedience—when you submit to be disciplined by His unchangeable will, so as to renounce inconstancy and changeableness and caprice and self-will: then you will steadily rest more and more securely, and more and more blessedly, in the unchangeableness of God.

For that the thought of God's unchangeableness is a blessed thought —who can doubt it? But take heed that you become of such a mind that you can rest happily in this immutability! Oh, as one is wont to speak who has a happy home, so speaks such an individual. He says: my home is eternally secure, I rest in the unchangeableness of God. This is a rest that no one can disturb for you except yourself; if you could become completely obedient in invariable obedience, you would each and every moment, with the same necessity as that by which a heavy body sinks to the earth or a light body moves upward, freely rest in God.

And as for the rest, let all things change as they do. If the scene of your activity is on a larger stage, you will experience the mutability of all things in greater measure; but even on a lesser stage, or on the smallest stage of all, you will still experience the same, perhaps quite as painfully. You will learn how men change, how you yourself change; sometimes it will even seem to you as if God Himself changed, all of which belongs to the upbringing. On this subject of the mutability of all things one older than I would be able to speak in better fashion, while perhaps what I could say might seem to someone very young as if it were new. But this we shall not further expound, leaving it rather for the manifold experiences of life to unfold for each one in particular, in a manner intended especially for him, that which all other men have experienced before him. Sometimes the changes will be such as to call to mind the saying that variety is a pleasure—an indescribable pleasure! There will also come times when you will have occasion to discover for yourself a saying which the language has suppressed, and you will say to yourself: "Change is not pleasant—how could I ever have said that variety is a pleasure!" When this experience comes to you, you will have especial occasion (though you will surely not forget this in the first case either) to seek Him who is unchangeable.

My hearer, this hour is now soon past, and the discourse. Unless you yourself will it otherwise, this hour and its discourse will soon be forgotten. And unless you yourself will it otherwise, the thought of God's unchangeableness will also soon be forgotten in the midst of life's changes. But for this He will surely not be responsible, He who is unchangeable! But if you do not make yourself guilty of forgetfulness with respect to it, you will in this thought have found a sufficiency for your entire life, aye, for eternity.

Imagine a solitary wayfarer, a desert wanderer. Almost burned by the heat of the sun, languishing with thirst, he finds a spring. O refreshing coolness! Now God be praised, he says—and yet it was merely a spring he found; what then must not he say who found God! and yet he too must say: "God be praised, I have found God—now I am well provided for. Your faithful coolness, O beloved well-spring, is not subject to any change. In the cold of winter, if winter visited this place, you would not become colder, but would preserve the same coolness unchanged, for the waters of the spring do not freeze! In the midday heat of the summer sun you preserve precisely the same coolness, for the waters of the spring do not become lukewarm!" There is nothing untrue in what he says, no false exaggeration in his eulogy. (And he who chooses a spring as subject for his eulogy chooses in my opinion no ungrateful theme, as anyone may better understand the more he knows what the desert signifies, and solitude.) However, the life of our wanderer took a turn otherwise than he had thought; he lost touch with the spring, and went astray in the wide world. Many years later he returned to the same place. His first thought was of the spring— but it was not, it had run dry. For a moment he stood silent in grief. Then he gathered himself together and said: "No, I will not retract a single word of all that I said in your praise; it was all true. And if I praised your refreshing coolness while you were still in being, O beloved well-spring, let me now also praise it when you have vanished, in order that there may be some proof of unchangeableness in a human breast. Nor can I say that you deceived me; had I found you, I am convinced that your coolness would have been quite unchanged—and more you had not promised."

But Thou O God, who art unchangeable, Thou art always and invariably to be found, and always to be found unchanged. Whether in life or in death, no one journeys so far afield that Thou art not to be found by him, that Thou art not there, Thou who art everywhere. It is not so with the well-springs of earth, for they are to be found only in special places. And besides—overwhelming security!—Thou dost not remain, like the spring, in a single place, but Thou dost follow the traveller on his way. Ah, and no one ever wanders so far astray that he cannot find the way back to Thee, Thou who art not merely as a spring that may be found—how poor and inadequate a description of what Thou art!—but rather as a spring that itself seeks out the thirsty traveller, the errant wanderer: who has ever heard the like of any spring! Thus Thou art unchangeably always and everywhere to be found. And whenever any human being comes to Thee, of whatever age, at whatever time of the day, in whatever state: if he comes in sincerity he always finds Thy love equally warm, like the spring's unchanged coolness, O Thou who art unchangeable! Amen!

BIBLIOGRAPHY
AND
INDEX

BIBLIOGRAPHY *

I. THE WORKS OF KIERKEGAARD
IN ENGLISH

1. L. M. Hollander, *Selections from the Writings of Kierkegaard.* 239 pp. University of Texas Bulletin No. 2326. 1932.
2. *The Diary of a Seducer* (from "Either/Or," Vol. 1), translated by Knud Fick. 173 pp. The Dragon Press (Ithaca, N. Y.). 1935.
3. *Philosophical Fragments*, translated and with an introduction by David F. Swenson. 105 pp. Princeton University Press. 1936.
4. *The Journals of Søren Kierkegaard:* A Selection, edited and translated by Alexander Dru. 603 pp. Oxford University Press. 1938.
5. *Purity of Heart Is to Will One Thing:* Spiritual Preparation for the Feast of Confession (Part One of "Edifying Discourses in Various Spirits"). Translated and with an introduction by Douglas V. Steere. 207 pp. Harper's. 1938.
6. *Purify Your Hearts!* (Same work as above.) Translated by A. S. Aldworth and W. S. Ferrie. 179 pp. Daniel (London). 1938.
7. *The Point of View for My Work as an Author* (including "Two Notes about 'The Individual'" and "On My Work as an Author"), translated by Walter Lowrie. 174 pp. Oxford. 1939.
8. *Fear and Trembling,* translated by Robert Payne. 192 pp. Oxford. 1939. (See also No. 13.)
9. *The Present Age* (latter part of "A Literary Review") and "Two Minor Ethico-Religious Treatises," translated by Alexander Dru and Walter Lowrie. 163 pp. Oxford. 1940.
10. *Christian Discourses* (including "Discourses about the Lilies and the Birds," "The High Priest—The Publican—The Woman that Was a Sinner"), translated by Walter Lowrie. 309 pp. Oxford, 1940. (See also No. 17.)
11. *Stages on Life's Way,* translated by Walter Lowrie. 472 pp. Princeton. 1940.
12. *For Self-Examination,* translated by Edna and Howard Houg. Augsburg. 1940. (See also No. 20.)
13. *Fear and Trembling,* translated by Walter Lowrie. 209 pp. Princeton. 1941.
14. *Repetition,* translated by Walter Lowrie. (With an essay, "How Kierkegaard Got into English," by W. L.) 200 pp. Princeton. 1941.
15. *Thoughts on Crucial Situations in Human Life:* Three Discourses on Imagined Occasions. Translated by David F. Swenson. 117 pp. Augsburg Publishing House (Minneapolis). 1941.
16. *The Sickness unto Death,* translated by Walter Lowrie, 231 pp. Princeton. 1941.

---

* The present edition retains the original Bibliography. For a more recent list of Princeton titles, see page ii.

17. *The Lilies and the Birds,* translated by A. S. Aldworth and W. S. Ferrie. Daniel (London). 1941.
18. *Concluding Unscientific Postscript to the "Philosophical Fragments,"* translated by David F. Swenson; completed and edited by Walter Lowrie. 579 pp. Princeton University Press and American-Scandinavian Foundation. 1941.
19. *Training in Christianity* (and the Edifying Discourse which accompanied it), translated by Walter Lowrie. 275 pp. Oxford, 1941; Princeton, 1944.
20. *For Self-Examination* and *Judge for Yourselves!* (and Three Discourses, 1851), translated by Walter Lowrie (except the final discourse, "God's Unchangeableness," translated by David F. Swenson). 243 pp. Oxford, 1941; Princeton, 1944.
21. *The Gospel of Sufferings* (Part III of "Edifying Discourses in Various Spirits"). Translated by A. S. Aldworth and W. S. Ferrie. Daniel (London). 1942.
22. *Edifying Discourses:* Volume I. Translated by David F. Swenson and Lillian Marvin Swenson. Augsburg. 1943.
23. *Edifying Discourses:* Volume II. Translated by David F. Swenson and Lillian Marvin Swenson. Augsburg. 1944.
24. *Either/Or: a Fragment of Life.* Volume I translated by David F. Swenson and Lillian Marvin Swenson; Volume II translated by Walter Lowrie. 387 pp, 304 pp. Princeton. 1944.
25. *The Concept of Dread,* translated by Walter Lowrie. 154 pp. Princeton. 1944.
26. *Kierkegaard's Attack upon "Christendom,"* translated and with an introduction by Walter Lowrie. 303 pp. Princeton. 1944.
27. *Edifying Discourses:* Volume III. Translated by David F. Swenson and Lillian Marvin Swenson. Augsburg. 1945.
28. *Edifying Discourses:* Volume IV. Translated by David F. Swenson and Lillian Marvin Swenson. Augsburg. 1946.
29. *Works of Love,* translated by Lillian Marvin Swenson. 330 pp. Princeton. 1946.

II. BOOKS ABOUT KIERKEGAARD
IN ENGLISH

1. Francis W. Fulford, *Søren Aabye Kierkegaard: A Study.* 75 pp. Privately printed, 1908 (?).
2. E. L. Allen, *Kierkegaard, His Life and Thought.* 220 pp. London. 1935.
3. John A. Bain, *S.K., His Life and Religious Teaching.* 160 pp. London. 1935.

4. Th. Haecker, *Søren Kierkegaard*. Translated from the German by Alexander Dru. 67 pp. Oxford. 1936.
5. Eduard Geismar, *Lectures on the Religious Thought of Søren Kierkegaard*; with an Introduction by David F. Swenson. 147 pp. Augsburg. 1937.
6. Walter Lowrie, *Kierkegaard*. 636 pp. Oxford. 1938.
7. M. Channing-Pearce, *The Terrible Chrystal: Kierkegaard and Modern Christianity*. 250 pp. Kegan Paul. 1940.
8. W. T. Rivière, *A Pastor Looks at Kierkegaard*. 231 pp. Zondervan (Grand Rapids, Mich.). 1941.
9. Walter Lowrie, *A Short Life of Kierkegaard*. 271 pp. Princeton. 1942.
10. David F. Swenson, *Something About Kierkegaard*. (Rev. and enl. ed.) 259 pp. Augsburg. 1941 and 1945.

III. IN PERIODICALS

1. Eduard Geismar, "Søren Kierkegaard" in *American-Scandinavian Review* 17: 591–599 (Oct. 1929).
2. Jean Wahl, "Hegel et Kierkegaard" in *Revue Philosophique* 112: 321–380 (Nov. 1931).
3. G. Cattani, "Bergson, Kierkegaard and Mysticism" (translated by Alexander Dru) in *Dublin Review* 192: 70–78 (Jan. 1933).
4. K. F. Reinhardt, "Cleavage of Minds: Kierkegaard and Hegel" in *Commonweal* 24: 523–524 (Oct. 2, 1936).
5. E. L. Allen, "Pascal and Kierkegaard" in *London Quarterly Review* 162: 150–164 (April 1937).
6. W. G. Moore, "Kierkegaard and His Century" in *Hibbert Journal* 36: 568–582 (July 1938).
7. F. Brandt, "Ce Qu'il y a de Réalité dans les Oeuvres de Søren Kierkegaard" in *Revue Philosophique* 126: 257–277 (Nov. 1938).
8. J. C. Mantripp, "Søren Kierkegaard" in *London Quarterly Review* 164: 237–243 (April 1939).
9. Henry Nelson Wieman, "Interpretation of Christianity" in *Christian Century* 56: 444–446 (April 5, 1939).
10. W. T. Rivière, "Introducing Kierkegaard" in *Christian Century* 56: 1164–1166 (Sept. 27, 1939).
11. R. W. Bretall, "Kierkegaard: a Critical Survey" in *The Examiner*, Vol. 11, No. 4 (Autumn 1939).
12. V. A. Demant, "S.K.: Knight of Faith" in *Nineteenth Century* 127: 70–77 (Jan. 1940).
13. J. S. Bixler, "The Contribution of Existenz-Philosophie" in *Harvard Theological Review* 33: 35–63 (Jan. 1940).

14. John Wild, "Kierkegaard and Classical Philosophy" in *Philosophical Review* 49: 536–551.

15. R. M. Pope, "Impression of Kierkegaard" in *London Quarterly Review* 166: 17–24 (Jan. 1941).

16. H. A. Reinhold, "S.K., Great Christian of the 19th Century" in *Commonweal* 35: 608–611 (April 10, 1942).

17. Paul Tillich, "Kierkegaard in English" in *American-Scandinavian Review* 30: 254–257 (Sept. 1942).

18. O. F. Kraushaar, "Kierkegaard in English" in *Journal of Philosophy* 39: 561–583, 589–607 (Oct. 8 and 22, 1942).

19. Karl Löwith, "On the Historical Understanding of Kierkegaard" in *Review of Religion* 17: 227–241 (March 1943).

20. Norbert Guterman, "Kierkegaard and his Faith" in *Partisan Review,* March–April 1943.

21. Philip Merlan, "Toward the Understanding of Kierkegaard" in *Journal of Religion* 23: 77–90 (April 1943).

22. E. M. Manasee, "Conversion and Liberation: a Comparison of Augustine and Kierkegaard" in *Review of Religion* 17: 361–383 (May 1943).

23. M. Channing-Pearce, "Repetition: a Kierkegaard Study" in *Hibbert Journal* 41: 361–364 (July 1943).

24. J. Durkan, "Kierkegaard and Aristotle: a Parallel" in *Dublin Review* 213: 136–148 (Oct. 1943).

25. G. O. Griffith, "Kierkegaard on Faith: a Study of *Fear and Trembling*" in *Hibbert Journal* 42: 58–63 (Oct. 1943).

26. Paul Tillich, "Existential Philosophy" in *Journal of the History of Ideas* 5: 44–70 (Jan. 1944).

27. W. H. Auden, "A Preface to Kierkegaard" in *New Republic* 110: 683–684 (May 15, 1944).

28. Douglas V. Steere, "Kierkegaard in English" in *Journal of Religion* 24: 271–278 (Oct. 1944).

29. G. E. Nicholson, "A Dramatic Approach to Christianity" in *Christendom* 9: 462–475 (Autumn 1944).

30. E. M. Dodd, "Kierkegaard and Schweitzer: an Essay in Comparison and Contrast" in *London Quarterly Review* 170: 148–153 (April 1945).

31. P. L. Holmer, "Kierkegaard, a Religious Author" in *American-Scandinavian Review* 33: 147–152 (June 1945).

32. Jean Wahl, "Existentialism: a Preface" in *New Republic* 113: 142–144 (Oct. 1, 1945).

33. D. G. MacRae, "The Danish Malady" in *Life & Letters Today* 47: 85–90 (Nov. 1945).

34. Richard McKeon, "The Philosophy of Kierkegaard" in *New York Times Book Review,* Nov. 25, 1945, p. 1.

35. M. W. Hess, "Kierkegaard and Isaac Penington" in *Catholic World* 162: 434–437 (Feb. 1946).
36. Hannah Arendt, "What Is Existential Philosophy?" in *Partisan Review* 13:34–56 (Winter 1946).

N.B. The excellent articles of Professor Swenson have been omitted from the above list, since they are all reprinted in his book, *Something about Kierkegaard* (Item II:10, above).

IV. A SELECT LIST OF WORKS
IN OTHER LANGUAGES

1. Georg Brandes, *S.K., ein literatisches Charakterbild.* 1879.
2. A. Bärthold, *Die Bedeutung der ästhetischen Schriften S.K.'s* 1879.—*Was Christentum ist.* 1884.—*Die Wendung zur Wahrheit.* 1885.
3. Henriette Lund (S.K.'s niece), *Mit Forhold til Hende.* 2nd ed. Copenhagen, 1904.—*Erindringer fra Hjemmet.* Copenhagen, 1909.
4. Th. Haecker, *S.K. und die Philosophie der Innerlichkeit.* 1913.—*S.K., Kritik der Gegenwart.* 2nd ed., 1922.
5. Harald Höffding, *S.K. als Philosoph* (übersetzt von A. Dorner & Chr. Schrempff). 167 pp. Stuttgart. 1922.
6. Karl Jaspers, *Psychologie der Weltanschauungen,* III (especially pp. 419–432). Berlin. 1925.
7. Werner Möhring, *Ibsen und Kierkegaard.* 187 pp. Leipzig. 1928.
8. Eduard Geismar, *S.K.: seine Lebensentwicklung und seine Wirksamkeit als Schriftsteller* (translated from the Danish by his wife and Frau Dr. Krieger). 1929.
9. Erich Przywara, S.J., *Das Geheimnis Kierkegaards.* 1929.
10. Frithiof Brandt, *Den Unge S.K.* 1929.—*S.K. og Pengene.* 1935.
11. Emanuel Hirsch, *Kierkegaard-Studien.* 3 vols., 1930–1933.
12. M. Thust, *Søren Kierkegaard.* 1931.
13. Karl Löwith, *Kierkegaard und Nietzsche; oder philosophische und theologische Überwindung des Nihilismus.* 32 pp. Frankfort, 1933.—*Von Hegel bis Nietzsche.* 538 pp. Zürich and N. Y. 1941.
14. Jean Wahl, *Études Kierkegardiennes,* 2 vols. Paris. 1938.

INDEX

NOTE: Italicized page numbers refer to material by editors, not directly by Kierkegaard. Distinctively Kierkegaardian terms and names have been set in capital letters. Mere passing references have not been included unless the subject or the fact of S.K.'s mention of it seemed to be of special interest. Some topics have been indexed more fully than others, and the number of references under each heading should not necessarily be taken as indicating Kierkegaard's relative interest in the subject, even within the confines of the present anthology.

Index